HEGEL'S *PHENOMENOLOGY*

McGill-Queen's Studies in the History of Ideas
Series Editor: Philip J. Cercone

1 Problems of Cartesianism
Edited by Thomas M. Lennon, John M. Nicholas, and John W. Davis

2 The Development of the Idea of History in Antiquity
Gerald A. Press

3 Claude Buffier and Thomas Reid: Two Common-Sense Philosophers
Louise Marcil-Lacoste

4 Schiller, Hegel, and Marx: State, Society, and the Aesthetic Ideal of Ancient Greece
Philip J. Kain

5 John Case and Aristotelianism in Renaissance England
Charles B. Schmitt

6 Beyond Liberty and Property: The Process of Self-Recognition in Eighteenth-Century Political Thought
J.A.W. Gunn

7 John Toland: His Methods, Manners, and Mind
Stephen H. Daniel

8 Coleridge and the Inspired Word
Anthony John Harding

9 The Jena System, 1804–5: Logic and Metaphysics
G.W.F. Hegel
Translation edited by John W. Burbidge and George di Giovanni
Introduction and notes by H.S. Harris

10 Consent, Coercion, and Limit: The Medieval Origins of Parliamentary Democracy
Arthur P. Monahan

11 Scottish Common Sense in Germany, 1768–1800: A Contribution to the History of Critical Philosophy
Manfred Kuehn

12 Paine and Cobbett: The Transatlantic Connection
David A. Wilson

13 Descartes and the Enlightenment
Peter A. Schouls

14 Greek Scepticism: Anti-Realist Trends in Ancient Thought
Leo Groarke

15 The Irony of Theology and the Nature of Religious Thought
Donald Wiebe

16 Form and Transformation: A Study in the Philosophy of Plotinus
Frederic M. Schroeder

17 From Personal Duties towards Personal Rights: Late Medieval and Early Modern Political Thought, c. 1300–c.1650
Arthur P. Monahan

18 The Main Philosophical Writings and the Novel *Allwill*: Friedrich Heinrich Jacobi
Translated and edited by George di Giovanni

19 Kierkegaard as Humanist: Discovering My Self
Arnold B. Come

20 Durkheim, Morals, and Modernity
W. Watts Miller

21 The Career of Toleration: John Locke, Jonas Proast, and After
Richard Vernon

22 Dialectic of Love: Platonism in Schiller's Aesthetics
David Pugh

23 History and Memory in Ancient Greece
Gordon Shrimpton

24 Kierkegaard as Theologian: Recovering My Self
Arnold B. Come

25 An Enlightenment Tory in Victorian Scotland: The Career of Sir Archibald Alison
Michael Michie

26 The Road to Egdon Heath: The Aesthetics of the Great in Nature
Richard Bevis

27 Jena Romanticism and Its Appropriation of Jakob Böhme: Theosophy – Hagiography – Literature
Paolo Mayer

28 Enlightenment and Community: Lessing, Abbt, Herder, and the Quest for a German Public
Benjamin W. Redekop

29 Jacob Burckhardt and the Crisis of Modernity
John R. Hinde

30 The Distant Relation: Time and Identity in Spanish-American Fiction
Eoin S. Thomson

31 Mr Simson's Knotty Case: Divinity, Politics, and Due Process in Early Eighteenth-Century Scotland
Anne Skoczylas

32 Orthodoxy and Enlightenment: George Campbell in the Eighteenth Century
Jeffrey M. Suderman

33 Contemplation and Incarnation: The Theology of Marie-Dominique Chenu
Christophe F. Potworowski

34 Democratic Legitimacy: Plural Values and Political Power
F.M. Barnard

35 Herder on Nationality, Humanity, and History
F.M. Barnard

36 Labeling People: French Scholars on Society, Race, and Empire, 1815–1848
Martin S. Staum

53 Nature and Nurture in French Social Sciences, 1859–1914 and Beyond
Martin S. Staum

54 Public Passion: Rethinking the Grounds for Political Justice
Rebecca Kingston

55 Rethinking the Political: The Sacred, Aesthetic Politics, and the Collège de Sociologie
Simonetta Falasca-Zamponi

56 Materialist Ethics and Life-Value
Jeff Noonan

57 Hegel's *Phenomenology*: The Dialectical Justification of Philosophy's First Principles
Ardis B. Collins

HEGEL'S *PHENOMENOLOGY*

The Dialectical Justification of Philosophy's First Principles

Ardis B. Collins

McGill-Queen's University Press
Montreal & Kingston • London • Ithaca

ISBN 978-0-7735-4060-6

Legal deposit second quarter 2013
Bibliothèque nationale du Québec

Printed in Canada on acid-free paper that is 100% ancient forest free (100% post-consumer recycled), processed chlorine free

This book has been published with the help of a grant from Loyola University Chicago.

McGill-Queen's University Press acknowledges the support of the Canada Council for the Arts for our publishing program. We also acknowledge the financial support of the Government of Canada through the Canada Book Fund for our publishing activities.

Library and Archives Canada Cataloguing in Publication
Collins, Ardis B.

Hegel's Phenomenology : the dialectical justification of philosophy's first principles / Ardis B. Collins.

(McGill-Queen's studies in the history of ideas ; 57)
Includes bibliographical references and index.
ISBN 978-0-7735-4060-6

1. Hegel, Georg Wilhelm Friedrich, 1770–1831. Phänomenologie des Geistes. I. Title. II. Series: McGill-Queen's studies in the history of ideas ; 57

B2929.C65 2013 193 C2012-906215-4

Typeset by Jay Tee Graphics Ltd. in 10/12 New Baskerville

This book is dedicated to the memory of those whose presence in my life created the person who could write it.

Edward Sullivan, C.S.B.

My undergraduate teacher and mentor,
who set me on the path of what he called the intellectual life.

Joseph Owens
Armand Maurer, C.S.B.
Edward Synan

My graduate professors and research directors,
who taught me to recognize and cherish the standards of good scholarship.

Emil Fackenheim

Who showed me the kind of philosopher and teacher I wanted to be,
and introduced me to a living, breathing, fascinating Hegel.

Contents

Acknowledgments

AFTER MANY YEARS AS A PARTICIPANT in Hegel studies, I find that a cliché has emerged in my conversations about Hegel: "No-one agrees with anyone else about Hegel." When I try to explain the comment, it usually comes out this way. Hegel is so difficult – his terminology and style so esoteric, his questions so uncompromising, his projects so complex and all-encompassing – that one cannot say anything helpful or interesting without taking a risk. And taking a risk inevitably affects in a personal, individual way the questions selected for special emphasis, the texts that are given privileged authority, the style used to make Hegel more accessible. Therefore, I wish to thank all the Hegel scholars whose work appears in this book as a challenge to my own. I have learned from you a host of questions that I might otherwise have left unnoticed. My way of addressing these questions may be different from yours, but I am grateful for the challenge that forced me to formulate my position with more care and precision. I hope that my difference serves you as well as yours has served me.

I express my thanks especially to the intellectual friends with whom Hegel discussions and debates became a kind of play, and who supported me and my Hegel work in various ways throughout the years – Marty DeNys, Tom and Janine Langan, John Burbidge, Stephen Houlgate, Bob Williams, John McCumber, George di Giovanni, Ken Westphal, Kevin Thompson, Adrian Paperzak. Pat Werhane, John Burbidge, and Ken Westphal said the word of advice that made me stop where I was in this endless project and start to finish it off. My gratitude for that word is profound. The community of Hegel scholars who form the Hegel Society of America has given me an intellectual home where Hegel is taken seriously in an atmosphere of mutual respect and good-natured diversity. The community of the Sheil Catholic Center at Northwestern University has given me a living experience of communal connection and commitment that could have taught Hegel a few things about spirit.

I am especially grateful to McGill-Queen's University Press for its willingness to consider and accept for publication a study of such length. This made it possible for me to honour the standards of careful textual work learned from the scholars of the University of Toronto's Mediaeval Institute, and to develop an interpretation appropriate to the subtlety and complexity of Hegel's thought. I acknowledge with gratitude the subsidy provided by McGill and Queen's universities which made this possible. I am grateful for the guidance provided by two anonymous scholars who evaluated the manuscript for the press, and especially for the required revisions that have given the book more coherence and completeness. I am also grateful to the editors of the press, especially Kyla Madden, whose guidance took the book through the various phases of publication and preserved throughout, as a shared concern with the author, a commitment to the intellectual integrity of the work. Kathryn Simpson, in her role as copy editor, helped me find the places where my explanations needed more careful articulation. She played the role of a reader sympathetic to Hegel but not caught up in the esoteric discussions of Hegel aficionados, which I hope has made me more effective in communicating with students and others pursuing a more general interest in Hegel's thought. I thank Ryan Van Huijstee for his exemplary patience as we made our way through all the details involved in producing this book.

I have received support for this work from my home institution, Loyola University Chicago, in the form of several research leaves and a book subvention, for which I am grateful. Several themes developed in this book appear in articles published earlier, but with a different focus. I have cited these in the appropriate places and have acknowledged permission granted by the publisher when the relation to the work of this book requires it.

My mother once said to me, "If you don't finish that book before I die, I'll come back to haunt you." I remember it now, fourteen years after she died, because it reminds me of all the friends and family who have cared about this project just because it was important to me: my faithful friends in Toronto and Chicago, my family in Texas. Thank you for feeling urgent about it for my sake. Your caring kept me going, and kept me conscious of the precious part of my life that transcends the work I do.

Abbreviations

Enz — *Enzyklopädie der Philosophischen Wissenschaften im Grundrisse* (1830) in *Gesammelte Werke*, ed. Wolfgang Bonsiepen & Hans-Christian Lucas (Hamburg: Felix Meiner, 1992), Band 20.
Citations refer to section numbers (§) common to all editions and English translations; Remarks (*Anmerken*) are indicated by *A*, Additions (*Zusätze*) by *Z* following the section number.
Quotes are taken from *The Encyclopaedia Logic*, trans. T.F. Geraets, W.A. Suchting, H.S. Harris (Indianapolis & Cambridge: Hackett, 1991), unless otherwise indicated.

PhR — *Grundlinien der Philosophie des Rechts*, ed. Johannes Hoffmeister (Hamburg: Felix Meiner, 1955).
Citations refer to section numbers (§) common to all editions and English translations; Remarks (*Anmerken*) are indicated by *A*, Additions (*Zusätze*) by *Z* following the section number.
Quotes are taken from *Elements of the Philosophy of Right*, ed. Allen W. Wood, trans. H.B. Nisbet (Cambridge & New York: Cambridge University Press, 1991).
Citations of the Preface refer to the Roman numeral ordering of the German text followed by the page numbers of the Nisbet translation indicated by N:

PhG — *Phänomenologie des Geistes*, eds. Hans-Friedrich Wessels & Heinrich Clairmont, according to the text of *Gesammelte Werke* Band 9, eds. Wolfgang Bonsiepen & Reinhard Heede (1980).
Hegel's Phenomenology of Spirit, trans. A.V. Miller (Oxford & New York: Oxford University Press, 1977).

Citations refer first to the numerical ordering carried over from *Gesammelte Werke* Band 9 followed by the paragraph number of the Miller translation thus: *PhG* 53/M ¶57.

WL — *Wissenschaft der Logik*: Die Lehre vom Sein (1832), ed. Hans-Jürgen Gawoll (Hamburg: Felix Meiner, 1990) according to the text of *Gesammelte Werke* Band 21, eds. F. Hogemann & W. Jaeschke (1985).

Wissenschaft der Logik: Die Lehre vom Begriff (1816), ed. Hans-Jürgen Gawoll (Hamburg: Felix Meiner, 1994) according to the text of *Gesammelte Werke* Band 12, eds. Friedrich Hogemann & Walter Jaeschke (1981)

The Science of Logic, trans. George di Giovanni (Cambridge: Cambridge University Press, 2010).

Hegel's Science of Logic, trans. A.V. Miller (London: Allen & Unwin, New York: Humanities Press, 1969).

Citations refer first to the Band number, followed by the numerical ordering carried over from *Gesammelte Werke*, followed by the page numbers of the Miller translation thus: *WL* 21:32-3/M 48-9. The numerical ordering of the *Gesammelte Werke* are reproduced in the di Giovanni translation.

Quotes are taken from the di Giovanni translation.

KrV A/B — Kant, I. *Kants Werke*, Akademie Textausgabe. Berlin/New York: Walter de Gruyter.

1903. *Kritik der reinen Vernunft*, 1. Auflage 1781, *Kants Werke*, Band IV (A)

1904. *Kritik der reinen Vernunft*, 2. Auflage 1787, *Kants Werke*, Band III. (B)

SCG — Aquinas, Thomas, *Summa Contra Gentiles*, Textus Leoninus, (Rome: Maretti, 1961-67).

On the Truth of the Catholic Faith, (Garden City, NY: Doubleday, 1955-57); (Notre Dame: University of Notre Dame Press, 1975).

Cited thus: *SCG* II, 12 (1-2). Numbers in parentheses refer to paragraph numbering in the English translation.

< > — Indicates an adjustment in the translation quoted.

PART ONE

INTRODUCTION

EVERY TIME A PHILOSOPHER USES the laws of logic to support or challenge a claim about the world of human experience, this philosopher assumes that the subject matter is or should be logical. Nature and the realities of life, however, seem to be very different from the stark, rigid rules of logic. Why should the abstract structures of thinking reveal anything at all about the varied and changeable world of natural happenings, or about human desires, feelings, aspirations, and life plans? What justifies the assumption that relations among concepts and propositions should reveal the true constitution of the real world or should determine the norms of action and social relations? G.W.F. Hegel's philosophy recognizes that such questions must be asked. It takes on the task of questioning, examining, and justifying the assumption that the realities of nature and human life are fundamentally logical.

It might seem at first that Hegel's questioning belongs to a tradition developed in early modern philosophy. Surely René Descartes, John Locke, David Hume, and Immanuel Kant have asked whether concepts and ideas reveal what reality truly is. Hegel's questioning, however, is more radical. It finds unexamined presuppositions even in the way modern philosophy formulates its questions. For example, Hegel challenges the way that modern philosophy questions the legitimacy of knowledge in general without questioning the very knowledge and principles that such a critique uses to address this question (*Enz* §10*A*). He challenges the way modern philosophy begins with a distrust that conceives knowledge as something isolated in itself, separated from reality, without asking whether this conception has any validity. Why can we not assume with equal justification that knowledge and reality are inseparable (*PhG* 53–6/M ¶73–6)? Hegel calls for a deeper questioning that does not depend on such unexamined assumptions about what knowledge is or what it is not, and that does not appeal to critical norms, principles, and proof procedures whose meaning and legitimacy have not been examined and justified. Hegel questions everything, demands proof of everything. He even questions the rules of proof itself: the way a proof defines the topic for investigation, and the basic principles of formal logic (*Enz* §1; *WL* 21:15–17/M 37–9). Thus, Hegel questions presuppositions that even philosophers seldom think to challenge. As a result, he must invent a whole new way of making a case, because he cannot take for granted the presuppositions that usually operate in proof procedures. The book introduced here will examine and explain the way Hegel formulates this radical questioning and what he proposes as a way of meeting the challenge posed by such questioning.

1

The Project and Its Strategy

IN THE NOVEL *Sophie's World* the philosopher repeatedly reminds Sophie to consider what a particular philosopher's aim is, because this makes it easier to follow his line of thought. "By this I mean," the philosopher says, "that we must try to grasp precisely what it is that each philosopher is especially concerned with finding out."[1] Sophie's philosopher, however, represents only one way in which philosophers study the history of philosophy. Philosophers take a different approach when they use contemporary questions and strategies to reveal what is significant in a philosophy that belongs to a different time and culture. The latter approach has the advantage of bringing a line of thought into our own time, making it more accessible to our own way of thinking. Sophie's philosopher also worries about how to bridge the gap between the great thinkers in the history of philosophy and those of us who belong to a different culture. He suggests, however, that we can accomplish this by identifying with the concerns of the philosopher we are studying. This approach has the advantage of expanding our philosophical horizons. Instead of absorbing what is different into our own way of thinking, we let what is different challenge our way of thinking with unfamiliar questions, strategies, and displays of evidence.

We can learn a lot from both of these approaches. Good conversation, after all, is a give and take affair in which each speaker relates the conversation to his or her own concerns and also surrenders to concerns voiced by the other participants. The project introduced here follows the recommendation of Sophie's philosopher. It focuses on the question, what is Hegel trying to do in the *Phenomenology of Spirit*. This approach is not the only good way to study Hegel's *Phenomenology*. It is, however, one good way to

1 Gaarder (1996), 30.

do it; and it is the way I have chosen for my contribution to the discussion of Hegel's philosophy. In my judgment, Hegel's own questions and way of addressing them deserve a prominent place in current philosophical conversation, because they challenge in a radical and imaginative way presuppositions we too often let pass unquestioned.

1 ORIENTATION AND LIMITS

There are two different ways of finding out what Hegel is trying to do in the *Phenomenology*. We can look at the way Hegel himself talks about what he is doing, or we can examine the way he actually does it. Each approach involves a large selection of texts different from those related to the other approach. In order to study the way Hegel actually carries out the task of the *Phenomenology*, we would have to study the main text of this work, and explain exactly how this complicated examination of experience makes its case. The main text of the *Phenomenology*, however, seldom provides a clear, fully analyzed account of its various moves. Often the text tolerates different interpretations that are in no way consistent with each other. What Hegel himself tells us about his own view of the work, therefore, provides much needed evidence for favouring one interpretation over another.

Hegel talks most explicitly about the task of the *Phenomenology* in the introductory essays of the *Science of Logic*, the *Encyclopaedia*, and the *Phenomenology* itself. But Hegel cautions us repeatedly about introductions. Introductions, he says, anticipate what is yet to be proved in the main text. They help us become familiar with the kind of work it will be. They do not justify any of its claims (*PhR*, Preface, XXIV/N: 23; *Enz* §19, 79; *WL* 21:27–8/M 43; 21:38–9/M 54–5; 21:44/M 59). Why, then, should we work with Hegel's introductions? Because these introductory essays tell us what Hegel thinks he has done in the main text. Hence, they provide a way of checking our interpretations of the main text against Hegel's own.

Moreover, these texts also introduce other questions that must be addressed in order to adequately investigate the main issue. The task of the *Phenomenology* raises questions about the relation between experience and thought, about how the knowledge and reality issue should be defined, about what can and cannot be presupposed in a critical examination of knowledge, about what counts as a legitimate justification procedure. The introductory essays of Hegel's major works, including the *Philosophy of Right*, provide the most explicit discussion of the way these issues are involved in the task of the *Phenomenology*. The *Phenomenology*, however, is an early work (1807). Hegel's other major works belong to a later period. Although the

Logic belongs to the period between 1812 and 1816, the introductory essays were revised in 1832. We must ask, therefore, whether the interpretation of the *Phenomenology*'s task in the later works is the same as the interpretation presented in the introductory essays of the *Phenomenology* itself. This question requires a full investigation of the way each work addresses the relevant issues.

This study of the *Phenomenology* begins, therefore, with an investigation that focuses on the way the introductory essays of Hegel's major works define the task and method of the *Phenomenology*. In order to address this issue adequately, the investigation does not limit its discussion to texts that explicitly consider the aims and method of the *Phenomenology*. It also explains the way this explicit discussion exposes other major issues and questions involved in what Hegel sets out to do in this work: the claim that philosophical thought is independent of experience; the claim that philosophical thought knows the true essence of the real; the analysis of dialectical proof procedure; the presuppositions of philosophy and the role of the *Phenomenology* in justifying these. In the process of considering these issues, the investigation asks whether Hegel's position remains the same in the early work and in the later works.

Thus, the book introduced here begins with a limited project, namely to collect, examine, and interpret texts that talk *about* the task proposed for the *Phenomenology* and the issues related to it, without examining how Hegel actually carries out the task in the main body of the text. In spite of its limits, however, this discussion of Hegel's introductory essays provides evidence that is crucial for any interpretation of the *Phenomenology* as a whole and even for reading and interpreting specific developments in the main text. The examination shows how Hegel himself interprets the aim of the *Phenomenology*, the method required for accomplishing the aim, the results produced, and their significance for Hegel's philosophy. Hence, the study of Hegel's introductions justifies preferential treatment for a certain interpretive approach to the main text of the *Phenomenology*. Moreover, the account of dialectical proof procedure that emerges in these essays can help us construct a fuller account of the various proofs developed in the main text when these are not fully articulated and analyzed in the main text itself. This analysis of dialectic also provides guidelines for favouring one possible interpretation over another when the main text is ambiguous.

By itself, however, the examination of the introductory essays produces an interpretation that is abstract and tentative. In order to fully appreciate the role of the *Phenomenology* in Hegel's philosophy, and make the best case for an interpretation of this role, we must examine the way Hegel actually carries out the task of the *Phenomenology* in a demonstration developed within the concrete dynamics of human experience. The best case requires mutual confirmation between what Hegel says in the introductory essays about the task, method, and results of the *Phenomenology* and what Hegel actually does in the long series of dialectical moves that supposedly develop the method and accomplish the task. My study of the *Phenomenology*, therefore, includes a study of the way Hegel carries out the task of the *Phenomenology* in the main text of this work. In order to keep the investigation manageable, however, the study of the main text focuses on selected parts, those that are most important for interpreting the principal role of the *Phenomenology* in Hegel's philosophy. The selection is governed by the way the study of Hegel's introductory essays identifies the task and method of the *Phenomenology*.

2 GENERAL STRATEGY

Scholars use different strategies for identifying the concerns of a philosopher. These strategies have in common a commitment to careful work on the philosopher's own texts. In order to fully appreciate what the philosopher is about, the investigator must be willing to read not only a small selection of texts, but all the texts that are relevant to a specific set of concerns. Moreover, the interpretation of the texts requires attention to the context. Taken out of context, a selection can be easily distorted by the investigator's pre-conceived notions or free associations. When studying Hegel, for example, the words 'universal' and 'contradiction' may not mean what most philosophically trained investigators would spontaneously associate with these words. My book on the *Phenomenology*, therefore, examines a large selection of texts and pays careful attention to context.

All effective strategies for identifying the concerns of a philosopher require careful attention to textual evidence. Some, however, add other strategies as well. Philosophers talk to each other, even across centuries. An investigation into the way other philosophers influenced a philosopher's thinking can often make sense of things in a philosopher's position that remain completely obscure without this background knowledge. If the philosopher was engaged in a dialogue with another philosophical position, creating a debate with the other position can expose subtleties in the way a philosopher handles philosophical issues and problems. In both approaches, however, the very thing that enriches the investigation can also hide or leave undeveloped the most innovative elements in a philosopher's position. For example, when we study Hegel by situating his thought in a dialogue with Kant, we discover issues and subtleties in Hegel's thought that we might not fully appreciate without the Hegel-Kant dialogue. If, however, Kant sets the agenda for the discussion, so that we study how well Hegel addressed Kant's questions, we may lose track of what Hegel's own agenda has to teach us.

My strategy in this book keeps Hegel's own agenda dominant in the investigation. If Hegel himself talks about his project by discussing other philosophical positions, my approach focuses exclusively on the way Hegel understands these positions. It does not consider the way these positions might be interpreted if examined on their own terms, or what they might reveal about Hegel's position if they were represented as an equal partner in a debate with Hegel. My approach also restricts its concern with background influences. It focuses exclusively on those that Hegel himself mentions in his discussions of issues related to the task of the *Phenomenology*. In a few places, I have set aside these restrictions. In these cases, I have compared Hegel's position to other philosophical positions in order to expose by similarity or contrast subtleties in the way Hegel handles a certain question. The comparison, however, focuses on the precise point in the other positions that identifies a significant element in the way Hegel's position resembles or differs from these. The comparison does not interrupt the focus on Hegel's concerns by discussing in detail the concerns of the other philosophers.

I readily admit that the strategies not used in this book have much to offer. I have simply chosen to make my contribution in a different way. My approach will, no doubt, give evidence for a Hegel that many contemporary thinkers find unattractive and implausible. I hope, however, that the investigation is careful enough and thorough enough to win this supposedly implausible Hegel recognition as a worthy opponent in contemporary debate. In my judgment, Hegel demands more than seems plausible, and claims more than seems plausible, because he questions more. If he teaches us nothing else, he might at least teach us what a fully justified position requires, so that we do not make exaggerated claims for more limited attempts. He might teach us, too, the difference between a debate focused on what proof requires and a debate focused on whether a particular proof meets the requirements. If Hegel fails to meet his own demands, this does not prove that the way the demands are formulated is mistaken. My approach in this book focuses primarily on how Hegel formulates what full justification requires and how the justifications developed would have to be interpreted in order to make a good case for meeting these requirements.

At this point in the history of Hegel research, the way to Hegel's own definition of his project must pass through a maze of careful and astute interpretations offering very different accounts of the *Phenomenology*'s project. These interpretations reveal that the project itself and the texts in which Hegel defines it involve a set of issues that can be arranged according to different priorities. Each arrangement gives us a significantly different view of what Hegel is trying to accomplish in the *Phenomenology*. These different views are based on good evidence, either in the form of issues that really belong to the task proposed for the *Phenomenology*, or in the form of texts in which Hegel talks about its aims and method. Therefore, we must address the questions raised by these interpretations in order to develop an account of Hegel's project that considers all the evidence, examines the issues in a thorough way, and brings to light the subtleties of Hegel's position.

In this book, however, I will try to explain and interpret Hegel's thought for as wide an audience as possible: experts in the study of Hegel's *Phenomenology* and *Logic*; Hegel scholars with expertise in other areas of Hegel's thought; students and philosophers familiar with Hegel in a general way; and students and philosophers just beginning the study of Hegel's thought. The study of Hegel's challenging, complicated, and innovative approach to philosophical issues requires concentrated attention, patient work with his esoteric terminology, and careful analysis of a long, drawn-out series of argumentative moves. The task becomes incredibly difficult if the reader must cope with this challenge while also addressing questions raised by the variety of interpretations and debates that have focused on Hegel's thought. Therefore, I have situated the discussion of the secondary literature in separate chapters, sections, and appendices, or confined it to the notes.[2] This allows the reader to move through my interpretation of Hegel's position and analysis of its demonstrations without the distraction and interruption of other philosophical positions and disagreements among interpreters. The book addresses the most relevant and challenging secondary literature, but separates the discussion of this literature from the presentation of Hegel's position in the introductions of the major works and in the demonstration developed in the main text of the *Phenomenology*.

2 The one exception to this strategy is the discussion of Alexandre Kojève's work on Hegel, since his interpretation of the master-servant relation has become so well known and so generally accepted as to be almost indistinguishable from Hegel's own, at least for those readers with only a casual or general familiarity with Hegel's thought.

3 STRATEGY: THE STUDY OF HEGEL'S INTRODUCTIONS

In the study of the introductory essays, the book selects texts from each of Hegel's major works where Hegel talks explicitly about the task of the *Phenomenology* or discusses issues involved in the way he defines the task. This examination discusses each work separately. In this way, the study examines each text as a coherent, self-enclosed context and allows each separate context to confirm or challenge the others. This part of the study is developed in Part Two (the *Philosophy of Right* and the *Encyclopaedia*), in Part Three (the *Science of Logic*), in Part Four (the Preface and Introduction of the *Phenomenology*), and in chapter 10 of Part Five (a review of the issues).

Interpretations of Hegel's project in the *Phenomenology* get their orientation from the texts that are the primary focus of the interpreter's research. Those whose work focuses primarily on the later works, especially the *Science of Logic*, study the task of the *Phenomenology* not as a project that has a significance of its own, but as a project that serves the needs of philosophy. Does the beginning of philosophy in logic require a justification of presuppositions that logic cannot provide for itself? Can the *Phenomenology* provide this justification, and if so how? Those whose work focuses primarily on the *Phenomenology* itself consider the text primarily as an examination of experience, one that begins within the isolated consciousness of the self and takes this consciousness through a long, rich, complicated tour of experience in its various forms. If these interpreters raise questions about the role of the *Phenomenology* in its relation to the *Logic*, their primary concern is the way experience itself, taken in all its variety and complexity, can show us that logic or rationality is the fundamental truth of real life experience.

The next chapter (Part One, chapter 2) identifies four different ways in which the task of the *Phenomenology* has been interpreted. It presents four models or paradigms that represent significant ways in which priority can be assigned to different parts of the evidence. The chapter selects one or several secondary sources to represent each model. After making a case for my own position by examining the introductory essays of Hegel's major works in Parts Two, Three, and Four, I will review these interpretive models in Part Five, chapter 11. This later account shows how my position differs from these, and explains why I think the evidence favours my interpretation.

The review of interpretive models shows that an emphasis on the later works focuses on the presuppositions of philosophy and the independent legitimacy of pure logical thought. Interpretations focused on the *Phenomenology* itself emphasize epistemological issues and the dynamics of experience. Interpretations based on a study of both works acknowledge a connection between the conclusion of the *Phenomenology* and the beginning of the *Logic*, but they disagree about what kind of connection it is. These differences raise two important questions: is there enough evidence to support an interpretation that integrates the *Phenomenology* into the later developments of Hegel's thought, and if so what does the evidence tell us about the connection between the early and later works. My aim is to address these questions. I begin the examination of Hegel's introductions with the later works. The examination focuses on texts in which Hegel discusses what philosophy is and what its presuppositions are. It examines these issues with the dominant concerns of the *Phenomenology* in mind. Since the *Phenomenology* examines the forms of experience, what do Hegel's later works say about the relation between philosophy and experience? When this question has been answered, the discussion shifts to the *Phenomenology* itself to compare its view of the phenomenological project with that of the later works.

4 STRATEGY: THE STUDY OF THE DEMONSTRATION DEVELOPED IN THE MAIN TEXT

The study of Hegel's introductions plays a crucial role in the study of Hegel's *Phenomenology*. These introductory essays provide good evidence for the way Hegel himself interprets the task and method of the *Phenomenology*, and they establish the legitimacy of accepting the *Phenomenology* as a source for interpreting the beginning concept of philosophy proper. They also provide a more explicit analysis of the proof procedure that governs the demonstration developed in the *Phenomenology* than is given within the main text itself. The study of the main text itself asks whether the interpretation of the *Phenomenology* developed in the introductory essays fits the way the *Phenomenology* describes and analyzes the different forms of knowing examined in the main text. If the texts tolerate conflicting interpretations, the strategy favours an interpretation that fits Hegel's own interpretation of his project in the introductory essays. In order to keep the project manageable, however, the study of the main text must be selective. The strategy that determines the selection favours those texts that are most important for explaining how the proof developed in the *Phenomenology* justifies the beginning principles of philosophical science.

The study of the main text begins with an examination and analysis of the key moves that define and justify the claims of reason, those developed in the "Consciousness" and "Self-consciousness" sections of the *Phenomenology* (Part Six). These sections provide the justification for the first and simplest definition of reason as Hegel interprets it, and Hegel's introductions provide ample evidence that according to Hegel the subject matter of philosophy is the rational. Moreover, much of the controversy among interpreters of Hegel's thought has its origin in disagreements about how Hegel identifies the rational, especially among those who favour a Kantian approach. The "Consciousness" and "Self-consciousness" sections are crucial for distinguishing Hegel from Kant on this question. Hence, my study of these sections follows each and every shift in the demonstration Hegel develops in this part of the *Phenomenology*. Each chapter in Part Six concludes with a separate section which explains the way my interpretation differs from Kantian interpretations of the proof procedure that operates in this demonstration.

In Part Seven, which covers the "Reason" and "Spirit" sections of the *Phenomenology*, the discussion must become more selective. This Part must provide some kind of continuity between the demonstration developed in the "Consciousness" and "Self-consciousness" chapters and the presuppositions of the demonstration that completes the project developed in the *Phenomenology*. My strategy for establishing this continuity focuses on the two major transitions developed in the "Reason" and "Spirit" sections, the transition from reason to spirit, and from spirit to religion. The examination analyzes carefully each of these transitional moves; but the discussion does not analyze each and every shift in the series of moves that leads up to these transitions. It treats these preliminary moves in a more summary way, just enough to expose the skeleton of the demonstration and to highlight certain themes that become crucial in the final moves of Hegel's phenomenological project. Part Eight returns to the strategy used in Part Six. It develops a thorough analysis of the demonstration developed from the account of conscience and the beautiful soul through the account of "Revealed Religion," into absolute knowing and the transition from phenomenology to logic.

The strategy for covering the "Reason" and "Spirit" sections of the *Phenomenology* focuses exclusively on the structure of its proof procedure, and this approach cannot do justice to the rich resources provided in these sections. A full appreciation of the experiences examined in these sections requires explicit knowledge of Hegel's sensitivity to the various cultures of his own time, and to the complex political, social, and ethical developments of European history. The best way to add this dimension to one's study of these sections is to consult the two best commentaries on the *Phenomenology*, namely, *Hegel's Ladder* by H.S. Harris and *Genesis and Structure of Hegel's* Phenomenology of Spirit by Jean Hyppolite. Harris provides a dense study that exposes in great detail the sources hidden behind the explicit text of the *Phenomenology*. Hyppolite provides a more streamlined, leaner commentary that discusses a select few of the influences affecting particular parts of the text. In order to keep my study of the *Phenomenology* focused on its role as an introduction to philosophical science, I do not enter into a dialogue with the commentaries published by Harris and Hyppolite unless they challenge in some way my own interpretation of the text.

The "Reason" and "Spirit" sections of the *Phenomenology* also provide resources for engaging in fruitful debates with other philosophical positions, or for developing a Hegelian approach to contemporary philosophical issues. Again in order to keep my study of the *Phenomenology* focused on its relation to philosophical science, I have limited my discussion of Hegel's debates with other philosophical positions to what Hegel himself addresses explicitly; and have focused exclusively on the ways in which these other positions play a role in Hegel's proof procedure. For the same reason, my study does not enter into any of the discussions that create a Hegelian approach to contemporary issues. It cites some of them. It addresses their concerns if my interpretation exposes a dimension of Hegel's thought that might contribute an additional perspective to these discussions. But these citations and comments appear only in the notes and appendices.

My selective approach to the main text of the *Phenomenology* has certain advantages. It keeps the skeleton of Hegel's argument clear and exposed, so that the forest does not get lost in the trees; and it keeps the discussion focused on the primary task of the *Phenomenology*. Moreover, the selection has a kind of completeness. It provides a careful analysis of all major transitions developed in the *Phenomenology*, those in which Hegel justifies the shift from one fundamental cognitive orientation to another that is fundamentally different. It carefully analyzes some moves that lead up to and justify the presuppositions governing these transitions, most notably those in the "Consciousness" and "Self-consciousness" sections, and provides a summary account of those developed in the "Reason" and "Spirit" sections.

My analysis of the demonstration developed in the *Phenomenology*'s main text preserves the policy of separating the discussion of secondary literature from the presentation of Hegel's position. Because of the vast literature devoted to the *Phenomenology*, in whole or in part, the strategy for discussing this literature must be selective. Discussions of the Kantian approach to the interpretation of the *Phenomenology* are contained in separate sections of the chapters in Part Six. A brief discussion of literature that is devoted to the role of contingency in Hegel's thought appears as an introduction to Part Seven. Lengthy discussions of relevant literature appear in the notes and appendices. The concluding chapter focuses on a set of readings in which the authors analyze precisely both the structure of absolute knowing, with which the *Phenomenology* ends, and the way this structure affects the structure of knowing with which Hegel's *Logic* begins.

5 STRATEGY FOR READING THIS BOOK

Students and philosophers familiar with Hegel's thought in a general way, and those who are just beginning the study of Hegel's thought, should begin by concentrating on the chapters that focus on Hegel's introductions. These chapters explain how Hegel distinguishes philosophy from other kinds of knowing, what kind of problems are involved in starting a philosophical project, and what seems to be required in order to justify the principles with which philosophy begins. In the context of these questions, Hegel begins to identify the role of the *Phenomenology*. This kind of introduction focuses primarily on the universal concerns that make the subject matter interesting and important, and only gradually introduces the more bewildering complexity involved in these concerns. It uses the readers' appreciation of a problem to support the study of Hegel's thought. Moreover, my study of Hegel's introductory essays discusses each work separately. Studies that jump around among different works and different contexts run the risk of confusing the reader and even misrepresenting Hegel's thought by losing the meaning provided by the context. My study of Hegel's introductory essays also does not use categories whose meaning depends on the way textbooks and contemporary philosophical discussions invent names for different schools of thought. Applying these categories to philosophical positions that belong to a different time and a different conversation adds an esoteric and foreign element which creates unnecessary confusion for those who are not initiated into this way of speaking. When the reader has finished the study of Hegel's introductions, he or she should be familiar with the general structure of Hegel's proof procedure, which will help clarify the way the chapters devoted to the *Phenomenology*'s main text interpret the shifts in the demonstration developed therein.

Students and philosophers just beginning the study of Hegel's *Phenomenology* would be well advised to skip the sections of my book devoted to the debates developed in the secondary literature, until they are more familiar with the texts in which Hegel himself explains the questions and problems this work is supposed to address. Students and philosophers with expertise in Hegel's thought, especially those whose study of Hegel focuses on the *Phenomenology* or the *Logic*, can certainly determine for themselves whether to read the chapters, sections, and appendices devoted to the secondary literature and in what sequence to read them. I strongly recommend, however, that all readers begin with the study of Hegel's introductions, since the full meaning and justification of my interpretation depends on the weight of evidence presented in this study.

6 SETTING THE SCENE

Hegel published the *Phenomenology of Spirit* in 1807, toward the beginning of his career as a philosopher. At the time of its publication, Hegel thought of the *Phenomenology* as the first part of his philosophy, which suggests that in some way the rest of his philosophy depends on it. Did he still think of it this way at the end of his life? We might claim, of course, that the phenomenological project is worth studying for its own sake, whether or not it plays a significant role in Hegel's later philosophical system. But then we could not look to the later works for help in understanding the task of the *Phenomenology*. Moreover, we would have to ask why Hegel changed his mind about the need for a phenomenological introduction to philosophy.

Several pieces of evidence suggest that Hegel did indeed change his mind about the role of the *Phenomenology*. The First Preface (1812) of the *Science of Logic* describes the *Phenomenology* as the first part of philosophy. But the Second Preface (1832) does not repeat this description (*WL* 21:8–9/ M 28–9; 21:10–20/M 31–42). The *Encyclopaedia* divides philosophical science into three parts: logic, philosophy of nature, and philosophy of spirit; it designates logic as the first part. Moreover, the *Encyclopaedia* introduces the philosophical project with a review of different positions on objectivity, not with a phenomenology of spirit. A radically abbreviated account of phenomenology appears in the *Encyclopaedia* not as an introduction to the whole philosophical project but integrated into the philosophy of spirit, the third part of Hegel's philosophical system (*Enz* §18; 25; 413–39). Finally, Hegel once described the *Phenomenology* as a "peculiar early work." John McCumber refers to this comment and asks whether this indicates that Hegel in his later works no longer endorsed the project developed in the *Phenomenology*.[3] These pieces of evidence give us reason to think that Hegel made some kind of adjustment to the way he conceived the task of the *Phenomenology*; but they provide no clear evidence for determining exactly what kind of adjustment this was.

3 McCumber (1993), 351 note 70. "Eigentümliche frühere Arbeit, nicht umarbeiten, – auf die damalige Zeit der Abfassung bezülich" (Editor's Note in *Phänomenologie des Geistes*, ed. Hoffmeister (1952), 578). See also Wolfgang Bonsiepen, "Einleitung," in *PhG*, L-LI.

Other questions arise if we consider several texts in which Hegel's later works explicitly discuss the task of the *Phenomenology*. These texts provide *prima facie* evidence that the Hegel of the later works thought of the *Phenomenology* as the introduction that justified the starting point of philosophy.

> In my *Phenomenology of Spirit*, which was for this reason described, when it was published, as the first part of the system of science, the procedure adopted was to begin from the first and simplest appearance of the spirit, from *immediate consciousness*, and to develop its dialectic right up to the standpoint of philosophical science, the necessity of which is shown by the progression. (*Enz* §25*A*)

> In the *Phenomenology of Spirit* I have presented consciousness as it progresses from the first immediate opposition of itself and the subject matter to absolute knowing. This path traverses all the forms of the *relation of consciousness to the object* and its result in *the concept of science*. There is no need, therefore, to justify this concept here (apart from the fact that it emerges within logic itself). It has already been justified in the other work, and indeed would not be capable of any other justification (*Rechtfertigung*) than is produced by consciousness as all its shapes dissolve into that concept as into their truth. (*WL* 21:32/M 48–9)

> We said in the Introduction that the *Phenomenology of Spirit* is the science of consciousness, its exposition; that consciousness has the *concept* of science, i.e. pure knowledge for its result. To this extent, logic has for its presupposition the science of spirit in its appearance, a science which contains the necessity, and therefore demonstrates the truth, of the standpoint which is pure knowledge and of its mediation. (*WL* 21:54–5/M 68–9)

These texts, from Hegel's later works, explicitly acknowledge that the standpoint of philosophy presupposes something, and that it depends on the *Phenomenology* for the "proof" or "justification" of this presupposition. If Hegel changed his mind about the role of the *Phenomenology* in his philosophical project, these texts show that this change did not set aside the *Phenomenology*'s role as a necessary introduction to philosophy. They also suggest a reason why he might change his mind about describing the *Phenomenology* as the first part of philosophy. The project that questions and proves what philosophy takes for granted must fall outside philosophy proper. In order to clarify the role that the *Phenomenology* plays in the philosophy articulated in Hegel's later works, therefore, one must look carefully at how Hegel defines the standpoint of philosophy and what it presupposes. This determines what the final result of the *Phenomenology* is supposed to be and provides a framework for discussing whether the work has or can achieve its purpose.

2

Interpretation Paradigms

THIS CHAPTER LOOKS AT FOUR MODELS for interpreting the relation between the *Phenomenology* and the *Logic*. It discusses briefly one or more representatives of each approach, in order to show how each interpretation might be articulated and supported. It also discusses the way the different paradigms implicitly challenge each other or the way other scholars have raised significant questions about them.

1 THE *PHENOMENOLOGY* BEGS THE QUESTION

The most negative interpretation of the *Phenomenology* dismisses the whole project because it cannot accomplish the task that Hegel assigned to it. According to Dieter Wandschneider, Hegel in the *Phenomenology* sets out to refute a whole series of positions that belong to the experience of consciousness, and this refutation supposedly justifies the move into the standpoint of logic. Wandschneider objects that the *Phenomenology* must use the fundamental principles of logic to refute the various positions that belong to the experience of consciousness. Hence, the legitimacy or truth of logic cannot depend on the demonstration developed in the *Phenomenology* because this demonstration presupposes the legitimacy of logic. The *Phenomenology* begs the question.

Logic, Wandschneider says, must get its justification from itself, not from the *Phenomenology*. Wandschneider acknowledges that Hegel himself develops no argument explaining how logic can accomplish this self-justification. Wandschneider himself supplies the argument. In order to make a case for denying the laws of logic, a position would have to use the laws of logic to prove the necessity of rejecting the laws of logic. A position denying the laws of logic contradicts itself, which proves that the denial is untenable.

If, however, denying the laws of logic is contradictory, then the opposite must be true. The laws of logic must be accepted as true.

Wandschneider asks whether what is necessary and unavoidable for thought can likewise be claimed for the actual, which exists outside thought. He answers that there is no way to deny the claim without appealing to what thought must accept as necessary. In order to demonstrate that the necessities of thought do not apply to actuality, a position must assume that what thought proves holds for actuality itself. Suppose that thought proves the following claim: the necessities of thought do not apply to the actual. If the necessities of thought do not apply to the actual, then the proof that they do not apply does not apply, and the necessities of thought do apply to the actual. Wandschneider concludes that logic proves itself to be absolutely and universally true, since no denial of its truth can be accepted as true; and this proof applies not only to thought but also to actuality.[1]

Wandschneider's claims show how the subtleties of the contradiction issue affect the way we go about discovering what Hegel's project is in the *Phenomenology*. Wandschneider interprets Hegel's whole position, including the *Phenomenology*, as dependent on the process of logical argumentation. According to this interpretation, the refutations developed in the *Phenomenology* use logical arguments to disprove various positions that belong to experience. In other words, these refutations apply logic to experience, and this proves their case against experience. The *Phenomenology*, therefore, cannot justify the standpoint of logic, since it uses logic to refute the forms of cognition that belong to experience. According to Wandschneider, logic justifies itself by proving that no claim can challenge it without falling into self-contradiction. The proof of logic is logic's own principle of contradiction.

2 THE *PHENOMENOLOGY* PROVES A NEGATIVE

Wandschneider's approach is only one way of interpreting the *Phenomenology* as an argument against false positions. Another approach claims that the *Phenomenology* argues against false positions by using their own principles against them. The *Phenomenology* shows how these positions collapse from within, and this clears away knowledge claims that challenge the philosophical standpoint. William Maker and Richard Winfield represent this interpretation.

1 Wandschneider (1985/86), 331–6.

Maker and Winfield begin with the structure of "consciousness," which is the kind of knowing examined in the *Phenomenology*. Consciousness takes the truth to be something other than knowing. Maker interprets this something other as "arbitrarily selected givens."[2] Both interpreters find in the basic structure of consciousness a certain presupposition about what knowing the truth requires; consciousness takes the truth to be the object in itself, the object as other. Consciousness knows the truth by overcoming the difference between itself and the other. It knows the other by becoming identified with it. Both interpreters take this to mean that consciousness cannot meet its own demands unless it knows the object as "identical in structure" with knowing itself (Winfield), as "nothing but its own structure of knowing" (Maker). According to Maker, knowledge cannot know what the object is in itself without reducing the object in itself to what the object is "for" consciousness.[3] But knowing the object as identical in structure with knowing itself collapses the otherness between knowing and known, which proves that knowledge in this form is not knowledge. The result is "complete indeterminacy." There is no knowing related to a known, no object giving definition to what the truth is. There is only the complete absence of all identifying determinations. According to Maker, this result proves "that it is a mistake to conclude that reason must be conditioned by any given factors." The *Phenomenology* demonstrates that the structure of consciousness itself is only "an arbitrary posit."[4] Maker interprets this as a positive result because it liberates thought to know in a different way. It shows that beginning without a presupposed given is possible.[5] Both he and Winfield insist, however, that there is no positive carryover from the *Phenomenology* to philosophy, no positive definition of truth derived from the final form of "consciousness."[6] Winfield puts it this way: "Since this result of the possible self-elimination of phenomenology has no distinction within it, it cannot refer back to any preceding ground or derivation. As such, it is really no result at all but a pure beginning taking nothing for granted."[7]

Stephen Houlgate provides another version of this interpretation. Houlgate agrees with the principal claims of the Maker-Winfield inter-

2 Maker (1994), 33.

3 Winfield (1989), 24; Maker (1994), 104, 129–31.

4 Maker (1994), 35–6.

5 Ibid., 92–3. See also Winfield (1989), 24–32.

6 Maker (1981), 381–97; (1982), 80–5; (1987), 286–90; (1990), 27–43, especially 38–9; (1992), 71–2; revised versions appear in (1994), see especially 30–7, 67–97, 100–6, 128–34. Winfield (1989), especially 16–32, 101–5. See also, Dove (1982), 28–9, 31–2.

7 Winfield (1989), 25.

pretation, which are: (1) that the beginning concept of philosophy is not deduced from or positively determined by the demonstration developed in the *Phenomenology*; (2) that the *Phenomenology* proves only the necessity of surrendering all presuppositions, all determinate claims about what thought or being are, and (3) that this collapses the distinction between knowing and what it knows, and hence philosophy begins without a knowledge structure of any kind. According to Houlgate, however, the *Phenomenology* ends with "a determinate conception of being as universal reason (*Begriff*) that marks the disappearance of the opposition between consciousness and its object."[8] The opposition between consciousness and its object belongs to the standpoint of consciousness; and by dissolving this fundamental distinction, consciousness demonstrates how the structure of consciousness as such negates itself. Philosophy begins, however, not with the negation played out in a form of consciousness, but with the abstract thought that positively asserts thought and being independent of all determinate conceptions of what they are. Houlgate claims that a thinker can get to this assertion in two different ways: by way of the *Phenomenology*, which demonstrates that the structure of consciousness as such collapses and thus calls for an act of abstraction that removes thought and being from all presuppositions about what they are; or a thinker can simply adopt a radical scepticism about all determinate conceptions of thought or being. Either way, philosophy begins with "the simple *unity* of thought and being – a unity that is initially no more than the indeterminate thought of sheer, immediate being."[9]

Both the Maker-Winfield interpretation of the phenomenological project and Houlgate's version of it reveal an ambiguity hidden away in Wandschneider's critique of the *Phenomenology*. Maker and Winfield argue that the kind of knowing examined in the *Phenomenology* wipes out its own claim to be a form of knowing. This exposes a contradiction in consciousness; "consciousness" both asserts itself as a form of knowing and negates itself as a form of knowing. This contradiction proves the necessity of rejecting the contradictory position. But this proof does not have to assume that the logical principle of contradiction, a principle of pure thought, determines what is true. It works by exposing a self-negating contradiction within experience or "consciousness" itself. The *Phenomenology* dismisses the claims of consciousness as untenable because consciousness negates itself as a form of knowing, not because consciousness violates the principles of logic. Houlgate's interpretation escapes completely the appeal to self-

8 Houlgate (2006), 162.

9 Ibid. For the whole discussion of these issues, see 144–50, 157–62.

defeating contradictory claims. Houlgate focuses on the way the final form of consciousness examined in the *Phenomenology* overcomes the otherness between consciousness and its object by finding its own rationality mirrored in what the object fundamentally is. Thus, the Maker-Winfield-Houlgate interpretation complicates the contradiction issue for Wandschneider. It shows how consciousness can negate its own claims without depending on the principles of logic.

Wandschneider, however, returns the favour. His interpretation complicates the issue for Maker, Winfield, and Houlgate. Wandschneider acknowledges the need to justify logic's reality claims, but denies that the *Phenomenology* provides the justification needed. So he substitutes one of his own. If it is impossible to deny that logic applies to the actual world, then its affirmation must be true. This strategy does not work, however, for Maker and Winfield. Even if the proof developed in the *Phenomenology* works as Maker and Winfield have interpreted it, the proof proves only a negative, that consciousness negates its own knowledge claims. It leaves undetermined the positive legitimacy of logic. According to Maker, the structure of consciousness is the structure of all knowledge based on presuppositions. This suggests that the *Phenomenology* proves the illegitimacy of presupposition-based knowledge as such, and therefore proves the possibility of a presuppositionless knowing. Wandschneider, however, assumes that logic begins as a study of logic, which means it has a definite subject matter that presumably plays a significant role in knowing what the truth is. The Maker-Winfield interpretation provides no way of proving this kind of positive truth claim. Indeed, it has no way of explaining why presuppositionlessness begins anything other than a thought experiment.

Houlgate's interpretation is more ambiguous. According to Houlgate, logic begins with what seems to be a positive claim. Thought thinks the unity of thought and being. Moreover, Houlgate acknowledges that this same unity of thought and being belongs to the concrete reality of absolute knowing, the form of consciousness in which the sameness of thought and being is revealed. If the move into the beginning of logic simply asserts the full meaning of absolute knowing, then the unity of thought and being has all the determinate meaning of the rationality exposed in the phenomenological examination of consciousness. Houlgate, however, denies this when he agrees with Maker that "the *Phenomenology* does not serve to deduce the concept of science by in any way predetermining or grounding the method, manner or nature of scientific cognition."[10] This seems to leave the unity of

10 Maker (1994), 72–3; Houlgate (2006), 162, note 24.

thought and being with no other meaning than being presuppositionless. How, then, can the unity of thought and being be anything other than the meaninglessness of presupposing nothing?

Franco Chiereghin recognizes this problem. Like Maker and Winfield, Chiereghin acknowledges that the *Phenomenology* brings consciousness to the beginning standpoint of philosophical science. He, too, identifies the beginning of the *Logic* without deriving any positive determination of its meaning from the *Phenomenology*. He, too, focuses on the constitution of the beginning as the collapse of all distinctions. Logic begins with a subject who simply decides to begin, and who thinks without being related to something else that it thinks. According to Chiereghin, however, this is an impossible beginning. The opening moves of Hegelian logic function as a failed attempt, a beginning that tries and fails to bring out of its thinking the thought of something positive and definite. The move into a definite, determinate meaning (*Dasein*) emerges from the rubble of a beginning that cannot begin. *Dasein* functions as a new beginning, a bastard first, determined not by what is implicit in the original beginning but by its failure.[11]

3 THE *PHENOMENOLOGY* AS HISTORICALLY CONDITIONED PEDAGOGY

The interpretations of the *Phenomenology* considered up to this point take the beginning of philosophical logic as their primary concern. They focus on what logic requires for the legitimacy of its truth claims. Interpreters who focus on the *Phenomenology* itself, however, define the issues differently. They see that the *Phenomenology* is about concrete experience. Hence, they conceive its task as one directed to a knower situated within experience. For these interpreters, the *Phenomenology* begins with what actually exists, the reality of experience, and it proceeds to show what this reality truly is. According to some, the primary task is pedagogical and historically conditioned. The *Phenomenology* teaches a knower situated within history to see that logic is fundamental to his or her own experience. If the *Phenomenology* reveals that this experience presupposes the structures and necessities of logic, this is not a problem. That is exactly what the *Phenomenology* is supposed to help us see. As examples of this interpretation, we will look at H.S. Harris and John McCumber.[12]

11 Chiereghin (2003). For explanations defending Hegel's claims for the opening moves of the *Logic*, see the following: Houlgate (2006), 263–83; Burbidge (1981), 37–42.

12 See also Pinkard (1990).

Hegel's Ladder, Harris's two-volume study of Hegel's *Phenomenology*, endorses both the titles that Hegel gave to this work. As a science of experience, Harris says, the *Phenomenology* situates us within the psychology of the singular self, the self's sense of its own consciousness, and exhibits therein "the conceptual structure of pure science."[13] As a phenomenology of spirit, the *Phenomenology* shows how an individual situated within his or her own experience and history belongs to the universal life of a spirit that encompasses all history and all selfhood. Thus, the *Phenomenology* demonstrates that the temporality of the singular self holds within itself eternity; and it conceives this eternity as the pure logic of philosophical science which is "the interpretation of its world by a rationally scientific community."[14] Harris intends to show that the *Phenomenology* is a continuous science in its own right, and that the logic developed in Hegel's philosophical system simply detaches this scientific, logical dimension from its embeddedness in concrete human experience.[15]

Harris explicitly uses this interpretation to challenge the Maker-Winfield claim that the *Phenomenology* accomplishes a purely negative task. According to the Maker-Winfield interpretation, the *Phenomenology* proves that knowledge in the form of "consciousness" is not knowledge; and this liberates the knower for a different kind of knowledge, knowledge as a completely self-determined science of logic. According to Harris, the domain of "consciousness," which is the domain of experience, is "the conceptual structure of pure science in a 'shaped' (or embodied) form."[16] The *Phenomenology* exposes the dynamics of logic at work in "consciousness" and thus shows the individual self that logic is the true spirit of the self's own situated experience. The *Science of Logic* articulates the same spirit detached from its embodiment in an individual's experience and historical context.

If, however, Harris's challenge to the Maker-Winfield interpretation is to succeed, it must provide a different interpretation of the way the *Phenomenology* makes its case. According to Maker-Winfield, the *Phenomenology* makes its case by convicting experience of a vicious, unproductive contradiction. It proves that knowledge in the form of "consciousness" or experience is not knowledge. This is contradiction in the form of an assertion that wipes out its own claims and thus clears the field for something completely different. According to Harris, however, the conflicts that move the

13 Harris (1997) I, 7.
14 Ibid., I, 131.
15 Ibid., I, xii–xiii, 8, 11, 14–16, 43, 110–14, 131.
16 Ibid., I, 8. See also I, 151 note 1.

Phenomenology through its various stages do not clear the field. Each one defines a new position by giving it a problem to solve: "A problem emerges in [the old framework] (and from it) for which it has no answer; and the new framework imposes itself as 'necessary' because it provides the answer – the best answer that is logically available and generally acceptable at that stage of cultural development."[17] Thus, the *Phenomenology* makes its way to the philosophical standpoint by showing how various problems that can be generated from experience reveal logical connections at work in it. The final conclusion does not set aside experience. It acknowledges what the *Phenomenology* has demonstrated, that experience is held together by a system of logical connections.

Harris acknowledges that the demonstration developed in the *Phenomenology* depends on a presupposition. The demonstration requires, he says, that we accept as "methodologically axiomatic" the "identity of the actual with the rational," which Harris interprets as "the cognitive process in which the 'object' is constituted."[18] If we accept this axiom, then knowledge as a phenomenon, i.e. knowledge as an existing reality, gives actual existence to the rational. By exposing the necessary development of this phenomenon, the *Phenomenology* takes us through the process whereby experience constitutes itself as rational. But then the *Phenomenology* begs the question. It proves that knowledge as an existing phenomenon is identical with truth by assuming this from the beginning. According to Harris's interpretation, the *Phenomenology* works out the full meaning of the axiom, but it does not justify the basic claim. Moreover, Harris assumes that knowledge as an existing reality is the current culture and its history, since this is the resource that provides the answers to the various problems exposed in the *Phenomenology*. This culture-specific dimension of Harris's interpretation has become a bone of contention in the literature devoted to the discussion of *Hegel's Ladder*.

Prior to the publication of *Hegel's Ladder*, Harris published *Hegel: Phenomenology and System*, which is a concise, summary statement of the general claims developed in *Hegel's Ladder*. In a review of this summary treatment, George di Giovanni focuses on a distinction Harris makes between time as such and the comprehension of one's own time. According to Harris in *Hegel: Phenomenology and System*, the *Phenomenology* shows us that the eternity of logic belongs to the conditions of any time, not just to a particular time.[19]

17 Ibid., I, 188.
18 Ibid., I, 183–5.
19 Harris (1994), ix, 99–100; di Giovanni (1997), 91–5.

In *Hegel's Ladder*, however, Harris says that the *Phenomenology* necessarily begins within the particular perspective of a particular time, the experience specific to Hegel's own time, which we resurrect by imaginative recollection. Harris's study of the *Phenomenology* shows how Hegel develops the full meaning of this experience, which involves conceiving time as comprehending a logic or spirit that is not time-bound.[20] If, however, the final concept develops the full meaning of a time-bound experience, why is the concept of a spirit that transcends time not limited to the way a particular historical context conceives itself? Why does it not show only that Western metaphysics must conceive itself in terms of an eternal logical spirit?

John Burbidge and Stephen Crites address the same issue by calling attention to Harris's preoccupation with sources. *Hegel's Ladder* identifies a formidable array of historical and literary materials that Hegel seems to be using as an essential element in his phenomenological examination of experience. According to Burbidge, *Hegel's Ladder* buries the *Phenomenology* in such an overwhelming display of Hegel's sources that Hegel's phenomenological project loses its immediate appeal to the reader's own experience. Without this immediate connection, the *Phenomenology* cannot do its job, since its task is to begin within the reader's own consciousness and show the reader how this leads to the *Phenomenology*'s final position. Harris says that the reader must recover, through memory and imagination, the cultural context that Hegel calls into play in the *Phenomenology*. Burbidge suggests that the *Phenomenology* needs a more immediate connection. To make its case, the *Phenomenology* needs the reality of my experience, not just the virtual reality of what I can imaginatively remember. How can a *Phenomenology* buried in the specifics of Hegel's own historical situation show the reader that the reader's own personal experience testifies to the truth of the *Phenomenology*'s final conclusion?[21]

Crites expresses the same criticism and expands it. Harris, he says, sets out "to demonstrate the logical coherence of the *Phenomenology*" by demonstrating "first, that every moment in the discourse follows necessarily and progressively from the preceding moment ... and secondly, that it does so not only logically but historically."[22] Crites claims that there is no evidence to prove Hegel's commitment to this strategy; and he points out how artificial and forced are Harris's attempts to find such logical/historical connections in the major transitions of the *Phenomenology*. According to Crites,

20 Harris (1994), 98–104. See also Harris (1997) I, 13–16.
21 Burbidge (2001–02).
22 Crites (2001–02).

the different chapters of the *Phenomenology* describe different areas of discourse. The project as a whole determines the role of each in relation to the others. It does not establish a linear progression from one to the other, nor was this ever Hegel's aim.[23] Moreover, because *Hegel's Ladder* identifies the linear progression with specific historical developments, it compromises the *Phenomenology*'s capacity to play a persistent, vital role in philosophical science. According to Crites, the *Phenomenology* must not only answer the needs of the historically-situated individual, who must use the *Phenomenology* as a "ladder" to the philosophical standpoint; it must also answer the needs of science itself which depends on the *Phenomenology* for a connection to the reality of concrete experience. If the *Phenomenology* describes an experience tied down to Hegel's historical context, it cannot connect philosophy to the living reality of an experience that has moved beyond this context.[24]

John McCumber provides an interpretation of the *Phenomenology* that acknowledges and works with this culture-specific issue. McCumber suggests that the Hegel of the later works dismissed the *Phenomenology* as outdated and no longer essential to Hegel's philosophy.[25] Yet McCumber himself develops an account of the phenomenological project. He interprets it as a pedagogical communication aimed at someone who resists it. From the perspective of one who resists, a challenge that attacks from without can be easily dismissed or ignored, because it looks so odd and alien. Successful communication must show that the need for a change is intrinsic to the resistant position itself. This depends on several conditions.

First, the communication must reveal problems generated from within the position. The *Phenomenology* accomplishes this by showing how the positions it sets out to change develop contradictions. Second, the communication must ask for a change in outlook that does no more than solve the problems generated from within the resistant position. A position resistant to change will adjust only to what it can see as a necessity that emerges from itself. Finally, both participants in the communication must have been acculturated by the same ethos. The communication succeeds by showing that the one who resists is really isolating his or her position from the larger context to which it belongs and within which it has its full meaning. McCumber suggests that this explains why Hegel dismissed the *Phenomenology* as "a peculiar early work," one belonging to an outdated set of conditions. Resistant positions belonging to a different set of conditions need a communication

23 Ibid., 97–105.

24 Crites (2002), 147–54.

25 McCumber (1993), 372 note 98.

adapted to their own acculturation. Thus, McCumber's position answers Burbidge's challenge by claiming that the *Phenomenology of Spirit* cannot provide an immediate connection with the current reader's experience. The current reader needs an updated phenomenological communication.

According to McCumber, phenomenology achieves its final result in absolute communication. In this position, the individual recognizes that "all possible standpoints to which she might come ... are not external to her but only various expressions of herself."[26] The individual loses her or his resistance to a new communication because the individual knows that a new standpoint can only reveal another dimension of her or his self.[27] If, however, phenomenological communication requires a cultural context shared by both participants, how does this carry the individual into a position of absolute communication, which opens up the individual to every possible standpoint? McCumber seems to provide an answer to this question in a different book, where he develops another account of Hegelian narrative. Here, McCumber says explicitly that Hegelian phenomenology depends on a condition.

Why, McCumber asks, does the recipient of the communication find self-contradiction intolerable? Why not dismiss the demand for consistency as the "hobgoblin of small minds"? Because contradiction puts the self at odds with itself, and this keeps the self from achieving its goal, the goal of self-consolidation. Phenomenology presupposes, therefore, the individual's commitment to the goal of self-consolidation. This, however, raises another question. What justifies this commitment to self-consolidation? McCumber answers for Hegel. The concept of self-consolidation sums up a long history of thought about freedom, and history shows that freedom is a good thing. Moreover, Hegelian philosophy appropriates all the intelligent critiques that have preceded it and rethinks them according to its own concept of self-consolidation. By doing this, it consolidates not only the individual but also the whole of culture. An individual situated within this historical context is necessarily committed to self-consolidation.[28] "All possible standpoints," therefore, seems to mean all those possible to an individual situated within this historical context. Why this should be accepted as absolute, however, remains unclear. Does not the tradition committed to

26 Ibid., 153.

27 Ibid., 151–4. McCumber says that this accounts for the difference between the *Phenomenology of Spirit* and the *Encyclopaedia* "Phenomenology." The "Phenomenology" of the *Encyclopaedia* communicates with an individual who has already reached absolute openness to all possible standpoints. Hence, the communication meets with no resistance (154).

28 McCumber (1989), 302–4.

self-consolidation leave out another quite plausible alternative suggested by McCumber himself? Why not consider the possibility of a commitment to self-diversification, or sum up the history of thought about freedom as a dynamic between self-consolidation and self-diversification, or consider the possibility that freedom as self-consolidation is not a good thing?

The culture issue complicates two other issues: the contradiction issue and the issue of presuppositions. Wandschneider, Maker, and Winfield interpret contradiction as the assertion and denial of the same claim, "P and not-P." They assume that the assertion of the claim wipes out the claim without remainder. The pedagogical approach challenges this. According to this interpretation, contradiction arises within experience as tensions and inconsistencies in the way an individual sees the world. This experience identifies a problem that sets parameters. By defining what is necessary for solving the problem, the contradiction yields a positive result. It determines what the new position must be. The problems emerge and are resolved, however, within a presupposed set of conditions. According to Harris, the *Phenomenology* presupposes the actual existence of experience and accepts as "methodologically axiomatic" the principle that the actual is rational and the rational actual. According to McCumber, phenomenology presupposes historical conditions whereby culture has become committed to self-consolidation. Neither Harris nor McCumber worry about this, since they see the *Phenomenology* as a project of bringing to consciousness the real truth about actually existing, historically conditioned experience.

Kenneth Westphal's response to *Hegel's Ladder* challenges Harris' interpretation by questioning the legitimacy and truth of this experience. The way knowing exists in history does not necessarily determine what true knowing is. Westphal describes *Hegel's Ladder* as a work that examines, fills out, probes, and analyzes the way the *Phenomenology* articulates and exhibits in experience a complex, intricate, organized conceptual structure. He commends Harris for producing a book that does this so well. Thus, he has no quarrel with the interpretation of the *Phenomenology* as a project that exposes the logic at the heart of experience, nor does he deny the need to identify Hegel's sources. But he asks for an analysis of how Hegel justifies his account of experience against others that might challenge its claims. What principles govern the proof structure? How does the proof avoid calling into play principles that are themselves in question?[29] Hegel insists that philosophical science must be "at once exoteric, comprehensible, and capable of being learned and appropriated by all" (*PhG* 15–16/M ¶13).

29 K.R. Westphal (1998b), (2000).

Harris takes care of this by showing how the claims of philosophical science belong to the "shared world-concept in the context of which we all think and communicate successfully."[30] Westphal's call for justification requires that this shared world-concept be proved, that its legitimacy be demonstrated, that evidence be presented to show why it necessarily commands the assent of every intelligence.

The pedagogical approach adds a new issue to the debate about what the *Phenomenology*'s project is. Does the *Phenomenology* depend on culture-specific experiences, specifically on experiences conditioned by Hegel's own historical situation? If so, how can the *Phenomenology* make its case to a reader who does not belong to this situation? If, however, we claim that the *Phenomenology* does not depend on Hegel's own situation, how do we explain the vast array of historical and literary references that one finds in the *Phenomenology*? Does the project need an updated phenomenology so that it can communicate with a current reader?

4 THE *PHENOMENOLOGY* AS EPISTEMOLOGY

Interpreters who focus on the Introduction to the *Phenomenology* find in Hegel's definition of the phenomenological project an astute appreciation of epistemological issues. How can any examination of knowledge, working as it must from within knowledge itself, judge whether or to what extent knowing is true? How can it avoid begging the question by presupposing the criterion according to which truth is determined? The epistemological interpretation is represented here by Hans-Friedrich Fulda, Kenneth Westphal, Robert Pippin and John McDowell, and Joseph Flay.[31]

30 Harris (1997) I, 43.

31 Forster (1998) acknowledges that the *Phenomenology* develops an epistemological justification of philosophical science, and that this justification belongs to the essential constitution of Hegelian science, not just to its historical situation. His analysis of dialectical implication, however, puts it more in the domain of the pedagogical interpretations. According to Forster, a form of consciousness develops a self-contradiction, which proves that it is untrue; and this justifies moving to a form of consciousness that holds the contradictory elements together without contradiction (compare to McCumber 1989, 302–4; Harris 1997, I, 188). Forster also interprets Hegel as endorsing a truth criterion based on *de facto* social agreement, which seems to make truth dependent on its situation within historical conditions (compare to McCumber 1989, 302–4). Finally, Forster, like Harris, claims that the moves in the *Phenomenology* from the very beginning in sense certainty are historical moves. All these issues have been articulated in the discussion of the pedagogical interpretation, and will be addressed in chapter 11 when this interpretation is reconsidered. For an argument directed explicitly to the specifics of Forster's book, see my review article (2003b).

4a The Phenomenology as a Systematic Introduction to Philosophical Science

Hans-Friedrich Fulda explains the role of the *Phenomenology* by distinguishing between a propaedeutic and a systematic introduction to philosophy. A propaedeutic functions as an educational project that teaches a subject how to enter the domain of philosophical discourse and think the truth as philosophy thinks it. It does not, however, address questions that challenge the truth claims of philosophy. According to Fulda, the introduction provided in the *Phenomenology of Spirit* is not just a propaedeutic. It demonstrates the necessary truth of philosophical thinking to a consciousness whose knowing does not attest to this truth. This demonstration is a necessity of science itself. Philosophical science asserts itself as truth. Science must prove its truth to the non-philosophical consciousness in order to prove its truth to itself, because it cannot know itself as truth unless it finds its truth appearing in its other.[32]

In a recent essay, Fulda acknowledges the significant advances in Hegel research that have developed over the past thirty-five years.[33] In order to address the questions posed by these developments, Fulda says, we need "precise formulations" of the program and procedure proposed for the *Phenomenology*, and these must be epistemological. Fulda limits his aim in the essay to providing "a corrective." He begins, therefore, by listing approaches that cannot be "the more adequate approach" needed.[34] It cannot be focused on the either/or of contemporary epistemology, i.e. either epistemological idealism or epistemological realism. Hegel can contribute to this discussion, but his own program cannot be adequately defined in terms of it. Nor can the program be focused primarily on theoretical knowledge, since the practical is equally important. It cannot focus exclusively on knowledge of objects. It must leave open the possibility that something might be real and yet not be an object that belongs to the world or to nature, that it might be something "world-transcendent" and "supernatural," or not. Finally, the program must leave open the question whether metaphysics in some form is or is not possible.[35]

Fulda supports this sweeping rejection of more specific, focused ways of defining the phenomenological program by calling attention to the minimalist way Hegel describes the program in the Introduction to the

32 Fulda (1965), 79–84.
33 Fulda (2008), 21–3.
34 Ibid., 23.
35 Ibid., 23–5.

Phenomenology: "Hegel, right at the beginning of the 'Introduction,' writes only in a very indefinite way about an 'actual cognition of what truly is'" (*PhG* 53/M ¶73).[36] According to this same text, the program proposed for the *Phenomenology* examines knowledge only as appearing, and even philosophical science is reduced to this status. The philosophical "we" that goes through the *Phenomenology* as a detached observer is itself only a consciousness that comes on the scene, happens, appears, and its role in the program is minimal. The observer consciousness must not interfere with the way the knowledge examined defines what it takes the truth to be, or with the way this form of knowing tests itself in an experience governed by this truth criterion. The moves to a new form of knowing must not go beyond what is contained in the experience that precedes it. The detached observer contributes nothing but its consciousness of the way a prior experience necessitates the form of knowing that follows it. As the observer consciousness moves through this connected development, however, it gradually develops a knowledge of the way the various forms of cognition, in virtue of their own internal principles and experience, necessarily connect themselves into a whole.[37]

This minimalist approach and uncompromising strict connectedness and continuity serve the primary and "most urgent" task assigned to the *Phenomenology*, which is "to understand how an epistemology of philosophical cognition gradually develops."[38] The *Phenomenology* must demonstrate how the self-knowledge of the human spirit, engaged in the experience of knowledge as it happens, is itself the development of philosophical knowledge. It must carry a consciousness embedded in the various forms of knowing as it appears into a decisive insight whereby it passes over "without alternative" from itself as knowledge appearing to philosophical science as actual knowledge.[39]

In his earlier book, Fulda provides a brief analysis of this "passing over." In its appearance, knowing involves an opposition between subject and object. In the absolute, this opposition is sublated, but not in a way that makes the opposition disappear. If there is no opposition between subject and object, knowledge as an appearance disappears. Fulda insists, however, that the move into the absolute does not destroy or do away with knowledge as an appearance. Rather this move into the absolute forms the opposites

36 Ibid., 25.
37 Ibid., 26–33.
38 Ibid., 25.
39 Ibid., 30.

into an identity within which the opposition is preserved.[40] Knowledge as an appearance passes over to philosophical knowledge as the true essence of this appearance, i.e. as that which appears in it. Fulda has doubts about whether the *Phenomenology* achieves its aim.[41] He insists, however, that the program aims at the passing over from appearing to actual knowledge at least as a possibility. The possibility that the aim might not be achieved or even achievable belongs to the openness of the program. Like its alternative, this outcome cannot be assumed; it must be proved.[42]

Stephen Houlgate, however, interprets the task of the *Phenomenology* in a way that challenges Fulda's claims. Houlgate represents the *Phenomenology* as a propaedeutic needed only by a consciousness incapable of surrendering all its presuppositions. All that is really necessary to begin philosophy is the resolve to consider thought as such with no presuppositions. The *Phenomenology* demonstrates to those incapable of this resolve that surrendering their presuppositions is a necessity implicit in their own ways of knowing.[43] Thus, Houlgate sticks to the negative aspect of the phenomenological program. It proves only the necessity of setting aside, surrendering, the presupposed truth criteria in the various forms of knowledge examined in the *Phenomenology*. Fulda insists on a positive as well as a negative dimension. According to his interpretation, the *Phenomenology* proves that the various forms of knowledge it examines are not what knowledge truly is, but belong to this truth as its appearance in experience.

4b The Scepticism Dilemma

Kenneth Westphal argues for a connection between the way Hegel defines epistemological questions and the way they are defined in the dilemma formulated by Sextus Empiricus.[44] Westphal analyzes Sextus's dilemma into four points. (1) The dilemma arises because there is a dispute about which criteria determine the legitimacy of knowledge claims. (2) First-order claims make claims about the way the world is. These claims, since they are subject to dispute, need a warrant or justification. (3) Second-order claims make claims about what knowledge is and the principles according

40 Fulda (1965), 88.

41 See Fulda (2008), 37–42.

42 Fulda (2008), 30.

43 Houlgate (2006), 144–50, 157–62.

44 K.R. Westphal claims that Hegel actually has Sextus Empiricus in mind, not just that Sextus helps us understand the epistemological importance of Hegel's project in the *Phenomenology* (Westphal 2000, 156–60).

to which it is distinguished from error. These claims provide the principles for judging the legitimacy of first-order claims. We justify what we claim about the world by appealing to a criterion that defines what establishes the legitimacy of knowing, e.g. the necessities of reason, or the evidence of sense experience, or coherence, or adequacy, etc. These second-order claims, however, also need a warrant or justification, since they are also subject to dispute. (4) Third-order claims make claims about what warrants or justifies second-order claims. Sextus's dilemma arises at the level of second-order knowledge. First-order claims can be settled by an appeal to second-order principles. But how do we prove the legitimacy of the second-order principles themselves? Either we dogmatically assume a criterion that determines what counts as real knowing, or we appeal to another criterion that determines the legitimacy of the criterion in question, and so on *ad infinitum.*

Westphal claims that Hegel, like Sextus, addresses the issue at the level of second-order claims, claims about what constitutes knowledge and the principles according to which the legitimacy of knowledge is measured. Hegel solves Sextus's dilemma by proposing an examination of knowledge in which the examiner remains neutral about criteria, allowing second-order claims to test their own presupposed principles. Westphal distinguishes, however, between two different ways in which this testing might be done. The testing might simply look at whether a theory of knowledge is self-consistent. If it is not, then it refutes its own claims. This kind of test, however, does not answer all the questions that need to be addressed. Even if a theory of knowledge is self-consistent, we can still ask whether it is true. Moreover, if two self-consistent positions stand opposed to each other, self-consistency will not determine which is true; self-consistency will not settle disputes among epistemologists. Westphal interprets Hegel as solving this problem by proposing a kind of test that does more than prove theoretical consistency. It tests a knowledge theory by the way it actually exists in real experience.[45]

According to Westphal, the *Phenomenology*, in order to have a problem for discussion at all , must take as given at least some *prima facie* capacity for knowing and for reflecting on what we know. The phenomenological project must assume that some kind of knowing goes on in us and that we have a terminology for articulating what this knowing is. Hegel avoids question-begging by finding in this *prima facie* knowing the capacity for self-criticism. Cognition carries with it a criterion, a set of second-order claims, according

45 Westphal (1998a), 76–85. See also, (1989a), chapter 6.

to which the truth of its knowing can be assessed. The intellectual tradition provides a whole array of alternative positions with different *prima facie* abilities, terminologies, and second-order claims. The *Phenomenology* examines the way these "forms of consciousness" measure up to their own internal expectations. But it keeps its distance, takes the position of an observer, remaining neutral regarding the second-order claims presupposed by the form of consciousness being examined.[46]

Each form of consciousness carries with it two kinds of second-order claims: claims that define what consciousness expects its object to be, and claims about what consciousness expects its own relation to the object to be. The *Phenomenology* examines what happens when a form of consciousness applies its expectations to the world and its own knowledge of the world. The expectations will certainly influence the way consciousness knows its object. But what the object and the knowing really are, apart from what consciousness expects them to be, has an impact on the experience. Hence, the examination can, and indeed does, bring to consciousness elements other than those that meet expectations. Westphal calls these "consciousness' mistakings." He distinguishes between two kinds of mistakings: aspects or features of the object that consciousness of the object includes, but not as a significant element in what consciousness expects the object to be; aspects or features of the object closely related to what consciousness expects the object to be, but not included in its consciousness of the object. The test consists in comparing expectations to results with regard to the object, with regard to knowledge, and with regard to the relation between object results and knowledge results. This brings to consciousness information about the world or about knowledge that provides a basis for revising the conceptions that determine what consciousness expects knowledge and the world to be.[47]

Westphal interprets the dialectical movement of the *Phenomenology* as a series of such tests. In a general analysis of Hegel's dialectic, he provides an analysis of dialectical procedure, and explicitly mentions the *Phenomenology* as an example. Dialectic begins with the simplest principle covering a whole domain of inquiry. It examines the relation between this principle and examples in its domain. This reveals the limits or inadequacy of the original conception. The conception does not cover the whole domain. It does not account for phenomena that its application to the domain of inquiry calls into play. This result justifies the shift to a more adequate conception.

46 Westphal (1989a), 91–2, 95–9, 130–1, 137.
47 Westphal (1998a), 85–94. See also, (1989a), chapters 7–9.

The new conception preserves the original conception within the limited domain revealed by the examination, and it also accounts for the features activated by the original conception but not captured by it. The new conception becomes the object of a new dialectical examination.[48]

Westphal provides a more precise analysis of these moves when he describes the *Phenomenology* as a "methodological scepticism." This form of scepticism commits itself to the view it seeks to criticize, rigorously applies its principles to the objects that belong to the domain identified by these principles, and thereby exposes both its positive features and its defects. This result provides a resource for designing a new form of consciousness. The new form "does not follow deductively from its predecessors." Rather, it emerges as "the best, simplest and most adequate set of principles for explaining both the successes and failures of the preceding form of consciousness and for systematizing the information about knowledge and its objects that it elicited."[49]

Westphal's study of the *Phenomenology* shows how the major parts of the book form "a sustained, complex argument for socio-historically grounded epistemological realism."[50] The argument takes the form of indirect proof. It attacks a view opposed to Hegel's own, usually one represented by a specific philosophical opponent, and uses the strategy of methodological scepticism to expose its strengths and defects. The argument then shifts to another view, usually represented by another philosopher's position.[51] According to the strategy of methodological scepticism, a particular position is selected for a specific place in the argument because it provides the best set of principles for integrating the various elements revealed in the test of the preceding position. Westphal provides an outline and a chart showing the layout of different opposing positions associated with specific parts of Hegel's book.[52] He represents the opening set of moves as an examination of "what is required to be conscious of objects."[53] Granting his analysis of dialectical procedure, we can assume that this question is supposed to identify the simplest principle defining the *Phenomenology*'s domain of inquiry, which is the domain of consciousness. The opponent

48 Westphal (1992).
49 Westphal (1989a), 134–5. See also 127.
50 Ibid., 154.
51 Ibid.
52 Ibid., 154–88. See also Westphal (2009b), 24–6, 28–9.
53 Westphal (1989a), 158.

view selected for representing this principle is naïve realism, also referred to as non-conceptual knowledge and concept empiricism.[54]

Westphal claims that Hegel's project depends on completeness. Hegel must prove that his examination of knowledge in the *Phenomenology* defeats all alternative claims about what knowledge is. In order to meet this requirement, the *Phenomenology* would have to cover the full capacity of the human spirit to reflect on its own knowing. Westphal has doubts about whether Hegel can claim this. Of course, Hegel has not considered every theory of knowledge that is logically possible. But he does not have to do that, since the real issue is not what is logically possible, but what is realistically possible, i.e. what is applicable to real experience. Westphal suggests, however, that there might be forms of consciousness not examined in the *Phenomenology* whose claims would carry a certain plausibility for real experience. The question remains, therefore, whether we can reconstruct Hegel's project to meet the challenge of such claims. Thus, Westphal's interpretation of Hegel's phenomenological project leaves it open-ended. Hegelian phenomenology must be prepared to deal with alternative accounts of knowledge that the *Phenomenology of Spirit* has not examined.[55]

As we have seen, Fulda rejects the kind of approach to the *Phenomenology* that Westphal takes. Westphal focuses on the way in which the *Phenomenology* supports the case for epistemological realism. Fulda acknowledges that the *Phenomenology* can make a contribution to this discussion, and indeed cites Westphal as having done just that.[56] Westphal himself acknowledges that his epistemological interpretation of the *Phenomenology* does not represent all the concerns addressed in this book. His only aim, he says, is to show that there is an epistemological argument developed in the *Phenomenology*.[57] He acknowledges, too, that he is trying to "reintegrate Hegel's theory of knowledge into main stream epistemology."[58] He defines the questions posed by epistemology thus: "Is there a way the world is regardless of how we think about it? If so, can we know the way the world is? Is knowledge a socio-historical phenomenon?"[59] Fulda seeks what he considers a more adequate view of the *Phenomenology*'s program and says that it, too, must be epistemological. He insists, however, that we must raise questions about exactly what

54 Westphal (1989a), 158; (1992), 98–9; (2009b), 6.
55 Westphal (1998a), 94–5.
56 Fulda (2008), 23 note 10.
57 Westphal (1989a), 154.
58 Ibid., ix.
59 Ibid., 1.

kind of epistemological question Hegel is asking.[60] He suggests that Hegel's program is minimalist in the beginning, leaving all kinds of questions open, undetermined, not even defined as questions. We do not begin by asking about "the way the world is regardless of how we think about it," because the question assumes that knowledge and reality are primarily about what the world is. Fulda's minimalist interpretation of the phenomenological program requires a beginning that leaves open the possibility that "what truly is" might not be objects in the world or even the world itself.[61]

There is also a subtle difference between the way Fulda and Westphal interpret dialectical moves. According to Westphal, the philosophical observer selects the simplest, most adequate set of principles capable of explaining and systematizing all the elements that have appeared in the test of the preceding view.[62] According to Fulda, the new view must contain nothing more than the experience of the preceding form.[63] If he is strict about this "nothing more," and his minimalism seems to require this, then the observer consciousness cannot interfere by contributing something of its own to the way the epistemology of cognition develops. The systematizing and integrity of the new form must belong to the preceding experience. The elements of the experience must connect themselves to each other, and integrate themselves into the set of principles that follows. The detached philosophical observer simply observes and recognizes the systematic integration that belongs to the preceding experience itself. This, of course, raises the question whether the consciousness engaged in the experience becomes conscious of the shift required by its own principles, and if not why not.

4c Completing Kant's Transcendental Deduction

Robert Pippin, in *Hegel's Idealism: The Satisfactions of Self-Consciousness*, defines the epistemological concerns of the *Phenomenology* in terms of Kant's transcendental deduction of the categories. John McDowell, influenced by Pippin's work on Hegel, develops another version of a Kantian approach to Hegel's thought. According to both Pippin and McDowell, idealism fails if it is subjective, i.e. if it represents knowing as a subject imposing its own conditions on an object with a different set of conditions. Both agree that

60 Fulda (2008), 23.
61 Ibid., 25.
62 Westphal (1989a), 135.
63 Fulda (2008), 31.

Kant's idealism fails because the unity of apperception does not determine all the conditions required for objectivity, since it does not determine the conditions required for an object to stand before consciousness in an intuition.[64]

Pippin begins by identifying the basic structure of Kant's transcendental deduction. According to Kant, experience cannot be the experience of an object unless a thinking subject has a conceptual scheme, a set of rules, according to which the subject can distinguish objects from the subject's subjective states of consciousness, and can discriminate among objects. Since these concepts are a pre-condition that makes experience of an object possible, they cannot be derived from or revisable by experience.[65] Pippin emphasizes the spontaneity involved in this. The experience of objects depends on thought's active engagement in unifying a given manifold according to thought's own conceptual scheme, and this means that all experience of objects belongs to the self-consciousness of thought.[66]

64 Pippin (1989), 8–9, 18–31. McDowell (2009), 72–9. McDowell acknowledges the limits of his approach. He says explicitly that Hegel does not begin with Kant, and that the transcendental element in Kant's critical philosophy cannot cope with the requirements of Hegel's idealism. McDowell claims only that approaching Hegel's idealism by way of Kant's concerns is at least one good way to develop an appreciation of Hegel's thought (McDowell 2009, 69, 81–2, 89). Pippin, however, seems to think that Hegel's concern with Kant's transcendental unity of apperception functions as the dominant concern in Hegel's idealism. He defends this approach by quoting the following text from Hegel's *Science of Logic*: "It is one of the profoundest and truest insights to be found in the Critique of Reason that the unity which constitutes the essence of the concept is recognized as the original synthetic unity of apperception, the unity of the 'I think,' or of self-consciousness" (*WL* 12:17–18). This quote belongs to the text that introduces the third and final section of the *Logic*. According to Pippin, this section provides "Hegel's most comprehensive statement of his own position," and Hegel structures the whole discussion that introduces it "by constant reference to, and often reliance on, Kant" (Pippin 1989, 17; see also 176, and 2011, 10). Pippin provides added evidence of Hegel's dominant concern with Kant's transcendental deduction in a chapter on two of Hegel's early writings: *The Difference Between Fichte's and Schelling's System of Philosophy* and *Glauben und Wissen* (*Faith and Knowledge*). This chapter explains how Johann Gottlieb Fichte and Friedrich Wilhelm Joseph Schelling develop and transform the transcendental deduction issue, and how Hegel's concern with the issue shows the influence of these developments without ever losing its focus on Kant's original insight (1989, chapter 4). Pippin acknowledges, however, that these Jena writings alone cannot provide an adequate understanding of the way Hegel finally transforms Kant's idealism into Hegel's own absolute idealism. For this, we must look to the *Phenomenology* and the *Science of Logic* (1989, 78–9). For an excellent in-depth study that examines the developments of Kant's thought in the period between Kant and Hegel, see di Giovanni (2005). See also Nuzzo (1994a, b).

65 Pippin (1989), 7–8; (2011), 7.

66 Ibid., 21.

According to Pippin, however, in order to claim objective validity for these concepts, Kant must provide a way of determining which logically possible pure concepts count as necessary conditions of objects, and this not only as necessary conditions of thinking an object, but even of there being any experience of objects at all.[67] According to Pippin's interpretation, Hegel's idealism appropriates Kant's fundamental insight. It focuses on the way Kant ties the necessary conditions of experience to a unity of self-consciousness that is completely independent of experience, so that the very possibility of knowledge itself is "relativised to" the requirements of such a subject.[68] Hegel must show, therefore, that the thinking subject's relation to an object depends on a general concept of what an object is, and that this implies a pure, empirically undetermined self-consciousness that takes the object to be such. In order to address the problem that Kant left unsolved, however, Hegel must show that the inadequacy of this conceptually formed self-consciousness can be exposed by simply describing the experience formed by this way of conceiving an object. This is the task of the *Phenomenology*.[69]

Pippin supports this interpretation of the *Phenomenology* with a Kantian interpretation of three key texts in the Introduction. In one text, Hegel says that consciousness of an object involves a twofold consciousness: consciousness of what consciousness takes the truth to be, and consciousness of the way that truth is known (*PhG* 59/M ¶85). Pippin finds in this statement something similar to the Kantian distinction between consciousness of the object and consciousness conscious of itself judging what the object is. He finds the same judgment structure in two other texts: the one in which Hegel says that consciousness is for itself its own concept and therefore "goes beyond itself" (*PhG* 57/M ¶80), and the one that describes consciousness as "relating itself to something from which it also distinguishes itself" (*PhG* 58–9/M ¶82). According to Pippin, consciousness relates itself to something by actively engaging itself in judging what the object is. Consciousness distinguishes itself from this something by judging it according to a criterion that belongs to what consciousness expects the object to be, an expectation that the object may or may not meet.[70] In later writings, Pippin explains how Hegel's version of an *a priori* self-consciousness can be revisable and yet not empirically determined. By being conscious of the way

67 Ibid., 8–9, 18–31.
68 Ibid., 31–9.
69 Ibid., 98–101.
70 Ibid., 102–15.

it pre-conceives what an object is, self-consciousness holds itself open to the possibility that its way of conceiving an object may not be what an object truly is. In other words, the concept is provisional, and its provisional status belongs to the very constitution of this self-consciousness. The validity of the concept depends on whether a self-consciousness committed to this way of conceiving objectivity can actually succeed in knowing an object that meets its requirements.[71]

Pippin interprets the task and strategy of the *Phenomenology* as an epistemological proof of the negative. Hegel begins with the opposite of the position he endorses. He begins with forms of consciousness committed to "realist" claims, which define knowledge as knowing what being is in itself, independent of all conditions that belong to the knowing subject. Then he demonstrates that this kind of presumption produces "inversions, paradoxes, and contradictions."[72] According to Pippin, this result proves that the minimum required for any experience at all, namely something definite or determinate to think, is impossible for a consciousness committed to "realist" interpretations of knowledge. Since the object cannot constitute itself as what satisfies the subject's need for something determinate to think, the subject must acknowledge that the constitution required comes from the subject.[73]

Even when this has been established, however, more is required. The *Phenomenology* must go through a whole host of mistaken ways in which the knowing subject actively structures the object according to the subject's own self-determined concepts, until it finds the one and only concept that finally satisfies the requirements of objectivity. This last Hegel calls absolute knowledge. The term "absolute knowledge" refers to "the conditions of human knowledge 'absolutized,' no longer threatened by Kant's thing-in-itself scepticism."[74] Hegel avoids the thing-in-itself issue by claiming that the necessary conditions of our experience are the necessary conditions "for the intelligible experience of any object."[75] These conditions identify "all that being can intelligibly be," which "counts as the knowledge of the thing-in-itself that Kant paradoxically denied."[76] This explains why Hegel's idealism transforms Kant's conception of a thinking subject from a subject related to empirical content given in sense intuition to self-conscious thought

71 Pippin (2011), 19, 25–6, 28, 38–9, 52–3, 55–61. See also Pippin (2005), 384–5, 398.
72 Pippin (1989), 167.
73 Ibid., 131–42, 146.
74 Ibid., 168.
75 Ibid., 39.
76 Ibid., 98. See also 83.

determining itself. Thought derives from itself, from its own independent, non-empirical concepts, "all that being can intelligibly be."[77] According to Pippin, Hegel assumes at the beginning of the *Logic* that the *Phenomenology* has already justified the claim that there must be a self-consciousness capable of autonomously determining possible objects.

At the end of *Hegel's Idealism,* Pippin identifies two problems that remain unresolved in Hegel's idealism. First, how do we explain the relation between thought determining itself and the host of empirical concepts that seem to be derived from the way the world is? Second, Hegel "stresses the 'identity' side of his own dialectical formula, and seems insensitive to what the 'difference' side ought to open up."[78] In other words, how do the self-determinations of pure thought govern investigations into the contingent details of the empirical world?[79]

John McDowell begins his version of the Kantian approach to Hegel by appropriating Pippin's analysis of the issues. McDowell points out, however, that Pippin does not explicitly address the space-time character of intuition. If space-time ordering persists as an *a priori* condition for relating objects to our subjectivity, then it counts as a condition of objects themselves only if we interpret objects themselves as objects given in our experience. Moreover, even if the free subjectivity of thought determines the possibility of bringing before consciousness something determinate to think, it does so by giving form to a content that is not determined by this free subjectivity. According to McDowell, idealism cannot avoid being a subjective idealism unless the free subjectivity of self-consciousness determines everything required for the knowledge of objects, and this means it must encompass everything that the object itself is, including its space-time ordering and empirical content.[80]

In a note, McDowell provides a helpful set of distinctions for clarifying the subtleties involved in his disagreement with Pippin. Transcendental idealism interprets the relation between subjectivity and objectivity as a subject-dominated relation. Subjectivity stands firm in its own autonomy. The conditions that belong to this autonomy determine the whole relation, and the conditions of objectivity are completely determined by the autonomous subject. Realism interprets the relation between subjectivity and objectivity

77 Ibid., 98–101, 108, 166–71. Pippin does not endorse Hegel's claim that the proofs developed in the *Phenomenology* prove necessity. He argues only for their plausibility (see 108).

78 Ibid., 259.

79 Ibid., 258–9.

80 McDowell (2009), 79–85.

as a relation dominated by the independent conditions of the object, with the subjectivity of the thinking subject completely defined by its relations to these conditions. Hegel's alternative, as McDowell interprets it, represents the relation between subjectivity and objectivity as one in which the conditions of both subjectivity and objectivity inseparably determine the necessary conditions of thought and the necessary conditions of the object, without either having priority over the other. This is what McDowell means when he describes Hegel's position as seeking equipoise between subject and object. According to this set of distinctions, Pippin's interpretation of Hegelian idealism is a transcendental idealism, because an autonomous thinking subject imposes the conditions of its experience on the object, and thereby reduces the conditions of objectivity to the conditions of the subject.[81]

McDowell offers a suggestion for how his interpretation of Hegelian idealism might handle the problems posed by Kant's transcendental deduction. If we conceive the space-time ordering of our experience not as the *de facto* character of our subjectivity but as "the independent layout of the world we experience," we could conceive space-time as a medium in which a free self-consciousness exercises its freedom and determines the objectivity of the experienced world. This conception would bring the domain of empirical research into the domain of free self-consciousness, since the self must learn from the experienced world the laws of the world's independent layout in order to act on the self's own freedom within this medium. Pippin's questions about how to fit empirical concepts into the free self-determination of self-consciousness would not arise. They arise for Pippin because he holds on to Kant's way of conceiving the freedom of self-consciousness, namely as a set of categories not derived from, or revisable by, experience.[82]

According to K. Westphal, Pippin's interpretation of Hegel's idealism involves a key assumption, namely that a condition required for an object to be an object of self-conscious experience must have its origin in the activity

81 Ibid., 80, note 5. McDowell is adapting for his own purposes a distinction made by Henry Allison between "conditions of the possibility of knowledge of things" and "conditions of the possibility of things themselves" (See Allison 1983, 13).

82 McDowell (2009), 85–8. McDowell acknowledges that the way this suggestion integrates empirical enquiry into the free self-determination of self-consciousness does not apply to the *Phenomenology*. According to McDowell, the *Phenomenology* examines different ways of conceiving "mindedness" in order to reveal to consciousness what its ordinary intellectual activity truly is, namely the free movement of the concept. Once this lesson has been learned, the development of thought can conceive the independent layout of the experienced world as the medium within which free self-consciousness exercises its self-determination.

of a knowing subject. Westphal challenges this assumption. It does not automatically follow that necessary conditions, just because they are necessary, must be produced in experience by the thinking activity of the knower. These conditions may be met by a structure that belongs to the world.[83] Westphal interprets McDowell's approach to Hegel as a realism similar to his own. This is not naïve realism, which takes the subject-object relation to be completely dominated by the object. It is rather what Westphal calls mental content externalism, which argues for distinct but interconnected roles for space-time ordering and the particular content elements of sense experience, for general concepts and the determinate elements of sense consciousness.[84]

The way that Fulda's minimalist approach challenges Westphal's approach applies in the same way to Pippin and McDowell. Fulda questions the tendency to let contemporary epistemology count as the whole domain of epistemological issues. The same question challenges the strategy that reduces epistemology to Kant's way of defining knowledge issues. For example, Pippin's interpretation of key texts in the Introduction to the *Phenomenology* takes for granted that when Hegel talks about consciousness conscious of what it takes the truth to be, he is talking about consciousness applying concepts in judgments. Fulda's minimalist approach requires that our interpretation of the phenomenological program preserve the open-ended, undetermined form of Hegel's text. What consciousness takes the truth to be belongs to the relation between consciousness and its object, and the project developed in the *Phenomenology* questions not only what consciousness takes the object to be but also what consciousness takes its relation to the object to be. Each form of knowing will have its own take on this relation; and according to Fulda's minimalist interpretation, everything assumed about this relation must emerge in the strict connectedness, continuity, and internally determined procedure of the phenomenological program. At the beginning of the program, therefore, Kant's way of defining the constitution of consciousness has no more authority than Aristotle's metaphysics, or Spinoza's ontology, or any other theory of knowledge.

Stephen Houlgate represents the case for ontology. He questions the way Pippin's Kantian approach compromises the reality status of logic. According to Houlgate, Pippin's interpretation transforms the being issue into "an object of thought" issue. It sets aside the ontological concern with being or reality *tout court* as a misconceived project that assumes a reality or being

83 K.R. Westphal (1999), 310–11. See also Westphal (1993).
84 Westphal (2006), 274–5, 286–90.

outside thought. Hegel supposedly replaces ontological concerns with a transcendental project that reduces all being questions to being-intelligible-to-thought questions, since being qualified in this way is all that being could "intelligibly" be.[85]

Houlgate's interpretation of the *Phenomenology* argues for a Hegelian idealism that can identify thought and being, and overcome the otherness of a reality out there, without reducing the possibilities of being to the possibilities of human self-consciousness.

> Hegel's analysis in the *Phenomenology* shows that, at all levels of consciousness prior to absolute knowing, consciousness remains in relation to something it regards as to some extent other than itself, be that something nature, other people, or God. However, the thinking which finally emerges in this process of transformation is one which knows that the ultimate truth or nature of things, which it had regarded as other than itself, is in fact identical with, constitutive of, and so to be found in and as, the true form of thought itself. But it also knows that it has to be released to this truth ... by relinquishing the self it has always regarded as its "own," and by gaining a new sense of selfhood in the truth it previously regarded as its "object" or "other" ... All of this perhaps sounds rather mystical; but all Hegel is trying to do is make sense of the relation between human thought and the rational structure of being – the rationality that informs and structures both nature and human thinking and is in that sense "absolute."[86]

According to Houlgate, human thought becomes a self-consciousness identified with being if and only if it surrenders the kind of claims that Pippin makes for it. Human thought knows its own identity with being by knowing itself as a participant in a rationality that is not limited to itself and does not originate in itself. The *Phenomenology* demonstrates that human thought belongs to a *logos* or rationality that it has in common with the otherness of nature.

The precise point of disagreement between Houlgate and Pippin, therefore, concerns which is primary, the rationality of human self-consciousness or the rationality of being. Does the rationality of being belong to and have its ground in the self-determinations of human thought; or does the rationality of human thought belong to and have its ground in the self-determinations of being? Thus, Houlgate says: "The only self that can know absolutely, in Hegel's view, is one that has allowed itself and its thinking to be determined – and so in a sense displaced and constituted anew – by whatever

85 Houlgate (2006), 137–43.
86 Houlgate (1994), 10.

the truth of reason or being determines itself to be … Absolute knowing is a thinking which coincides with its 'object,' not because it has absorbed its object into itself or taken its object up into thought, but because it has relinquished any distinct identity or selfhood of its own into which it could conceivably absorb another, and has allowed itself to be determined by its 'object,' the truth."[87]

4d Testing the Presuppositions of Everyday Life

Joseph Flay, in *Hegel's Quest for Certainty*, begins as K. Westphal does, with the problem of disputed truth claims. He, too, asks how knowledge can prove that its claims are true without appealing to a truth criterion whose legitimacy must be presupposed. He, too, focuses on Hegel's strategy of internal critique, whereby different forms of knowledge are examined according to their own presupposed truth criteria. Flay, however, gives a different account of how the *Phenomenology* begins and what it must presuppose from the outset. Every work, he says, must presuppose some problem that sets the agenda for the discussion to follow. Otherwise the work would have no focus, no direction. He contends that the case is compromised only if the solution to the problem determines *a priori* the shape of the argument, not if the definition of the problem shapes it. The *Phenomenology* begins, therefore, with a problem to solve. The definition of the problem, but not its solution, functions as a presupposition for the whole project. The *Phenomenology* gets its problem from an encounter between the philosophical tradition and "the natural attitude of ordinary, non-reflective consciousness."[88]

By the natural attitude, Flay means the kind of consciousness involved in coping with the world, going about our everyday tasks. By the philosophical tradition, he means the tradition of thoughtful reflection aimed at knowing the "ultimate truth about ultimate reality." From the beginning right up to Hegel's own time, philosophy pursued its aim as a task removed from the concerns of everyday life. Everyday life focused on the finite, concrete things that are immediately accessible. Philosophy sought the underlying principle or ground that gave these ordinary things meaning or intelligibility, a principle available only to reflection, not to non-reflective consciousness itself. If, however, philosophy claims that its principle is the underlying principle of real everyday life, the natural attitude can demand that this be demonstrated in everyday life itself. Moreover, in Hegel's time, Kant's

87 Ibid., 11.
88 Flay (1984), 5.

philosophy dominated the philosophical scene, and Kant's philosophy challenges thought's claim to know what is absolutely true. According to Flay, Hegel begins the *Phenomenology* with the absolute posed as a problem. How can philosophy prove that it knows the "ultimate truth about ultimate reality"; and how can it demonstrate to the consciousness involved in the reality of living that philosophy's truth grounds that reality and makes it intelligible? These questions define the problem that the *Phenomenology* is supposed to solve. Hegel derives the formulation of the problem from his dialogue with the philosophical tradition and from the challenge posed by the alienation of the natural attitude.[89]

The *Phenomenology* begins with sense certainty, the immediate experience of whatever happens to stand before consciousness. Flay describes sense certainty as "the natural attitude in its most unreflective state ... where access to reality is simply taken for granted."[90] In this consciousness, no questions arise about whether or not sense experience knows the reality of things. The *Phenomenology* must start here, Flay says, because it must prove the legitimacy of questioning this immediate access; and it must do so by finding the question within sense certainty itself. Thus, the *Phenomenology* begins with the natural attitude pure and simple, completely immersed in its relation to the reality of everyday life; and it demonstrates, by a dialectic developing within the subject matter itself, that everyday life itself raises the questions addressed by philosophical reflection.[91]

Flay analyzes the dialectic of the *Phenomenology* by distinguishing between two thematics: the world as thematized by someone unreflectively engaged in everyday life, and an attitude or standpoint presupposed in this unreflective engagement, but thematized by philosophy. This attitude or standpoint, which Flay also calls a presupposition-set, defines what someone in the natural attitude assumes about the relation between subject and object, thought and what it thinks, agent and the field of action. By thus defining certain epistemological and ontological assumptions at work in the natural attitude itself, the standpoint or presupposition-set connects the natural attitude to the reflections of philosophy. Everyday moral life, for example, thematizes the world by asking whether a proposed way of acting is right or wrong. Someone engaged in this experience assumes unreflectively that moral questions are appropriate for human agents and refers such questions to some presupposed principle of moral authority – a

89 Ibid., 1–13.
90 Ibid., 14.
91 Ibid., 13–18.

personal maxim, socially defined moral principles, church teachings, the dictates of conscience. Philosophy reflectively thematizes these unreflective presuppositions.

According to Flay, Hegel's project in the *Phenomenology* undertakes a justification of philosophy's absolute standpoint by examining the relation between the natural attitude's "unthematized" presupposition-sets, thematized by philosophy, and the reality of unreflective everyday experience. The examination consists in determining whether "the real world we know in the natural, unreflective attitude of the everyday" would be possible if these presuppositions were actually true of it.[92] If "truth-value gaps, contradictions, inappropriatenesses and anomalies of various sorts occur within the situations where they should not," then the presupposition fails. It does not render intelligible "those real circumstances which constitute our actual experience, knowledge, and action."[93] Hence, the standpoint is not "the absolute standpoint," i.e. the standpoint that gives us access to reality. By carefully reflecting on how the presupposition-set fails, we can formulate a new presupposition set that "compensates" for the inadequacy and thus provides a more adequate account of the "praxis taken to be definitive."[94]

Flay's interpretation of the project developed in the *Phenomenology* contains subtleties that must be highlighted. First, the interpretation sets up the experience of unreflective everyday life as a reality standard. It tests a standpoint, a presupposition-set, by whether it makes sense of and is appropriate to experience in the natural attitude. The standpoint that adequately or fully renders this experience intelligible gives us access to reality. Does this mean that the unreflective experience of everyday life can somehow be distinguished from what the presupposition-sets make of it? If not, how does the unreflective experience of everyday life provide a reality check for these presuppositions? According to Flay, a presupposition-set fails the test if its thematizing produces contradictions and anomalies of various sorts. If, however, these contradictions and anomalies indicate a distortion, why assume that the distortion has its origin in philosophical reflection and the presupposition-sets it thematizes? Why dismiss the possibility that the distortion might be produced by the way everyday experience deals with reality? According to Flay's own account, in Hegel's time philosophy and the natural attitude were alienated from each other, each viewing the other as perverse, turning the world upside down. Philosophy sees the natural attitude

92 Ibid., 24.
93 Ibid., 27.
94 Ibid., 26.

as a distortion, just as the natural attitude sees philosophy as a distortion. Hegel's *Phenomenology*, Flay says, takes up this alienation as a problem to be solved.[95] The problem is not solved, however, by dismissing from the outset philosophy's claim that the natural attitude is a distortion and has no access to what the truth really is.

Flay's interpretation also assumes that the *Phenomenology*, from the beginning, is looking for an absolute standpoint, a standpoint that leaves nothing in our experience 'unthematized' or anomalous. Flay does not see the talk of an absolute standpoint as a preliminary statement of what the *Phenomenology* will eventually prove; he interprets it as a determining factor in the examination of experience. The examination judges that a presupposition-set is inadequate because it does not meet the requirements of an absolute standpoint. Thus, two criteria are operating in the examination: the specific presupposition-set being examined and questioned, and the unquestioned assumption that absoluteness is the measure of a presupposition-set's legitimacy and adequacy.

At the end of his book, Flay acknowledges this unquestioned presupposition and reformulates it. The presupposition assumes that everyday life is a totality, a whole, and that the principle of its intelligibility must make sense of it as a whole. But everyday experience, Flay contends, does not justify presupposing that the principle of its totality or wholeness and the principle of its intelligibility must be the same. The way in which we can move seamlessly from one framework to another, e.g. from being a handyman to visiting with a friend to playing a concerto, challenges this presupposition. Although conscious of these experiences as one and all my own (the principle of totality), I use a different presupposition-set in each one (the principles of intelligibility). Flay finds in the natural attitude itself the presupposition that everyday life is a whole. He claims that Hegel falls into this unexamined, unquestioned, unjustifiable presupposition because of his faithfulness to the natural attitude. The aim of accommodating philosophical reflection to the unreflective presuppositions of everyday life is Hegel's undoing.[96]

K. Westphal, like Flay, interprets the *Phenomenology* as beginning with a problem to solve. But according to his interpretation, the *Phenomenology* gets its problem from Sextus's dilemma. This problem does not set up absoluteness as a standard. It simply requires a non-question-begging strategy for justifying second-order claims about knowledge, claims that justify first-

95 Ibid., 8–10.

96 Ibid., 249–67. See also 49–50.

order claims about the world. Only the dialectical proofs worked out in the *Phenomenology* can determine whether these second-order claims are a plurality of different criteria, or one comprehensive integrating system of criteria, or some other arrangement. The answer is not presupposed from the beginning. According to Westphal's interpretation, therefore, the *Phenomenology* tests a criterion by how well it handles its own domain. The phenomena not accounted for come into experience associated in some way with what a consciousness committed to the criterion expects its object to be. Thus, they belong to the domain that the criterion itself identifies as its own, and yet they are not captured by it. Applying this to one of Flay's examples, the presupposition-set for being a handyman calls into play phenomena that belong to being a handyman, and yet the proposed presupposition-set for being a handyman does not account for these phenomena. According to Westphal, Flay's interpretation mistakes distributive claims for totalizing claims. Sense certainty claims to know, to have access to, particulars. Hence, wherever a particular shows up in experience, sense certainty claims access to it. This does not mean that it expects to know this domain of objects as an integrated totality.[97]

5 CONCLUSION

My study of the *Phenomenology* begins with a study of the essays in which Hegel introduces his major works. This part of the book aims at identifying the way Hegel himself defines the project developed in the *Phenomenology*. The review of the interpretation paradigms identifies a set of questions and issues that the study of Hegel's introductory essays should address.

First, the study must look for clues to the way Hegel himself formulates the primary question the *Phenomenology* is meant to answer; and ask whether the formulation hides unjustified, unquestioned presuppositions. Second, the study must ask whether the object investigated in the *Phenomenology* is non-philosophical consciousness engaged in the experiences of life (the pedagogical interpretation) or a philosophically thematized version of this consciousness (Flay, Westphal, Pippin, McDowell). Third, the study of Hegel's introductions must ask how Hegel himself interprets the status of the knowing examined in the *Phenomenology*. Is it a collection of false positions whose illegitimacy must be exposed (Maker-Winfield-Houlgate), an appearance in which truth manifests itself but not the truth itself (Harris), or a knowing whose truth status is a completely open question, to be

97 K.R. Westphal (1999), 307–10.

determined by the examination developed in the *Phenomenology* (Fulda)? The study must also ask whether the *Phenomenology* is required for proving the truth of philosophical science (Fulda, Westphal, Pippin, McDowell, Flay), or only provides a way of initiating the knower into the philosophical way of thinking (Harris, McCumber, Houlgate). If it proves the truth of philosophical science, then it must address the completeness problem formulated by K. Westphal. The whole domain of experience must show that nothing in the realm of experience can satisfy what experience itself requires for its truth, and also demonstrate that philosophical science, beginning with logic, somehow meets this requirement. In order to address the first three issues, the study of Hegel's introductions must pay close attention to the way Hegel himself defines the requirements of the procedure according to which the *Phenomenology* develops its examination of knowledge. This involves collecting clues to the way Hegel defines the role of dialectic and contradiction, the criterion issue, the subjectivity-objectivity issues; and it must ask how these affect the culture-specific status of experience. Finally, the study must look for clues to the way the *Phenomenology* handles the issues raised by Pippin and McDowell regarding empirical data, space-time ordering, empirical research, and the difference dimension of knowledge.

PART TWO

THE FREEDOM OF PHILOSOPHICAL THOUGHT

THE STUDY OF HEGEL'S INTRODUCTIONS covers Parts Two, Three, Four, and Five. This study focuses on two questions. First, how does Hegel himself define the task and method of the *Phenomenology*, and how does he interpret its relation to the philosophical system? Second, does the interpretation of the *Phenomenology* in Hegel's later works remain consistent with the interpretation provided in the introductory essays of the *Phenomenology* itself? The study of the interpretation paradigms in Part One identifies certain issues that have provoked debate and disagreements among scholars who have published discussions relevant to these questions. The study of Hegel's introductions addresses these issues first by concentrating on Hegel's texts, without interrupting the discussion by referring to the debates among the different interpreters. Part Five returns to the interpretation paradigms examined in chapter 2, and explains how the evidence developed in the study of Hegel's introductions affects these interpretations.

Part Two examines the way Hegel defines the standpoint of philosophy in the introductory essays of the *Philosophy of Right* and the *Encyclopaedia*. We shall see that Hegel's way of defining philosophical science determines the questions that must be asked about the role of the *Phenomenology* in Hegel's philosophical thought. It makes sense to connect the way this issue is developed in the *Philosophy of Right* and the *Encyclopaedia* because each work discusses the character of philosophical science by covering the same fundamental issues in a similar way. Each text identifies philosophical thought as pure thought, detached from its involvement in and dependence on other forms of knowing. Each text acknowledges that pure thought must turn back to experience and know its independent thought determinations as the true essence of empirical reality. Each analyzes the proof procedure developed in philosophy, and this exposes philosophy's presuppositions and raises questions about how these can be justified.

The *Encyclopaedia* considers briefly the role of the *Phenomenology* in the justification of philosophy's beginning presuppositions. It also substitutes an examination of three positions on objectivity in the introductory role originally assigned to the *Phenomenology*, and it comments briefly on the relative merits of each approach. We must identify precisely, therefore, the way each approach operates in this role, and ask whether Hegel favours one approach over the other, and if so why.

Part Two begins by focusing on the introductory essays of the *Philosophy of Right* and the general introduction of the *Encyclopaedia*, discussing each work separately. This strategy allows each text to develop its position strictly by itself and on its own terms, so that each can serve as an independent confirmation of the other. When this has been done, the discussion turns to the *Encyclopaedia*'s examination of the three positions on objectivity. The chapter devoted to this text focuses on those parts of the examination that confirm, expand, or challenge the issues identified in the previous two chapters, and those that touch on other questions that will be introduced in the chapters on the introductory essays of the *Science of Logic* and the *Phenomenology*.

3

The Philosophy of Right

1 PHILOSOPHY AS PURE THOUGHT

Hegel begins the Preface to the *Philosophy of Right* by insisting on the special character of philosophical knowing. The philosophy of right, he says, presupposes a kind of proof (*Beweis*) that is different from every other way of knowing (*Erkenntnis*) (*PhR* Preface IV/N:10). Hegel elaborates on this claim by distinguishing a philosophy of right from three other ways of knowing what right is. Subjective conviction knows what is right by consulting the individual's own independent feelings. According to this way of thinking, the individual must not be bound by what 'everybody thinks,' what the community believes, what the state declares. The individual must form his own opinions, follow her own sense of what is right. Hegel objects that this way of knowing reduces truth to contingent, arbitrary feelings. It asserts as true what the individual happens to find convincing and thus makes truth particular to this knower. This reduces the truth to a chaos of conflicting opinions. No conviction can set aside any other, since the fact that a person feels convinced gives equal justification to any and every claim (*PhR* Preface VIII–XVI/N:12–18; §2*A*).

Hegel also considers another kind of subjective knowing, one that distinguishes "a world beyond," an ideal ought to be, from the actual social world. According to this way of thinking, the legitimacy of an actual state depends not on what the state itself is but on how it measures up to an ought that is different from it. Hegel objects that this way of knowing cannot call itself philosophy. Philosophy, he says, seeks knowledge of the rational, and the rational is actual. An ought distinguished from the actual state exists only in "a one-sided and empty ratiocination." In other words, thought in this ideal form derives its definition of the ought from a form of reasoning that keeps itself aloof from the real world (*PhR* Preface XVIII–XXII/N:20–2).

Knowledge existent in the established social order, in "public laws and in public morality and religion," escapes the arbitrariness and chaotic conflict of individual subjective convictions and also the unreality of an ought distinguished from the world as it is. In the Preface, Hegel acknowledges that these public ways of representing what is right declare and know the truth of the matter. In the Introduction, he says that established ways of representing what is right may or may not be true. But in both texts, Hegel's main point is unambiguous. Even if established ways of representing what is right express what right truly is, they lack the form of philosophical thought because they have the form of something given. They articulate what happens to be accepted as right by the external positive authority of the state, by mutual agreement among human beings (*die Übereinstimmung der Menschen*), by the felt convictions of the people and the spirit of the community that corresponds to them. Philosophy requires the form of science, which knows the truth as a demonstrated necessity. The philosophy of right must show that its claims about right are completely justified (*gerechtfertigt*), that right must be what philosophy takes it to be (*PhR* Preface VII/N:11; §2*A*).

Yet not every form of demonstration meets the requirements of philosophy. Certain forms of knowledge give themselves the external form of science by beginning with a definition and by showing how the claims of the science follow necessarily from this definition. But they justify the definition itself by deriving it from etymology or by abstracting it from particular cases. It conforms to a generally accepted way of speaking, or it expresses a generally accepted way of representing what is being defined. Thus, the definition that justifies the conclusions of the science rests on what is given in the culture. Even if the science succeeds in proving that its conclusions follow necessarily from the definition of the subject matter, it does not prove that this definition identifies the way the subject matter must be conceived (*PhR* §2*A*).

Hegel makes the same point again when he distinguishes between the historical and philosophical study of law. Historical explanation demonstrates how particular legal institutions came to be as a result of certain historical conditions, and this shows how laws have developed in time. Hegel distinguishes philosophy from this kind of explanation by pointing out that what is "grounded in and consistent with the prevailing circumstances and existing legal institutions" is not necessarily right. Moreover, even if it is right, its historical emergence as a result of "the circumstances, eventualities, needs, and incidents" of the time does not prove that it is right. We might, for example, explain Hitler's rise to power by showing how the humiliation of Germany after the First World War contributed to it. We might explain the existence of slavery in the colonies of the American South by demonstrating that a plantation economy was dependent on it. This does not prove that Hitler's rule or slavery in the Southern colonies were right. They may have been quite consistent with the circumstances and existing legal institutions and yet "wrong and irrational in and for themselves" (*PhR* §3*A*). Thus, Hegel distinguishes between philosophical justification and historical explanation. Historical explanation shows that a legal institution answers to requirements established by what is given in the culture of the time, and Hegel acknowledges the legitimacy of such studies. But he insists that they do not qualify as philosophical justification. Philosophical justification questions not only a given legal institution but also the cultural conditions that explain and account for it. It asks whether these established cultural conditions are right.

Thus, Hegel distinguishes the philosophy of right from culture-based knowledge of various kinds. Neither the existence of certain practices, institutions, and accepted ways of representing what right is, nor a consensus among human beings, nor demonstrations dependent on definitions or conditions given in the culture of the time can meet the requirements of philosophical knowing. Philosophy must prove its claims without appealing to the authority of these established ways of knowing. Hegel describes this independence of culture-based knowledge as thought set free, thought beginning from itself. Thought detaches itself from what is given and proves its claims by deriving them from the necessities of thought itself (*PhR* Preface VII/N:11). Hegel insists, however, that this independence does not reduce philosophical thought to the independent thought of an isolated individual or to thought itself isolated in itself and set apart from the real world. Therefore, an interpretation of Hegel's position on the distinctive character of philosophy, as elaborated in the introductory essays of the *Philosophy of Right*, must avoid two extremes: the reduction of philosophy to culture-based knowledge; and the reduction of philosophy to the necessities of the thinking subject.

2 THE RATIONAL IS ACTUAL AND THE ACTUAL RATIONAL

How, then, does Hegel's account of philosophical knowing, as articulated in the introductory essays of the *Philosophy of Right*, keep philosophy free from all dependence on culture-based knowledge without reducing it to the necessities of the thinking subject? Philosophy maintains its independence of culture-based knowledge by asking whether what actually exists in the culture is rational. Philosophical thought does not let what is given in the culture function as a standard (*Maßstab*) or criterion (*Kriterium*) according to which the truth of philosophical concepts is measured. On the contrary, philosophical thought judges the truth of cultural representations according to its concept of the rational. The philosophy of right, for example, asks whether established ways of representing what is right are truly right and rational; it responds to the question by comparing these cultural representations to the concept that identifies the rationality of right.

But philosophical concepts are not the thoughts of a thinking subject isolated in itself and detached from the realities of external existence. Philosophical concepts identify the rationality that is the nature, the essential truth, of what is. Thus, culture-based knowledge and philosophical knowing know the same real world. But culture-based knowledge knows this reality as a given, a state of affairs or way of thinking that happens to appear in external existence (*die äußerliche Erscheinung*). Philosophy knows the real as rational, and rationality is its nature or true essence. Therefore, cultural consciousness does not know the real truth of the matter even when the content of cultural representations corresponds to the content of the philosophical concept. For cultural consciousness, the content belongs to the givenness of the world, to reality as what makes an appearance in external existence. For philosophy, the same content belongs to the rationality that is the nature and true essence of what appears.

Hegel restricts the word "actuality" to this essential dimension of what exists. He dismisses everything else as "transitory *existence* [*Dasein*], external contingency, opinion, appearance without essence, untruth, deception, etc" (*PhR* §1*A*). When, therefore, he says in the Preface that the rational is actual and the actual is rational, he claims rationality not for everything that happens to exist but only for that which gives reality to the rational. Philosophy knows the truth of the real world by focusing on the rationality that is its essence and distinguishing this from the contingencies that happen to exist with it. Philosophy can do this because it has a concept of real rationality that does not depend on what is given in the *de facto* reality of the world. Yet this concept has a legitimacy for the real world that the isolated thought of a thinking subject cannot claim.

In two places, Hegel introduces another complication in his account of philosophy's relation to the given circumstances of the real world. "For since the rational, which is synonymous with the Idea, becomes actual by entering into external existence [*Existenz*], it emerges in an infinite wealth of forms, appearances, and shapes and surrounds its core with a brightly coloured covering in which consciousness at first resides, but which only the concept can penetrate in order to find the inner pulse, and detect its continued beat even within the external shapes. But the infinitely varied circumstances which take shape within this externality as the essence manifests itself within it, this infinite material and its organization, are not the subject matter of philosophy" (*PhR* Preface XX/N:20–1). Reason becomes actual in external existence; and the proliferation of forms, the endless variety of circumstances, belong to the conditions of external existence. Therefore, the rational becomes actual in an endless variety of forms, shapes, and circumstances. But the specific determination and arrangement of these circumstances do not belong to the subject matter of philosophy. Philosophy does not have to prove that the circumstances in which the rational makes its appearance must be exactly this specific set of circumstances. Indeed philosophy should leave such matters alone; they are none of its concern. Thus, the subject matter of philosophy, which is the rationality of the real, necessarily exists in specific circumstances whose specific determination philosophy itself cannot explain. The rationality of the real is subject to certain conditions that cannot be derived from the necessities of reason itself.

Moreover, these conditions play a role in philosophical procedure. Philosophy proves the necessity of the concept. This is its principal task. But then it looks for what corresponds to the concept in our language and cultural representations. Thus, there is a moment in philosophical thought when it turns to cultural experience and thinks the rational by recognizing it in the concrete realities of the given cultural world. But philosophy does not derive its concepts from the culture; it does not depend on cultural ways of thinking for its principles. Nor does the proof of its truth depend on its correspondence to established cultural forms. On the contrary, a lack of correspondence proves the untruth of the cultural forms and calls for an adjustment in cultural representations.[1] "In philosophical cognition ... the chief concern is the *necessity* of the concept, and the route by which it has become a *result* [is] its proof and deduction. Thus, given that its *content* is necessary *for itself*, the second step is to look around for what corresponds to it in our <representations> [*Vorstellungen*] and language ... But [our representation] is so far from being the measure and criterion of the concept which is necessary and true for itself that it must rather derive its truth from the concept, and recognize and correct itself with the help of the latter" (*PhR* §2*A*).

1 For a careful commentary on the "rational is actual" formula, see Peperzak (1987), comment on paragraph 13, 92–103.

3 PHILOSOPHICAL PROOF PROCEDURE

The Preface and Introduction to the *Philosophy of Right* give us several clues to the character of philosophical knowing. Two concern procedure, the other concerns subject matter. Philosophy knows the truth as a demonstrated necessity, and its demonstrations meet all the requirements of properly scientific knowledge. Hegel says that certain non-philosophical ways of knowing have the external form of science because they begin with a definition of the subject matter and justify their claims by relating them to the definition. This tells us that the form of scientific knowing begins with a definition and uses the definition to prove its claims. If, however, a form of knowing generates the definition itself from given ways of speaking or from a general pattern derived from given examples, then it does not meet all the requirements for scientific knowing. Philosophy, which is properly scientific knowing, demonstrates the necessity of the definition, not just the necessity of what follows from the definition (*PhR* §2*A*).

The philosophy of right, as a part of philosophy, accepts the concept of right from what precedes it in the development of Hegel's philosophical system. This prior development produces the concept of right as a result and is the proof that justifies it. The proof of the concept does not belong to the philosophy of right itself. The philosophy of right takes the concept as given, assumes its legitimacy, and concentrates exclusively on developing a full articulation of what the concept itself proves about what right is. Philosophy itself, however, does not take the concept as given. Philosophy proves it, but does so by deriving it from a prior concept that defines a different part of philosophy (*PhR* §2).

What, then, is the concept that defines the subject matter of the whole philosophical project? What concept determines the shifts from one part of philosophy to another, from one philosophical concept to another? In the introductory essays of the *Philosophy of Right*, Hegel identifies the general character of philosophy as knowledge of the rational. He describes philosophical procedure as a process that demonstrates the rationality of the subject matter, which he also calls its "logical spirit" (*PhR* Preface V/N:10; §31+*A*). This suggests that the concept of the rational or logical defines the subject matter of the whole philosophical project, and that the concept of right is a way of conceiving the rational. This suggestion is confirmed by the way Hegel talks about "what is rightful and rational (*rechtlich und vernünftig*)" and what is "contrary to right and irrational (*unrechtlich und unvernünftig*)" (*PhR* §3*A*/N:29). Therefore, the philosophical study of a particular subject matter begins with a concept that identifies the rationality of the subject matter. The concept of right as the actualization of freedom identifies what constitutes the rationality of right (*PhR* §27, §29). Philosophy produces this concept as the necessary result of a prior philosophical demonstration, which proves the legitimacy, the necessity, of conceiving the rational in this way. The philosophical developments prior to the philosophy of right prove the necessity of conceiving the rational as the actualization of freedom. Thus, philosophy justifies scientifically, with complete necessity, even the definitions that identify what the subject matter of a philosophical science is.

As we have seen, Hegel distinguishes philosophy from the kind of thought that remains isolated within itself and detached from the real world. Philosophy, he says in the Preface, seeks knowledge of the rational, and the rational is actual (*PhR* Preface XIX/N:20, XX/N:21). In the Introduction, Hegel defines the rational as the concept actualized in the real world, which he calls the Idea. Moreover, the concept identifies the nature of the subject matter (*der Natur der Sache*) and what is truly essential (*das wahrhaft Wesentliche*), which Hegel distinguishes from the way the concept happens to appear in the circumstances of history. Philosophical concepts, therefore, are not mere concepts. They are not thoughts detached from the real world. As concepts of the rational, they identify the nature, the true essence, of the real world (*PhR* §1*A*, §3*A*/N:30).

Philosophy maintains its scientific character within each philosophical science by letting its beginning concept determine and justify all its claims. Hegel insists that this procedure must not depend on given circumstances or the application of the concept to external material. A philosophical science does not work up a full account of its subject matter by adding to the defining concept what it finds given in the external world. Hegel also insists that philosophical procedure does not depend on a method that the thinking subject brings to the process. Philosophy does not give a rational account of its subject matter by imposing on its object a rationality derived from the thinking subject. Philosophy brings to consciousness the rationality immanent in its beginning concept. Even the concept's relation to its own actualization must be proved in this way. Philosophy "develops the Idea" by demonstrating that the concept itself demands its actualization in the real world. Thus, a philosophical science begins with a concept that identifies the subject matter as a form of reason. The science gives a full account of the subject matter by bringing to consciousness determinations derived from the concept itself and nothing else. Hegel calls this "the method whereby the concept, in science, develops out of itself and is merely an *immanent* progression and production of its own determinations" (*PhR* §2, §31+*A*).

The immanence of the development depends on its dialectical structure. In the Introduction to the *Philosophy of Right*, Hegel gives no more than a suggestive sketch of the way the concept develops dialectically. Still this sketch provides good evidence against certain ways in which Hegelian dialectic has been interpreted. The principle that governs the concept's self-development "not only dissolves the particularizations of the universal but also produces them." This production of differences involves the generation of "an opposite and limiting factor." The concept demands a relation to what stands opposed to it; and this relation shows the concept limited to itself and excluding something else. But this generation of an opposite also produces a "*positive* content." Hegel clarifies this production of a positive content by distinguishing "the higher dialectic of the concept" from dialectic of another kind, which he calls dialectic in a negative mode (*PhR* §31+*A*).

In the negative mode, dialectic takes up some given object or proposition in order to show that its opposite can be deduced from it. Negative dialectic concludes from this result either that the object or proposition in question cannot be true, or at least that the object or proposition can be no more than an approximation of the truth. The higher dialectic of the concept differs from this in three ways. First, the process of deriving an opposite from the concept is not imposed on the subject matter by the way a thinking subject "dissolves and confuses it." It arises rather from "the *very soul* of the content." "This development of the Idea as the activity of its own rationality is something which thought, since it is subjective, merely observes, without for its part adding anything extra to it" (*PhR* §31*A*). Thus, it belongs to the very nature of the concept itself that it be opposed and limited by an other. Second, the production of an opposite does not wipe out the concept or compromise its truth. Rather it derives from what is "immanent" in the concept itself something positive, something more. This alone, Hegel says, makes it possible for the process to be "a *development* [*Entwickelung*] and immanent progression." The generation of an opposite belongs to what the concept itself means and hence adds to what the concept is and what we know about it. Third, the necessary connection between the beginning concept and its opposite both dissolves and produces the particularizations of the universal. The universal governs the whole dynamic between the opposites. This dynamic identifies each opposite and distinguishes it from the other. Thus, the universal dissolves the isolation of each opposite in itself by connecting each to the other in the same defining process. But the universal also produces their particularization by deriving their difference from the dynamic they have in common (*PhR* §31*A*).

Hegel says that the way in which conceptual development proceeds should be familiar from logic (*PhR* §2A, §31). He says that his account of this development in the *Philosophy of Right* will assume that the reader can fill in the details of the argument from a prior acquaintance with scientific method which has been fully explained in the *Science of Logic* (*PhR* Preface V/N:10). But he also insists that philosophy must allow the concept of the subject matter to determine its own development: "To consider something rationally means not to bring reason to bear on the object from outside in order to work upon it, for the object is itself rational for itself ... the sole business of science is to <bring to consciousness> this work which is accomplished by the <rationality> of the thing [*Sache*] itself" (*PhR* §31*A*). Applying this to the *Philosophy of Right*, the science of right does not bring a pre-conceived set of rational principles to the investigation of right and judge questions of right according to these principles. Rather, it brings to consciousness the rationality implicit in the concept of right, which identifies the subject matter that the science of right investigates.

What, then, does Hegel mean when he says that the *Philosophy of Right* assumes a familiarity with scientific method that has been worked out in the *Logic*? As we have seen, the philosophy of right gets its beginning concept, the initial concept of right, from the philosophical development that precedes it in Hegel's philosophical system. This process develops the concept of the rational or logical. The concept of right, therefore, carries with it, as immanent in it, the movement that has developed the concept of the logical or rational and produced the concept of right as a result. But the philosophy of right must rethink these developmental moves as developments determined by the concept of right. This will bring to consciousness the logical spirit immanent in the concept of right itself.[2]

2 A significant debate has developed about the status of logic in the *Philosophy of Right*. Allen Wood and Frederick Neuhouser detach Hegel's social theory from its relation to the claims of Hegel's *Logic* (Wood 1990, 1–6; Neuhouser 2004–05; 2000, 1–16). William Dudley argues against Neuhouser that detaching Hegel's social theory from what comes before, which determines and justifies its point of view, and from what comes after, which corrects its limitations, gives us a somewhat distorted view of Hegel's position (Dudley 2004–05). David Kolb claims that an interpretation of the *Philosophy of Right* demands an explicit investigation of the way the categories of the *Logic* operate in the demonstrations developed in the *Philosophy of Right* (Kolb 2004–05). I am claiming that Hegel's philosophical procedure requires explicit attention to the way the beginning concept of the *Philosophy of Right* is determined by the dialectical moves that precede it in Hegel's system. But I am also claiming that Hegel himself rejects an approach that applies logical categories in an external way to the demonstration developed in the *Philosophy of Right*. The moves in the demonstration must be determined by the concept of right. If the determinations implicit in this concept correspond to the categories of Hegel's logic, this must be demonstrated within the *Philosophy of Right* itself.

4

The Encyclopaedia: *General Introduction*

THE INTRODUCTORY ESSAYS OF THE *Encyclopaedia*, in the process of discussing the character of philosophical science, raise questions about how philosophy begins. They propose two different ways of addressing this question: the approach developed in the *Phenomenology of Spirit*, and the examination of three positions on objectivity, developed in the *Encyclopaedia* itself. We begin our study of the *Encyclopaedia* with the more general discussion developed in the Introduction and in the introductory sections of the part entitled "Preliminary Conception." This more general discussion examines first the way the *Encyclopaedia* identifies philosophical science, acknowledges its relation to experience, and analyzes its procedure. We then discuss how this way of defining philosophical cognition raises questions about its starting point, and what the *Encyclopaedia* has to say about the role of the *Phenomenology* in addressing this issue. In the following chapter (chapter 5), we consider the *Encyclopaedia*'s alternative approach through an examination of three positions on objectivity.

Hegel identifies philosophy in a general way as a form of thinking. Thinking, however, is active in everything human; thinking gives the human its human character. Philosophy differs from this humanizing thought activity, and is also one with it: "This distinction is connected with the fact that the human import of consciousness, which is based on thinking, does not appear in the form of thought straightaway, but as feeling, intuition, representation – which are forms that have to be distinguished from thinking itself as form" (*Enz* §2). This statement sets the agenda for the whole discussion of philosophy in the Introduction. In this text, Hegel focuses on the way philosophical thought becomes detached from other forms of human consciousness while remaining related to them as the same thought appearing in another form.

1 THE LIBERATION OF PHILOSOPHICAL THOUGHT

Feeling, intuition, and representation belong to experience. Experience is consciousness conscious of a content attached to its sense of self (*selbst dabei sein*). We experience something by having it present in our consciousness of ourselves (*der Gewißheit seiner selbst*). Thus, we experience colour by feeling our eyes filled with the sense of colour. We experience sound by feeling our ears filled with the sense of sound. We experience our duty by feeling obliged by it. We experience God by feeling God's presence in our faith, our conscience, and our worship (*Enz* §7*A*, §8). Experience gets its content from intuition. Hegel describes this content as present (*präsenten*), immediately at hand (*unmittelbar Vorhandenen*), the found (*Gefundenes*), the given (*das Gegebensein*) (*Enz* §7, §12+*A*). Representation adds to intuition the sense of the content's presence "in me," its being my experience, which gives the different elements a loose kind of unity. The elements are strung together as one and all mine, my experience (*Enz* §20*A*). Thus, experience knows its content as what happens to be present, what it finds given to it, what happens to arise in consciousness, and hence as "altogether contingent" (*Enz* §12). Hegel calls attention to the all-pervasiveness of experience. Everything in consciousness – even spiritual contents like God and right, even thoughts and concepts like singular and universal – belong to experience. When we think something – duty or right or absolute, universal or essence or ground – we become conscious of ourselves thinking it. Whatever the content, we find ourselves immediately conscious of it, and hence it arises in consciousness as given and present in our sense of ourselves (*Enz* §8).

Experience, however, does not accept all contents as equally important. It distinguishes what is really important in the given content from what just happens to exist. Hegel makes this point when he reconsiders the formula articulated in the *Philosophy of Right*: "What is rational, is actual, and what is actual, is rational" (*Enz* §6*A*). In common life, he says, anything that exists gets the name "actual." But even ordinary feeling, which Hegel identifies with experience, is more discriminating than this. Even experience distinguishes the actual from the random or fortuitous, the kind of existence that might just as well not be, which is no better than the possible. Thus, a farmer dismisses a random day of mild weather in the middle of an Ontario winter. The day exists, of course. But for a farmer, it might just as well not exist. The farmer knows from experience that this mildness does not "actually" belong to the complex system that determines the seasons for planting and for reaping. Also, when citizens of a country honour the nation's flag, they honour the institutions, laws, and national fellowship that the flag symbolizes. The flag's size, the material out of which it is made, its situation outside the third-floor window of a court house in Dayton, Ohio might just as well not be. For the patriotism of the citizens, these details are irrelevant, dismissible, not essential. When, therefore, Hegel says that the actual is rational and only the rational is actual, he does not mean that every detail of the existing world is rational. The actual is not identical with everything that happens to exist. The actual identifies what is really important in the existing world, what is not fortuitous or random or temporary or irrelevant. The actual is the real truth, not just a transitory appearance; and even experience can distinguish the actual from what merely exists (*Enz* §6+*A*).

Hegel begins to work out the distinction between experience and thought by distinguishing between form and content. Content is the particulars, the determinate characteristics (*die Bestimmtheiten*), of our feelings, images, representations, aims, duties, thoughts, concepts. Hegel insists that thought and experience have the same content. But the form, the way each is conscious of the content, is different. Hegel begins his account of this difference by referring to an old belief, the belief that in order to know the true constitution of an object we must think it over (*darüber nachdenken*). We think over or reflect on what appears immediately to consciousness in order to focus on what is essential, important, the real issue, the truth of the matter (*Enz* §5, 7).[1] But as we have seen, even experience discriminates between what is really important and what just happens to exist, between the actual and what might just as well not be. How does thinking something over do this differently? Thinking over (*Nachdenken*) looks for what is universal and necessary. Experience can discriminate between the actual and what merely exists by remembering what usually happens. A farmer can distinguish between the season for planting and a series of mild winter days by just remembering his past experience. Thought needs necessity. It needs to know what the subject matter must be, what is always there because it is essential. Thought distinguishes the actual from what merely exists by distinguishing what is necessary from what just happens to be the case (*Enz* §7).

Hegel describes two forms of thinking over or reflection. One form, the form characteristic of empirical science, goes beyond experience by identifying general classifications and laws in the apparently fortuitous flow of events. Empirical science does not remain rooted in the particulars of immediate experience and their contingency. It rethinks the data

1 See also *Enz* § 21*A*, 22.

of experience as manifestations of what is universal and necessary (*Enz* §7).[2] Empirical science, however, does not completely satisfy the needs of thought. Hegel gives two reasons for this. First, empirical science relates the universal to the particulars in a way that is external and contingent. It brings different particulars under a general category or law, and applies this universal in the same way to different instances. It does not derive the differences from the universal, so that the universal explains why this differentiation is necessary. Second, empirical science relates the particulars to each other in the same external and contingent way. The particulars belong to the same universal because each one manifests the same pattern, not because the universal necessitates a connection between them.

In biology, for example, the genus identifies the same set of characteristics repeated in different species. But nothing in the internal constitution of the genus requires its differentiation in just these ways. Nor does the universality of the genus integrate the different species with each other. So also physics observes the way heavy bodies move toward the center of the earth, and discovers a pattern that repeats itself with the force of necessity. Hence, it rethinks a given pattern as a law that operates with necessity in the motions of bodies on earth. But physics simply accepts the definition of the law from what it finds given in experience, a certain proportion between distance and velocity. It does not explain why motion must have these two factors, or why distance and velocity must go together, or why their association has to have this proportion. It simply 'finds' a universality and necessity with this constitution given in experience. Thus, empirical explanations mix the form of universality and necessity with the givenness of empirical material and retain much of the contingency and randomness characteristic of the given. Hegel suggests that thought cannot be satisfied unless it knows a universal that determines its own differences and by doing so determines their necessary relation to each other. Only in this way can thought free itself from the contingency of the given (*Enz* §9).[3]

Philosophy comes into being as thought's dissatisfaction with empirical consciousness. Thought thinks the empirical as not giving thought what it needs to know. This establishes a negative relation between thought and its origin within experience. Because thought does not find in the empirical the kind of necessity it needs, thought turns away from what is simply there, a fact given in experience, and "finds its first satisfaction in itself" (*Enz* §12).

2 See also *Enz* §9*A*, 12. Compare to David Hume, *An Enquiry Concerning Human Understanding*, Section VII.

3 See also *Enz* §7*A*.

Thought, Hegel says, needs "to give satisfaction to its highest inwardness, to thinking, and to make thinking into its object" (*Enz* §11).

Hegel stops at this point to explain how the negative relation between thought and experience exemplifies the ambiguous relation between immediacy and mediation. He develops a more careful discussion of this issue in the examination of the three positions on objectivity, which we consider in chapter 5, and in the introductory essays of the *Logic*, which we consider in Part Three. Here, in the general introduction to the *Encyclopaedia*, he mentions it only briefly. Since, however, it is meant to explain a dominant issue in this text, I will provide a preliminary clarification at this point, promising a more thorough explanation in chapter 5 and Part Three. Hegel's discussion of mediation and immediacy depends on a certain way of understanding relations. It is helpful to think of "mediation" as a relation that exists in the subject matter itself, not just in the way we think about it. In order to understand Hegel's use of the term, it is also necessary to allow for negative relations, i.e. the subject matter itself really engaged in excluding something, not just the investigator thinking "A is not B" by comparing "A is A" and "B is B." The term "immediacy," when used in contrast to "mediate" or "mediation," refers to the way a subject matter stands alone, identified by what it is in itself, not identified by any relations, positive or negative, to anything else.

Hegel introduces the mediation-immediacy issue here to describe the way thinking becomes independent of experience by separating itself from sensible feeling and intuition. Thought makes itself independent "by means of" its dissatisfaction with and rejection of what is given to sense and intuition. In other words, thought is engaged in a relation to experience. It seeks in experience what is universal and necessary. But the universality and necessity that it finds there is not the kind of universality and necessity that satisfies its need to know. Hence, its relation to experience turns into a negative relation. Thought pushes off from experience, becomes actively engaged in separating itself from experience. Hence, its independence of experience is mediated by, dependent on, its engagement in a negative relation to experience. But the mediation produces immediacy. Thought's negative relation to experience, its rejection of experience as not satisfying its need for absolute necessity, separates thought from its relation to experience and thereby brings it back to itself standing on its own, preoccupied only with its own necessary determinations (*Enz* §12*A*).

Hegel calls this detached form of thought philosophical science, which is the second form of thinking over or reflection. In logic, philosophical reflection articulates the laws and categories proper to thought in its purity and freedom (*Enz* §12).[4] Hegel distinguishes the logic of philosophical reflection from two other kinds of logic. He distinguishes it first from formal thinking, which has as its object the determinations and laws of thought that it finds given in the way we think. Hegel's logic does not observe the way thought operates and discover universal categories and necessary laws governing these operations. In Hegelian logic, thinking gives itself its determinations and laws as a "self-developing totality" (*Enz* §19*A*).[5] It thinks thought itself as a self-necessitating subject matter, one that accounts for its own determinations and thus accounts for itself in every way. This kind of object and this way of knowing the object satisfies thought's need for necessity. It derives the categories and laws of thought not from what it finds given in the way we think, but from the necessities implicit in what the subject matter, the thinkable or logical, itself is.

Hegel also distinguishes the logic of philosophical reflection from the subjectivity of the thinker. Thinking something over is the act of a thinking subject; it is my act. Thinking, however, requires freedom from everything other than the self-determination of thought itself. Thought derives its content from what the subject matter itself determines, and the subject-matter of logic is thought itself. Hence, a thinking subject, my thinking, must be free from all the subject's particular characteristics and states. The subject must act as the universal subject matter itself determining its own content. The subject thinks thought deriving its content from what thought itself must be, and thus it brings to consciousness the true essence of its object (*Enz* §23+*A*).

But which object? Does logic bring to consciousness the true essence of independent thought or the true essence of empirical realities? Hegel says that philosophy and experience have the same content. They differ only in form, in the way they know the content. But he also says that thought derives its content from itself. In order to do this, thought thinks without depending on experience; thought focuses on itself, a subject matter that is independent of experience. How, then, can it have the same content as experience? In order to answer this question, Hegel distinguishes his own definition of philosophy from other ways of identifying what philosophy is. According to one point of view, philosophy is about ideas and ideals and these are nothing but phantoms or fantasies. According to another point of view, ideas and ideals identify an excellence, an ought, that either exceeds what reality can be or lacks what it takes to become actual in the

4 See also *Enz* §19.
5 See also *Enz* §82*A*.

real world. When Hegel defines philosophy as the self-development of pure thought, he is not talking about thought developing ideas that are nothing but thoughts, nor about thought developing the idea of an ought that cannot be realized. He is talking about thought articulating the determinations of a rationality that defines not only the true essence of thinking but also the true essence of the real world. The rational is actual, and the actual is rational (*Enz* §6+*A*).[6]

2 THE RATIONAL IS ACTUAL AND THE ACTUAL RATIONAL

In order to know this truth, philosophy cannot remain isolated within itself. For a content to be accepted as true, Hegel says, the knower must experience it, feel it identified with the knower's sense of self. Hegel calls this the principle of experience. "The principle of experience contains the infinitely important determination that, for a content to be accepted and held to be true, man must himself be actively involved with it (*selbst dabei sein müsse*), more precisely, that he must find any such content to be at one and in unity with the certainty of his own self. He must himself be involved with it, whether only with his external senses, or with his deeper spirit, with his essential consciousness of self as well. This is the same principle that is today called faith, immediate knowing, revelation in the outer [world], and above all in one's own inner [world]" (*Enz* §7*A*). If, therefore, rationality is the true essence of thinking and also the true essence of the real world, then the knower must experience it as such. Thought must confront sense intuitions, images, religious faith, empirical classifications and laws, and show how these are manifestations of its own concepts, its own idea, its own necessities. Hegel even says that the agreement between philosophical thought and experience serves as at least an external test (*wenigstens aüßeren Prüfstein*) of philosophical truth, although he does not explain what he means by an external test. The "at least" suggests that the external test will not do the whole job. It will not prove everything that must be proved. Certainly it does not prove what the necessary determinations of rationality are. Philosophical thought demonstrates what the rational is by letting the subject matter itself determine what it is. Experience, therefore, cannot disprove philosophical claims by forcing philosophical thought to adjust its claims and take care of appearances. The truth is not some third thing produced by a mutual adjustment between thought and experience. The truth is uncompromising pure thought deriving its categories and laws from what

6 See also *Enz* §3, 9.

thought itself is. But philosophy must also know this truth as the rationality of the actual, and this is where an external test might have a role to play. If an independent thought determination cannot also belong to the reality of experience, then it cannot pass the external test of philosophical truth. Hegel suggests this when he says, "Indeed, this accord can be viewed as an outward touchstone, at least, for the truth of a philosophy; just as it has to be seen as the supreme and ultimate purpose of science to bring about the reconciliation of the reason that is conscious of itself with the reason that is, or actuality, through the cognition of this accord" (*Enz* §6). Hegel does not say that science aims at knowing an already established reconciliation of reason as self-thinking thought with reason actualized as a world. He says rather that science aims at bringing about this reconciliation (*hervorzubringen*) by knowing the accord between philosophy and experience. In other words, philosophy is reason as self-thinking thought, and experience is "reason that is, or actuality." If, therefore, philosophical thought does not identify the empirical appearance that corresponds to its independently developed thought determinations, then philosophical thought cannot pass the externality test. It cannot know itself as the rationality of what exists outside pure thought, and hence it will not bring about the reconciliation of reason as self-thinking thought with reason actualized as a world.

How, then, does philosophy know this accord between its own pure thought and the actual world of experience? Hegel answers this question by talking about the relation between philosophy and empirical science. Empirical science brings to light certain universal principles and necessities operative in experience, which shows that experience itself belongs to thought. Experience has the universality and necessity characteristic of thought itself. This challenges thought to develop a positive relation between itself and experience, so that thought can claim as its own the universality and necessity that empirical science discovers in the empirical world. Philosophy meets the challenge by demonstrating that the necessities operative in experience belong to the necessary structure of thought. Empirical science discovers universal principles and necessary laws given in experience. Philosophy rethinks these necessities by deriving them from the necessities of pure thought. Thus, philosophy demonstrates that the necessities of rational thought and the necessities of experienced realities are the same rationality.

Hegel insists that there can be no philosophy without experience, just as there can be no eating without food. When we reflect, we think over what we experience. When we think philosophically, we think about the content of experience. Philosophy even appropriates for its own purposes the laws of empirical science. But philosophical thought, like eating, is ungrateful. Like eating, it does not acknowledge, respect, or preserve the givenness of what it has received. It absorbs its food into the dynamics of its own system. Philosophy does not justify its concepts, its Idea, or its demonstrations by appealing to what is given in experience. It rethinks the content of experience, including the classifications and laws of empirical science, by deriving them from the categories and necessities of pure thought.

Hegel calls this *a priori* thinking. Because of its Kantian associations, however, we must pay attention to the way Hegel's use of the term here differs from the way Kant uses it in his critique of understanding. Hegel will be more explicit about this difference in his later discussion of positions on objectivity. But even here, where critical philosophy is not mentioned, Hegel gives the term *a priori* a meaning that must not be confused with Kant's transcendental analytic. Hegel is not talking about thought bringing its *a priori* forms into the given content of experience in order to provide the synthesis necessary for objectivity in experience. Hegel is talking about thought detached from its involvement in experience, thought deriving the content of experience from thought's own internal necessities, which transforms experience into "the presentation and imitation (*Nachbildung*) of the activity of thinking that is original and completely independent" (*Enz* §12+*A*). In other words, philosophical thought knows the empirical world as thought's own rationality playing out its own internal dynamics in the form of a reality presented to thought as a replica of itself.[7]

There are, of course, problems involved in this claim. If philosophy knows the realities of experience one way and experience knows the same realities a different way, why should we accept philosophy's way of knowing as the real truth of the matter instead of the way experience knows it? The *Encyclopaedia*, at least in the general introduction considered here, suggests that this claim depends on thought's need for the necessity that empirical knowledge does not provide. And the necessity thought seeks is one that identifies and explains experienced realities themselves. Empirical science discovers that certain associations operate in experience with the force of necessity. Philosophy needs to know why these associations are necessary. We can, however, repeat the same question as a challenge to this answer. What justifies the assumption that what thought needs determines what reality truly is? Why not accept that reality has no more necessity than what empirical science discovers? We shall see Hegel providing a better response to these questions when he asks about how philosophy begins, when he

7 See also *Enz* §3, 9.

examines the three positions on objectivity, and especially in the introductory essays of the *Logic* and the *Phenomenology*.

Even in this part of the *Encyclopaedia*, however, Hegel acknowledges that the actual existence of the rational in the realities of experience involves some complicated associations. Philosophical thought cannot completely transform empirical knowledge into the rationality of pure thought. Hegel acknowledges this when he distinguishes his encyclopaedia from "other, ordinary encyclopaedia." Ordinary encyclopaedia include the "positive sciences." Hegel talks about two kinds of "positive" science. A science that is completely "positive" merely brings together bits of information. Philosophy has nothing to do with such sciences. Some "positive" sciences, however, have a rational ground and a rational beginning. For example, the science of jurisprudence works with legal principles, natural science investigates nature, and history studies the existence of the human spirit in time. Nature, social law, and the historical development of the human spirit have their ground in reason; and hence they belong to the subject matter of philosophy. But natural science, jurisprudence, and history focus on the way these rational concepts and their ground belong to the contingencies of empirical singularity - details of law left undetermined by the concept of the rational, natural phenomena determined by chance or the play of circumstances, historical developments determined by contingent events and the arbitrariness of free choice. Thus, although the subject matter and its development belong to the necessities of reason, the empirical sciences deal exclusively with the conditions proper to its empirical appearance (*Enz* §16+*A*).

Hegel makes the same point again when he distinguishes philosophy from forms of knowledge that address ought questions. Hegel acknowledges the legitimacy of these questions. The contingent, transitory ways in which the rational makes its appearance are not always as they should be. Conditions and institutions that have been important for a time or in a limited sphere might not be appropriate for another time or sphere. Hence, it is right to raise questions about these matters. But Hegel insists that such concerns must not be mistaken for real philosophical issues. Philosophy is concerned with the rational. This means that it is concerned with experience and the actual, because the rational is actual in experience. But the rational exists as the essential element in empirical reality, and only as such is philosophy concerned with it. The task of judging how well contingent details conform to this essence does not belong to philosophy. Thus, Hegel identifies legitimate ought questions with the kind of knowledge that deals with the contingencies of experience. Like jurisprudence, natural science, and history, this kind of knowledge has its own domain, a domain in which philosophy has no place (*Enz* §6*A*).

Finally, Hegel deals with the same issues in a different way when he distinguishes between two ways in which philosophical science comes into being. In the form of "external history," different philosophies governed by different principles emerge at different times. Thus, philosophy appears diversified in a contingent sequence of different philosophical positions. But the history of philosophy shows that philosophy is one spirit gradually developing a knowledge of what it is, and the principles that ground each particular philosophical position are different branches of philosophy as a whole. The positions that come later in the series emerge as the result of the preceding ones. Hence, the later positions are more concrete, more fully developed, richer in content, because they hold within them the different philosophical principles that have preceded them in the historical sequence. Hegel adds a qualifier here. The philosophy latest in time is the most concrete, the most fully developed, the richest in content "provided that it does deserve the name of philosophy" (*Enz* §13). The qualifier seems to acknowledge that renegade philosophies can appear in history, philosophies whose principles do not fall in with the development established by preceding philosophical positions. Hegel does not hold himself responsible for integrating into the historical development of the philosophical whole everything in history that calls itself philosophy.[8]

This qualifier, however, does not solve every problem. Indeed, it raises some difficulties. In the *Philosophy of Right*, Hegel explicitly denies that historically necessitated results can justify philosophical claims. We must ask, therefore, whether the *Encyclopaedia* account of philosophy's historical development conflates historically and philosophically necessitated results. Also, if it is possible for a philosophy to fall out of line with philosophy's development in history, according to what principle do we distinguish between what does and does not belong to this development? Hegel suggests his answer to these questions when he distinguishes between the development of thinking "presented in the history of philosophy" and "the same development ... presented in philosophy itself." In philosophy itself, thought develops "purely in the element of thinking," "freed from that historical outwardness." In philosophical science, thought is free from every determination but its own. It develops according to its own necessities. This development takes the form of a unity opening up into distinctions held together as a whole. The necessity of the differences depends on

8 This interpretation is confirmed later in *Enz* §86*Z2*.

their being developed from what the unity of the whole requires of itself (*Enz* §14). If, therefore, the history of philosophy is the same development in the form of outwardness, then the reality outside thought mirrors the necessities that thought develops from within its own self-determination. This is the principle according to which we select from history what belongs to thought's self-development. Hegel's concern with the history of philosophy, therefore, does not have to address philosophical positions exactly as they were proposed. Rather, it aims at identifying in them what the necessities of thought have determined. Philosophy knows the rational by knowing the accord between independent, self-determined thinking and the necessary determinations of the empirical world.

What, then, is the truth status of all these realities that do not belong to the subject matter of philosophy? If philosophical truth requires the actualization of thought's independent determinations in the realities of experience, then the involvement of the rational in the contingencies of the surrounding context belongs in some way to what the truth is. We shall continue to ask this question as we continue the study of Hegel's introductions, in order to show how the problem continues to haunt Hegel's project. We shall see Hegel address the issue briefly in his examination of the three positions on objectivity, and deal with it more thoroughly in the main text of the *Phenomenology*.

3 PHILOSOPHICAL PROOF PROCEDURE

In the introductory essays of the *Encyclopaedia*, Hegel gives a brief, preliminary description of the procedure according to which philosophy demonstrates what is involved in the self-determination of independent thought. He warns, however, that this description is an anticipation of what must be proved within logic itself. The preliminary account gives us a preview of where the necessities of thought will lead (*Enz* §19*A*, 79*A*).

According to Hegel, every logical reality has three aspects: the abstract or understandable (*verständige*), the dialectical or negatively rational, and the speculative or positively rational (*Enz* §79). Understanding holds to fixed determinations that stand firm in their difference from others. It takes each determination by itself, identifies this determination in terms of itself alone, and keeps the determination separated from other determinations. Thus, understanding thinks with precision, carefully and relentlessly focusing on what identifies a determination, and allowing no mingling with anything else (*Enz* §80). In the Addition to the section in which Hegel identifies understanding, we find evidence that Hegel in his lectures talked about the rather complex way in which this thinking with precision plays a role in thinking rationally. As a form of thinking, understanding gives universality to what it thinks. Understanding thinks a content common to many, a universal, and thereby holds together different things under one identifying determination. Hegel calls this universality abstract, because understanding keeps the content of the universal strictly distinguished from all particulars that might accompany it, and hence it thinks a determination repeated without variation in different instances. But understanding contributes to rational thinking its fixed, precise meanings and content differentiation. Understanding's universals may be abstract, because they do not contain the differentiation that distinguishes different instances of the same determination. But these universals are not indeterminate. They have a definite content strictly distinguished from other definite contents. Without understanding's insistence on precision and fixed meanings, philosophy and all forms of theory and practice would fall into vague, indeterminate ways of thinking (*Enz* §80*Z*).

Dialectical thinking shows how the fixed determinations of understanding pass over into their opposites. Hegel explains this development by distinguishing the dialectical moment in philosophical procedure from dialectics, from reflection, and from scepticism (*Enz* §81+*A*). Dialectics functions as an external art form. The dialectician deliberately produces confusion and the appearance of contradiction in a concept. Addition #1 indicates that Hegel in his lectures described Socratic irony as an example of dialectics. Socratic irony is subjective. It depends on the cleverness of the dialectician, and the slow wit of the one with whom he converses. Thus, Socrates, through clever questioning, manipulates the one who is questioned into conclusions that contradict the claims this speaker made at the beginning of the conversation. Dialectical philosophical procedure differs from this because it derives the transition into an opposite from the meaning of understanding's finite determinations, not from the way a thinker gets trapped by the manoeuvres of another thinker. Hegel offers Plato's *Parmenides* and Kant's antinomies as examples of proper philosophical dialectic. In the *Parmenides,* Plato "deduces the Many from the One" while maintaining that the Many by its very nature "determines itself as the One." Kant's antinomies "exhibit how each abstract determination of the understanding, taken simply on its own terms, overturns immediately into its opposite" (*Enz* §81*Z*1).

Reflection acknowledges that understanding's isolated determinations are necessarily connected to their opposite. But it persists in thinking that validity belongs to the determination in its isolation. Addition #1 describes two forms of cognition that conform to this description of reflection. Ordinary consciousness acknowledges that understanding's concepts are limited by other, opposed concepts. It deals with this state of affairs by adopting a "live and let live" attitude. It accepts each of understanding's fixed, limited determinations for what it is by itself, unconnected to the opposite, which allows other, opposed determinations to be what they are in the same disconnected, isolated way. Human beings are living things; human beings are also things that die because external conditions kill them off. The negation that opposes a human being's life is conceived as nature's own independent way of being. So also, red is red; its not being green is simply green being green. Thus, this form of reflection reduces the opposition between one determination and another to A is A and B is B. Dialectical philosophical procedure differs from this attitude because it finds that understanding's fixed, limited determinations carry the seeds of their negation within their own nature. Human life itself moves toward death. Red by being red determines itself as not other colours.

Sophistry also acknowledges that understanding's isolated determinations are connected to their opposites. But sophistry holds to one of these, and argues from this fixed, isolated determination to the negation of whatever stands opposed to or limits it. For example, I am free, and a consequence of being free is my right to overrule or dismiss social norms that restrict my freedom. Philosophical dialectical procedure differs from this because it exposes and acknowledges the limitations of all one-sided, finite determinations. Their very one-sidedness and precision negates any claims they might make against other determinations whose claims restrict and challenge them. My freedom requires realization in an inter-subjective world. Precisely by being limited to me, this freedom negates any claim it might make against the freedom of others realized in the same world, or against any social laws established to keep the world open to the freedom of all.

According to Hegel, scepticism is dialectic as understanding interprets it, namely as a negative result isolated from all its connections. The Additions indicate that Hegel amplified this explanation by distinguishing scepticism proper from other negative attitudes toward knowledge. According to the Additions, scepticism is not the kind of doubt typical of modern philosophy. Modern doubt either distrusts the claims of finite understanding in the hope of finding among these something that cannot be doubted, or it denies the validity of the supersensible while accepting the validity of sense experience. Scepticism proper is the "high ancient scepticism" exemplified by Sextus Empiricus, which rests in "complete despair about everything that the understanding holds to be firm" (*Enz* §81 *Z2*). Philosophical dialectical procedure, like high ancient scepticism, exposes the self-negation implicit in everything finite. Precisely because a determination has a definite content, fixed and isolated from other contents, precisely because this content determines it as restricted to what it is, the determination identifies itself as not the whole truth. But philosophical dialectical procedure differs from scepticism because scepticism sticks to the negation as negation, as the untruth of all finite claims, whereas philosophy knows that the negation is also positive.

Proper philosophical dialectic has a positive as well as a negative result because the negation is determinate. In the dialectical moment of philosophical procedure, the negativity of the opposite, its not being the original concept, emerges as a result of what the original concept is. Thought follows the meaning of the concept into the self-negation that is implicit in it. The transition to an opposite, therefore, develops a determinate negation. It preserves the positive content of the original concept and connects the concept to a negation whose whole meaning is derived from and given specific content by this connection. Hence, the move does not deny the original concept or cancel it out. On the contrary, it asserts the concept's fuller meaning. It expands what thought thinks in the concept by including the negation that connects the concept to its opposite (*Enz* §81*A*, 82*A*).

Determinate negation determines the speculative or positively rational move in philosophical procedure: "The speculative or positively rational apprehends the unity of the determinations in their opposition, the affirmative that is contained in their dissolution and in their transition" (*Enz* §82). Speculative thought thinks something positive. It affirms something. What does it affirm? It affirms that the original concept and its negation are one truth. But how is this unity conceived? It is conceived as a unity "contained in" the dissolution and transition of the opposites, a unity of the determinations "in their opposition." The original concept dissolves its rigid, isolated self-definition. Its identifying determination carries the concept into the opposite that negates it. So also the opposite, as the determinate negation of the original concept, dissolves its separation from what it negates. It derives what it is from the negating that connects it to what it negates, and hence from its being involved in an opposition relation to it. This connection unifies the opposites "in their opposition." Both belong to the same process and both get their not-being-the-other from this process. Thus, speculative thought does not get rid of the opposition or neutralize it. Speculative thought thinks the unity implicit in the opposition. It asserts the unifying principle that governs the dynamic between the opposites and thus identifies them as mutually exclusive members of the same truth (*Enz* §82+*A*+*Z*).

4 THE BEGINNING PRESUPPOSITIONS OF PHILOSOPHY

The rigorous immanence of philosophical procedure makes the whole project dependent on the necessity of the original concept. How, then, does philosophy prove the necessity of its beginning concept, the concept of the rational or logical? According to the *Encyclopaedia,* philosophy begins in experience. Thought moves to the philosophical standpoint by becoming dissatisfied with empirical knowledge. Thought needs complete necessity, and experience does not provide it. In order to satisfy this need, thought separates itself from experience and withdraws into the internal dynamics of thought itself. Conceiving the truth project in this way involves two presuppositions. First, it assumes that thought withdrawn into itself, thought detached from its involvement in the givens of the empirical world, has access to a rationality that is common to both thought and being. Thus, it conceives thought itself not as the thinking of the thinking subject but as the rationality in which this thinking is rooted and which it has in common with the real world. Second, the *Encyclopaedia* describes philosophy as thought demanding necessity. Entering the domain of philosophy, therefore, involves a commitment to the demand for complete necessity. This commitment is accomplished in the decision to make thought itself the subject matter of a science. The decision, however, does not establish the legitimacy of the demand. Philosophy presupposes this legitimacy. It assumes that necessity is not only what thought needs but also what the true essence of reality is.

Hegel recognizes the problem at the outset. Philosophy, he says, does not have the same advantages as other sciences. Other sciences take their object from a given representation, and assume that the beginning of the science and its method are already established. Biology, for example, is a life science. As such it assumes that there is life in nature and begins with the generally accepted understanding of what life is. This general representation of life focuses the investigation on a certain subject matter, which determines what does and does not belong to the process that provides a more adequate account of what life is. Sociology is a social science. It accepts the actual existence of social relations and begins with the generally accepted understanding of what counts as social. Both sciences assume that the method of the empirical sciences is valid. Hegel acknowledges that philosophy, too, begins with representations, because it begins within experience.

Philosophy shares its objects with the content of religious experience. Both religion and philosophy seek truth in the highest sense, in the sense that God and God alone is the truth. Both seek the truth of the finite, of nature and the human spirit, in the infinite, absolute reality of God. Hence, we come to philosophy with its objects already familiar to us from religious experience. But familiarity is not enough. Philosophical thinking demands that "the necessity of the content be shown, and the very being, as well as the determinations, of the ob-jects should be proved (*beweisen*)" (*Enz* §1).

If, however, philosophy requires a demonstration of necessity, then it disallows all presuppositions and assurances, both about the determinations of its objects and their reality. Philosophy cannot simply accept familiar ways of thinking about nature or the human spirit, and use these to develop further claims about these realities, as other sciences do. It cannot accept assurances from religion about a truth that transcends all finite restrictions and gives to everything finite its ultimate true meaning (*Enz* §1). This raises questions about how thinking embedded in and committed to accepted representations or ways of thinking becomes converted to a philosophical attitude. The demand that nothing be accepted without proof of its necessity calls for a certain detachment, a questioning attitude toward all representations and asserted ways of thinking.

Philosophy, Hegel says, must show ordinary consciousness the need for philosophy's own approach. In other words, philosophy must show ordinary consciousness why familiar representations or ways of thinking must be questioned, why a proof of their necessity and validity must be demanded; or philosophy must somehow call forth this questioning within ordinary consciousness itself. In its relation to religion, philosophy must show that thought operating on its own, without dependence on religious representations, can demonstrate the necessity of religion's object; and if differences emerge between the way religion represents the truth and the way philosophy demonstrates its necessity, philosophy must justify its claims against those of religion. Speaking generally, philosophy must justify the way thought's need for necessity challenges the familiar representations operating in experience and adjusts them to its own requirements (*Enz* §4).

Hegel insists, however, that every beginning is a presupposition (*Enz* §1). Hegel says this in the context of a discussion that talks about the way sciences identify the subject matter to be investigated and the method for investigating it. Other sciences undertake an investigation by presupposing a generally accepted representation of the subject matter and an accepted method for developing a fuller understanding of what the subject matter is. Philosophy cannot begin with a representation and methodology taken from what is familiar and generally accepted. But philosophy must begin with some kind of presupposed concept, since it cannot undertake an investigation without an object to be investigated, and it cannot focus the investigation on this object without a beginning concept of what it is. Moreover, if philosophical methodology derives its various moves from the way understanding identifies a determination, then even methodology depends on some kind of presupposed concept of philosophy's object.

Philosophy, however, differs from other sciences because its subject matter is not something other than thought that thought must presuppose as the object of investigation. The subject matter of philosophy is thought itself. Thought, therefore, can give itself its object by asserting itself as the object of investigation. Thought achieves the philosophical standpoint by simply resolving to think about thought itself. Philosophy begins with a decision, a free act of thinking. How, then, does philosophy come up with the definition of its beginning concept? It begins with the concept that identifies what is minimally required to make thought itself the object of investigation. It begins with thought conceived as immediate, prior to all its determinations, thought simply being, prior to the development of any positive or negative predicates (*Enz* §86+*A*+*Z*1).[9] Philosophy will demonstrate that this immediacy is itself mediated. The development of its beginning concept eventually proves that thought in its immediacy is the result of what has been developed from it. Philosophy comes full circle. Its necessary moves bring it back to the original concept, and this transforms the immediacy of the concept into a result, a mediated immediacy. Thus, the beginning concept is an unmediated beginning only for the subject who begins the philosophical project. Thought as the object of philosophy develops in a continuous circle. But the thinking subject, the one who undertakes the philosophical project, must make a beginning (*Enz* §17).[10]

Hegel has shown, however, why neither the decision to think about thought itself nor the circularity of philosophy's conceptual development can solve the real problem involved in philosophy's beginning concept. Developing the internal necessities of the concept that defines the subject matter of philosophy gives us a disciplined, thorough, fully articulated knowledge of what thought is. The philosophical return to the beginning concept redefines the beginning as a concept situated within a circular process, and it redefines the process as an integrated, self-contained whole. But why should we accept this as anything more than a thought experiment? We suppose thought left to its

9 See also *Enz* §78. Compare to *PhR* §33*A*.
10 See also *Enz* §84.

own internal self-necessitating devices, and then we observe what develops. Why is Hegelian philosophy anything more than this?

In order to address this question, we must examine the ambiguous way in which Hegel talks about mediation and immediacy when he considers the way thought begins philosophical science. Philosophy's beginning position is the immediacy of pure thought, thought concentrated only on itself. But this position is mediated by thought rejecting experience as not the necessary truth that thought seeks. In other words, the immediacy of thought, thought isolated in itself and separated from all mediating relations, depends on and is mediated by the negative relation that liberates thought from its involvement in experience. Philosophical thought assumes, however, that thought developed according to its own internal necessities exists as the true essence of the empirical world. The legitimacy of this assumption depends on what provokes the separation of thought from experience. If experience itself demonstrates that its own truth depends on the internal dynamics of independent thought, then we can legitimately assume that what thought reveals about itself also reveals the fundamental truth of the empirical world. If, however, thought separates itself from experience because of some need that thought itself brings to experience, which is what the Introduction to the *Encyclopaedia* suggests, then the internal dynamics of independent thought provide nothing more than a full articulation of what this need involves. The fundamental question remains unanswered. Why assume that what thought needs identifies what empirical reality is?

Hegel gets to this question indirectly. Philosophy has as its object the same infinite, absolute reality that religion knows as God; and like religion, it knows this infinite as the true essence of nature and the human spirit. How do we know that human thought, which is finite, is capable of knowing a truth that is infinite and absolute? Hegel says that philosophy itself must justify its claim to know with necessity an infinite, absolute truth. Philosophical thought itself must demonstrate its ability to know absolute objects, presumably by actually accomplishing it (*Enz* §10). Any other kind of proof would be "an un-philosophical one, and it could not be more than a tissue of presuppositions, assurances, and argumentations (*Räsonnements*), i.e., of contingent assertions, against which the opposite assurances could be made with the same right" (*Enz* §10). Philosophy, however, proceeds by developing the necessities of pure thought. If it does not assume that the necessities of thought are also the necessities of reality, then it produces the idea of the infinite only as a condition of thinking, not as absolute truth.

Hegel acknowledges, however, two other ways in which the same question has been addressed. Critical philosophy claims that before we engage in the project of knowing God or the essence of things, we must first examine the knowing instrument. We must ask whether this instrument is capable of knowing these "absolute objects," because if it is not, the whole project would be pointless. Thus, critical philosophy begins by entertaining the possibility that knowing might be incapable of knowing "the essence of things." Hegel says that this strategy turns cognition away from its concern with objects and focuses on cognition itself, which he refers to as "the formal aspect." Critical philosophy turns away from cognition's concern with the content of what it knows and focuses on the form that cognition gives to it (*Enz* §10*A*).

Once this move is made, Hegel's question becomes my question. Kant's critical philosophy certainly shows that the form of thought can develop an idea of God as the absolute condition of all finite determinations. But this idea belongs only to the form of knowing. It conceives the conditions required to give thought the form of completeness and coherence required by reason. But what reason demands proves only what is implicit in the form of thought. It proves nothing about objects, whether we conceive these as the content of experience or the reality of things outside consciousness.[11] From the perspective of critical philosophy, Hegelian philosophy might demonstrate its ability to conceive the conditions required for absolute truth without proving that these conditions belong to empirical reality. Even if philosophy proves that the internal dynamics of independent thought necessitate thought's involvement in experience, this does not prove that this thought-determined relation to experience reveals the true essence of experience itself.

Hegel attacks the strategy of critical philosophy by pointing out that a critique of knowledge is itself a kind of knowing. In order to carry out the project of examining the knowing instrument, critical philosophy would have to use the instrument whose knowing capacity has been questioned. It would have to engage in a knowing project before it has proved that knowing is capable of the project. According to Hegel, Reinhold tries to avoid this difficulty by beginning philosophy with a hypothetical thesis, continuing with this thesis until the procedure somehow reaches the origin or source of truth (*Urwahre*).[12] Hegel points out that this procedure is no different from the usual way of developing an investigation. Something is

11 *KrV*, A298–311/B355–68; A321–40/B377–98; A567–83/B595–611.

12 Hegel refers here to Karl Leonhard Reinhold (1758–1823). For an excellent explanation of Reinhold's role in the philosophical developments that influenced Hegel's thought, see di Giovanni 1985, 9–20; 2005, chapters and sections 3.3, 4.2, 4.5, 6.3, 7.2.

proposed as a beginning definition of the subject matter, and the investigation uses this definition to justify its claims. Reinhold's approach shows that such justifications are nothing but hypotheticals, i.e. they prove only what must be true *if* the original provisional definition is true. This insight, however, serves only to expose the inadequacy of the usual approach (*Enz* §10*A*).

Hegel's objection to the procedure he attributes to Reinhold tells us something important about the procedural requirements Hegel is imposing on himself. The objection claims that philosophy cannot begin with a provisional assumption or an appeal to empirical evidence, since this would ground the necessary truth of philosophy in a supposition that may or may not be true. But Hegelian philosophy begins with the decision to think about thought set free from experience. It gets its beginning concept, the concept of the logical or rational, from this resolution. It proceeds by demonstrating what necessarily follows from this concept. Hegel can begin philosophy with this free act of thinking if all he needs for the object of philosophy is thought as such. If, however, the object of philosophy is thought as a rationality whose necessities reveal the true essence of the actual, then Hegel must either posit thought so defined as a hypothetical philosophical thesis, a strategy he rejects in his critique of Reinhold, or he must find a way to prove the thesis.

5 THE ROLE OF THE PHENOMENOLOGY

Hegel in the *Encyclopaedia* recognizes that this problem must be addressed and indicates that the *Phenomenology of Spirit* deals with it: "In my *Phenomenology of Spirit*, which was for this reason described, when it was published, as the first part of the system of science, the procedure adopted was to begin from the first and simplest appearance of the spirit, from immediate consciousness, and to develop its dialectic right up to the standpoint of philosophical science, the necessity of which is shown by the progression" (*Enz* §25*A*). In the Introduction, Hegel calls experience "immediate consciousness" (*Enz* §12). The *Phenomenology* begins with experience. Moreover, it begins as a "first and simplest appearance," without complicating procedures or complex content structures. It begins with experience reduced to the minimum required for it to appear at all. The *Phenomenology* proceeds dialectically, and its dialectic proves the necessity of the philosophical standpoint.

The introductory essays of the *Encyclopaedia* persistently insist on strict necessity, in contrast to necessities that depend on what just happens to be accepted in familiar ways of thinking, or necessities that just happen to be operative in the dynamics of empirical reality, or just happen to be the categories and rules according to which thought thinks. It seems obvious that in these texts the word "necessity" refers to what unconditionally must be, a necessity in no way dependent on what only happens to be the way things are, or only happens to be what people accept as true or valid, or only happens to be the way thought thinks. When, therefore, the same texts attribute "necessity" to the *Phenomenology*, we should accept the word as carrying the same force. Moreover, by saying that the *Phenomenology* proceeds dialectically, Hegel suggests a procedure akin to scepticism. Whether he has in mind the dialectical procedure of scepticism as a negative science or the dialectical move in philosophical procedure, he refers to a dialectic that derives the negation of a position from the internal necessities of the position itself. In other words, dialectic demonstrates that what has been asserted as true negates its own claims to truth. The *Phenomenology* begins with experience reduced to the first and simplest way in which it appears, and hence in the form that experience must first and foremost be. The *Phenomenology* proceeds by exposing dialectical negations implicit in experience itself, and this process demonstrates the necessity of shifting into the philosophical standpoint. Thus, the *Phenomenology* shows that experience, examined according to its own internal necessities, requires the rejection of its own claims to truth.

Hegel goes on to say that the "development of consciousness" in the *Phenomenology* might seem to be "restricted just to what is formal," but that the *Phenomenology* could not stick to "the formal aspect" (*Enz* §25*A*). Hegel refers to "the formal aspect" in his discussion of critical philosophy. This phrase describes the way critical philosophy turns cognition away from its concern with objects and focuses it on cognition itself (*Enz* §10*A*). Hegel also refers to form distinguished from content when he distinguishes the form of thought from the form of intuition and representation. Both know the same content, but the form of knowing it is different (*Enz* §2). The *Phenomenology* seems to be a project that focuses cognition on the form of knowing proper to experience, distinguished from the content of experience. But the philosophical standpoint, Hegel says, is "in itself" (*in sich*) a form of knowing conjoined to (*zugleich*) the richest and most concrete content. Since the philosophical standpoint emerges from the *Phenomenology* as a result, philosophy presupposes "the concrete shapes of consciousness, such as morality, ethical life, art, and religion" (*Enz* §25*A*). Hence, it was not possible to demonstrate the necessity of the philosophical standpoint by focusing exclusively on the formal aspect of consciousness. It was necessary to examine forms of consciousness for which the object of experience has some of the same concrete content as the concrete parts of the philosophical system.

This text in the *Encyclopaedia* supports limited claims, but they are worth noting. Hegel says here that the *Phenomenology* begins within immediate consciousness or experience; and he acknowledges that the philosophical standpoint depends on the *Phenomenology* for proof of its necessity, that this standpoint emerges as the result of a dialectic developed in this work. Thus, the Hegel of the *Encyclopaedia* acknowledges that the necessity of the philosophical standpoint must be demonstrated, and that it must be demonstrated by deriving it from a dialectical procedure in which experience negates its own truth claims. Moreover, Hegel says that philosophy "presupposes" (*voraussetzen*) the concrete content of morality, social life, art, and religion, and for this reason the content must be included in the *Phenomenology*'s project. This suggests that the concrete content that philosophy develops from the beginning concept of its subject matter is the same content that appears in the phenomenological examination of experience. When philosophy begins with the concept of the rational or logical, it takes for granted that this concept identifies the fundamental truth of experiential content as well as the fundamental truth of the formal cognition structures embedded in this content. The *Phenomenology* exposes the dialectical implications of experience, an exposition that develops "behind its back," i.e. without becoming explicit in the experience itself. This exposition demonstrates the necessity of rethinking the content of experience as a content that belongs to the necessities of pure thought.

None of these points are compromised by Hegel's decision to use a different approach in the *Encyclopaedia*. The *Encyclopaedia* introduces the philosophical standpoint by describing "the positions available to thinking with respect to objectivity" (*Enz* §25). But Hegel says that this approach is troublesome or inconvenient (*das Unbequeme*), because it is merely historical and argumentative (*räsonierend*) (*Enz* §25A). In the Introduction, Hegel calls experience "immediate and argumentative consciousness (*das räsonierende Bewußtsein*)" (*Enz* §12). He describes the history of philosophy as the development of thought in its externality, in the form of "a contingent succession" without the necessary connections that integrate the succession into a whole (*Enz* §14+A). By using the same terminology to describe the way the *Encyclopaedia* gets us into the philosophical standpoint, Hegel suggests that this approach has the form of experience. It describes the development of philosophy as something given in the experience of its history. It does not expose the dialectical necessity determining the developments that appear in the history it describes, nor does it present the final position as a necessary result of these developments. In other words, the *Encyclopaedia*'s approach does not demonstrate necessity as the *Phenomenology* supposedly does.

6 CONCLUSION

Both the *Philosophy of Right* and the *Encyclopaedia* identify philosophical thought by distinguishing it from knowledge based on subjective convictions, established customs and ways of speaking, arguments derived from generally accepted definitions and historical states of affairs. The *Encyclopaedia* develops the same theme in a more general way by distinguishing philosophical thought from all forms of experience, including even the forms of thought developed in the empirical sciences. According to both works, the subject matter of philosophy is the rational, and philosophy knows the rational by developing the necessities of pure thought without depending on what it finds given in experience.

Yet both texts also distinguish philosophical thought from thought focused on an ought, a norm, that is completely removed from the domain of real experience. Both texts insist that philosophical thought must turn back to experience and know the necessities of pure thought actualized, made real, in experience. Both texts develop the rational is actual theme by distinguishing the essential element in the realities of experience from the contingent, transitory, irrelevant details that accompany it. The term "actual" refers only to the essential element, and the term "rational" refers to the way this element corresponds to the rationality of pure thought. Philosophical thought knows the truth by knowing the rational actualized in experience. Philosophy provides a norm for judging whether existing states of affairs are what their own rational essence requires them to be; but an ought whose excellence makes it incapable of becoming actualized in experience does not belong to the rationality that is the subject matter of philosophy.

This way of identifying what philosophy is raises three questions. First, exactly how does philosophy justify its conception of the rational? To put it another way, how does philosophy develop the necessities of pure thought without depending on what is given in experience? Second, what justifies the assumption that what corresponds to the necessities of pure thought identifies what the realities of experience essentially are? Third, since the rational element actualized in experience is embedded in contingent and transitory details, do these details belong to the truth of experience and to the way philosophy knows this truth?

Both the *Philosophy of Right* and the *Encyclopaedia* answer the first question with an analysis of philosophical proof procedure. Philosophy derives its conception of the rational from a threefold dynamic: a beginning concept that identifies the subject matter; the development of an opposite from what is implicit in this concept; a positive result in which the concept and its opposite are conceived as differences within the same truth. *The Encyclopaedia* introduces the term "determinate negation" to identify the way the opposite emerges from what it opposes and remains attached to it and defined in terms of it. The *Philosophy of Right* describes the positive result as a universal that both unifies particulars and necessitates their diversification. The *Encyclopaedia* describes it as the unity of the opposites in their opposition, indicating that the unity not only preserves the opposites but also preserves the opposition between them. Hegel refers to this procedure as dialectic. Both the *Philosophy of Right* and the *Encyclopaedia* distinguish philosophical dialectic from the kind of dialectic in which a thinking subject dismisses a proposition by creating confusions and contradictions. The *Encyclopaedia* also distinguishes philosophical dialectic from sophistry and scepticism, both of which get stuck in the negative results of dialectic.

The analysis of philosophical proof procedure calls for a discussion of how philosophy justifies the beginning concept that determines and justifies the determinate negations and positive results developed from it. The *Philosophy of Right* says that its beginning concept, the concept of right, is justified by a prior demonstration belonging to a different area of philosophical investigation. This answer raises questions about the concept that defines the subject matter of the whole philosophical project. How is the beginning concept of the rational justified, and what justifies the assumption that the rational identifies the true essence of real experience? The general introduction to the *Encyclopaedia* offers three different answers to this question. First, since philosophical thought has as its subject matter the rationality of thought itself, it can begin by simply resolving to think thought as such. This, however, leaves unquestioned and unproved the reality status of philosophical thought, its being true of what is actual in the realities of experience. The narrative developed in the general introduction suggests that the move out of experience into independent thought is governed by thought's need for necessity, which raises the same question, why what thought needs reveals what reality essentially is. Second, the *Phenomenology of Spirit* begins with the first and simplest appearance of knowing, immediate consciousness, and follows its dialectic to the point where it demonstrates the necessity of the concept that defines the subject matter of philosophy. This approach aims at providing the necessity demanded by thought. Third, the *Encyclopaedia* examines three positions on objectivity in order to lead the reader into the philosophical standpoint. Hegel acknowledges that this last is a less satisfactory approach than the one developed in the *Phenomenology*.

In the process of discussing the question, how does philosophy begin, the *Encyclopaedia* introduces a question that provokes a response in which Hegel rejects certain ways of providing an introduction to philosophy. According to the *Encyclopaedia*, philosophy and religion have the same content. Philosophy seeks the absolute truth, the infinite that religion knows as God. How do we know that human knowledge is capable of knowing the infinite? Critical philosophy says that before we become engaged in trying to know the infinite we have to do a critique of knowledge to find out if we are capable of knowing it. But Hegel objects that this involves questioning what knowledge can do while taking for granted the legitimacy of the critic's norms and judgments. Reinhold proposes a strategy that begins with a hypothetical thesis and develops it until it reaches the source of truth. But Hegel objects that this reduces the whole development to a hypothetical case. Hegel says that only philosophy can prove that human knowledge can know the infinite. But that depends on the possibility of finding a way to begin the process that is neither an unproved hypothesis, nor a critical point of view with unquestioned, unexamined critical principles, nor an arbitrary decision that assumes without question the reality status of pure thought.

The *Philosophy of Right* and the general introduction to the *Encyclopaedia* do not provide a fully developed position on the philosophical status of the contingent, transitory elements of experience. Do these elements have any role to play in the way philosophy knows the realities of experience? The general introduction to the *Encyclopaedia* suggests that these contingencies belong to other areas of knowledge, not to philosophy. It also suggests a correspondence between philosophy's development in the externality of its history and its development according to the internal necessities of philosophical thought. The legitimacy of these suggestions, and their consistency or inconsistency with each other remain open questions at this point.

5

The Encyclopaedia: *Three Positions on Objectivity*

THE *ENCYCLOPAEDIA* TAKES US INTO the philosophical standpoint by examining three positions on objectivity: naïve metaphysics, empiricism and critical philosophy, immediate knowing. As we have seen, Hegel acknowledges the limitations of this "historical" approach, calling it more troublesome than the approach developed in the *Phenomenology*. A closer look at the *Encyclopaedia* alternative, however, exposes more serious problems than its historical status. Hegel brings his own presuppositions to the examination of each position. He tells us what each contributes to true cognition and how it fails; and his own position functions as the criterion that determines these judgments. By examining the way Hegel works his way through the three positions, therefore, we will learn more about the way Hegel identifies the philosophical standpoint. We will find helpful clues to the complex issues involved in making a philosophical beginning. We will learn how to distinguish Hegel's position from the positions of other philosophers. We will not find ourselves involved in a procedure that demonstrates the necessity of accepting as true the philosophical standpoint as Hegel has conceived it.

The strategy governing our discussion of the three positions focuses exclusively on what the discussion reveals about Hegel's own position. We will consider the three positions as Hegel himself understands them, concentrating on the way his interpretive bias reveals the subtleties of the philosophical standpoint that Hegel himself accepts as true. We will not consider how these accounts of objectivity might be represented if we examined them on their own, independent of Hegel's own point of view. Nor will we develop a debate between Hegel and the philosophers represented in these accounts. We will concentrate on the way Hegel uses his own interpretation of the three positions to demonstrate what is required and what must be rejected in what he takes to be the true position.

Hegel's discussion of the three positions on objectivity proceeds chronologically. As a result, it addresses various complicated questions in a piecemeal way, which makes it difficult to recognize and appreciate the coherent position exposed in these scattered clues. I shall handle this difficulty by organizing the discussion according to the themes introduced in the chapter on the *Philosophy of Right* and the chapter on the *Encyclopaedia*'s general introduction: the rational is actual issue; the definition of philosophy's beginning concept; the problem of philosophical presuppositions; scientific proof procedure and the justification of the philosophical standpoint. The discussion of each issue will bring together clues scattered throughout Hegel's discussion of the various positions on objectivity, so that the coherent position developed in these clues can be exposed and appreciated.

This chapter will make more use of the Additions than the previous chapter. A strategy governs this use. Since the Additions are derived from student notes, no interpretation of Hegel's position will depend on Additions alone. They will be used only to clarify and perhaps elaborate a claim confirmed by something in the text that Hegel himself published, the main text or the Remarks. Please note that citations indicate Remarks with an *A* (*Anmerken*), and Additions with a *Z* (*Zusätze*) to honor the original language of the text.

1 THE RATIONAL IS ACTUAL AND THE ACTUAL RATIONAL

In the discussion of the three positions on objectivity, the rational is actual question becomes the thing-in-itself issue. Hegel begins by endorsing the basic position of traditional pre-Kantian metaphysics. He describes this position as a naïve belief that thought can go straight to the object, and can know what objects truly are simply by thinking about them (*Enz* §26). This belief rests on a presupposition: "This science regarded the thought determinations as the fundamental determinations of things; and, in virtue of this presupposition, that the cognition of things as they are in themselves results from the thinking of what is, it stood at a higher level than the later critical philosophising" (*Enz* §28). Pre-critical metaphysics presupposes a sameness between thought determinations operating in thinking and these same determinations as the fundamental truth of what exists in itself and apart from thinking. Hegel endorses this presupposition, and in doing so explicitly sides with the old metaphysics in opposition to Kant's critical philosophy. Indeed he describes the procedure characteristic of the old metaphysics in a way that resembles the description of his own approach articulated in the *Encyclopaedia*'s general introduction. Pre-critical metaphysics, like Hegelian philosophical reflection, takes the content of sense experience and intuition and rethinks it as a thought content. Thus, Hegel says that pre-critical metaphysics is capable of "authentic speculative philosophising" (*Enz* §27).

Hegel calls the traditional position naïve, however, because it is unaware of the opposition (*Gegensatz*) between thought in itself and thought opposed to itself (*in und gegen sich*) (*Enz* §26). This way of speaking suggests that the position Hegel endorses as the true position will have to preserve the fundamental presupposition of the old metaphysics while also acknowledging some kind of opposition between thought in itself and thought set off from itself as a thing-in-itself. Things in themselves, therefore, are not just an other distinguished from thinking; they are an other set off from, opposed to, thinking. It is not clear at this point what kind of opposition this might be: an opposition established by an object existing separately, detached from its relations to knowing; some characteristic that does not fall in with and mirror what thought is; or both. By finding the opposition missing in traditional metaphysics, however, Hegel suggests that the otherness of "things in themselves" is more radical than is acknowledged in the traditional distinction between the thought determinations of thinking and the same thought determinations as the fundamental truth of real things.

Hegel also criticizes traditional metaphysics because it reduces its objects to the limited content of a general thought determination, without the capacity to draw out of this generality the rich, diversified content characteristic of what we encounter in experience. Moreover, this metaphysics accepts uncritically the way thought determinations are conceived and the legitimacy of these conceptions for knowing the truth of things. As a result, thought can run away into any kind of theory without coming up against anything that determines whether or not the theory is true. Empiricism restores concrete content by focusing cognition on the content given in sense perception; and it gives stability to knowledge claims by supporting them with what is immediately present in sense experience (*Enz* §37–8).

Empiricism converts a perpetually changing stream of content elements into experience by finding a kind of universality and necessity operating in the panorama of perceptual objects. Experience is composed of two elements: an endless display of content elements separated out into single characters (the material element), and the universality and necessity that form these into some kind of pattern. Empiricism, however, accepts as true only what can be proved by sense experience. Its universals are really nothing more than sense contents that show a resemblance to each other, and its necessities are nothing more than the way things usually happen.

Universality and necessity, therefore, "appear to be something unjustified, a subjective contingency, a mere habit, the content of which may be constituted the way it is or in some other way" (*Enz* §39). Because empiricism accepts as true only what sense experience can prove, empiricism must limit its truth claims to the way objects make themselves known in sense experience, and hence it rejects all supersensibles. But sense experience presents common characteristics and regular associations only as what usually appears. It does not know the reasons why things must be the way they are, why they cannot be otherwise. Hence, what feels to us like universality and necessity does not belong to objects as a commonality or connection they must have. It just feels that way because we are accustomed to a pattern that appears with regularity in our experience.

Hegel identifies two significant contributions that empiricism makes to the way truth must be conceived. On the object side, empiricism insists on the reality principle. What is true must be actual. It cannot be something beyond the real that only ought to be. Truth "must be there (*dasein*) for our perception." On the subject side, empiricism brings to the concept of truth "the important principle of freedom ... namely that what ought to count in our human knowing, we ought to see for ourselves, and to know ourselves as present in it" (*Enz* §38*A*). When, therefore, Hegel says that the actual is rational and the rational is actual, he is talking about the actuality of what is present to perception. The truth that reason is must exist in sense experience. Moreover, knowing the truth must have an experience dimension, because a knower must be free to accept as true only what his or her sense of self attests to as true.

Hegel faults empiricism, however, for depending on the empirical as given, and hence as contingent facts, for denying the supersensible, and for limiting cognition to general forms that remain restricted to their commonality, with no principle that determines the diversity contained within this commonality. According to Hegel, this means that what belongs to experience has no objectivity or truth (*Enz* §38*A*, 39*A*). In order to have objectivity and truth, what exists in experience must exist there with strict universality and necessity, and this requires a knowable supersensible element with a principle that can convert its generality into the determinate content of the differences that belong to it.

Critical philosophy, like empiricism, takes experience to be the only legitimate basis of knowledge, finds in experience a manifold of single sensible content elements (the material element) organized by universal, necessary relations (the formal element), and finds in perception, taken by itself, only contingent facts, only what happens to be the case. Critical philosophy differs from empiricism, however, in the way it explains the fact that universal, necessary relations appear in experience. Instead of dismissing universality and necessity as a subjective response to certain repeated patterns that appear in the given content, critical philosophy takes universality and necessity to be essential determinations of experience. Without universality and necessity, experience would be a stream of variable and subjective states of consciousness, consciousness feeling its own sensations. Universal, necessary relations give to sense experience an objective dimension, something that belongs to the necessities of the object rather than to the particular conditions of the subject whose experience it is. Since the content of perception cannot provide the universality and necessity required for this objectivity, critical philosophy explains its presence in experience as a synthesis derived from the spontaneity of thinking, whose judgments organize the data according to *a priori* concepts of understanding (*Enz* §40). The unity of the thinking subject (the transcendental unity of apperception) operates as a "determinate ground" for this plurality of concepts. The same "I think" makes different kinds of judgment governed by different categories or rules. In this way, the unity of the thinking subject diversifies itself in the different categories of judgment, and thereby forms the content given in perception into an objective synthesis. In this synthesis, the subject knows the manifold as an experience belonging to one selfsame thinking subject (*Enz* §42+Z1).

Critical philosophy acknowledges that the validity of *a priori* concepts must be proved. But the proof focuses exclusively on the subjectivity-objectivity issue. It proves the objectivity of understanding's *a priori* concepts by demonstrating that they are universal and necessary determinations of experience. Experience of objects is not possible without them. But this proof absorbs experience "in its entirety" into the subjectivity of the thinker. All the content of experience, all its determinate relations, as well as the distinction between the thinking subject and the object it thinks, belong to the subject, which leaves nothing for the objectivity that stands opposed to the subject except an empty thing-in-itself. Hegel goes on to say that thinking "in spite of its objectivity, is interpreted as a merely subjective activity" (*Enz* §41).[1]

Several Additions give evidence that Hegel in his lectures sorted out more carefully his position on this part of Kant's critique. According to the first of these, Hegel supports Kant's disagreement with the orientation of ordinary consciousness. Ordinary consciousness takes the sensible to be an independent object, something that exists on its own, and thought

1 See also *Enz* §43, 44+A, 46A.

depends on this independent object for what it thinks. According to Kant, what is given in perception is an unstable panorama of subjective feelings and moods, whereas thought thinks what is essential to a subject matter and thereby brings stability into experience. Instead of the way I feel about something, which belongs to the contingent state of the subject's consciousness, thought thinks determinations that belong to the universal, necessary conditions of objects. Hegel disagrees with Kant, however, about the reality-objectivity status of these thought determinations: "according to Kant, thoughts, although they are universal and necessary determinations, are still only our thoughts, and are cut off from what the thing is in-itself by an impassable gulf. On the contrary, the true objectivity of thinking consists in this: that thoughts are not merely our thoughts, but at the same time the in-itself of things and of whatever else is ob-jective" (*Enz* §41 *Z2*). At this point, the Addition identifies three different meanings for the term "objectivity." First, objectivity means what is externally present (*äußerlich Vorhanden*), distinguished from what is subjectively supposed or imagined. Second, objectivity means what Kant means by it, namely what is universal and necessary in experience distinguished from the contingencies, particularities, and subjectivity of sensation. Third, objectivity means what Hegel means by it in the text quoted above, a thought product that exists in itself. Hegel distinguishes this form of objectivity from what is only our thought, which is thought not existing in itself, and from what only exists in itself (matter), which is thought not existing as a thought determination.

Thus, the Addition introduces a new subtlety into the position Hegel takes on the reality question. In the preceding chapter, we saw the *Encyclopaedia* discussing the reality issue as the reality of experience. In the discussion of the second position on objectivity, we see Hegel distinguishing his own position on the objectivity of thought from the Kantian interpretation of what experience is. According to Hegel, Kant absorbs the whole of experience, including its objectivity, into the subjectivity of a thinking subject. Hegel insists that true objectivity requires thought determinations existing as something "in itself." Later, in Hegel's own text, Hegel defines thing-in-itself as "ob-ject, inasmuch as abstraction is made of all that is for consciousness, of all determinations of feeling, as well as of all determinate thoughts about it" (*Enz* §44*A*). In other words, the term "thing-in-itself" refers to a reality not confined to mutual relations between what is given in perception and what is imposed on the given by the synthetic activity of thought. The universal, necessary determinations of pure thought are objective only if they belong to the reality of what exists in itself, on its own, set off from relations to the thinking subject.

Hegel makes the same point in a different way when he talks about the status of objects as "mere appearances." Kant reduces the content of perception to the subjective way in which what appears affects consciousness. Thought gives objectivity to this content by organizing the data according to the *a priori* determinations of the thinking subject. But these same conditions of objectivity depend on the content given in perception, since they function only as forms of this content. In other words, the categories are synthesizing concepts that have no meaning or function without a given content to be synthesized. Experience, therefore, is constituted by two different kinds of subjectivity: the subjectivity of thought's *a priori* concepts applied to the subjectivity of the appearances given in sensation (*Enz* §43).

As we have seen, there is evidence that Hegel in his lectures supported Kant's opposition to the way ordinary consciousness assumes that the sensible exists as an independent reality. In another Addition, however, we find that this support must be qualified (*Enz* §45*Z*). According to Hegel, Kant is right to claim that objects immediately presented to consciousness, i.e. those given in perception, have the status of mere appearances. Why? Because "they do not have the ground of their being within themselves, but within something else." But Hegel disagrees with Kant about what this something else is. When Kant says that the objects of consciousness are mere appearances, he means that "for us," for our cognition, objects are mere appearances, because "what they are in themselves remains for us an inaccessible beyond." All we can know about them is the way they appear to us, what they are in relation to our sensation, and the way our thinking makes sense of it. According to Hegel, as this Addition represents him, objects immediately presented to our cognition are "mere appearances" precisely because what they are in themselves has its ground in something other than themselves, namely in the universal divine Idea: "This interpretation must also be called idealism, but, as distinct from the subjective idealism of the Critical Philosophy, it is absolute idealism ... [which] forms the basis of all religious consciousness. This is because religion, too, regards the sum total of everything that <exists> (*was da ist*), in short the world before us, as created and governed by God" (*Enz* §45*Z*).[2] Whatever Hegel means by the universal divine Idea, it is more akin to religion's belief in a creator God than to a product of human thought.

Another Addition makes the same point when it criticizes Kant's transcendental unity of apperception: "it is not the subjective activity of self-

2 See also *Enz* §60Z1.

consciousness that introduces absolute unity into the multiplicity in question; rather, this identity is the Absolute, <the true> (*Wahrhafte*) itself. Thus it is the goodness of the Absolute, so to speak, that lets <singulars> enjoy their own selves, and it is just this that drives them back into absolute unity" (*Enz* §42*Z*1). Thus, whatever Hegel means by "the Absolute, the true itself," it is not the "subjective activity of self-consciousness." Moreover, whatever else Hegel means by the absolute, he conceives it as a principle that posits singulars in all their isolated singularity and drives them back to unity from within this singularity. Singulars do not get their unity from a unifying activity that belongs to thought but not to the singulars themselves. The true that unifies singulars exists in and exists as what singulars are in themselves, which isolates each one in itself; and the unity of these develops out of this singularity.

Hegel's discussion of Kant's antinomies reveals another nuance in Hegel's position on the rationality of the actual. Kant demonstrates that reason proves the necessity of attributing to the same subject opposite predicates. Hegel acknowledges this as a profound insight. Hegel objects, however, to the way Kant resolves the antinomies. As Hegel sees it, Kant was reluctant to acknowledge that the world is infected with contradiction, and hence Kant claims that the contradiction belongs not to the world but to the way reason thinks. The contradiction, Hegel insists, emerges from the content of the categories themselves, not just from the way reason applies them. According to Hegel, Kant fails to see that antinomies are found "in all objects of all kinds, in all representations, concepts and ideas. To know this, to be cognizant of this property of ob-jects, belongs to what is essential in philosophical study" (*Enz* §48*A*). According to Hegel, then, contradictory opposition is not an inevitable, irresistible failure of reason. Rather, it is the property of objects, of all objects; and it is a property of thoughts, of "all representations, concepts and ideas"; and philosophy does what is proper to its way of thinking when it knows contradiction as a property of objects (*Enz* §48+*A*+*Z*).

Thus, Hegel's discussion of critical philosophy repeats the opposition theme introduced in the discussion of traditional metaphysics. Hegel calls traditional metaphysics naïve because it does not acknowledge the opposition between thought thinking and thought determinations existing as the truth of things in themselves. The critique of the antinomies talks about a contradiction structure fundamental to all objects and all thoughts. Opposition exists not only between thinking and things in themselves but also within the objectivity of real things and within the subjectivity of representations, concepts, and ideas.

If, then, we look back at the various contexts in which Hegel's criticism of Kant distinguishes Hegel's idealism from Kant's, we find Hegel repeatedly objecting to the way Kant confines the determinations of thought and the determinations of experience to the subjectivity of our thinking and our experience. These objections speak to the necessity of giving reality its due. Objectivity requires not only an object distinguished from the thinking that thinks it, but also an object set apart from its own relations to that thinking. Moreover, even the status of things as "mere appearances" belongs to this independent objectivity. Things are "mere appearances" because they have their ground in something else; this something else is neither Kant's empty, inaccessible thing-in- itself, nor the Kantian transcendental unity of apperception. Things are "mere appearances" of something more fundamental that the one-sidedness of pure reason and the one-sidedness of independent objectivity have in common. And this common principle takes the form of contradictory opposition.

2 THE BEGINNING CONCEPT OF PHILOSOPHICAL SCIENCE

The examination of the three positions on objectivity addresses the issue of philosophy's beginning concept by asking how the infinite is conceived. Hegel criticizes traditional metaphysics because it thinks the objects of reason – e.g. soul, world, God – as subjects in a judgment. These judgments identify these subjects by attaching thought determinations to them in the form of immediately given predicates: the soul is simple; the world is contingent; God is infinite. The old metaphysics thinks these thought determinations as understanding does, restricting them to the precise content that belongs to their isolated meaning; and it accepts them without asking whether in this detached form they can be true to what they themselves are. As a result, traditional metaphysics, like understanding generally, does not allow the predicates to pass over into their opposites. Even the predicate "infinite" becomes a finite determination, because it excludes the finite and all the definite determinations derived from contents limited by and set off from other contents. When the old metaphysics thinks the infinity of God, therefore, it reduces God to an abstract universal, "being" conceived without any definite way of being. The truth, according to Hegel, must be infinite "within itself"; it must derive from itself everything that truth is (*Enz* §28*Z*). In other words, knowing the truth requires a cognition in which thought derives the truth of the finite, with all its restrictions and diversity, from what the infinite is within itself (*Enz* §28+*A*+*Z*). Only thus is the infinite not restricted by what is other than itself.

Hegel's brief discussion of Kant's transcendental dialectic makes the same point again. According to Kant, reason moves beyond the limited concepts and judgments of understanding to produce ideas of what is not conditioned or restricted by anything else. Reason conceives soul as the thinking subject to which all the determinations of thought belong, world as the unity to which all objects belong, God as the sameness of all reality or being (*Enz* §47–9). In each idea, reason thinks the unconditioned by thinking all limited determinations as contained within a selfsameness, so that the selfsame leaves nothing out that could condition or restrict it. According to Kant, as Hegel represents him, this pursuit of the unconditioned is really the unity of apperception making its own selfsameness the object and purpose of its thinking. Thought seeks to be completely at one with itself in its thinking of the object (*Enz* §45).

Critical philosophy, however, conceives the unity of reason only as an abstract unity. It conceives the selfsameness and unconditionedness of thought as a unity set off from the diversification of thought distributed in understanding's empirical cognitions. Hence, the unity of thought remains indeterminate, without content. It does not derive the content of its thinking from itself. Rather it thinks a content given in perception, and thinks its own *a priori* determinations as relations immersed in this content. If reason necessarily seeks the complete unification of this diversity in the selfsameness of the unconditioned, and Kant concedes that it does, then thought must turn away from its ties to experience and let itself think what cannot belong to experience. Hence, it thinks ideas that cannot be exemplified in experience, and it thinks a unity that cannot derive from itself the concrete content of experience. In other words, reason thinks the infinite only as beyond the finite, as the not-finite; and by thinking in this way it thinks the infinite as restricted and limited by its not being something else (*Enz* §45+*Z*, 46, 49, 52+*Z*).

Hegel finds in Kant's *Critique of Judgment*, however, an idea that qualifies as authentic speculative thinking. In this his third critique, Kant develops the idea of an intellectual intuition giving itself a purpose. Hegel sees in this idea a way of integrating the universality of pure reason with the diversity and contingency of empirical reality. Hegel describes this "intuitive understanding" as "an understanding in which the particular, which is contingent for the universal ([i.e. the] abstract identity) and cannot be deduced from it, would be determined through this universal itself; and this is experienced in the products of *art* and of *organic* nature" (*Enz* §55). The idea preserves the contingency of empirical particulars. It does not conceive them as necessarily implied in and hence deducible from the abstract selfsameness of the universal. Rather it conceives them determined by the universal as a purpose it gives to itself (*Enz* §55+*A*).

Hegel acknowledges that in this idea, and only in this idea, Kant's philosophy becomes speculative thought. According to Hegel, as we have seen, speculative thought thinks the positive connection in which opposites belong to the same truth. Kant's idea of intuitive understanding, or inner purposiveness, conceives a positive connection between the universality of thought and the contingent particulars of experience, between the subjectivity of thinking and the objectivity of empirical reality.

Even so, Hegel finds fault with Kant's idea of intuitive understanding. According to Kant, Hegel says, the idea of intuitive understanding is "a principle of judging that belongs only to our understanding" (*Enz* §58), and the unity conceived in it is taken up only as it happens to appear in experience. Hegel objects because Kant does not see that the unity of the universal and the particular conceived in this idea is the true, indeed is truth itself (*Enz* §56). Truth itself is the universal intuitive understanding that derives from itself the particulars of empirical reality by producing them as a purpose. According to Kant, the concept of the good, the final purpose of the world, belongs to our practical reason, and so this concept conceives the unity of thought and being only as "the correspondence of the state of the world, and of what happens in it, with our morality" (*Enz* §60). If we conceive it without restriction, Hegel says, then "the Idea would be that the universality that is determined by reason – the absolute final purpose, the good – is made actual in the world, and this through a third, through the might that itself posits this final purpose and realises it – i.e., it is made actual by God, in whom, since he is the absolute truth, those antitheses of universality and singularity, of subjectivity and objectivity are resolved and declared to be not self-standing and untrue" (*Enz* §59). The final purpose of the world becomes actual through a rationality that is neither the one-sided subjectivity of Kantian self-consciousness nor the one-sided objectivity of a world opposed to it, but a third in which these opposites do not stand apart in their independence of each other.

Thus, Hegel not only rejects the way Kantian idealism reduces the objectivity of empirical objects to a form that does not reach the independent otherness of being, he also rejects the way critical philosophy restricts our notions of absolute being and the highest good, so that thought thinks only what is appropriate to our thinking and our morality. Whatever Hegel means by God, it cannot be confined within the rationality of our thinking and our action. The term "God" refers to a truth that overcomes the divisions typical of our rationality and posits a purpose appropriate to this overcoming. For Hegel, truth conceived as intellectual intuition giving itself a purpose does not belong to the conditions of our reason. Rather it stands as what is absolutely true, the truth that religion aspires to when it believes in God.

Hegel introduces the third position on objectivity, associated primarily with Friedrich Heinrich Jacobi, as a reaction to problems posed by critical philosophy. According to Hegel, Jacobi accepts critical philosophy's description of thinking, and as a result acknowledges that thinking cannot think the infinite. To think is to understand one thing by relating it to something else that accounts for it. Hence, thinking demands an explanation for every explanation. If heat explains why metal expands, something else must explain why heat is present to make the metal expand. Otherwise, the presence of heat becomes unintelligible, something that just happens for no reason. Thus, thought makes everything finite by thinking it as mediated by something else. Thought thinks whatever it thinks as not the whole truth. Any thought that tries to conceive the whole truth thinks nothing more than an "all" or "also" with no determinations or content of its own, the simple togetherness or aggregate of realities set apart from and limited by each other. The third position asserts, however, that the human spirit knows the truth, and knows it not in the distorted form of finite determinations, but in the fullness of truth that God is. Since the mediations of thinking cannot grasp such truth, the cognition that knows the truth must be immediate knowing or faith (*Enz* §62*A*, 63).[3]

Hegel hastens to add that this is not the faith of Christianity. Christian faith has the authority of a community, a church, whereas the faith of immediate knowing appeals to the authority of "one's own subjective revelation." Moreover, Christian faith has a content articulated in an objective

3 Hegel mentions various ways in which critical philosophy rules out the possibility of thinking the infinite. Thinking operates only within the limited sphere of subjectivity, and hence it does not think or know objective reality in its independent existence, set apart from its relations to the thinking subject. Within this limited sphere of subjectivity, reason thinks the infinite as an abstract, formal identity, and hence neither the manifold content of experience nor the diversification of thought in the categories belong to this thought. In the form of understanding, thought thinks its objects as conditioned and mediated by the synthesis that connects each content element to others within the same synthetic unit, and by being assigned to different categories, which limits the object to one set of possible determinations rather than others. Thus, critical philosophy represents thought in all its forms as thought restricted, leaving something out: subjectivity excluding the objectivity of what exists externally and in itself; reason thinking the infinite by excluding the concrete content and diversified categories of understanding's empirical judgments; understanding thinking objects by relating them to other determinations (*Enz* §61–2).

system of doctrines, whereas for immediate knowing "the way a content is found within consciousness, and is a fact in it" determines the truth of it (*Enz* §63*A*). The third position takes as its truth criterion the fact that a certain content is present in consciousness as a representation identified with the certainty of its truth. Truth, therefore, does not depend on the nature of the content, but on the way the content is present in "my" consciousness. For example, a person believes in God because this person feels the presence of God in his or her consciousness. This belief does not depend on whether the content of the belief, the way God is defined or conceived, makes sense or is supported by evidence. Rather, the believer accepts the existence of God as true because that is the way it feels in the believer's experience.

According to the third position, immediate knowing knows "that the Infinite, the Eternal or God, that is [present] in our *representation* also *is* – that within our consciousness the certainty of its *being* is immediately and inseparably combined with our *representation* of it" (*Enz* §64). Hegel describes this immediate knowing as "the transition ... from the subjective Idea to being," which indicates that his use of the word "being" (*Sein*) refers to a reality that is not merely subjective. Immediate knowing knows the content of the infinite inseparably united with the consciousness of its being; and being here refers to a reality beyond the "subjective Idea."

Hegel compares Jacobi's immediate knowing position to Descartes' *cogito*. Descartes' *cogito* does not describe a sequential move from a starting point to a conclusion. There is no middle term connecting the ego thinking to the ego existing. Rather, the consciousness of thinking is immediately identified with the consciousness of thinking existing, and in a way that makes its existence indubitable. So also the philosophy of immediate knowing claims that its consciousness of the infinite represented is immediately and indubitably identified with the consciousness of the infinite existing. Indeed, this philosophical standpoint makes similar claims for its consciousness of the subject's body and its consciousness of external things. The representation of these is present in consciousness inseparably identified with the certainty of their existence (*Enz* §64+*A*, 69, 76). Immediate knowing, therefore, is a fact of consciousness, "a psychological phenomenon," an experience (*Erfahrung*). Consciousness knows immediately, in the experience of its own state of consciousness, the existence of its own body, the existence of external things, and the existence of the infinite, eternal God (*Enz* §65–6). Hegel gives this position on objectivity a qualified endorsement: "When philosophy attempts to prove a unity of this sort, i.e., when it wants to show that the nature of thought or of subjectivity implies that they are inseparable from being or from objectivity, then (whatever the status of such proofs may be) philosophy must in any case <be satisfied to see it maintained and shown> that its propositions are also facts of consciousness and hence that they are in agreement with experience" (*Enz* §64*A*).

This qualified endorsement allows us to use Hegel's analysis of immediate knowing's intuition to reveal more fully what Hegel means when he claims that the philosophical standpoint conceives the truth as the unity of thought and being:

For what is asserted from this standpoint is that neither the *Idea*, as a merely *subjective* thought, nor a mere *being* on its own account (*für sich*), is <the truth> [*das Wahre*]; For being on its own account (*für sich*), any being that is not that of the Idea, is the sensible, finite being of the world. But what is immediately asserted by this is that the Idea is <the truth> only as *mediated* by being, and, conversely, that being is <the truth> only as *mediated* by the Idea. What the principle of immediate knowing rightly insists on is not an indeterminate, empty immediacy, abstract being, or pure unity on its own account (*für sich*), but the unity of *the Idea* with being. (*Enz* §70)[4]

Being "for itself," "mere being," being not mediated by "the Idea" refers to being by itself, not interpreted by a true concept; this is the *de facto* existence of the sensible world. The third position rejects this as not what the truth is. But the third position also rejects "the Idea," the true conception of being, if it is taken as a "mere" subjective thought, without the being "for itself" of this thought. Immediate knowing insists that its intuition knows the infinite not only as represented in a thinking subject but also as existing in its own reality. Immediate knowing, Hegel says, "rightly insists on" this way of conceiving the truth.

4 The term "Idea" (*die Idee*) requires some explanation. Hegel distinguishes his use of the term from the way some philosophies interpret it, and from the way we use "idea" in ordinary life. In these ordinary ways of speaking, "idea" refers to concepts, i.e. to any thought that in some way identifies an object; "idea" might also refer to representations, i.e. to any image or law that presents to consciousness a set of perceptions. Hegel, following Kant, restricts his use of the term Idea to thought thinking unconditional truth. Hegel rejects, however, the way Kant interprets Idea as a thought restricted to the conditions of the thinking subject, without validity for thinking objects. According to Hegel, the Idea is the "adequate concept," the concept that thinks the whole and unqualified truth and knows this thought to be actualized as the independent, external, objective reality of being (*WL* 12:173–7\M 55–60). Most English translations indicate that Hegel is using the term *Idee*, rather than the term *Begriff* (translated "notion" or "concept") or the term *Vorstellung* (translated "representation" or "idea"), by beginning the English word "Idea" with a capital letter.

Hegel finds fault with the immediate knowing position, however, by probing the way it appeals to the experience principle. In the examination of empiricism, Hegel talks about the experience principle as the subjective side of sense experience. According to this principle, what the subject accepts as true must be present in the subject's sense of self. In other words, it must be directly experienced. In the discussion of the immediate knowing position, Hegel talks about experience as the subjective side of a supersensible cognition. This suggests that the supersensible truth proved by philosophy cannot be accepted as true unless the knower also experiences the presence of this truth in the knower's sense of self. In other words, if philosophy proves that the subjectivity of thought is one with the objectivity of being, this unity cannot be accepted as true unless the result of the proof is also directly experienced.

Hegel's appeal to the experience principle becomes even more suggestive when we consider the way Hegel compares the third position's intuition of the infinite to Descartes' *cogito*. Descartes' *cogito* is the thinker's own "I think." The knower, by thinking, knows the content that characterizes this thinking and in the same act knows indisputably the actual existence of this thinking. Comparing the intuition of the infinite to this kind of immediate cognition suggests that the intuition knows the actual existence of the infinite as somehow involved in the existence of the knower's own consciousness. Belief in God, however, involves bigger claims than those supported by Descartes' *cogito*. Descartes' *cogito* asserts its own thinking as indisputable evidence of its own actual existence. All other claims depend on the mediated cognitions developed from this starting point (*Enz* §76–7).[5] The immediate knowing position asserts its intuition of the infinite, and this alone, not as indisputable evidence of the believer's own finite existence but as the certainty of God's existence – God who is infinite, not finite. Since, however, immediate knowing asserts its subjective conviction as truth, it takes for granted that the certainty, the conviction, present in my consciousness must be present in the consciousness of everyone. Everyone must be convinced as I am of God's existence (*Enz* §71).

What, then, have we learned about the philosophical standpoint from Hegel's examination of the three positions on objectivity? We have learned first that philosophical thought thinks a truth that is all-encompassing,

5 In order to expand the limited claim supported by the *cogito* into claims about the causal principle, the existence of God, and the existence of a world outside thought, Descartes moves beyond immediate intuition into a demonstration process. See *Meditations on First Philosophy*, III.

unconditioned, infinite. Philosophical knowing stands within the perspective of the whole truth. We have learned, too, that philosophy does not conceive the infinite as traditional metaphysics does, as a transcendent being set apart from the finite. The traditional conception thinks the infinite with all the reality and determinations of the finite excluded, and thus does not conceive truth all-encompassing, unrestricted, unlimited. Philosophy conceives the infinite as the unconditioned condition that determines all finite realities. It does not, however, conceive this condition as an empty, abstract unity that leaves undetermined the differentiation that belongs to finite realities. Indeed, Hegel insists that the infinite must be conceived in a way that determines even the contingencies of empirical reality. He suggests that Kant's idea of intuitive purposiveness, akin to religion's doctrine of a creative, provident God, shows us the correct way to conceive the infinite, because this idea avoids the problem of trying to deduce contingencies. Philosophy conceives an infinite that determines the contingent as the realization of a purpose, not as a deduced implication.

The examination of the immediate knowing position teaches us to think pure thought not as a thinking isolated in the subjectivity of the knower, but as thought existing in itself, in its own reality; and it teaches us to think the being of the infinite not as the givenness of sensible reality, but as a reality identified with pure thought. This introduces the experience principle into the conception of the infinite. The philosophical standpoint presupposes an immediate knowing in which the knower experiences his or her subjectivity identified with the thought and being of infinite truth, so that the immediate experience of one's own existence qualifies as universal, unqualified truth.

3 PHILOSOPHICAL BEGINNING AND THE PROOF ISSUE

As we have seen, Hegel says that the experience claimed by immediate knowing corresponds to the fundamental claim that philosophy sets out to prove, namely that the subjectivity of thought is one with the objectivity of being. Hegel rejects the immediate knowing position, however, because it excludes mediation; and he characterizes this excluding posture as a rejection of philosophy. Immediate knowing, without the mediation of a demonstration or proof, finds itself reduced to a personal conviction with no claims on the consciousness of anyone else. Moreover, any personal conviction will do. Since truth is tested only by the way the subject experiences the content of his or her consciousness, any desire or interest or purpose that a subject believes in takes on the authority of truth. There is no way of distinguishing between a personal conviction that is immoral or evil and one that is right and good (*Enz* §72).

There are two ways of establishing the universality of a truth claim based on my experience. One is the universal agreement (*consensus gentium*) approach. According to this approach, "my" experience is true because everyone agrees with it: "But the need of thinking to know that what shows itself as *universally* present is *necessary* is still not satisfied by the *consensus gentium*" (*Enz* §71*A*). The universal agreement approach does not meet thought's need for necessity. Even if we could show that everyone has the same conviction, the same content present in consciousness with the same certainty, this would not prove that the experience must be accepted as true. It would prove only that universal agreement on the matter happens to be the case. Thus, Hegel distinguishes between universality without necessity and a universality based on necessity. General agreement just happens. It does not prove that what everyone thinks or believes or experiences must be true. Only what is universal because it is necessary provides the necessity demanded by thought.[6] Moreover, even if universal agreement could qualify as a satisfactory proof, the approach would fail for belief in the infinite, the Eternal or God, because there are in fact people who do not believe in God (*Enz* §71+*A*). Hegel suggests another way of establishing the universal legitimacy of 'my' experience. But we will postpone consideration of this alternative until we have examined Hegel's analysis of the mediation-immediacy issue.

In the process of discussing mediation and immediacy, Hegel develops a complicated, subtle position on the structure of proof. The discussion begins with a critique of traditional arguments for the existence of God. In this critique, Hegel distinguishes between the proof procedure of understanding and the proof procedure of reason. Understanding proves something by demonstrating that some other determination necessitates it. Hence, the proof depends on a presupposition. It accepts as true a certain determination, and then shows how this truth implies the necessity of what

6 Hegel's argument against the *consensus gentium* theory of truth applies with equal force to the way Forster (1989) interprets Hegel's own theory of truth. "According to this theory, it is a necessary and sufficient condition of a claim's truth that it be agreed upon by an enduring continual consensus" (69). If "enduring continual consensus" is a sufficient condition of truth, then the mere fact that such a condition exists is enough to establish its truth. Hegel denies this when he says that even if absolutely everyone agreed, this would not prove truth. The fact that people happen to agree is a contingent state of affairs. It does not prove that what they agree about has the necessity required for truth. Truth requires a consensus established by knowing that the content of the truth claim must be true.

is to be proved. This kind of proof, Hegel says, produces conclusions that are always mediated. The cognition expressed in the conclusion knows its object by means of and in terms of the object's relation to the evidence that proves it. As a result of this procedure, understanding engaged in proving the existence of God falls into either pantheism or dualism. Pantheism conceives God as "the immediate substance of his world" and thus conceives the infinite only as what the finite belongs to or exists in. God becomes one selfsame thing whose properties are all the various finite determinations given in the world presented to understanding. Dualism conceives God as the world's other. It attributes to God various finite determinations, e.g. justice, benevolence, wisdom, power. Then it denies that these are the same in God as they are in their finite form, which reduces God to the empty concept of being "something else." Understanding knows the infinite only as not-the-finite (*Enz* §36*A*).

Hegel distinguishes the proof procedure of reason from the proof procedure of understanding in his account of pre-Kantian metaphysics, where it is developed in an Addition (*Enz* §36*Z*), and also when he discusses Kant's critique of the traditional arguments for the existence of God, where the same points are made in Hegel's own text (*Enz* §50*A*). Reason, like understanding, takes as its starting point something other than the infinite. It begins with something immediate, something accepted as "what simply is." Reason proves, however, that this starting point is not immediate, that it is posited, originated, mediated by a ground; and this proves that God, conceived as ground, "must be considered to contain mediation sublated within himself, hence to be genuinely immediate, original, and resting upon himself" (*Enz* §36*Z*).

Hegel's point about proper proof procedure becomes clearer and more subtle if we compare the move into a ground to a representative example of the way effect to cause arguments work in traditional metaphysics. Therefore, we will make an exception here to our strategy of focusing exclusively on the way Hegel in this part of the *Encyclopaedia* represents the three positions on objectivity, and will look directly at the way Thomas Aquinas works with arguments for the existence of God. Aquinas begins one of his arguments by accepting as true the fact that things come to be and pass away, and by inferring from this that they cannot account for their own existence. This is the argument from contingency. From this starting point, Aquinas demonstrates the existence of an uncaused first cause, a necessary being, a being whose being does not depend on anything else. He derives from this demonstration other claims about what God is. God is creator, the originating cause of everything real in the world of created things, including the limitations that distinguish them from each other, the details that isolate them in their singularity, and the relations that organize them into a world order.[7] Moreover, according to Aquinas, relations between God and the created world exist as real relations in created things but not in God, because relations involve some kind of dependence, and God cannot be conceived as dependent on finite realities.[8]

Aquinas' strategy seems to fulfill everything that Hegel is claiming for rational proof: a demonstration proving that the starting point is itself mediated by its dependence on a ground, a ground conceived as not mediated by its relations to anything else, and as the originating principle of the starting point with which the proof begins. Hegel's attitude toward traditional metaphysics would lead us to believe that he would reject Aquinas' argument as a proof procedure in the form of understanding. What, then, distinguishes the proof procedure of Aquinas' demonstration from the proof procedure that Hegel endorses as rational proof? The *Encyclopaedia* Addition suggests that Hegel is aware of the question: "The main thing here is that a proof, as it is envisaged by the understanding, is the dependence of one determination on another … So we can see at once that what must emerge is something distorted, since God is supposed to be precisely the sole ground of everything, and thus not to depend on anything else" (*Enz* §36*Z*).

If we credit traditional metaphysics with supposing God to be "the sole ground of everything, and thus not to depend on anything else," which is certainly Aquinas' position, then Hegel's objection focuses on the distorted way in which understanding's proof procedure makes known this ground. This kind of proof gives us knowledge of God by means of, mediated by, the role God plays in our explanation of the world: as what explains the existence of things that do not have to exist; as what explains the order

7 See Collins (1990), especially 512–17, for a more complete account of Aquinas' position, full citations supporting my interpretation, and a discussion of the way Aquinas' position is related to questions raised in Hegel's *Phenomenology of Spirit*.

8 "Now, these relations which refer to God's effects cannot possibly exist in Him really. For they cannot exist in Him as accidents in a subject, since there is no accident in Him, as was shown in Book I. Neither can they be God's very substance, because, as Aristotle says in the *Categories*, relative terms are those 'which in their very being refer somehow to something else' (6a 36); so that God's substance would then have to be referred to something else. But that which is essentially referred to another depends upon it in a certain way, since it can neither be nor be understood without it. Hence, it would follow that God's substance would depend on something else extrinsic to it, so that He would not be, of Himself, the necessary being, as He was shown to be in Book I. Therefore, such relations do not really exist in God" (Aquinas, *SCG*, II 12 [1–2]).

observable in the world of finite things; as what fulfills human nature's orientation toward a purpose. Although Aquinas denies that relations between God and the world really exist as mediations in God's own reality, he nevertheless admits that our knowledge of God is limited to the way in which relations between the world and God make God known. Our knowledge of God knows the absolute ground in its relation to what it grounds; or takes the form of negative theology, which conceives God as not revealed in these relations, indeed as transcending all human ways of thinking. Thus, the traditional proofs do not give us a concept of the divine being as it is in itself.[9]

With this in mind, let us look closely at the way Hegel in the Addition describes rational proof.

> When we say, "Consider nature, for it will lead you to God, and you will find an absolute final purpose," this does not mean that God is mediated, but only that we make the journey from an other to God, in the sense that God, being the consequence, is at the same time the absolute ground of what we started with, so that the position of the two is reversed: what appears as the consequence also shows itself to be the ground, while what presented itself as ground to start with is reduced to [the status of] consequence. And that is precisely the path of rational proof. (*Enz* §36*Z*)

If rational proof is supposed to avoid the distortion that is typical of understanding's proof procedure, then it must somehow take thought beyond conceptions that identify the ground in terms of its relations to what it grounds. Rational proof must take thought into a concept that actually thinks the immediacy of the ground in itself and in the self-determination that derives from itself what it grounds. This seems to be what Hegel means when he says that the mediations exposed in rational proof demonstrate a ground in which mediation is sublated.

Hegel's critique of traditional metaphysics introduces two different ways in which we might understand the presupposition issue. Hegel distinguishes between mediation as a presupposition for knowing and mediation as a presupposition for being. Knowledge of God presupposes, depends on, is a consequence of what we learn from the way nature reveals itself to us. The knowledge produced by the move from nature to God, however, demonstrates that the being or reality of nature presupposes, depends on, is a consequence of the reality of the ground that God is. In the domain of knowing, therefore, the knowledge of God presupposes, depends on,

9 Aquinas, *SCG*, I 30 (4); II 11, 13–14; III part I, 49 (9).

is a consequence of what we know about nature. In the domain of being, nature presupposes, depends on, is a consequence of its ground, which is God (*Enz* §36*Z*, 50*A*).[10] Hegelian proofs differ from traditional proofs of God's existence because Hegel's proofs do not persist in this opposition between the priorities of knowing and the priorities of being. Traditional proofs end with a concept of the ground that depends on what the ground must explain in the evidence that leads up to it. As a result, knowing persists in a form that is inadequate to the truth revealed in the proofs. Hegel's proof procedure moves on to a concept of the ground in its independence and immediacy, so that the ground is conceived not as a relation to what has led up to it, but as something in itself. This serves as the starting point for a knowing that derives from its knowledge of the ground knowledge of what depends on the ground, which gives knowing a form that is adequate to the truth exposed by the proof procedure. The critique of traditional proofs for the existence of God, therefore, shows Hegel proposing a proof procedure that develops according to the following steps: (1) the initial move from the immediacy of a starting point to proof of its dependence on a ground, (2) which proves that the starting point is not immediate but mediated, rooted in something other than itself as its ground, (3) which proves that the ground itself is not mediated, dependent on, or defined by what proves it, (4) but stands on its own, in itself, as the self-determining originating principle of everything that preceded it in the proof.

We have seen a similar description of proof procedure in the *Encyclopaedia*'s general introduction. The version developed in the general introduction, however, focuses on a proof developed within the philosophical standpoint. Philosophy begins with the decision to focus on thought, thought in itself detached from its involvement in experience, thought proposed as a subject to be investigated prior to the exposition of its determinations. Hegel identifies this beginning as thought in the form of immediacy. Philosophy demonstrates that thought in its immediacy depends on, is mediated by, all the thought determinations that philosophy finds necessarily implied

10 Hegel's discussion of the proofs in the *Vorlesungen über die Beweise vom Dasein Gottes* belongs to the project that develops the full meaning of the logical or rational within the framework of philosophical science (see especially the Tenth Lecture, 275–6, Hodgson trans. 94–6). The critique of the proofs in the *Encyclopaedia*'s discussion of the three positions on objectivity belongs to the concern with how to establish and justify the concept with which philosophical science begins, the concept that identifies what kind of project it is. Hence, the *Encyclopaedia*'s discussion suggests that the proof required for justifying Jacobi's intuition of the infinite is not a cosmological argument that depends on the concept of the contingent, but a proof developed from the examination of consciousness as such.

in it. The subject involved in the philosophical investigation must begin with thought in its immediacy. But the investigation proves that the object investigated is not immediate, but involved in and dependent on a circle of connected determinations (*Enz* §17).[11]

When, however, Hegel talks about proof in connection with traditional proofs for the existence of God, is he talking about philosophy demonstrating the necessary determinations of pure thought, or is he talking about a proof that demonstrates the legitimacy of the philosophical standpoint? Demonstrating the necessary determinations of pure thought addresses the question, what is the identifying content of pure thought. In other words, what is the logical or rational? Demonstrating the legitimacy of the philosophical standpoint addresses the question, why must we accept the determinations of pure thought as anything more than a thought experiment. In other words, why assume that the necessities of pure thought are also necessities of the real?

Hegel's examination of the immediate knowing position focuses on the proof required for establishing the objective legitimacy of an intuition that identifies the standpoint of philosophy. Hegel's examination of the third position does not challenge the way this position exposes the inadequacy of mediate knowledge, or the way it claims for immediate knowing knowledge of the truth. Hegel's objection focuses exclusively on the way the third position separates immediate knowing from mediation: "This standpoint is not content when it has shown that mediate knowing, taken in isolation, is inadequate for the [cognition of] truth; its peculiarity is that immediate knowing can only have the truth as its content when it is taken in isolation, to the exclusion of mediation" (*Enz* §65).

Hegel challenges this disjunction first by disputing its factual claims. He begins by describing the way an educated human being achieves immediate knowing as a result of the most complicated, mediated process. A mathematician learns the truths of mathematics through a step-by-step process of demonstration. Having been through the process, however, he experiences the principles revealed by it as something immediately, intuitively known. Before studying geometry, I might be able to think the content that belongs to the statement "the sum of the angles of a triangle equals two right angles." I experience the content differently after I have made my way through the mathematical proof. As a result of this process, my experience of the content becomes immediately identified with the certainty of its truth. So also, we learn certain skills, like driving a car or riding a bicycle, through a step-

11 See also *Enz* §84.

by-step training process. In the end, however, we just immediately know how to do it. Whatever claims may be made for religious faith, innate ideas, intuitive moral convictions, an immediate sense of how to do things or what will work, all these depend on some kind of educational process that brings this knowledge to consciousness; and "it is sheer mindlessness not to know that when the necessity of education is granted, it is just the essential requirement of mediation that is expressed" (*Enz* §67*A*). The educational process demonstrates the connection between what is immediately known and what produces the certainty, the conviction, the know-how involved in the knowing. The fact that we experience our knowledge as immediate and intuitive, therefore, does not prove that the knowledge excludes mediation (*Enz* §66–7).

Hegel attacks the third position again by exposing a negative mediation within the content of the intuition itself. Immediate knowing claims that its intuition knows the content and being of God and the divine; and it acknowledges that this involves "an elevation above the sensible and the finite, as well as above the immediate desires and inclinations of the natural heart" (*Enz* §68). The movement ends in an intuition of what God and the divine are. But it arrives at this intuition by means of a movement that detaches consciousness from its involvement in the sensible, the finite, and the self's given desires and inclinations. The immediacy of the intuition that knows God presupposes the mediation of the process whereby consciousness becomes separated from its consciousness of what is not God.

Finally, Hegel finds mediation within immediate knowing itself. Immediate knowing claims that its intuition experiences thought identified with being and being identified with thought. This involves the mediation of distinct determinations. If thought were not mediated by being, it would be the isolated subjectivity of the thinker. If being were not mediated by thought, it would be the givenness of sensible realities. This mediation, however, is not a mediation with or through something else. Rather, it is a mediation enclosed within the selfsame truth (*sich in sich selbst beschließend*), an original togetherness independent of, unmediated by, any external connecting principle (*Enz* §69).

> But it is quite mindless not to see that the unity of distinct determinations is not just a purely immediate, i.e., a totally indeterminate and empty unity, but that what is posited in it is precisely that one of the determinations has truth only through its mediation by the other; or, in other words, that each of them is mediated with the truth only through the other. – It is thereby shown to be a *factum*, that the determination of mediation is contained in that very immediacy ... (*Enz* §70)

> ... a content can only be [re]cognised as <the truth> (*das Wahre*), inasmuch as it is not mediated with an other, i.e., is not finite, so that it mediates itself with itself, and is in this way both mediation and immediate self-relation all in one. (*Enz* §74)

Knowing God as unlimited, unqualified truth requires a cognition that does not identify the truth in a way that sets it off from other truths, since this would involve knowing infinite truth as finite. Knowing the truth requires some kind of unmediated knowing. Since, however, a completely unmediated knowing also fails, knowing the truth involves some kind of mediation, but not the kind that relates unqualified and unlimited truth to something other than itself that qualifies and limits it. Cognition accomplishes the requisite kind of mediated immediacy by knowing the truth as self-related or self-mediated, and this is to know God as spirit. Spirit identifies truth as a self knowing itself through its other self (*Enz* §74).[12]

According to Hegel, therefore, the intuition of infinite truth involves three kinds of mediation: (1) the mediation of a proof that produces the certainty of its truth; (2) the mediation that detaches cognition from the sensible; (3) mediation within the intuition itself and in the determinations

12 K. Westphal (1989b) criticizes Hegel's argument against Jacobi's position because the argument is governed by Hegel's own principles rather than those of Jacobi himself. I agree with this representation of Hegel's strategy. Since, however, I am concerned here with probing the evidence for clues to Hegel's own position, I have no objection to this approach for the present discussion. My disagreement with Westphal's analysis of Hegel's argument against Jacobi focuses on the following claim: "if Hegel's ontological holism were true, 'immediate knowledge' would be utterly impossible" (148). Westphal represents Hegel's ontological holism thus: "If things are mutually interrelated in Hegel's way, then in order to determine the properties of one thing and so to determine the content of the knowledge of that thing, one must articulate the connections between that thing and other things" (148). Westphal explains how Hegel applies this way of thinking to the relation between the infinite and the finite (*Enz* §74). Hegel says that "the general nature of the form of immediacy," would isolate the infinite in itself and exclude the finite, which would give it the form of the particular. The infinite would be known as this and not that, infinite and not finite. Hegel's analysis of rational proof, however, shows how Hegel can give Jacobi's position a qualified endorsement without compromising the relational dynamics of his holism. According to Hegel, the mediation of the finite proves itself rooted in an infinite ground. This result demonstrates that the finite world has no actuality of its own, but rather belongs to the reality of the infinite, as its manifestation; and the infinite has the mediation of the finite sublated within itself as the ground from which finite determinations are derived. Thus, the immediacy of the ground is more fundamental than the determinacy of mutual relations between different things. "Jacobi did not [re]cognize ... that, in its mediation, [essential thinking] sublates mediation itself" (§50A). For Hegel, therefore, immediate knowing is not impossible. But it must be proved in a demonstration that exposes the way the mediation of the finite retreats into infinity as its ground and thereby sublates the mediation.

that logic and the whole of philosophy expose as implicit in it. In the critique of traditional proofs for the existence of God, Hegel rejects the proof procedure typical of understanding, which produces a concept of the infinite that identifies it by its relation to the finite. Hegel endorses instead the procedure of rational proof. When, therefore, Hegel insists that philosophy must prove the objective truth of the third position's unproved intuition, he is asking for the kind of retreat into a ground provided by rational proof.

Like traditional proofs, rational proof begins with finite realities, and demonstrates their dependence on the infinite as their ground. But it "sublates the mediation." The step-by-step process that produces both the concept of the infinite ground and the certainty of its real existence also produces an immediate intuition that knows the infinite in itself, on its own, instead of conceiving it as a reality related to something other than itself. This shift into immediate cognition transforms the way thought conceives the relation between the infinite and the finite. It conceives the infinite as a reality that stands on its own, mediated by no relations to something other than itself. It conceives the relation between the infinite and the finite as self-mediation, the infinite related to its other self, which is what Hegel means when he says that the infinite is spirit.

In the discussion of empiricism and critical philosophy, however, Hegel insists that the cognition of finite realities must accept the data of sense experience as an essential element in the knowledge of objects. In the examination of empiricism, too, he talks about the experience principle as the demand that what a subject accepts as true must be present in the subject's sense experience. If, therefore, Hegel's proof procedure begins with sense experience, then it begins with what is immediately present in the isolated consciousness that is "my" experience. From this starting point, the procedure demonstrates that the reality of sense experience depends on a ground that does not belong to the reality of sense experience itself. Thus, the procedure involves not only the positive mediation that demonstrates the truth of the philosophical standpoint but also the negative mediation that detaches philosophical thought from its involvement in the sensible.

In Hegel's critique of the immediate knowing position, Hegel suggests that the experience principle also applies to the supersensible ground. If a proof demonstrates that the truth of finite, sensible realities is a supersensible ground, and if what a subject accepts as true must be present in the subject's sense of self, then the experience of the subject's rootedness in this ground must be present in the subject's sense of self. I must experience the certainty of its reality in the immediate experience of my own. In the examination of the third position, Hegel's discussion of the education process suggests that the truth of the experience depends on a movement through a process, a mediation that produces within the subject the certainty of its truth. Not just any mediation, however. The universal truth status of my experience, whether sensible or supersensible, depends on a procedure that answers thought's need for necessity.

We have seen Hegel reject the *consensus gentium* strategy because a universal consensus has the status of what happens to be the case; it does not provide the kind of necessity demanded by thought. But Hegel also mentions a second way in which a truth claim based on personal experience could establish the universal legitimacy of its claim, namely by examining the nature of consciousness itself. This examination, however, involves a "laborious meditation, which is the only way to find out what is universal in and for itself in this consciousness" (*Enz* §71*A*). Hegel suggests here that we might establish the universal truth of a claim based on "my" experience by deriving the claim from what consciousness as such must be. This would honour the experience principle, which makes the subject's own experience a necessary condition for accepting something as true, while also demonstrating a necessary sameness between this subject's experience and the experience of any and every consciousness. This alternative makes the comparison to Descartes' *cogito* even more suggestive. The examination would begin within the subject's immediate experience of its own consciousness, an experience immediately identified with the experience of its own existence. The examination would identify in this experience the determinations that belong to the nature of consciousness as such. If the examination were to show that consciousness as such is rooted in the infinite as its ground, then the conscious subject would experience the necessary existence of the infinite as one with the experience of its own existence; and it would know this experience as one with the necessary determinations of every consciousness. In the discussion of the three positions on objectivity, Hegel raises no objections to this alternative, and so allows it to stand as an open possibility (*Enz* §76).

The proof procedure suggested by all these clues, therefore, would begin within the isolated consciousness that is "my" sense experience, proceed to identify within "my" experience what belongs to the nature of consciousness as such, and would conclude by demonstrating that the nature of consciousness as such necessarily involves its dependence on an infinite supersensible ground that is the unity of thought and being. In this way, the proof brings the isolated consciousness that is "my" experience into an experience that knows its own existence identified with the existence of the infinite.

4 BEGINNING WITHOUT PRESUPPOSITIONS

Hegel concludes his critique of the third position by challenging its fundamental claims as arbitrary presuppositions. The immediate knowing position assumes that immediacy and mediation are opposed and completely independent of each other. Immediate knowing must be completely free of mediation and mediated knowing must be completely incapable of immediacy. Hegel has already suggested an alternative to this either/or, namely a self-mediated immediacy, whose very conceivability reveals that the dichotomy between immediacy and mediation, intuition and demonstration, can be questioned. But Hegel does not let himself assert his own position against the third position. Instead he questions the strategy of beginning with presuppositions. Committing oneself to the project of philosophical science, he says, requires the surrender of all presuppositions and arbitrary assurances, whether these are taken from representations or from thinking. Philosophical science itself must determine the meaning and validity of all representations or thoughts, as well as all either/or dichotomies that might be supposed in them (*Enz* §78).

We have ample evidence, however, that Hegelian philosophy itself begins with a presupposition. It presupposes the legitimacy of assuming that the determinations of pure thought are the determinations of being, the real, what exists. Hegel's critique of the immediate knowing position makes it clear that Hegel demands proof of this assumption. Without it, conceiving the truth as the unity of thought and being becomes itself a subjective, arbitrary assertion. What, then, does Hegel mean when he insists on a presuppositionless beginning for philosophy? We must be careful to distinguish two different ways of interpreting this question. Certainly philosophy must begin without presupposing a specifically articulated analysis of what the logical or rational is. We cannot assume a system of categories, a set of logical principles or rules. We begin with the concept of pure thought identified with being, but without any presuppositions about the concrete constitution of this truth. Philosophy itself must demonstrate what the necessary determinations of the rational are. The beginning concept, however, presupposes the legitimacy of conceiving truth as thought identified with being. What, then, does Hegel mean when he insists on a presuppositionless beginning for philosophy?

We can make sense of this if we apply Hegel's analysis of rational proof to the question. Rational proof is a retreat into a ground. It begins with something we know, and it demonstrates that what we know is rooted in and dependent on a ground. Asserting the truth of the ground, therefore, presupposes, depends on, the proof that exposes its status as the ground of something we know. The proof proves, however, that what we began with presupposes, depends on, the ground. The proof demonstrates the presuppositionless status of the ground by showing that everything else in the proof presupposes the ground. Philosophy begins without presuppositions because it begins with what a proof has exposed as the ground that everything else in the proof presupposes.

A proper introduction to philosophical science, therefore, must clear away all presuppositions about what the logical or rational is, and also all presuppositions that challenge the assumption that truth is the unity of thought and being. Hegel suggests that scepticism as a negative science might accomplish this clearing away, since scepticism exposes the negativity within all forms of cognition. Hegel rejects this approach for several reasons.[13] Scepticism as a way of getting into philosophy is redundant, Hegel says, since dialectical scepticism belongs to philosophical procedure itself. Philosophy itself exposes the negativity within all finite forms of cognition whereby their claims to knowledge are overturned. Moreover, scepticism would have to "find the finite forms empirically and unscientifically, and to take them up as given." Beginning with this approach would make philosophy dependent on the *de facto* comprehensiveness of knowledge claims proposed and overturned so far, which may or may not cover all the ways in which knowledge resting on a presupposition might be claimed (*Enz* §78*A*).

Hegel's objection implies that philosophical thought must begin as thought liberated not only from all presuppositions exposed so far, but from all possible ways in which cognition might depend on a presupposition. This suggests that the negation of all presuppositions must be derived from a principle that identifies presupposition-based cognition as such and thus covers all possible ways in which such knowledge claims might be proposed. We might ask at this point whether examining the nature of consciousness, as Hegel has suggested, would count as an examination of presupposition-based cognition as such. If so, then a proper introduction to the philosophical standpoint would examine the nature of consciousness and thereby cover at least all the essential factors involved in proposing a knowledge claim that depends on a presupposition.

13 All of Hegel's objections are directed to scepticism in the narrow sense, which rejects all "finite" forms of cognition, not to the kind of scepticism that dismisses as dogmatic any philosophy that supports a definite thesis.

5 CONCLUSION

Hegel's examination of the three positions on objectivity adds complexity and precision to the themes introduced in the introductory essays of the *Philosophy of Right* and the general introduction to the *Encyclopaedia*. Comparing naïve metaphysics, empiricism, and Kantian idealism adds precision to Hegel's interpretation of the rational-is-actual theme. Hegel accepts the way metaphysics knows the forms of thought as the true essence of things, rejects the way Kantian idealism isolates the relation between subject and object within subjectivity, and insists that the rational is actual in an objectivity that exists in itself, set off from its relations to consciousness. Hegel adds complexity to the rational-is-actual theme, however, by endorsing the way both empiricism and Kantian idealism acknowledge the particulars of experience as a necessary and essential element in objectivity. By endorsing Kant's idea of intellectual intuition giving itself a purpose, Hegel shows that he is looking for a way to derive given particulars from the universality and necessity of rational thought without doing it by deduction. The examination of empiricism and Kantian idealism also repeats the experience principle introduced in the general introduction of the *Encyclopaedia*. Hegel insists yet again that a knowing subject has the right to acknowledge as true only what can be immediately experienced with the certainty of its truth. He acknowledges that the immediate knowing position, with its intuition of the infinite, honours this principle by providing the experienced certainty of truth conceived as the unity of thought and being.

The *Encyclopaedia*'s critique of the immediate knowing position expands significantly Hegel's position on the presuppositions of philosophy and the proof required for the justification of these presuppositions. Hegel associates the immediate knowing position with the standpoint of philosophy, and endorses the way this position conceives the truth as the unity of thought and being distinguished from the given immediacy of sense realities and from the isolated subjectivity of thought. This suggests that the pure being with which philosophy begins is thought existing as what being truly is. The critique of the immediate knowing position, however, demands a proof that demonstrates the legitimacy of this beginning concept. The immediate knowing position, by conceiving the truth as an immediacy that excludes all mediation, appeals to an experience isolated within the subjectivity of the knower. Without a proof, this experience has no way of justifying a claim to universal, objective truth, no way of showing that it holds for all reality and all knowers.

The *Encyclopaedia* suggests that a truth claim based on personal experience might be able to establish the universal validity of its claims by demonstrating that the experience belongs to the nature of consciousness as such. This kind of proof would focus on what is essential to a consciousness kind of cognition, and hence its results would hold for all knowers engaged in a consciousness form of knowing. Thus, the *Encyclopaedia* acknowledges that the beginning concept of philosophy must be proved, and suggests that the proof required would examine consciousness as such, which is the name Hegel gives to experience. The general introduction to the *Encyclopaedia* says that the *Phenomenology of Spirit* proves the necessity of the philosophical standpoint in a dialectical demonstration that begins with immediate consciousness. We must ask, therefore, whether Hegel considers the *Phenomenology* to be an examination of consciousness as such. We must also ask how the *Encyclopaedia*'s call for a proof of philosophy's beginning concept squares with its statement that philosophy can begin by simply resolving to consider thought as such. Finally, we must ask how the discussion of these issues affects Hegel's claim that the beginning of philosophy is both mediated and immediate.

The critique of traditional proofs for the existence of God, included in the discussion of the three positions on objectivity, provides the most explicit clues to the way Hegel addresses these questions in the *Encyclopaedia.* In this discussion, Hegel rejects a proof procedure that ends with a concept that defines the infinite in terms of its relation to the finite. He calls for a procedure that shifts into a concept that thinks the infinite in itself. Yet the same text insists that the legitimacy of the concept must be proved, that without proof immediate knowing becomes subjective and arbitrary. By describing the proof procedure as a retreat into a ground, the *Encyclopaedia* makes sense of this ambiguity. The mediation involved in proving the truth of the concept that identifies the standpoint of philosophy turns into a negative mediation, because it proves that the philosophical standpoint belongs to a domain different from the derivative truth that retreats into it; and this negative mediation demonstrates the necessity of thinking the ground as independent of, not mediated by, what it grounds. Hence, philosophy begins with a simple resolve to examine thought as such. A beginning of this kind focuses on pure knowing in itself, without the positive mediation that identifies it as the truth of consciousness, and without the negative mediation that separates pure knowing from its involvement in consciousness. If we compare this kind of proof to traditional proofs for the existence of God, which the *Encyclopaedia* invites us to do, Hegelian proof demands a shift from the traditional position, which conceives God in terms of what the infinite explains in the finite, to a position that conceives the infinite in itself and thus takes us into the whole-truth perspective of God.

PART THREE

THOUGHT VS. EXPERIENCE

In the introductory essays of the *Science of Logic*, Hegel again discusses the standpoint of philosophy, its procedure, and its presuppositions. Here, too, he talks about the relation between philosophy and experience. But the emphasis is different in the *Science of Logic*. The position Hegel develops in the *Philosophy of Right* and the *Encyclopaedia* focuses on an ambiguity in the relation between philosophy and experience. Philosophical thought develops its concepts without depending on experience, and yet philosophical thought must know itself in experience. In the introductory essays of the *Logic*, Hegel exposes a fundamental opposition between philosophy and experience and defines the task of the *Phenomenology* in terms of this opposition.

6

The Challenge of Empirical Consciousness

THE SECOND PREFACE OF THE *Logic* and its Introduction begin as the *Philosophy of Right* and the *Encyclopaedia* begin, with a discussion of the relation between thought and experience. The *Logic*'s Second Preface does not use the term *Erfahrung*. But it refers to sensations, intuitions, representations, what is "inward," which corresponds to what the *Encyclopaedia* identifies as experience. The *Logic* also mentions expressions generally known (*Allbekanntes*) in the culture, just as the *Philosophy of Right* refers to culture-based knowledge of various kinds; and what is given in the culture belongs to the experience of social life and the representations in which a culture expresses itself (*WL* 21;11–12/M 33). Moreover, like the *Philosophy of Right* and the *Encyclopaedia*, the *Logic* distinguishes between thought embedded in experience, thought separated from experience, and thought recognized in experience.

1 LOGIC EMBEDDED IN EXPERIENCE

The discussion begins with a description of "natural thinking." Logic, Hegel says, is so natural to human beings, so characteristic of their humanness, that it permeates even their relations to physical nature. What we feel in our senses, what we perceive or desire or need, what we find ourselves driven to, we experience in a logical form. The logical character of this experience comes from linguistic representation. Everything "inner," everything a person makes his or her own, is represented and articulated in language. Language names our intuitions, our needs, our creations; it articulates their connections. In the process, it gives them a logical form. It represents them as things with common names, as particulars within a universal, as things distinguished from their properties, as relations of dependence or mutual exclusiveness. The category may be explicitly expressed as a logical category, or it may remain hidden and mixed with other elements. But all language explicitly or implicitly involves articulating a content in the form of a logical category. By transforming a content into language, we represent it as an object that corresponds to the way we think.

Logical categories, therefore, are as familiar as the language we use. We express the determinations of thought in everything we say. Natural thinking, however, does not focus on the categories of thought as such. It uses them unconsciously, instinctively, to deal with the content of life, to create and exchange representations for the organization of information, the satisfaction of needs, the pursuit of interests, the fulfillment of purposes. The universality of the categories provides a system of abbreviations for the overwhelming number and diversity of singular things. The connection between thought categories helps us understand relations among objects. Thus, the determinations of thought operate in natural thinking as forms attached to a content. According to this way of thinking, thought serves our need to understand and deal with something else, the content of experience (*WL* 21:10–15/M 31–6; 21:27–8/M 43–4).

2 LOGIC LIBERATED FROM EXPERIENCE

According to the Second Preface, the logic current in Hegel's own time calls attention to the separation of thought from content by detaching thought determinations from their involvement in the concerns of life. Formal logic reduces the determinations of thought to forms without content, ways of thinking without something to think, abstract rules that must depend on something other than thought for what thought thinks according to these rules. Formal logic, however, does not satisfy the need for truth. Truth, Hegel says, is the explicit object and aim of logic. Logic knows its subject matter only if it knows the forms of thought as "the *logos*, the reason of that which is, the truth of what we call things" (*WL* 21: 17/M 39). Again he says, "when we speak of things, we call their nature or essence their concept, and this is only for thought" (*WL* 21:14/M 35). Thus, the *Logic* as well as the *Encyclopaedia* defines "concept" as a thought that knows the essence or nature of things (*WL* 21:13–18/M 35–9).

Hegel repeats this theme in the Introduction to the *Logic*, where he supports the claims of ancient metaphysics against the thinking current in his own time. The current thinking takes the position that sense perception provides the content and reality for knowing, and that thought on its own produces nothing but phantoms or fancies (*Hirngespinste*). This, Hegel says, reduces truth to a subjective knowing, a knowledge of the way the object appears, which leaves unknown the nature of the thing itself (*Sache selbst*). Ancient metaphysics, he insists, has a better conception of truth. According to this conception, thought knows the truth of things by giving them the form of thought. Thinking and its determinations do not impose on things a form external and alien to what they are. On the contrary, by thinking things in a form proper to thought itself, thought brings before itself their essence and truth. The true nature of things and the determinations inherent in thought have the same content. By abstracting from the concrete concerns of life, therefore, logic does not empty itself of content. Rather, it focuses on the content that belongs to the real truth of the matter. Logic has as its content and subject matter (*die Sache*) the determinations of thought, and these determinations are the essence of reality. Thus, in the Introduction to the *Logic*, as in the Second Preface, Hegel repeats the claims of the *Encyclopaedia*. The *Logic* as well as the *Encyclopaedia* endorses traditional philosophy's claim that thought knows the true essence of things themselves by knowing their correspondence to the forms of thought. The *Logic* as well as the *Encyclopaedia* couples this endorsement with a rejection of the Kantian claim that thought knows only the way a thing appears to knowing, which leaves unrevealed what a thing is in itself (*WL* 21:29–30/M 45).

In the *Logic*'s Second Preface, Hegel emphasizes the way logic sets thought free, a dominant theme in the introductory essays of the *Philosophy of Right* and the *Encyclopaedia*. In linguistic experience, the thinking subject instinctively conforms to a set of laws, feels itself driven by necessities that seem to be given or imposed. Moreover, experience leaves the laws of logic isolated from each other. By following these laws as they are given in experience, thought finds itself fragmented, unstable, confused, torn between different laws and different categories without a stabilizing system of connections to guide it. Finally, experience leaves the soul of things, the real truth of the matter, differentiated from the "reality relative to it," the body, in which it appears. Experience does not know how what appears belongs to what the object fundamentally is. Philosophical logic brings to consciousness the laws of thought and distinguishes these laws from the given particulars of experience; it reveals what is proper to thought itself. It also knows the necessary connections that make these laws different determinations of the same logical spirit. Thus, the thinking subject comes to know the logical necessity operative throughout the contingencies of experience and hence knows how experience is ruled by thought. The instincts operative in experience and the objects given in experience come to light as manifestations of thought itself. The soul of things, the real truth of the matter, becomes manifest in its body; the essence of what is shows itself in the reality that relates it to consciousness. Thus, thought is liberated from instinctive thinking and a foreign content. Thought knows it all as its own logical spirit, and thus knows itself as self-governed and free (*WL* 21:15–16/M 37).

3 THOUGHT RECOGNIZED IN EXPERIENCE

Truth requires this explicit self-recognition. Truth is not fully actual in the mere existence of the logical as the true essence of what is. The logical must know itself as such. Truth is accomplished, it becomes actual, only if the logical spirit exists as thought knowing itself to be the truth of what is: "The most important point for the nature of spirit is the relation, not only of what it implicitly is *in itself* to what it *actually* is, but of what it *knows itself* to be to what it *actually* is; because spirit is essentially consciousness, this self-knowledge is a fundamental determination of its actuality" (*WL* 21:15–16/M 37). Here again, as in the *Encyclopaedia*, Hegel insists that knowledge does not just know the truth, it accomplishes the truth. The truth becomes actual only in the knowing that actually knows the spirit of its own logical thinking as the truth of what is. The Introduction to the *Logic* describes the educational process that accomplishes this actualization.

When we study logic with no great experience of the other sciences, Hegel says, we take it to be one science among others, a detached preoccupation with the rules of thinking. This detachment leaves the other sciences on their own. As a result, they have worked on their content as a subject matter that is completely independent of logic. The study of logic, however, by forcing consciousness to concentrate on what is remote from the sense intuitions, purposes, feelings, and representations of experience teaches consciousness to recognize rational structures. As a result of this discipline, consciousness becomes adept at recognizing the rational element in the various sciences. When our knowledge of the other sciences is more fully developed, we recognize that logic is not an abstract system detached from the concrete particulars of experience. Rather, it holds all these particulars within itself because the logical or rational is what they essentially are. Thus, we come to know the particulars of experience not as a content other than and given to thought, but as determinations of the logical or rational, which is the structure of thought itself. Thought focuses first on the determinations of thought by themselves, apart from their involvement in the concrete, so that it can then recognize in its knowledge of concrete objects what is proper to thought itself (*WL* 21:41–3/M 57–9).

Thus, the *Logic* repeats a point stressed in the *Encyclopaedia*. Thought in its freedom, thought developed according to its own independent determinations, logic in its true form does not remain detached from experience. It achieves its aim by knowing the truth, and knowing the truth is knowing its own determinations as the true essence of experience. In the *Logic* and in the *Encyclopaedia*, Hegel makes this point explicitly by talking about the way the freedom of pure thought knows its own determinations in the material presented by the non-philosophical sciences, whose investigations operate within experience.

4 ORDINARY PHENOMENAL CONSCIOUSNESS

Hegel makes one point in the Second Preface of the *Logic* that introduces a new dimension to the discussion of thought and experience. Logic as natural thinking, which is logic embedded in experience, treats the forms of thought as forms without content, ways of thinking that depend on something other than thought for what they think. In the Introduction to the *Logic*, Hegel examines more carefully this separation of form and content, thought and what it thinks; and by doing so, he exposes a fundamental opposition in the relation between thought and experience.

The Introduction begins by asking about the concept of logic. The concept of a science defines its subject matter; and the subject matter of logic is "thinking in general." The Introduction begins, therefore, with questions about the definition that determines how logic investigates "thinking in general." The discussion considers first the concept of logic that has prevailed up to Hegel's own time. According to this concept, thinking is a form abstracted from all content, the form of knowing abstracted from what it knows. This kind of logic, Hegel says, has its foundation in "the determinations that constitute the nature of our ordinary, phenomenal (*erscheinenden*) consciousness" (*WL* 21:29/M 45). Ordinary phenomenal consciousness assumes that the materials of knowing exist on their own in a world apart from thought. The object of thought by itself is complete; it can be itself with or without its relation to thought. However, thought by itself is an empty form, the indeterminateness of thinking without the definiteness of what it thinks. Hence, thought cannot be fully itself, it cannot really think, unless it fills itself with a content provided by what is other than itself, the object. Thought comes to the content of knowing as an external form, a form not proper to the content itself.

Hegel describes two views of what thought knows in this form-content relation. One view does not articulate in any definite way the difference between matter and form, object and thought. It simply assumes that thought must overcome the difference by making its thinking agree with the object. Thought knows the truth by accommodating itself to what the object is. The second view assumes that the difference between thought and its object is insurmountable. Thought accommodates itself to an object constituted by thought itself, by the way thought receives content and the way thought forms the content received into something intelligible. Hence, thought knows what its receptivity and formative activity have made of the object, not what the object itself is in itself and on its own. The "thing-in-itself," in its otherness and independence of thought, remains a "beyond" to which thought has no access (*WL* 21:28–9/M 44–5).

Although the second view bears a marked resemblance to Kant's critical philosophy, Hegel does not treat it as a particular philosopher's view. He treats it as a structure that belongs to human consciousness as such. The Kantian point of view articulates one view that can be derived from the structure of ordinary phenomenal consciousness. Hegel even describes the same view again under the name "ordinary common sense" (*gemeiner Menschenverstand*). This version of ordinary consciousness assumes that thoughts are "only" thoughts. It dismisses the independent thought of reason, reason concerned only with itself, as generating nothing but fantasies. "Common sense" keeps its feet on the ground. It never forgets that thought has no content or reality of its own, that thought gets whatever truth it has from its relation to sensuous reality. Since, however, sense perception reveals only the way thought is affected by what is other than itself, thought knows only a subjective truth. It knows the object as it appears to thought, not as it is in itself (*WL* 21:29–30/M 45–6).

According to Hegel, then, this common sense view shares with the more nebulous, indefinite version of ordinary consciousness the same fundamental presuppositions. Both presuppose the separation of thought and its object. Both assume that thought comes to its content as an empty form that does not belong to the content itself. Both assume that truth depends on the content and is in no way derived from thought. Hence, Hegel calls the separation of thought and object, form and content, the separation of "certainty" and truth. The object or content, which is the truth, is independent of and other than thought, which is only the certainty, the consciousness of or assent to the truth (*WL* 21:28/M 44).

The presuppositions of ordinary phenomenal consciousness are not only the presuppositions of formal logic but also the presuppositions of natural thinking or natural logic, which is thought embedded in experience. Natural logic uses logical categories to organize and manage the content of life. But natural thinking does not know these categories, these determinations of thought, as the essence or nature of the content. Natural thinking assumes that logical categories, expressed in linguistic representations, serve thought's concern with something other than thought. Thus, natural thinking, in its preoccupation with the content of life, presupposes the relation between thought and content that identifies ordinary phenomenal consciousness. Thought embedded in experience takes on the structure of ordinary phenomenal consciousness.

It is important to notice the precise way in which Hegel questions the presuppositions of ordinary phenomenal consciousness. He does not claim that these presuppositions are illegitimate for ordinary phenomenal consciousness itself. On the contrary, he says that they "constitute its nature." But he challenges the claim that the same presuppositions hold for reason: "However, when these prejudices are carried over to reason, as if in reason the same relation obtained, as if this relation had any truth in and for itself, then they are errors, and the refutation of them in every part of the spiritual and natural universe is what philosophy is; or rather, since they block the entrance to philosophy, they are the errors that must be removed before one can enter it" (*WL* 21:29/M 45). Philosophy does not refute or set aside the presuppositions of ordinary phenomenal consciousness itself. It refutes or sets aside the error of attributing these presuppositions to reason. At this point in the discussion, Hegel leaves the status of ordinary phenomenal consciousness itself undetermined. Here he focuses on the constitution of philosophy. Thought cannot be philosophical unless it liberates itself from the presuppositions of ordinary phenomenal consciousness. These same presuppositions belong to natural logic, which is thought embedded in experience. Hence, thought cannot be philosophical unless it separates itself from its involvement in experience.

As we have seen, the *Encyclopaedia* makes the same claim. Thought begins within experience. It becomes philosophical when it separates itself from experience. According to the *Encyclopaedia*, the impetus for this separation is a need that belongs to thought itself, the need for truth which is equated with the need for necessity. The Introduction to the *Logic* talks about the separation of thought from experience in a different way. It introduces a general form of cognition, ordinary phenomenal consciousness. This form of cognition presupposes a definition of truth that stands opposed to the way philosophical science defines it. Philosophical science assumes that thought separated from experience, thought developed according to its own independent necessities, reveals the truth of what is. Ordinary phenomenal consciousness assumes that the truth of what is exists as an object separated from and independent of thought. Natural thinking, which is thought embedded in experience, belongs to this form of cognition. Thus, thought involved in experience is committed to a definition of truth that stands opposed to the way truth is conceived by philosophical thought. How, then, do we justify the move from thought involved in experience to thought separated from experience, a move that gives up one way of defining the truth and endorses its opposite? The *Science of Logic* discusses the beginning concept of philosophy in terms of this question.

5 ABSOLUTE BEGINNINGS

In the Introduction to the *Encyclopaedia*, Hegel distinguishes between what a philosophical beginning requires and what a non-philosophical science can take for granted. In the introductory essays of the *Science of Logic*, he develops a more thorough account of the same issue. In other sciences, he says, the subject matter of the science is different from the method used to investigate it. Biology, for example, uses an empirical method to study life in natural things. But the empirical method does not belong to the subject matter itself. Biology uses the method to investigate something else. Moreover, non-philosophical sciences derive the content of the subject matter from other concepts and materials. Biology, for example, uses the concepts of matter, locomotion, and cause-effect in its study of physical life. Finally, non-philosophical sciences use generally accepted forms of argumentation to make a case for their claims. Logic, however, studies the laws of thinking, and hence it cannot take its method or its way of arguing from what is generally accepted. Logic itself must determine what the laws of thinking are. Moreover, even the concept of the logical cannot be adopted from what is generally accepted. Logic itself must investigate what the logical is (*WL* 21:27–8/M 43). It seems, therefore, that logic must make an absolute beginning, which Hegel defines thus: "The beginning must then be *absolute* or, what means the same here, must be an abstract beginning; and so there is *nothing* that it may *presuppose,* must not be mediated by anything or have a ground, ought to be rather itself the ground of the entire science" (*WL* 21:56/M 70).

"Absolute" and "abstract" here seem to mean disconnected, isolated, not dependent on something else, since an absolute or abstract beginning has no ground, depends on nothing presupposed, is not mediated by anything. Logic cannot presuppose the legitimacy of a method or way of arguing. It cannot even presuppose a generally accepted definition of its subject matter. It seems, therefore, that logic must simply assert a definition of its subject matter and thus make an absolute beginning.

But Hegel also talks about absolute beginnings for the non-philosophical sciences, and explains why philosophy cannot begin in this way. A science makes an absolute beginning when it begins with a precise definition of what anyone would acknowledge as the subject matter of this science. The beginning is absolute because it is not produced as a result of a demonstration or argument. It is simply asserted as what no one would dispute. But such definitions contain nothing more than a precise articulation of what is familiar and generally accepted. Someone can always challenge them by describing a case in which one or more of the terms in the definition mean something different. On the basis of this counter example, the challenger can demand an adjustment in the definition of the science and a corresponding adjustment in the science itself.

Then an argument develops about what should and should not be included in the science. For example, does political science include political theory, or does theory belong only to political philosophy? Does the subject matter of biochemistry or biological anthropology belong to the subject matter of biology? Is clinical psychology really a science? There is no way to settle these disputes. Since the definition of the science depends on no justification process, it can only be asserted as a historical claim: this definition expresses what is in fact the accepted way of understanding the subject matter and aims of the science. But this is exactly what the counter example challenges. The challenger presents a case in which the definition would not be acknowledged as the accepted way of defining the subject matter of the science. The argument can be settled only by arbitrarily deciding what evidence to accept and what evidence to dismiss. Making an absolute beginning, therefore, involves making an arbitrary beginning. The original definition of the science gets its legitimacy from the arbitrary decision (*Willkür*) to accept the evidence on one side of a dispute and to reject the evidence on the other side (*WL* 21:32–3/M 49).

Yet Hegel talks about an absolute beginning for logic, and he never rejects it as illegitimate. Moreover, he describes it as a resolve (*Entschluß*), a choice (*Willkür*). We decide to do logic, to consider thought as such. Why does Hegel propose this kind of beginning for logic and yet dismiss as arbitrary the way non-philosophical sciences do it? How does the absolute beginning Hegel rejects differ from the absolute beginning he accepts? The absolute beginning Hegel rejects chooses what evidence to accept and what evidence to dismiss in the debate about how to articulate with exactness the familiar, generally accepted definition of the science. The absolute beginning Hegel endorses chooses to do logic. When Hegel proceeds to articulate the definition of logic with more exactness, he does not choose between contrary sets of evidence supporting contrary definitions. He simply rules out any definite articulation of the beginning concept that identifies the subject matter of logic. Logic cannot get its beginning definition of thought as such by distinguishing it from or comparing it to something else, or by analyzing its constitution, or by deriving it from a ground. Definitions determined in this way are mediated; they depend on what the subject matter is distinguished from, compared to, constituted by, the result of. Hegel concludes from this that logic's beginning is absolute in the sense of being abstract. The concept of pure thought begins logic with no predicates whatsoever; it begins as pure being (*WL* 21:56/M 70; 21:61–2/M 74–5).[1]

6 PHILOSOPHY VERSUS ORDINARY PHENOMENAL CONSCIOUSNESS

When Hegel says that logic can make an absolute beginning, he talks about two different issues. How can the beginning definition of the subject matter be thought so that all its determinations are developed within the science of logic itself, so that none are presupposed in the beginning definition? This is the question that provokes the claim that logic begins with the abstract thought of pure being. Thus, Hegel says: "It also follows that what constitutes the beginning, because it is something still undeveloped and empty of content, is not yet truly known at that beginning, and that only science, and science fully developed, is the completed cognition of it, replete with content and finally truly grounded" (*WL* 21:58/M 72). But Hegel also talks about how we get into the position of doing logic rather than some other science; and this involves a choice. We simply choose to do logic. In order to make this choice, however, we must decide between alternatives. If we decide to do Hegelian logic, then we reject the definition of truth implicit in ordinary phenomenal consciousness and choose a definition of truth that stands opposed to it. If we choose to do formal logic, then we reject the

1 I shall not address all of the controversial questions that this thought of pure being raises for the study and interpretation of the *Logic*'s opening moves. My concern focuses on the problem of getting into philosophy rather than the problem of getting on with it. My interpretation of the relation between the *Phenomenology* and the *Logic* will probably have some significance for the way the *Logic*'s opening moves are interpreted. But I will leave to other scholars the task of determining exactly how this plays out in the development of the *Logic*'s categories. For a good review of the issues involved in the opening moves of the *Logic*, consult the following: Burbidge (1981), 38–42; (1992), chapter 2; (2006), 38–41; Chiereghin (2003); Houlgate (2006), chapter 14.

definition of truth presupposed by Hegelian logic and choose a definition of truth that fits the presuppositions of ordinary phenomenal consciousness. Either way, we choose between truth as an object separated from and independent of thought and truth as thought developed according to its own independent necessities (*WL* 21:33–4/M 49–50).

We can look at Hegel's two issues another way as well. Every science has an ambiguous relation to its subject matter. It begins by presupposing the general definition that identifies what the science investigates. But it also produces this concept as a result in the sense that it demonstrates and articulates its full meaning. For example, biology begins as the study of natural life; and it proceeds to investigate exactly what life is. Ethics begins as a study of moral norms; and it proceeds to investigate what these norms are. Hegelian philosophy has a similarly ambiguous relation to the concept of pure thought or logic. It begins by deciding to philosophize, by resolving to focus on the logical, the purely rational, pure thought determinations; and it produces as its result a full articulation of what the logical is (*WL* 21:27/M 43).[2] When, therefore, Hegel works on the problem of letting logic itself determine what the logical is, he is asking how this science works out the full meaning of its subject matter. But Hegel is also concerned with a different question.

By undertaking the study of a certain subject matter, a science takes for granted the legitimacy of the concept that determines the focus of the investigation. If we grant the legitimacy of defining physical processes as living, then we can use the concept of life to develop a fuller and more adequate understanding of how life functions in the natural order. If we grant the legitimacy of defining human action as governed by moral norms, then we can use the concept of a moral norm to work out what these norms should be; we use as the starting point of ethical arguments the role that moral norms play in human action. But if we do not justify defining physical processes as living or human action as moral, then we leave open the possibility that biology or ethics are preoccupied with something that is simply unreal and hence are not real knowledge.

The same conditions hold in the case of logic. If we grant the legitimacy of a science that focuses on the logical, the rational, thought as such, then we can use the concept of thought as such to develop a fuller and more adequate knowledge of its laws and categories. But if we do not prove the legitimacy of this concept, then we leave open the possibility that logic is preoccupied with an empty, meaningless construct. This problem haunts

2 See also *WL* 21:29–30/M 45; 21:33–4/M 49–50; 21:48–9/M 63.

even the absolute beginning that presupposes no determinations derived from distinctions, comparisons, analysis, or relation to a ground. By deciding to do logic, we assume that logic is real knowledge, that it is not a knowing of nothing; and this means that the object known, the pure rationality of thought, is not empty and meaningless. Hegel explicitly worries about this. If, by focusing on pure thought determinations, logic detaches thought from the content that gives it meaning, then "good sense" rightly relegates it to the status of a school exercise. But Hegel insists that logic has a content of its own. It knows the categories of pure thought; and these categories are the essential content of everything we know. Thus, logic begins by assuming that the pure forms of thought are not empty notions but the essential content of what truly is (*WL* 21:10–18/M 31–40).

Yet this assumption is not indisputable. The presuppositions of ordinary phenomenal consciousness, natural thinking, and formal logic stand against it. If, therefore, logic does not prove the necessity of the concept that provides the beginning definition of its subject matter, then logic begins with an arbitrary choice. By deciding to do logic, we simply decide to accept the claims on one side of the disagreement and to reject those on the other side. According to Hegel, this is exactly what is wrong with absolute beginnings in the non-philosophical sciences: "In this method of beginning science with a definition, no mention is made of the need to demonstrate the *necessity* of its *subject matter,* and hence the necessity of the science itself" (*WL* 21:33/M 49).

In the *Encyclopaedia,* Hegel says that philosophy begins with a free act of thought. Thought decides to think about itself. Philosophy gives itself an object by thinking its own thought (*Enz* §17). It would be tempting to conclude from this that logic begins with the thinking subject's own thought and hence has direct access to its object. We could then claim that the real content of logic is immediately evident. The object of logic is the real thought we find existent in ourselves. In the *Science of Logic,* however, Hegel refuses this option, which he describes as "beginning with the 'I.'" He opens the discussion by proposing two reasons why this approach seems appropriate for philosophy. First, philosophy looks for a truth that can be the origin of everything that follows; and philosophy needs a principle that can account for all its own determinations. Second, it looks for "something with which one is already acquainted, and even more than just acquainted, something of which one is *immediately certain.*" If the beginning of philosophy cannot depend on anything else, precisely because it is the beginning, then philosophy must begin with something immediately accessible. Moreover, this immediately accessible truth must carry with it a legitimacy that goes beyond the subjective feelings of a particular subject. It must be true for everyone, not just for me. The "I," "this immediate consciousness of the self," seems to fulfill all these requirements. It needs nothing else to make it available and familiar. We know immediately our self conscious of itself. Everything else we know belongs to this ego as a content distinguished from the ego itself, and is therefore contingent. The particular state of consciousness that knows this content may or may not be reproducible in other thinkers. But the structure of a self immediately conscious of itself, its knowing immediately its own identity with itself, demands the assent of every "I" and without the mediation of any other knowing (*WL* 21:62–3/M 75–6).

Hegel challenges this claim to immediacy. The "I" purged of its content, the ego identified only with itself, the abstract "I" pure enough to be the source of all its own determinations, is not immediately at hand (*nicht unmitelbar vorhanden ist*) in every individual, is not "the familiar, ordinary 'I' of our consciousness to which everyone immediately links science." The thinking subject has direct access only to ordinary consciousness, the ego of empirical self-consciousness, which is conscious of itself as "the most concrete of all things," "as an infinitely manifold world." This is the "I" involved in intuitions, representations, and the practicalities of life, the self of ordinary (*gewöhnlichen*) phenomenal consciousness, which Hegel suggests by repeatedly referring to it as "ordinary (*gewöhnliche*) consciousness." Before this ego can become the beginning of philosophy, it must separate itself from its content and become conscious of itself as the abstract ego, the empty "I am I," in which the difference of subject and object disappears. If, however, philosophy begins by simply demanding that the individual ego assume this position, then it reduces the beginning of philosophy to an arbitrarily chosen (*willkürlicher*) standpoint, "a subjective postulate," or even to an empirical state of consciousness that may or may not be found or produced in each and every thinker (*WL* 21:62–4/M 76–7).

Thus, the *Logic* repeats the objection Hegel develops in the *Encyclopaedia*'s critique of the immediate knowing position. Thought asserting itself as the empty "I am I" and immediate knowing asserting itself as the intuition of the infinite have the same status. In this form, thought becomes an esoteric experience, a knowing isolated in the subjectivity of one knower's thinking. The *Logic*, like the *Encyclopaedia*, insists that the truth status of isolated pure thought must be proved. The *Logic*, however, tells us exactly what kind of proof is required: "before it proves itself as a valid demand, the progression of the concrete 'I' from immediate consciousness to pure knowledge must be demonstratively exhibited within the 'I' itself, through its own necessity" (*WL* 21:63/M 76). Hegel calls this an objective movement, in contrast to the subjective postulating of the abstract ego. In order to make the beginning of philosophy a truth that is true for every thinker, we must begin with the ego that is immediately at hand for everyone, the concrete ego of ordinary consciousness. We must demonstrate that the move into the position of pure knowing is necessitated by this ego.

Hegel's argument against beginning with the "I" applies as well to his own claim that logic can begin with a choice, the simple resolve to focus on pure thought. A simple resolve moves the thinking subject into the position of pure knowing as an arbitrarily chosen standpoint, a subjective postulate, or even an empirical state of consciousness that may or may not be found or produced in each and every thinker. Moreover, this simple resolve requires that thought separate itself from its embeddedness in ordinary consciousness. In the *Encyclopaedia*, Hegel calls this kind of move a mediation. Philosophy defines its beginning position by negating, separating from, experience; and hence pure thought is mediated by the separation relation that sets it free from its involvement in empirical cognition (*Enz* §12). In the *Encyclopaedia*'s examination of the immediate knowing position, Hegel also says that the philosophical standpoint has no objectivity without proof. Hence, the freedom of pure thought, which is the standpoint of philosophy, is mediated by the proof process that produces this independence.

In the *Science of Logic*, Hegel says again that the separation of thought from experience depends on a demonstration. Here, however, he tells us more explicitly what kind of demonstration is required. The demonstration must show that the ego of ordinary consciousness necessitates the freedom of philosophical thought. The beginning of logic presupposes the legitimacy of treating thought as though its content and truth did not depend on its involvement in the ordinary consciousness of experience. If thought gets to this presupposition by simply deciding to make the assumption, the beginning of logic depends on a negative mediation; thought withdraws into itself by rejecting experience as not the real truth of the matter. If thought gets to the presupposition by demonstrating that the ego of ordinary consciousness necessitates it, the beginning of logic depends on a positive mediation. Thought withdraws into itself by demonstrating that experience itself requires it. How, then, can Hegel accept the legitimacy of an unmediated, absolute beginning? In the *Science of Logic*, this problem provides the framework for Hegel's discussion of the relation between logic and the *Phenomenology*.

7

The Justification of Logic

IN THE *ENCYCLOPAEDIA*, Hegel says that the *Phenomenology of Spirit* proves the necessity of the philosophical standpoint (*Enz* §25*A*). In the introductory texts of the *Science of Logic*, he develops a fuller and more careful account of this claim. Moreover, he repeats this discussion three different times: in the first section of the Introduction entitled "General Concept of Logic"; in the second section of the Introduction entitled "General Division of the Logic"; and in the essay entitled "With What Must the Beginning of Science Be Made." All three texts identify the subject matter of phenomenology as a form of cognition that Hegel calls "consciousness." All three describe this form of cognition in a way that corresponds to the structure of ordinary phenomenal consciousness. Ordinary phenomenal consciousness separates certainty from truth, thought from object, form from content (*WL* 21:28–9/M 44–5). Consciousness begins as an opposition between itself and the object (*WL* 21:32/M 48). Consciousness separates certainty from object, certainty from truth, subjectivity from objectivity, form from content (*WL* 21:33–4/M 49–50; 21:45/M 60; 21:55/M 69). Also, Hegel refers to the phenomenology of consciousness as "the science of manifested (*erscheinenden*) spirit," which repeats the term used to describe ordinary phenomenal (*erscheinenden*) consciousness (*WL* 21:54–5/M 68–9). Both "consciousness" and "ordinary phenomenal consciousness" refer to consciousness in the form of an appearing. The *Phenomenology*, therefore, has as its subject matter the same ordinary phenomenal consciousness that operates in the content of life. Natural thinking, which is thought embedded in experience, belongs to this form of cognition. Whatever else *erscheinenden* means here, it means at least the cognition that appears in experience.

1 THE *PHENOMENOLOGY* AS PROOF

The first section of the Introduction describes the role of the *Phenomenology* as a justification (*Rechtfertigung*), proof (*Beweis*), deduction (*Deduktion*) that has the concept of science as its result, that demonstrates (*aufgezeigt*) the necessity of this concept and therefore of the science itself. Thus, Hegel uses strong words to describe the way the concept of scientific thinking, which defines the subject matter of logic, depends on the *Phenomenology*. The *Phenomenology* justifies the concept, proves it, demonstrates the necessity of conceiving thought in this way. The *Phenomenology* begins, he says, with consciousness in its immediate form, the immediate opposition between consciousness itself and its object. The *Phenomenology* moves from this starting point through every way in which consciousness is related to its object until the movement reaches absolute knowing. This development shows that absolute knowing is the truth of consciousness in all its forms. They all lead into absolute knowing as what these forms of consciousness truly are. This truth dissolves the separation of certainty and truth, and thus liberates cognition from the opposition that belongs to the fundamental structure of consciousness. As a result, knowledge must be conceived not as consciousness conceives it but as knowing set free from the way consciousness conceives it, not as the separation of certainty and truth but as a truth that is one with certainty and a certainty that is one with truth.

> [Pure science] contains *thought in so far as this thought is equally the <thing>* (*die Sache*) *as it is in itself*; or the *<thing> in itself* in so far as this *is equally pure thought.* As *science*, truth is pure self-consciousness as it develops itself and has the shape of the self, so that *<in and for itself being is the known concept, but the concept as such is in and for itself being>* (*an und für sich Seiende gewurßter Begriff, der Begriff als solcher aber das an und für sich Seiende ist*). (*WL* 21:33–4/M 49)

Thus, the *Phenomenology* proves the necessity of setting aside the way consciousness conceives the truth, and of accepting the way logic conceives it. Moreover, the *Phenomenology* does not use the questionable strategies that we saw Hegel use in the *Encyclopaedia*. The *Phenomenology*, as the Introduction to the *Logic* describes it, does not appeal to a need that thought brings to experience, the need for necessity. The *Phenomenology* does not judge the forms of experience by determining the way they measure up to or fall short of what Hegelian philosophy expects the truth to be. The *Phenomenology* demonstrates a necessity implicit in the kind of cognition that belongs to experience itself. Thus, the Introduction says that the concept of science emerges in consciousness, that it arises out of, is the result of, the phenomenological movement through the various forms of consciousness. It says that all the forms of consciousness "dissolve into that concept as into their truth," just as they are all resolved into absolute knowing as their truth. Both absolute knowing, which is the end of the *Phenomenology*, and the concept of science, which is the beginning of logic, are the same truth (*WL* 21:32–4/M 48–9).

The way in which the Introduction talks about this truth suggests that it emerges from the phenomenology of consciousness with a definition that is both negative and positive. The phenomenological movement proves what truth is not. It is not what consciousness takes it to be, an object separated from the certainty that knows it. But the phenomenological movement also proves what truth is: "truth has become equal to certainty and this certainty to truth." Similarly, logic presupposes thought's liberation from the opposition in consciousness; logic presupposes that the separation of certainty and object has been dissolved. But it also begins with "*thought in so far as this thought is equally the <thing>* (*die Sache*) *as it is in itself*; or the *<thing>* (*die Sache*) *in itself* in so far as this *is equally pure thought*." Thus, Hegel talks about the truth at the end of the *Phenomenology* and at the beginning of logic in the same positive-negative way. This truth overcomes and hence negates the opposition in consciousness, which is the opposition of thought and being; and it thinks the positive that follows from this, namely the sameness of thought and being (*WL* 21:33–4/M 49).

The section entitled "General Division of Logic" supports this interpretation. Pure knowing, which is the principle of logic, knows that the opposition between a subject isolated in itself (*für sich*) and an object isolated in itself (*für sich*) has been overcome. This is the negative definition of pure knowing. But the text immediately restates the definition in a positive form. Pure knowing knows that the pure concept (the concept as pure thought) is true being (the concept as object), and that true being is the pure concept (*WL* 21:45/M 60).

2 THE AMBIGUITY OF LOGIC'S ABSOLUTE BEGINNING

In the first section of the Introduction, however, the discussion of the *Phenomenology*'s role contains an ambiguity. According to this text, the concept of science needs no justification in logic because the *Phenomenology* provides the justification, and indeed this concept cannot be justified in any other way than by its emergence in consciousness. But the text also says that the concept "emerges within logic itself." Since Hegel mentions both claims in the same text, he seems to endorse a position in which both can be maintained (*WL* 21:32–3/M 48–9). What he says at the beginning of the Introduction can help us sort this out: "Logic, therefore, cannot say what it is in advance, rather does this knowledge of itself only emerge as the final result and completion of its whole treatment" (*WL* 21:27/M 43). This statement refers to one side of the ambiguity we discovered in the discussion of absolute beginnings. Logic produces as its result the concept of science fully articulated, its whole meaning developed. In this sense, logic demonstrates what the logical is, and thus the concept of scientific thought emerges within logic itself. But the beginning concept that emerges as a result of the *Phenomenology* defines the project as a science of logic. It provides the minimal definition that focuses the investigation on what logic is rather than on what consciousness is.

This interpretation is confirmed by the way the section entitled "General Division of Logic" talks about the relation between logic and the phenomenology of consciousness: "In the philosophical treatment of division, the concept must show that it itself holds the source of the determinations. But in the Introduction, the concept of logic was itself presented as the result of a science <lying beyond> it (*jenseits liegenden Wissenschaft*), and hence as equally a *presupposition* here. Accordingly, logic was defined as the science of pure thought" (*WL* 21:44–5/M 60). The divisions of logic follow from the concept of logic. But the concept of logic itself is the result of a preceding science. Logic gets its definition as the science of pure thought from the result of the preceding science in which the opposition in consciousness is overcome. This definition determines the developments that reveal the complex structure of pure thought.

The essay "With What Must the Beginning of Science Be Made?" explicitly refers to the Introduction when it discusses the way the beginning of logic depends on the phenomenology of consciousness. In the essay, however, Hegel discusses the beginning of logic as a mediation-immediacy issue. This is where we must look, therefore, for his answer to the absolute beginning problem. He begins the discussion by referring to what he has already said in the *Encyclopaedia* (*Enz* §12*A*). Mediation and immediacy are inseparable; each needs the other. Hence, everything, including the beginning of logic, contains both (*WL* 21:53–4/M 67–8). How, then, does Hegel work out a position in which the beginning of logic is both mediated and immediate? In order to answer this question, we must sort out the different ways in which Hegel uses the mediation-immediacy terminology in the same brief text.

3 THE MEDIATION-IMMEDIACY ISSUE

Logic begins "in the element of a free, self-contained (*für sich*) thought, in pure knowledge." An element is a milieu, an environment appropriate to a subject, like the cultural life that suits our taste. The element appropriate to logic is one that presupposes "thought that is free and for itself," thought thinking itself, "pure knowledge." The science of logic itself works out a scientific account of what pure knowing is. But the element of thought thinking itself determines what question is being asked. It puts thought into the position of investigating what pure knowledge is, and this establishes the philosophical standpoint. Four times in the same brief text, Hegel refers to pure knowing as the result of a prior science, the science of phenomenal consciousness. All four instances describe the beginning of logic as a knowing that presupposes this result. One says explicitly that the exposition of consciousness demonstrates "the necessity, and therefore demonstrates the truth of the standpoint which is pure knowledge." The beginning of logic is logical because it belongs to this standpoint, this preoccupation with thought thinking itself. The logical element itself, however, is "mediated, for pure knowledge is the ultimate and absolute truth of consciousness." The *Phenomenology* proves the necessity of the logical element, the element defined as pure knowledge, by demonstrating that consciousness requires pure knowledge as its own truth. Thus, we know the truth of pure knowledge by means of the exposition developed in the *Phenomenology*; the concept of pure knowledge is mediated (*WL* 21:54–5/M 68–9).

This mediation, however, sets itself aside, sublates itself, by bringing about the immediacy of pure knowing. Mediation has a double meaning here. It refers to the way the concept of pure knowledge depends on the exposition of phenomenal consciousness. But mediation also refers to the way all forms of phenomenal consciousness are mediated forms of cognition, because they depend on relations to something other than consciousness for what they are conscious of. If, therefore, the phenomenology of consciousness demonstrates that phenomenal consciousness has its truth in a form of knowing that lies beyond the whole domain of phenomenal consciousness, then it proves the necessity of conceiving true knowledge as not-mediated, not related to something other than itself as phenomenal consciousness is. The mediation that derives the beginning concept of logic from the exposition of phenomenal consciousness demonstrates the necessity of conceiving knowledge as not mediated by its relation to a truth that is other than itself.

Hegel uses the term "simple immediacy" to express this. Simple immediacy refers immediacy to the mediation that it negates. It describes the unity of pure knowing conceived as the absence of all distinctions. "Pure knowledge, thus withdrawn into this unity, has sublated every reference to an other and to mediation; it is without distinctions and as thus distinctionless it ceases to be knowledge; what we have before us is only *simple immediacy*. Simple immediacy is itself an expression of reflection; it refers to the distinction from what is mediated. The true expression of this simple immediacy is therefore *pure being*" (*WL* 21:55/M 69). In logic, thought does not think something else; it thinks itself. Yet even thought thinking itself distinguishes between thought as thinking and that same thought as the object of thinking. If, however, thinking and what it thinks belong to the same truth, if they are distinctions within the same truth, then the concept that conceives what they fundamentally are must think a unity that is prior to and the principle of their differentiation. The science that conceives knowledge in this way, therefore, must begin with a concept that does not distinguish knowing and known, precisely in order to think the unity from which the distinction is derived. Knowledge "ceases to be knowledge" in the sense that pure knowledge thinks the unity that precedes the distinction between knowing and what it knows (*WL* 21:54–6/M 68–70).[1]

This interpretation is confirmed by what Hegel says in the Introduction under the heading "General Division of Logic." Here he repeats what he said earlier in the Introduction. The concept of logic presupposes the preceding science of consciousness from which it emerges as a result. This result defines logic "as the science of pure thought – the science that has pure knowledge for its principle." This knowing knows that the opposition in consciousness has been overcome. In consciousness, subject and object are self-contained and separate. Pure knowledge knows them as inseparable. But in this very knowing, it also knows them as distinct: "This unity also constitutes the logical principle as *element*, so that the development of the distinction which is from the start present in it proceeds only *inside* this element" (*WL* 21:45/M 60). The differentiation of knowledge into subject and object, thinking and what it thinks, belongs to pure knowledge as a difference immediately present in its unity. Pure knowledge collapses the separation of subject and object into an undifferentiated unity, only to develop

1 "This pure being is the unity into which pure knowledge returns ... Or again, inasmuch as pure being is to be considered as the unity into which knowledge has collapsed when at the highest point of union with its objectification, knowledge has then disappeared into this unity, leaving behind no distinction from it and hence no determination for it" (*WL* 21:59/M 73).

the same differentiation again as pure knowledge distinguished from itself. Thus, the Introduction describes the unity with which logic begins in the same way that the essay "With What Must the Beginning of Science Be Made?" describes the simple immediacy in which knowledge "ceases to be knowledge." Both texts describe this undifferentiated unity as the principle or source of the difference that constitutes knowledge. The Introduction explicitly identifies this difference as the opposition in consciousness rethought as a difference contained within the unity of pure knowledge. This confirms the interpretation of simple immediacy as a unity that does not do away with the differences in consciousness, but only rethinks them as inseparable. By beginning with their unity in one principle, logic can think the differences as pure knowing differentiated from itself.

The same text that describes the simple immediacy of logic's beginning concept also describes a beginning of logic with a different kind of immediacy.

> But if no presupposition is to be made, if the beginning is itself to be taken *immediately*, then the only determination of this beginning is that it is to be the beginning of logic, of thought as such (*für sich*). There is only present the resolve, which can also be viewed as arbitrary (*Willkür*), of considering *thinking as such* (*al solches*). The beginning must then be *absolute* or, what means the same here, must be an abstract beginning; and so there is *nothing* that it may *presuppose*, must not be mediated by anything or have a ground, ought to be rather itself the ground of the entire science. (*WL* 21:56/M 69–70)

The simple resolve to consider thought as such means that logic begins with pure being. Thought simply thinks itself being, without thinking any determination that distinguishes it from something else, or any differentiation of determinations within itself. Pure being, Hegel says, is "the unity into which pure knowledge returns" (*WL* 21:59/M 72).

Thus, Hegel develops a threefold way of conceiving the beginning of logic. First, the beginning concept of logic, thought as such or pure knowledge, presupposes its emergence in consciousness. This is the beginning as mediated, conceived as the truth of consciousness. Second, this mediation sublates itself; it sets up the result of the mediation as not mediated. The emergence of pure knowledge as a result of finite knowing or consciousness sets up pure knowing as not a consciousness kind of knowing; consciousness has its truth not in consciousness itself but in pure knowledge, or thought as such. This is the beginning as not-mediated; its emergence in consciousness separates it from consciousness. Third, logic begins with the resolve to consider thought as such, to begin with thought simply being. This is the beginning cut off from all mediation, even the mediation involved in negating the opposition in consciousness. In this resolve, logic makes an absolute beginning. The beginning, however, is not without reasons or justification. It asserts what the mediation and the mediated immediacy have proved. The exposition of consciousness proves that thought as such is the real truth of the matter, and that this truth is not a consciousness kind of knowing. Thus, it proves that thought as such is properly conceived as thought liberated from its relation to consciousness, thought standing in itself, on its own, not conceived in terms of consciousness. The account of scientific procedure that Hegel develops in the *Science of Logic* confirms this interpretation.

4 SCIENTIFIC PROCEDURE: THE ROLE OF THE BEGINNING CONCEPT

The Introduction to the *Science of Logic* makes it clear that philosophical science cannot begin with its method in place. The philosophical standpoint begins with logic and logic has as its subject matter scientific thinking itself. Logic itself must determine what scientific knowledge is and what constitutes scientific procedure (*WL* 21:27/M 43). We have seen, however, that the philosophical standpoint involves certain presuppositions, that these presuppositions are challenged by ordinary consciousness, and that logic depends on a prior demonstration proving the necessity of setting aside this challenge. The *Phenomenology of Spirit* provides this demonstration. The phenomenological project, therefore, falls outside philosophy proper, since philosophy presupposes its results. This means that the phenomenology of consciousness, articulated in the *Phenomenology of Spirit*, precedes the science that determines what scientific thinking is. What, then, is the status of the demonstration developed in the *Phenomenology*? We have seen Hegel repeatedly refer to the *Phenomenology* as science, the science of consciousness and the science of manifested spirit. How can the phenomenology of consciousness be science if the project of determining what science is presupposes the results of this phenomenology?

In the introductory essays of the *Science of Logic*, Hegel insists repeatedly that the procedure developed in the *Phenomenology* is scientific in the same sense that philosophy itself is scientific. Indeed, he says that the procedure to be followed in the *Logic* has already been developed in the *Phenomenology*. He says this in the First Preface, in the Introduction, and in the essay "With What Must the Beginning of Science Be Made?" (*WL* 21:8/M 28; 21:37–8/M 53–4; 21:57–9/M 71–2). He says it every time the introductory essays of the *Logic* analyze the dynamics of scientific procedure. We shall assume, therefore, that everything these essays say about scientific procedure applies not only to philosophy proper but also to the phenomenology of consciousness. The most important texts make this explicit.

The introductory essays of the *Logic*, like those of the *Philosophy of Right* and the *Encyclopaedia*, distinguish philosophical method from the methods of the other sciences by deriving it from the concept of the subject matter itself. The philosopher does not bring a method to the investigation and produce results by applying the method to the subject matter. Philosophy allows the concept of the subject matter to determine its own development. In this way, philosophy demonstrates that its procedure is necessitated by the subject matter itself. The subject matter itself requires development in just this way. The concept with which the procedure begins, however, must do no more than define the minimal conditions for focusing an investigation on this particular subject matter. This restriction ensures that everything the science claims about its object follows from the minimum that must be assumed to be concerned with the object at all. The beginning concept itself, which identifies the science as a science of this subject matter, gets its justification from something outside of and prior to the science itself. Within the science, the beginning concept is a presupposition (*WL* 21:7–8/M 27–8; 21:27/M 43; 21:39–40/M 55; 21:55/M 69).[2]

Hegel explicitly applies this description to the phenomenology of consciousness as well as to the science of logic. Logic begins with the concept of thought as such reduced to the minimum conditions for focusing on thought withdrawn into itself and separated from its involvement in ordinary consciousness. This concept determines the development that fully articulates what thought as such is. The minimal concept of thought as such, or pure knowledge, is presupposed in logic and justified by the exposition of consciousness developed in the phenomenology of consciousness. The phenomenology of consciousness begins with "the first immediate opposition of itself and <its object>" which is "empirical sensuous consciousness" (*WL* 21:32/M 48; 21:55/M 69). In other words, the science of consciousness begins with the minimal conditions required for identifying cognition as a form of consciousness. It begins with the opposition that separates consciousness from its object. Taken according to these minimal conditions, consciousness is consciousness-of, unmediated by any other knowing; its object is the immediately given datum of sensation, the simple *etwas* confronting consciousness as an "other" that it is conscious of. From

2 See also *Enz* §1; *PhR* §31.

this starting point, the science of consciousness goes through all the various forms of consciousness and thus gives a full articulation of what consciousness is. The science comes to an end in the claim that the real truth of consciousness is cognition in another form, cognition as pure knowledge or thought as such (*WL* 21:32–3/M 48–9; 21:54–6/M 68–9; 21:57–8/M 71).

Hegel says explicitly that within the science of consciousness, the beginning form of consciousness is a presupposition (*WL* 21:55/M 69). A presupposition requires a justification provided by something outside the science itself. What is there outside the science of consciousness that can justify the form of consciousness with which it begins? Hegel suggests the answer to this question when he criticizes the approach that begins philosophy with the "I" of pure thought. The "I" that is immediately accessible, Hegel says, is not the "I" of pure thought but the "I" of ordinary consciousness (*WL* 21:62–4/M 76–7). We know that consciousness is not an empty, meaningless notion because we are immediately conscious of ourselves existing within it. Of course, the science of consciousness cannot begin with all the concreteness of this ego, all its complex relations and linguistic representations. But to identify its minimal conditions, we do not have to detach ourselves from what is immediately accessible, as we do when we withdraw into the "I" of pure thought. We can identify the minimal conditions of consciousness by looking at what appears immediately in experience. We simply focus on the form of consciousness that reduces appearing in experience to its minimal conditions. The immediate presence of a sense datum to consciousness provides this minimal form of consciousness. Thus, the phenomenology of consciousness begins with the minimal conditions for making the reality of cognition immediately evident. This cognition actually appearing is all we need to justify taking it seriously as some kind of real knowing.

5 SCIENTIFIC PROCEDURE: DIALECTIC, UNDERSTANDING, AND REASON

The introductory essays of the *Logic* describe the scientific development of a beginning concept in ways that correspond to the descriptions provided in the *Philosophy of Right* and in the *Encyclopaedia*. In the *Logic*, however, the descriptions probe the issues and analyze the procedure more thoroughly. In the *Science of Logic*, as in the *Philosophy of Right* and the *Encyclopaedia*, Hegel distinguishes scientific procedure from the kind of dialectic that aims only at destroying the position attacked. Destructive dialectic proves that a position is worthless by showing that it can be used against itself.

The dialectic has no positive result. It develops no better knowledge of the truth. It simply dismisses a claim to truth by showing that it is in conflict with itself. This kind of dialectic assumes that dialectical conflict does not belong to the subject matter itself. It operates as a strategy the dialectician uses to expose the worthlessness of a position.

Kant, however, demonstrated that dialectic belongs to the necessary structure of thought as such; and Hegel considers this a great advance over the arbitrariness of the dialectician's manipulative strategy. According to Kant, thought inevitably comes into conflict with itself, necessarily falls into contradiction, when it moves from understanding to reason. Kant, however, does not break free of the assumption that dialectical conflict, which Hegel also calls contradiction, is a sign of untrue, untenable thinking. Reason seeks a principle that finally and completely accounts for the objects of understanding. It assumes that objects are a reality outside and independent of thought and thus must be accounted for as such. When reason makes this assumption, it proves contradictory conclusions. According to Kant, this demonstrates the illegitimacy of trying to think an unconditioned condition, which Hegel calls the infinite, as a condition of things in themselves (*WL* 21:40–1/M 55–6).[3]

According to Hegel, however, the conflict that Kant has discovered in reason arises from the way understanding knows its objects, and hence the contradiction belongs to experience itself, not just to thought thinking the object as a thing-in-itself. Understanding defines the object. It identifies the determinations that make the object what it is and thereby separate it from what it is not. Thus, understanding thinks the finite. It identifies the limits of its object by setting up the other as a restriction, a truth, that the object does not contain within itself. This brings the other into the same defining process with what excludes it and is restricted by it. Thus, thought necessarily moves beyond the determinations that separate objects and thinks their connection. This is the move to reason. Reason transcends the limitations of understanding by connecting the defined, delimited object to the opposite whose otherness belongs to its defining and delimiting. Reason comes into conflict with itself because it thinks the finite as infinite; it thinks the finite within the connection that transcends its limits and includes its opposite. It is important to notice here that reason would not be in conflict with itself if it did not preserve the contradictoriness, the necessary non-identity, of the opposites it connects. According to Hegel, the connections

3 See also Kant, *KRV* A296/B352–A298/B355; A497/B525–A502/B530; A506/B534–A507/B535.

of reason do not suppress the necessary non-identity of objects; they make it possible. The necessary non-identity of objects presupposes definitions that identify not only what the objects are, but also what they cannot be. This necessary separation of one from the other, this defining of one in opposition to the other, is exactly what connects them (*WL* 21:29–31/M 46–7).

Thus, Hegel describes the Kantian move from understanding to reason as a move from the limiting definitions of understanding to the inclusive unity of rational thought. In the First Preface of the *Logic*, Hegel gives his own account of dialectic using this same terminology (*WL* 21:8/M 28). Understanding develops fixed determinations. Its definitions keep the object contained within itself; they identify only what it is. Reason dissolves the fixity of these determinations; it moves between them and thus brings them into the same defining process. But this same negative reason is positive, "because it generates the universal and comprehends the particular therein." By moving between the fixed determinations of understanding, dialectical reason establishes a process that they have in common. This establishes a common principle, the principle governing the movement that connects the definitions of understanding. As a result, the definitions of understanding take on a different status. They do not stand on their own, isolated from each other. They arise from the connecting process and hence are determined by the universal principle that governs this process.

At this point, Hegel reverses the direction of the discussion. Having introduced the universal principle in a positive form, he describes the definitions of understanding and the process of dialectic in terms of the universal from which they are derived. By making this shift, he describes a new way of thinking that is justified by the dialectical development of understanding. Once reason demonstrates that the objects of understanding belong to the same definitive process, the same truth, our way of knowing what they are must change. In order to know the real truth of the matter, we must think the objects of understanding as determinations derived from the universal. After describing the move from understanding to dialectic to reason, therefore, the First Preface shifts into an analysis that begins with the universal generated by this process.

The universal that holds the determinations of understanding within itself negates its own simplicity and thereby establishes the fixed, separating determinations of understanding. These determinations do not exist on their own, apart from and indifferent to each other; and the universal is not something under which they are subsumed. The universal derives the determinations of understanding from itself. Hence, what exists in them is not each object by itself, but the universal dividing off from itself and existing in opposition to itself. If, however, the separating determinations of understanding are derived from the same principle and are determinations of it, then the opposition dynamic that arises from the way each is itself and not the other also belongs to this principle. The universal not only negates its simplicity and establishes the differences of understanding, it also negates these differences by connecting them and thus re-establishes the sameness of the truth played out in them. The universal is a dynamic between the diversification of unity and the unification of diversity. The fixed definitions of understanding belong to this dynamic, are derived from it, and operate within it as both separating and connecting determinations.

This analysis reveals two different demonstrative processes at work in Hegelian scientific procedure. The first procedure begins with understanding, derives from its definitions the necessity of dialectical connection, and concludes from this that the determinations of understanding depend on a universal principle. The second procedure begins with the universal, derives from it the necessity of separating definitions, derives from these the necessity of connecting these definitions, and in virtue of this connecting returns to the simplicity of the universal. The second procedure asserts nothing more than what has been proved in the first, namely that the necessary non-identity of understanding's fixed definitions belongs to a process in which each connects itself to the others in the process of setting itself off from them.

Although the First Preface begins by describing philosophical procedure as something carried out by understanding and reason, it also insists that this is a procedure determined by the subject matter itself: "This spiritual movement, which in its simplicity gives itself its determinateness, and in this determinateness gives itself its self-equality – this movement, which is thus the immanent development of the concept, is the absolute method of the concept, the absolute method of cognition and at the same time the immanent soul of the content" (*WL* 21:8/M 28). The subject matter has the structure of understanding; it identifies itself by what it is in itself. The subject matter proves itself dialectical by connecting itself to the opposite from which it distinguishes itself. Hegel describes this dynamic as a move from understanding to negative reason to positive reason, which is also the way he describes it in the *Philosophy of Right* and the *Encyclopaedia*. But then he suggests that this procedure leads to a follow-up procedure that thinks the universal generated by positive reason as what the first procedure showed it to be, namely a common principle determining itself as a differentiating and connecting process played out between the fixed determinations of understanding.

Following this analysis, Hegel says explicitly that the same procedure operates in the *Phenomenology of Spirit.* With consciousness as its subject matter, the *Phenomenology* demonstrates that the self-development of this subject matter is governed by the "pure essentialities which constitute the content of logic" (*WL* 21:8/M 28). This establishes the standpoint of pure knowing. Pure knowing thinks the pure essentialities of logic as the spirit or principle governing the self-development of consciousness. This is the first procedure. The second follows from it. Thought must shift to a procedure that thinks the pure essentialities of logic as what the *Phenomenology* shows them to be, namely the logical spirit whose independent self-development determines the development of consciousness.

6 SCIENTIFIC PROCEDURE: DETERMINATE NEGATION AND RETREAT INTO A GROUND

The account of scientific procedure in the *Logic*'s First Preface only suggests the interpretation I have developed in the previous section. Texts in the Introduction and in the essay "With What Must the Beginning of Science Be Made?" explain the inference structure of scientific procedure and this confirms the interpretation by showing why the shift to a follow-up procedure is necessary. The Introduction begins with a description of scientific procedure explicitly applied to the moves in the *Phenomenology.* The *Phenomenology* examines cognition in the form of "consciousness." This involves showing how each form of consciousness "dissolves itself in being realized" and thus results in its own negation (*WL* 21:37–8/M 54). The phrase "in being realized" is important. Hegel is saying that each form of consciousness succeeds. It realizes what it expects knowing to be. It becomes conscious of the truth it is looking for. But in the process, it dissolves itself, which brings about its own negation. What does "dissolves itself" mean?

Hegel explains by referring to the principle of determinate negation. A determinate negation belongs to the specific content that it negates. If, for example, consciousness succeeds in knowing the object as something in itself and independent of its relation to consciousness, then determinate negation is the negation of the object as something with this kind of independence. This negation does not negate all knowing. It negates only the kind of knowing that expects the object to be independent of its relation to consciousness. If this form of consciousness "dissolves itself in being realized," then it succeeds in knowing the object as something independent of its relation to consciousness, and this very knowledge negates this independence.

Hegel calls this joining of the concept to its negation "the self-contradictory." We must not, however, let the language of contradiction mislead us. Just because Hegel uses this term does not prove that he has in mind the kind of contradiction that asserts and denies exactly the same claim. Indeed, the very text in which Hegel describes determinate negation and calls it "self-contradictory" supports a different interpretation.

> The one thing needed to *achieve scientific progress* ... is the recognition of the logical principle that negation is equally positive, or that what is self-contradictory does not resolve itself into a nullity, into abstract nothingness, but essentially only into the negation of its *particular* content; or that such a negation is not just negation, but is the negation of the <determinate subject matter> (*bestimmten Sache*) which is resolved, and is therefore determinate negation; that in the result there is therefore contained in essence that from which the result derives – a tautology indeed, since the result would otherwise be something immediate and not a result. Because the result, the negation, is a *determinate* negation, it has a *content*. It is a new concept but one higher and richer than the preceding – richer because it negates or opposes the preceding and therefore contains it, and it contains even more than that, for it is the unity of itself and its opposite. – It is above all in this way that the system of concepts is to be erected – and it has to come to completion in an unstoppable (*unaufhaltsemem*) and pure progression that admits of nothing extraneous. (*WL* 21:37–8/M 54)

In order to be a result, and not an immediacy, the new concept must contain the preceding concept together with the development of the opposite as its result. The new concept is "richer" because it contains the original concept together with its opposite. Thus, the contradiction expands the original concept, adds something else to it. The kind of contradiction that completely wipes out a position remains within the limits of the original concept and both affirms and denies it.

It is important to notice, too, that the new concept asserts nothing more than the preceding concept together with the negation of this concept, a negation justified because it is developed from the necessary implications of the concept itself. When, therefore, Hegel talks about resolving a contradiction, he does not mean that we get rid of it or neutralize its contradictory opposition. He means that we endorse the necessary connection between the opposites. If, therefore, the procedure introduces "nothing extraneous," then the new concept contains nothing more than the connection to the opposite that has developed in the original concept (*WL* 21:37–8/M 54). This means that the new concept not only preserves both opposites within a unity, it also preserves the opposition between them.[4]

But why call this self-contradiction? It seems to be an opposition relation, a connection between different elements, not the positing and negating of the same. The essay "With What Must the Beginning of Science Be Made?" answers this question. The essay describes scientific procedure as a retreat into a ground, and it explicitly applies this description to both the *Phenomenology* and the *Logic*. The procedure begins with the concept of the subject matter. It proceeds by developing correct inferences from this concept. Thus, all developments arise from the necessary implications of the original concept and come back to it as that which persists and gets full articulation in these developments. The continuous, necessary line of development proves that the same principle drives the connections between all the various forms of the concept. This principle accounts for or grounds the whole dynamic in which the concept is fully articulated, and hence all the various forms of the concept are this one principle determining its own development. If, therefore, the demonstration proves that the concept involves a necessary connection to its opposite, then both the concept and its opposite belong to the same ground. One and the same concept determines itself as divided against itself in these opposites (*WL* 21:57–8/M 71–2). Hegelian self-contradiction certainly is an opposition relation between different elements. But the opposition that differentiates the elements has its ground in the selfsame concept, and hence puts the concept in opposition to itself.[5]

The structure of a retreat into a ground explains the direction shift suggested by the *Logic*'s First Preface. It also explains how the beginning concept of philosophy can be both mediated and immediate. Since the *Phenomenology* is a retreat into a ground, its process of coming to know the truth moves in a reverse direction to the truth itself. Coming to know begins

4 Wandschneider's rational reconstruction of Hegel's dialectic makes the same general point that I am making here. He, too, insists that nothing external to the dialectic can determine the new concept. He also claims that the new concept from the beginning is determined as the sameness of opposites (Wandschneider, 1991).

5 Hegel talks about contradiction and ground in different contexts. In the introductory essays of the *Logic,* he uses the terms to describe the general structure of scientific procedure, which anticipates the way the development of a beginning concept determines the full articulation of what it means. This analysis applies to Hegelian dialectical procedure throughout the whole philosophical system and even within the examination of ordinary phenomenal consciousness in the *Phenomenology*. Hegel also talks about contradiction and ground as particular categories within the science of logic. For several good discussions of contradiction as a logical category, consult the following: di Giovanni (1993); Wolff (1986), (1999); Pippin (1978).

with what has been derived from the ground; and it uses its knowledge of the derivative truth to prove, to ground, its knowledge of the ground itself (*WL* 21:57–8/M 71). In order to know the truth in its proper form, therefore, knowledge must reverse its direction and derive its knowledge of what is determined by the ground from its knowledge of the ground. In order to begin this process, knowledge must assert the ground as immediate, i.e. as not derived from or dependent on its relation to anything else, because this is what the retreat into a ground proves it to be. Thus, Hegelian procedure always begins with what is both mediated and immediate: mediated, because we come to know the concept by way of what is derived from it; immediate, because we come to know it as ground and hence must assert it as the source not the result of what it grounds. Hegel says that the beginning of logic belongs both to logic and to consciousness: "A beginning is *logical* in that it is to be made in the element of a free, self-contained (*für sich*) thought, *in pure knowledge*; it is thereby *mediated*, for pure knowledge is the ultimate and absolute truth of *consciousness*" (*WL* 21:54/M 68).[6] The phenomenological examination of consciousness retreats into pure knowledge as its ground; and this justifies the concept of pure knowing, which defines the subject matter of logic. Hence, the concept with which logic begins is mediated by being "the absolute truth of consciousness." But logic must assert this concept as ground. Hence, logic begins with the concept of pure knowledge in its immediacy, cut off from all determining relations, in order to think it as the source, not the result, of the forms of consciousness through which its necessity has been proved. This positing of pure knowledge as ground gives logic an absolute beginning that escapes the arbitrariness of simply choosing to focus on thought as such (*WL* 21:32–4/M 48–9; 21:44–5/M 60; 21:53–9/M 67–72).[7]

This interpretation fits the way Hegel talks about the relation between the *Phenomenology* and the *Logic* in the part of the Introduction devoted to the "General Division of Logic." The concept of logic is the result of a science outside the science of logic (*jenseits liegenden Wissenschaft*), i.e. the *Phenomenology of Spirit*. This other science overcomes the opposition "between a subjective for-itself being and a second, objective for-itself being" (*WL* 21:45/M 60, translation mine). The *Phenomenology* has demonstrated that the opposition between subject and object has its ground in a principle or spirit common to them both. This retreat into a ground necessitates a shift into a procedure in which thought asserts the common principle as

6 See also *WL* 21:32–3/M 48–9; 21:44–5/M 60–1.

7 See also *PhG* 366-7/M ¶680; 429–30/M ¶802.

the beginning concept of logic, and thinks the opposition in consciousness as a differentiation derived from this concept.

The account of philosophy as a retreat into a ground begins and ends with brief comments on the way Reinhold addresses the question 'how does philosophy begin.' Here again, as in the *Encyclopaedia*, Hegel talks about a position that begins philosophy with a truth that is hypothetical and problematical. Here again he approves Reinhold's interest in the question; but he rejects Reinhold's claim that the beginning of philosophy has the status of "an arbitrary and temporary assumption" or "seems to be an arbitrary and tentative presupposition ... of which it is subsequently shown that to make it the starting point was indeed the right thing to do" (*WL* 21:58/M 72). Hegel rejects the provisional, hypothetical approach because according to Hegel, the beginning is itself a kind of ground. The process of coming to know the truth begins with the concept of the subject matter to be investigated. This concept provides the ground, basis, or foundation of the process that brings knowledge to the point of acknowledging the truth in which the subject matter has its ultimate ground or foundation. Hence, the truth revealed at the end of the process emerges as a result of the beginning. If the beginning is provisional and arbitrary, then what follows from it as a result will be equally provisional and arbitrary (*WL* 21:56–9/M 70–2).

If, however, the beginning concept of philosophical science governs the demonstration that proves the truth of the ultimate ground, and if the process of coming to know the truth does not depend on any provisional acceptance of its beginning principle, then everything depends on the independent legitimacy of the beginning concept. How is this legitimacy established? According to various texts, scattered throughout the introductory essays of the *Logic*, the *Phenomenology* demonstrates the legitimacy, the truth, of the concept with which philosophical science begins.

7 THE INDETERMINACY OF THE BEGINNING CONCEPT

The *Logic*, like the *Encyclopaedia*, names the beginning concept of philosophy "pure being" and interprets this to mean thought asserted without any determinations whatsoever. Like the *Encyclopaedia*, too, the *Logic* insists that this indeterminacy has the content of thought identified with being. The *Logic* explicitly refers to this content as the content of pure knowledge.

This pure being is the unity into which pure knowledge returns, or if this knowledge, as form, is itself still to be kept distinct from its unity, then pure being is also

> its content. It is in this respect that this *pure being*, this absolute immediate, is just as absolutely mediated. However, *just because* it is here as the beginning, it is just as essential that it should be taken in the one-sidedness of being purely immediate. If it were not this pure indeterminacy, if it were determined, it would be taken as something mediated, would already be carried further than itself; a determinate something has the character of an *other with respect to* a first. (*WL* 21:59/M 72)

"Pure knowledge" in the *Logic* names the concept of science derived from and justified by the science of manifested spirit developed in the *Phenomenology*. Philosophy begins, therefore, with thought identified with all the content exposed in the *Phenomenology*'s examination of consciousness or experience. The beginning concept of philosophy, however, conceives this content as the undifferentiated unity in which all the differences and determinations exposed in the *Phenomenology* have their ground. Philosophy proper will develop the content again as determinations of the undifferentiated pure thought with which philosophy begins. But the content belongs to the beginning concept of philosophy because the *Phenomenology* has exposed this concept as the ground of the content that belongs to experience (*WL* 21:57–9/M 71–2).

8 CONCLUSION

The introductory essays of the *Science of Logic* repeat themes developed in the *Philosophy of Right* and the *Encyclopaedia*, provide a fuller articulation of the issues involved, and explicitly connect these issues to the task and method of the *Phenomenology*. Like the *Encyclopaedia* and the *Philosophy of Right*, the *Logic* discusses the way philosophy identifies the necessities of thought existing in the experience of everyday life and knows them as the true essence of what is. The *Logic*, however, analyzes experiential knowing as a domain with its own knowledge structure and its own knowledge claims, and explains how this kind of knowing challenges the claims of logical thought. Phenomenal consciousness takes the truth to be other than and separate from consciousness itself, and dismisses pure thought as thought without truth, as mere thought. The *Logic* states that philosophical science begins with thought in itself identified with being in itself, which states unambiguously what the *Encyclopaedia*'s analysis of the immediate knowing position suggests. According to the *Encyclopaedia*, the immediate knowing position rightly seeks "the unity of the Idea with being," and it distinguishes this from the immediate givenness of sense realities and from the isolated subjectivity of thought. This suggests that thought as the Idea is the defining character of independent being. According to the *Logic*, therefore, pure logical thought takes the truth to be the unity of thought and being, and phenomenal consciousness opposes this way of conceiving the truth by taking the truth to be other than and separate from the consciousness that knows it. How, then, can philosophy justify its standpoint against the challenge of phenomenal consciousness?

The *Logic*, like the *Encyclopaedia* and the *Philosophy of Right*, rejects the strategy of beginning a philosophical science with a concept derived from generally accepted definitions of the subject matter. The *Logic*'s discussion of absolute beginnings analyzes the logistics of this unacceptable strategy. Questions can always be raised about whether this really is the accepted way of defining the subject matter, and arguments that address these questions determine the answer by arbitrarily accepting evidence on one side of the issue rather than the other. The *Logic* also repeats Hegel's rejection of the strategy attributed to Reinhold. According to both the *Encyclopaedia* and the *Logic*, philosophy cannot begin with a concept that provisionally or hypothetically identifies what the truth is and allows the philosophical investigation developed from this hypothesis to prove its truth. The *Logic* adds to these rejected strategies the strategy that begins with the "I." This strategy assumes that consciousness is immediately available to itself, and that it has the status of truth because every consciousness, every "I," has the same identifying character. Hegel rejects this approach because the "I" that is immediately available to consciousness is consciousness engaged in the differentiated content of experience, not the "I" withdrawn into the abstract structure of thought thinking itself.

These rejections develop a common theme. They argue against various attempts to begin philosophy without deriving its beginning concept from some other kind of knowledge. Yet both the *Encyclopaedia* and the *Logic* say that philosophy begins with the resolve to consider thought as such. How can this kind of beginning meet the challenge posed by phenomenal consciousness? How can philosophy defend its claim that thought focused on itself knows the truth, if phenomenal consciousness, which has the reality status of experience, claims that thought knows the truth only if it knows what an object outside thought independently is?

The *Encyclopaedia* suggests that the proof required for the justification of philosophy's beginning concept would examine consciousness as such, and states in another place that the *Phenomenology* demonstrates the necessity of the philosophical standpoint. The *Science of Logic* puts these two statements together in an unambiguous and repeated set of claims that define the role of the *Phenomenology*. These claims describe the task of the *Phenomenol-*

ogy as an examination of consciousness. They identify consciousness as a form of knowing in which thought is related to an object that is other than thought itself; and they say that the examination of consciousness begins with this structure in its simplest, minimal form. Thus, the *Logic* identifies "consciousness" with the structure of phenomenal consciousness, and identifies the subject matter of the *Phenomenology* as consciousness as such.

The *Logic* explicitly and repeatedly claims that the examination of consciousness developed in the *Phenomenology* produces the concept of pure knowledge as its result, and like the *Encyclopaedia*, it talks about a retreat into a ground that justifies the beginning concept of philosophy. The *Logic*, however, explicitly identifies this procedure with the examination of consciousness in the *Phenomenology*. Philosophy does not displace experience. Philosophy rethinks it according to a principle that experience itself derives from its own necessary development. Pure knowledge is the ground exposed in absolute knowing at the end of the *Phenomenology*. Pure knowledge knows itself as the ground, the fundamental principle and source, of the dynamics played out in phenomenal consciousness. The *Phenomenology* proves that experience is a derivative truth rooted in pure knowledge. This proves the necessity of rethinking the whole domain of experience by beginning with its ground and deriving the dynamics of experience from the necessities implicit in this ground. Hence, the *Logic*, like the *Encyclopaedia*, talks about a beginning that simply resolves to examine thought as such. A beginning of this kind focuses on pure knowledge in itself, without the positive mediation that identifies it as the truth of consciousness, and without the negative mediation that separates pure knowing from its involvement in consciousness. This immediate, independent beginning, however, depends on a proof that demonstrates its truth and justifies its immediacy and independence.

Because philosophy begins with the unity of thought and being asserted as a ground, this beginning concept has a special kind of indeterminacy. Both the *Logic* and the *Encyclopaedia* claim that philosophy begins with the indeterminacy of being; but both also insist that the indeterminacy is not empty, that it has content. An Addition in the *Encyclopaedia* distinguishes the indeterminacy of this beginning concept from the indeterminacy derived from and mediated by the negation of all determinations (*Enz* §86*Z*). According to the *Logic*, pure being conceives the content of pure knowledge, indeed the content of all being, compressed into an undifferentiated unity (*WL* 21:58/M 72). Since the concept of pure being is conceived as the ground of phenomenal consciousness in all its forms, this concept contains implicitly all the content of the derivative truth.

Like the *Philosophy of Right* and the *Encyclopaedia*, the *Logic* describes a scientific procedure that begins with a concept of the subject matter and develops its necessary implications in a series of determinate negations. All three works distinguish this procedure from the kind of dialectic that manipulates a position or claim into a self-defeating contradiction and thus dismisses it as untenable. Determinate negations remain attached to what they negate. They connect the negated concept to its opposite, and justify the move to a concept that endorses the whole dynamic. The result of a determinate negation asserts the original concept together with the negation that emerges as its necessary outcome; and the new concept conceives this connection as one truth within which the original concept and its opposite play out their opposition. Both the *Logic* and the *Encyclopaedia*'s discussion of the second position on objectivity make it clear that the result of a determinate negation not only conceives the opposites as one truth, it also preserves their contradictoriness within this one truth. Both texts criticize the way Kant neutralizes the opposition between antinomies, instead of acknowledging, as true philosophy does, that rationality involves contradiction and that contradiction is fundamental to every concept, representation, and thing. Both texts use the language of contradiction to explain the dynamics of determinate negation. The original concept and its opposite belong to the same dynamic. Hence, they are governed by the same necessity, the same truth. In them, this truth breaks up into the same truth opposed to itself.

Both the *Encyclopaedia* and the *Science of Logic* explain scientific procedure in this way. The *Logic*, however, repeatedly insists that the *Phenomenology* follows the same procedure. Moreover, both texts say that the *Phenomenology* begins with the immediacy of sense consciousness, the simple consciousness of a sense datum. As the simplest form of consciousness, this structure identifies the minimal structure of consciousness as such, and hence belongs to the fundamental structure of any and every form of consciousness. By deriving all moves in the science of consciousness from the necessary implications of this minimal structure, the *Phenomenology* justifies a conclusion that has the universality of truth; it holds for all knowers.

PART FOUR

THE *PHENOMENOLOGY* SPEAKS FOR ITSELF

PART FOUR EXAMINES WHAT THE *Phenomenology* itself says about its task and method, and relates this to the other issues we have seen associated with this question in the later works. The introductory essays of the *Phenomenology* discuss the task of the *Phenomenology* in three ways: as a project that answers the needs of Hegel's time; as a project that overcomes a division in knowledge; as a critique of knowledge.

8

The Phenomenology of Spirit: *Preface*

THE PREFACE TO the *Phenomenology* reviews the cultural conditions of Hegel's own time; and it raises questions about the task and method of the *Phenomenology* in terms of these conditions. This approach introduces the issue of historical conditionedness. Is the *Phenomenology* a culture-specific project? Does its strategy for addressing the knowledge question have legitimacy only for Hegel's own time and culture?

1 THE SPIRIT OF THE TIMES

According to Hegel, the spirit of his own age differs significantly from the spirit of an earlier time. The older culture confidently assumed that it was one with essential truth; it looked for this truth not in the present world, the world immediately confronting us, but in its relation to a divine presence beyond this world. For those who belonged to this culture, the present or empirical world was murky, confused, limited, whereas the presence beyond was clear, rich in thoughts and images, infinite. Hence, the present world, the world of experience, held no interest for them. It offered little in the way of inspiration and enlightenment. Giving this world persistent, concentrated attention was a task forced upon them against their inclination. Only after a long and gradual development, therefore, did they discover in the murkiness and confusion of the empirical a clarity that had once been found only in heavenly things. This development established the legitimacy of projects focused on the present as such, also called "experience." Once this happened, however, participants in the culture became absorbed in empirical matters, so much so that they had to be pressured into taking an interest in higher concerns.

Hegel sees the spirit of his own time as one that has passed beyond the preoccupation with experience to a spirit that is dissatisfied with it. This spirit of dissatisfaction recognizes the limits of empirical knowledge; and it expects philosophy to raise it above these limits by revealing a truth that has ultimate significance. Hegel uses the term "absolute" to describe the philosophy of his time; and in this context, he associates the term "absolute" with a truth in which all is one, all belongs to the same truth. According to Hegel, the philosophy of his time conceives the absolute as a unity without diversity, and it dismisses as untrue the kind of knowledge that insists on diversity. Hence, it rejects knowledge in the form of understanding. Understanding renders the empirical intelligible by developing precise and dependable definitions of its differences, and by exposing in its variability relations that stand firm. Understanding handles differences, gives them a stable form. But it does not overcome the differences by knowing the one truth that is the fundamental truth of everything. Absolute philosophy, therefore, dismisses knowledge in the form of understanding, because a knowing mediated by definitions and relational principles keeps the truth divided in different contents. Absolute philosophy asserts as truth what is completely one and selfsame; and this requires a form of knowing that is also one and selfsame, an immediate intuitive knowing (*PhG* 11–13/M ¶6–8; 13–14/M ¶10).

Thus, philosophy tries to satisfy the culture's need for something more profound and important than the here and now by offering an intuition of the absolute that holds itself aloof from the diffuse variety and variability of the empirical world. But the cultural consciousness feels deprived by philosophy's lack of content, and especially by the loss of understanding's concepts and laws, which give order and stability to this content. Moreover, philosophical intuition has no way of communicating its knowledge to others. Only what is "completely determinate," Hegel says, is also "exoteric, comprehensible (*begreiflich*) and capable of being learned and appropriated by all" (*PhG* 15–16/M ¶13). Hegel associates the "completely determinate" with the form of understanding, which indicates that the determinate involves differentiated content rendered intelligible by precise definitions and stable relations. Through this content, the thought of one thinker relates itself to the thought of another. A form of knowledge that does not articulate itself in the distinctions of understanding remains isolated in the simple intuiting of the knower (*PhG* 15–16/M ¶13–14).

Absolute philosophy tries to appropriate the content of the empirical world by showing that the absolute is present in the data of experience. But this strategy reduces the absolute to an abstract universal. An abstract universal repeats exactly the same form in each of its instances. It does not account for the differences that distinguish one instance from another. It does not explain why the universal must be differentiated from itself in these different contents. So also absolute philosophy finds the same formula repeated in the diversity of empirical data, a formula that supposedly defines the sameness of all things in the absolute. But this philosophy does not explain why this formula appears in different contents. It does not show that the differentiation of the content is determined by the absolute and hence belongs to it. The absolute just happens to appear in these different ways. Consequently, the differentiated content of experience challenges philosophy's claim to absolute truth by presenting it with something it cannot explain. In philosophy's appropriation of experience, the differences of the empirical world persist as something other than and opposed to the unity and selfsameness of the absolute. Philosophical intuition tries to get around this problem by claiming that the differences are not really true, that the real truth is their identification with what is absolutely self-identical. It dismisses those who cannot see this as thinkers incapable of thinking absolutely.

Hegel objects. There was a time, he says, when the mere possibility of conceiving something in a different way was enough to refute a knowledge claim. Empirical knowledge actually exists. It knows something. It thinks a rich variety of content rendered intelligible by understanding's concepts and laws. Absolute philosophy cannot explain why a content that can be definitely known should be dismissed; and it provides no alternative account that derives the content from a source other than experience itself. In Hegel's time, therefore, knowledge is divided into two opposed forms. Empirical knowledge knows the rich variety of experience rendered intelligible by understanding. But it fixes things in their differences and has no thought for their integration in one truth. Philosophical intuition knows the truth as absolute self-identity, 'A = A.' But the intuition lacks the rich content of experience, which makes it "esoteric," incapable of being communicated to others (*PhG* 16–18/M ¶15–16).

Hegel explains this state of affairs as a product of history. Individuals exist rooted in a culture. This culture exists as the individual's "inorganic nature." It exists outside the individual organism, but is an essential dimension of the individual's own life. Participants in a culture become educated by appropriating this inorganic nature. Through education, they come to experience the values and definitions of the culture as their own way of thinking. In the process, they give its objective content the form of subjective self-consciousness. Individuals become conscious of their own way of thinking as typical of the context in which they live. Individual self-consciousness becomes a culture's consciousness of itself. In the movement of history, different cultures emerge. Each culture gets its particular character or spirit by focusing the consciousness and life of the culture on one facet of spiritual life, which Hegel identifies with the way it knows the truth. Other determinations of spiritual life, other ways of knowing the truth, exist in the culture only as blurred features not fully developed. In the movement of history, as the nature of knowledge becomes more and more explicit in the life of the culture, the simpler undeveloped forms of spiritual life recede into the background. The main thing in simpler cultural forms persists in the more developed forms as a trace. It belongs to cultural memory. Hence, an individual who lives in a more advanced culture appropriates the simpler, less developed forms of knowledge by appropriating what belongs to cultural memory. Since civilization has already mastered these forms and seen through them, since the knowledge of their limits is explicit in the culture, the individual moves through them as material already prepared and made easy. Thus, the individual appropriates the developments of history by appropriating what is existent and familiar in his or her own culture.

According to Hegel, history has already brought itself to the point where the various cultural spirits have become aspects of one and the same spirit. A cultural spirit actually exists in which each dominant spirit of a former culture has become a facet of the present culture rather than the definition of the whole. The present culture focuses the consciousness and life of the culture not on one or the other of these previous ways of knowing, but on the whole to which they belong. This brings history to the concept of science. Thus, Hegel associates the concept of science with a way of knowing that conceives the truth as a unity to which all prior ways of knowing belong as only a facet or aspect. He also distinguishes the concept of science from its actuality. The concept conceives the whole in the principle whose unity and sameness makes it a whole. Actuality brings out of this unity the different forms of knowing in which it develops what it is. Hegel compares this to the acorn and the oak. In the acorn, the tree exists in an undeveloped, implicit form. Only when it has been articulated in a strong trunk, spreading out into different branches, adorned by a mass of foliage does it become the actual tree (*PhG* 24–6/M ¶28–9).

In the culture of Hegel's time, scientific knowing exists only as absolute philosophy's intuition of the absolute, which is nothing more than the immediate thought of complete unity or self-identity. The culture remembers, however, a knowledge full of content and intelligibility (*Verständlichkeit*), the kind of knowing characteristic of understanding. This kind of knowledge spreads out to cover the differentiated material of experience, and gives it the form of thought by organizing it according to concepts and stable relations. Philosophical intuition offers something more, because it offers a truth that knows the true meaning and essence of it all. But by setting aside the differentiated content of experience and understanding, it separates the concept of science from its actuality. It thinks the fundamental truth in itself instead of thinking it as the foundation of the concrete knowledge operative in preceding cultures. For science to become actual, this thought must become articulated and developed in the different forms of knowing preserved in cultural memory. It must think the one and selfsame as a principle originating, necessitating, its own differentiation in these different ways of knowing (*PhG* 14–15/M ¶11–12; 16–17/M ¶15; 21–2/M ¶24; 25–6/M ¶29).

Hegel introduces here a significant clue to his position on the relation between philosophy's beginning concept and experience. An intuition that separates its cognition of absolute truth from the diversified and organized content of experience separates the concept of science from its actuality. Experience, therefore, gives reality to the truth conceived by philosophy. Hegel also acknowledges here two different ways in which this actualization makes itself manifest: "It is the whole which, having traversed its content in time and space, has returned into itself, and is the resultant simple <concept> of the whole. But the actuality of this simple whole consists in those various shapes and forms which have become its moments, and which will now develop and take shape afresh, this time in their new element, in their newly acquired meaning" (*PhG* 14–15/M ¶12). History has made its way through the content of the truth until it arrives at a culture that conceives the truth as the "simple <concept> of the whole." This is the move from derivative truths to their ground. The concept of the whole truth having been produced by this development, these same derivative truths must now be rethought as moments, facets, of the whole. This is the move from the concept of the ground to the reality and organization of experience known now as realities actualizing the concept of the whole.

2 STRATEGY FOR MEETING THE CHALLENGE OF EMPIRICAL KNOWLEDGE

Before science can undertake this actualization process, however, it must acknowledge the limitations of philosophical intuition. It must recognize that conceiving the truth as an unmediated unity is only a beginning. It conceives the principle from which everything else follows. But it thinks only the principle, the originating source, not the completed whole. It thinks the concept of science, but not its actuality (*PhG* 21–2/M ¶24). Moreover, the beginning has a presupposition (*die Voraussetzung*). Science requires a consciousness that dwells in the element of science. Science must be the "aether," the inorganic nature, the cultural context in which this consciousness recognizes its own way of thinking. In other words, science requires a consciousness that is already committed to the concept of science, one that conceives the truth as a whole whose unity and selfsameness is the principle or ground of all knowing. Consciousness requires of science, however, a demonstration showing that this whole is present as the individual's own knowing: "Conversely, the individual has the right to demand that Science should at least provide him with the ladder to this standpoint, should show him this standpoint within himself. His right is based on his absolute independence, which he is conscious of possessing in every phase of his knowledge; for in each one, whether recognized by Science or not, and whatever the content may be, the individual is the absolute form, i.e. he is the immediate certainty of himself and, if this expression be preferred, he is therefore unconditioned being" (*PhG* 22–3/M ¶26; 29–30/M ¶36).

We see here another articulation of the experience principle, repeated several times in the *Encyclopaedia* (*Enz* §7*A*; 38*A*; 64*A*). As a free person, the individual has the right to experience the truth as something attested to by his or her own consciousness. Like the *Encyclopaedia*, too, the Preface to the *Phenomenology* connects the experience principle to the reality issue. Science must be acknowledged by the individual's immediate experience because the self's immediate certainty of itself has the status of "unconditioned being." The individual self immediately conscious of its own consciousness, whatever the content may be, has the status of what exists, what simply is, unqualified by any determinate way of being. If science does not know itself in this element of immediate self-consciousness, it does not know itself as the truth of what is real. Thus, the Preface to the *Phenomenology*, like the *Encyclopaedia*, casts experience in the role of the real, and insists that pure thought or science must know itself in the reality of experience. Moreover, like the *Encyclopaedia*, the Preface to the *Phenomenology* represents the turn to experience not only as what reveals the truth but also as what accomplishes the truth. The truth becomes actual as philosophical science knowing itself in the otherness of experience.

The Preface to the *Phenomenology* also focuses on a nuance that gives fuller meaning to a discussion in the *Encyclopaedia*'s examination of the immediate knowing position. According to the *Phenomenology*'s Preface, not only must philosophical thought find its own determinations functioning as the true essence of experience, it must also find each individual's immediate experience attesting to this truth. The *Encyclopaedia* describes the immediate knowing position as an intuition that knows immediately the unity of thought and being; it compares the intuition to Descartes' *cogito.* The *Encyclopaedia* acknowledges the importance of an experience that confirms philosophy's conception of what the truth is (*Enz* §64*A*). It insists, however, that the experience must find a way to demonstrate that the isolated experience of a knowing subject has the status of a universal, objective truth, a truth that all knowers must know as true (*Enz* §67–8+*A*). The Preface to the *Phenomenology* represents the project developed in the *Phenomenology* as doing just that. The *Phenomenology* demonstrates that the standpoint of philosophical science belongs to and exists in the immediate experience of an individual consciousness conscious of itself existing. Like the *Encyclopaedia,* the *Phenomenology* acknowledges that individual self-consciousness must be led into the philosophical standpoint through a process of education that exposes the presence of philosophical science within the individual self's immediate sense of its own being (*PhG* 22–4/M ¶26–7). In Hegel's time, world history has already worked its way into this position. The individuals of Hegel's time, therefore, can work their way into it by appropriating the historical development preserved within their culture (*PhG* 25–6/M ¶29).

3 THE PROBLEM OF HISTORICAL CONDITIONEDNESS

This reading of the Preface to the *Phenomenology* examines the texts and arguments supporting pedagogical interpretations of the *Phenomenology.* According to this reading, the *Phenomenology* addresses individuals situated within a certain historical situation. Its task is to educate them. In the Preface, becoming educated refers to the process whereby individuals appropriate the cultural context in which they exist. As pedagogy, therefore, the *Phenomenology* teaches the individuals of Hegel's time how to make their own the concept of knowledge as a whole that has emerged from the developments of history. According to this interpretation, the individual relives the process whereby concepts of knowledge belonging to previous cultures have proved the necessity of moving beyond these concepts to more adequate conceptions of what knowledge is. The process ends with the concept of science, which defines what Hegel's own culture takes knowledge to be.

This interpretation of the *Phenomenology* brings with it several problems. First, does the *Phenomenology* prove anything to an individual not situated in Hegel's time or in Hegel's historical tradition? The *Phenomenology* supposedly demonstrates that the concept of science exists as the fundamental principle of the individual's own knowing, and thereby demonstrates that the unity and selfsameness of the whole is the fundamental truth of all knowing. If, however, the individual does not belong to Hegel's historical tradition, then the development relived in the *Phenomenology* will not be recognizable as the individual's own. As a result, the individual will become conscious of himself or herself as one not identified with the kind of knowing that is governed by the concept of science; and this challenges the claim that the concept of science is the principle of all knowing. Second, if the *Phenomenology* does nothing more than integrate individuals into a given historical development, then it shows that the concept of science is the way a particular historical tradition must conceive true knowledge. It does not show that the necessities of this tradition are the necessities of knowledge itself. The phenomenological project makes the tradition exist as a culture conscious of itself. But it does not show that this self-consciousness knows what knowledge truly is. Interpreted thus, the Preface to the *Phenomenology* is at odds with what Hegel in the later works says about scientific procedure, which the introductory essays of the *Logic* explicitly and repeatedly attribute to the *Phenomenology* as well as to philosophy proper.

The *Logic* explicitly distinguishes the proof developed in the *Phenomenology* from "historical" arguments dependent on the familiar, accepted way of representing the subject matter (*WL* 21:32–3/M 48–9). The *Philosophy of Right* says that proofs dependent on historical conditions do not justify philosophical claims; they prove only what fits a given situation (*PhR* §3*A*). Thus, a proof that demonstrates how prior historical conditions have necessitated a certain way of thinking does not satisfy the requirements of the procedure that the *Phenomenology* shares with philosophy. Historical necessity proves that a certain way of thinking is necessitated by a given historical situation. It does not prove that the given historical situation defines the necessary conditions of knowledge.

The *Encyclopaedia* takes an even stronger position when it says that the universality demanded by philosophy cannot be mere universal agreement, even if it could be shown that every single person shares the same conviction. Philosophy requires the universality established by necessity. It must know that the conceptual context within which everyone thinks and communicates is necessarily true (*Enz* §71). We can apply this same objection to the *Phenomenology*. Even if we could demonstrate that the history reviewed in the *Phenomenology* includes the whole history of humankind, the demonstration would not prove that this historical development reveals what knowledge must be.

Yet the introductory essays of the *Logic*, and at least one section of the *Encyclopaedia*'s Introduction, claim that philosophy depends on the *Phenomenology* for a justification of its beginning concept (*WL* 21:32–4/M 48–9; 21:44/M 60; 21:54–5/M 68; *Enz* §25*A*). If the beginning concept does not have the same kind of necessity as that required of philosophy itself, then everything that follows from this concept will be compromised. Also, the *Encyclopaedia* suggests that we might prove the objective truth of immediate knowing's intuition of the infinite by demonstrating that this experience of the infinite belongs to necessities implicit in the nature of consciousness as such (*Enz* §71*A*). The text insists, however, that the examination would have to isolate within conscious experience those elements that belong to the universal determinations of consciousness as such. This condition rules out any examination of consciousness specific to a certain culture or tradition.

Does this mean that the early Hegel's interpretation of the *Phenomenology*'s task and method does not call for the same kind of strict necessity and universality as that required by the interpretation developed in the introductory essays of the later works? The next section responds to this question by taking a closer look at the texts of the Preface that support the historical-pedagogical reading, and other texts addressing the same issues. This will show that Hegel's historical talk belongs to a more complicated account of the *Phenomenology*'s task.

4 HISTORICAL AND PHILOSOPHICAL NECESSITY

The Preface to the *Phenomenology* insists on the difference between philosophy and history just as the *Encyclopaedia* does (*Enz* §16+*A*): "As regards historical truths – to mention these briefly – it will be readily granted that so far as their purely historical aspect is considered, they are concerned with a particular existence, with the contingent and arbitrary aspects of a given content, which have no necessity" (*PhG* 31–2/M ¶41). If, therefore, philosophical truth appears in history, it must be governed by a kind of necessity that historical truths do not have. The Preface to the *Phenomenology* says that Hegel's time is ripe for science, and describes the historical conditions that account for this readiness. But the Preface introduces this discussion with a distinction. It distinguishes external necessity from inner necessity. Inner necessity belongs to the nature of knowledge itself. What knowledge is demands that it take the form of science. External necessity belongs to the way in which time develops sequentially the existence of different knowledge forms. Because time has brought into being different cultural spirits in a certain sequence, knowledge must become science at a certain time, namely in Hegel's own time. Hegel says that the external necessity is the same as the inner. Thus, the Preface to the *Phenomenology*, like the *Encyclopaedia*, distinguishes between the externality of history and the inner necessity of knowledge itself (*Enz* §13–14). The inner necessity determines what knowledge must be. The external necessity determines when knowledge becomes what it must be.

What does this tell us about the relation between the nature of knowledge and its existence in time? It suggests the following: that the nature of knowledge determines the sequence according to which different forms of knowledge appear in different times; that this differentiation is necessitated by what knowledge essentially is; that philosophical science, which unifies the different forms of knowledge in the unity of its own absolute knowing, appears in time as a result of temporal conditions determined by the nature of knowledge itself. If this is Hegel's meaning, then the time is ripe for science because the nature of knowledge has displayed in time all the reasons why the essence of knowledge requires that it take the form of science (*PhG* 11–12/M ¶5; 14–15/M ¶11).

When Hegel describes the spirit of his own time, therefore, he describes not only what is typical of a certain culture but also what belongs to the structure of knowledge itself. He describes a culture in which philosophy and empirical knowledge stand opposed to each other. Empirical knowledge asserts itself as a knowledge full of content and intelligibility (*Verständlichkeit*). Against this knowledge dispersed in the differentiated content of experience, absolute philosophy asserts its intuition of the absolute, which knows itself immediately identified with absolute truth. But Hegel restates this historical confrontation as the opposition between the element of consciousness and the element of science. Each inverts the position of the other, turns it upside down, and thus constitutes itself as the other's opposite. Consciousness is in its element, it is at home with itself, when it knows objective reality as an other that is not consciousness itself and knows consciousness itself as not objective reality. Thus, science, which is thought preoccupied only with itself, appears to consciousness as thought without an object, thinking without the reality of actually knowing something. Science, however, assumes that thought and being are one. Knowing the object truly involves knowing it as not other than thought. Therefore, science judges that consciousness, by insisting on the opposition between itself and its object, loses the real truth of both (*PhG* 17–18/M ¶16; 22–4/M ¶26).

The *Logic* describes the same opposition as "ordinary phenomenal consciousness" challenging the presuppositions of pure knowing (*WL* 21:27–30/M 44–6; 21:32–4/M 48–9; 21:54–6/M 68–70). The *Encyclopaedia* describes an encounter in which thought has become separated from experience, withdrawn into itself. Empirical knowledge, organized by the concepts and laws of understanding, challenges thought to develop a positive relation between itself and experience, so that thought can claim as its own the intelligibility that understanding discovers in the empirical world (*Enz* §12). Thus, Hegel describes the same opposition between consciousness and pure thought in the Preface to the *Phenomenology* and in his later works.

The Preface exposes the same historical ambiguity in the individual's need for "a ladder to the standpoint of science." The need is a necessity of knowledge itself, not just a need specific to individuals in a certain culture. Consciousness exists as the individual's immediate sense of self, and this consciousness is conscious of itself as absolutely independent. Hegel interprets this independence in several ways. First, consciousness is the "I" in which the whole is completely dismembered (*in der absoluten Zerrissenheit*), each "I" free and separate from its connections within the whole. Consciousness belongs only to the one whose consciousness it is. Even if I see blue and you see exactly the same blue, my seeing it is not your seeing it. Second, consciousness knows itself as a subject set off from its object. Being-conscious-of is conscious of being different from what it is conscious of. This is the structure Hegel sometimes refers to as natural consciousness, which the *Logic* calls ordinary phenomenal consciousness or just consciousness. If, therefore, science expects the individual's consciousness to acknowledge that all knowing belongs to one and the same whole, then science must show that this whole is present as the exclusive individual's own knowing. Since this exclusive sense of self is also knowing in the form of consciousness, a knowing set off from what it knows, science must show that scientific knowing takes the form of consciousness. This is what Hegel describes as science providing the individual with a "ladder to the standpoint of science" (*PhG* 22–4/M ¶26–7; 26–7/M ¶32; 29–30/M ¶36).

The *Phenomenology*'s main task, therefore, is not to educate the individual about his or her cultural history. The primary task is to demonstrate that the whole element of consciousness has its roots or ground in pure thought thinking itself. The element of consciousness has two general determinations: first, the alienation or otherness of consciousness and its object; and second, the isolated sense of self exclusive to each individual. Every form of knowing with these determinations belongs to this element, whether or not it belongs to the history of thought reviewed in the *Phenomenology*. The *Phenomenology* provides a ladder to the standpoint of science by showing the individual that his or her singular consciousness, isolated in itself and dependent for its object on an independent other, belongs to a universal knowing that integrates all knowledge into a whole.

5 PHENOMENOLOGY AS SCIENCE

In the Preface, Hegel calls the task of the *Phenomenology* a science. He describes scientific procedure in general as the "necessary expansion" of a content into an organic whole, and the scientific procedure of the *Phenomenology* as "the path by which the <concept> of knowledge is reached," "a necessary and complete process of becoming," which encompasses "the entire sphere of <mundane> consciousness in its necessary development" (*PhG* 28–9/M ¶34). Since the *Phenomenology* is a science, it does what scientific procedure does. It expands a content into an organic whole, and it does so by developing the necessary connectedness of the content. Hegel calls the content of the *Phenomenology* the element of immediate existence (*des unmittelbaren Daseins*), which he identifies with consciousness. The *Phenomenology* expands the element of immediate existence, which is the whole sphere of consciousness, into an organic whole. This development, Hegel says, takes us to the concept of knowledge. The concept of knowledge, therefore, conceives the simplicity of the whole. It identifies knowledge as the simplicity that integrates the whole sphere of consciousness into one and the same knowing.

This interpretation is confirmed by the way Hegel talks about the relation between the spirit of science and the phenomenological development of consciousness. Consciousness is the element in which the spirit of science "explicates its moments," "becomes alienated from itself," "returns to itself from this alienation," and "becomes a property of consciousness" (*PhG* 29–30/M ¶35–7). The full meaning of this becomes clear only when the *Phenomenology* reaches its final conclusion. At this point, it tells us at least that the *Phenomenology* does not do away with consciousness. Rather it reveals what consciousness essentially is. The necessary development of consciousness shows that its different forms and the radical exclusivity of each conscious self are one whole; and the principle of this whole is the simplicity of pure knowledge, which is the concept of science.

The Preface reinforces this interpretation by denying explicitly and repeatedly that the *Phenomenology* is a purely negative project. In the Preface to the *Phenomenology* – as in the *Philosophy of Right*, the *Encyclopaedia*, and the *Science of Logic* – Hegel distinguishes between scientific procedure and the reasoning that simply refutes a position. The reasoning that adopts the purely negative approach belongs to the "I." The "I" brings the negative to the investigation by using its skill to refute or destroy the position. This approach reduces the negated position to a dead end. It proves that the position is simply false. The truth cannot be found here. Look for the truth elsewhere. Scientific procedure, also called conceptual thinking (*begreifenden Denken*), is "the immanent movement and determination of the content." This procedure develops the negation from the content itself, and hence is a determinate negation. This kind of negation does not set aside what it negates. It negates the restricted meaning of the content, connects it to other determinations, and eventually integrates it into a meaning constituted by the whole process (*PhG* 42/M ¶59). At the end of the *Phenomenology*, the content of consciousness has been developed into a connected whole. This result negates the restricted meanings of consciousness in its various forms; and it positively establishes the unifying principle of the whole as their true essence. Thus, the *Phenomenology* follows the necessary development of an element that turns out to be the spirit of science appearing and becoming actual. The different ways of knowing that appear in the consciousness element are negated as fixed differences. But they persist as positive and necessary aspects of the whole movement that is the life of truth itself. Moreover, the life of truth itself distinguishes the simplicity of its identity with itself from its diversification in forms of consciousness, different cultural spirits, and the exclusivity of each conscious self (*PhG* 27–9/M ¶33; 30/M ¶38; 34–5/M ¶47).

But this is only the beginning. The *Phenomenology* demonstrates the necessity of conceiving consciousness as first and foremost the spirit of knowledge as a whole. The otherness between the "I" and its object turns out to be knowledge as a whole distinguished from itself. This result puts knowledge in a different element. It now conceives knowledge not primarily as consciousness, which knows its object as other than itself, but in the "form of simplicity which knows its object as its own self." This Hegel calls the element of "the True in the form of the True" (*PhG* 30/M ¶37). When knowledge reaches this point, it is in a position to conceive the different forms of knowing as one and the same truth determining its own differentiation. This is the work of logic or speculative philosophy (*PhG* 28–30/M ¶34–7).

This dynamic corresponds to the way Hegel describes the relation between the *Phenomenology* and philosophical science in his later works. According to the *Logic*, the *Phenomenology* retreats into a ground, and this produces the concept of science. The *Phenomenology* proves the legitimacy of conceiving knowledge as pure knowledge by demonstrating that pure knowledge is the ground in which the whole development of consciousness has its source. Hence, the concept of science or pure knowledge belongs to the element of consciousness as its result, as what it proves. What it proves, however, requires that the whole process be rethought as determined by and derived from pure knowledge; and this is the task of philosophy. Philosophy rethinks the whole development of consciousness as the unity of pure knowledge determining its own differentiation (*WL* 21:32–4/M 48–9; 21:44–5/M 60; 21:53–9/M 67–72). The *Encyclopaedia*, in its discussion of the three positions on objectivity, also describes the proof required for establishing the standpoint of philosophy, and analyzes it as a retreat into a ground (*Enz* §36*Z*, 50*A*). The Preface to the *Phenomenology* does not use ground terminology. But it describes the same dynamic in other words. Moreover, in the "Religion" section of the *Phenomenology*, Hegel explicitly describes the phenomenological development of consciousness as a retreat into a ground (*PhG* 366/M ¶680).

The *Encyclopaedia*'s general introduction describes the move into philosophical thought in terms of the relation between experience and philosophy, which is a primary concern in the Preface to the *Phenomenology*. According to the *Encyclopaedia*, thought begins in experience. But experience does not meet thought's need for necessity. This need for necessity separates thought from experience and sets up its development within thought itself. But thought must turn back to experience and recognize its determinations in experience. This turn back to experience reconciles thought with its own actuality (*Enz* §2, 6, 11–12). So also according to the *Phenomenology*'s Preface, the development of knowledge begins within experience, i.e. within the domain of consciousness. The *Phenomenology* provides a disciplined account of why the necessities of experience itself require thought's separation from experience and its development according to the necessary determinations of thought itself. But the Preface, like the *Encyclopaedia*, says that experience is the actuality of science. To separate the unity and selfsameness of thought from the diversity of experience, as the intuition of the absolute does, separates the concept of science from its actuality (*PhG* 14–15/M ¶12). The *Phenomenology* makes its way through what will turn out to be the spirit of truth itself actualized in experience.

9

The Phenomenology of Spirit: *Introduction*

IN THE INTRODUCTION TO the *Phenomenology*, Hegel examines yet again the opposition between experience and "science." This account, however, defines the issues in terms of the epistemological questions raised by early modern philosophy. It asks whether we must examine critically the capacities and limitations of our knowing powers before engaging in a significant knowledge project aimed at substantive truth claims. In the process of addressing this question, Hegel redefines the critical project and provides his most explicit analysis of dialectical procedure. Most important of all, he changes the focus of epistemology's reality question. Epistemology asks whether human knowledge can know reality as it truly is. Hegel sets up a procedure that makes it possible to examine critically different ways of defining the reality expectations of knowledge. Exactly what kind of reality is knowledge trying to know? If different forms of knowledge have different reality expectations, how do we determine and evaluate not only whether the expectation has been met but also whether the right reality question has been asked?

1 THE NATURAL ASSUMPTION

It seems "natural," to assume, Hegel says, that we must first understand the nature and limits of the instrument or medium through which we discover the truth before we become involved in actual knowing. This is "natural" because without this critique we might mistake the limited capabilities of the instrument or medium for a knowing that knows what the truth itself is; or we might use a form of knowing unsuited to the subject matter. Hegel identifies presuppositions hidden in this mistrust of knowledge. It assumes (1) that the truth is on one side and knowing is on the other, (2) that knowledge functions as a means, either as an instrument used for gaining access to the truth or as a medium through which the truth makes contact with our knowing, (3) that knowing is real and yet is isolated in itself and separated from the truth, (4) or that it can know only a certain kind of truth and not absolute truth, and (5) that "that there is a difference between ourselves and this cognition" (*PhG* 53–5/M ¶73–5). Hegel uses the term "absolute" here interchangeably with "what truly is"; and later he says explicitly that its meaning has not yet been determined (*PhG* 74–5/M ¶75). Therefore, I will interpret "absolute" here as a vague reference to the concern for truth. The mere fact that the word "absolute" appears in this context justifies nothing more definite than this.

If we look briefly at the way the critiques of early modern philosophy analyze the epistemological question, we can explain how Hegel makes the leap from the natural assumption to a rather complicated and subtle collection of presuppositions. Both Descartes and Locke acknowledge that raising questions about what we can and cannot know leaves unaffected the certainty with which we know the ideas that belong to our thinking. I may be in doubt about whether a reality corresponding to my ideas exists outside thought. But I am in no doubt at all about the reality of my thinking these ideas.[1] Kantian critique develops a complicated analysis of the structures involved in the relation between thinking and an object thought. This kind of critique also acknowledges that the content of what we think manifests a connection to something outside thought that provides this content. But Kantian critique denies that this connection reveals anything at all about what this external something is in itself.[2] Thus, these philosophers assume that knowing can be related to a known, it can actually know some objective content, without being related to what a real thing is. This assumption takes for granted that knowing can be real and still be separated from the truth, and hence that knowledge is on one side and truth on the other; or it assumes that we can know only a certain kind of truth, the truth of an object isolated within the subjectivity of the knower.

1 Descartes, *Meditations* II, 28–9; III, 34–7. Locke, *Essay Concerning Human Understanding*, book IV, chapter I §2; chapter II, §14.

2 Kant, *KrV* A42/B59–A43/B60; B66–8 II; B129–42 (§15–19); B146–8 (§22); B163–5 (§26). For an astute examination of the content issue as it affects Hegel's critical appropriation of Kant, see K. Westphal (2003), 65–71.

In these presuppositions, we recognize the structure that the *Logic* attributes to "ordinary phenomenal consciousness," that the Preface to the *Phenomenology* calls natural consciousness, and that both texts attribute to the element of consciousness. "Ordinary phenomenal consciousness," "natural consciousness," and the element of consciousness all take the truth to be something other than consciousness itself. Consciousness is true if it succeeds in being conscious of what this other really is (*PhG* 17–18/M ¶16; 22–4/M ¶26; 56/M ¶78; 58–9/M ¶82; *WL* 21:28–30/M 44–5). Perhaps Hegel calls the distrust of knowledge "a natural assumption" because it presupposes the structure of "natural consciousness."[3] It assumes that "consciousness," rather than "science," has identified what knowledge fundamentally is.

The otherness between cognition and truth accounts for the tendency to conceive cognition as a means, a medium or instrument, whereby we gain access to the truth. We need a means only if truth is not knowable as it stands, only if it becomes knowable by means of what cognition contributes to the knowing relation. Since access to what truly is depends on the way cognition alters this truth, cognition cannot set aside these adjustments without surrendering its access to the truth. By retaining them, however, cognition knows the truth not as it is in itself but only in the altered state that makes it available to knowing. If, therefore, the examination of knowledge begins with a mistrust of cognition, which implicitly assumes that cognition and truth are fundamentally separate and independent, then the examination determines the way the question will be answered by the way the question is posed (*PhG* 53–4/M ¶73–4).

If we try to get around this problem by claiming that the knowing instrument brings the truth closer but makes no adjustment in what the truth is, "[the absolute] would surely laugh our little ruse to scorn, if it were not with us, in and for itself, all along, and of its own volition. For a ruse is just what cognition would be in such a case, since it would, with its manifold exertions, be giving itself the air of doing something quite different from creating a merely immediate and therefore effortless relationship" (*PhG* 53–4/M ¶73). Hegel does not say here that the absolute is with us from the start. He says that *if* it allowed itself to be known just by being brought closer, then it would have to be with us from the start. Otherwise, bringing it closer would accomplish nothing.[4]

3 Compare to Kant, *KrV* A3/B7–A4/B8. See also Hegel, *Enz* §415.

4 I am challenging the way Harris has interpreted this text (1997, I, 166).

Hegel might have Reinhold in mind here. In the *Difference Essay* (1801), which belongs to the same period of Hegel's career as the *Phenomenology*, Hegel represents Reinhold's position thus:

> We can see that [Reinhold's] Absolute in the form of truth is not the work of Reason, because it is already in and for itself something true and certain, that is, something cognized and known. Reason cannot assume an active relation to the Absolute. On the contrary, if Reason were active in any way, if the Absolute were to receive any form through it, the activity would have to be viewed as an alteration of the Absolute, and an alteration of the arch-true would be the production of error. So [for Reinhold] philosophizing means absorbing into oneself with absolute passive receptivity something that is already [in and by itself] fully completed knowledge ... According to that convenient habit of thought, the union of reflection and the Absolute in knowledge takes place in perfect accord with the Ideal of a philosophical utopia in which the Absolute itself readies itself for being something true and known, and surrenders itself for total enjoyment to the passivity of a thinking which only needs a mouth agape ... When the entire business of a philosophy is reduced to wishing to be nothing but a problematic and hypothetical trial and prelude, the Absolute must necessarily be posited as arch-true and known; – for how else could truth and knowledge issue from the problematic and hypothetical?[5]

This text helps us understand the objections Hegel raises in the *Logic* and the *Encyclopaedia* against Reinhold's hypothetical strategy. Since the result depends on a truth provisionally accepted, it infects the result with the same provisional status. If we accept the provisional condition, we must accept the truth that follows from it. If we do not accept the provisional condition, the development of this condition into a result will not establish the truth of the result. Unless, of course, we assume that the truth of the result has already surrendered itself into our knowing in the provisional beginning. But if this assumption is accepted, why bother with the process of producing the truth as a result?[6]

Whether or not the Introduction to the *Phenomenology* refers to Hegel's earlier attack on Reinhold, a careful reading of the text does not support interpretations that read the reference to an absolute with us from the start as if it were Hegel's own position. Hegel is considering the way someone might try to solve the problems involved in the natural assumption by representing the critical examination of knowledge as simply bringing the truth closer. Hegel reduces this defence to the following disjunction: either the

5 Hegel, *Differenzschrift*, 85–6; Harris-Cerf translation, 184–5.

6 For a discussion of Reinhold on his own, see di Giovanni (1985), 9–19.

truth of knowledge can be questioned because the truth is really other than knowledge, in which case truth would resist any attempt to know it that did not change it into something suitable for our knowing capacity; or the truth is not really other than knowledge, in which case truth is immediately and unquestionably present in knowledge and a critical examination of knowledge is unnecessary. According to Hegel, the second alternative implicitly assumes that the absolute is with us from the start. Hence, this alternative does not solve the problems involved in the natural assumption; it simply proposes a strategy based on the opposite assumption. The natural assumption takes for granted that truth is other than knowledge and inaccessible without some kind of adjustment. A critical examination of knowledge that only brings the truth closer assumes that truth is with us from the start (*PhG* 53–4/M ¶73–4). We shall see that Hegel himself endorses neither of these alternatives.

The natural assumption also presupposes a distinction between "ourselves" and the cognition that functions as a means to the truth. By proposing an examination of the knowing instrument, we assume that we can make our own knowledge an object. In other words, we take for granted the possibility of distinguishing between knowledge as an object examined and the knowing that undertakes the examination (*PhG* 53–4/M ¶74). Hegel identifies this presupposition without explaining it. What he says later, however, could explain it. He asks how we can undertake an examination of knowledge without presupposing a criterion that defines what knowledge essentially is (*PhG* 57–8/M ¶81). How else can we judge whether, or to what extent, the cognition under examination really counts as knowing? The criterion problem makes sense of the natural assumption's distinction between "ourselves" and the knowledge being examined. The natural assumption assumes that we can examine knowledge and that we are in a position to make judgments about it, which involves knowing what the criterion is. The cognition being examined is relegated to a different position; it may or may not measure up to what the criterion requires of it.

2 PHILOSOPHICAL SCIENCE CHALLENGES THE NATURAL ASSUMPTION

After identifying the presuppositions implicit in the natural assumption, Hegel introduces "science" as a challenge to these presuppositions. Science expresses its assurance that its own scientific knowing is one with absolute truth. This reveals a hidden, unjustified premise in the way the natural assumption raises questions about the reliability of cognition. Just by claiming that its knowing is situated within absolute truth and thus has direct access to it, science dismisses as untrue the presumed otherness between knowing and truth that is implicit in questions about the reliability of our knowing powers. This shows that the natural assumption can be questioned, that it stands in need of justification. Indeed, science questions the whole domain of natural consciousness, which includes every kind of knowing that takes the truth to be something other than consciousness itself. As a mere assurance or conviction, however, science itself is just a claim. Other forms of knowing committed to the presuppositions of the natural assumption express the assurance, the conviction, that the claims of science have no legitimacy. This shows that the claims of science can be questioned, that they also stand in need of justification. "One bare assurance is worth just as much as another" (*PhG* 55–6/M ¶76).

Hegel describes the status of both positions as "the appearance of knowing" or "phenomenal knowledge," and also as simply "being"; and he associates this condition with existing alongside an other. Each form of knowing simply appears, is there. Since each dismisses the other as without truth, each keeps itself separated from the other. This lets the other stand apart as a different, opposed form of knowing whose very existence challenges the opponent's claim to be what knowledge essentially is. It is important to notice that in this text Hegel does not focus on the historical situation in which this appearing occurs. He equates knowing as an appearance with knowing as a mere assurance. "The appearance of knowing" means making a claim, expressing a conviction. Knowing in this form is simply posited, asserted; it simply is. This describes the general condition of knowing as a reality. Knowing at any time, in any set of historical conditions, becomes existent by being asserted or posited. Hegel suggests that science might try to overcome its status as an appearance by demonstrating that other forms of cognition are manifestations of science itself. In this way, science would liberate itself from the challenge posed by a form of knowing that is not science. Other forms of knowing would be imperfect preliminary versions of science itself. But Hegel rejects this strategy because it would leave science in the form of an appearance. Science would remain a mere assurance. It would simply assert its conviction that science itself is the true form of knowing and that other forms of knowing are its imperfect manifestations (*PhG* 54–6/M ¶76).

With this, Hegel makes clear that some of what the Preface says about the relation between science and consciousness does not belong to the beginning framework of the *Phenomenology*. The Preface describes the element of consciousness as the actuality of science, as its appearing, as the objectification in which the spirit of truth knows itself. Appearance here means the spirit of truth standing before knowing as an object known (*PhG* 29–30/M ¶36).[7] Hegel says explicitly, however, that the Preface provides only a preliminary outline of what must be justified by a full exposition (*PhG* 17–18/M ¶16–17). The Introduction explicitly rejects a strategy that assumes from the beginning the standpoint of science and interprets other forms of knowing in terms of science. This rejection applies to any way in which science might presuppose its own fundamental claim as the framework according to which every other kind of knowing is interpreted. If the examination of knowledge in the *Phenomenology* assumes from the beginning that the forms of consciousness are the actuality of science, then this examination remains caught in the arbitrariness of science as an appearance. The Introduction, therefore, introduces a different meaning for knowledge as an appearance, which refers to a way of knowing that simply exists, makes a claim, asserts itself. If this appearing turns out to be truth appearing to itself, the *Phenomenology* must prove it, not assume it.

By challenging science as an appearance, Hegel acknowledges that a critical examination of knowledge is necessary. We cannot legitimately assume that our knowledge is one with the truth and get on with the task of knowing what truly is. But Hegel also challenges the kind of critique that begins with the natural assumption, since it presupposes the otherness of knowledge and truth and thus predetermines the conclusion that knowledge cannot know truth as it is in itself. This confrontation between science and natural consciousness redefines the whole critical project. Scepticism about the whole domain of natural consciousness liberates knowing from its commitment to natural representations, thoughts, meanings. The appearance of science brings about this liberation. By challenging the assumption that knowledge is other than truth, science challenges any form of cognition that receives its truth from something else, from what is given as natural. The existence of natural consciousness, however, reduces science itself to a mere assurance or claim, which makes it necessary for the critic to remain detached about the presuppositions of science as well.

This double doubt separates us from every criterion according to which we might judge the truth of knowledge: from every criterion that identifies truth as something other than knowledge itself; from every criterion that identifies truth as not other than knowledge itself (*PhG* 54–6/M ¶76; 55–6/M ¶78). Thus, Hegel begins the examination of knowledge with a distinction between "ourselves" and our own knowing, just as the natural

7 See also *PhG* 14–15/M ¶12; 22–4/M ¶26–7; 25–6/M ¶29; 30/M ¶38; 34–5/M ¶47.

assumption does. Hegel's version, however, leaves critical cognition with nothing but its detachment. Everything else belongs to the cognition that must prove itself, justify itself. If, however, an examination of knowledge cannot presuppose any criterion that defines what knowledge truly is, how can it determine whether or not the knowledge being examined measures up to what is required of it?

3 THE STARTING POINT

The key to Hegel's strategy is the starting point. Hegel begins with knowledge as an appearance, and he associates knowing-as-an-appearance with knowing as a mere assurance, knowledge merely asserted or claimed (*PhG* 54–6/M ¶76). What do we know about knowledge from its mere appearance as an actually existent cognition? We know only that it is a consciousness-of directed to what it is conscious of. In other words, the conditions of knowledge making an appearance are the bare-bones conditions of knowing related to a known, a consciousness conscious of something (*etwas*) (*PhG* 56–8/M ¶80; 58–9/M ¶82). Hegel refers to these conditions in minimal terms: the "fact that consciousness knows an object at all" (*PhG* 59–60/M ¶85). Thus, Hegel begins with consciousness related to what it is conscious of, without assuming, as early modern critique does, that this relation is isolated within the subjectivity of the knower and may or may not reveal something existing outside the knowing relation.

In the structure of knowledge as an appearance, the object has a double status. Since consciousness is pure consciousness-of, it depends on something that is other than consciousness itself; it depends on what consciousness is conscious of. Since this other must provide what consciousness itself lacks, namely a term or 'what' in which the consciousness relation is completed, the object must be what it is without deriving what it is from its relation to consciousness. Take, for example, being conscious of blue. Blue is what the object is in itself; blue is blue. Being conscious of blue does not make it blue. It just is blue. Since, however, consciousness completes its being-conscious-of only by being conscious of the object, the object's relation to consciousness makes known what the object is in itself and outside this relation (*PhG* 58–9/M ¶82; 58–9/M ¶84–5). Being conscious of blue makes known to consciousness what blue is. Without this or some such revelation, consciousness ceases to be conscious of an object. Thus, both being blue (the object in itself) and being known to be blue (the object "for" consciousness) belong to the mere fact that consciousness is conscious of blue (*PhG* 58–9/M ¶82; 58–9/M ¶84–5). The object in itself is not something hidden behind the object for consciousness. The object in itself is the content of the object for consciousness that pure consciousness-of cannot get from itself.

This analysis of knowledge as an appearance also describes the structure that the *Logic* attributes to "ordinary phenomenal consciousness," that the Preface to the *Phenomenology* calls natural consciousness, that both texts attribute to the element of consciousness, and that the Introduction finds in the presuppositions of the natural assumption. Cognition in this form takes the truth to be other than knowing (*PhG* 17–18/M ¶16; 22–4/M ¶26; 53–5/M ¶73–5; *WL* 21:28–30/M 44–5). Thus, Hegel translates the fundamental structure of consciousness, natural consciousness, and ordinary phenomenal consciousness into the minimal conditions required for knowing to appear, to be an existing cognition.

Hegel is not the only philosopher to find this rudimentary structure at the base of all experience. Fichte, Jacobi, and Jean-Paul Sartre describe in the same way the fundamental relation between consciousness and what it is conscious of; they, too, treat it as a structure immediately evident in experience. This lends some credibility to Hegel's claim that the determinations of phenomenal knowledge immediately present themselves in exactly this way (*PhG* 58–9/M ¶82). These other philosophers, however, do not agree with each other about what this experience means; and Hegel takes a position that both resembles and differs from their way of interpreting it. I will briefly compare the different positions, therefore, in order to explain more precisely what Hegel is and is not claiming when he introduces this structure as a beginning framework for the *Phenomenology*. In order to keep the discussion focused on the main issue, the comparison will not examine the influence that Fichte and Jacobi might have had on the way Hegel formulates the starting point of the *Phenomenology*; nor will it discuss the influence Hegel might have had on Sartre.[8] The comparison will also not discuss the way Fichte, Jacobi, and Sartre develop this structure into fully articulated positions. The comparison focuses exclusively on the way they interpret the basic structure, and on the way these different interpretations of the same rudimentary experience expose subtleties in Hegel's position.

The discussion of Fichte's analysis focuses on Book Two of *The Vocation of Man*. In Book One, Fichte demonstrates that his self belongs to a natural system and is governed by its forces. In Book Two, he starts over in order to

8 Hegel is certainly aware of Jacobi and of Fichte's *The Vocation of Man* during this period of his career, since both are discussed in *Glauben und Wissen* (Sections B and C), which was published in 1802.

see whether the evidence used in Book One really demonstrates the necessity of the conclusion. He looks at what happens in knowledge and asks whether anything in our knowing supports the claim that we know a world outside ourselves. The examination begins by focusing on immediate perception, e.g. seeing a red color or feeling a smooth texture.[9] In the process of describing exactly what goes on in this experience, Fichte makes the same point Hegel makes:

> I am always conscious only on the condition that *that which is conscious* and *that of which there is consciousness* appear distinct from each other ... my consciousness first becomes possible with and through their separation ... beyond that consciousness there is no consciousness ... That separation is the condition, it is the result of consciousness as such ... That there is a consciousness ... the foundation is in the subjective itself; that just this is seen is something for which it depends on the objective, on which it is fixed, and by which it is, as it were, swept away. The objective on the other hand contains the foundation of its being within itself. It is in and for itself, it is as it is because it just happens to be so.[10]

According to Fichte, therefore, consciousness must be conscious of something distinguished from itself, in order for consciousness to exist at all. The subjective side of the relation accounts for there being a consciousness, a perceiving. But the subjective side depends on the objective side for the content of its perceiving. The perceiving side is swept away in its relation to what it perceives. The content perceived, however, is what it is because of itself, not because of its being perceived. This corresponds to what Hegel calls the object in itself distinguished from the object "for" consciousness. Both Hegel and Fichte, therefore, derive the distinction between the object "for" consciousness and the object in itself from the way consciousness depends on a content that cannot be derived from its relation to consciousness. Both claim that this structure identifies the necessary conditions for consciousness to appear. Without it, consciousness does not exist.

Fichte analyzes the consciousness of some content into three different elements. First, consciousness perceives itself in a certain condition, e.g. feeling a red or smooth or sweet sensation. Second, consciousness has an intuition of red or smooth or sweet as a property of a thing outside itself. Third, consciousness thinks the thing outside itself as the cause of its sensation. The immediate consciousness of externality, Fichte claims, is rooted in the immediate intuition that consciousness has of itself. Just by being

9 Fichte (1987) 28–32; (1981) II–200–75 to II–204–83 (215–19).
10 Ibid., 48–9; (1981) II–225–130 to II–226–132 (236–7).

conscious, I am conscious of myself. Subject and object are the same. But in order to be thus conscious of myself, myself as object must be separated from myself as subject. Consciousness experiences this separation as space. The perception of a sensible thing belongs to this fundamental structure. Without the experience of spatial separation, perceiving would collapse subject and object into each other. Perceiving red, for example, would be a way of seeing, a condition of sight, feeling one's sight filled with a red sensation. In order to have a perception *of* red, red must be separated from the perceiving, held out in front of it as an other that it is conscious of. Consciousness gets this separation from the intuition of space. It locates the sensible content in another part of space, and thus perceives it as something outside the perceiving self. This separation, however, belongs to the innate constitution of all knowing, and is only a separation of consciousness from itself. Knowing is the separation of subject and object in the same consciousness. Thus, there are two different forms of immediate consciousness: the sensation of being in the condition of perceiving in a certain way; and the immediate intuition of being spatially separated from what consciousness is conscious of.[11]

Thought relates the two. It conceives the sensation as a way of being affected, and infers a force that causes the sensation. It conceives this force with a twofold determination: one whereby the force determines itself as having a particular determination, e.g. being red; the other whereby the force affects consciousness in a particular way, e.g. causing perception to see red. Thus, Fichte projects the distinction between the object in itself (being red) and the object for consciousness (being perceived as red) onto a hidden force conceived as the cause of sensation. By thinking the sensation as caused by a hidden force, thought ties the condition of the perceiver to something separated from the perceiving and thus connects the content of a particular sensation to the intuition of something experienced as separated from the sensing self.[12] According to Fichte, therefore, the immediate consciousness of some content proves nothing about a reality outside knowledge. Indeed, it leaves open the possibility that there is no world outside knowledge, that knowledge is only knowledge, a dream about nothing but dreaming.[13]

11 Ibid., 45–52; (1981) II–222–122 to II–240–162 (233–47).

12 Ibid., 37–45; (1981) II–212–101 to II–222–122 (225–33); (1987), 52–60, (1981) II–230–140 to II–240–162 (240–7).

13 Ibid., 60–4; II–240–162 to II–247–178 (247–52). Although Fichte does not stay with this conclusion, his escape from it depends on other evidence, not on the immediate consciousness of some content.

Jacobi and Sartre draw exactly the opposite conclusion from the same evidence. Jacobi says:

> I experience that I am, and that there is something outside me, in one and the same indivisible moment ... But strain your whole attention once more, I pray you, and collect your being at the point of a simple perception, so that you might become once and for all aware ... that the I and the Thou, the internal consciousness and the external object, must be present both at once in the soul even in the most primordial and simple of perceptions – the two in one flash, in the same indivisible instant, without before or after, without any operation of the understanding.[14]

The experience is completely unmediated. No representations, no concept of cause and effect, no inferences connect the consciousness of oneself to the consciousness of the external object. The "I" simply experiences the object in its externality, and thus experiences the object's distinction from consciousness itself. This, Jacobi says, "must be present ... even in the most primordial and simple of perceptions." He adds later: "for our human consciousness (and let me add right away: for the consciousness of each and every finite being) it is necessary that besides the thing that does the sensing, there is also a real thing which is sensed. We must distinguish ourselves from something."[15] According to Jacobi, then, the experience that distinguishes consciousness from an external object is the necessary and fundamental condition of all finite consciousness. Representations and concepts are derived from reflection on this original experience, and they depend on it for their truth. For example, Jacobi argues for the objective truth of the representation "extended being" by probing the implications of the original experience. In this experience, the sensing self experiences itself distinguished from what is sensed. Hence, the self's immediate experience of its own reality is inextricably tied to the reality of an other from which the self distinguishes itself. This proves that "extended being," i.e. one being outside another, exists "not just ideally, but in actuality."[16] According to Fichte, the immediate experience of consciousness related to an other depends on and is derived from thought applying the concept of causal connection to this experience, which detaches the relation between consciousness and what it is conscious of from whatever might actually exist

14 Jacobi (1787), 64; (1994), 277.

15 Ibid., 111; (1994), 293.

16 Ibid., 111–12; (1994), 293–4. "It is necessary that besides the thing that does the sensing, there is also a real thing which is sensed. We must distinguish ourselves from something. Hence, two actual things outside one another, or 'duality'" (1994, 293; 1787, 111).

outside knowledge. According to Jacobi, the concept of extended being depends on and is derived from the immediate experience of consciousness related to an other. Since Jacobi claims that the reality of what is sensed belongs to the immediate experience of consciousness related to an other, a concept derived from this experience knows what is actual, not just what belongs to knowledge closed up within itself.

Sartre, like Hegel, begins with the bare-bones structure of consciousness. Consciousness is consciousness of something. Sartre considers two opposite ways in which this basic structure might be interpreted. Either consciousness constitutes the object, or consciousness is a relation to a reality that transcends the relation to consciousness. Sartre explicitly argues against the first alternative, that consciousness constitutes its own object. Consciousness is nothing more than being-conscious-of. Without some definite content to complete it, without something to be conscious of, consciousness is not conscious at all. It simply disappears. Consciousness cannot give this content to itself. Being-conscious-of has no content. Even if consciousness is conscious of itself, Sartre argues, it must be conscious of some definite quality – red, rough, long, loud – in order to be conscious at all; this quality cannot be derived from pure consciousness-of. Sartre, like Jacobi, treats this as a being issue, not an epistemological issue. Consciousness exists conscious of something. This consciousness cannot exist at all without being conscious of some content that being-conscious-of cannot get from itself. Hence, the existence of the object as a transphenomenal being is given with the existence of consciousness. Sartre explicitly distinguishes transphenomenal being from noumenal being. Noumenal being is hidden behind appearances. Transphenomenal being is the appearance itself whose being cannot be reduced to its appearing. What appears to consciousness is what it is in itself. Consciousness of red necessarily involves not only red being perceived but also red being red.[17]

For all practical purposes, Fichte, Jacobi, and Sartre find the same structure in the fundamental experience of consciousness conscious of some content. Even Fichte acknowledges that we have an immediate experience of externality, and that we experience space, which is the condition of externality, as the separation of a sense content from the consciousness that is conscious of it. Moreover, both Fichte and Sartre explicitly acknowledge the double status of the object, which is a major factor in Hegel's account. Hegel distinguishes between the object as something in itself and the object as "for" consciousness, both of which fall within consciousness

17 Sartre (1957) (1994), Introduction, section V: "The Ontological Proof."

(*PhG* 58–9/M ¶82; 58–9/M ¶84). Fichte, too, acknowledges that the content perceived is what it is because of itself, not because of its being perceived. Sartre uses the terminology Hegel uses, the object in itself and for consciousness, and explicitly distinguishes this from a noumenal thing-in-itself hidden behind appearances. Finally, Fichte, Jacobi, and Sartre, like Hegel, identify the fundamental experience structure as a necessary condition for consciousness to appear at all.

Fichte, however, overrules the fundamental experience, consciousness conscious of something, by appealing to an immediate intuition of the self's consciousness of itself, "I am I." From this intuition, he derives a space condition and interprets it as consciousness separated from itself. Based on these moves, he re-interprets the fundamental experience as a relation situated within the self's consciousness of itself. He also isolates his discussion in an epistemological framework. Because knowledge provides no evidence that there is a world outside knowledge, everything becomes unreal, a dream of dreaming. Jacobi sticks to what he finds in the experience itself. Based on the experience itself, 'myself' is the sensing side of the experience. I am conscious of myself as a relation to an other. Nothing in this dynamic justifies the claim that perceiving and what it perceives are the same consciousness distinguished from itself, only that there is a relation between them. Sartre adds to this an explicit argument against the kind of claims that Fichte makes. There is no immediate intuition of the self's identity with itself, "I am I." Consciousness is conscious of itself only in its relation to an other, a content, that it is conscious of.

Finally, Jacobi's and Sartre's interpretations of the fundamental experience differ from Fichte's in a way that redefines the whole issue. Fichte assumes that the real world is the world existing outside knowledge, if such exists. Jacobi and Sartre recognize that consciousness itself is real, and its reality is manifest in our being conscious of something. This reality is inextricably tied up with the reality of whatever consciousness is conscious of, not as an inaccessible thing-in-itself, but as a real content situated within the experience relation. What exists is consciousness conscious of something. This is the real world immediately manifest in the most rudimentary consciousness. The externality of the world falls within this experience as one dimension of its reality. To conceive a world that falls outside this reality merely abstracts the externality element in the experience relation, separates it from its relations, and projects it into some unknown realm outside knowledge.

How, then, does this brief look at Fichte, Jacobi, and Sartre help us explain more precisely the way Hegel interprets the rudimentary structure of consciousness? It identifies several questions that must be asked in order to clarify Hegel's position. Is Hegel undertaking an examination of knowledge as primarily an epistemological project? If so, then the project asks how we determine whether or not our knowledge is true, which is also Fichte's question. Does Hegel, like Jacobi and Sartre, restrict his interpretation of the rudimentary structure to the relational dynamic manifest in the structure itself? This would allow him to address the externality issue from within experience, without falling into the presuppositions he objects to in a critique determined by the natural assumption. Does Hegel, like Jacobi and Sartre, set out to examine the reality of experience rather than the conformity of knowledge to a real world that is other than knowledge? If so, then the project asks what the reality of experience is, not whether or not it can know some truth external to itself? For Jacobi and Sartre, the externality of the real falls within the reality of experience.

As we have seen in the preceding section, Hegel clearly and explicitly takes a stand against the kind of critique that begins by looking at knowledge as if it were something set apart from truth. Hegel also acknowledges that both the object in itself and the object for consciousness are within consciousness; and his interpretation of this structure simply ignores the question of a thing-in-itself outside knowledge that may or may not be accessible to knowledge. Instead, Hegel says that the subject matter of the *Phenomenology* is knowledge as an appearance, which he describes as knowledge that simply is. Thus Hegel says: "By the former assurance, Science would be declaring its power to lie simply in its being; but the untrue knowledge likewise appeals to the fact that it is, and assures us that for it Science is of no account ... It is for this reason that an exposition of <knowledge appearing> (*des erscheinden Wissens*) will here be undertaken" (*PhG* 55–6/M ¶76). It seems, therefore, that the *Phenomenology* sets out to examine the being of experience.

Moreover, Hegel preserves the externality of the object within the existence of cognition, just as Jacobi and Sartre do. Thus Hegel says:

> Consciousness simultaneously distinguishes itself from something, and at the same time relates itself to it, or, as it is said, this something exists for consciousness; and the determinate aspect of this relating or of the being of something for a consciousness, is knowing. But we distinguish this being-for-another from being-in-itself; whatever is related to knowledge or knowing is also distinguished from it, and posited as <being> outside of this relationship. (*PhG* 58–9/M ¶82)

Hegel insists that the distinction between the object's relation to knowing and the object posited outside this relationship falls within consciousness and "is already present in the very fact that consciousness knows an object at all" (*PhG* 59/M ¶85). Because the object provides a content that being-conscious-of does not have, consciousness is conscious of the object as something with a content of its own, a content not derived from its relation to consciousness. For Hegel, therefore, externality is the content's independence of its relation to consciousness, which consciousness knows by being in need of this independent content in order to be conscious at all. Since, however, consciousness is conscious of this content, consciousness also knows it as something related to consciousness. Thus, Hegel, like Jacobi and Sartre, interprets the rudimentary structure of consciousness as a relational dynamic to which the externality of objects belongs.

4 THE PRESUPPOSITION STATUS OF THE STARTING POINT

In the *Logic*, Hegel acknowledges that the rudimentary structure of consciousness is a presupposition in the *Phenomenology* (*WL* 21:54–5/M 69). We can locate this presupposition if we compare the starting point of the *Phenomenology* to the analysis of phenomenal consciousness in the *Encyclopaedia*'s "Philosophy of Spirit." In the *Encyclopaedia*, Hegel derives the distinction between consciousness-of and what it is conscious of from the developments of the actual soul (*Enz* §411–14). As soul, the human spirit feels itself living in and forming the determinations of its immediately given, external, physical being. As consciousness, the human spirit distinguishes itself from these determinations, holds them before itself as objects, and thus becomes the consciousness of something. Thus, Hegel in the *Encyclopaedia* acknowledges that the starting point of phenomenology in the philosophy of spirit involves a presupposition derived from a preceding set of moves. Why, then, does he not treat the starting point of the *Phenomenology of Spirit* in the same way?

The role of phenomenology in the *Encyclopaedia* differs from the task of the *Phenomenology of Spirit*. The *Encyclopaedia* belongs to philosophy proper, and develops according to the procedure of philosophical science. This procedure begins with the concept of science, which is the unity of thought and being. Scientific procedure develops a full articulation of this concept's necessary implications. These implications carry thought into the concept of spirit, and eventually show the necessity of conceiving spirit as phenomenal consciousness. In the philosophy of spirit, therefore, the task is to show how the separation of consciousness from what it is conscious of develops within the rational whole and how it is determined by the beginning concept of the logical or rational. The task of the *Phenomenology of Spirit* is to justify the concept of the logical or rational with which the *Encyclopaedia* begins. The *Phenomenology of Spirit*, therefore, must begin with a legitimacy that does not depend on anything developed within the system of philosophical thought, since the *Phenomenology* justifies the concept on which everything in the system depends. But the *Phenomenology* itself assumes from the beginning a cognition structure in which consciousness experiences the content side of experience as an other set off from and independent of the consciousness-of side of experience. What justifies this presupposition?

Sartre can help us find Hegel's answer to this question. According to Sartre, as we have seen, if there were no distinction between being conscious of and some independent something that consciousness is conscious of, then consciousness would simply disappear. Even Fichte acknowledges that there is no consciousness without the distinction between consciousness and what it is conscious of. Taking a suggestion from the *Encyclopaedia*'s philosophy of spirit, we might say that without this distinction, a human being would be completely identified with and absorbed into its life functions, with no distance that allows him or her to be conscious of this life.[18]

With these suggestions in mind, let us look carefully at the clues to Hegel's answer provided by the Introduction to the *Phenomenology*. After describing the abstract structure of knowledge as an appearance, Hegel says: "Just what might be involved in these determinations is of no further concern to us here. Since our object is <appearing> knowledge [*das erscheinende Wissen*], its determinations too will at first be taken directly as they present themselves; and they do present themselves very much as we have already apprehended them" (*PhG* 58–9/M ¶82). Consciousness-of dependent on something other than itself for what it is conscious of identifies the minimal conditions for knowledge to appear at all. Without it there is no knowing related to something known. Unlike Fichte, however, Hegel does not try to explain the experience in terms of an *a priori* space condition. Nor does he accept it as an established truth that can justify other claims about knowledge and reality, as Jacobi and Sartre do. The *Phenomenology* gets its starting point from the given fact that "knowing something" happens. Knowing, not just living, shows up as a real experience. The *Phenomenology* begins with the bare-bones structure of this experience, with the minimal conditions required for "knowing something" to appear. Whatever else this involves remains to be seen; and what remains to be seen does not leave the bare-bones structure unchallenged.

18 Compare to Marx (1968), 514–18; (1994), 62–4.

Hegel preserves the epistemological question within his examination of experience as an existing cognition. The *Phenomenology* asks whether knowledge as an appearance conforms to what knowledge truly is. Instead of assuming a world separated from experience that knowledge may or may not know, it addresses the world of experience itself and asks whether it lives up to its true essence (*PhG* 54–6/M ¶76–7). Moreover, Hegel does not define the critical project by relating the world of experience to the critic's questions and methodology. Instead, he finds the critical question within the fundamental structure of experience itself. Cognition conceived as nothing more than being conscious of something requires that the object be what it is (the object-in-itself) and that what it is be known (the object-for-consciousness). This demand functions as the criterion that consciousness imposes on itself just by being conscious of the object. Consciousness expects the object to be something with a content of its own made known to consciousness (*PhG* 58–9/M ¶82; 59–60/M ¶84–5). According to Hegel, this self-critique will show that cognition in this form fails to meet its own demands, and this result begins a process that will demonstrate the untruth of consciousness in all its various forms (*PhG* 55–6/M ¶77–8).

5 THE PHENOMENOLOGY AS SCIENCE

In the Introduction to the *Phenomenology*, Hegel acknowledges the ambiguity involved in attributing scientific status to the project developed in the *Phenomenology*. The *Phenomenology* has as its subject matter knowledge in its appearing (*das erscheinende Wissen*), whereas science is "free and self-moving in its own <proper> (*eigentümlichen*) form" (*PhG* 55–6/M ¶77). Science has the form of a knowing that knows itself identified with what is absolutely true. It develops its determinations within the framework of this assurance. Knowledge in the form of what appears simply exists, with its truth status undetermined. Even science has this form when it comes on the scene as a simple assertion, because other forms of knowing that dismiss its truth claims also exist. If, therefore, the *Phenomenology* examines knowledge in order to determine the truth status of appearing cognitions, then it does not work within the framework of a knowing assured of its truth. How, then, can it be science? Hegel answers that the *Phenomenology* has a scientific status for two reasons: it goes through an educational process that takes consciousness into the standpoint of science; and the process develops according to a scientific procedure (*PhG* 54–6/M ¶76–8).

Hegel describes the *Phenomenology*'s procedure as natural consciousness moving "through the series of its own configurations as though they were stations appointed for it by its own nature," as a "necessary progression and interconnection of the forms of unreal consciousness" (*PhG* 55–6/M ¶77; 56–7/M ¶79).[19] Because of this necessity, the way to science is itself already science, and hence, in virtue of its content, is the science of the experience of consciousness (*PhG* 61–2/M ¶88). Thus, the Introduction describes the *Phenomenology*'s procedure in ways that correspond to the descriptions of scientific procedure in the *Logic* and in the Preface to the *Phenomenology*.

Like the *Logic*, the Introduction describes a movement determined by the "nature" of the subject matter itself. Like the *Logic* and the Preface, it equates science with a procedure driven by necessity and describes the *Phenomenology*'s procedure as a necessary movement. Like the Preface, the Introduction describes the expansion of a content into an organic, i.e. "interconnected," whole (*PhG* 28–9/M ¶34; WL 21:7–8/M 27–8; 21:27/M 43; 21:32–3/M 48–9).[20] Moreover, Hegel refers to the rudimentary structure of consciousness, which is the starting point of the *Phenomenology*, as the concept of consciousness. "Consciousness, however, is <for itself> the <concept> of itself" (*PhG* 57/M ¶80). Consciousness makes its fundamental definition known to itself just by being conscious of something. Thus, the *Phenomenology*, like any scientific investigation, begins with the concept of its subject matter.

The Introduction, however, suggests something about the *Phenomenology*'s beginning concept that we have not seen in the other descriptions of scientific procedure. This concept is not a thought whose legitimacy must be proved by a prior demonstration. This concept is the reality that consciousness itself is. Consciousness identifies itself for itself just by being conscious of something. There is no question of dismissing this concept as a meaningless notion that refers to nothing real. Moreover, the concept that consciousness itself is identifies consciousness as "something that goes beyond limits, and since these limits are its own, it is something that goes beyond itself" (*PhG* 57–8/M ¶80). Consciousness of something relates being-conscious-of to an other that completes it, to a 'what' that provides a content for it to be conscious of. Thus, consciousness thrusts itself toward a truth that it is not; and this will move it beyond itself until it rests in that truth (*PhG* 56–8/M ¶80).

19 See also *PhG* 61–2/M ¶89.
20 See also *Enz* §1; *PhR* §31.

6 SCIENTIFIC PROCEDURE

The Introduction describes the way the *Phenomenology* develops the concept of consciousness by referring to the principle of determinate negation. The examination of consciousness exposes the untruth of consciousness. But this is not "a merely negative procedure." The negation is determinate. It does not negate all knowing. It negates the specific form of knowing whose untruth has been exposed. Moreover, the negation emerges as the result of what it negates, as implicit in it and necessarily determined by it. Hence, it must be taken as "the result of that from which it emerges," "a result which contains what was true in the preceding knowledge." This defines a new form of consciousness, one identified by the old form explicitly known as bringing about its own negation (*PhG* 56–7/M ¶79; 59–60/M ¶86; 61–2/M ¶87). Here we have the crucial elements identified in the *Logic*'s account of scientific procedure: determinate negation; the result that contains that from which it results; and the old form of the concept in unity with its negation or opposite (*WL* 21:37–8/M 54).

The subject matter of the *Phenomenology*, however, brings with it added complications. As we have seen, the rudimentary structure of consciousness distinguishes between what the object itself is and this object's relation to consciousness, with the object in itself functioning as the truth that gives consciousness something to know. By making this distinction, consciousness sets itself up as a self-critical dynamic. Hegel describes this dynamic as a comparing of concept and object; and he offers two different ways of using the terminology. We could use the term "concept" to represent the way we know the object, and the word "object" to represent what the object itself truly or essentially is. According to this way of defining the terms, consciousness tests its knowledge by demanding that the "concept" correspond to the "object." But we could also use the term "concept" to represent the true essence of the object, and the word "object" to represent this essence as it is "for another," i.e. the object as known or "for" consciousness. According to this way of defining the terms, consciousness tests its knowledge by demanding that the "object" correspond to its "concept." Hegel says that these two procedures are evidently the same. If we look carefully at the difference between the way the terms are defined, the sameness in the procedure turns out to be this: consciousness tests itself by seeing whether the way the object is known ("concept" according to the first articulation, "object" according to the second) corresponds to the truth or essence of the object ("object" according to the first articulation, "concept" according to the second). Since both factors fall within consciousness itself, this means that consciousness tests the way it is conscious of the object by what it expects the truth to be (*PhG* 58–9/M ¶84).

Hegel says later that knowledge is essentially knowledge of the object, and that the object belongs essentially to this knowledge. I take this to mean that knowledge is essentially directed to whatever it expects the truth to be. In the rudimentary structure of consciousness, for example, consciousness takes the object to be a content that provides consciousness with something to be conscious of; and it relates to this content as something belonging to the object in itself, on its own, independent of its relation to consciousness. This determines what consciousness looks for in its experience, and the way it is conscious of what shows up in experience. Consciousness looks for an independent content that completes the consciousness-of relation by providing something for consciousness to be conscious of. If what shows up in experience fails to meet these expectations, consciousness experiences it as not the real truth of the matter; and this deflects consciousness to something else in search of what provides a content in which to rest. Thus, the comparing of concept and object happens within experience itself, not as some reflection after the fact, nor as a critique that calls upon its own independent criteria and judgments. Consciousness provides a truth criterion within its own dynamic, and measures itself against this criterion by being conscious of the object in terms of what it expects the truth to be (*PhG* 59–60/M ¶85).

If, however, this self-critical dynamic develops a determinate negation, what happens to the criterion, the truth expectation that belongs to the negated consciousness? The criterion, Hegel says, belongs to the knowledge and is negated along with it. In the beginning structure of consciousness, for example, knowledge is consciousness of an object as something with its own independent content. A determinate negation remains attached to what it negates. It negates what the negated specifically is. Hence, the determinate negation of a knowledge defined as consciousness of an independent content negates not only the way consciousness knows an independent content but also its essential orientation toward the truth in this form. Consequently, the new form of consciousness justified by this development will have a different orientation. It will look for a different kind of truth. It will impose different requirements on its experience of the object.

The Introduction articulates the transition to a new form of consciousness thus:

> Hence it comes to pass for consciousness that what <previously was for it the in itself is not in itself, or that it was only in itself for consciousness>.[21] Since consciousness thus finds that its knowledge does not correspond to its object, the object itself does not stand the test; in other words, the criterion for testing is altered when that for which it was to have been the criterion fails to pass the test; and the testing is not only a testing of what we know, but also a testing of the criterion of what knowing is. (*PhG* 59–60/M ¶85)

> Consciousness knows something; this object is the essence or the in-itself; but it is also for consciousness the in-itself. This is where the ambiguity of this truth enters. We see that consciousness now has two objects: one is the first in-itself, the second is the being-for-consciousness of this in-itself ... But as was shown previously, the first object, in being known, is altered for consciousness; it ceases to be the in-itself, and becomes <for it such that> it is the in-itself only for consciousness. And this then is the True: the being-for-consciousness of this in-itself. Or, in other words, this is the essence, or the object of consciousness. This new object contains the nothingness of the first. (*PhG* 59–60/M ¶86)

These texts leave themselves open to various interpretations, not all of them consistent with each other. Before considering these ambiguities, however, we should notice one subtle but unambiguous concern revealed in the second text. Hegel is careful here to keep the new object restricted to the negative result of the first. What consciousness took to be the in-itself shows itself as "not in itself" and to be "the being-for-consciousness of this in-itself." The new form of consciousness takes the truth to be (1) the first object, (2) as not in-itself, (3) as the in-itself for consciousness.[22] This confirms in one respect the way the *Logic* describes the *Phenomenology*'s procedure. Nothing extraneous enters into the development: no hidden premises, no principles not derived from the dialectical development itself. The transition to a new object simply asserts the original object together with its negation (*WL* 21:37–8/M 53–4).

The Introduction articulates the negation, however, in an ambiguous way. What consciousness took to be the in-itself turns out to be the in-itself only for consciousness. What does this mean? With Fichte in mind, we might interpret "in-itself only for consciousness" to mean that the object

21 "Es wird hiemit dem Bewußtsein, daß dasjenige, was ihm vorher das an sich war, nicht an sich ist, oder daß es nur für es an sich war." (*PhG* 59–60) Note that the German uses the definite article "*das*" with *an sich* only in the first instance. After that, the term *an sich* can be interpreted as an adjective. Miller translates it as a noun throughout the passage.

22 See also *PhG* 60–2/M ¶87.

of consciousness is nothing but a projection of conditions that belong to consciousness itself. This interpretation, however, does not fit what "only for consciousness" means when the Introduction talks about the way the *Phenomenology* will end: "In pressing forward to its true existence, consciousness will arrive at a point at which it gets rid of its semblance of being burdened with something alien, with what is only for it, and some sort of 'other,' at a point where appearance becomes identical with essence, so that its exposition will coincide at just this point with the authentic Science of Spirit" (*PhG* 61–2/M ¶89). Here Hegel associates "what is only for it" with "some sort of other" with the burden of "something alien." What is only for consciousness, therefore, refers to an other as the real truth of the matter, something that remains in itself, something alien not fully absorbed in what it is for consciousness. The *Phenomenology*'s examination of consciousness ends when it reaches a form of knowing in which the object's true essence is completely revealed in the way the object exists for consciousness. The determinate negations leading up to this end, therefore, expose the way what a form of consciousness takes the truth to be refers to an other as its true essence and thus justifies the shift to a new form of consciousness with a different truth expectation. The process ends with a form of consciousness in which the truth expectation is met, what consciousness expects the truth to be stands revealed without referring itself to something other that is its true essence.

The way the *Logic* describes the *Phenomenology*'s procedure fits this interpretation of determinate negation. According to the *Logic*, the *Phenomenology* shows how each form of consciousness "dissolves itself in being realized" (*WL* 21:37–8/M 54). Consciousness realizes itself by actually knowing what it takes the truth to be. The rudimentary structure of consciousness, for example, takes the truth to be what the object itself is, independent of its relation to consciousness. This form of consciousness realizes itself by actually knowing what constitutes the object's independence of consciousness. Suppose, however, that this knowledge also reveals that the object's independence of consciousness refers to something other than itself as its true essence. This would show that the object's independence of consciousness is only the way the essence appears in experience, not what this essence is in itself. Thus, the consciousness that takes the truth to be the object's independence of consciousness negates this truth expectation precisely by fulfilling it. This justifies the shift to a new form of consciousness, one that knows the object's independence of consciousness as not its own true essence, but only the being for consciousness of this essence.

7 THE ROLE OF THE OBSERVER

The Introduction distinguishes between two different ways in which the shift from one form of cognition to another is accomplished. The consciousness situated within the knowledge being examined does not develop. It persists as a divided consciousness with different, even conflicting, truth expectations. If it moves from one form of cognition to another, it does so because it experiences a different kind of knowledge that challenges its usual way of looking at things, and this experience persuades consciousness to abandon the old way and commit to the new. This, Hegel says, is what we usually think of as experience (*Erfahrung*). But Hegel gives experience a new meaning by applying it to what goes on in the one who remains uncommitted to the truth expectations of the cognitions being examined. The observer consciousness knows the necessary connection whereby one form of knowing gets its structure and definition from the self-negation of another. Hegel insists that the knowledge examined and the knowledge developed in the examiner have the same content. But only in the observer does knowledge develop as a connected whole governed by the same concept. This, Hegel says, "is what experience has made of it" (*PhG* 60–2/M ¶87–8). Hence, it is the observer's knowledge that overcomes the challenge of different, conflicting forms of experience governed by different, conflicting truth expectations. Only the observer's knowledge produces as its result the concept of "science," which is the concept of a spirit that governs, grounds, and operates in the whole distribution of different knowledge forms. If the observer observes a form of cognition that corresponds to this concept of science, only the observer knows it scientifically, because only the observer knows its necessary development from the rudimentary concept of knowledge as an appearance.

Thus, Hegel introduces the role of the "we" that simply observes as different forms of consciousness test themselves against their own truth expectations. From the beginning, Hegel makes it quite clear that the forms of consciousness examined in the *Phenomenology* do not themselves develop. Consciousness in one form does not turn itself into consciousness in another form. Rather, the one who undertakes the examination observes the self-negation implicit in each form of consciousness, and knows how this negation necessitates a shift to a different form of consciousness with different truth expectations. The necessity is not causal. It does not produce the shift. It justifies the shift by showing that it follows necessarily from the way the previous form of consciousness has exposed its true meaning. Hegel says that only the observer knows these necessary implications. He does not say why. I suggest that this is because only the observer is uncommitted to the truth expectations operating in the knowledge being examined. What a form of consciousness expects the truth to be belongs to its essential orientation. Everything that falls into its experience is experienced in terms of this expectation. If something does not fit, consciousness will reject it as unessential or untrue. Only the observer is in a position to be conscious of the way the essential orientation of consciousness itself contributes to its experience of the object.

Hegel's redefinition of the critical project, however, allows the observer nothing more than what can be learned from this detached position. The observer knows how the knowledge being examined belongs to the necessary implications of the concept with which the investigation begins, nothing more. "Thus in the movement of consciousness there occurs a moment of being-in-itself or being-for-us which is not present to the consciousness comprehended in the experience itself. The content, however, of what presents itself to us does exist for it; we comprehend only the formal aspect of that content, or its pure origination" (*PhG* 61–2/M ¶87). Origination (*Entstehen*) refers to the way a positive result emerges from a determinate negation, and hence is limited to the way the negation develops within the experience negated by it. The observer consciousness must not re-interpret the experience by contributing something of its own. It must simply acknowledge the new element exposed in the determinate negation, precisely as the determinate negation exposes it. "But not only is a contribution by us superfluous, since <concept> and object, the criterion and what is to be tested, are present in consciousness itself, but we are also spared the trouble of comparing the two and really testing them, so that, since what consciousness examines is its own self, all that is left for us to do is simply to look on" (*PhG* 59/M ¶85).

8 THE REALITY ISSUE

The observer's empty detachment has significant repercussions for the epistemological concerns of the *Phenomenology*. In the beginning, the form of consciousness being examined expects the truth to be a reality existing apart from consciousness, and hence we observe a form of experience concerned with becoming conscious of the object as an external reality. The self-critical structure of experience, however, with its openness to determinate negation, introduces the possibility that other forms of experience may seek a different kind of truth, and this may change the role that reality plays in knowledge questions.

We may, for example, find ourselves observing a form of consciousness that asks whether moral actions succeed in producing a world governed by moral principles. In this case, the truth question does not ask whether consciousness knows what external reality is on its own independent of its relation to consciousness. It asks whether external reality meets the expectations of moral consciousness. Morality experiences the world's externality, its independence of the relation to consciousness, as indifference to moral principles and hence as a condition at odds with what this form of experience expects the truth to be.[23] In the *Phenomenology*, experiences of this kind belong to an epistemological project. The *Phenomenology* asks about the truth of knowledge. Only certain forms of knowing expect the truth to be what reality is outside and independent of our knowing. If certain determinate negations demonstrate the necessity of changing what knowledge expects the truth to be, then these same negations demonstrate the necessity of adjusting the way knowledge asks the epistemological question, and the way it defines the role of external reality in the answer that meets its expectations.

The Introduction addresses the reality issue in a different way when it identifies the subject matter to be investigated in the *Phenomenology* and talks about what the investigation makes of it. The *Phenomenology* examines knowledge in the form of what appears, cognition simply existing, its truth status yet to be determined. Hegel uses the term "knowledge appearing" (*das erscheinende Wissen*), which Miller translates "phenomenal knowledge," interchangeably with the term "natural consciousness." Knowledge appearing in its bare-bones, abstract structure is consciousness conscious of an object as something other than and independent of its relation to consciousness. The examination of knowledge developed in the *Phenomenology* takes this form of knowledge "through the series of its own configurations as though they were the stations appointed for it by its own nature, so that it may purify itself for the life of the Spirit, and achieve finally, through a completed experience of itself, <knowledge of what it is in itself>" (*PhG* 55–6/M ¶77).[24] Thus, the *Phenomenology* goes through steps determined by the nature of natural consciousness itself. Through a long and complicated series of determinate negations, this process exposes what is implicit in the structure of knowledge as an appearance. The completion of this process shows that the form of knowing with which the process began was only a beginning concept of knowing, not yet realized in all its determinations

23 Consider, for example, *PhG* 324–5/M ¶599–600.

24 Translation adjusted using the Baillie translation.

and complexity. Only at the end does natural consciousness exist as a complete experience of what it is.

The complete experience of what it is, however, demonstrates that natural consciousness is not real knowledge. "But since it directly takes itself to be real knowledge, this path has a negative significance for it, and what is in fact the realization of the <concept> counts for it rather as the loss of its own self; for it does lose its truth on this path ... this path is the conscious insight into the untruth of <appearing> knowledge (*das erscheinende Wissen*), for which the supreme reality is what is in truth only the unrealized <concept>" (*PhG* 56–7/M ¶78). When, at the end of the *Phenomenology*, the full meaning of its beginning concept has been exposed, knowledge as an appearance will show itself as not in itself what knowledge really and truly is.

PART FIVE

REVIEW OF THE ISSUES

PARTS TWO, THREE, AND FOUR HAVE STUDIED the way the introductory essays of Hegel's major works interpret the task and method of the *Phenomenology*. This study focuses on four issues: the subject matter and presuppositions of philosophical science; philosophy challenged by the claims of empirical consciousness; the requirements of scientific procedure; the scientific justification of philosophy by the phenomenological examination of empirical consciousness. We are now in a position to review the evidence provided in each text separately, and to address questions raised about the relation between the *Phenomenology of Spirit* and the logical starting point of Hegel's philosophical system.

10

The Consistency of Hegel's Position

THIS CHAPTER REVIEWS THE EVIDENCE provided in the introductory essays to show that the Hegel of the later works and the Hegel of the *Phenomenology* maintained the same position on the issues addressed in my study of these texts.

1 THE RATIONAL IS ACTUAL AND THE ACTUAL RATIONAL

All three of Hegel's later works – *Philosophy of Right, Encyclopaedia,* and *Science of Logic* – claim that philosophical thought thinks the necessities of thought itself and develops these without depending on what is given in or established by experience in its various forms. All three explicitly distinguish philosophical principles from what is established or given in an accepted way of thinking, whether this takes the form of socially established norms, or generally accepted definitions, or mutual agreement among human beings, or justifications derived from historical states of affairs. The *Encyclopaedia* also distinguishes philosophy from empirical science, which accepts as given the regularities and necessities that appear in experience. Both the *Encyclopaedia* and the *Science of Logic* describe a process whereby thought detaches itself from experience, and both identify thought in this detached position as philosophical thought. All three of the later works, however, explicitly distinguish philosophical knowledge from thought isolated in itself, whether in an individual or universal form. They distinguish philosophy from any knowledge that depends on the subjectivity of the individual thinker, because individual subjectivity does not have the universality, necessity, or communicability required for truth. Even when the *Encyclopaedia* accepts the way Jacobi's intuition of the infinite identifies the truth, it rejects the way this intuition depends on the isolated subjectivity of the knower. The later works also distinguish philosophical thought from an ideal ought that cannot be actualized in the real world (*Philosophy of Right* and *Encyclopaedia*), and from the Kantian interpretation of knowledge, which isolates the subject-object relation within the subjectivity of thought (*Encyclopaedia* and *Logic*).

There is a consensus among the later works, therefore, that philosophical thought develops its necessary, rational determinations without depending on experience, and yet is not pure thought isolated in itself. All three of the later works insist that philosophy knows the truth by knowing its independently developed, rational determinations as the true essence of objects existent in the real world. The *Philosophy of Right* talks about reality as external existence, which could be read as a reference to the objective world, the world outside the conscious self. The *Encyclopaedia*, however, is unambiguous. Reality is experience. It is the conscious self encountering the givenness of what is ready to hand. According to the *Encyclopaedia*, reason is actual not in a world outside the conscious self but in the experience to which both self and world belong. From this point of view, "external existence" would have to mean the reality of experience that thought leaves behind when it withdraws into itself.

Both the *Science of Logic* and the *Encyclopaedia* address the reality issue by asking how philosophical science begins. According to both texts, philosophical science begins with the concept of pure thought identified with being. Both texts clarify what this means by distinguishing the being determination from sensuous existence, and by distinguishing the thought determination from the subjectivity of the thinker. Philosophical science begins with the independent reality of being conceived as identical with and identified by the rationality of pure thought. If, however, philosophy knows the truth by recognizing its own independent thought determinations as the true essence of real experience, then thought identified with being means thought identified with what the reality of experience fundamentally is. The *Science of Logic* adds another dimension to this issue when it shows how the fundamental structure of experience opposes and challenges the concept that identifies the domain, the element, of philosophy. Hence, the consensus position articulated in Hegel's later works raises the question, what justifies the presupposition implicit in philosophy's beginning concept, that philosophical thought knows the true essence of a reality whose fundamental structure stands opposed to the principle that governs the whole philosophical project.

The introductory essays of the *Phenomenology* analyze the relation between philosophy and experience in the same way. The Preface, like the introductory essays of Hegel's later works, represents the element of consciousness, which is the element of experience, as a reality that is preserved within the spirit of philosophical science. Truth works out its self-articulation in the element of consciousness. Experience gives actuality to the spirit of truth (See especially *PhG* 14–15/M ¶12; 29–30/M ¶35–7; *Enz* 25*A*). The *Phenomenology*, like the *Logic*, defines the phenomenological project in terms of an opposition between the standpoint of philosophical science, which defines knowledge as the unity of thought and being, and the standpoint of consciousness, which defines knowledge as consciousness of a truth that is other than consciousness itself. The Preface to the *Phenomenology* discusses the opposition between philosophy and natural consciousness in terms of historical conditions. Like the *Encyclopaedia*, however, it distinguishes between internal necessity, determined by what the concept of the subject matter requires, and the externality in which this necessity makes its appearance in history. Both the Preface and the Introduction to the *Phenomenology* identify in the historical situation an issue rooted in the fundamental structures of human knowing. Both also raise objections to science as an appearance on the scene in the same way that the *Encyclopaedia* criticizes the immediate knowing position. Like Jacobi's intuition of the infinite, absolute philosophy's intuition of absolute truth takes the form of an isolated subjective conviction whose truth cannot prove its universality by being communicable to others.

2 THE ROLE OF THE *PHENOMENOLOGY*

According to all three of the later works, philosophy differs from other sciences because its methodology is determined by the necessities implicit in the beginning concept, which defines the subject matter of the science, and because philosophy demonstrates the necessity of the beginning concept itself. Philosophy proves that a certain way of conceiving the subject matter is the way it must be conceived. The *Philosophy of Right*, of course, gets its beginning concept from the demonstrations developed in the preceding parts of the philosophical system. If, however, philosophy proves its beginning concepts, then it must also prove the concept with which the whole system begins. How, then, does philosophy prove the necessity of its beginning concept, which is the rational or logical conceived as thought identified with being? According to the *Encyclopaedia*, thought becomes committed to this concept through a double determination. Driven by the need for necessity, thought separates itself from its involvement in experience because experience does not provide the kind of necessity thought demands. This detachment accomplished, thought resolves to focus on thought in itself, pure thought, and to develop what follows from this way of conceiving true knowing. This account, however, leaves us with another question. Since thought's need for necessity is not derived from or satisfied by experience, why assume that what thought needs determines what experience fundamentally is?

Both the *Encyclopaedia* and the *Logic* acknowledge that the beginning concept of philosophy depends on, is mediated by, a proof developed from the necessities of experience itself. The *Encyclopaedia* suggests and the *Logic* states that the beginning concept of philosophy depends on a demonstration that examines consciousness as such, which is the name Hegel gives to experience. Both texts describe this proof as a retreat into a ground that sublates the mediation. The proof begins within what depends on the ground and demonstrates the necessity of thinking the ground as independent of, not mediated by, what it grounds. Hence, both texts point out that the proof involves a negative mediation that separates the more fundamental truth, the ground, from the kind of knowing that provides the evidence by which we make our way to this truth. The *Logic* says explicitly that this evidence is provided by the *Phenomenology*'s examination of consciousness, which proves the legitimacy of conceiving the truth as not a consciousness kind of knowing. The *Encyclopaedia* says that the proof begins with finite reality and makes its way to a ground that is not finite but infinite. It points out that immediate knowing achieves its intuition of the infinite by separating consciousness from its involvement in the finite. The *Encyclopaedia* suggests that an examination of consciousness as such might be the kind of proof required for this retreat into a ground, and in another place it says that the *Phenomenology of Spirit* proves the necessity of the philosophical standpoint (*Enz* 25*A*).

Finally, both the *Encyclopaedia* and the *Logic* talk about a beginning that simply resolves to examine thought as such. A beginning of this kind focuses on pure knowing in itself, without the positive mediation that identifies it as the truth of consciousness, and without the negative mediation that separates pure knowing from its involvement in consciousness. The *Encyclopaedia*'s critique of traditional proofs for the existence of God provides the most explicit clue to the role this pure immediacy plays in Hegel's account of the way philosophy begins. In the *Encyclopaedia,* Hegel rejects a proof procedure that ends with a concept that defines the infinite in terms of its relation to the finite. He calls for a procedure that shifts into a concept that thinks the infinite in itself. Yet the same text insists that the legitimacy of the concept must be proved, that without proof immediate knowing becomes subjective and arbitrary. By describing the proof procedure as a retreat into a ground, both the *Encyclopaedia* and the *Logic* make sense of this ambiguity. A proof that examines the nature of consciousness as such demonstrates that consciousness is a derivative truth, a truth dependent on a more fundamental truth. In order to know the truth in its proper form, therefore, we must think the more fundamental truth isolated in itself, and then demonstrate how it grounds the forms of cognition that belong to consciousness.

The Preface to the *Phenomenology* assigns to absolute philosophy the role of representing the concept of philosophical truth that comes on the scene isolated in itself, asserted as an intuition that claims for itself immediate identification with absolute truth. This Preface situates absolute philosophy's truth claim between two challenges. The whole domain of experiential knowledge claims for itself the status of real knowledge. This claim challenges absolute philosophy to show that its truth is present in experiential knowledge itself and belongs to this cognition as its truth. The Introduction to the *Phenomenology* explains why the challenge cannot be met by simply interpreting experience according to the unproved principles of absolute philosophy itself. The proof must begin within the element of consciousness, which is the element of experience, develop a demonstration governed by principles proper to experiential cognition, and thus demonstrate that absolute philosophy's intuition is the truth of experience itself. The Preface to the *Phenomenology* also challenges the isolated intuition of absolute philosophy by representing it as an empty concept whose content is not yet fully developed. Thus, the introductory essays of the *Phenomenology*, like the introductory essays of the *Encyclopaedia* and the *Logic*, represent the task of the *Phenomenology* as a demonstration that begins within experience, retreats into the concept that identifies the element of philosophical science, and proves that this concept is the truth of experience itself. Like the introductory essays of the later works, those of the *Phenomenology* also represent the beginning concept of philosophical science as a concept whose full meaning is yet to be developed by philosophical science itself.

3 PROOF PROCEDURE

All three of Hegel's later works give an account of the way philosophy maintains complete necessity in the investigation of its subject matter. According to all three, philosophy proceeds by drawing out the implications of the beginning concept in a completely immanent movement. Every shift belongs to the subject matter as the development of its original concept. Nothing other than what is necessitated by this concept functions as a contributing factor in the demonstration. All three texts describe this development as the concept generating its own opposite. All three distinguish this generation of an opposite from another kind of dialectic, one in which a thinking subject manipulates a concept into contradicting itself, and concludes from this that the concept is untenable. In Hegelian philosophical procedure, the generation of an opposite is the result of what the concept itself is; and this development has a positive result. The procedure does not dismiss the concept as untenable. It expands the concept to include the connection to its opposite.

The *Encyclopaedia* and the *Logic* analyze the generation of an opposite as a determinate negation. Determinate negations remain attached to what they negate. They connect the negated concept to its opposite. They justify the move to a concept that endorses the whole dynamic between the opposites. The result of a determinate negation asserts the original concept together with the negation that emerges as its necessary outcome, and it conceives this connection as one truth within which the original concept and its opposite play out their opposition. Both the *Logic* and the *Encyclopaedia*'s discussion of the second position on objectivity make it clear that the result of a determinate negation not only conceives opposites as one truth, but also preserves their contradictoriness within this one truth. Both texts criticize Kant's way of resolving antinomies instead of acknowledging, as true philosophy does, that rationality involves contradiction and that contradiction is fundamental to every concept, representation, and thing. Both texts use the language of contradiction to explain the dynamics of determinate negation. The original concept and its opposite belong to the same dynamic. Hence, they are governed by the same necessity, the same truth. In them, this truth breaks up into the same truth opposed to itself.

Both the *Encyclopaedia* and the *Science of Logic* explain scientific procedure in this way. The *Logic*, however, repeatedly insists that the *Phenomenology* follows the same procedure. The *Encyclopaedia* suggests this when it calls the *Phenomenology*'s procedure a dialectic of consciousness. But the *Logic* explicitly and repeatedly analyzes the dynamics of scientific procedure and applies it to the *Phenomenology*. The *Phenomenology* itself confirms this. The Introduction to the *Phenomenology* describes the same determinate negation procedure. The negation emerges as a "result" implicit in and determined by what it negates. The negation remains attached to what it negates, as the negation of a specific form of knowing. The negation determines a new form of knowing in which the previous form is preserved together with the negation.

The *Logic*, the *Encyclopaedia*, and the *Phenomenology* describe in slightly different ways the form of consciousness with which the exposition of consciousness begins. The *Encyclopaedia* says that the *Phenomenology* begins with the "first and simplest" appearance, which is immediate consciousness (*Enz* §25*A*). The *Logic* says that the *Phenomenology* begins with "empirical, sensuous consciousness," which is immediate knowledge properly speaking (*WL* 21:55/M 69). The Introduction to the *Phenomenology* says that consciousness is for itself its own concept. Consciousness presents the concept of itself just by appearing, by being conscious of something. The Introduction calls this structure the "abstract determinations" of consciousness, sets aside whatever else consciousness may be as of no concern at the beginning of the project, and says that the determinations of phenomenal knowledge will be taken "at first" just as they immediately present themselves (*PhG* 58–9/M ¶82). The *Phenomenology*'s Introduction does not explicitly say that these determinations immediately present themselves as sense consciousness. But the *Phenomenology* begins its exposition of consciousness with sense certainty. It describes sense certainty as "immediate knowledge itself," because it does not depend on, is not mediated by, any relations between different cognitions or different objects (*PhG* 63–4/M ¶90–1). Moreover, Hegel attributes to sense certainty the same structure that he attributes to the concept of consciousness in the Introduction. Sense certainty is a knowing completely dependent on its relation to the object, whereas the object is what it is independent of any relation to knowledge (*PhG* 63–4/M ¶93). Thus, the exposition of consciousness begins with sense consciousness as the way in which knowledge as an appearance "immediately presents itself." Sense certainty is consciousness of something reduced to these determinations and no others. Thus, the *Phenomenology*'s description of its starting point fits the way the later works describe it.

4 ISSUES MORE PROMINENT IN THE *PHENOMENOLOGY*

The *Phenomenology*'s account of its own task and method introduces two crucial issues that do not appear in the later works, although both are suggested in one or the other of them. Only the Preface to the *Phenomenology* discusses the structure of consciousness in terms of the isolated independence of the ego (the "I"). The structure of consciousness involves not only an otherness between consciousness and its object but also a consciousness conscious of itself as "me" and no one else. No matter what the content that consciousness is conscious of, being conscious of it is isolated in the one self whose sense of self it is. The *Phenomenology* begins within this isolated sense of self. Its task is to demonstrate to consciousness that its true essence is the whole, the one spirit, to which all knowing belongs. Accomplishing the task, however, proves the truth of a whole that can hold itself together in "absolute dismemberment," because the whole must survive its division in the isolated self of each and every consciousness (*PhG* 27–8/M ¶32).

The *Encyclopaedia* touches on the same issue when it talks about the experience principle, which acknowledges the individual's right to accept as true only what the individual's own experience attests to as true. But the *Encyclopaedia* does not acknowledge the isolated experience of the individual as an essential element in the structure of consciousness, nor does it acknowledge the necessity of the truth becoming "dismembered" in the isolated individuality of consciousness. The *Science of Logic* touches tangentially on the same theme. It talks about the ego, the "I," of experience, which is the only form in which the "I" is immediately accessible. Finally, both the *Encyclopaedia* and the *Logic* describe the beginning of logic as a resolve, a decision, to focus on thought thinking itself. A resolve brings the independence of self-commitment into the philosophical project. It integrates the isolated self into the universality of philosophical knowing, and it transforms the universality of logic into something "I" have decided to do.

The *Phenomenology* also pays more attention to the epistemological dimension of its project than the later works do. Both the *Encyclopaedia* and the *Science of Logic* talk about the need to demonstrate the necessity and truth of philosophy's beginning concept, which is a claim about what knowing is. The *Encyclopaedia* mentions in an aside the way Kant and Reinhold raise questions about the legitimacy of our knowing; and this Remark bears a strong resemblance to the way the Introduction to the *Phenomenology* talks about the natural assumption (*Enz* §10*A*). But only in the Introduction to the *Phenomenology* is the phenomenological project analyzed as a strategy for dealing with the issues introduced by the mistrust of knowledge; and only here is determinate negation analyzed as a self-critical dynamic implicit in the forms of consciousness.

The way Hegel transforms the critical project, however, involves an attitude toward what reality is, and this attitude is repeated in the *Encyclopaedia*. Reality for the epistemology of Hegel's *Phenomenology* is not a world outside knowledge that it may or may not know. Reality is experience itself to which the externality of the world belongs. In the *Encyclopaedia*, too, experience plays the role of the real. Experience is the reality to which thought must return out of the independent development of its own necessities. Thought must know its independent determinations in the reality of experience. The rational is actual in experience. The Preface to the *Phenomenology* adds a nuance to this claim. Philosophical thought becomes real in the individual self conscious of its own experience attesting to the truth of philosophical science.

Thus, the *Phenomenology*'s account of its task and method includes a dimension that Hegel's later works do not explicitly consider. This added dimension, however, belongs to an overall account of the project that is the same as the account given in the later works. In my judgment, the review of Hegel's introductory essays demonstrates that the way Hegel interprets the task and method of the *Phenomenology* remains consistent throughout his career and in a variety of texts.

5 AN ISSUE IDENTIFIED ONLY IN THE INTRODUCTIONS OF THE LATER WORKS

All three of Hegel's later works describe the way thought knows the rational as the true essence of empirical objects, and thus recognizes a correspondence between the realities of experience and the rationality of thought itself. In the discussions of the rational-is-actual formula, the *Philosophy of Right* and the *Encyclopaedia* distinguish the actual, which is the rational element in what exists, from the contingencies that accompany it; and the *Encyclopaedia* acknowledges that these contingencies do not belong to the subject matter of philosophy, that they are the proper objects of other sciences. The *Encyclopaedia*'s discussion of the second position on objectivity, however, endorses the way both Kant and the empiricists acknowledge the particulars of experience as a necessary and essential element in objectivity. In this same discussion, Hegel also acknowledges as truly speculative Kant's idea of an intellectual intuition whose purposiveness can be conceived as determining the particulars of the real world without deducing these details from the necessary implications of a concept. Finally, in both the *Philosophy of Right* and the *Encyclopaedia*, Hegel attributes a normative function to pure thought. Pure thought identifies the rational element in the reality of experience, and uses this as a norm for judging whether the existing state of affairs is or is not as it should be. The discussion of Kant's teleological judgment suggests that Hegel expects the rational norm to function not only as a principle for judging what exists but also as a ground, a purpose, that derives the non-rational contingencies of the real world from the rationality of an agent. We shall see this issue developed in the main text of the *Phenomenology*.

6 SORTING OUT TEXTUAL PROBLEMS

In chapter one §6, I introduced several ambiguities in texts from Hegel's later period that raise questions about the way the later works interpret the role of the *Phenomenology* in the Hegelian philosophical system. First, the *Phenomenology* itself describes its project as the first part of science; the later works do not. Second, the *Encyclopaedia* does not begin with a *Phenomenology*; it begins by reviewing different positions on objectivity. Third, an abbreviated phenomenology appears as part of the *Encyclopaedia*'s philosophy of spirit. Finally, the later Hegel once referred to the *Phenomenology* as "a peculiar early work."[1] We are now in a position to assess this evidence.

Whatever the later Hegel may have meant by calling the *Phenomenology* "a peculiar early work," he did not mean that it could be set aside as no longer essential to his philosophical project. As we have seen in Part Three, the 1832 version of the *Logic*'s introductory essays develops a fully articulated position on the role of the *Phenomenology*. In these texts, Hegel repeatedly insists that the concept of philosophical science, which identifies pure knowing as the subject matter of logic, gets the proof of its necessity and truth from the exposition of consciousness in the *Phenomenology*. He says explicitly that the domain of logic can be justified in no other way. Although the later Hegel does not acknowledge the *Phenomenology* as the first part of science, this does not change his basic position. It simply indicates a change in the way he uses his terminology. In the later works, Hegel distinguishes between "science" and "scientific." He reserves the term "science" for knowledge committed to the presuppositions of philosophy, which begins with logic. He uses the term "scientific" for the procedure followed in philosophy proper and in the *Phenomenology* as well.

Moreover, the *Encyclopaedia* says explicitly that the *Phenomenology* was called "the first part of the system of science" because of its procedure, which began with immediate consciousness and developed its dialectic "right up to the standpoint of philosophical science, the necessity of which is shown by the progression." In the same text, Hegel says that the way the *Encyclopaedia* begins, with an examination of different positions on objectivity, "has the even greater inconvenience that it can only be conducted <historically> (*historisch*) and argumentatively (*räisonierend*)" (*Enz* §25*A*). In the *Logic*'s discussion of absolute beginnings, Hegel analyzes more explicitly a beginning that is *historisch* and *räisonierend* (*WL* 21:32–3/M 49). An investigation begins with a definition of its subject matter, and this definition governs the way the investigation makes its case. The beginning is "absolute" because it is simply asserted, not justified by a proof. The beginning is historical if the definition simply asserts what is generally accepted. In other words, it

1 Editor's Note in *Phänomenologie des Geistes*, ed. Hoffmeister (1952), 578. See also Wolfgang Bonsiepen, "Einleitung," in *PhG*, L–LI.

accepts what has become the generally accepted way of defining the subject matter. The beginning is argumentative (*räisonierend*) because the claim that the definition is generally accepted can be challenged. An argument develops about which definition is generally accepted. Thus, all participants rely on simple assertions and on what does or does not have credibility with general opinion. None of this is acceptable for the beginning of philosophical science. Philosophical science must justify its beginning concept by proving the necessity of its truth, and the *Phenomenology* provides this justification. As we have seen, Hegel examines the three positions on objectivity by taking his own definition of objectivity for granted, and by showing how the three positions fit or fail in comparison with this definition. The examination assumes the truth of Hegel's position as if it were generally accepted, and it allows this assumption to function as a criterion according to which the other positions are judged. We have examined a great deal of evidence in the *Science of Logic* to show that Hegel expects a more disciplined, thorough proof for the beginning of philosophical science. Moreover, the *Encyclopaedia* itself says that the *Phenomenology* provides necessity, while the *Encyclopaedia*'s alternative introduction to philosophical science provides only an argumentative approach.

There is also no evidence that the abbreviated phenomenology developed in the *Encyclopaedia*'s philosophy of spirit is supposed to be an alternative to the *Phenomenology*. The philosophy of spirit, and phenomenology as part of it, belong to the element of philosophical science. As such, they develop within the framework of philosophy's presuppositions. Pure knowing, developed according to its own internal necessities, demonstrates that knowing in the form of consciousness belongs to these necessities. The *Phenomenology of Spirit* belongs to the element of consciousness, which challenges the presuppositions of philosophy. The task of the *Phenomenology* is to show how consciousness, taken on its own terms, proves the necessity of shifting into the presuppositions of philosophy.

11

Interpretation Paradigms Revisited

IN THIS CHAPTER, I WILL EXPLAIN how the interpretation I have developed from the study of Hegel's introductions fits or challenges the interpretations described in chapter 2 of Part One.[1]

1 RE: THE *PHENOMENOLOGY* BEGS THE QUESTION

Dieter Wandschneider dismisses the *Phenomenology* because it cannot accomplish the task that Hegel assigned to it. The *Phenomenology* cannot demonstrate the truth of logic because it uses logical principles, especially the principle of contradiction, to set aside the claims of experiential cognition. Wandschneider substitutes an alternative way of justifying the starting point of Hegel's philosophy. He shows that any attempt to deny the laws of logic or to deny their validity for knowledge of the actual world falls into absurdity, which proves that the opposite must be true.

Hegel's own defence of his project shows that it is Wandschneider, not Hegel, who begs the question. Wandschneider's argument assumes that what thought cannot conceive, or what it conceives as absurd and untenable, cannot be true of the real world. But according to Hegel, this correspondence between the laws of thought and the real world is exactly what must be proved. Wandschneider does not take into account the possibility that an argument based on pure logic cannot decide the issue one way or the other, because what must be proved is the relevance of pure logic to the real world. Hegel's own interpretation of the *Phenomenology* describes a procedure that does not beg the question. According to the introductory essays of the *Logic* and the *Phenomenology*, the *Phenomenology* follows the

1 For complete citations, see the corresponding sections of chapter 2.

procedure necessitated by its own subject matter, which is empirical cognition or consciousness. It defeats the claims of experience not by using the principles of pure logic but by letting experience disprove its own claims.

Some interpretations of Hegel's procedure, however, will not withstand Wandschneider's challenge. Hegel tells us that the *Phenomenology*'s procedure negates consciousness in all its forms, and that this develops because each implies its own opposite. If we interpret this development as a contradiction, and interpret contradiction as proof that the concept is untenable, then we import into the argument the way some logics define the principle of contradiction. We assume that contradiction is the assertion and denial of exactly the same claim, and that contradiction is *ipso facto* false. The more benign version of this interpretation acknowledges that in Hegelian procedure the emergence of a contradiction calls for a new concept in which both opposites are preserved, but without the contradiction.[2]

Hegel's accounts of determinate negation, however, do not support either of these interpretations. Hegel repeatedly rejects the kind of dialectic that manipulates a concept into a self-defeating contradiction, one that wipes out the whole concept and comes to a dead end. Hegel insists that determinate negations prove the necessity of preserving the negated concept together with its negation. Moreover, his accounts acknowledge that the opposition between the concept and its opposite is preserved within the unity that holds them together. Determinate negation does not prove that a concept is absurd or untenable. It proves only that the concept is not the whole truth, that it belongs to a dynamic with its opposite; and this proves that the concept has in common with its opposite the principle that governs both their opposition and their necessary connection. The *Logic* calls this principle "self-contradiction." Finally, in the *Encyclopaedia*'s critique of Kant's antinomies, Hegel says explicitly and unambiguously that antinomy, which he equates with contradiction, belongs to "objects of all kinds" (*Enz* §48*A*). The *Logic*'s discussion of Kantian antinomies makes the same point (*WL* 21:40-1/M 56).

2 Peter Steinberger gives us the most careful and deliberate example of this interpretation (Steinberger 1988, 61–8). In the process of developing his own analysis, Steinberger criticizes Michael Rosen's view (1982) that Hegelian dialectic is non-inferential; and he criticizes Hans-Georg Gadamer (1976) for being non-specific about exactly how the dialectical inferences operate (80–3). I agree with these objections. I consider Hegel's view inferential. Hegel himself refers to philosophical and phenomenological procedure as *richtige Folgerungen* (*WL* 21:58/M 71). I have also tried to be specific about the way I am interpreting Hegel's dialectical inferences. However, I disagree with Steinberger because he does not preserve the full force of contradiction in his analysis of Hegelian dialectic.

2 RE: THE *PHENOMENOLOGY* PROVES THE NEGATIVE

The Maker-Winfield interpretation of the *Phenomenology* depends on a certain way of reading Hegel when he says that the collapse of otherness between knowing and what it knows "ceases itself to be knowledge" (*WL* 21:58/M 69). Maker and Winfield interpret this to mean that the consciousness form of knowledge examined in the *Phenomenology* cannot meet its own knowledge requirements without collapsing the distinction between knowing and its object. As a result, knowledge becomes no knowledge at all, a knowing that connects with nothing known.

In chapter 7, I have examined the texts that supposedly support the Maker-Winfield interpretation. Because so much depends on the way the principal text is determined by its context, I will respond to the Maker-Winfield interpretation first by quoting the context and situating the crucial text within it.

> A beginning is *logical* in that it is to be made in the element of a free, self-contained thought, *in pure knowledge*; it is thereby *mediated*, for pure knowledge is the ultimate and absolute truth of *consciousness*. We said in the Introduction that the *Phenomenology of Spirit* is the science of consciousness, its exposition; that consciousness has the *concept* of science, that is, pure knowledge, for its result. To this extent, logic has for its presupposition the science of spirit in its appearance, a science which contains the necessity, and therefore demonstrates the truth, of the standpoint which is pure knowledge and of its mediation ... but in logic the presupposition is what has proved itself to be the result of that preceding consideration, namely the idea as pure knowledge. *Logic* is the *pure science*, that is, pure knowledge in the full compass of its development. But in that result the idea has the determination of a certainty that has become truth. (*WL* 21:54–5/M 68–9)

This text clearly shows Hegel identifying the result of the *Phenomenology* with the beginning concept of logic, referring to both as *das reine Wissen*, "pure knowledge." It also shows Hegel claiming that the concept of pure knowledge with which logic begins is the result of the *Phenomenology*, and depends on it as the proof of its truth. Finally, the second part of the text says that "the idea" as pure knowledge, which is the result of the science of consciousness, is logic's presupposition and "has the determination of a certainty that has become truth," whereas the full development of this is the science of logic itself. This is the context in which the crucial text for the Maker-Winfield interpretation is situated.

> But in that result the idea has the determination of a certainty that has become truth; it is a certainty which, on the one hand, no longer stands over and against a subject

matter confronting it externally but has interiorized it, is knowingly aware that the subject matter is itself; and, on the other hand, has relinquished any knowledge of itself that would oppose it to objectivity and would reduce the latter to a nothing; it has externalized this subjectivity and is at one with its externalization ... Pure knowledge, thus *withdrawn* into this *unity*, has sublated every reference to an other and to mediation; it is without distinctions and as thus distinctionless it ceases to be knowledge; what we have before us is only *simple immediacy*. (*WL* 21:55–6/M 69)

In this text the unity without distinctions that "ceases to be knowledge" is "the certainty which has become truth" of the preceding text, which describes the beginning concept of logic derived from the result of the *Phenomenology*. Thus, the collapse in which "knowledge ceases to be knowledge" belongs to "the certainty which has become truth" with which the *Logic* begins.

When Hegel begins the *Logic*, he is talking about a unity into which the distinction between knowing and its other "withdraws," a unity conceived as the ground presupposed by this distinction. Hence, he insists that the distinction will emerge again as a result implicit in and determined by the ground (*WL* 21:58–60/M 72–3). The move from the *Phenomenology* to the *Logic* does not wipe out the distinction between knowing and known that characterizes the forms of knowing examined in the *Phenomenology*. It retreats into the ground of this distinction, and reconceives the elements as differences within the same *logos* or rationality.

Moreover, a close look at Hegel's texts challenges the way the Maker-Winfield interpretation conceives the presuppositionlessness of logic. In the last text quoted above, Hegel repeats a theme developed in the *Encyclopaedia*'s examination of the third position on objectivity. The *Encyclopaedia* says: "What the principle of immediate knowing rightly insists on is not an indeterminate, empty immediacy, abstract being, or pure unity <for itself>, but the unity of *the Idea* with being" (*Enz* §70). Hegel analyzes this unity into two distinct determinations. According to his interpretation, immediate knowing does not assert being without qualifying it, since this would refer to the givenness of sensuous existence. Nor does immediate knowing assert the Idea without qualifying it, since this would refer to the subjectivity of thinking. Rather immediate knowing asserts the unity of distinct determinations: being as Idea and the Idea as being. Hegel preserves immediacy and unity in this mediation by conceiving it as a mediation that remains within the selfsame (*sich in sich selbst beschließend*), i.e. it does not depend on any relation to an other (*Enz* §69, 70, 74). In the *Logic* text quoted above, Hegel says that pure knowing has "internalized the object (*ihn innerlich gemacht hat*)," and has also given up its own subjectivity set apart from the object. Logic begins with being that is not just being, but being in the form of knowledge, the Idea, and not just the subjectivity of knowing, but knowing, the Idea, in the form of being.

Thus, philosophical science, which begins with logic, has a definite subject matter distinguished from other ways in which a subject matter might be conceived: being in the form of pure knowing, not the immediate givenness of sensuous existence; knowing in the form of being, not the knowing of a thinking subject. In another place, the *Logic* describes the subject matter of philosophy as "the *logos*, the reason of that which is, the truth of what we call things" (*WL* 21:17/M 39). When, therefore, the *Encyclopaedia* describes philosophy as thought separated from and independent of experience, it means thought withdrawn into the determinations it shares with the true essence of what is. This is the significance of the formula, the rational is actual and the actual rational. To undertake an investigation of this subject matter presupposes a great deal. It assumes that the logical is not a meaningless notion, and that the development of its necessary implications is not just a school exercise. It assumes that logical thought can develop its own necessary determinations and know thereby the true essence of reality. This presupposes the unity of thought and being in the logical or rational. The *Phenomenology* is supposed to prove the necessity and truth of this presupposition by demonstrating that the real world of cognitive experience refers itself to the logical or rational as its true essence. Philosophy, therefore, does not begin without presuppositions.

Hegel's account of determinate negation also challenges the Maker-Winfield interpretation. If the *Phenomenology* negates the forms of consciousness in a series of determinate negations, as Hegel clearly claims, then consciousness does not wipe itself out. Rather it articulates what it is in a series of moves that preserve each negated form of knowing together with a necessary connection to its opposite. The unity of opposites, therefore, does not assert and deny the same claim and collapse as an incoherent absurdity. It conceives the opposites as differences derived from the common principle that governs the opposition dynamic to which they both belong. Hegel's analysis of the retreat into a ground shows how this would work in the transition from the *Phenomenology* to the *Logic*. According to the *Logic*, the science of consciousness, like philosophy proper, retreats into a ground. It follows the determinations of consciousness back into their ground, which is pure knowledge. Thus, the phenomenological development of consciousness grounds our knowledge that pure knowledge is the true essence of consciousness. But this knowledge proves that the determinations of consciousness are derivative truths, and that pure knowledge is their principle or ground. Therefore, in order to think what the

Phenomenology has proved about consciousness, we must reverse direction. We must assert the *Phenomenology*'s result, which is pure knowledge, as the principle or beginning, and we must think the determinations of consciousness as determinations derived from this principle. This means we must think pure knowledge as a "simple immediacy," cut off from all dependence on these determinations. This "simple immediacy" is the unity that collapses the distinction between knowing and what it knows. Thinking it as a distinctionless unity, therefore, means only that the unity of subject and object is thought as the ground of their differentiation in consciousness, not that the differentiation in consciousness is not a real difference or not a real knowing.

In defence of his position, Maker challenges those who oppose his negative interpretation of the *Phenomenology*'s task to make sense of the following: "that logic begins without presuppositions while the *Phenomenology* is nonetheless the presupposition for the *Logic*, further, that the concept of science or logic cannot be in any way predetermined and that nonetheless the *Phenomenology* is the deduction of the concept of science."[3] My examination of the mediation-immediacy issue in the *Logic* and in the *Encyclopaedia* answers this challenge. A retreat into a ground begins with something known that will be exposed in the demonstration as dependent on a ground. Hence, knowledge of the ground depends on, is mediated by, the evidence provided by what depends on the ground. In order to justify the claim that logic is the ground of all truth, Hegel begins with what is immediately accessible, namely our involvement in our own consciousness, our own experience. Examining this on its own terms, following it through its own determinate negations, he proves that the reality of experience has its ground in the logical or rational. Asserting the truth of logic, therefore, depends on, is mediated by, the demonstration developed in the *Phenomenology*. This mediation identifies logic as that which grounds the reality of experience. It conceives logic in terms of what it grounds.

The demonstration proves, however, that experience has its truth not in itself but in something other than itself, namely in thought liberated from its dependence on experience. This separates logic from experience, not by dismissing experiential consciousness but by locating its truth in something other than experiential cognition itself. Hegel identifies this move as a negative mediation. It conceives logic as not-consciousness, not-experiential cognition, thought separated from experience. Since, however, both mediations prove that logic is the ground, the foundation, of the

3 Maker (1994) 72.

cognitive reality examined in the *Phenomenology*, they also prove that undistorted knowledge of the truth requires a shift into a reversed set of priorities. The ground must now be asserted as ground, as the beginning; and the cognitive reality must be reconceived as derived from and determined by the ground. Philosophy begins, therefore, with logic in its immediacy, as not dependent on its relation to anything else, because philosophy takes the logical to be the ground of everything. This presupposes, however, the legitimacy of asserting it as ground. The assertion would be completely subjective and arbitrary without a demonstration of its truth. We have seen Hegel make this point explicitly in the *Encyclopaedia*'s critique of the third position on objectivity.[4]

Finally, chapter 8 shows how the Preface to the *Phenomenology* confirms this interpretation. Scientific procedure expands a concept into a whole, which proves the necessity of conceiving the simplicity of the whole as the determining principle of all the differences that lead up to it. Thus, the Preface describes the domain of consciousness as the reality in which the spirit of truth diversifies itself and gives itself actuality. The *Phenomenology* does not take us through a long, complicated journey only to show us that the whole process is a dead end. It takes us through limited ways of knowing to show how they constitute a connected experience rooted in an integrating principle or truth.

Although Houlgate agrees with the principal claims of the Maker-Winfield interpretation, his version of it requires a separate response. Houlgate acknowledges some kind of correspondence between the form of consciousness in which the *Phenomenology* completes its project and the beginning of the *Logic*. The *Phenomenology* ends with a form of consciousness that conceives being as universal reason. This dissolves the fundamental distinction between knowing and what it knows because it conceives both the knowing and the known, both thought and being, as the same rationality. Logic begins with "the simple *unity* of thought and being – a unity that is initially no more than the indeterminate thought of sheer, immediate

4 Tom Rockmore claims that the *Logic*, by beginning without presuppositions, rests on faith in reason: "Hegel shows that if thought is to know being, we must presuppose a prior unity between thought and being. Hegel's philosophical solution to this enduring problem hence is based on the need to have faith in the ability of reason to know, although that is neither demonstrated nor demonstrable, but merely necessary" (1986, 157). If Hegel's philosophy begins as Maker-Winfield interprets it, then Rockmore's point is well taken. I am claiming that Hegel does indeed begin the *Logic* by presupposing a prior unity between thought and being. But Hegel also states repeatedly that the *Phenomenology* demonstrates the necessity and truth of this concept.

being."[5] According to Houlgate's interpretation, therefore, the *Phenomenology* ends with the unity of thought and being in the form of a consciousness conscious of its own rationality in an other; and logic begins with the unity of thought and being in the form of an indeterminate thought thinking the pure immediacy of being. Yet Houlgate agrees with Maker that "the *Phenomenology* does not serve to deduce the concept of science by in any way predetermining or grounding the method, manner or nature of scientific cognition."[6]

Houlgate's concern here seems to focus on the need to derive the determinations of thought and being from the beginning concept of philosophical science, and from no other source. The study of Hegel's introductory essays shows that this is a legitimate concern. Hegel defines scientific procedure as a demonstration that begins with a minimal concept of the subject matter and derives the full development of the subject matter from the method and necessary inferences implicit in this concept, without introducing anything extraneous. Hegel also insists, however, that the beginning concept itself must be justified by a demonstration that is prior to and presupposed by the development of this particular subject matter. Within the philosophical system, for example, the philosophy of right begins with a minimal concept of right, and derives the full development of this concept from the necessities implicit in the concept itself. The beginning concept of right, however, is a presupposition in the philosophy of right. It gets its justification from prior demonstrations developed in the preceding parts of philosophical science.[7] Hegel explains the relation between the *Phenomenology* and the *Logic* in a similar way. Logic begins with the unity of thought and being conceived with no determinate predicates. The science of logic itself demonstrates what the logical or rational is. The *Phenomenology*, however, justifies the beginning concept of the logical or rational by demonstrating that the reality of experience, which is a consciousness form of knowing, retreats into a ground (*WL* 21:54–5/M 68–9; 21:57–8/71–2). The *Phenomenology* demonstrates how consciousness as such negates itself, but only as not in itself its own truth, as having its truth in a ground that is not a consciousness form of knowing. The *Phenomenology* does not predetermine the method of philosophical science, and it does not predetermine the predicates or structures of the logical or rational. It does determine and justify conceiving the truth as the unity of thought and being. Without

5 Houlgate (2006), 162. For the whole discussion of these issues, see 144–50, 157–62.

6 Maker (1994), 72–3; Houlgate (2006), 162, note 24.

7 See chapter 3, §3.

this justification, the indeterminate thought of immediate being is just an arbitrary, subjective intuition, like Jacobi's intuition of the infinite.

3 RE: THE *PHENOMENOLOGY* AS HISTORICALLY CONDITIONED PEDAGOGY

The pedagogical approach, more than any of the others, appreciates the way the *Phenomenology* addresses the individual situated within her or his own experience. Moreover, this approach explicitly works with the cultural and historical conditions that belong to this experience. Both the *Logic* and the Preface to the *Phenomenology* support this emphasis and indicate the precise way in which Hegel is committed to it. In the *Logic*, Hegel identifies two different ways in which the "I" might provide a starting point for philosophy. He rejects the "I" that supposedly knows immediately its own identity with itself, "A = A." This "I", he says, is not immediately accessible. We are immediately accessible to ourselves only as an ego immersed in experience. At this point, Hegel explains exactly what is required in order to get to the ego separated from experience. The process begins within the immediate consciousness of the concrete ego, and it shows how the move into pure knowing emerges as a necessity of this ego. In other words, the *Phenomenology*'s examination of the concrete ego demonstrates that pure knowing, which is the beginning of logic, is the true essence of the individual situated within his or her own experience.

The Preface to the *Phenomenology* shows us another dimension of this immersion in the individual's experience. The *Phenomenology* works within the separate, isolated individuality of each person's exclusive consciousness. No matter how common the content, the consciousness of the content is mine and mine alone. The Preface insists that the *Phenomenology* must demonstrate the spirit of science at the heart of this exclusivity. By doing so, it demonstrates the spirit of the whole broken up in absolute dismemberment. Thus, both the *Logic* and the *Phenomenology* claim that the spirit with which philosophy begins exists within the stuff of experience. The task of the *Phenomenology* is to sort through the concrete, diverse panorama in which we exist, and to demonstrate the logic at work within it. Moreover, this is the reality to which philosophy must return in order to do what the *Encyclopaedia* requires of it, which is to know the rationality of pure thought existent in the concrete stuff of experience.

The concrete stuff of experience, however, includes our immersion in a culture and its history, which includes the history of philosophy. The Preface to the *Phenomenology* even introduces the project as something demanded by the spirit of Hegel's time. Hegel scholars like H.S. Harris, Terry Pinkard, and Kenneth Westphal have identified specific cultural sources in which Hegel finds the various structures of knowing examined in the *Phenomenology*.[8] John McCumber claims that the phenomenological project belongs to a historical tradition committed to self-consolidation. What role do these cultural forms play in the science of consciousness? My position on this question is determined by the demands of Hegel's scientific procedure. In Parts Two, Three, and Four, I have examined Hegel's descriptions of scientific procedure both as the procedure of philosophy itself and as the procedure of the *Phenomenology*. Both discussions clarify what is expected of the *Phenomenology*.

Scientific procedure begins with a concept that defines the minimal conditions for focusing an investigation on a particular subject matter. The beginning concept itself requires justification. This justification must prove that the subject matter must be conceived as the concept defines it, and that the concept defines a subject matter that cannot be dismissed as a meaningless notion. The science develops a full articulation of what the subject matter is by developing the necessary implications of this defining concept. Nothing extraneous is added to this demonstration. No external method is imposed on it. Everything is determined by the necessities of the beginning concept. In this way, the procedure proves that its developments and conclusion are necessitated by the subject matter itself.

The introductory essays of the *Philosophy of Right* and the *Encyclopaedia* take the subject matter of philosophy to be what is articulated in the formula, the actual is rational and the rational actual. The *Logic* describes this subject matter as "the *logos*, the reason of that which is, the truth of what we call things" (*WL* 21:17/M 39). Philosophy begins, therefore, with the concept of the logical or rational, and it exposes the full meaning of this concept by developing its necessary implications. This procedure makes philosophical thought independent of what is given in the objective reality of the natural and social worlds, in the subjective reality of "my" convictions, "my" experience, even everyone's experience. Philosophy asks whether these realities are true to their rational essence. By articulating what is necessarily involved in this essence, philosophy distinguishes the true essence of what is from the contingencies and unessential particulars that accompany it.

The *Philosophy of Right* and the *Encyclopaedia* indicate, however, that philosophical thought knows the truth by recognizing its own necessities embedded in the circumstances of real experience. The *Encyclopaedia* and

8 H.S. Harris (1997); Terry Pinkard (1994); Kenneth Westphal (1989a; 1998c; 2000a).

the Preface to the *Phenomenology* talk about parallel developments in the history of philosophy and in philosophy as pure thought thinking itself. Hegel takes this into account by situating the dialectical development of his philosophical concepts within recognizable empirical realities, including philosophical positions belonging to real history. Hence, an interpreter of Hegel's philosophical texts must be careful to distinguish between what Hegel intends as necessary determinations of reason and what belongs to the culture-specific environment in which Hegel finds these determinations actualized. The same problem faces the interpreter of the *Phenomenology*.

Philosophy gets the justification of its beginning concept from the *Phenomenology*'s examination of consciousness. This examination must prove that the rational or logical is not a meaningless notion, and that it must be defined as the *Logic*'s beginning concept conceives it. The *Science of Logic* says explicitly and repeatedly that the *Phenomenology* is an example of scientific procedure, the same procedure that develops in philosophical logic. Indeed, the *Logic* repeatedly describes the specific way scientific procedure operates in the *Phenomenology*. The *Phenomenology* justifies the beginning concept of logic, therefore, by deriving it from a scientific demonstration.[9]

If, however, the *Phenomenology* must satisfy the requirements of scientific procedure, then it must begin with a concept of its subject matter, not with principles taken from what is generally accepted in the history of a particular culture (McCumber), or with the imaginative recollection of a specific cultural experience (H.S. Harris). Moreover, the concept of the *Phenomenology*'s subject matter cannot be justified by an appeal to culture-specific evidence, since scientific procedure disallows this kind of concept justification. Finally, a phenomenological argument based on a culture-specific starting point cannot justify the beginning concept of philosophical science. The *Logic* explicitly rules out justifications of philosophy's beginning concept that appeal to what is generally accepted in the culture.

The subject matter of the *Phenomenology* is knowing in the form of consciousness, which is knowing as an appearance. The *Phenomenology* must begin, therefore, with the concept of this subject matter. The beginning concept of consciousness conceives it as consciousness of something (*etwas*) reduced to its minimal conditions in immediate sense consciousness. The *Logic* says that this immediate consciousness is immediately accessible. We know immediately, just by being conscious of something, that consciousness exists. Hence, consciousness cannot be dismissed as a meaningless notion. Moreover, consciousness disappears if the rudimentary structure

9 See chapter 7, §4.

is not there. Therefore, consciousness, knowledge as an appearance, must be conceived as this rudimentary structure defines it. The concept of consciousness is justified by the evidence of its actual appearing.

As the science of consciousness, the *Phenomenology* must develop its examination of knowledge from the necessities of its beginning concept. The way Hegel describes the logistics of this procedure does not fit the way the pedagogical approaches have interpreted phenomenological dialectic. According to Harris and McCumber, a way of thinking runs into problems, falls into contradictions, wanders into anomalies; and the problem to be solved determines and justifies the move to a new way of thinking that resolves the difficulty. This interpretation assumes that problems have to be solved, contradictions and anomalies eliminated. According to the *Logic*, however, scientific procedure introduces nothing extraneous when it moves from one way of thinking to another. A way of thinking by asserting itself connects itself to its own opposite. This necessitates the move to a new way of thinking that asserts the original way of thinking together with the necessary connection to its opposite that has emerged from it. The new way of thinking does not solve the problem by getting rid of the opposition. The new way of thinking expands the original concept to include its necessary connection to the opposite. Thinking the unity of opposites simply acknowledges that the opposites get their opposition from a dynamic to which they both belong.

The forms of knowing examined in the *Phenomenology*, however, exist in the stuff of experience and the contingencies of history, including the history of philosophy. Hegel acknowledges this by describing the forms of consciousness and their developments as they appear in the empirical-cultural situation. If, however, the *Phenomenology* follows a procedure as strict as that of philosophy itself, then it, too, must sift through the stuff of experience, expose what belongs to the conceptual necessities of its subject matter, and distinguish this from the contingencies, the unessential particulars, the culture-specific circumstances in which Hegel finds it actualized.[10] Kenneth Westphal himself says that Hegel's sources function only as exemplifications

10 By taking this position, I do not deny the value of studies like those of H.S. Harris and Terry Pinkard, which show us the richness of the cultural world in which Hegel is working out his project. Harris, Pinkard, and Kenneth Westphal have identified sources that help us recognize the experiences, the issues, the complications that appear in the various forms of consciousness examined in the *Phenomenology*. My concern, however, focuses on the strategy Hegel proposes for exposing the dialectical necessities that demonstrate the truth of the concept that identifies the subject matter of philosophical science.

of what belongs to the constitution of human consciousness as such.[11] My work on Hegel's proof procedure supports this claim.

Both John Burbidge and John McCumber, however, raise a good question when they ask whether the *Phenomenology* can continue to communicate to a reader of our time. Harris addresses this issue by saying that we resurrect and recall the experience specific to Hegel's own time. We relive it, and in this way the demonstration developed in the *Phenomenology* can carry us into the way Hegelian philosophy conceives the truth. I think we can make a stronger case for Hegel if we allow more flexibility. The *Phenomenology* is supposed to take care of what the *Encyclopaedia* calls the experience principle. Conscious beings have a right to demand that Hegel show them within the singularity and exclusivity of their own consciousness the necessity of acknowledging the truth as Hegel's philosophy conceives it. According to my interpretation, this task is driven by the discipline of Hegel's proof procedure. The *Phenomenology* retains its immediate appeal to the reader's own experience because it begins with a structure that is fundamental to any form of experience, and it articulates nothing but the necessary implications of this structure. When the *Phenomenology* moves beyond this starting point, it must meet two requirements. First and most important, it must limit the new form to the claims and attitudes justified by the preceding determinate negation. Second, it must describe and name an experience in which these claims and attitudes become recognizable. As long as the first requirement is strictly met, the project can take care of the second requirement with a certain amount of imaginative flexibility. Indeed, even when we confine ourselves to Hegel's own selections, we would do well to acknowledge in them a certain loose appropriateness.

If we take Hegel's analysis of determinate negation seriously, and interpret Hegel's transitions according to its requirements, then we must be careful not to make a case for an interpretation that depends on the associations the named experience might have in our own experience or even in the culture of Hegel's own time. The mere fact that Hegel uses certain names to indicate experiences in which the necessary structures of experience appear does not justify claiming that all the possible meanings and connotations of these names can be attributed to the experience being examined, or that the experience being examined exhausts what the name might mean if transferred to another context or framework. The name selected must have some association with the area of experience that corresponds to what the procedure requires, in order to help us locate and

11 K.R. Westphal (1998a), 84.

recognize the way this experience appears in our own knowing. But the rules of phenomenological procedure determine and limit the meaning of a name when applied to this experience.[12] This granted, I see no reason why in our time we could not find equally or even more appropriate experiences for showing how the necessary structures of experience belong to our own consciousness, as long as the selection honours the rules of Hegel's proof procedure.

The interpretive approach I am proposing also addresses one of the questions raised by Stephen Crites. Crites criticizes Harris for claiming that the moves in the *Phenomenology* must be historically as well as logically necessitated. According to Crites, there is no evidence that Hegel was committed to this strategy. In Parts Two, Three, and Four, I have demonstrated that Hegel's own account of scientific procedure insists on strict, dialectical necessity. Dialectical necessity, however, belongs to the internal meaning of a concept. Hegel says that the externality of history mirrors this development, but only because and insofar as the internal necessities have appeared in history. The meaning of the concept determines the development, not the historical circumstances in which the concept appears. Hegel says so explicitly (*PhG* 31–2/M ¶41).[13] According to my interpretation of these clues, the developments implicit in what the beginning concept means function as selection criteria. They determine what parts of history can be legitimately included in an account of the concept's development in time.

Finally, my interpretation addresses the justification issue raised by Kenneth Westphal. First, the beginning concept of the *Phenomenology* does not depend on the culture of Hegel's time. In any culture at any time knowing must appear as knowing related to a known, consciousness conscious of something. Time belongs to this concept only in the most general sense, as the condition of making an appearance, of becoming existent in the sequence of heres and nows that simply is. Thus, the *Phenomenology* begins with time as such, not with the specifics of Hegel's own time. Second, the concept that governs the demonstration developed in the *Phenomenology* identifies the structure of knowing as an appearance, knowing asserting a claim. Hence, it defines the minimal conditions for any alternative knowledge claim that might challenge Hegel's position. If the *Phenomenology* demonstrates that its results follow necessarily from these conditions, then

12 Compare to *WL* 12:130–1/M 708–9.

13 See also *Enz* §16+*A*.

it proves that its claims are implicit in any knowledge that might be asserted to challenge it.

Even so Hegel calls the beginning concept of the *Phenomenology* a presupposition. How does he justify this presupposition? He addresses the issue both as a truth question and as a problem of access. Although the *Logic* argues explicitly against beginning with the ego as absolute ground, Hegel finds the ego of experience immediately accessible. By beginning with knowledge as it immediately appears, knowledge as a phenomenon, the *Phenomenology* begins with this immediately accessible form of knowing. Thus, the beginning concept of the *Phenomenology* is not just something we think about. It defines an actual reality within which we exist. Our access to our own experience places us in real conditions, and truth belongs to these conditions as both a question and a demand. The beginning concept of the *Phenomenology*, therefore, has the legitimacy of real life; it defines experience as a lived truth project. Moreover, the *Phenomenology* begins with conscious life reduced to its minimal conditions. In the beginning, the truth project is defined only by what consciousness must be in order to appear at all. Scientific procedure requires that the development of this beginning concept maintain strict necessity and immanence. Everything must be determined by the necessities implicit in the concept itself, without any appeal to external presuppositions or premises. If these requirements are met, the real life legitimacy of the beginning concept will carry over to the concept that the *Phenomenology* produces as a result. Because the logical is the truth of "consciousness," it is the truth called for by the reality of conscious life itself.

4 THE *PHENOMENOLOGY* AS EPISTEMOLOGY

My response to the various epistemological interpretations of the *Phenomenology* focuses on the following questions: how to begin; what counts as reality; the logistics of dialectical procedure; the completeness issue. As we have seen in the Introduction to the *Phenomenology*, Hegel is suspicious of epistemological approaches that begin with knowledge as a problem. Thus, Hegel challenges the way epistemological questions are usually formulated. If epistemology begins by asking whether or with what limitations knowledge knows what exists outside and independent of knowledge, then epistemology takes for granted that knowledge and reality are separated from each other, and that this separation is more fundamental than any unity or coordination that might obtain between them. Why is it not equally legitimate to assume that knowledge and reality are the same, and to ask whether there is also some kind of otherness between them? Hegel points out that when philosophical science comes on the scene, it challenges the usual way of asking the epistemological question by simply asserting that its knowledge is immediately identified with what reality fundamentally is, and hence it makes no sense to assume some kind of otherness that might keep knowledge separated from what exists. Thus, Hegel shows his sensitivity to the way beginning with a problem can hide unjustified presuppositions. We must keep this in mind as we look again at the epistemological interpretations of Hegel's *Phenomenology*.

4a The Phenomenology as a Systematic Introduction to Philosophical Science

Hans Friedrich Fulda explicitly rejects interpretations of the *Phenomenology* that represent the phenomenological project as a propaedeutic. A propaedeutic simply initiates a thinker into philosophical ways of thinking. According to Fulda, the *Phenomenology* is supposed to prove the truth claims of philosophy to a knower whose knowledge does not endorse these claims. Fulda also insists that this proof is a necessity of philosophical science itself, because philosophy knows its truth in its other. My study of Hegel's introductory essays provides ample support for Fulda's interpretation. First, it supports Fulda's claim that philosophy must know itself in its other. The discussion of the 'rational is actual' formula in the *Philosophy of Right* and the *Encyclopaedia* shows Hegel repeatedly insisting that thought independently developed in philosophical science must know itself actualized in the reality of experience. In the introductory essays of the *Logic* and the *Phenomenology*, Hegel describes a fundamental opposition between the fundamental structure of consciousness, which is the structure of experience, and the fundamental structure of philosophical knowing. If, therefore, philosophical thought must know itself actualized in experience, it must know itself actualized in a reality whose fundamental structure is other than, indeed opposed to, the structure of philosophical thought itself. Philosophical science depends on the proof developed in the *Phenomenology*, because the phenomenological project proves that the rationality of philosophical thought is the true essence of experience, which is philosophy's other.

Second, the study of Hegel's introductory essays supports the way Fulda insists on a minimalist interpretation of the procedure according to which this proof is developed. Although Fulda acknowledges that Hegel's *Phenomenology* can serve as a resource for the debate between epistemological realism and epistemological idealism, he insists that Hegel's project in the *Phenomenology* cannot be *adequately* defined in terms of this debate. The *Phenomenology* has as its object knowledge as appearing, happening, coming on the scene. Philosophical science itself has the same status. It just makes an appearance, comes on the scene alongside other forms of knowledge that oppose and challenge it. An adequate interpretation must develop careful, precise formulations of the procedure according to which the various ways in which knowledge appears take their place in the development of the project. Each move must be completely determined by the experience that precedes it, with nothing added that is extraneous. The "we" who observe must remain strictly detached, adding nothing to the demonstration process. The approach, therefore, must have no predetermined philosophical opponents or allies. It must not dismiss from the outset epistemological realism, or epistemological idealism, or metaphysics, or the possibility that there might be a reality that transcends nature and the human world.

Hegel's introductory essays repeatedly analyze scientific procedure as just such a minimalist, open-ended procedure developed with strict necessity, with no hidden, unexamined, unjustified premises. The procedure begins with a minimal concept of the subject matter, a concept justified by a prior scientific procedure; and it demonstrates how a negation emerges from the necessary implications of this concept. This result justifies a move into a new concept that preserves the previous concept, the negation emerging from its necessities, the opposition between the concept and its opposite, and their necessary connection. The new concept adds nothing to the preceding experience except the recognition that the preceding truth negates its isolation in itself and belongs to a complex unit with its opposite. The unifying principle that defines the new concept has no content other than the integration demonstrated by the necessary implications of the preceding concept.

According to Fulda, this minimalist, strictly necessary procedure carries the observer consciousness into a knowledge of experience integrated into a whole. This knowledge passes over without alternative into philosophical knowledge in which the opposition characteristic of experience is preserved within a unity, and experience is known as this unity appearing in experience. The Preface to the *Phenomenology* describes the result produced by the phenomenological project in exactly this way: as the development of a whole, as absolute truth actualized in experience. This Preface criticizes the detached empty universality of absolute philosophy as an abstract universal separated from its actualization. The analysis of the retreat into a ground, developed in the introductory essays of the *Logic* and in the *Encyclopaedia*'s examination of the three positions on objectivity, explains the structure of this actualization and the mediations involved in proving it.

Since the study of Hegel's introductory essays supports the way Fulda defines what an adequate interpretation requires, my interpretation of the project developed in the main text of the *Phenomenology* adopts the kind of minimalist, open-ended, strictly necessary approach recommended by Fulda.

4b The Scepticism Dilemma

Kenneth Westphal defines the task of the *Phenomenology* by distinguishing between first order and second order knowledge claims. First order claims make claims about the world. Second order claims provide a principle according to which we judge the validity of first order claims. According to Westphal, Hegel attacks the knowledge question at the level of second order claims. In other words, the *Phenomenology* examines the second order principles according to which we judge the legitimacy of our first order claims about the world. This approach to Hegel's project has the advantage of concentrating on the criterion issue; and this is certainly where the primary focus should be. In order to judge, however, whether my interpretation of the criterion issue is consistent with his, I would need a fuller analysis of the term "world." It is possible that a fuller description of what the term includes might reveal that my interpretation is making the same point in a different way.

Several suggestive factors have contributed to the way I interpret the object of first order claims in Hegel's project. Hegel's starting point in the *Phenomenology* bears a remarkable similarity to Jacobi's original experience, which takes reality to be the whole relation between knowing and what it knows. For Jacobi, as we have seen in chapter 9, the reality of an external object is given with the reality of the experience that is conscious of it. So also the *Phenomenology*'s rudimentary concept of consciousness, constituted by the minimal conditions required for knowledge to appear, includes within its dynamic structure an object that is independent of its relation to knowing; and this independence functions there as the measure of truth. This is not an object outside knowledge that consciousness may or may not know. The independence of the object is a factor in its being known. It provides the "what" that consciousness is conscious of, and hence is given in the reality of an actual cognition. For Hegel's epistemology, reality is the whole dynamic knowledge structure, with the independence of the object as only one facet.

Moreover, if the rudimentary knowledge structure develops a determinate negation, then knowledge and truth will have to be conceived differently, which will change the way epistemology asks its questions. Suppose, for example, that the rudimentary form of knowledge as an appearance eventually proves that the independence of the object negates its own truth status, that its truth turns out to be not what it is in itself but what it is in its relation to the conscious self. Epistemology would then ask whether knowledge knows the independence of the object as a reality essentially related to the conscious self, which is the exact opposite of the question posed by the original rudimentary structure and by epistemology as it is usually conceived.

According to my interpretation, therefore, the epistemology of Hegel's *Phenomenology* focuses on the reality of experience and how well it measures up to its own true essence. This approach seems to be confirmed by the *Encyclopaedia* and the Preface to the *Phenomenology*, where Hegel identifies the reality issue with experience. Thought or spirit is actualized in experience. Thought or spirit knows itself in the reality of experience. Hence, Hegelian epistemology does not ask whether knowledge is true to a world separated from knowledge. It asks whether experience is true to itself. Moreover, this examination of experience begins not with a problem taken from the history of philosophy, but with the concept that defines the minimal conditions for focusing an investigation on experiential consciousness. The *Phenomenology* begins with sense certainty, which functions as the form of consciousness in which experience is restricted to the minimal conditions of its concept. As the science of consciousness, the *Phenomenology* must develop its examination of knowledge from the necessities of this beginning concept.

Westphal's analysis of phenomenological dialectic acknowledges some of the factors that I find in Hegel's account of scientific procedure. According to Westphal, applying a concept to experience calls into play factors that belong to the concept's domain but that the concept does not capture. This result calls for a new concept that acknowledges the limitations of the original concept, expands the domain to which it belongs, and thus captures the "additional information" associated with it but not captured by it. The shift to a new concept acknowledges the way the concept shows its own limitations and its association with something more that it fails to capture. The new concept expands the original concept to cover this something more.

My own interpretation adds to this an analysis of the way the "something more" belongs to a determinate negation. A form of consciousness has a fundamental orientation toward a certain kind of object, and it relates to everything it is conscious of in terms of this orientation. If, therefore, something more shows up in experience, it will be experienced in terms of the concept that has failed to capture this something more. Moreover, according to the *Logic*'s account of scientific procedure, the additional information must be a necessary and immanent development of the original concept. Determinate negation is the key to this necessity and immanence. A concept by being what it is necessarily connects itself to its opposite. The additional information appears as what the concept excludes or opposes, as "not-A" to the concept's "A," rather than as additional information, "B." Thus, the concept expands to include the whole dynamic between the concept and its opposite. In this way, the development remains immanent to and a necessary outcome of what the original concept means. A form of consciousness by being what it is, by being actually conscious of the truth as this form of consciousness conceives it, necessarily develops into a consciousness of this truth's necessary relation to its opposite. This necessitates the move to a form of consciousness that is conscious of the dynamic between the first truth and its opposite.

My interpretation of the shift to a new concept differs from Westphal's, however, because it interprets differently the role of the observer consciousness. Westphal takes the position that the philosophical observer selects the simplest set of principles for explaining adequately the successes and failures of the preceding experience. In my judgment, the Introduction to the *Phenomenology* supports Fulda's interpretation of the observer consciousness, which requires that the consciousness of the observer contribute nothing of its own. Fulda's minimalist approach restricts the observer to observation only. The study of the Introduction to the *Phenomenology* supports this minimalist interpretation of the observer's role, and hence my interpretation is committed to the same approach. According to this interpretation, the observer consciousness must follow the way the developments of the preceding experience determine the integration of the diverse elements. This preserves the strict necessity called for by Hegel's analysis of his dialectical procedure. The integration belongs to the preceding experience itself, not to the way the observer consciousness integrates its various elements.

My interpretation and Fulda's also differ from the indirect proof approach that Westphal uses. According to Westphal's approach, Hegel's project commits itself to a view it aims to challenge, and uses the principles of this view to expose the positive features and defects involved in it. This approach is appropriate for showing how Hegel can challenge other philosophical positions. For showing how Hegel proves the truth of philosophy, however, a radically minimalist approach, with its open-ended, strictly necessary procedure provides a more powerful argument, if it succeeds.

The minimalist approach also addresses the problem of completeness introduced by Westphal. Hegel must prove, he says, that the *Phenomenology*'s examination of knowledge defeats all alternative accounts of knowledge. Westphal expresses some doubt about whether Hegel can anticipate and take care of all possible alternatives. The texts of the *Logic*, however, define the project somewhat differently. According to the *Logic*, the *Phenomenology* is a science of consciousness, not an examination of knowledge in general. As a science, the project must begin with a concept that defines the minimal conditions for focusing an investigation on this subject matter, which means it begins with conditions that apply to every possible alternative account of knowledge in the form of consciousness. Moreover, if the science develops according to the strict requirements of scientific procedure, then it develops the necessary implications of its beginning concept; and these implications will belong to the basic conditions of any consciousness form of knowing. Finally, if the science of consciousness proves that the defining concept of consciousness or experience necessitates a shift from an experience form of knowing to the independence of pure thought, then it will prove that this shift is the necessary outcome of any and every form of consciousness or experience.

4c Completing Kant's Transcendental Deduction

Robert Pippin argues for a Kantian approach to the interpretation of Hegel's thought by using a strategy similar to my own. He examines a variety of texts to show the legitimacy of giving preferential status to a certain way of interpreting Hegel's project. Pippin's investigation looks at a set of texts different from the ones that I have used to support my own interpretation; and he concludes from these that Hegel's appropriation of Kant provides the most appropriate framework for interpreting Hegel's concerns, procedure, and positions. The work I have done in this book challenges Pippin's case based on the evidence provided in the introductory essays of Hegel's major works, especially the *Encyclopaedia*.

In the *Encyclopaedia*, Hegel criticizes Kant's critical philosophy because it reduces the otherness between thought and its object to the otherness between subjectivity and objectivity, and thereby absorbs the whole of experience, including the otherness of the object, into the subjectivity of thought. Objectivity is reduced to a relation, the object "for" consciousness. Hegel misses in this the true otherness of a thing-in-itself, which Hegel defines thus: "The *thing-in-itself*… expresses the ob-ject, inasmuch as *abstraction* is made of all that is for consciousness, of all determinations of feeling, as well as of all determinate thoughts about it" (*Enz* §44*A*). Pippin's interpretation of Hegel conceives objectivity as an object constituted by the spontaneity of thought, an object conceived as all that being could *intelligibly* be. This notion of objectivity also remains confined within a subjectivity-objectivity formulation. According to Pippin's interpretation, the object counts as a thing-in-itself because the way thought constitutes it is all that being *as an object of human thought* could be. Hegel is demanding more than this. He expects objectivity to be what being is on its own, set off from its relation to consciousness, set off from what it is only "for" consciousness, even if consciousness has the form of thought.

This notion of objectivity explains why Hegel sides with pre-critical metaphysics against Kant on the thing-in-itself issue. "[Pre-critical metaphysics] regarded the thought-determinations as the *fundamental determinations of things*; and, in virtue of this presupposition, that the cognition of things as they are *in themselves* results from the *thinking* of what *is*, it stood at a higher level than the later critical philosophising" (*Enz* §28). According to Hegel, pre-critical metaphysics assumed that thought could go directly to things and could know things in themselves by knowing the determinations of thought as the fundamental truth of things. We must interpret Hegel's endorsement of this assumption according to Hegel's explicit definition of thing-in-itself, since both the endorsement and the definition belong to the same context, which is the *Encyclopaedia*'s examination of the three positions on objectivity. If thing-in-itself means what a thing is on its own, independent of all relations to knowledge, then the presupposition of pre-critical metaphysics, as Hegel interprets it, claims that intelligibility belongs to things because of what they are in their own independent constitution, not because human thinking gives them an intelligible constitution; and he considers this presupposition to stand "at a higher level than the later critical philosophising." In other words, Hegel endorses the traditional claim that to be is to be intelligible.

Kenneth Westphal makes this same point. He criticizes Pippin for not considering the possibility that the necessary conditions of being an object might belong to the world. Pippin does consider this possibility, however, when he discusses Hegel's project in the *Phenomenology*. According to Pippin, the first part of the *Phenomenology* demonstrates that when a form of knowing assumes that the determinations of objects belong to what the object independently is, knowing gets tangled up in inversions, paradoxes, and contradictions. Pippin interprets this to mean that the object thus conceived cannot satisfy what thought needs in order to have an object that makes sense, an object that is thinkable. Inversions, paradoxes, and contradictions demonstrate that this way of conceiving an object is what an object intelligible to thought cannot be.

Hegel's discussion of Kant's antinomies, in the *Encyclopaedia* and in the *Logic*, challenges this interpretation. Hegel praises Kant for recognizing that reason inevitably develops contradictions. He criticizes Kant for failing to recognize that antinomies are not mistakes that reason makes; they are the fundamental structure of all objects, concepts, and representations. If contradiction is fundamental to all concepts as well as to all objects, then contradiction belongs to the fundamental intelligibility of being. According to Hegel, contradictions expose the untruth of cognition not because contradiction is unintelligible, but because contradiction exposes the fundamental opposition dynamic at the heart of what the object is. As we have seen, Hegel's analysis of determinate negation, in a variety of texts and contexts, makes this point again and again.

My interpretation of Hegel's proof procedure also challenges the way Pippin interprets the analysis of the consciousness structure in the Introduction to the *Phenomenology*: "Consciousness simultaneously *distinguishes* itself from something, and at the same time *relates* itself to it" (*PhG* 58–9/M ¶82). According to Pippin's Kantian interpretation, this refers to consciousness as an act of judging that has its own norms distinguished from the object judged according to these norms. Interpreting the text this way deprives the *Phenomenology* of a starting point that fits the demands of Hegelian scientific procedure; and it misconceives the status of the truth criteria according to which the *Phenomenology* tests the various forms of consciousness examined. Hegelian scientific procedure begins with a concept of the subject matter to be investigated, a conception limited to the minimal conditions required for the investigation to be focused on this subject matter; and it requires proof that this is the right way to conceive it and that the conception is not an empty notion. A minimal interpretation of the consciousness structure fits the text and provides a minimal definition of consciousness, the subject matter to be investigated in the *Phenomenology*. According to this interpretation, the *Phenomenology* does not have to assume anything more than consciousness conscious of some content (*etwas*). This seems to be an obvious requirement for any kind of knowing to actually happen; and as something that actually appears it cannot be dismissed as an empty notion. Finally, the Introduction to the *Phenomenology* refers to the consciousness structure as a concept: "Consciousness, however, is for itself the concept of itself" (*PhG* 57/M ¶80, translation mine). Thus, the minimal interpretation of the consciousness structure provides a beginning concept for the *Phenomenology* that reduces what is presupposed to a minimum, and a minimum with significant credibility. Everything else the *Phenomenology* must prove.

If, however, I insist on this kind of minimalism in the starting point, I must also acknowledge that the *Phenomenology* cannot rule out from the beginning the possible legitimacy of Pippin's interpretation. Pippin does not claim that the Introduction's analysis of the consciousness structure defines the structure of consciousness with which the investigation begins. He describes the beginning in sense certainty in a way that fits my minimal interpretation of the consciousness structure described in the Introduction, which I claim is also the structure of sense certainty. The case for or against Pippin's interpretation depends, therefore, on the way the demonstration in the *Phenomenology* is developed. I will address this question in Part Six, chapter 12.

The *Encyclopaedia*, however, provides some clues to what Hegel means when he says that philosophical science begins by conceiving the truth as the unity of thought and being, a concept justified by the science of consciousness developed in the *Phenomenology*. The *Encyclopaedia*'s discussion of the three positions on objectivity repeatedly criticizes Kant for reducing truth to the conditions of *our* understanding, *our* practical reason, the limitations of *our* reason. Hegel repeatedly insists against this that truth transcends the limits of our knowing. He articulates this objection using religious ways of speaking. But Houlgate's way of articulating it works just as well. Our thinking becomes identified with the truth if and only if it becomes integrated into the fundamental truth of being, which is not reducible to the limited capabilities of human knowing left to its own devices. We know the truth by knowing the *logos*, the logicality or rationality, in which both our thought and the independent reality of objects have their common ground.

McDowell suggests an interpretation of Hegelian philosophy that seems to conceive the rational as a ground common to the independence of thought and the independence of the object. He points out that knowledge cannot qualify as absolute truth unless it includes within it an explanation of space-time ordering and empirical content. Consequently, he conceives the rational as an equipoise between the concepts of pure thought and the space-time ordering and empirical content of independent objectivity. This, he suggests, would integrate empirical concepts and the contingencies of experience into the rational. The introductory essays of the *Encyclopaedia* provide evidence that could support some aspects of McDowell's suggestion. According to the Introduction, empirical science exposes necessities that appear in the dynamics of experience, and this calls philosophical thought back to the task of thinking the rational actualized in the reality of experience. The examination of the Kantian position on objectivity endorses Kant's notion of inner purposiveness as a way of deriving the particulars of experience from the practical operations of rational thought, so that these contingencies belong to the rational without being derived deductively from the necessities of the rational. This supports McDowell's suggestion that the world has its own given content and space-time ordering which empirical science makes known, and which rational agents must take into account in their free self-determined actions.

McDowell does not address, however, one of the questions raised by the role of empirical content in the rationality of the object. In the discussion of the traditional position on objectivity, Hegel mentions that traditional philosophy fails to recognize that within the correspondence between thought and object there is also an opposition between thought and object. We must ask, therefore, how this opposition belongs to the correspondence between thought and its object.

4d Testing the Presuppositions of Everyday Life

Joseph Flay addresses the criterion issue by distinguishing the unreflective experience of everyday life from the way philosophy thematizes this experience in presupposition sets. According to his interpretation, philosophy tests its thematizing against the reality of everyday life experience. If the presupposition set provokes contradictions and anomalies, this shows that the presuppositions must be rejected. A presupposition set that makes the experience of everyday life intelligible gives thought access to reality and thereby demonstrates its truth.

My interpretation agrees with Flay's about how to identify the reality concerns in Hegel's knowledge questions. These questions ask about the reality of experience, not about the reality of a world outside experience. Some forms of experience expect the truth to be an object independent of its relations to cognition. But this way of defining the truth belongs to a particular form of experience, and the independence of the object exists within the experience as a given content that cannot be derived from the consciousness-of side of the experience. My interpretation differs from Flay's, however, in the way it interprets the status and function of the truth criteria tested in the *Phenomenology*'s examination of knowledge. As I read the Introduction to the *Phenomenology*, the truth criteria belong to the basic structure of experience itself. They are not reflections on or interpretations of what is going on in experience. They are expectations operating in the way consciousness experiences the object. Sense certainty senses the object as a given content that provides something to be conscious of. Perception senses the panorama of data as separate things. Experience tests itself. It does not test some philosophical thematizing that reflects on and interprets experience. If the test exposes an untruth, the untruth belongs to experience itself, not to the way philosophy thematizes it.

My interpretation of Hegel's procedure in the *Phenomenology* also challenges Flay's interpretation. According to Flay, a way of thinking runs into problems, falls into contradictions, wanders into anomalies; and the problem to be solved determines and justifies the move to a new way of thinking that resolves the difficulty. Thus, Flay assumes that problems must be solved, contradictions and anomalies eliminated. According to the *Logic*'s account of scientific procedure, however, a concept develops a necessary connection to its own opposite, and the new concept redefines the original concept by expanding it to include this necessary connection. The problems that arise by determinate negation are not resolved; they are endorsed.

Finally, Flay's interpretation of the *Phenomenology* assumes that the absolute, at least as a problem, is with us from the start. From the beginning, the demand for absolute intelligibility, the ultimate meaning of all reality, functions as a demand or criterion according to which the forms of consciousness are judged. According to my reading, Hegel's text does not support this. The Preface and the Introduction to the *Phenomenology* both talk about an encounter between natural consciousness and absolute philosophy, also called science. But this discussion makes limited claims. The appearance of science makes it possible for us to distinguish ourselves from our involvement in the presuppositions of natural consciousness because it shows that these presuppositions can be questioned. But this does not allow us to question natural consciousness by demanding absoluteness of it. It does not allow us to question natural consciousness at all. It only makes possible the standpoint of a detached observer, so that we can observe natural consciousness questioning itself. Moreover, the opposition between natural consciousness and science shows that absolute philosophy itself can be questioned, which means that its assumption about what knowledge essentially is cannot be presupposed. Thus, Hegel says:

> For an examination consists in applying an accepted standard, and in determining whether something is right or wrong on the basis of the resulting agreement or disagreement of the thing examined; thus the standard as such (and Science likewise

> if it were the criterion) is accepted as the *essence* or as the *in-itself*. But here, where Science has just begun to come on the scene, neither Science nor anything else has yet justified itself as the essence or the in-itself; and without something of the sort it seems that no examination can take place. (*PhG* 57–8/M ¶81)

PART SIX

THE PROOF OF REASON

AT THIS POINT, we have completed the first part of the project developed in this book. This first part examines the way Hegel himself, in the introductory essays of his major works, interprets the aim of the *Phenomenology*, the method required for accomplishing it, the results produced, and their significance for Hegel's philosophical project. We turn now to an examination of the way Hegel actually carries out the task of the *Phenomenology*. This examination adopts a strategy governed by the demands of Hegel's dialectical proof procedure. If a text tolerates different, incompatible interpretations, my strategy accepts those that remain faithful to Hegel's scientific procedure. This preference is justified by the preceding study of the introductory essays, which reviews the evidence supporting my interpretation of Hegel's scientific procedure and its applicability to the *Phenomenology*.

Part Six begins the study of the *Phenomenology*'s main text with an examination of the proof developed in the "Consciousness" and "Self-consciousness" sections of the *Phenomenology*. In these sections, Hegel proves that reason is the fundamental truth of both the independent objectivity of the world and the independent subjectivity of thought. In the process, he justifies the beginning concept of the rational.

12

Consciousness and the Transition to Self-consciousness

THIS CHAPTER FOCUSES on the way the transition from consciousness to self-consciousness determines the necessary connection between consciousness focused on the independent content of an object and consciousness that knows itself as the truth of the object. Because this part of Hegel's phenomenological project has received a lot of attention, and because it has been used to ground the Kantian interpretation of this project, my explanation of its various moves must work with the details of Hegel's text. In order to keep the discussion clear and manageable, I will interpret the dialectical moves of the "Consciousness" section without engaging the details of the interpretations I am challenging. In this part of the discussion, I will only address explicitly the general problems that my interpretation is trying to avoid. At the end of the chapter, I will discuss more carefully some of the interpretations that represent the move into self-consciousness as a shift into a Kant-type unity of apperception.

1 THE BEGINNING FRAMEWORK

Hegel begins the examination of consciousness with a form of knowing that he calls sense certainty. The account of sense certainty begins with an analysis of its structure and the presuppositions implicit in it. In this analysis, Hegel uses the first person plural, "our" and "we," in two ways: what we must assume in order to stand within the sense certainty experience, and what we know as a detached observer. As a consciousness situated within sense certainty, we must be completely receptive. Consciousness in sense certainty depends on no mediations, no representations derived from other experiences or thoughts derived from thinking about experience.

Sense certainty simply lets the object be whatever it is and present itself as such, without altering anything. This total passivity isolates consciousness within a singular experience. Nothing that connects the experience to some other consciousness has a role to play in sense certainty. Thus, sense certainty reduces consciousness to the mediation involved in its relation to the object. Consciousness has no other determination than to be conscious of. It has no character or function of its own. It does not interpret, compare, select, or organize what it is conscious of. It passively receives the way the object affects it. Hence, its knowing is completely dependent on the object's being whatever it is.

The object, too, is unmediated. The object stands before sense certainty simply being whatever it is. No mediating relations within it or between it and other things complicate the object's relation to consciousness. The object is simply this something standing before this consciousness. Because, however, sense certainty has no other determination than its being receptive to the object, sense certainty takes the object to be the essential element in knowing. Knowing occurs when consciousness apprehends, takes in, what the object is. Moreover, if consciousness in sense certainty is completely receptive, altering nothing, then what it receives cannot depend on consciousness itself. Hence, sense certainty takes the object to be independent of knowing. The object is what it is whether or not it is known (*PhG* 63/M ¶90–1; 63–4/M ¶93).

Hegel's description of sense certainty corresponds in every way to the abstract determinations of consciousness described in the Introduction. As a completely receptive consciousness, sense certainty reduces consciousness to a pure relation, a pure consciousness-of. The object that completes the relation, what consciousness is conscious of, does not depend on its being "for" consciousness. The object just is whatever it is, independent of its being known. Moreover, sense certainty and the abstract determinations of consciousness define the truth in the same way. Truth is whatever the object is in itself, on its own, independent of its relation to consciousness. Finally, the account of sense certainty, like the analysis of abstract consciousness, sets aside as of no concern whatever else might be associated with consciousness in this its minimal first form (*PhG* 58–9/M ¶82; 63/M ¶90). Thus, beginning with sense certainty is not just a plausible way to begin. It is the structure that reduces to its minimal conditions what is required for any kind of knowing to appear, which provides the minimal definition of the subject matter to be investigated in the *Phenomenology* and also establishes the reality status of the subject matter as a real experience that cannot be dismissed as an empty notion.

As we have seen in the chapter on the Introduction to the *Phenomenology*, the observer consciousness that follows and articulates the implicit inferences exposed in the *Phenomenology* contributes nothing of its own. It remains detached, uncommitted, to any of the truth criteria that operate in the forms of consciousness examined. It simply observes the dynamics that belong to the experience observed, articulates the negative implications embedded in its presuppositions, and keeps track of the necessities that justify shifting from one form of experience to another. If the observer knows more than the form of consciousness being examined, this can only be because the observer knows the way negations implicit in the preceding forms of consciousness have justified its presuppositions. If the procedure remains true to the way Hegel has proposed it, then the observer must not add any criteria or interpretive baggage to the proof developed in the examination (*PhG* 59–60/M ¶84–5; 60–1/M ¶87).

Yet even here, at the very beginning, Hegel says that we – the observers – know the structure of sense certainty in a way that is not the same as sense certainty's own experience of its knowing. If the observer's consciousness begins with no other determinations than its relation to the knowing it observes, how can the observer know something about this knowing that the consciousness involved in the knowing does not know? In order to answer this question, we must distinguish our object as a consciousness situated within sense certainty's experience from our object as a detached observer of this experience. Situated within sense certainty, our consciousness focuses on what it is conscious of as this something immediately presents itself. Standing back in the position of a detached observer, we focus on the whole relation between knower and known as this relation immediately presents itself. As a detached observer, therefore, we know that consciousness is mediated by its relation to the object, and also that the object is mediated by its relation to consciousness. We know this because our object is the reality of experience. The object belongs to this reality as something known, and hence its existence presents itself to us as something related to knowing. Thus, Hegel says that the object is in sense certainty through something else, i.e. through consciousness. This does not mean that we, the observers, have already dismissed the object's status as something independent of knowing. It means only that whatever the status of the object turns out to be, it presents itself to our observation only as a factor in experience and hence as involved in a relation to consciousness. If the object is independent of its relation to knowing, that independence exists for us within the reality of experience; and for us that independence cannot be the only essential element, since we are asking about what experience is, not just about what the object of experience is. Moreover, as a detached observer, we know that consciousness determines experience by being oriented toward a certain kind of truth. It colors its own experience by being conscious of the object according to a certain truth expectation. Sense certainty determines its experience of the object by assuming that the object is what it is independent of its relation to knowing. Hegel says explicitly that the observer will examine sense certainty according to the way sense certainty defines itself, not according to the way we in the observer's position define it (*PhG* 63–4/M ¶92–3).

2 SENSE CERTAINTY: DIALECTICAL DEVELOPMENT

Hegel begins the examination of sense certainty by translating the object "simply being" into here and now (*PhG* 64–5/M ¶95).[1] We must not jump to the conclusion, however, that this introduces into the analysis notions of space and time. To begin with, sense certainty has no other determination than to be consciousness conscious of something immediately presented to it. Hegel's use of the terms "here" and "now" remains faithful to this limited determination if we interpret it as the experience of the object as just being there before consciousness.

First Move. In the first move, Hegel asks sense certainty "What is this." What does sense certainty experience in its consciousness of what is presented to it here and now? Suppose it answers "Now is night," and "Here is tree" (*PhG* 64–5/M ¶95; 65–6/M ¶98). Right away we must tread carefully. Night and tree refer to complicated things, characterized by a whole cluster of characteristics. Calling them night and tree also involves using words that apply not only to this one experience of night and tree but also to other experiences of night and tree. If Hegel begins the *Phenomenology* with consciousness reduced to its minimal conditions, how can he allow sense certainty to talk about anything as complicated as night and tree and to use general terms for a singular experience? Hegel's procedure requires that we observe a form of consciousness testing itself in a real experience. The test must allow consciousness to take in whatever content shows up. But consciousness takes it in according to the demands of the truth criterion that gives consciousness its fundamental orientation. Sense certainty expects the truth to be something that simply is whatever it is. Sense-certainty tries to know this truth by letting the object present to consciousness whatever it is, without manipulating it in any way. Night and tree in a

1 See also *PhG* 63/M ¶90–1.

sense-certainty experience, therefore, refer to contents that just show up here and now before consciousness. As long as Hegel's account of sense certainty treats them as such, as long as it does not assume that such things are complex units or instances of a general definition, Hegel's procedure remains uncompromised.

Hegel suggests that we test the truth of the experience by writing it down. Then he adds: "a truth cannot lose anything by being written down, any more than it can lose anything through our preserving it" (*PhG* 64–5/ M ¶95). Writing down what the here and now is, therefore, functions only as an attempt to preserve the experience; and the problems that emerge as a result of the writing-down have to do with preserving the experience. Nothing in Hegel's account of this move authorizes us to project onto sense certainty anything else we might associate with the use of language. Sense certainty uses language as a way of preserving an experience. Hence, our questions about the use of language here must be limited to this role. If sense certainty tests itself according to its own truth expectations, then preserving the experience must somehow be implicit in these truth expectations. How so?

Sense certainty expects the truth to be something that simply is whatever it is, a singular something not determined by its relations to anything else. Sense certainty knows this truth by remaining passive, letting the object present itself without altering it in any way. In order to test this knowing, sense certainty must ask whether what presents itself here and now to consciousness is simply itself being what it is, with no negatives, relations, or changes into something else. If it does, then the here and now presented immediately to consciousness should persist as just what it is. Preserving it by writing it down should not affect it.

But it does. For the consciousness preserved in writing, now is night and here is tree. For the consciousness presently going on, now is day and here is house. Moreover, the first experience written down persists while a different experience is happening. This brings to consciousness a negative dimension in sense certainty. The experience currently going on experiences the content of its here and now as not the content of the here and now preserved in writing. The present consciousness experiences day as not night and house as not tree. Thus, what presents itself here and now does not present itself as simply being whatever it is. It presents itself as "a simplicity (*Einfaches*) such that it is neither This nor That, a *not-This*, and is with equal indifference This as well as That" (*PhG* 64–5/M ¶96). What presents itself here and now to consciousness persists only by being and not being what each of its different heres and nows are. Hegel calls this a universal.

Again, we must not jump to conclusions. The use of the word "universal," even when it defines a universal as being indifferently any of its various instances, does not prove that Hegel is talking about universal concepts here. Hegel is not talking about thought at all. He describes rather a universality in the way the object of consciousness is sensed. Different contents present themselves immediately to consciousness. Throughout this presentation, the object simply being, being there before consciousness, persists. It persists, however, not as this singular something, but as a mediated simplicity, a series of different contents strung together as a continuing here and now. If, therefore, the object is left to itself, to be whatever it is on its own, then it shows itself in a way that negates its claim to be what sense certainty expects the truth to be. Left to itself, the object keeps negating what it is by becoming something else. In order to know the object simply being what it is, consciousness must hold on to one here and now by itself. Now is day being day and here is tree being tree because day and tree are what I mean.

Hegel says that this reverses the priorities in the relation between knower and known. At first, sense certainty lets the object define the whole knowledge relation. Knowing is consciousness carried away by what the object is. With the development of the continuing here and now, however, sense certainty shifts into a posture that gives consciousness the essential position. Knowing is the object meant, the content held by its relation to consciousness. This complicates the sense certainty experience, but does not negate its fundamental orientation. Consciousness still expects the truth to be a content that simply is what it is – day being day, tree being tree, blue being blue. Consciousness is still conscious of something with a content of its own not derived from its relation to consciousness. But in order to become conscious of this something simply being what it is, consciousness cannot depend on the object left to its own devices. Hence, sense certainty shifts away from the object's independence and focuses on what consciousness is conscious of or means. Thus, the full complexity of the consciousness-of structure becomes explicit. Sense certainty's experience of its own knowing is conscious of the object's double status, an independent content simply being whatever it is (the object in itself) and this same content related to consciousness as what consciousness means (the object for consciousness) (*PhG* 65–6/M ¶99–101).

Second Move. What consciousness means, however, develops the same kind of instability as the object. The "I" for whom now is day and here is tree vanishes in another "I" for whom now is night, not day, and here is house, not tree (*PhG* 65–6/M ¶101; 67/M ¶104).[2] "What does not disappear in all this is the "I" as *universal*, whose seeing is neither a seeing of the tree nor of this house, but is a simple seeing which, though mediated by the negation of this house, etc., is all the same simple and indifferent to whatever happens in it, to the house, the tree, etc." (*PhG* 66–7/M ¶102). Consciousness seeing tree is conscious of this seeing as not seeing house. Each seeing is mediated by the negation of the others. This is what establishes the universality of the "I." The "I" persists, does not disappear, because the seeing not now going on persists as a consciousness negated by what consciousness now sees. Consciousness sees house and in the experience knows this seeing as not the seeing of tree that the "I" once was. Thus, the "I" develops into a simplicity identified with different sensings focused on different sensed contents.[3] What consciousness means, like what the here and now is, negates its own claim to be what sense certainty expects the truth to be.

Again, however, the negation complicates sense certainty without negating its fundamental orientation toward a singular something simply being what it is. This kind of object still belongs to the experience. But in order to know it as the truth that sense certainty takes it to be, consciousness must separate the singular from its involvement in the continuity of what consciousness means, just as it had to separate this something from its involvement in the continuity of what the here and now is. What consciousness means must be caught and held by its relation to this object, and the object must be caught and held by its relation to this consciousness. Sense certainty shifts to a posture that takes knowledge to be consciousness and its object isolated in a single intuition (*PhG* 66–7/M ¶103–5).

2 Hegel refers to this other "I" both as "another 'I'" and as "myself at another time." Hegel seems to use these as alternative ways of saying the same thing. It makes sense in this context to talk about myself at another time as "another consciousness," because consciousness here has no other determination than what it is conscious of. Being conscious of night is not the same consciousness as being conscious of day (Kant talks in the same way about this kind of consciousness [*KrV* B 134]). But it makes no sense at all in this context to interpret "another consciousness" as someone else's consciousness. Sense certainty is a consciousness situated within immediate experience. I cannot experience someone else's experience. The other consciousness could report the experience to me. But this would get us involved in inter-subjective communication, and nothing in the rudimentary structure of sense certainty justifies a leap into inter-subjective communication. Moreover, even inter-subjective communication would not make it possible for one consciousness to actually experience what the other consciousness experiences, such that each sensing would be the same consciousness taking on different contents. Yet this is exactly the way Hegel describes the instability of consciousness here.

3 Compare to Locke, *Essay*, book II, chapter 27, especially §13–14.

Third Move. In his description of sense-certainty's first two moves, Hegel describes the here as something with a definite content, tree or house. Even his description of the now suggests the experience of what day looks like as distinguished from what night looks like. The account of the third move, however, seems to focus on the experience of being here and being now. Yet Hegel begins the third move by introducing the consciousness to be examined as a pure intuiting of day and tree; and he returns to tree and house in the chapter's concluding remarks (*PhG* 67/M ¶104–5; 69–70/M ¶109). I shall begin the explanation of the third move, therefore, by summarizing the analysis of its here-now dynamics. I shall then review the here-now dynamics by including the concrete content of the experience.

Consciousness becomes engaged in an isolated consciousness-of pointing to, focused on, this now. But in the process of pointing it out, consciousness becomes focused on what has been. Hence, consciousness rejects as untrue its pointing out the now as what is and intuits it rather as what has been. This, however, points out what is not, and sense certainty expects the truth to be what is. Hence, consciousness rejects as untrue its pointing out what has been and intuits the now as what is. Hegel restates this dynamic in terms of a this and its other. Consciousness asserts as truth a this, sets aside this truth in favour of an other, then sets aside the other and returns to the first. Hegel clarifies this with examples. A day contains many hours within the same day. An hour contains many minutes within the same hour. A simple now is not a "this something" simply being what it is, but a plurality of nows taken together as the same now, "something that is reflected into itself, or a simple entity which, in its otherness, remains what it is: a Now which is an absolute plurality of Nows" (*PhG* 67–8/M ¶106–7). "Reflected into itself" refers to the way the simple now, a day or an hour, is a plurality of nows belonging to each other. Hegel calls this a universal, not the universality of a generality identified indifferently with each and all instances, but the universality of a connected whole composed of different elements.

The dynamic of the here develops in the same way (*ebenso*), Hegel says. Consciousness points out this here. But pointing it out involves becoming conscious of different heres: above-below, right-left, before-behind. Moreover, each of these in turn involves an above-below, right-left, before-behind. Each here vanishes in the others. "What is pointed out, held fast, and abides, is a negative This, which is negative only when the Heres are taken as they should be, but, in being so taken, they supersede themselves; what abides is a simple complex of many Heres ... the pointing out shows itself to be not an immediate knowing, but a movement from the Here that is meant through many Heres into the universal Here which is a simple plurality of Heres, just as the day is a simple plurality of Nows" (*PhG* 68–9/M ¶108).

Let us look now at the confusions in this account. In his description of sense certainty's first two moves, Hegel describes the here as something with a definite content, tree or house. This way of describing the experience focuses on the separateness of the different heres and nows, on tree as not house and night as not day. The abstract analysis of the third move, however, seems to reduce the whole sense continuum to an uninterrupted series of spatio-temporal points. The now shows itself in experience as passing but remaining the same, a passage of time. The here shows itself as a set of position-points spread out but not separated. If, however, we review the dynamics of the third move by including the concrete content of the experience, the result seems to be more consistent with the first two moves as well as with sense certainty's truth criterion.

Sense certainty looks for the truth as a singular something being what it is. In order to grasp this truth, consciousness must become conscious of an isolated time unit like day or an isolated space unit like tree or house. The third move begins with this kind of consciousness. In the process, however, consciousness becomes conscious of the very singularity of the object as internally universal, related, mediated. The object must hold together different heres and nows so that the object can isolate itself from other heres and nows that are not this singularity. The hours of a day must turn in on themselves, belong to each other, in order to be day isolated in itself and separated from night. A set of position-points must turn in on themselves, belong to each other, in order to be this spread out something, e.g. tree, isolated from other sets of position-points that are a different spread out something, e.g. house. If we interpret it this way, the dynamic of sense certainty remains faithful to the demands of sense certainty's truth criterion. The dialectic isolates the object without depending on anything outside the object itself. The mediation that isolates it in itself belongs to the internal constitution of the object. Thus, sense certainty realizes itself. It succeeds as a singular experience of a singular something simply being what it is. But in realizing itself, sense-certainty resolves itself. The singularity of the experience dissolves in a consciousness that moves through a multiplicity of times and position-points held together as the same something, and this develops so that consciousness can separate the object from other somethings in the same here and now field. Thus, the thisness that isolates the object in what it is turns out to be not singular but universal, a simplicity or sameness common to and constituted by many. This universality does not dismiss or prove wrong the singularity of the sense certainty experience. Rather universality as the sameness of different times and position-points turns the object in on itself and thus establishes its being singular, i.e. its being only itself. This mediation adds another dimension to the truth of sense certainty. Consciousness of a singular something just being itself involves consciousness of what it is separating itself from what it is not.

What, then, is the role of sense content in sense certainty's here and now display? The sense content is what holds the different times and positions together in sense certainty's experience. Consciousness senses the light of day holding together a multiplicity of hours, which isolates day in itself and separates it from the dark of night. Sense certainty senses the colours and textures and shape of the tree holding together different position-points, which isolates the tree in itself and separates it from other position-points held together by the colours, textures, and shape of the house. The content of this day turns the hours of the day in on themselves, so that they belong to each other and are not dissolved in the endless continuity of times; the content of this tree covers different position-points turned in on themselves, so that they belong to each other and are not dissolved in the endless continuity of positions.[4]

4 In his account of sense certainty, Hegel repeatedly calls attention to the way language transforms the differentiated data of experience into a generality that does not distinguish one thing from another. We use words like "this," "singular," "individual" to mean the immediately sensed something with all the particulars that are unique to it. But the words say only what can be said of any and all sensed somethings. They do not say what ties the experience down to a something that nothing else is. Sense certainty insists on the sensed particulars, not the empty generalities. But Hegel says that language is truer, because it says what the real truth of sense certainty is (*PhG* 64–5/M ¶97; 69–70/M ¶110). If, however, these comments are taken too literally, then they indicate a departure from the rigors of Hegel's phenomenological procedure. The dialectic of sense certainty does not prove that the true essence of the sensed singular is its being the same as every other sensed singular. Hegel says explicitly that sense certainty turns away from this indifferent universal to concentrate on what isolates each here and now in itself. Sense certainty finally negates itself by showing that the object stands fast in itself, resists being lost in the continuity, because of its internal mediation and universality. Sense certainty's final conclusion, therefore, does not set aside as untrue the orientation to sensed particulars identifying a something differentiated from other somethings. Rather it reveals the internal, self-isolating structure operating in these particulars (*PhG* 65–6/M ¶99; 70/M ¶110). Hegel restates this result at the end of the chapter and explicitly distinguishes it from the way language functions in sense certainty, "But if I want to help out language ... by pointing out this bit of paper, experience teaches me what the truth of sense certainty in fact is: I point it out as a 'Here,' which is a Here of other Heres, or is in its own self a 'simple togetherness of many Heres'; i.e. it is a universal" (*PhG* 70/M ¶110).

3 PERCEPTION AND THE SELF-IDENTITY CONTRADICTION

Perception takes as its truth criterion the results of sense certainty's experience. Like sense certainty, perception expects the object to be something with a content of its own that provides consciousness with something to be conscious of. The object is what it is whether or not consciousness knows it. In order to know the truth, therefore, perception simply apprehends, allowing the object to be what it is without any alteration. Unlike sense certainty, however, perception expects the object to be a plurality of heres and nows held together as a self-identical thing. Moreover, because the self-identity has a plurality within it, perception acknowledges the possibility that consciousness can get caught in the diversity and lose the selfsameness (*PhG* 71/M ¶111; 73–4/M ¶116).

When perception tests its expectations in experience, the experience exposes a complicated opposition dynamic involved in the self-identity of a thing. Perception senses the singular as an identifying content, e.g. white, spreading out over different position-points and persisting through a passage of time. But the content belongs to a context that extends beyond the singular; white belongs to a field of colors. When, however, perception shifts to a consciousness of the larger context, it finds that the sense content exists in the larger context as a particular content set off from others, e.g. white set off from black, green, blue, and other colours as well as from other whites in other heres and nows. Perception comes back to the original content as a singular that excludes. In the separated singular, perception experiences a plurality of contents identifying the same thing. As a result, perception perceives the disintegration of the thing into its component elements, each element identified with its own character alone, unrelated to what the other contents are. Consciousness becomes conscious of white, and tart, and cubical. This result returns consciousness to sense certainty in the form of what consciousness means. Consciousness is conscious of a stream, a continuity, of different content elements referred to or meant. As we have seen in the examination of sense certainty, however, consciousness in this form cannot focus on what the object is unless it becomes conscious of the object stabilized by holding together different heres and nows in the same here and now (*PhG* 74-5/M ¶117).

Perception, therefore, returns to its original starting point now conscious of the object's relation to consciousness in a disintegrated collection of sense contents. Since perception expects the truth to be a self-identical thing, it discounts the experience of non-identical, unrelated sense contents. This disintegration manifests the way the object appears to consciousness. The object itself is a simple, selfsame thing set off from other things. Without properties, however, the object would be indistinguishable from everything else in the continuity of sense contents. Being a one that excludes identifies indiscriminately all the heres and nows in the continuum. Perception, therefore, cannot become conscious of what the object itself is in itself unless it takes the plurality of properties as the identifying content of the object itself.

Moreover, the object cannot have a self-identity of its own unless it has a plurality of properties. One property alone identifies the thing not as something in itself, but as an element in the whole panorama of sense data. As such the thing would be dissolved in contrast relations to other elements, and would belong to the endless continuity of heres and nows slipping away into other heres and nows, like a piece in a cosmic abstract painting. In order to appreciate Hegel's point here, consider two paintings, a Mondrian and a Klee, hanging next to each other in a museum. Each painting contains within itself mutually exclusive colors and shapes. Yet the reds and yellows of the Mondrian identify the same self-identity, the same thing. So also if the objects of perception were identified by only one content element, they would be absorbed into a set of contrast relations constituting the whole field of perceptual data, which would not account for our experience of one thing not being another thing, a tree not being house, the Mondrian not being the Klee hanging next to it. In order to perceive the self-identity of one thing as not the self-identity of another, each self-identity must be identified by a cluster of content elements belonging to each other and not to the larger context of perceptual data that surrounds it.

Consciousness perceives this belonging by perceiving the properties overlapping and characterizing the others: "All these many properties are in a single simple 'Here,' in which, therefore, they interpenetrate; none has a different Here from the others, but each is everywhere, in the same Here in which the others are. And, at the same time, without being separated by different Heres, they do not affect each other in this interpenetration ... since each is itself a simple relating of self to self it leaves the others alone, and is connected with them only by the indifferent Also" (*PhG* 72-3/M ¶113). Hegel identifies here a set of relations different from contrast relations. Contrast relations identify a content by the way it opposes and excludes other contents. The plurality of properties within the same self-identity keeps each property isolated within its own character: white is white, tart is tart, cubical is cubical, etc. Each is simply what it is without opposing or setting itself off from the others. Yet they "interpenetrate." Perception perceives them together in the same here and now. The perception of white perceives cubical in the same intuition of what stands here and now before consciousness, without moving to another here and now that transforms the first into what is not but has been here and now. Moreover, perception is conscious of white as the colour that characterizes a cubical shape, cubical shape as the shape of a white colour, tart as the taste that characterizes a white cubical shape. In a more complex perception, it perceives the configuration of red and yellow shapes in an abstract painting as the character of a continuous rectangular shape of a certain thickness. Without this plurality of properties mutually characterizing each other, the separateness of a thing could not be perceived.

If, however, perception attributes only the plurality to the object, then the object disintegrates. It loses the selfsameness that identifies the different properties with each other and keeps the object stabilized in a content of its own. It slips again into the stream of content elements that consciousness refers to or means. Consciousness of an object with a content of its own, therefore, involves focusing on a set of content elements set off from other content sets in the field of perceptual data. The object does not get lost in the continuum because it takes to itself its own properties, compresses their difference into the same here and now, and excludes all content-sets that do not belong to this one (*PhG* 75-7/M ¶119–23).

Perception tries to preserve the isolated independence of the object by reducing the negation, the not-being-the-other, to two positives. Consciousness is conscious of a thing as not-the-other by being conscious of "A as A" and "B as B." In other words, perception tries to experience the exclusivity of things without perceiving the negative excluding relation as a real relation in the object itself. The strategy fails, however, because the very character of a thing determines its not being the other. By being white-tart-cubical, salt determines itself as not the red-tart-oval character of the apple. Perception tries again by distinguishing what is essential from what is necessary but not essential. White-tart-cubical identifies what the self-identity of salt is. Not being red-tart-oval is necessarily implied in white-tart-cubical, but does not identify the self-identity itself. This strategy also fails. If the essential character of salt, its being white-tart-cubical, posits the necessity of its not being the red-tart-oval apple, then the negative relation that excludes the identifying character of the apple belongs to the essential character of salt (*PhG* 77–8/M ¶123–5).

Thus, the self-identity of a thing involves a contradiction. What the object itself is necessarily determines the thing as not-being anything else. Hence, the object's independent, unconnected being necessitates its distinguishing relations to what it is not. By being salt, salt necessarily distinguishes itself from other things in the properties white, tart, and cubical. But the relatedness that brings the object out of its separateness and independence identifies the object precisely as not other things. Thus, the object's relation to other things establishes its opposite, the object's unrelatedness and independence. This gives us the first form of Hegelian contradiction, which I shall call the self-identity contradiction (*PhG* 77–80/M ¶123–31).[5] The self-identity contradiction introduces a set of Hegelian technical terms: being-for-itself (*für sich Sein*) refers to the object isolated in itself and excluding what is other than itself; being-for-another refers to the object identifying itself in relation to an other (*PhG* 78–80/M ¶126–30).

A careful examination of the self-identity contradiction shows that Hegel is not talking about the assertion and denial of exactly the same claim. Contradiction here is a dynamic structure in which each opposite turns into the other. Independence and separateness necessarily involve a relation to something else as what the thing is not; relation to something else as what the thing is not necessarily involves determining the thing as separate and independent. The contradiction resolves itself into the unity of opposites in a dynamic of separating and relating. Thus, it expands the original concept to include both what the thing itself is and the relation whereby it sets itself apart from other things.

The separation and relation dynamic, however, is a structure without content. It identifies indiscriminately the independence of any and every object. In order to identify the independent reality of a definite object, an object with a content of its own, the structure must play itself out in a set of properties belonging to this one thing. Hegel's account of perception argues this point explicitly when it explains why the plurality of properties must belong to the object. A thing cannot be perceived as this unit distinguished from others unless it has a collection of particular properties that distinguish its unity from that of other things. Yet the essential structure of the independent unit, which is the structure of separating and relating, does not determine that the properties must be any particular set of properties. Thus, perception cannot know the truth of its object unless it becomes conscious of a universal structure embedded in a set of particulars whose particular content and configuration is not derived from the universal structure itself. The particulars by themselves are not the truth of the object. But as specific determinations of the object's essential struc-

5 Note especially the following: "the object is in one and the same respect the opposite of itself: it is for itself, so far as it is for another, and it is for another, so far as it is for itself" (*PhG* 78/M ¶128).

ture, as particular modes in which separating and relating exist in a singular thing, the particulars belong necessarily to what the object itself is (*PhG* 75–6/M ¶119–20; 80–1/M ¶131; 82–3/M ¶134).

4 UNDERSTANDING AND THE SYSTEMATIC WHOLE CONTRADICTION

Now let us look at the way the self-identity contradiction governs the move to a new concept. As we have seen, Hegel describes his procedure as "an unstoppable (*unaufhaltsemem*) and pure progression that admits of nothing extraneous" (*WL* 21:38/M 54). I take this to mean that the resolution of a contradiction involves no hidden premises. The move to a new position does not assume that contradictions are self-evidently false, and conclude from this that the original position is untenable. Nor does it assume that contradictions must be resolved, and hence move to a position that solves the problem, one that holds the opposites together without contradiction. The move to a new position simply endorses the contradiction by conceiving the necessary connection between the original concept and its opposite.[6] Thus, the form of experience that follows perception, which Hegel calls understanding, endorses perception's self-identity contradiction. Understanding knows its object as the separating and relating dynamic of force expressing itself. Hegel develops understanding's truth criterion from what is implicit in this dynamic and thus preserves not only perception's determinate negation but also the positive result precisely as the result of this negation.[7]

Let us see, then, how perception's self-identity contradiction becomes transformed in a form of consciousness that accepts the whole contradiction dynamic as what the object of perception shows itself to be. Instead of the static, isolated thing of perception, understanding perceives a dynamic force playing off other forces. A force gives itself content by expressing itself in certain particulars that differentiate it from other forces. For example, dynamic energy identifies itself as the power of a body in motion to overcome resistance. The expression of force preserves the being-for-another of perception. A force establishes its independence by referring the particulars of its expression back to itself. The expression expresses what is withdrawn

6 Dieter Wandschneider's rational reconstruction of Hegel's dialectic makes the same general point that I am making here. He, too, insists that nothing external to the dialectic can determine the new category. He also claims that the new category from the beginning is determined as the sameness of opposites. See (1991), 227–42; (1992), 37–41.

7 Compare to *PhG* 56–7/M ¶79.

into itself, the "force of," the "power to," the "capacity for." Overcoming resistance expresses the "power to" overcome resistance. Force withdrawn into itself preserves the being-for-self of perception. Hegel refers to the dynamics of a single force as "the first universal" (*PhG* 87–8/M ¶142).

The dynamics of one force, however, activates the opposite dynamic in other forces. Dynamic energy by making itself manifest as the power of a body in motion to overcome resistance absorbs its other into its own self-identity dynamics. Dynamic energy identifies itself in relation to what resists it, and identifies resistance only as the other of dynamic energy. Resistance belongs to the self-definition of dynamic energy itself as its negative. Thus, dynamic energy appropriates the whole relation, defining the whole, including the force opposed to it, in terms of dynamic energy itself. Since, however, a force expresses itself precisely as not the other, this force negates its being-for the other and returns to itself as what excludes the other. By relating itself to and separating itself from another force, the force "seduces," calls forth, the positive identity of its other. Dynamic energy returning to its isolation in itself becomes identified as the other's negative, and the other expresses itself in a set of particulars that identify what it positively is. Static force expresses itself as the power of a body at rest to resist the energy exerted against it. The identity originally identified only as an opposite becomes the dominant identity that identifies the other in terms of itself, e.g. static force and an other that exerts itself against static force. Thus, the second force appropriates the whole relation and identifies the whole, including the force opposed to it, in terms of itself. But static force also expresses itself as not the other, and hence separates itself from its being-for the other, returning to itself as what excludes the other; and this calls forth the being-for-another of the first force. Thus, each force is dissolved in a dynamic with other forces (*PhG* 82–8/M ¶134–41).

Since the play of forces follows necessarily from the self-identity structure that identifies what perception takes the truth to be, it affects the whole field of perceptual objects. Everything in the field of perception appears as a process in which separateness turns into relation and relation turns into separateness. Perceptual objects make an appearance, and in this appearance refer to others; and these others refer to what refers to them, so that nothing stands firm as the truth of what is. Consciousness knows the truth, therefore, by knowing perceptual objects as only appearances. Consciousness does not simply apprehend or take in what the object is. Consciousness understands the necessity that governs the appearance of perceptual objects and connects them to other appearances. The real truth, therefore, is not perceptual realities themselves, but the necessity or law that governs the connections that operate in them. Hegel calls this "the second universal" (*PhG* 87–8/M ¶142; 89–90/M ¶146–8). At this point, understanding moves beyond what stands immediately before consciousness.

> The first universal would be Force driven back into itself, or Force as Substance; the second, however, is the *inner being* of things *qua* inner, which is the same as the <concept> of Force *qua* <concept>. This true essence of Things has now the character of not being immediately for consciousness; on the contrary, consciousness has a mediated relation to the inner being and, as the Understanding, *looks through this mediating play of Forces into the true background of Things.* The middle term which unites the two extremes, the Understanding and the inner world, is the developed *being* of Force, which, for the Understanding itself, is henceforth only a vanishing. (*PhG* 87–8/M ¶142–3)

Consciousness as understanding perceives the way the play of forces dissolves the independence of different forces in the universality of a connected field, and thus reduces the play of forces to "appearances as appearances," i.e. a perceived play of forces referring itself to an inner force that does not stand immediately before consciousness. The meaning of the word "concept" here is limited to this mediated relation that carries understanding's thought into the inner truth of an independent perceptual field standing before consciousness.

Hegel's account of understanding keeps shifting between the dynamic involved in a single appearance of law-governed connection and that involved in the whole system. My interpretation of the account will distinguish the two issues and explain how they come together in the same experience. Understanding takes the truth to be an inner necessity that governs the play of forces. In order to know this truth, understanding thinks different objects as the different factors of a law. The real truth of the matter, however, is not the law itself, but the principle that identifies the factors of a law as differences within one and the same necessity. Without this sameness, the factors would fall apart as disconnected appearances. The results of the perception dialectic together with its fuller development in the play of forces has invalidated this way of taking perceptual data. Hence, understanding rejects as untrue the experience of perceptual objects as disconnected factors. It thinks the factors of a law as differences derived from and referred back to a simple force. Thus, it thinks the regular proportion between distance and velocity as the law of motion, and it thinks the force of gravity as the common ground that accounts for their constant association. It thinks the appropriateness between the drawing power of lodestone and the susceptibility of iron and steel as the law of magnetism, and it thinks magnetic force as the common ground that accounts for their necessary connection. Understanding knows the true essence of what appears by knowing the different factors of a law as the same force distinguished from itself (*PhG* 92–3/M ¶152).

The same way of thinking applies to the system as a whole. The lawfulness of appearances appears in different contents, e.g. the law of electricity, the law of motion, the law of magnetism, the law of thermodynamics. In this form, law is determinate; it breaks up into different laws and different instances of the same law. If, however, everything in the perceptual world belongs to a law-governed dynamic, then there must be a law to cover the association of different laws, and even to govern the differentiation of the same law in different instances. The order of law dissolves into an indefinite number of laws, a law to cover each and every appearance. Understanding, however, takes the truth to be a system of laws that remains invariable throughout all the relations and differences of the perceptual world. Without this stability, law dissolves into a random, disconnected, unaccountable association of appearances, which understanding must reject as untrue. Understanding takes the truth to be an inner necessity governing all associations in the perceptual world, a presupposition justified by the perception dialectic. Understanding, therefore, thinks all laws as one law, the law of universal attraction. Every appearance manifests an invariable law, which is itself compelled by other laws according to an invariable law, and in every law the necessity of order and connection, the law of attraction, reappears (*PhG* 90–2/M ¶149–50).

In order to know this truth, understanding in a process of explanation distinguishes the law as a unifying force from the diversity in which it appears. Thus, understanding thinks the regular proportion between distance and velocity as the law of motion governed by the force of gravity. It thinks the appropriateness between the drawing power of a magnet and the susceptibility of iron and steel as magnetic force (*PhG* 90–3/M ¶148–52). But this leaves the diversity of appearances without a ground. The simplicity of force does not explain why distance is coupled to velocity, or why the proportion between them is exactly this proportion, or why the particular constitution of loadstone gives it the power to attract objects with a particular metallic constitution. Indeed it does not even explain why the simplicity of force appears as different factors. Yet the move to simple force is determined by the way the separating and relating dynamic of perceptual objects retreats into a unifying connecting force that operates in them. Hence, simple force must explain not only the sameness of the dynamic to which different factors belong but also the differentiation played out in this dynamic. Understanding must think simple force as that which determines the necessary difference and opposition between different forces; and this cancels the distinction it previously made between simple force and diverse appearances (*PhG* 91–5/M ¶150–4).

At first, understanding attributes the movement played out in explanation only to the way understanding knows the object, not to the object itself. Understanding distinguishes the unity of the perceptual field from its diversity, and then cancels the distinction. The perceptual field itself remains integrated. But understanding cannot persist in this strategy. In the process of explanation, understanding knows the inner truth of the objective order as that which necessitates the diversity and opposition of appearances and makes itself manifest therein. Thus, understanding thinks the diversity and instability of appearances as inherent in simple force itself, and it thinks the simplicity of simple force operating in the diversity and opposition of appearances. Simple force sets itself off from the diversity of appearances by operating as a connecting force that negates the differences and absorbs everything into the selfsameness of an integrated whole. Simple force cancels the distinction by necessitating its own diversification in the opposition and exclusivity of forces opposing each other (*PhG* 95–7/M ¶155–6).

Hegel describes the result of this development as an inverted world. The confusing way in which Hegel talks about the inverted world becomes more understandable if we remember the dynamics involved in perception's self-identity contradiction, which is carried over into the way understanding is conscious of the play of forces. One identity by being what it is sets itself off from what it is not. For example, dynamic energy expresses itself as the power of a body in motion to overcome resistance. Thus, the whole self-identity dynamic, including the other that it excludes, is identified by one of the identities involved in the dynamic. The identity excluded takes its determination from being the other of the dominant identity, e.g. dynamic energy and what resists dynamic energy. But the dominant identity by setting itself off from its other returns to its separation from the other, and this identifies it as not the other. Dynamic energy is identified as what exerts itself against static force. Thus, the being-for-self of one identity calls forth the positive identity of its opposite, and thus reduces the first force to an other, an opposite, identified by what it opposes. Static force expresses itself as the power of a body at rest, and transforms dynamic energy into what exerts itself against the power of a body at rest. The identity originally identified only as an opposite becomes the dominant identity that identifies the other in terms of itself.

By making and cancelling the distinction between the unity of force and the diversity of appearances, the objective system identifies the play of forces with the selfsameness of a unifying force, and in the process turns the world upside down by identifying the selfsameness of force with the play of forces. As the ground of appearances, force becomes identified as that which determines the content of appearances. This content, however, shifts around. Understanding finds itself positing as an inner force the content of one participant in the play of forces, e.g. dynamic energy, only to have the dominance shift to the opposite participant, e.g. static force. This seems to be what Hegel means when he describes the dynamics of the objective system thus:

> Expressed in determinate moments, this means that what in the law of the first world is sweet, in this inverted in-itself is sour, what in the former is black is, in the other white. What in the law of the first is the north pole of the magnet is, in its other, supersensible in-itself, the south pole; but what is there south pole is here north pole. Similarly, what in the first law is the oxygen pole of electricity becomes in its other, supersensible essence, hydrogen pole; and conversely, what is there the hydrogen pole becomes here the oxygen pole. (*PhG* 97/M ¶158)

Moreover, the diversity of forces set off from each other keeps turning into the sameness derived from their involvement in the same separation and relation dynamic governed by the same force; and their involvement in the same separation and relation dynamic keeps turning into the diversity and opposition derived from this dynamic. The same force governs their necessary connection and their necessary non-identity (*PhG* 96–8/M ¶157–9).

Making and cancelling the distinction between the unity of force and the play of forces dissolves the objective system in a threefold contradiction. One form of the universal identifies the whole as the same connecting force unaffected by the diversity and opposition of the perceptual world. Hegel refers to this universal as the tranquil kingdom of laws and also as the tranquil, tautological universal. But by determining different forces as the same force, the universal determines them as differences derived from the simplicity of force itself and thus becomes the necessity of division and opposition within the same force. This is the force of division and opposition, which I will call the divisive, self-opposed universal. Differences exist, however, as a play of forces that integrates different forces into a single dynamic of separating and connecting. Hence, the force of division and diversification cancels its own division and self-opposition. Throughout its divisions and oppositions, one and the same connecting force persists unchanged. Thus, each form of the universal, by determining the objective order in one way, requires its determination in the opposite way. The contradiction dissolves the opposites into the opposition dynamic played out between the unification of diversity and the diversification of unity, and thus the opposites become factors in the same dynamic whole. This is what it means for a contradiction to resolve itself (*PhG* 91–2/M ¶149–50; 95–101/M ¶155–62).[8]

But understanding's systematic whole also involves another contradiction. By making and cancelling the distinction between simple force and diverse appearances, the system establishes a necessary connection between the necessary structures of objectivity and the givenness of perceptual particulars. Simple force has no particular content of its own from which the particulars of empirical laws could be inferred. It contains only the universal structure of the unity and diversity dynamic. This structure cannot appear as the essential truth of real differences without becoming embedded in the particulars that distinguish different realities from each other. Thus, simple force takes on whatever content experience provides in the appropriate kind of configuration, which is any content that can be thought according to the structures of the unity and diversity dynamic. As Hegel himself says, this is an explanation that explains nothing. It simply rethinks experienced facts as specific determinations of the unity and diversity dynamic. Moreover, in order to think simple force as the truth of appearances, understanding must think the empirical content as the content of force itself. Simple force is that which determines this content, that which appears as this content. The universal, necessary structure of the object's independent reality requires a content whose specifics are not determined by the necessary structure itself (*PhG* 89–90/M ¶146–7; 94–6/M ¶154–5).[9] Thus, understanding's systematic whole involves a necessary connection between the necessity of the unity-diversity structures and the contingent givenness of the particular content in which these structures make their appearance.

As we have seen, a contradiction resolves itself when the contradictories become pure opposites, i.e. when everything that identifies each contradictory is absorbed in a necessary relation to the other. This reduces the opposites to their participation in a dynamic common to both. But the contradiction between the necessary structures of understanding's dynamic whole and the contingency of their particular content does not resolve itself in this way. The necessary structures require some kind of diversification in particular content; and the determinacy of the content, its being dis-

8 See also Collins (1990), 533–8.

9 See also *PhG* 75–6/M ¶119–20; 80–1/M ¶131; 82–3/M ¶134.

tinguishable from other contents, requires some kind of relation to other contents. But the specific character of the particulars and the particular configuration in which they are associated persist as independent givens, not determined by their involvement in the unity-diversity structures. The contradiction remains unresolved.[10]

The third contradiction necessitates the shift from object-dominated consciousness to subject-dominated self-consciousness. The process of explanation makes and cancels the distinction between the inner truth of things (simple force) and its appearance in the play of forces. Cancelling the distinction demonstrates the necessity of thinking the integrating force of the objective system as nothing more than the unification-diversification dynamic played out in the field of perceptual data. Simple force anchors perceptual data in an independent system of mutual, integrating relations. This is what prevents its dissolution in a stream of different contents that consciousness refers to or means. This same force makes itself known to consciousness in the unification-diversification dynamic played out in appearances. Cancelling the distinction between simple force and diverse appearances, therefore, also cancels the distinction between the independence of the objective system and its relation to consciousness. Thus, the independence of the objective system shows itself as necessarily identified with the system's relation to consciousness (*PhG* 94–7/M ¶154–7; 100–2/M ¶163–5).

5 THE TRANSITION TO SELF-CONSCIOUSNESS

If we take seriously the proof procedure that Hegel describes in the introductory essays of his major works, then the transition from consciousness to self-consciousness must depend on a determinate negation that emerges in consciousness. Hegel calls such transitions "correct inferences" that depend on "nothing extraneous" (*WL* 21:38/M 54; 21:58/M 71). Hence, nothing that does not belong to the internal dynamics of the negation can determine the move from one set of presuppositions to another, not even the assumption that contradictions cannot be true. According to the Introduction to the *Phenomenology*, the determinate negations that emerge in its examination of experience must remain faithful to the truth criterion that belongs to the form of experience being examined (*PhG* 58–9/M ¶83–4).

10 In the "Philosophy of Nature," Hegel explicitly refers to this kind of contradiction as an unresolved contradiction (*der unaufgelöste Widerspruch*) (*Enz* §248A). See also §247–8, §250–1.

Finally, determinate negations are both negative and positive. They negate the original presupposition taken by itself; but they also justify this presupposition in connection with the opposite emerging from it (*WL* 21:38/M 54; *PhG* 56–7/M ¶79).

The contradiction involved in this connection has the form of an opposition dynamic in which each opposite is reduced to its opposition relation to the other. The original presupposition exposes a connection to the opposite implicit in what it is, and the opposite takes the form of a negation tied to and identified in terms of what it negates. Each opposite is a pure opposite, completely identified by its opposition to the other, so that only their mutual relations in the same dynamic identify what they are. This result justifies asserting as the new truth criterion a principle that identifies the sameness of the dynamic itself and determines the opposites as differences within its sameness. The principle involves a contradiction because it identifies the mutual exclusiveness and hence necessary non-identity of the opposites, and in the process identifies their necessary sameness as members of the same mutually constituting dynamic (*WL* 21:38/M 54).

With this proof procedure in mind, let us examine the way Hegel describes the transition from consciousness to self-consciousness. Consciousness takes the truth to be what the object is on its own and independent of its relation to consciousness. Consciousness in the form of understanding knows the object's independence as a system of self-identity relations, the play of forces, governed by a tranquil kingdom of laws formed into a systematic whole by a unifying connecting force. But this way of understanding the objective order necessarily involves identifying the unifying force with its opposite, namely a force that determines the diversity and oppositions operating in the appearances derived from simple force. This result exposes understanding's determinate negation: the unity of the objective system negating its diversity, and the diversification of the system negating its unity. Holding the opposites together, therefore, calls for a fundamental principle conceived as a unity driven by the necessity of breaking up into differences, existing as the self-isolating dynamic that separates these differences from each other, which in the process connects them to each other, and thus brings them back to unity through a dynamic inherent in their diversity. Life presents itself to consciousness in this self-differentiating, self-unifying form. Consciousness knows the objective system as a system of forces governed by the universal force of attraction. Self-consciousness knows the objective system as a life system governed by a life force. Life is the name for whatever drives the contradiction in understanding and determines its opposites as the same self-differentiating, self-unifying process:

"each [opposite] is the opposite of itself; each has its 'other' within it and they are only one unity. This simple infinity, or absolute <concept>, may be called the simple essence of life ... whose omnipresence is neither disturbed nor interrupted by any difference, but rather is itself every difference, as also their supersession; it pulsates within itself but does not move, inwardly vibrates, yet is at rest. It is self-identical, for the differences are tautological; they are differences that are none. This self-identical essence is therefore related only to itself" (*PhG* 99–100/M ¶161–2).

The "Understanding" chapter ends and the "Self-consciousness" section begins with an analysis of the life system. Life appears in the diversity of individual organisms separated from each other in a common continuum. Hegel calls this continuum a unity that immediately is, time/space, inorganic nature, and nature's independence (*Selbständigkeit*). Because living things belong to this element, they belong to the external, independent existence of the objective order. By living off this element, organisms take its hidden life-support into their own organic process and thus make it actually appear as living. One and the same life repeats itself in different singulars. This is the tranquil selfsameness of the universal. But life identified with different organisms becomes a connected system of life against life. In the process of life, each organism relates itself to a life that is not its own, and in this relation maintains itself as a separate life set off from and opposed to the other. This is the divisive, destabilizing universal. But the process of life against life negates the life of each and every organism, absorbs it into the ongoing process of life, and thus brings life back to its undisturbed identity with itself. This undisturbed selfsameness makes itself actual in individual organisms, and the process begins again (*PhG* 105–7/M ¶169–71).[11] Thus, Hegel describes the object of self-consciousness as a life process that holds together the opposites that emerge in understanding. Moreover, the object described preserves not only their necessary connection but also their opposition.

Understanding's determinate negation, however, has another dimension. Understanding accepts certain presuppositions justified by the examination of sense certainty and perception. Consciousness of an object with a content of its own involves a self-identity dynamic in which the object

11 Compare to *PhG* 97–9/M ¶159–60; 101–2/M ¶164–5). It is important to notice here that the life system does not identify the whole as a single organism in which the parts are subordinate to the whole and the whole is conceived as some kind of world soul. Hegel describes here a life system, which includes an inanimate environment, separate organisms, and diversity dominating unity as well as unity dominating diversity.

presents itself as a cluster of properties held fast by a separation and relation dynamic between itself and other property-sets. The examination of perception has also exposed in the object a separation and relation dynamic between what the object is in itself and what it is for consciousness. The examination moves with perceiving consciousness through every aspect of the perceived thing, and in the process finds itself conscious of the object as a thing appearing to consciousness. It also tries out a distinction that attributes unity to the thing in itself and the plurality of properties to the way the thing appears to consciousness, then reverses the distinction; and in each case, perception finds that it must attribute to the thing in itself what it has taken to be the way the thing appears to consciousness. Thus, perception introduces into the consciousness framework consciousness of the object as an object independent of its relation to consciousness together with this same object making itself known to consciousness. The being-for-self/being- for-another dynamic operates not only between thing and thing but also between thing and consciousness (*PhG* 74–8/M ¶117–23).

Understanding introduces the distinction between the object-in-itself and the object-for-consciousness in another form. Perceptual consciousness perceives the play of opposition between the independent identity of one thing and that of another. Understanding thinks this appearance of diversity and opposition as a unified, stable system of laws; and it takes this unity and stability to be the real truth of what appears to perception. Thus, understanding overrules the way objects present themselves to consciousness. It takes perceptual data to be only the way the truth appears, not what the truth itself is. At first, understanding takes this truth to be a supersensible world distinguished from the world as it appears in experience. In the process of explanation, however, understanding cancels this distinction. Explanation distinguishes the unity of force from the diversity of appearances and then cancels the distinction by thinking the unity of force as the explanation of appearances. This shows that the tranquil kingdom of laws is not a supersensible world, but a set of connections operating within the diversity and fluctuations of the sensible world. In other words, explanation collapses the distinction between what the objective system is in itself and what the system is for consciousness. In the process of redefining the dynamics of the objective system, understanding's determinate negation identifies the independent objectivity of the system with the system relating itself to consciousness. If, therefore, life is the principle that drives the objective system, then life must also include the role that being for consciousness plays in the completion of the system. And this fits the way Hegel describes the beginning form of self-consciousness.

Hegel describes the object of self-consciousness as an objective system that determines its own constitution and belongs to its own independent time/space. But the process of this self-constitution demonstrates that every way in which life exists as an object is not life itself but one of its differentiations. Even its constitution as a universal system is differentiated into an opposition between the unification of diversity and the diversification of unity. Hegel concludes from this that nothing in the objective world "contains all these moments as superseded within itself" (*PhG* 107/M ¶172). Nothing in the system lives in all the rest so that their life is really its own. Since, however, everything in the system lives by its connection to other members of the system, life lives in the objective order as one, selfsame life differentiated from itself. Whose life is it? What life supersedes all facets and forms of the objective life system by reducing them to facets and forms of itself?

Only consciousness, "for which Life exists as this unity" (*PhG* 107/ M ¶172). All the forms and facets of the objective life system exist for consciousness as differences within its consciousness of life as one whole. Life as an independent objective order, therefore, negates itself as not the essential determination of its own life and exists as what it truly is only by being "for" consciousness. Since, however, this being "for" consciousness is what life makes of itself, consciousness knows itself in this object only as another form of the same life. The life system refers itself to consciousness as an other that the life-world is not, but also as an other for which the life-world exists and in which it completes itself. In order to know the truth, therefore, consciousness must know the world as the conscious self's own life existing as an independent reality outside the self. Consciousness of an other turns out to be self-consciousness (*PhG* 104–7/M ¶169–74).

The move from consciousness to self-consciousness changes the way the phenomenological examination of knowledge defines the reality issue. Self-consciousness does not completely set aside the way consciousness defines the reality question. It still expects the object to be a reality that is independent of consciousness. But self-consciousness also expects this independent object to show itself as negated. This negation has two facets. It negates the independence of the object as not in itself its own truth; and it refers the object to the independence of the conscious self as the other, the something else, in which the object's truth is found. Thus, the self-negation of the objective system expands the structure of reality to include not only the objective system itself but also the system's necessary relation to consciousness and consciousness itself in which the relation is completed. For self-consciousness, the whole object-subject dynamic constitutes what exists.

Knowing reality as it truly is means knowing it as an object-subject dynamic whose dominant element is the conscious life of the self. The objective life system becomes what it truly is by constituting itself as a system existing for the conscious self.

6 THE KANTIAN INTERPRETATION

A significant group of contemporary commentators interpret the transition from consciousness to self-consciousness as a Kantian move. According to this interpretation, the process of explanation and the account of the inverted world show that the objective order is an order of intelligibility constituted by the activity of understanding itself. The otherness of the object persists, but not as an independent object with its own self-determined constitution. Thought's other gets its constitution from thought itself. Those committed to the Kantian interpretation support their position by interpreting the confusions of the inverted world as proof of the negative. These confusions supposedly show that we get trapped in an untenable position if we assume that an objective system gets its necessity and order from a supersensible reality outside thought.

Some supporters of the Kantian approach claim that this confusion justifies turning to thought itself as the only alternative explanation of the order and necessity required for the intelligibility of objects.[12] Others claim that this turn to thought is determined by the dynamics of understanding itself; the process of explanation exposes the objective system's dependence on the activity of thought itself.[13] Harris claims that throughout the examination of consciousness the observer consciousness knows that the object-dominated orientation of consciousness is a mistake. According to Harris, we, the philosophical observers, know "that 'universality' is an activity of the perceiving mind (which has identified the *Ding*, and placed it as an essence in an *intellectual* context)"; that the real order of space and time is "*constituted* by thought"; that it is a mistake for understanding to think that the truth of the perceptual world is a supersensible world out there; that "the observing intellect is the place of this world (and the only place that it has)."[14] We know this because we observe how a form of consciousness

12 Pippin (1989), 131–46; Pinkard (1994), 40–4.

13 Flay (1984), 77–80; (1970), 676–7; (1998), 149–50. De Nys (1995); (1982). Harris (1997), I 300–8.

14 Harris (1997), I 239, 263.

brings its own truth criterion to the experience and thereby determines the way it is conscious of the object.[15]

If, however, we consider the descriptions of proof procedure offered in the introductory essays of Hegel's major works, we find that the Kantian interpretations fail to meet several of its requirements. First, the restrictions of determinate negation, with its "correct inferences" that depend on "nothing extraneous" (*WL* 21:38/M 54; 21:58/M 71), do not allow a move that simply dismisses a position because it develops oppositions and inversions. Dismissing the position assumes that oppositions, contradictions, inversions cannot be true. According to Hegel, however, the result justified by a determinate negation must assert the original position together with its opposite; and he calls this a self-contradiction (*WL* 21:38/M 54). Moreover, in the *Encyclopaedia* and in the *Logic*, Hegel criticizes Kant for not realizing that contradiction is fundamental to all concepts, representations, and realities, and that it emerges from the content of what we know, not just from its form (*Enz* §48*A*; *WL* 21:30–1/M 46–7). In the preceding section, I have demonstrated how the inverted world can be interpreted according to the requirements of determinate negation.

Second, the restriction Hegel imposes on the observer consciousness rules out Harris's interpretation. In the Introduction to the *Phenomenology*, Hegel says that the philosophical observer knows exactly the same content as the consciousness being examined. The observer consciousness adds to this only what can be learned from observing the necessary connections between the determinate negation of one form and the beginning presuppositions of the next form. This leaves us in no position to judge whether the presupposed criteria of the consciousness being examined are or are not correct, except as this is revealed by the self-critique operating in the consciousness being examined (*PhG* 61/M ¶87). What, then, do we observe in the development of sense certainty and perception that justifies introducing an activity whereby consciousness gives the object its essential constitution?

We know that the object involves a relation to consciousness, which gives consciousness a role in what the object is. But this role, as revealed in sense certainty and perception, is strictly limited. Consciousness is an other to which the truth of the object, its differentiation within the universality of the here and now, makes itself known; and the object returns from this relation back into itself. Thus, the object plays off the otherness of consciousness as a being-for- self/being-for-another dynamic, just as it plays off the

15 Ibid., I 239.

otherness of other objects. A being-for- self, Hegel says, is conditioned by the other, because it needs the other in order to identify itself as differentiated from it. Hence, the other becomes essential to it.[16] But as long as consciousness as the object's other is defined exclusively by the way the object develops itself, consciousness has no content of its own, only its determination as an other completely absorbed by its relation to what the object is. Between object and object, perceptual data provide a given content for the other. But between object and consciousness, no content for consciousness has yet emerged (*PhG* 82/M ¶132).[17]

Harris' interpretation also suggests that we, the philosophical observers, recognize in sense certainty and perception an intellectual context, structures constituted by thought, although the consciousness being examined does not realize this. If, however, the examination of consciousness respects the orientation of the form of consciousness being examined, then what emerges in the experience should be interpreted according to the expectations of the cognition that is being tested. According to my interpretation, consciousness begins with the minimal structure required for knowledge to appear, a pure consciousness-of dependent on the object for what it is conscious of. This is what justifies interpreting the first truth criterion as what the object is in itself, on its own, independent of its relation to consciousness; consciousness cannot appear without something other to complete it by giving it something to be conscious of. In order to preserve this orientation, at least until it reorients itself, I have interpreted what emerges in the content presented to sense certainty and perception as necessities and connections that belong to and are sensed in what stands immediately before consciousness. The universal here and now belongs to a sensed continuity of sense data arranged in certain ways. The universality of the self-identical perceived thing belongs to a unit with different qualities, and this universality is sensed as qualities belonging to each other by overlapping and characterizing each other (*PhG* 71–2/M ¶113). I have interpreted "essential" and "non-essential" in the third move of perception according to perception's own expectations. "Essential" refers to the unity, the sensed overlapping

16 This is enough to account for what Hegel says about what we know that perception itself does not yet know. We know that both the object and consciousness are equally essential, that the universal is the truth of both (*PhG* 71/M ¶111).

17 "For us, this object has developed through the movement of consciousness in such a way that consciousness is involved in that development and the reflection is the same on both sides, or, there is only one reflection. But since in this movement consciousness has for its content merely the objective essence and not consciousness as such, the result must have an objective significance for consciousness."

and mutually characterizing set of sensible qualities, that holds the properties together as a separate set and thereby identifies the separate self-identity of the thing. This is what perception expects the object to be, and hence what perception would experience as what the object truly is. "Necessary but not essential" refers to the relatedness that connects the separate property-set to other property-sets, which perception tries to experience as distinguished from the thing's separate self-identity. Interpreted in this way, which keeps the examination strictly contained within the domain defined by the truth expectations of sense certainty and perception, the universals and necessities that emerge in these forms of cognition belong to the way the content of sense experience constitutes itself. They do not require or justify a re-interpretation of sense experience that derives these universals and necessities from consciousness conceived as a knowing with principles of its own.

The strongest argument for the Kantian interpretation claims that the process of explanation exposes understanding actively involved in the constitution of the objective system. This argument, however, does not remain faithful to understanding's truth criterion. At first, understanding attributes the explanation dynamic only to the way understanding knows the object, not to the object itself. In itself, the objective order is the tranquil, tautological selfsameness of simple force. Understanding knows this selfsameness, however, through a movement, the process of explanation, in which thought distinguishes simple force from its appearance in disconnected diverse phenomena and then rethinks these diverse phenomena as one and the same force. Understanding finds, however, that it must attribute the explanation dynamic to the object itself (*PhG* 87–9/M ¶142–5; 94–6/M ¶154–6; 100–2/M ¶163–4). The Kantian interpretation assumes that the dynamic attributed to the object is understanding's own activity of explaining. My interpretation claims that the dynamic attributed to the object is the process of making and cancelling the distinction between the unity of force and the diversity of appearances. I base my claim on Hegel's insistence that the examination of experience must remain faithful to the truth criterion that belongs to the experience being examined. If understanding finds that it must attribute to the objective system itself making and cancelling the distinction between the unity of force and the diversity of appearances, this must be interpreted according to understanding's own truth expectations.

The dialectical development of perception and understanding demonstrates that becoming conscious of the object as something with a content of its own depends on the self-identity connections that keep the content of experience from perpetually slipping away in the indifferent continuum that is neither this nor that and is this as well as that. Understanding makes and cancels the distinction between the unity of force and the diversity of appearances in order to become conscious of this connectedness. Understanding distinguishes the unity of force from the diversity of appearances in order to become conscious of the connecting force that integrates these differences into the sameness of a whole. Understanding cancels the distinction in order to become conscious of the connecting force as that which determines the differences and lives in them. Understanding must attribute to the objective system itself the process of making and cancelling the distinction between the unity of force and the diversity of appearances because an object standing firm with a content of its own, which is the truth criterion of consciousness, depends on a connectedness that makes it possible for the object to have a content of its own. Without this connectedness, the field of perceptual data dissolves into free-floating elements that consciousness means. Thus, when understanding attributes the explanation dynamic to the object, it gives the dynamic the same independent, objective status as the tranquil kingdom of laws: "The Understanding thus learns that it is a law of appearance itself, that differences arise which are no differences, or that what is selfsame repels itself from itself; and similarly, that the differences are only such as are in reality no differences and which cancel themselves; in other words, what is not selfsame is self-attractive. And thus we have a second law whose content is the opposite of what was previously called law, viz. difference which remains constantly selfsame" (*PhG* 96/M ¶156). The unity of force distinguishes itself from the diversity of appearances by connecting different forces and laws in the same connected system, thereby negating their diversity. The same force cancels the distinction by existing in and existing as their diversity, thereby negating its own unity.

Kenneth Westphal interprets the whole movement of consciousness as a kind of transcendental argument, and in this sense his interpretation can be included here as a kind of Kantian interpretation. Westphal does not claim, however, that Hegel's account of consciousness reduces the intelligibility of the object to something "constituted" by thought. According to his interpretation, Hegelian epistemology is a realism that is also anti-sceptical. There is "a way the world is that does not depend upon what we say, think or believe about it"; and we can know how the world is in its independence of what we say, think, or believe.[18] Westphal's transcendental analysis of

18 Westphal (2006), 274. In this article, Westphal develops a subtle analysis of the difference between his "realist" interpretation of Kant and Hegel and McDowell's.

the consciousness dialectic has a Kantian dimension because it claims that consciousness knows what the object in itself is by bringing to experience certain *a priori* concepts: space-time, self-identity, causal interaction. Consciousness begins with a form of cognition that expects knowledge to be an immediate, direct, "non-conceptual" sense cognition (sense certainty); and Hegel's account of sense certainty, perception, and understanding shows that space-time, self-identity, and causal interaction cannot be derived from sense experience. The possibility of sense experience depends on the application of concepts derived not from experience (concept empiricism) but from thought.[19]

Westphal's book-length study of Hegel and Hume on perception provides an extensive, careful, text-based example of how this realistic transcendental approach interprets the perception section of the *Phenomenology*. In this study, Westphal interprets Hegel's examination of perception as an argument against concept empiricism.[20] The study sets out to show how Hegel's examination of perception proves that perceiving a thing with many properties is not possible without judgments based on understanding's *a priori* conceptions. In order to pinpoint precisely my disagreement with this interpretation, I must distinguish the different claims involved in it. Westphal's explanations of the specific moves in Hegel's account of perception are careful and in my judgment correct. My disagreement focuses exclusively on the conclusion derived from these moves. This conclusion can be analyzed into three different claims. First, it claims that perceiving a thing with many properties is not possible for perception. Second, it claims that consciousness of a thing with many properties depends on an act of understanding. Third, it claims that the act of understanding is a cognitive judgment based on *a priori* conceptions. I disagree only with the third claim; but this disagreement is based on different ways of supporting the first and second claims.

My study of Hegel's *Phenomenology* focuses on the claims Hegel makes for his scientific procedure, which means that I must preserve a strict, minimalist approach that allows nothing to play a role in Hegel's demonstration unless it becomes strictly necessary. My approach to Hegel's account of perception, therefore, tests Hegel's claims for his procedure by interpreting shifts in the dialectic as the most minimal changes possible, and by keeping the observer consciousness from contributing anything whatsoever to the demonstration. Hence, I interpret the moves in sense certainty and percep-

19 Westphal (2009b).
20 Westphal (1998c), especially chapter 2, §9–14.

tion as moves that preserve the object as an object of sense experience. In my judgment, sense certainty does not have to use *concepts* of space-time, self-identity, or causal interaction. I do not need a concept to experience the difference between sweet and sour, or the difference between my sensation of sweet right now from my sensation of sour before. Nor do I need a concept to experience the way red has a round shape and a tart taste whereas white has a cubical shape and a sweet taste. Hegel's account of perception can remain confined within sense experience: (1) as a parade of different sensed contents broken up by the experience of contrasting contents, such as sweet-sour, rough-smooth, round-cubical; (2) as contents overlapping and characterizing others, such as a cubical white shape tasting sweet; and (3) as sets of overlapping contents not belonging to other sets, such as cubical white shape tasting sweet not being the experience of round red shape tasting tart.

Perception cannot, however, integrate the separateness and relatedness of the perceived object. I agree with Westphal's interpretation about this. According to my interpretation, however, this is not because its integration cannot be perceived without an appeal to *a priori* concepts. Rather perception expects the truth to be the separate self-identity of a thing, and hence it experiences as not true the way this separateness dissolves into distinguishing relations to other things. Understanding begins with perception's opposites integrated in the experience of force expressed and withdrawn into itself. Hegel acknowledges explicitly that this experience preserves the immediacy of perception. Why can understanding have this experience if perception cannot? Because understanding has a different truth expectation. It takes the truth of the perceived object to be the integration of its separateness and relatedness into the same self-identity, and hence it does not reject as untrue the way separateness turns into relatedness and vice-versa. The move into what exists only for understanding emerges not in the integration of the opposites internal to a single perceived thing, but in the way objects of perception develop a play of forces that reduces the whole perceptual field to a connected whole whose true essence is the inner not-perceived connecting force (*PhG* 87–8/M ¶142–3).

Even in this, however, consciousness preserves its complete dependence on the object. It does not judge the object according to its own concepts. It follows the way the dynamics of the perceptual field refers itself to an inner connecting force and thus presents itself as the appearances of this force. Understanding's consciousness of the sensed relations between different forces shows each and every object in the perceptual field negating its independent status by relating itself to other objects, so that the whole experience collapses the diversity of the field into the experience of a connected whole. According to my interpretation, therefore, the system of laws and the connecting force are not concepts applied to the sense data. They are supersensible principles that the mutual exclusivity and negativity displayed in perception brings to consciousness. Interpreted thus, the dialectic remains true to the object-dominated criterion that operates in the consciousness dialectic. Nothing so far established in the examination of consciousness makes the move to *a priori* concepts strictly necessary.

I do not deny that Hegel will eventually demonstrate the legitimacy of defining truth as a correspondence between the principles of independent thought and structures that operate within the objective world. I think a good case might be made for Westphal's point of view if it were situated within the framework introduced by the transition from self-consciousness to idealism. In order to preserve the integrity of Hegel's scientific procedure, however, my interpretation of Hegel's project postpones the introduction of *a priori* concepts until the demonstration justifies the concept of reason in which both the independence of thought and the independence of the objective world have been explicitly established. According to my minimalist approach, the consciousness developed in sense certainty, perception, and understanding has no content of its own. Its only determination is its relation to the object. In this relation, the object shows itself dependent on necessary connections revealed in the way the object presents itself to consciousness as an appearance that refers to an inner, hidden connecting force (*PhG* 74–5/M ¶117; 78–80/M ¶129–30; 87–90/M 143–7; 104–5/M ¶168).

7 AMBIGUITIES IN THE TEXT

Several comments that Hegel makes at the conclusion of the understanding dialectic seem to support the Kantian interpretation. Understanding, he says, finds explanation satisfying because in explanation understanding deals only with itself (*PhG* 100–1/M ¶163). Moreover, the "necessary advance" through the various forms of consciousness, which the phenomenological observer knows and the consciousness under examination does not, shows "that not only is consciousness of a thing possible only for a self-consciousness, but that self-consciousness alone is the truth of those shapes" (*PhG* 101–2/M ¶164). Finally, Hegel says that there is nothing behind the world of appearance "unless *we* go behind it ourselves, as much in order that we may see, as that there may be something behind there which can be seen" (*PhG* 102/M ¶165).

These texts, however, will tolerate my interpretation just as well. Understanding in explanation deals only with itself because it becomes engaged in a being–for-self/being-for-another dynamic with the objective system. In the process of explanation, understanding goes out to the object and becomes conscious of it as the appearance of a supersensible force. Thus, understanding takes the form of a consciousness identified by its relation to something other than itself, being-for-another; the object takes the form of an object that takes to itself the diverse appearances that relate it to consciousness, being-for-self. The object in itself dominates the dynamic between itself and its other. But explanation, like the play of forces, reverses direction. It thinks the unity of force as the ground of appearances, which transforms the objective system into being-for-another; and this transforms consciousness itself into a being-for-self turned back to itself by the object's relation to it. Consciousness becomes the dominant participant in the dynamic between the other and itself. Thus, Hegel begins the account of self-consciousness by describing the objective life system as having no being-for-self within itself, as referring to consciousness as its being-for-self (*PhG* 107/M ¶172). Understanding in explanation deals only with itself not because its thinking gives the objective system its internal constitution, but because understanding finds itself dealing with a system whose self-constituting otherness identifies itself as being-for consciousness.

Moreover, this dynamic between consciousness and its object corresponds to the abstract structure of consciousness described in the Introduction to the *Phenomenology*, the structure that belongs to it simply by being conscious of something (*etwas*), the structure with which the examination of experience begins. Consciousness is a pure relation to whatever the object is, pure consciousness-of; and the object is simply whatever provides consciousness with something to be conscious of. The distinction between the object-in-itself and the object-for-consciousness is implicit in this bare-bones knowing. Because consciousness has no other determination than its relation to what it is conscious of, consciousness cannot provide the content that completes the relation. Hence, it is conscious of the object as something that does not derive what it is from its relation to consciousness. Since, however, consciousness is also conscious of this something, consciousness relates to the object not only as something independent of consciousness but also as something made known to consciousness. Implicit in this structure is a certain truth expectation. Consciousness expects the object for consciousness to reveal what the object in itself is. In the process of explanation, this is achieved. Explanation knows the connecting force that identifies what the objective system is in itself as a force identified with the data in which the system is made known to consciousness.

This interpretation fits the way the *Science of Logic* describes the scientific procedure that operates in the *Phenomenology*: "each [form of consciousness] dissolves itself in being realized ... and thereby has gone over to a higher shape ... Because the result, the negation, is a determinate negation, it has a content. It is a new concept but one higher and richer than the preceding – richer because it negates or opposes the preceding and therefore contains it, and it contains even more than that, for it is the unity of itself and its opposite" (*WL* 21:37–8/M 54). Understanding realizes itself. It meets the requirements imposed by the beginning concept of consciousness. It knows the object's independence of consciousness, and knows it as a reality surrendered, revealed, in the object's relation to consciousness. But in the process of realizing itself, understanding resolves itself. The very independence of the object identifies itself as a relation to consciousness.

Thus, self-consciousness is the unity of consciousness and its opposite. Consciousness takes the truth to be the object's independence of consciousness; its opposite knows this independence as self-negating. In the new form of consciousness, therefore, the object's necessary relation to consciousness must emerge as a result of the object's independent self-constitution. Hegel describes the first form of self-consciousness in just this way. Life develops itself as a unifying force that absorbs everything into the ecological system, only to negate this unification by splitting up in the individual life forms supported by the system, only to negate this diversification by living as each life form's relation to the environment, which integrates different life forms into the ecological system. This diversification-unification dynamic negates everything within it as not by itself the truth of what is, and thus brings out of itself the relation to conscious life which knows the life system as a whole.

Thus, "consciousness of a thing is possible only for a self-consciousness" because consciousness cannot know the independent constitution of a thing without knowing the dynamic whereby the objective order dissolves into a unification-diversification dynamic that transforms its independent reality into being-for-another; and the other is consciousness. "Self-consciousness alone is the truth of those shapes" because the dialectical development of sense certainty, perception, and understanding completes itself in this transforming determinate negation (*PhG* 101–2/M ¶164). At this point, it is not clear what Hegel means when he says that there is nothing behind the world of appearance "unless *we* go behind it ourselves, as much in order that we may see, as that there may be something behind there which can be seen" (*PhG* 102/M ¶165). Hegel hastens to add, however, that we cannot at this point go behind appearance, that this can be done only after the *Phenomenology* has demonstrated what consciousness knows in knowing itself. The opening moves of self-consciousness, which we shall consider in the next chapter, will expose a dimension of self-consciousness that might make sense of this text.

Finally, the Introduction to the *Phenomenology* describes the transition to a new object thus:

> Hence it comes to be for consciousness that what for it was previously in-itself is not in-itself, or that it was only in-itself for consciousness. (*PhG* 59–60/M ¶85, translation mine)

> But, as was shown previously, the first object, in being known, is altered for consciousness; it ceases to be the in-itself, and becomes something that is in-itself only for consciousness. And this then is the True: the being-for-consciousness of this in-itself. Or, in other words, this is the essence, or the object of consciousness. This new object contains the nothingness of the first, it is what experience has made of it. (*PhG* 59–60/M ¶86)

When Hegel introduces self-consciousness, he repeats this description of the move to a new object: "this in-itself turns out to be a mode in which the object is only for an other" (*PhG* 103/M ¶166). The Kantian interpretation tempts us to read these texts as dismissing the independent status of the object, reducing it to a being-for consciousness that consciousness mistakenly took to be something independent and in-itself. According to my interpretation, the object's independent being (being-in-itself) turns out to be a way in which the object determines itself as "for" consciousness. Its independence of consciousness remains; the objective order persists as a reality that exists in itself and determines its own constitution. But this independent reality develops as a system that completes itself by relating itself to consciousness. Both consciousness and self-consciousness assume that the objective order exists on its own, with its own laws, independent of its relation to consciousness. What distinguishes consciousness from self-consciousness is the status or importance attributed to this objective being-in-itself. Consciousness assumes that what the object is in-itself defines what is essential and primary. Self-consciousness assumes that what the object is in-itself is not the primary truth of the object. For self-consciousness, the essence or primary truth of the object is the being-for-consciousness of this object-in-itself.

The sameness between consciousness and its object that follows from this interpretation differs significantly from the self-consciousness of the

Kantian interpretation. According to the Kantian interpretation, consciousness knows its own ways of thinking either as the essential determination of an object constituted by thought itself or at least as concepts that expose the true essence of a reality independent of thought. This leaves the otherness of the object tame and pliable. What thought determines or exposes according to its own requirements does not fight against what understanding demands of it; or if it does, this resistant element belongs to what is not important, not essential to the truth of what is. If, however, we interpret the move to self-consciousness according to the demands of Hegel's scientific procedure, then the object's independence of its relation to consciousness *transforms itself* into a being "for" consciousness. The negation is determinate. It emerges as a result of what it negates and remains attached to it. The object remains an other set apart, following its own laws, not limited to what thought can make of it. The self expects this object to negate itself, to determine itself as an object "for" consciousness, and thus to establish a sameness between the object and the self. But because this sameness depends on the object as other than and independent of the self, the seed of resistant otherness remains. Thus, "we" the philosophical observers, who have seen the necessary development of self-consciousness from object-dominated consciousness, know from the beginning what self-consciousness itself must learn, namely that the object's resistance to self-consciousness, and the independence that this manifests, must reassert itself. Hegel says so explicitly (*PhG* 104–5/M ¶168; 107–8/M ¶175).

13

Self-consciousness and the Transition to Idealism

IN THIS CHAPTER, we will look at the way Hegel's phenomenological examination of self-consciousness makes a case for the beginning presuppositions of reason. Hegel articulates these presuppositions in his account of idealism. I shall offer here an interpretation of self-consciousness governed by the demands of Hegel's proof procedure. This approach shows how the *Phenomenology* again expands and redefines the reality claims of cognition.

1 THE BEGINNING STRUCTURE OF SELF-CONSCIOUSNESS

Self-consciousness begins as desire. We have seen how the objective life system is the determinate negation of understanding's object; life expands this object to include the tranquil universal necessarily connected to the divisive, inverted world universal. Desire is the determinate negation of what understanding assumes about consciousness itself. Understanding takes the truth to be an independent objective system, and it takes knowing to be consciousness as a pure relation to this independent truth. In the determinate negation, the independence of the objective system identifies itself with its being for consciousness and thus turns consciousness back to itself. In order to experience this truth, therefore, the self must experience the natural system as a system that refers itself to the conscious self. Desire provides this kind of experience. The objective life system, operating according to its own laws, produces objects that the self finds suitable to its self. Desire experiences plants and animals as food, water as drink, air to breathe, caves as dwellings, the male or female of the species as sex partner. As a pure relation to, desire-for, what is produced by the independent operations of the objective order, desire preserves the form of consciousness. It is conscious of something other than consciousness itself, something with a content of its own. Desire, however, is conscious of this otherness together with its negation, as an other referred to the self's consciousness of its wants and needs. Desire experiences what the object truly is, therefore, in the experience of desire satisfied. Desire satisfaction takes the object out of its role in the independent objective system and integrates it into the life of the self (*PhG* 107–8/M ¶174–5).

Hegel distinguishes desire as the determinate negation of understanding from the ordinary desires of an animal organism. Life negates life in three different ways. First, one determinate life form negates another; organisms distinguish themselves from other organisms and from the inorganic environment. Second, the "inorganic universal nature of life" negates the life of individual organisms. Organisms die in the natural course of things: in storms, floods, earthquakes, as victims of predators, by natural deterioration. Both kinds of negation operate within the objective life system. Self-consciousness as desire differs from these because it negates life from outside the objective system. It seeks an experience in which the independence of the whole objective system is negated, and its existence for the conscious self takes over as its true essence.

It is important to notice that three essential factors identify the beginning structure of self-consciousness: first, the self's status as the truth of the whole objective life system, as the conscious life for which the whole system exists; second, the determinate negation status of the self, which identifies the self in terms of its attachment to and negation of the objective life system; third, the self's status as an independent, conscious life, outside the objective life system. Self-consciousness cannot experience what it expects the truth to be unless all of these factors are preserved in the experience. Desire satisfaction gives the self the experience of itself as that for which the products of the natural system exist, and so preserves the first factor. In order to experience the world as "for" the self, desire must remain attached to the independent content of the objective system and be continually engaged in absorbing this content into its being "for" the self. Hence, desire reveals the self as a negation attached to and identified in terms of what it negates, which preserves the second factor. But desire cannot experience the object as something identified by its relation to the self without also becoming conscious of itself as something identified by its relation to the object. Self-conscious desire experiences itself as a self engaged in mutual relations between itself and its other, and so desire fails to give the self an experience of the self as an independent, conscious life outside the objective life system. Self-consciousness expects the truth to be the self in itself, with the objective order reduced to being for another, i.e.

for the self. According to this expectation, the self is not one element in the relation between self and world; the self is the truth of the whole relation. Self-consciousness cannot experience what it takes the truth to be, therefore, unless the experience of the world's being-for the self also gives the self an experience of its own independence, its own being-in-itself. Self-consciousness must confront an objective life system that negates itself. The natural order, in its independence, must transform itself into what exists for the self (*PhG* 107–8/M ¶175).

Hegel gives us very little to go on when he makes the next move. We must unpack his argument from two brief statements:

> Since the object is in its own self negation, and in being so is at the same time independent (*selbstständig*), it is consciousness ... But this universal independent nature in which negation is present as absolute negation, is the genus as such, or the genus as self-consciousness. Self-consciousness achieves its satisfaction only in another self-consciousness. (*PhG* 107–8/M ¶175)

The first part of the text assumes that only consciousness can qualify as an object that is both independent and "in its own self negation." The second part identifies the negation as the simple genus. "Simple genus" refers to consciousness as the negative essence that knows the diversified life of the objective order as a life negated and unified by its being "for" consciousness. Only another self-consciousness engaged in the negation of the objective life system can play the role of life presenting itself as an independent reality negating its own claim to truth. Only in its relations to another self-consciousness does the objective life system stand before a conscious self as an independent reality negating its own truth status (*PhG* 107–9/M ¶175–7).

In the discussion of the transition from consciousness to self-consciousness, we considered a text in which Hegel says that there is nothing behind the world of appearance "unless we go behind it ourselves, as much in order that we may see, as that there may be something behind there which can be seen" (*PhG* 102/M ¶165). This makes more sense now that the examination of self-consciousness has expanded the dynamic between self and world to include the world situated between one self-consciousness and another. Self-consciousness expects the truth to be an objective life system existing for a self-consciousness outside the system. Left to itself, however, the objective system does not show itself in its true form. The truth becomes manifest only if the objective existence of the system includes its relation to a self-consciousness. Self-consciousness, therefore, must play a double role. It must maintain its position as an independent subject for which the objective order exists, and it must exist as the true essence of the objective system that presents itself to another self-consciousness. Thus, the objective system cannot reveal anything hidden behind its appearances unless a self gets behind the world of appearances and gives it a significance beyond itself, the significance of belonging to the life of a conscious self. This is self-consciousness in its objective role. In its subjective role, self-consciousness cannot see the real truth of the objective system unless self-consciousness sees itself standing behind the appearances as the system's true essence. None of this requires a transcendental interpretation. Self-consciousness does not have to claim that human thought gives nature its organizational structure; nor does it have to presuppose *a priori* concepts operating as necessary conditions for the possibility of knowing objects. Self-consciousness gives the objective order a significance beyond itself simply by expecting the organization and processes that understanding finds operating in the objective system to function as a dynamic that identifies the system as a world existing "for" the self (*PhG* 108–9/M ¶177).

2 THE PRESTIGE BATTLE

In order to give nature its true form, self-consciousness must detach itself from its involvement in the objective life system, and must take as its own the fundamental power or force that drives the system. Self-consciousness must assert itself as both independent of nature and its master. The self accomplishes this independence and mastery by showing itself willing to throw away its existence as a natural living thing, to risk life by wielding as the self's own nature's power over life and death, and to risk life for nothing but the prestige of demonstrating that this self is not attached to life. Self-consciousness asserts its independence in a battle to the death with another self-consciousness. If, however, each self-consciousness asserts the same independence and mastery, how can the one know itself in the other? The truth expectations of self-consciousness allow for no generalization of self-consciousness. The other's self cannot be my self just by being another instance of self-consciousness. Nor is there here any justification for assuming a shared social life, a shared language, or a moral principle that grounds one self's recognition of another as the same life distinguished from itself.[1]

1 Hegel does mention here the "I" that is "We" and the "We" that is "I," which belongs to the concept of spirit. But he also admits that in this its first form, self-consciousness does not yet know what spirit is. We must learn how self-consciousness at this point knows itself in another self by identifying an experience appropriate to the beginning presuppositions of

At this point in the phenomenological development of cognition, the self's only determinations are derived from its consciousness of life; and consciousness is nothing more than a consciousness-of, which experiences the object as mine, an experience exclusive to me (*PhG* 110–11/M ¶187).[2]

When, therefore, self-consciousness brings into the structure of truth its relation to another self-consciousness, the whole issue of mine and not yours arises. Self-consciousness refers the whole differentiated distribution of natural life to the self's sense of itself as my consciousness, my experience, which excludes the other self's sense of its own consciousness or experience. How, then, can a self stand before another self-consciousness as an other in which this self-consciousness knows itself? A self-consciousness knows itself in another self both negatively and positively: negatively by being conscious of the other as an opponent and hence as not myself, positively by being conscious of the way the other is conscious of me. I know myself as the master of nature in another self acknowledging me as such. But this same self challenges my claim by opposing its claim to mine (*PhG* 109–10/M ¶178–84).

The prestige battle, however, does not reveal the truth that self-consciousness is after. While the battle rages, the combatants conquer nature by dismissing natural life as not important and by wielding nature's power as their own; and each recognizes the other as a worthy opponent, engaged in a battle not for the petty satisfactions of food or territory or sex, but for recognition of their status as a self that is not attached to life. But one of them must die. When he does, the winner loses the recognition provided by the opponent, who now belongs to the independence and indifference of nature and its processes (*PhG* 111–12/M ¶188). This experience shows that "life is as essential to [self-consciousness] as pure self-consciousness" (*PhG* 112/M ¶189).

The transition to a new form of self-consciousness, as well as the determinate negation of this new form itself, become more manageable if we pay attention to a clue Hegel gives us. Hegel compares the prestige battle to the play of forces (*PhG* 110/M ¶184). In the account of the play of forces, each force focuses the whole dynamic on itself, with the other force reduced to a factor in what the dominant force is. This sets up one force

---

self-consciousness, which are derived from the determinate negation of consciousness, and by examining the way the sketchy beginning structure of self-consciousness exposes its full meaning in a sequence of determinate negations belonging to self-consciousness itself (*PhG* 108–9/M ¶177).

2 See also *PhG* 63/M ¶91; 65–6/M ¶100; 74–5/M ¶117.

as being-for- itself, reduces the other force to being-for this other, and thus integrates the otherness of the second force into the being-for-itself of the dominant force. The second force becomes a factor in the way the first force constitutes its own exclusive singularity. The second force, however, does not lose its otherness or its status as force. It functions as the resistance required for the self-constitution of the first force. The second force operates as the other that turns the first force back to itself. Thus, the otherness of the second force belongs to the full articulation of what the first force is (*PhG* 83–6/M ¶136–8).

So also in the prestige battle, one self-consciousness maintains its status as a self-consciousness by playing off another self-consciousness. Each self focuses the whole battle on itself, with the opponent self reduced to its role in the first self's self-consciousness. Each self's being-for-itself calls into play another self's being-for-another (*PhG* 110/M ¶184–5). This opposition dynamic necessarily results in one self securing its claim to truth by reducing the other self to a dead self, a thing of nature. But just as the subordination of one force by another does not set aside the otherness of the subordinate force, or its status as force, so also the victory of one combatant in the prestige battle does not set aside the otherness of the defeated self or its status as a self-consciousness. Rather the defeat redefines the role of the other self as another self-consciousness integrated into the being-for-self of the dominant self. The otherness of the subordinate self-consciousness must be reconceived as a self-consciousness necessarily connected to its own death. The subordinate self-consciousness dies to its self and becomes integrated into the self-consciousness of the dominant self (*PhG* 112–13/M ¶189).[3]

3 MASTERY AND SERVICE[4]

Both the dominant and the subordinated self-consciousness belong to the same set of presuppositions. Both remain committed to the truth criterion of self-consciousness. Self-consciousness expects the truth to be self-consciousness in its subjective role. The world exists in its true form when it shows itself as a system existing and operating for a self outside and

3 Hegel says explicitly that the subordinate self "is a self-consciousness" (*PhG* 114/M ¶194).

4 Michael Hoffheimer (2001) has made a good case for not translating this discussion as master-slave. The word 'slave' suggests institutional slavery. Hegel uses a different German word (*Sklaverei*) when he talks about institutional slavery. In the discussion of self-consciousness, he uses the word *Knechtschaft.*

independent of the system. Both mastery and servitude acknowledge that truth belongs to the master self, whose willingness to risk life establishes the self's independence of nature, and who makes nature the self's own by appropriating nature's power over life and death. Servitude belongs to self-consciousness in its objective role. The servant self remains attached to life, completely overwhelmed by fear of the master's power over life and death. As a self-consciousness, however, the servant self acknowledges mastery as the true essence of life. Servitude, therefore, identifies itself with the truth by completely surrendering the servant's whole self to the master. The servant self identifies itself as the master's man. Serving the master is the servant's whole life. The servant's work belongs to this surrender. The servant produces an objective world adapted to the master's desires, and does so as a manifestation of what self-consciousness expects the truth to be, namely nature existing for an independent self-consciousness. Thus, the servant's work operates as an extension of the master's mastery (*PhG* 112–13/M ¶190–1; 114/M ¶194; 115–16/M ¶196).

Hegel stresses the permanence derived from a world transformed by servitude. The servant does not appropriate the world as his own, does not integrate its satisfactions into his own conscious life. The servant's work leaves the objective world standing on its own, now adapted to its true form, which is its existence for an independent self-consciousness. If the world serves the servant's natural desires and needs, it does so at the master's discretion, as the master's world. Thus, servitude negates the world's indifference to self-consciousness without making its independence disappear. Moreover, servitude integrates the negativity of self-consciousness into "the permanent order of things." The objective order stands before the master as an independent system whose driving force is self-conscious work adapting the system to its being for a self. In the process, it exposes another way in which self-consciousness establishes its independence of the objective world. Work liberates the servant-self from the fear of nature by struggling with and conquering nature's alien form, leaving a world tamed and ready to show itself as the master self's own world (*PhG* 114–16/M ¶195–6).

Work, however, shifts dominance in the master-servant relationship from mastery to servitude. The servant self confronts a world whose integration into the life of self-consciousness has been produced by the servant's own act. Moreover, mastery now appears as a status produced by the servant's work. The master confronts a world that shows itself as the master's world only because the servant's work and service has transformed it into the master's world. The master-servant dialectic begins with the servant identified as the master's man, a factor in the master's self-consciousness. It ends with the master identified as a mastery that the servant both serves and brings about, a factor in the servant's self-consciousness (*PhG* 114/M ¶192–3; 114–16/M ¶195–6).

Alexandre Kojève's interpretation of this result claims that it proves the truth of the servant's self-consciousness and negates the truth of the master's self-consciousness. According to this interpretation, the master's role is necessary only so that the self-consciousness of the working servant can develop; all subsequent moves in the dialectic develop the self-consciousness of work, not mastery.[5] But Hegel says explicitly that the master-servant dialectic negates both the self-consciousness of mastery and the self-consciousness of servitude (*PhG* 117–18/M ¶199). He says, too, that if the self-consciousness of the worker self is not completely absorbed by its fear of the master, the work does not function as a confrontation with the negative power of nature, which the servant encounters in the master's willingness to risk and take life. Without this confrontation, work is just "a skill which is master over some things, but not over the universal power and the whole of objective being" (*PhG* 115–16/M ¶196). In other words, without the relation to mastery, the worker self knows itself only as a skill that works with nature, not as a self who rules the whole system and gives it its reason for being. Servitude conquers nature because it operates as the master's mastery operating in the servant's work.

When addressing the issues raised by Kojève's interpretation, it is important to remember that master and servant function in the *Phenomenology* as factors in a certain way of conceiving what counts as essential and true in the dynamics between self-consciousness and nature. We are not talking about particular individuals in a particular set of circumstances. We are examining a form of knowledge as this has been defined and justified by determinate negations originating in the abstract structure of consciousness. In other words, Hegel's account of the mastery-servitude dialectic describes a form of knowing implicit in the necessary conditions of experience. It examines the experience involved in knowing the natural world as a world existing for the conscious self. The master-servant dialectic demonstrates that this experience necessarily takes two forms: self-consciousness knowing itself as a consciousness isolated in itself, separated from its own relations to nature (mastery); self-consciousness engaged in relations to nature, and integrated into natural existence as the negativity that gives the world its being-for self-consciousness (servitude). Mastery is self-consciousness withdrawn into itself, the subjectivity of conscious life knowing itself as set off

5 See especially Alexandre Kojève (1947), 173–5, 179; (1969), 45–7, 52.

from the world of nature. Servitude is self-consciousness integrated into the objectivity of the natural world, as a force that gives it its true form.

Here again the dynamic of the play of forces can help us appreciate the way the dynamic of self-consciousness operates. In the play of forces, each force constitutes itself by positing its own constitution in opposition to the other, which reduces the other to what the posited force is not. Dynamic energy posits itself by exerting itself against resistance, which reduces its other to what dynamic energy is not. But in order to be something else, the resisting force must posit something that it is, e.g. static force. This gives resistance a constitution of its own opposing dynamic energy, which reduces dynamic energy to what static force is not. But the force that static force resists must have a constitution of its own in order to be something other than static force, which shifts back to the dominance of dynamic energy. Thus, the dominance of one force shifts into the dominance of the other, which in turn shifts back to the dominance of the first. The whole play of forces dissolves its factors into the shifting dynamic between different forces (*PhG* 85–8/M ¶137–41).

Self-consciousness operates in a similar way when it shifts from the dominance of mastery to the dominance of servitude. The master-servant dialectic begins with mastery in the dominant position. Self-consciousness isolated in itself by its willingness to risk and take life derives from itself its mastery of nature by putting the fear of the lord into the servant self. As a result, the otherness of the servant self becomes defined by the master's self-consciousness. By acknowledging the master as the true self, and surrendering his own claims to this status, the servant manifests his self as a factor in the self-consciousness of mastery. In order to fulfill its role in the master's self-consciousness, however, servitude must have a constitution of its own. The servant self exposes its constitution in work. Work integrates self-consciousness into the dynamics of the objective world, as a force operating in the permanent order of things, and thereby produces the world as the master's world. Thus, mastery becomes a factor in the self-consciousness of servitude. It is what the servant's work produces through the servant's own act. But mastery still has a constitution of its own that distinguishes it from servitude. Mastery manifests this constitution as a willingness to risk and take life, which isolates self-consciousness in itself and separates it from its relations to the natural world. Mastery belongs to servitude as the self-consciousness that the servant-self is not; mastery is the self who does not transform the natural world through work. Servitude belongs to mastery as the self-consciousness that the master-self is not; servitude is the self who does not risk life and wield as its own nature's power over life and death.

The full significance of this result becomes more explicit if we translate it into the essential elements of self-consciousness. Mastery is self-consciousness isolated in itself and deriving from itself its relations to the natural world; servitude is self-consciousness involved in the natural world and deriving from this involvement its independence of the natural world. Each opposite shows itself as necessary to the other, and neither stands firm as the true essence of the whole interchange. Thus, the dynamic between conscious life and the natural life system dissolves into a play of opposites that negates everything in life as not what life truly is. Like the play of forces, the play of opposition between opposed forms of self-consciousness reduces the opposites to appearances, representations, that manifest something else as their true essence. This justifies a new form of self-consciousness. In this new form, self-consciousness takes the truth to be something other than the conscious life of the self. This other transforms the necessary connection between the opposite forms of conscious life into the self-same principle distinguished from itself (*PhG* 116–17/M ¶197; 117–18/M ¶199).

4 STOICISM-SCEPTICISM

The determinate negation of the mastery-service dynamic introduces self-consciousness in the form of thought. Hegel introduces this form by distinguishing the sameness and otherness of thought from the sameness and otherness of self-conscious life. Mastery begins as a self-consciousness set off from the natural world itself and from the servant self attached to the natural world. Mastery knows itself in an otherness not derived from or determined by mastery itself. Servitude knows itself in a thing it produces, but knows self-consciousness in the master self who is not the servant's self. We, the philosophical observers, however, have seen all these differences dissolve into life connecting itself to some other life. We know from this that self-consciousness must be redefined as a sameness that remains the same throughout all of life's differences and changes. The true essence of life remains the same self-consciousness in all the various facets of life. Self-consciousness, therefore, must find the truth in its own detachment from the tensions, diversity, and dependencies of life, and in what corresponds to this detached self-consciousness in the objective world. Thus, consciousness becomes two-layered. Consciousness involved in life satisfies desire, risks life, masters nature, or fears it and works on it. Consciousness detached from all this is thought.

Hegel associates this detached self-consciousness with stoicism, and he explicitly calls attention to the way stoicism reinstates the objective as an equally essential component in what the truth is. Prior forms of self-consciousness expected the truth to be a consciousness set apart from the objective order, a consciousness achieving its truth by suppressing the otherness of the objective order. Stoic thought accepts the otherness of the object, but knows it in the form of thought. This form is the object's own, not one imposed on it by the self. But like the subject's true form, it involves a withdrawal from the overt dynamics of life. The truth of the objective world is not the threat, violence, conflict, and tensions of life. The truth of the objective world is what makes the world intelligible to thought. Stoicism calls this correspondence between free thought and the intelligibility of being "the true" and "the good" (*PhG* 116–18/M ¶197–9).

This result introduces the knowledge issue in a new form. In order to know the truth, stoic thought must know itself, its world, and other self-conscious individuals in a way that gets beyond the alienated otherness produced by the dynamics of life. In the process, thought must detach itself from the restrictions generated by this alienation: the restrictions of space-time imposed by nature, the restrictions of singularity imposed by the challenge of other self-conscious individuals, the restrictions of a particular role determined by the individual's relations to other individuals. Stoicism, therefore, takes as its truth criterion a knowing not limited to a particular time, place, and way of life, and not confined to what a singular consciousness knows as true. It expects the truth to be what must be true not only of the particular world to which the individual thinker belongs, but also of every world. It assumes that the claims of thought must be acknowledged not only by other individuals living in the same world, but by anyone, anywhere, anytime. By detaching itself from the restrictions of life, stoic thought detaches itself from the conditions of temporal, individualized existence.[6]

Thought, however, becomes liberated by leaving out the multiplicity and conflicts of life. The freedom of stoic thought, Hegel says, lets natural existence go free (*frei entlassen*). Thought abandons life to its own devices, leaves it free to be unaffected by what thought requires of it. Hence, life remains other than thought, indifferent and alien to it; and thought itself is only an abstract structure. This abstract structure provides the bare-bones

6 Hegel will show in his account of unhappy consciousness, that the singularity of the self and its space-time limitations belong to the conditions of human life, because humans are objects of sense certainty (*PhG* 124/M ¶212; 125–6/M ¶217). I have assumed, therefore, that the detachment of stoic thought and the negativity of scepticism includes detachment from and negation of life's space-time conditions, although these are not explicitly mentioned in Hegel's account of stoicism and scepticism.

definition of what knowing the truth is. According to this concept, knowing the truth is thinking the intelligibility of the object, or thought thinking the object as something that corresponds to or is attuned to thought. Although this concept conceives a differentiated truth, thought thinking itself in an independent diversified other, the concept does not contain the reality and content of life, with all its tensions and conflict. Yet self-consciousness in the form of thought assumes that thought is the true essence of life. In order to know the truth, therefore, thought must become involved in the conditions of life and make them appear in their true form (*PhG* 118–19/M ¶200–1).

Stoic detachment sets thought up as a self-consciousness "complete in itself," a knowing that knows only what corresponds to itself, and hence does not require anything else for the fulfillment of what it is. This independence makes it possible for thought to begin with itself, to derive from itself the determinations of life. At this point in the phenomenological examination of knowledge, however, thought has no positive content of its own from which the content of life might be derived. Its only determination is the selfsameness that distinguishes it from the differences and tensions played out in the particulars of real life experience. Thought, therefore, makes the truth manifest in the realities of life by deriving from its independence a negation that attacks life experience in each of its elements, makes each one appear in its untruth, and thus absorbs them all into the same thought process. Thought becomes scepticism. Stoic thought takes the form of a tranquil, tautological selfsameness. This kind of universality gives difference a form that creates no conflict or tension; the same truth remains unaffected by its differentiation in the dynamic between self and world. Sceptical thought transforms this undisturbed universality into a unity established by negating differences. Sceptical thought negates everything in life that would set itself up as a stable, unchangeable truth, and absorbs it into the ongoing process of thought thinking itself alone as the only persistent, unchangeable truth (*PhG* 118–19/M ¶202).

But in order to do this, thought must become involved in what it negates; it must live the contingency and confusion of life as unessential and untrue. Scepticism accomplishes this by self-consciously exposing all the problems we have observed in the preceding determinate negations. Sceptical thought enters its own object-dominated cognitions and brings to consciousness their contradictions. The conflicts that emerged in sense certainty, perception, and understanding appear here as thought self-consciously unsettling its own experience of the truth as an independent objective order. Thought lives a single life entangled through desire and work in the ongoing process of life and death, contingently appearing at a particular time in a particular place, opposed by the forces of nature and the threat of other self-conscious individuals. It lives a particular role, like master or servant, compelled by commands, expectations, laws governing relations between one self-consciousness and another. And it knows every facet of this existence as contingent, vulnerable, unimportant. Thus, thought gives itself existence in the contingencies and conflicts of life, and makes each one appear as a different manifestation of the same thought-driven negativity (*PhG* 119–20/M ¶203–5).

In the process, thought becomes identified with what it rejects as untrue. Thought knows itself as the isolated singular consciousness that is me and no other, a consciousness belonging to a particular time and place, immersed in whatever particulars happen to show up in perceptual experience, carried along by the necessities of nature and desire, compelled by expectations belonging to its life with others, preoccupied with actions and productions determined by these expectations; and all the while thought dismisses this life as pointless, as not at all what life truly is. Thus, thought knows itself lost in what is not its self. Yet by losing its self in the contingencies and conflicts of life, thought "converts itself again into a consciousness that is universal and self-identical; for it is the negativity of all singularity and all difference" (*PhG* 120–1/M ¶205).

In the transition from consciousness to self-consciousness, we saw the reality factor of cognition expanded to include the whole dynamic between self-consciousness and its object. In the account of stoicism and scepticism, we see Hegel explicitly acknowledging this in the way he analyzes the relation between thought and life. Detachment from life separates thought from reality (*Dasein*). Scepticism is the realization (*die Realisierung*) of thought, the actual experience (*die wirkliche Erfahrung*) of free thought (*PhG* 119/M ¶202).[7] Thus, Hegel introduces the thought versus reality issue as a thought versus experience issue, which is also the way he defines it in the *Encyclopaedia.* Thought becomes actual, it becomes real, in the whole dynamic between consciousness and the field of empirical data, between self-conscious life and the objective life system, between desire and work, mastery and servitude. Self-consciousness knows the truth by making it all appear in the form of thought. In the process of thinking the untruth of life's various forms, sceptical thought becomes negatively involved in and identified with the concrete conflicts and tensions of life, conscious life as well as the life of the objective life system. This involvement transforms the different forms of life into the same thought differentiated from itself in

7 See also *PhG* 121/M ¶206.

them. "The differences, which in the pure thinking of self-consciousness are only the abstraction of differences, here become the entirety of the differences, and the whole of differentiated being becomes a difference of self-consciousness" (*PhG* 119/M ¶202).

Hegel says explicitly and with some emphasis that thought's sceptical involvement in life identifies thought itself with the singularity of the conscious self. Because sceptical thought derives its independence and truth status from its negative involvement in life, independent thought persists as the thought of this singular self. When, therefore, thought gives itself reality as the negation of life, it also negates the self's isolated singularity. Even thought becomes untrue when it is limited to the thought of a singular self. Yet thought lives; and because it lives, it is trapped in the singularity of this self (*PhG* 120–1/M ¶205; 121–2/M ¶207). This development gives us the knowledge question in its most challenging form. How can a cognition isolated within the consciousness of this individual make claims that must be acknowledged not only by other individuals living in the same world but by anyone, anywhere, anytime? How can a knowing focused on a world that belongs to a particular time, place, and way of life claim that what is true of this world is true of every world? Sceptical thought can only pose the question, not give the answer. Thought in this form achieves its liberation by being involved in life. It sets itself apart by becoming negatively involved in what it thinks as untrue, distorted, unstable; and this negativity is its only determination. Hence, the universality and timelessness of sceptical thought has no content or existence of its own. It exists in and defines itself in terms of what it negates – the thinker's isolated individual self-consciousness, a life tied to nature, a life that belongs to a particular time, place, and environment.

5 UNHAPPY CONSCIOUSNESS

In the transition from sceptical thought to unhappy consciousness, Hegel gives us one of his most explicit accounts of the way determinate negation works. A self-consciousness committed to the presuppositions of scepticism keeps the contradictories apart. It takes the truth to be the selfsameness of thought thinking itself, and so it thinks its own sceptical thinking as the true essence of real life experience. This same scepticism also knows its own thought involved in and identified with the break up of life in non-identical forms of living. But scepticism keeps these contradictory ways of thinking separated from each other. It does not acknowledge the way each turns itself into the other. The shift to the next form of self-consciousness adds nothing. It simply moves to a form of self-consciousness that acknowledges what is already exposed in scepticism. It brings together scepticism's different ways of thinking, acknowledges the way they turn into each other, and accepts the contradiction between them as what the self is. Moreover, Hegel explicitly calls attention to the rigors of the shift. Unhappy consciousness begins with "the duplication of self-consciousness within itself ... not yet in its unity; the Unhappy Consciousness is the consciousness of self as a dual-natured, merely contradictory being" (*PhG* 121–2/M ¶206). Unhappy consciousness begins with the results of scepticism in their contradictoriness. This alone has been justified by the scepticism dialectic. Whatever else Hegel claims about the truth expectations of unhappy consciousness must emerge from this starting point (*PhG* 121–2/M ¶206–7).

Unhappy consciousness acknowledges the contradiction that is its very self. Hegel describes this contradiction in terms of the changeable and the unchangeable. Thought freed from the dynamics of life is unchangeable. Free thought does not keep turning into its opposite, as life does. Thought stands firm. It remains selfsame, in the thinking subject and in the intelligibility of the object. Unhappy consciousness, like scepticism, takes this stable, unchanging form of thought to be the essential thing. But unhappy consciousness cannot stand firm in its true self. Its unchangeable thought depends on its involvement in life for its liberation from life. In unhappy consciousness, unchangeable thought turns itself into thought engaged in the instability of life, and then comes back to its unchangeableness as a result of its negative involvement in the changeable. Thus, the changeableness of unhappy consciousness takes the form of unchangeable thought changing into changeable thought, and changeable thought changing into unchangeable thought (*PhG* 122–3/M ¶208–9).

Hegel works out the presuppositions of unhappy consciousness by talking explicitly about the role of singularity. Unchangeable thought derived from the negation of real life experience becomes infected with singularity, because real life experience belongs to a singular self. Thought liberating itself from life is a singular self-consciousness thinking its way out of the restrictions of its singular existence. Thus, thought knows itself as my thought and no-one else's even while it acknowledges that knowing the truth requires a thought not limited to me. Moreover, unhappy consciousness knows nothing more about the truth than what this negation of singularity reveals. This limited knowledge reveals what the truth of unhappy consciousness requires. Truth requires a thought not limited to the thought of a singular self, and not compromised by the limiting conditions of life. Unhappy consciousness expects the truth to be universal, all-encompassing thought thinking itself. But unhappy consciousness knows that its own thought does not have this kind of universality. Its thought belongs to a singular self dependent on its involvement in life's alien conditions to establish its independence of those conditions. Truth, therefore, belongs to another being whose unchangeable thought exists in itself, uncompromised by its opposite.

This conception of the truth, however, differs from the benign, undisturbed selfsameness and universality of stoic thought. Stoic thought detaches itself from the singularity of the self and the divisiveness of its life experience. The shift into scepticism acknowledges the necessity of making this self-thinking thought exist in real life. Hence, unhappy consciousness, appropriating the developments implicit in scepticism, conceives the unity and universality of thought as a truth that can, and indeed must, exist in the singularity and diversity of life. In other words, it conceives an unchangeable truth other than unhappy consciousness itself but appropriate to it, a truth that can exist in the dynamics of unhappy consciousness and reconcile its contradictory opposites. Unhappy consciousness expects the truth to be timeless, all-encompassing thought existing as the thought of a singular self involved in the spatio-temporal conditions of the natural world. By becoming thus identified with the contradictory opposites that divide unhappy consciousness against itself, universal, unchangeable thought transforms these opposites into the selfsame unchangeable truth. Unhappy consciousness takes the truth to be a singular self, a human being, identified with the timeless, all-encompassing, unchangeable thought that transcends the limitations and instability of unhappy consciousness itself. Hence, we might call this truth a divine self or God-man. Unhappy consciousness itself becomes true by becoming one with the thought and life of this divine self (*PhG* 123–4/M ¶210–11; 124–5/M ¶213; 125/M ¶216).[8]

Hegel describes the way the truth of unhappy consciousness is accomplished by repeating the dynamics of servitude and mastery reproduced as a dynamic between the divided self of unhappy consciousness and the self of the God-man.[9] In yearning and devotion, pious action, and asceticism, unhappy consciousness tries to experience its own thought and life completely negated and surrendered to this divine self-conscious individual.

8 Burbidge (1992) explains why the account of unhappy consciousness should not be interpreted as a reference to historical Christianity. My own interpretation, like his, takes unhappy consciousness to be implicit in the general structure of self-consciousness and hence not limited to the experience of medieval Catholicism.

9 For a description that helps us appreciate how it feels to be engaged in the experience of unhappy consciousness, see Crites (1998), 290–303.

Yearning and devotion absorb the self of unhappy consciousness into a relation in which it stretches out toward a self separated in time and place from the self that yearns for it (*PhG* 124–5/M ¶214; 125–6/M ¶217). Pious action represents the desires and work of unhappy consciousness as gifts received from the divine self. By giving thanks, unhappy consciousness brings the experience of the divine other into the divided self's sense of itself (*PhG* 126–8/M ¶218–22). Asceticism transforms the divided self's sense of itself into the experience of its own untruth. The self lives its life as a life completely negated. A religious superior represents his or her commands as the will of the divine self made manifest. By obeying these commands and letting them rule the self's whole life, the ascetic surrenders his or her thought to the divine self. The negation of life belongs to this surrender. The ascetic gives up property and enjoyment, speaks an alien incomprehensible language, becomes immersed in the self's dependence on natural life, and lives this as wretchedness and degradation. All this transforms the life of the ascetic self into recognition of the divine self as the true self-consciousness that the ascetic self is not; and the mediator represents for the ascetic the otherness of the divine self acknowledging the surrender (*PhG* 128–31/M ¶223–30).

The restrictions of Hegel's proof procedure, however, make it necessary to re-conceive the thought and life of the divine self and bring it back into the thought and life of human cognition. The move to a form of thought that transcends human cognition depends on what is implicit in the contradictory dynamic of human cognition itself. This dynamic shows that detached thought and thought immersed in life roll over into each other; what each opposite is necessitates its changing into its opposite. This demonstrates that the dynamic is driven by a connecting principle, and the connecting principle identifies the opposites as differences within an integrated dynamic structure. In order to know the principle that identifies the unity and selfsameness of the structure, self-consciousness distinguishes the unity principle from the divisiveness of what it unifies. Since, however, self-consciousness justifies the unity principle only as what grounds or accounts for the connectedness of the divided self, self-consciousness must cancel the distinction. It must re-conceive the self-sameness of thought and life in the divine self as a selfsameness identified with the contradictory opposites of unhappy consciousness. This immanence identifies human cognition as the selfsameness of thought persisting throughout the opposition dynamic between detached thought and thought immersed in life. Unhappy consciousness experiences this return move as the mediator or religious superior assuring the ascetic self that its life has been reconciled to the divine self. The assurances of the mediator give the ascetic individual the experience of being taken up into the universality of the true self (*PhG* 132/M ¶231). "It is no longer I who live, but Christ who lives in me."[10]

6 THE TRANSITION TO REASON

In order to make sense of the transition from unhappy consciousness to reason, we must look carefully at certain subtleties introduced in the account of unhappy consciousness. First, unhappy consciousness complicates the form-content issue. Hegel introduces the form-content issue in the examination of understanding. In the play of forces, form is the dynamic between being-for-self (separation) and being-for-another (relation). Content is the properties overlapping and belonging to each other, e.g. white colouring a cubical shape (the exclusive one), and these same properties involved in contrast relations to other properties in the field of sense data, e.g. a white cubical shape showing itself as not the red round shape in a different place (the also). Thus, content is the particulars in which the necessities of the form operate (*PhG* 82–3/M ¶134–5; 86–7/M ¶140). We concluded the explanation of the understanding dialectic by pointing out an unresolved contradiction that Hegel himself does not discuss, namely the contradiction between the necessities of the dynamic form and the contingency of the particulars in which the form operates. The form must exist in the particulars. But it does not necessitate any specific collection of particulars. Self-consciousness carries along this form-content issue in the constitution of the objective life system and in the particulars of self-conscious desire. The dynamic forms of life operate in these particulars without determining exactly which particulars they have to be. When, therefore, unhappy consciousness brings life into the dynamics of thought, the givenness of life's particulars also becomes part of the process.

Also, unhappy consciousness conceives the form of life as thought's opposite. Unhappy consciousness gets its opposites from scepticism; and scepticism vacillates between detached thought, which thinks objective reality only as an intelligibility attuned to thought, and thought immersed in life, which thinks what is alien to thought precisely as such. Scepticism's involvement in life brings into the thought process the contingent particulars in which the necessities of objective and subjective life become real. Unhappy consciousness conceives the transcendent truth of the divine self as the reconciliation of the opposites exposed in scepticism. Thought

10 Galatians 2:20.

thinking the objective world as an intelligible world and thought thinking the same world as alien and unintelligible now belong to the selfsame truth. As a result, the whole complicated content of life, with all its contingencies and conflicts, belongs to universal thought thinking itself. But unhappy consciousness conceives this reconciliation as not what human thought can accomplish. The rich content of life is completely intelligible only in transcendent, unchangeable truth identified with the life of a singular self-consciousness.

Unhappy consciousness also redefines the role of reality in knowledge. The complete surrender of the human self to the divine self reduces human self-consciousness to a thing: "[Unhappy consciousness] has the certainty of having truly divested itself of its 'I,' and of having turned its immediate self-consciousness into a Thing, into an objective existence (*gegenständlichen Sein*)" (*PhG* 130–1/M ¶229). In order to fully appreciate the significance of this, we must remember that thought belongs to unhappy consciousness as well as mastery and servitude, desire and work. Thought as human thought remains trapped in the singularity of the human self, dependent on its involvement in a human life conditioned by nature and the challenge of other self-conscious individuals. The whole complicated dynamic between thought as stoic detachment and thought as the sceptic's negativity belongs to unhappy consciousness, which has now been re-conceived as objective being (*gegenständlichen Sein*). In unhappy consciousness, the whole subject-object, thought-life dynamic belongs to objective existence, and objective existence has its truth in a form of thought distinguished from this reality. Thus, the *Phenomenology* introduces the distinction between pure thought and the reality of experience.

Self-consciousness, like consciousness, ends with a distinction made and cancelled. Unhappy consciousness vacillates between thought thinking an intelligibility attuned to itself and thought thinking the unintelligibility of life's particulars, spatio-temporal contingencies, self-nature tensions, and conflicting individualities. The move to a transcendent self-consciousness distinguishes the selfsameness of the opposites from their diversity and opposition. The move back from the transcendent self to the human self cancels this distinction by thinking each opposite played out in unhappy consciousness as the same principle distributed in different realities. Thus, self-consciousness develops its own version of the determinate negation that connects a tranquil, tautological universal with a divisive, self-opposed universal. This justifies the move from self-consciousness to reason. Reason assumes that the opposites negating each other in the dynamics of unhappy consciousness are the same rationality distinguished from itself (*PhG* 131–3/M ¶230–3).

Hegel tells us later that reason has no religion, because the rational self knows itself in what is immediately present to it, not in a reality that transcends itself and its world (*PhG* 363/M ¶673). But the *Phenomenology* justifies the presuppositions of reason by coming to them from the dynamic of religious self-consciousness (*PhG* 130–2/M ¶230–1). This reveals two necessary conditions hidden away in the rational attitude. The first is a surrender condition. Human thought can assume that its independent thinking knows universal truth only if the dominance of human subjectivity in the relation between self and world has been negated. Human thought must surrender to a form of thought that includes within its universality not only the independent subjectivity of human thinking but also the way both nature and human life maintain their independence of this subjectivity.

Thus, Hegel says that the transition to reason restores object-dominated consciousness to an essential role in knowing what the truth is: "There appeared two aspects, one after the other: one in which the essence or the True had for consciousness the determinateness of being, the other in which it had the determinateness of being only for consciousness. But the two reduced themselves to a single truth, viz. that what is or the in-itself, only is insofar as it is for consciousness, and what is for consciousness is also in itself or has intrinsic being" (*PhG* 132–3/M ¶233). Rationality belongs to the independent reality of the objective order, to the way the world is, regardless of the way we think about it. Our thinking does not determine the way the world is, nor does it dominate the relation between self and world. But the way the world is and the way we think are governed by the same rationality. The world's independent truth and our own are in some way a shared truth. By thinking rationally, therefore, we can know the world; and we can know what it is as a world independent of the way we think about it.

The transition from self-consciousness to reason also involves a reality condition. Reason acknowledges that knowledge must exist in and be identified with the reality of human experience. But reason assumes that the thinking individual has become identified with a rationality that transcends the limits of his or her singularity, attachment to life, and specific spatio-temporal situation.

7 IDEALISM

Hegel tells us in the *Science of Logic* that scientific procedure retreats into a ground, and he explicitly refers to the way this procedure operates in the scientific development of consciousness, which is the task of the *Phenomenology*

(*WL* 21:57–8/M 71–2). In chapter 7, I have explained how this procedure makes sense of the ambiguous way in which Hegel talks about a mediated beginning which is nevertheless immediate. The process that exposes the necessary implications of a concept demonstrates that the concept identifies something rooted in and determined by something other than itself. Our knowledge of the ground is mediated, because it depends on what we know about something derived from the ground. The proof proves, however, that what we started with depends on the ground, not the other way around. In order to know the truth in its proper form, therefore, we must conceive the ground as prior to, and hence not mediated by, what depends on it. We must assert the ground as a principle independent of the concept that leads us into the ground, and then see how what has been exposed as a derivative truth emerges from the necessary implications of the ground.

The *Phenomenology*'s examination of consciousness and self-consciousness shows how these forms of experience retreat into reason as their common ground. At the end of the self-consciousness dialectic, reason is a result dependent on, mediated by, what consciousness and self-consciousness prove themselves to be. But the demonstration proves the necessity of reversing the priorities, since it shows that reason is the fundamental, originating principle governing the dynamics of consciousness and self-consciousness. This reversal must also take a form appropriate to the method and task of the *Phenomenology*. The *Phenomenology* examines ordinary phenomenal consciousness, which is cognition engaged in experience. The various truth criteria that emerge in this examination are tested by the way each appears in experience. In order to make the shift from self-consciousness to reason, therefore, Hegel must look for an experience in which reason asserts itself immediately, without deriving its claims from any other knowledge, so that reason can be experienced as not derivative but foundational. He finds this experience in idealism.

According Hegel's account of idealism, thought asserts itself by itself, without explanations and without content, since all explanatory principles and identifying content must be known as what reason derives from itself. To begin with, reason asserts itself immediately, without demonstration, as the truth of all reality. Thought posits itself thinking itself ("I am I"), and thus knows itself as a thinking reality, thought being, which Hegel calls the simple category (*PhG* 132–4/M ¶231–5). Being, however, does not mean being in general, or being as a reality distinguished from consciousness:

> the category means that self-consciousness and being are the same essence, the same, not through comparison, but in and for themselves. It is only the one-sided,

spurious idealism that lets this unity again come on the scene as consciousness, on one side, confronted by an in-itself, on the other. But now this category or simple unity of self-consciousness and being possesses difference in itself; for its essence is just this, to be immediately one and selfsame in otherness, or in absolute difference. (*PhG* 134–5/M ¶235)

The sameness of self-consciousness and being does not mean that the same rational structure is repeated in each. It means that they are the same identity. Each belongs to the rationality of the other. Self-consciousness and being together are what exists, the in-itself. This selfsame identity is also for-itself; rational self-consciousness knows the rationality of its other as one in being with self-consciousness itself. Thus, the term "being" in the account of idealism refers to the ground that the subjectivity of thinking and the objectivity of the intelligible have in common (*PhG* 134–5/M ¶235).

We see here the same way of talking about the unity of thought and being that we saw in the *Encyclopaedia*, when Hegel compares the third position on objectivity to Descartes' *cogito*.[11] Like Descartes' *cogito*, immediate knowing knows not just being as an object of thought, but the real being of its own knowing. But Descartes' *cogito* knows only its own limited being. The *cogito* of the immediate knowing position asserts itself identified with the infinite, and hence the certainty of its own existence is also the certainty of the infinite existing. Hegel's account of idealism in the *Phenomenology* describes a form of reason with the same kind of immediacy and a similar kind of self-importance. Idealism asserts itself identified with the fundamental truth of all reality. Unlike Jacobi's immediate knowing position, however, idealism asserts itself as thought, not belief; and it expects its self-positing to posit not only its own thought existing but also its own thought deriving from itself all reality.[12]

11 See chapter 5, §2.

12 Cinzia Ferrini interprets Hegel's phenomenological account of idealism as an engagement with issues raised by Kant's, Fichte's, and Schelling's idealism. She situates the discussion of these issues in the context of Hegel's encounter with the same issues in other works, both early and late. She explains Hegel's analysis of idealism by focussing on idealism as an empty, abstract thought that fails because it cannot derive from itself the concrete determinations of the empirical world (Ferrini 2009a; see also Dahlstrom 2006–07, 41–3; Russon 2004, 118). Although I do not deny that these issues are involved in Hegel's phenomenological account, I interpret them according to the requirements of Hegel's proof procedure. This gives the abstractness of idealism the form of a self identified with the immediacy of a ground. As the certainty of being all reality, self-consciousness simply asserts itself, like a Cartesian *cogito*, and expects to have the dynamics that have retreated into it immediately appear as its consequence.

In the process of positing itself being, thought appears to itself in a plurality of categories. This plurality appears as given. Thought does not demonstrate why these ways of thinking rather than others show up in our thinking. When thought thinks, these different ways of thinking appear. Since, however, thought as reason takes itself to be the truth of all reality, thought thinks these differences as not different from the simplicity of thought itself. Hence, it thinks the differences as species of thought, with the simplicity of thought as the genus that remains the same in each and all the different ways of thinking. Idealistic thinking integrates the multiplicity of its categories by negating their difference and recognizing them as one and all "mine"; all the differences belong to one thought, one unity of apperception. Thus, thought, like perception's self-identical thing, forms its multiplicity into a singularity separated from what is not itself. It takes to itself its own differences and excludes whatever is not its own. The individuality of the self appears in the form of thought.

The singular, Hegel says, is "the transition of the category from its <concept> (*Begriff*) to an external reality (*äußern Realität*)" (*PhG* 135–6/M ¶236). In other words, thought thinking itself necessarily identifies itself as an exclusive individual, and in virtue of this connects itself to an other, to what is not its own; and it derives what this other is from what thought thinking itself must exclude. Thought thinking itself in terms of unity and difference distinguishes itself from an other that is also conceived in terms of unity and difference. As other, however, the unity and difference take the form of an opposite. Thought persisting as the same unity of apperception in all its different thought categories posits itself in an opposition connection to a simplicity that remains uninvolved in the differences that belong to it, and thus leaves them spread apart, disconnected, each isolated in itself. Hegel uses the term "thing" to express this excluded, opposed simplicity, "whether the Thing is called an extraneous impulse, or an empirical or sensuous entity, or the Thing-in-itself, it still remains in principle the same, i.e. extraneous to that unity" (*PhG* 137/M ¶238). The constitution derived from what consciousness excludes identifies "thing" as a simple undifferentiated something that appears as an unconnected variety of data (*PhG* 134–6/M ¶235–6).

The thing, however, belongs to self-conscious thought itself as an other conceived in terms of thought, as the opposite of thought's own way of being both a unity and a plurality. Thought thinks itself as the unification of diversity in the unity of apperception. Thought thinks its opposite as the diversification of simplicity in unconnected data. Moreover, thought appropriates the other by thinking it as an other identified by what relates it to thought itself. It thinks the differences belonging to the thing as the thinking subject's own sensations and representations, and it thinks these according to the categories of thought itself. Thought, therefore, shows itself as a necessary connection between opposite forms of thought: the tranquil unity of thought thinking different categories or ways of thinking as one and all its own unity of apperception; thought distributed in the isolated data presented by something extraneous to, excluded by, thought's tranquil self-sameness. Thought thinks the whole opposition dynamic as thought thinking itself: "Consciousness, however, as essence is this whole process itself, of passing out of itself as simple category into a singular individual, into the object, and of contemplating this process in the object, nullifying the object as <different> (*unterscheidnen*), appropriating it as its own, and proclaiming itself as this certainty of being all reality, of being both itself and its object" (*PhG* 136/M ¶237).

This dynamic, however, contains something that remains resistant to the claims of thought thinking itself. There is a diversity in the experience that thought does not derive from itself. Self-conscious thought finds its various categories involved in a wealth of particulars whose differences are not determined by these different ways of thinking. Thought makes the particulars its own by thinking them as "my" sensations and representations and by organizing them according to its own thought categories. But the result of this appropriation leaves the full array of differences unexplained, since the differentiation of the categories falls far short of the differentiation displayed in the particulars of sensation and representation.

Idealism, therefore, develops a contradiction. The simplicity of thought thinking itself asserts itself as the truth of all reality. This very self-assertion brings into play an experience in which thought thinks itself differentiated in various categories or ways of thinking, a difference in which thought remains the same unity of self-consciousness throughout all the differences. But this tranquil, transparent selfsameness necessarily connects itself to its opposite, because the very thought of its own selfsameness excludes the full development of difference in the array of particulars thought in the various categories. Yet these particulars actually appear. They exist in real experience. Indeed, they appear in experience as a reality inextricably connected to thought thinking itself. But thought must dismiss them as not true, not essential, because they appear precisely as not included in what reason takes the truth to be, namely thought thinking itself. Since, however, they belong to what reality is, thought thinking itself must dismiss itself as not true, because it does not appear to itself as what it claims to be. In idealism, thought does not appear to itself as all reality.

Hegel compares this to the contradiction of sceptical thought, except that scepticism is negative and idealism is positive. Sceptical thought knows itself as essence and truth by demonstrating the untruth and unreality of what appears to be other than and independent of thought. Idealistic reason knows itself as essence and truth by thinking as "mine" the particulars derived from what is foreign and alien to thought. In both cases, thought thinks itself as the essence of the object by directing itself to an alien, indifferent other. In the case of idealism, which relates positively to this foreign element, reason returns to the presuppositions of perception and understanding, forms of consciousness dependent on an object that is completely independent of and indifferent to consciousness. According to the presuppositions of idealistic reason, however, thought thinking what is alien and indifferent to thought does not know the truth, because idealism presupposes the claim that reason is the truth of all reality (*PhG* 136–7/M ¶238).

This development justifies the beginning presuppositions of what Hegel calls "actual reason," which in its first form is reason as observation. Actual reason exists within the framework of idealism's presuppositions. In actual reason, however, the commitment to reason's truth criterion is not overt, but hidden and unconscious. It operates in the way rational knowers carry out their investigations. In actual reason, too, the certainty of being all reality exists together with its determinate negation – the return to a foreign object, the kind of object appropriate to perception and understanding. For actual reason, the reality of reason is a task. Reason becomes actually "what is" only when thought actually knows the rationality of what appears when thought thinks itself. Only then does reality actually exist as thought thinking itself. The account of reason as observation, therefore, examines not nature itself or self-consciousness itself but the rational study of both. Reason brings its rational expectations to experience and gives itself reality by bringing to consciousness the rationality of experience (*PhG* 137–8/M ¶239–43).

Hegel retrieves here a factor exposed in the dialectic of consciousness and self-consciousness, but without much explicit discussion. In the development of perception and again in the development of understanding, Hegel shows how knowledge of the object knows the particulars of perceptual reality only as carriers of essential structures. Neither things, nor forces, nor laws explain why their particulars must be these particulars. Particulars are necessary, because a thing, a force, or a law is nothing other than the organization of particulars. But why a thing or force or law has these particulars rather than some other set of particulars remains unexplained; they are simply accepted as given and known according to the necessary structures of objectivity. When the objective order is redefined as the life-world of self-consciousness, this mixture of necessary structures and contingent particulars goes with it and is carried along all the way through the various shifts in the examination of self-consciousness. Idealism conceives pure thought as a plurality of categories in which the differentiation of reality and even the externality of the object belong to the tautological sameness of thought thinking itself. But this concept determines itself only as a dynamic between unity and differentiation. It does not explain why the unity of thought and thing must be differentiated in the particular ways that actually appear. Even the differentiation of thought in a plurality of categories remains a given; it just happens that we think this way.

The consciousness version of perception and understanding expects the truth to be an independent object. Hence, these forms of experience can accept the structures of independent objectivity without accounting for the particulars that belong to these structures. According to the presuppositions of reason, however, thought thinking itself is the truth of all reality. If, therefore, thought thinks itself and its object in given particulars, without exposing the rationality of these particulars, then thought does not think itself as the truth of all reality. Reason becomes the truth of all reality only when it actually thinks as thought thinking itself everything that belongs to reality, including the given species of thinking and the particulars of perceptual experience. Hence, reason makes itself actual by discovering the rational structure of unification and diversification in the particulars of experience and given ways of thinking. Moreover, because reason assumes that reason is the true essence of all reality, reason as observation does not remain passive or purely receptive in this search. It seeks and expects to find in its objects structures that mirror the structures of reason, and it actively selects or works on the material in order to make the object appear in rational form (*PhG* 137–8/M ¶240–2; 167–8/M ¶299–300).

8 THE KANTIAN INTERPRETATION REVISITED

After explaining Hegel's account of the transition from consciousness to self-consciousness, I argued against various Kantian interpretations of this move. Since, however, the interpretation of this transition determines the opening moves of self-consciousness, significant Kantian interpretations of these moves have appeared in recent studies of Hegel's *Phenomenology*. In this section, I will consider two of these in order to explain how my interpretation of the transition from consciousness to self-consciousness challenges Kantian interpretations of desire, the prestige battle, and the master-servant dialectic. I will also explain how my non-Kantian interpretation of the transition from consciousness to self-consciousness accords with the Kantian elements in the transition from self-consciousness to reason and idealism.

Frederick Neuhouser interprets the transition to desire and recognition as a transcendental argument that accepts as its starting point the Kantian interpretation of the transition from consciousness to self-consciousness. "The second and more plausible alternative is to see recognition not as presupposed by the concept of desire but rather as the necessary condition of an even earlier stage of the dialectic, namely, self-consciousness' initial view of itself as the merely formal unifier of its representations."[13] Neuhouser argues that both desire and recognition belong to a search for the conditions that make possible the experience in which the self is conscious of itself as this "formal unifier of its representations." He interprets this self-knowing as the self conscious of itself as a self set apart in its own isolated independence.[14] Neuhouser's more recent interpretation of mastery-service continues this way of conceiving the normative element in self-consciousness.[15]

If, however, we interpret the transition from consciousness to self-consciousness as a determinate negation, then Neuhouser's interpretation loses the negation's attachment to what it negates. As a determinate negation, self-consciousness enters the dialectic as the other in which the objective life system completes what it is. The self's independence of life is derived from the objective life system negating itself as not its own truth, which turns into the positive determination that its truth is its being "for" the self. Neuhouser's interpretation conceives the independence of the self by itself, and looks for the conditions that make an experience of this isolated independence possible. My interpretation conceives the independence of the self in terms of its derivation from the dynamics of the objective life system. A form of self-consciousness fails if its independence loses the experience of itself as the truth of the natural world. Hence, the self engaged in a battle to the death does not satisfy the truth expectations of self-consciousness, because the winner finds himself confronted by a corpse that belongs to the natural world's indifference to the self; and the master does not satisfy these same truth expectations because he finds himself

13 Neuhouser (1986), 257.
14 Ibid., 258.
15 Neuhouser (2009).

dependent on the servant's work for transforming the independent objective world into a world existing for the master.

McDowell offers a more radical Kantian approach to the opening moves of self-consciousness. According to McDowell, understanding ends with "an antithesis between empirically accessible reality and the subject consciousness."[16] In order to keep the focus on this problem, McDowell interprets the prestige battle and the master-servant dynamic as an "allegory" that represents the struggle between a single subject's independence of empirical reality and the same subject "aware of being determined by the empirically given milieu in which it lives its life."[17] The primary task of self-consciousness is to overcome the alien otherness between these two opposed ways of being a conscious self. In the self-consciousness of the prestige battle and the master-servant relation, the self experiences its engagement in empirical reality as something alien to its independence. The allegory represents this experience of alienation; the master plays the role of the thinking subject's independence of empirical conditions, and the servant represents the same self immersed in empirical conditions.[18] McDowell asks how a literally other self-consciousness helps to resolve the tension between the independent self and the self engaged in empirical reality.[19] I answer that the other self functions as the independent otherness of the natural world preserved within the dynamics of self-consciousness. In this role, a literally other self-consciousness presents itself to the subject self (1) as the unifying life and being-for-self integrity of the objective life system, (2) as the natural world negating itself as not in itself the truth, and (3) as the world referring itself to the subject self as that for which it exists and in which it has its truth.[20] McDowell's interpretation focuses exclusively on the internal dynamics of the subject self and loses the independent otherness of the natural world as an essential component in the dynamics of self-consciousness.

Thus, my interpretation of the transition from consciousness to self-consciousness challenges not only the Kantian interpretation of the transition itself but also the way the Kantian approach interprets the opening moves of self-consciousness. I must admit, however, that Hegel obviously has Kant in mind when he explains the move from self-consciousness to reason. The

16 McDowell (2009–10), 33.
17 Ibid.
18 McDowell (2003a, 2003b, 2006, 2009–10).
19 McDowell (2009–10), 57.
20 For another critique of McDowell's interpretation, see Houlgate (2009–10) and Pippin (2011) chapter 4.

analysis of idealism, which introduces reason, uses technical terms that are typical of Kant's and Fichte's approach to epistemological questions. I insist, however, that Hegel's account of idealism transforms Kant's and Fichte's epistemology into a conception of reason that is fundamentally different from the way Kant and Fichte conceive it. There are presuppositions in Hegel's account of idealism that do not belong to the epistemology of Kant and Fichte; and Hegel is fully justified in allowing these presuppositions to determine the way the examination of idealism develops, since they are justified by the determinate negations of consciousness and self-consciousness. The *Phenomenology*'s task is to expose the necessary implications of its beginning concept, not to engage in a dialogue with Kant or Fichte. This means that Hegel must remain faithful to what his procedure requires for the demonstration of a necessary implication. Kant and Fichte belong to the project only insofar as their thought fits the demands of this procedure.

The structure of idealism that Hegel describes resembles Pippin's Kantian interpretation of Hegel. The otherness of the thing-in-itself belongs to the structure of thought itself; and thought appropriates this otherness by thinking it as "my" sensations and representations organized according to the categories of thought. Idealism dismisses as unessential the particulars given in sensation, except as vehicles for the necessary structures of objectivity. Thus, idealism, like Pippin's interpretation of Hegel, might say that the object constituted by thought is all that being could *intelligibly* be. Moreover, idealism would go further and claim that intelligibility is all that being can be, since reason, the rational, is the truth of all reality.

There are, however, two important factors in Hegel's account that challenge Pippin's interpretation. First, Hegel demonstrates the legitimacy of idealism's claims by deriving them from the determinate negation of unhappy consciousness. As we have seen, this brings into the presuppositions of reason a surrender condition. Human thought cannot legitimately claim that its own conditions reveal the true essence of being unless human thought has surrendered its self-consciousness to a rationality that transcends what human thought by itself is. The rationality of the human subject is not the truth of all reality. The rationality of being, to which both subject and object belong, is the truth of all reality. Human thought must surrender itself to the truth of reason, which is the common ground of both the independent subjectivity of self-consciousness and the independent objectivity of the world. This is a surrender condition exactly like the one described by Houlgate in his account of logic's reality status.[21]

21 See the discussion of the Pippin-Houlgate debate in chapter 2, §4c.

Second, Hegel demonstrates the limits and untruth of idealism by exposing a contradiction implicit in it. The sameness in otherness accomplished in idealism connects thought necessarily to what it cannot think as its own. In order to claim everything as its own, idealism must dismiss as unessential the particular ways in which both thinking and the object make themselves manifest. Hegel insists that these particulars belong to reality. If thought cannot think them as particulars determined by thought itself, thought cannot assert itself as the truth of all reality. Thought cannot legitimately assume that what is intelligible to thought is all that being can be.

PART SEVEN

THE DIALECTICAL DEVELOPMENT OF REASON

PART SEVEN FUNCTIONS AS A LINK between the first form of reason and the last form of spirit. The strategy for the interpretation of consciousness, self-consciousness, and the transition into reason examines every move of the demonstration that eventually defines and justifies the beginning presuppositions of reason. In Part Eight, I will resume this strategy, at least for the most important moves in the demonstration that completes the task of the *Phenomenology*. Part Seven, however, covers a large part of Hegel's text, in which Hegel examines areas of experience governed by radically different cognitive norms, and in the process moves through an overwhelming number of dialectical shifts, and addresses issues that have provoked a great deal of controversy. Hence, the strategy for this Part must be more selective. The strategy that governs the selections focuses on two themes that emerge in the transition from self-consciousness to reason. We shall see that both of these themes continue to the very end of the *Phenomenology*, and play an important role in the way the end justifies and determines the transition into the beginning of philosophy.

The first theme focuses on the way the examination of consciousness and self-consciousness conforms to the analysis of a retreat into a ground developed in the introductory essays of the *Encyclopaedia* and the *Logic*. It shows how object-dominated consciousness examined according to its own criterion necessarily transforms the object's independence into an independence identifying itself as a relation to, a being-for, the conscious self. It shows how subject-dominated self-consciousness examined according to its own criterion necessarily transforms its independence into an independent self necessarily identifying itself as a relation to and engagement in the independence of the objective order.[1] Thus, each opposite determines itself as a transition into the other, which is the way the general introduction to the *Encyclopaedia* describes the move from the negative result of dialectic to the positive content of the speculatively rational (*Enz* §82).

The shift into the immediacy of reason corresponds to the way a retreat into a ground reverses priorities. The examination of consciousness and self-consciousness proves that these forms of knowing are derivative truths whose common ground is a rationality that determines both their differentiation into opposites and their unification in the same mutual dynamic. In the process of coming to know this truth, consciousness and self-consciousness have priority, because our knowledge of reason depends on our knowledge of consciousness and self-consciousness. In the domain of the truth we come to know, reason has priority, since it is the ground that determines what consciousness and self-consciousness truly are. In order to know the truth in its proper form, therefore, we must assert reason in its immediacy, as a truth that depends on nothing other than itself, since it is the ground in which consciousness and self-consciousness have their origin.[2]

Part Seven develops the retreat into a ground theme by focusing on two crucial transitions: the transition from reason to spirit, and the transition from spirit to religion. Each chapter provides a careful analysis of the determinate negations that govern the final moves in the transition that is the chapter's major focus. Each covers the shifts leading up to each transition with brief summaries that expose the general outline of the demonstration.

The second theme focuses on the contingent circumstances, temporary determinations, irrelevant details associated with the rational in the realities of experience. In the discussion of the rational-is-actual formula, the *Philosophy of Right* and the general introduction of the *Encyclopaedia* call attention to these contingent particulars. Both texts mention non-philosophical ways of knowing whose task it is to study the particular patterns and laws operating in these details, or to devise ways of organizing them so that they are appropriate to the rational necessities that exist in them.[3] According to the *Encyclopaedia*, these ways of knowing investigate those features of things derived from their empirical singularity (*Enz* §16+*A*).

1 See chapter 13, §6.

2 See chapter 5, §3 and chapter 7, §6 for a discussion of the way Hegel's introductions analyze scientific procedure as a retreat into a ground.

3 See chapter 3, §2 and chapter 4, §2 for the discussion of these claims.

The examination of consciousness in the main text of the *Phenomenology* shows how the necessary relational forms of the objective world are necessarily involved in particulars that are not determined by these forms. The examination of self-consciousness carries along this particularity element in the objects of desire, the servant's work, the instability created by scepticism, and the asceticism of unhappy consciousness. All of these engage the relational forms of the natural world embedded in the contingent particulars of the objective system. Self-consciousness also finds these particulars in itself, in the particular desires that attach the self to the objects of the natural world. In chapter 13, we have seen how idealism exposes a necessary connection between thought thinking objective reality according to the categories of thought itself and thought thinking the same reality as an alien other whose given particulars do not manifest the necessity and relational integrity demanded by reason. At this point, the contingent element associated with the necessities of the objective order becomes an explicit factor in the way consciousness tries to know what objects truly are.[4]

Reason asserts itself as the truth of all reality. Hence, it expects its experience to manifest a world that mirrors the rationality of thought itself. It also acknowledges the contingency that characterizes the way the object spontaneously presents itself to consciousness. Hence, reason conceives its own relation to the object as thought actively engaged in exposing the rationality of the objective order. The truth criterion presupposed in a form of consciousness colours the way it becomes conscious of its object. If, therefore, reason finds itself confronted by a natural world that frustrates its search for rational order in the real particulars of this world, then reason will experience these particulars as reason's opposite, as the irrational. We shall see that reason as observation finds itself confronted by just such a resistant element, and Hegel calls it the irrational (*Unvernunft*). Thus, the theme that focuses on the distinction between the actual and the contingencies and particulars that accompany it becomes transformed into a discussion of the opposition dynamic between the rational and its opposite. In the process, the contingency element takes on a dialectical function that will transform the issue yet again into the opposition between rational thought and the radical independence of nature.[5]

4 See chapter 13, §7.

5 A condensed, preliminary version of the irrationality theme developed here and in subsequent chapters appears as an article published in *Dialogue: A Canadian Philosophical Journal*. See Collins (2000a). Reprinted here with the permission of the publisher.

Part Seven begins the development of this theme here, with a brief consideration of a study by Will Dudley in which he identifies and analyzes the irrationality theme in Hegel's philosophical works.[6] Dudley begins his discussion of the irrationality issue by citing texts from the *Logic* in which Hegel identifies the irrational (*vernunftlos*) as that which lacks concept (*begrifflos*). He then distinguishes two ways in which Hegel defines the condition of being without concept. The first is the abstract universal. An abstract universal has no content that identifies it. It is simply an indeterminate unity. "Consequently, if we find that any given particular or collection of particulars does happen to be affiliated with an abstract universal, this affiliation must simply be accepted, without reason, and is hence irrational."[7] The second way of being without concept is abstract determinacy. An abstract determinacy has a definite content, a set of particulars that identify what it is. But the set is not determined internally, by the nature of the entity. Rather the particulars are drawn from a collection of particulars that remain external to what the entity is, and hence there is no reason why it has this set of particulars rather than some other (*WL* 12:39–41).[8]

The examination of consciousness in the *Phenomenology* provides examples of both these irrational structures. The self-identical thing, which is the object of perception, is an abstract determinacy. It has a set of particulars that identify what it is. But these particulars belong to the field of perceptual properties, and are simply drawn off the field by the unity that holds them together in a shared space and thus constitutes them as a separate set. The unity that unites and separates them does not explain why the set must be these particulars rather than some other set; and the properties themselves do not explain why they must be associated with each other. They are just found to be arranged that way. The unconditional universal, which is the object of understanding, is an abstract universal. It has no content of its own that explains the content of determinate laws. It is simply an indeterminate unity that posits whatever

6 Dudley (2003–04). See also the following sources for a discussion of the way the necessity of contingency emerges in the *Science of Logic*: Burbidge (2007), chapter 2; di Giovanni (1992); Houlgate (1995).

7 Dudley (2003–04), 28.

8 Ibid., 26–30. Dudley cites a variety of texts to support his analysis of the irrational and the condition of being without concept. The text from the *Logic* that I have selected and cited at this point, however, provides a coherent, efficient discussion that supports Dudley's analysis and also refers beyond the *Logic* to the way this condition appears in nature and the human spirit.

happens to appear in a certain configuration. It is an explanation that explains nothing (*PhG* 95–96/M ¶155).[9]

In the examination of self-consciousness, these structures appear again. The prestige battle and the master-servant dialectic play out the contingency and arbitrariness of an abstract determinacy. The independent self functions as a separate entity fighting to claim the content of the objective world as its own, with the arbitrary result that whoever wins takes all. But this result shifts around so that the same content appears as a relation to the loser's work as well as to the master's desires. For the independent self, the content of the self remains external. It belongs to the externality of the natural world. It is not derived from the internal constitution of the conscious self. Stoicism and scepticism have the structure of an abstract universal. Stoic thought detaches itself from the content of the life-world and thus becomes indeterminate. Scepticism makes this indeterminacy manifest by becoming actively engaged in exposing the untruth of the life-world.[10]

The retreat into reason as ground requires that the whole consciousness-self-consciousness dialectic be repeated as a reality derived from and determined by reason. If, therefore, the irrational structures persist, they will be experienced in terms of reason and thus explicitly as irrational. For the development of the irrationality theme, Part Seven selects texts in the "Reason" and "Spirit" sections of the *Phenomenology* that provide clues for understanding how the irrationality issue identified by Dudley emerges within the internal dialectic of experience. If irrationality belongs to the structure of the rational as Hegel finally identifies it, then the phenomenological project that justifies the beginning concept of the rational must show why the irrationality issue emerges as a necessity in the way experience retreats into a ground. Part Seven focuses primarily on the highlights that show how the irrationality issue changes its definition and structure as the *Phenomenology* moves through the forms of reason and spirit.

9 See chapter 12, §2–4.
10 See chapter 13, §2–4.

14

Reason, the Irrational, and the Retreat into a Ground

REASON MAKING ITSELF actual begins as observation. This form of reason takes for granted that objects standing immediately before consciousness are rational, although it does not have in mind any well-formed concept of what reason is. It instinctively seeks in the object a universal of some sort that identifies what the object truly is, and it assumes that some such unifying, explanatory principle is there to be found. Hence, the observational sciences do not stand back and let the object present itself as it may. Rather they manipulate objects, run experiments, judge what evidence is relevant and what evidence is not, in order to expose the rational structure operating in the given constitution of the world (*PhG* 137–8/M ¶239–43).

1 REASON AS THE OBSERVATION OF NATURE[1]

Reason begins by retracing the moves through perception and understanding, not in an attempt to become conscious of a separately existing thing, but rather to become conscious of the element that renders things comprehensible, intelligible. It describes and classifies perceived particulars in order to expose patterns and consistencies in the way these particulars identify and distinguish things, which provokes the search for laws that govern the mutual relations whereby sets of properties mutually exclude each other (*PhG* 139–42/M ¶246–8). This absorbs observable things into

1 Cinzia Ferrini provides an excellent study of the "Reason as Observation" section of the *Phenomenology* (Ferrini 2009b). This study takes the reader through the various moves into different areas of empirical research, identifies the particular scientific theories that belong to the experience that Hegel has in mind, and refers to other Hegel texts that clarify the way Hegel is interpreting the issues. Section 1 of this study covers the observation of nature.

a continuity with other things, so that their distinctive character belongs to the relational dynamic that connects them to other things. Reason uses experiments to isolate the necessary element that governs these relations. But this distinguishes the universal, intelligible element from what is available for observation. We cannot directly observe gravity, only the patterns and associations of the particulars governed by it. In order to observe the rational element in objects, therefore, reason as observation shifts to the observation of organic nature. The life of the organism itself forms its different functions into a separate whole and controls its relations to other organisms and to the inorganic environment, and all this is observable. The inorganic environment – earth, air, water, climate – provides a shared, continuous context for individual organisms, becomes absorbed into them as life supporting elements, and also dissolves them into itself in the life and death process of life. Reason as life science, therefore, searches for laws that govern the relations between organisms and the environment (*PhG* 144–6/M ¶253–5).

Hegel introduces an explicit discussion of the irrationality factor in the account of the life sciences. At one point, reason tries to find rational order in the internal dynamics of the individual organism. Reason observes (1) the system that operates within the organism itself (sensibility), (2) the system that reacts to things outside the organism (irritability), and (3) the system that reproduces the life of the organism within the organism itself and in its offspring (*PhG* 150–1/M ¶265–8). But these systems manifest no necessary law governing their association with each other. Variations in food assimilation (which belongs to sensibility), in reactions to carrying heavy loads (which belongs to irritability), in the number and kind of offspring (which belongs to reproduction) show no necessary correspondence to each other. Reason must take the systems as given (*Vorhanden*), as simply there (*Dasein*); and as such they fall apart like indifferent properties that happen to be associated (*PhG* 154/M ¶275).[2]

In the process of making this point, Hegel says that these systems "sink to the level of common properties," and show themselves as indifferent to each other. When observation tries to find a law in some kind of consistent quantifiable variation, it loses completely the connectedness that integrates differences into a rational whole. Instead of manifesting the unity of relation, Hegel says, they "manifest the freedom of Nature released (*entbundne*) from the control of the concept"; instead of demonstrating the determina-

2 Chris Lauer (2006–07), 57–65 provides a careful and helpful summary of the teleological arguments developed in the observation of organic nature.

tions of the concept, they manifest "the irrational (*unvernünftiges*) here-and-there-play on the scale of contingent magnitude" (*PhG* 154/M ¶275). These quotes suggest that particulars manifesting no necessary connectedness in their associations give observational reason the experience of nature as a reality set apart, on its own, independent of its involvement in rational thought relations. The alien character of the objective world, introduced in the dialectical results of idealism, shows up as the concrete experience of nature resisting observational reason's search for rational order.[3]

The search for rationality in the life process eventually focuses not on the particular features of different organic elements, but on the general dynamic that operates in these particulars. The life of the organism lives in different parts and functions, and holds them all together as the same life. This dynamic isolates the organism in itself setting it off from everything that does not belong to its own life; and this establishes a numerical difference between different organisms, each constituted by the same self-isolating, self-unifying dynamic. Life appears as a genus repeated in and identified with the singularity of each living thing. In the generic structure of life, therefore, reason observes a kind of rational order. Within the individual organism, the same life lives in all the organism's different parts and functions. In the genus, the same life dynamic is repeated in each and every living thing.

The observable necessities of life, however, do not explain all that belongs to what reason observes in living things. The same set of properties appearing in some organisms and not others arranges singular living things into groups and thus makes life appear as different species. The generic structure of life does not account for these differences. It simply happens to appear in these various ways. Moreover, organisms are at the mercy of contingent and destructive forces that do not operate organically, like storms, earthquakes, floods, drought, fire. The generic structure of life exists in the context of a natural element whose operations do not belong to the

3 Daniel Dahlstrom rightly asks "what are we to make of these appeals to something like a surd factor to discredit certain conceptions of rationality?" (Dahlstrom 2006–07, 46). Dahlstrom suggests that the persistence of this "surd factor" in the subsequent developments of the *Phenomenology* might compromise Hegel's claim that the rational is actual and the actual rational (45–8, 51–3). Dahlstrom acknowledges a possible answer to his questions by referring to Will Dudley's analysis of impure reason (see Dudley 2003–04). I am in the process of developing an interpretation that will claim that some kind of non-rational factor does indeed persist to the very end of the *Phenomenology*, and that it plays a dialectically necessary role in the constitution of rationality. In this chapter, I call attention to developments in Hegel's text that confirm some of Dudley's claims.

generic structure of life. Hence, reason does not find in its observation of life a ground that determines all the differences and thus integrates them all into the selfsameness of a unifying principle (*PhG* 163–6/M ¶291–7). The examination of observational reason shifts, therefore, into the observation of self-consciousness.

2 REASON AS THE OBSERVATION OF SELF-CONSCIOUSNESS[4]

Reason looks for rationality by observing the way self-consciousness unifies nature in relation to itself and thus posits itself as the universal persisting through all nature's differences (*PhG* 189–90/M ¶341). Reason expects to find in this self-positing a necessity that determines the differentiation of self-consciousness, within itself and in its relations to the external world, and brings this differentiation back to the unity of self-consciousness. The observation begins, therefore, by observing thought thinking itself, and it finds thought differentiated in the laws of thought (*PhG* 167/M ¶298).

Hegel's account of this observation is full of anticipations that describe what thought and its laws turn out to be when philosophy becomes adequate to the task of investigating it. Since, however, each form of consciousness must measure itself against its own criterion, these anticipations do not belong to the examination of reason as observation, and cannot legitimately play a normative role in the way observational reason demonstrates its own limitations. Hegel indicates this by calling us back to the way thought appears to "observation qua observation." He contrasts this to knowing, which moves through various thoughts, exposing their necessary connection to each other. Observation treats thought not as the movement of knowing but as what exists. For observation, thought is simply there, like any other being presenting itself to consciousness. As such, it displays thought thinking in different ways according to different laws. These different laws are simply found or given, not developed from a principle or concept. For observation, therefore, thought presents itself as a collection of disconnected necessities operating in the same self-consciousness; and the unity of self-consciousness is not a universality integrating different thoughts into the same thought, but a singular self who happens to be the consciousness in which these thoughts occur (*PhG* 167–9/M ¶299–300; 189–90/M ¶342).

4 See Ferrini (2009b), section 2 for her study of reason as the observation of self-consciousness. Harris provides a helpful summary of reason as the observation of self-consciousness at the beginning of his commentary on the text. See Harris (1997), volume I, 553–6.

Reason as observation runs into similar problems when it tries to find rationality in the dynamics between self and world. The self as an immediately given observable object has a peculiar determinateness, a set of particulars that identify this self's individual character (*PhG* 171/M ¶310). This character expresses itself in various ways – the line and shape of the body, posture and body language, behaviour, speech, work, handwriting. All these are contingently related to the self-consciousness they signify, and hence none of them presents to observation self-consciousness itself, which reason at this point takes to be the unifying purpose of the world's differences. Either self-consciousness becomes absorbed into the world's conditions or remains hidden behind the signs in which it expresses itself. If it becomes absorbed into the world's conditions, it succumbs to the world's un-integrated divisions. If it remains hidden behind its own physical manifestations, self-consciousness remains detached from the world whose purpose it is supposed to be (*PhG* 171–80/M ¶310–22).

Reason tries to get around this detachment by finding self-consciousness existent as an inert, dead thing. Hegel talks here about phrenology, which tries to read the character of the self from the shape of the skull (*PhG* 183–8/M ¶331–8). It is important to notice that Hegel finds this just as absurd as we do. Indeed, its absurdity is exactly Hegel's point. "In fact, from whatever side we look at the matter, there is no necessary reciprocal relation at all between them, nor any direct indication of such a relation. If, all the same, the relation is still to exist, what remains and is necessary to form it is an irrational (*begrifflose*), free, pre-established harmony of the corresponding determination of the two aspects" (*PhG* 185/M ¶335). In phrenology, observational reason shows itself at its worst and reveals what it really is, namely the disgracefulness (*Schmählichkeit*) of thought without concept (*begrifflosen*) (*PhG* 189/M ¶340; 191/M ¶345).[5]

Hegel repeats here the same point he made in his examination of the life sciences. In the earlier account, we have seen Hegel associate the term "concept" with the term "irrational" (*unvernünftiges*) when he describes the freedom of nature as "Nature released (*entbundne*) from the control of the concept" (*PhG* 154/M ¶275). In the context of reason as observation, "concept" refers to the rational, and "irrational (*unvernünftiges*)" refers to what the concept does not control. When, therefore, Hegel talks about phrenology as "unconceptual (*begrifflosen*) thought," he is talking

5 Michael Quante (2008) explains Hegel's critique of psychology, physiognomy, and phrenology, and shows how it challenges contemporary action theory and exposes presuppositions that persist in present-day philosophy of mind.

about rational thought finding itself in what the concept does not control. In other words, reason finds itself presented as reason's opposite, a thing without conceptual, rational form. "What merely *is*, without any spiritual activity, is, for consciousness, a Thing, and, far from being the essence of consciousness, is rather its opposite ... From this point of view it must be regarded as a complete denial of Reason to pass off a bone as the actual existence of consciousness" (*PhG* 187–8/M ¶339). Moreover, the account of phrenology, like the account of the life sciences, associates the irrational element with being as something released, set free, from the demands of thought. "But when Reason is presented as its own self and its opposite, and is held fast in the entirely separate (*einzelnen*) moment of this asunderness (*Auseinandertretens*), it is apprehended irrationally (*unvernünftig*)" (*PhG* 191–2/M ¶346). In phrenology, or some similar attempt at finding self-consciousness existing as an inert, dead object, reason is captured by the otherness of its opposite, and hence knows itself in the form of the irrational.

3 THE IRRATIONALITY ISSUE REDEFINED

In the introduction to Part Seven, we considered two forms of the irrational that Dudley finds identified in Hegel's philosophical works. Both forms appear in reason as observation. Whenever reason tries to explain the panorama of particulars that are immediately observable, it finds itself forced to infer an inner unifying principle that explains them. But the inner turns out to be an abstract universal. Reason knows it only as whatever arranges observable particulars as they happen to be arranged, and all attempts to find its unifying necessity manifested in these arrangements fails. Observational reason finds a trace of rationality in the life dynamic that forms the singularity of each organism, and in the genus that repeats itself in each living individual. It fails, however, to find a rational order that integrates the given particulars of the species and the contingencies of inanimate nature into the selfsameness of the genus. The species has the form of an abstract determinacy. Explanations that appeal to the constitution of the species simply accept as given the content that identifies it.

The observation of self-consciousness fares no better. Self-consciousness as a given reality presented for observation shows itself as contingently associated contents: a collection of logical principles presented as the way an individual self happens to think; words or other physical expressions contingently associated with a self that either remains hidden and detached from its manifestations or falls apart in their disconnectedness; self-consciousness reduced to inert physical formations arbitrarily associated with certain psychological characteristics. Even when observing the given reality of self-consciousness itself, therefore, reason finds itself confronted by contingent associations instead of the unifying, relational integrity demanded by conceptual thought.

The terminology of the irrational discovered by Dudley also appears in Hegel's discussion of reason as observation. The term *unvernünft* describes the way the particular properties of the organism are unconnected, indifferent to each other. They just happen to be associated, with no concept to explain why. Hegel says that this condition manifests nature released from the control of the concept (*Begriff*). The term *begrifflos* describes the way phrenology reduces self-consciousness to the givenness and otherness of a thing. When reason apprehends itself in this form, Hegel says, it apprehends itself irrationally (*unvernünftig*). Thus, the *Phenomenology* follows the same pattern as the texts Dudley cites from Hegel's philosophical works. It identifies the irrational as being without concept.

The *Phenomenology*, however, adds a dimension to the irrational that Dudley does not mention. According to Hegel, the way the concept gets lost in a given, unexplained display of particular contents and arrangements manifests something essential about nature. Nature is free, released from the control of concepts, and as such it lets itself go in a manifold that cannot be tamed by conceptual explanations (*PhG* 154/M ¶275). The principal text cited by Dudley also interprets the non-conceptual diversity of particulars as the way nature manifests its independence of reason:

> This is the impotence of nature, that it cannot abide by and exhibit the rigor of the concept and loses itself in a blind manifoldness void of concept. We can wonder at nature, at the manifoldness of its genera and species, in the infinite diversity of its shapes, for wonder is without concept and its object is the irrational (*das Vernunftlose*). It is <nature set free (*freigegeben*) to indulge in this diversity>, since nature is the self-externality of the concept. (*WL* 12:39)

In phrenology, reason knows itself as a thing that belongs to this uncontrolled element in nature. From this point on, therefore, the irrationality issue is developed in several different forms: (1) the indeterminacy of the abstract universal, (2) the abstract determinacy of given particulars, and (3) nature confronting the rational self as an opposite, a reality not controlled by the self's rationality.

4 THE TRANSITION TO PRACTICAL REASON

Reason as the observation of self-consciousness takes the truth to be a world conceived as existing for a self. Thus, the rational observer knows the objective world as a world inhabited by other self-conscious individuals and defined in terms of them. This form of rationality culminates in a kind of knowing that collapses the distinction between the inner and the outer in a way that resembles a similar move in understanding. The inner self, like simple force, has the same content as its appearance. The inner self has no other determination than to be the simplicity that determines itself as the given non-conceptual irrational properties presented to observation – a given determinate character, expressed in body language, behaviour, speech, work, handwriting, the shape of the skull. Reason as observation finds self-consciousness presented to it as a thing. The inner spirit of self-consciousness manifests itself as the otherness, givenness, in-itself independence of objective being. In the process, self-consciousness, as the unifying principle of the objective world, determines the whole objective order as an independent system presenting itself to the subjectivity of the rational observer. The shift into the next truth criterion, therefore, must preserve the negated together with its negation. It must preserve the world as an independent objective world of self-conscious individuals together with the negation of this world's indifference to the thinking subject. Reason as self-actualizing self-consciousness takes the truth to be the independent world of self-conscious individuals existing for the individual subjectivity of the conscious self. In other words, self-consciousness here takes the truth to be a social world that acknowledges the individual self as the world's defining purpose. Hegel tells us explicitly that this form of reason will repeat the moves developed in the self-consciousness of life. He says, too, that this development retreats into spirit as its ground (*PhG* 192–3/M ¶347–8).

5 THE SELF-ACTUALIZATION OF SELF-CONSCIOUSNESS[6]

Hegel introduces self-actualizing self-consciousness by anticipating its retreat into spirit, which in its proper form is the spirit of a people. As the result of the transition from observational reason, however, spirit is still defined as the inner self of a singular self-consciousness. Moreover, this

6 Terry Pinkard provides an imaginative description of the experiences covered in this part of the "Reason" section (Pinkard 1994, chapter 4, section 2). The description effectively communicates both the feel of each experience and the rational framework embedded in it.

individual spirit finds itself confronted by the otherness of a ready-made, established world. The self takes the truth of both self and world to be the self's own individual spirit, and it takes this truth to be already implicit in the world as given. In order to know this truth, the self must expose the agreement between its inner spirit and the spirit of the world by actualizing its inner spirit in the world (*PhG* 196/M ¶356).

Pleasure and Necessity. Reason as the actualization of self-consciousness begins as self-conscious desire transformed by the presuppositions of reason. In its rational form, self-consciousness does not try to get rid of the world's otherness, as self-conscious desire does, since reason expects rationality to be the true essence of both independent objectivity and independent subjectivity. But reason as the actualization of self-consciousness expects independent objectivity to exist as a world focused on and appropriate to the spirit of this individual self. Hence, the individual self dismisses forms of knowledge that investigate the world's independent reality and constitution, and rejects forms of life that demand the individual's integration into the established ways of the social world. The individual simply takes pleasure in it. In the feeling of pleasure, the individual experiences the world as something appropriate to the individual's own spirit (*PhG* 198–9/M ¶360–2).

Having achieved this, however, the self finds itself realized not only as what corresponds to the self's own individual spirit, but also as a participant in an alien spirit. The other who gives pleasure belongs to the world and its ways, which the individual has dismissed as not important. By living in the enjoyment of the other, the individual finds his or her self defined in terms of this world, absorbed into it, subject to whatever fate the ways of the world impose upon him or her. Thus, individual self-consciousness in the process of experiencing the world as its own world becomes necessarily connected to the opposite, which is the experience of itself as a self overwhelmed and distorted by the spirit that operates in the ways of the world (*PhG* 199–201/M ¶362–5).[7]

7 Hegel uses the language of life and death here to indicate that pleasure and necessity reproduces in rational form the dynamics of self-consciousness engaged in the prestige battle. In the dynamics of pleasure and necessity, the world challenges the self by absorbing the individual's spirit into the independent dynamics of the world itself, just as death in the dynamics of self-consciousness absorbs the individual into the independent processes of nature. In the process of taking the world as its own, the individual loses his or her self in the necessity that operates in the ways of the world.

The Law of the Heart. The determinate negation of this result holds the opposites together (*PhG* 201/M ¶366).[8] The new form of reason acknowledges that these opposites are the same spirit, that the subjectivity of self-consciousness itself is the necessity that governs the objective world. Since, however, this selfsameness does not appear in the actual ways of the world, the individual's felt sense of self must actualize itself as the universal spirit of the world by acting against the established ways of the world. Thus, this form of self-consciousness asserts itself as a felt law, the law of the heart, whose aim is to transform an alien and indifferent world into a world ruled by the individual's own spirit. Self-consciousness achieves its aim by opposing and dismissing the authority of established rulers, replacing it with the law of the individual's own free spirit. Moreover, the self acts here not only for itself but for the world. Taking its own spirit to be the true essence and purpose of the world, the self sees itself as liberating all who belong to the world by getting rid of the alien authority that oppresses them (*PhG* 201–3/M ¶367–71).

Acting on this presupposition, however, transforms the law of the heart, which belongs to the self's individuality, into a reality that is independent of the self and belongs to the world's universality. The individual's own law becomes integrated into a world that encompasses the self-consciousness of other individuals. These others resist the individual's law of the heart because it is someone else's law, not their own. For them, the individual's free spirit has the form of an established authority that must be resisted so that their free spirit can take over. It does not matter whether an individual's own spirit agrees with the content of the ordinance or not. Any law offends if it takes the form of a law that confronts the individual as an independent necessity imposed on him or her. Thus, self-consciousness discovers that the world is not a dead, indifferent universal thing. The world is a world alive with the self-consciousness of individuals actualizing their spirits in it. But the world does not present itself as a self-conscious spirit that agrees with the individual's law of the heart. It presents itself rather as self-consciousness gone mad, a hostile world of warring individualities in which each individual perverts the spirit of others and finds its own spirit perverted by

8 Note the similarity here to the description of determinate negation in the Logic: "but the realization of this End is itself the setting-aside (*Aufheben*) of the latter" (*PhG* 199–200/M ¶362); "At issue [in the *Phenomenology*] are shapes of consciousness, each of which dissolves itself in being realized (*selbst auflöst*)" (*WL* 21:37–8/M 54).

them. This hostility and perversion is the law of individuality itself operating as the universal spirit of the objective world (*PhG* 203–8/M ¶372–9).[9]

Virtue and the Way of the World. The determinate negation of reason as the law of the heart preserves the law of the heart together with its negation. The self knows itself divided against itself. Its actualization in the world confronts the self as a spirit rejected, negated, perverted by the other individualities living in that world. Moreover, the self recognizes this hostility and perversion as the law of individuality itself. Hence, the determinate negation of this experience is the law of individuality negated. The new form of experience takes the truth to be the self's own virtue, which rejects the warlike spirit of its own individuality and dismisses the warlike spirit of the world. The virtuous self acknowledges as truth a tranquil universal spirit in which individuality is sacrificed, and all live by the same spirit (*PhG* 207–8/M ¶380–1).

Thus, the virtuous self distinguishes between the world as it actually appears in the dynamics of social existence and the world in itself, the true essence that is its inner, hidden truth. Truth, as this form of reason conceives it, is not actual as things stand. It becomes actual only if the virtuous self acts to bring about a world in which individuals actually live and manifest a shared spirit at peace with itself, a spirit that shows itself as the virtuous self's own spirit.

Action calls upon the self's gifts, powers, and capacities to effect a change in the world. Gifts, powers, and capacities also exist in the way of the world, since individuals who belong to the world use these to actualize their own individual spirit. Thus, these instruments of action (gifts, powers, capacities) have no status of their own. They work at the disposal of a free individual who determines whether their use is virtue or vice, in service to a universal spirit at peace with itself or a universal spirit divided against itself.

9 The dynamics of the law of the heart reproduces in rational form the dynamics of mastery and servitude. In the self-consciousness of mastery and servitude, mastery functions as the self's independence of the natural world, which corresponds to the subjectivity of the law of the heart. Servitude functions as this same mastery operating in the servant's work, which transforms nature into the master's world and thus becomes a permanent mastering force in the dynamics of this world. Servitude corresponds to the law of the heart operating as the world's law. The work of the servant transforms mastery's law into a law that exists as the servant's own act, which corresponds to the law of the heart absorbed into a world focused on the independent subjectivity of other hearts. For mastery and servitude, however, existence as a dimension of the world's order is a subordinate factor in the master's mastery. Reason as the law of the heart acknowledges the necessity of transforming itself into a law that belongs to the world's independent objectivity, and takes itself to be acting not only for itself but also for the world.

Either way, action depends on individuality identifying itself with particulars that belong to the individual's given constitution. Moreover, the self must act against the world's current state of affairs, which is dominated by the exclusive, self-focused, being-for-self dynamics of perverse individuality. Yet virtue assumes that the tranquil universal spirit is already implicit in the existing world. Hence, the self cannot be serious about trying to change the world. It expects rather that virtuous action will activate the world's own true spirit, and this spirit will give virtue the victory over vice (*PhG* 208–11/M ¶381–6).

Virtue, however, cannot win. If it becomes a real action, it takes the form of an individual's gifts, powers, and capacities released into the dynamic of worldly existence. The world sees these as mere objects to be used, resources for the self-interested, self-focused, self-serving projects of competing individualities. Hence, the spirit that virtue activates is none other than the way of the world. The virtuous self may announce its lofty purpose, denounce the world's ways, proclaim itself the world's saviour. But those who belong to the way of the world know how to spin out explanations that "demonstrate the presence of self-interest in every action" including virtue's own (*PhG* 213–14/M ¶392). Moreover, virtue's champion cannot say specifically and definitely what the true spirit of the world is, because this spirit has no content, is indeed nothing more than that which negates, and thus unifies, the world's divisions and differences. Hence, the unifying spirit of the world becomes actual only if it actually lives in and lives as individuals using their gifts, powers, and capacities to produce a world that expresses the same fundamental spirit living at the heart of each one's individuality. Virtue asks for the sacrifice of individuality, but individuality is a necessary condition for actuality.

Thus, virtue's distinction between what the world is in itself and what it is in the ways of the actual world turns out to be no distinction at all. The unifying spirit of the world, the world in itself, is simply a spirit that exists as the inner self of individuals and becomes actual in their self-actualizing action. Virtue conceives this inner self of individuals as the same spirit remaining at one with itself in each individual's self-actualization. Vice conceives this same inner self as a selfish, self-obsessed spirit that expects the world, including the self-actualization of other individuals, to revolve around him or her. If, however, virtue's unifying spirit is nothing more than the same spirit existing as the fundamental spirit of different individuals, then individuality's self-focused, self-concerned being-for-self simply manifests this spirit identified with the individuality of those who share it. Virtue's unifying spirit is only the unity aspect of the social world. Vice's spirit of individuality is only the individuation aspect of the same social world (*PhG* 209–14/M ¶385–93).[10] "With this lesson in mind, the idea of bringing the good into existence by means of the sacrifice of individuality is abandoned; for individuality is precisely the actualizing of <in itself being> (*Ansich-seienden*), and the perversion ceases to be regarded as a perversion of the good, for it is in fact really the conversion of the good, as a mere End, into <actuality> (*Wirklichkeit*): the movement of individuality is the reality of the universal" (*PhG* 213/M ¶391).

The form of consciousness defined by the determinate negation of virtue and the way of the world acknowledges the necessary connection between the in-itself of virtue and its being-for-others in the way of the world. It takes the truth to be action itself in which the inner universal spirit of the individual actualizes itself in the individuality dynamic that constitutes the actual world, and becomes a self existing for others. The whole aim of this self-consciousness is to express itself and thus make explicit the spirit it shares with others (*PhG* 198/M ¶359; 212–13/M ¶389).

In the account of virtue and the way of the world, the irrational element re-enters the explicit formulation of what consciousness expects the truth to be. The dynamics of virtue show that reason cannot become actual without becoming absorbed into the individuality dynamic in which the self expresses itself to others. In order to become involved in this dynamic, the virtuous individual must use the particular talents, powers, and capabilities given in his or her physical and psychological constitution. These belong to the given particulars that a self happens to have. Moreover they function as the vehicle in which the individuality of the self expresses itself in the world, and thereby becomes connected to the given particulars in which other self-conscious individuals have expressed themselves. Thus, the individuality issue, which asks how the singularity of the self belongs to the universality

10 Virtue and the way of the world reproduces in rational form the self-consciousness of stoicism and scepticism. Like stoicism, virtue conceives the truth as a universal good detached from the division between self and world that separates the independent conscious subject from self-consciousness integrated into the independent dynamics of the objective world. Like stoicism, virtue reinstates independent objectivity to the status of something essential. For both, the independent objectivity of the world and the independent subjectivity of the conscious self are equally essential in the determination of what the truth is; and both conceive this shared truth as an un-actualized, hidden truth. Like stoicism, virtue is at a loss to say exactly what this hidden truth and goodness is. Like scepticism, virtue cannot negate the divisions of real experience without becoming identified with these same divisions. As a form of reason, however, detached self-consciousness acknowledges that the world's truth already exists as a hidden truth in the actual world. Scepticism sets out to negate and discredit the world of actual experience; virtue sets out to expose the good that already belongs to it.

of reason, becomes connected to the irrationality issue, which asks how the non-conceptual, not-rational given arrangements of particulars belongs to the universality and necessity of the rational.

6 SELF-CONFIDENT INDIVIDUALITY

The determinate negation of virtue and the way of the world transforms the relation between self-consciousness and the world. The individual does not assert his or her self as a spirit set off from the world, does not act to bring the world into conformity with the inner self of the individual. Rather the individual knows his or her self rooted in a spirit that comprehends this individual's self and the world of other self-conscious individuals as well. Action activates, exposes, makes explicit the given, implicit sameness of spirit already established between self and world. Individuality, Hegel says, takes itself to be real in and for itself: in itself as the hidden, inner spirit of the individual's social world; for itself as this same spirit manifested as a reflection of the individual's own spirit. I shall call this form of reason self-confident individuality, because the individual here is confident that the spirit expressed in her or his action already fits with the spirit that belongs to the field of action.

Hegel's account of self-confident individuality returns to the terminology of idealism. It describes this form of reason as "the certainty of being all reality," as "the category which has become aware of itself," as having "the category as such for its object" (*PhG* 213–15/M ¶394–5). In idealism, "the category means this, that self-consciousness and being are the same essence, the same, not through comparison, but in and for themselves ... But now this category or simple unity of self-consciousness and being possesses difference in itself; for its essence is just this, to be immediately one and selfsame in otherness, or in absolute difference. The difference is, but is perfectly transparent, and a difference that is at the same time none" (*PhG* 134–5/M ¶235).

The determinate negation of virtue and the way of the world brings the category into the diversity and givenness of concrete experience. Virtue's tranquil universal spirit exists in and exists as the individuality of the self using its given constitution of gifts, powers, and capacities to actualize itself; and it actualizes itself in a world alive with the self-actualization of other individuals acting through their own given constitution of gifts, powers, and capacities. Self-confident individuality takes itself to be a given set of particulars, an "original determinate nature," living in an element appropriate to it. Hegel describes this as a universal permeated with individuality, i.e. a world of gifts, powers, and capacities activated by individual agents.

In self-confident individuality, the category takes the form of action for its own sake. The individual acts in order to become actively engaged in a sameness of spirit already established in the given constitution of the self and its world. We might say that the individual simply acts out his or her belonging to the spirit that self and world have in common. In the process, however, the belonging is reversed, and the sameness of spirit belongs to the individual self as something exclusively its own. Hegel compares this to an animal that lives by "steeping its entire nature" in the specifics of its element (earth, air, or water) and yet maintains its separateness and individual integrity by giving this element the form of its own singular living. Self-confident individuality maintains its separateness and individual integrity within the spirit shared between self and world by giving the shared element the form of the individual's own singular doing (*PhG* 215–17/M ¶396, ¶398–9).

For example, a talented musician finds herself in a world full of concerts, music schools and mentors, musical compositions, musical genius, radio and television stations broadcasting musical performances, businesses producing music scores or musical instruments. The individual demonstrates that this world is her own by becoming actively involved in the world of music – as a music student, as a performer of musical compositions, as an appreciative listener, as a purchaser of music scores and musical instruments, perhaps as a music teacher or composer. Thus, the individual does not construct a world that suits her interests. She participates in a world that suits her interests. Her musical talent makes the world of music her own, and the world's music makes her one of the world's own. Her active participation, however, gives the element of music the form of her own exclusive individuality. Music is transformed into her music, a musical activity that she and she alone does.

First move. Self-confident individuality repeats the elements belonging to the preceding forms of rational self-consciousness, but within a framework that cancels their isolation by conceiving them as a movement within the same universal spirit. The same spirit becomes divided in the different factors of action: proposed end, given circumstances, means used, end accomplished. In the objectivity of the world, a universal spirit exists as a set of circumstances that attract the individual's interest; the world is full of musical activities that speak to the individual's musical nature. In the subjectivity of the agent, the same spirit exists as a proposed end or purpose; a musical individual aims at a career in music. In the movement from a proposed end to its actual accomplishment in the world, the agent makes use of a talent appropriate to the circumstances; a musical individual uses her musical talent to become a participant in the music world. In the accomplished work, the individual's spirit becomes integrated into the independent objectivity of the world; the musical individual becomes actively engaged in the world of music – as a concert performer, published composer, teacher in a music institute, music critic, producer or sponsor of musical events, music enthusiast. By becoming thus identified with the dynamics of action, a universal spirit emerges from what is exclusively the individual's own (the proposed end) into the otherness of the public world, so that the individual self explicitly knows the independent reality of the world as the individual's own personal spirit (*PhG* 216–20/M ¶399–404).

Second move. The accomplished work, however, reveals the limitations of the individual's original determinate nature. The work expresses the particular way in which this individual identifies with the spirit he or she shares with the world. For example, the world in which the musical individual becomes actively involved also exists as a world of literature, the plastic arts, architecture, and dance. The world of the arts is also a world of industrial production, empirical science, communications, sports, health care. Even the world of music exists as more than this one individual's work. As a violinist, she has talents and concerns that are different from those of cellists and pianists, vocalists, players of the flute, the oboe, or the drums. As a performer, her talents and concerns differ from composers, conductors, music critics, producers of music paraphernalia, and the music audience. Her character and style set her apart even from other violinists. Thus, the specific content of an individual's work orients the world to her particular interests, talents, and style, represents the world as her doing, and thus focuses the world on her as different from others.

For another individual, therefore, the work does not express the world's orientation toward his particular character and interests. It does not give him a consciousness of the world as his element, his place, a world that answers to what he is and what he has done. To accomplish this, he must change the orientation of her work so that it is focused on his interests and his particular character. She becomes an element in his world. If he is the conductor of an orchestra, he will expect her to adapt her performance so that it fits his interpretation of the music. If he is a communications expert, he will assign her work and her world to the margins of his world, as entertainment perhaps (*PhG* 220–2/M ¶405–6).

In this encounter with the activity of other determinate natures, the action comes apart. Its different factors do not retain the necessary connection required for preserving the unity and selfsameness of the spirit that operates in them. The question arises whether the end proposed by the agent really expresses the true essence of the spirit shared between self and world, since other individuals active in the world manifest this shared spirit in terms of their own, different determinate natures. For example, if the shared spirit of self and world acknowledges the importance of education, is this cause well served by an individual's esoteric music project? Would it not be better served by medical research, the development of energy resources, or engineering projects. It becomes contingent, too, whether the means used to accomplish the purpose are suitable for manifesting the spirit shared between self and world. For example, even if the shared spirit acknowledges the need to develop cleaner fuels, redirecting corn crops to fuel production may not be the best way to do it, since this tends to drive up the cost of food. Finally, it becomes contingent whether the accomplished purpose realizes the true spirit shared between self and world, since what happens may be just as favourable to a purpose untrue to the spirit as one that is true to it. For example, an education policy that focuses on test scores may inhibit the full development of a child's intelligence instead of fostering it (*PhG* 222/M ¶407).

Hegel analyzes this disintegration of the action's factors in two ways. He says that the content of the factors and their contingent association can be compared to sense certainty and perception (*PhG* 223–4/M ¶410–11).[11] Perception's thing with many properties falls apart because the particular content of the properties does not necessitate their belonging to each other. These particulars just happen to occur in an overlapping cluster, which reduces thinghood to their contingent association, releases the properties from their ties to each other in a separate unity, and lets them float free in the here and now continuity appearing as a field of perceptual data. So also self-confident individuality's proposed end, real circumstances, means used, and work accomplished do not have a particular content that necessitates their belonging to the same action. They just happen to be associated that way. This releases the components of the action from their attachment to the inner spirit of the individual and lets them loose in the world of other active individuals. Perception, however, takes the truth to be the self-sameness of a thing, and self-confident individuality takes the truth to be action persisting as the selfsame spirit throughout its various components. If, therefore, the content does not show the selfsameness that each form of experience expects the truth to be, then each must look for the selfsameness not in the content but in the form that holds the content together.

11 For the discussion of sense certainty and perception, see chapter 12, §2–3.

Perception finds self-identity in the dynamic between separateness and relatedness. A thing through its properties relates itself to other things, and in the process distinguishes itself from these others by holding on to the properties as one and all exclusively its own. Self-confident individuality finds selfsameness in action as such. Whatever the content of the proposed end, the circumstances of the action, the means used, and the work accomplished, all belong to the individual agent as what he or she does.

Here again, we find Hegel developing the irrationality theme. When Hegel introduces the term "irrational," he uses the same way of speaking to describe the constitution of organisms as that used to analyze the "also" of perception – different properties existing together in "mutual indifference" (*PhG* 72–3/M ¶113; 75–6/M ¶120; 154/M ¶275). In these cases, the irrational is a set of particulars existing together in the same unit, even though nothing about the content of each particular requires its association with the others or manifests a necessary coordination with the others. In the account of self-confident individuality, Hegel explicitly compares the break-up of the self's original determinate nature to sense certainty and perception. Self-confident individuality imposes a necessary connection on the different factors of its action. Its purpose, means used, accomplished work, and given circumstances all manifest the same original determinate nature. Like the properties of perception, however, their involvement in the surrounding context does not preserve this unity. They fall apart in their relations to the differences encountered in the world, so that the rational integration of the action becomes irrational in its accomplishment.

The account of self-confident individuality also repeats again the connection between the irrational as a contingent association of particulars and the irrational as the independence of the objective world. The disintegration of self-confident individuality's action surrenders the individual's purpose into the independent dynamics of the world. The individual experiences the antithesis between doing and being. What the individual sets out to do runs up against the otherness of the world, which absorbs the individual's action into a reality that goes its own way, preserving its independence of the agent. The work "vanishes" in the world (*PhG* 220–2/M ¶405).

Third move. Self-confident individuality, however, takes this very independence of the world to be another dimension of the spirit that becomes actual in the self's action. This form of self-consciousness does not set out to negate the world's otherness, as did mastery and scepticism, or to negate the alien way in which this otherness exists, as did the law of the heart and virtue. It sets out to preserve within the selfsameness of the self's action the concrete diversity and being-for-others that constitutes the world's otherness. Even the way the world takes over the individual's project and relates it to the purposes of other agents must somehow belong to the individual's own action. What really matters here is not the particular purpose the individual sets out to accomplish, but the general purpose of bringing to light the sameness of spirit that exists between this self-confident individual and the other individuals who share the world with him or her (*PhG* 221–2/M ¶406; 222–3/M ¶408–10).

Self-confident individuality shifts its focus. In the pursuit of a particular purpose, the individual is not concerned about whether or not the purpose accomplished corresponds to the way the individual has anticipated and willed it. The individual's main concern is to transform the given attunement between self and world into something the individual wills as her or his own. At this point, self-confident individuality takes the true essence of its action to be not a specific aim, but the general aim of manifesting the individual's deliberate identification with the world. Hegel calls this general concern *die Sache selbst*, which Miller sometimes translates as "the matter in hand" (what the real aim is) and sometimes as "the heart of the matter" (the true essence of what is done), and Pinkard translates as "the real thing."[12] *Die Sache selbst*, however, can be viewed in two significantly different ways, depending on which side of the attunement gets primary emphasis. The self-confident individual agent focuses on the way the world reflects the individual's own personal spirit. For the individual in this role, any component of the action can function as its true essence if that component identifies the action as the individual's own doing.

At this point, Hegel reviews all the different strategies an individual might use to take possession of what happens in his or her world. Even if the proposed purpose fails, the individual has willed it, has done something about a situation, instead of standing idly by. If the purpose is opposed by others or gets absorbed into their projects, the individual's work has provoked their actions, and hence their actions belong to what this individual has done. If something happens that belongs to the individual's interests, the individual claims it as his own, even if he has done nothing to make it happen. If something of historical significance happens, something in no way related to an individual's concerns, the individual appropriates it by becoming a partisan either supporting or opposing it. Even if the individual does nothing at all, becomes in no way active, the individual appropriates what happens by claiming it as his good luck, or as what she deserves. Another strategy identifies doing nothing with what reality allows as a real possibility.

12 See Miller ¶409–20; Pinkard (1994), 119.

"I did nothing" becomes "there was nothing I could do." Thus; everything in the individual's world becomes focused on the agency, whether active or inactive, of the individual's distinctive self.

What makes this possible, however, is the way self-confident individuality conceives the universality of spirit shared between self and world. Like sense certainty's universal here and now, the universality of spirit is conceived as indifferently this as well as that, but also neither this nor that, since its identification with one does not prevent its identification with the other even though the one is not the other. Any component of the individual's action can identify the true spirit shared between self and world, and any component can be dismissed as not belonging to what the true spirit essentially is (*PhG* 223–6/M ¶411–14; 226/M ¶416).

There is a certain dishonesty in all this. The individual supposedly acts in order to manifest the sameness of spirit shared between self and world. The individual's strategy, however, gives primary importance to the way the world in its otherness exists for and reflects the self of this individual. Thus, the individual takes as the essential component of the action whatever brings the individual back to his or her self, i.e. whatever makes the world appear as a reality that belongs to the individual's own spirit. The others who share the individual's world, however, see it differently. They expect the individual to act for the sake of identifying his or her self with the world's spirit. The musician looks for a way to experience the world as a world related to her music and whatever accompanies it in her personal constitution. Those who share her world expect her to care more about belonging to and supporting the world's causes than about her own self importance. The world's spirit has its own importance independent of this self's involvement in it. Music is more important than any one individual's attachment to it; medical research is more important than music.

When, therefore, an individual carries out a project in the world, other individuals engage in a strategy aimed at absorbing the project into the independent dynamics of the world. They point out that what he has done, they have already accomplished; or if they have not, they make it their own project by helping with it, improving it, or integrating it into their own plans and purposes. The individual resists this takeover by redirecting the project to his self, showing interest not so much in the project itself as in the gratification given by its being this individual's endeavour. The others accuse the individual of dishonesty. They were given to believe that the individual cared about the cause, when he was really only engaged in ego satisfaction, caring only about claiming the project as his own accomplishment. If, however, they withdraw from the project and concentrate on their own affairs, they find that this individual does not stick to his own projects, but gets involved in assisting, improving, appropriating theirs.

All of this interference is necessitated by what self-confident individuality expects the truth to be. Individuality in this form takes itself to be rooted in a spirit that also exists as the world's own spirit. The musician, for example, knows her spirit to be the spirit of music, and hence asserts her musicianship as the true spirit of the world as well. In order to know the truth, therefore, the individual must experience the world's spirit as this individual's own. Since, however, the world's spirit is constituted by the actions of other individuals with the same truth expectations, they must appropriate the individual's project in order to experience the world as a spirit that answers to who they are and belongs to what they do (*PhG* 225–7/M ¶415–18).

Hegel analyzes this result in terms of content and in terms of form. Here again the comparison to perception clarifies Hegel's interpretation of self-confident individuality. In the transition from perception's self-identical thing to understanding's play of forces, Hegel analyzes the separation and relation dynamic between forces in terms of form and in terms of content. In terms of form, the being-for-self separateness of one force necessarily turns itself into a being-for-another relatedness to another force. By expressing itself, this force (A) distinguishes itself from another force (not-A), which identifies the other (not-A) in terms of this force (A). But this being-for-self exclusiveness inevitably turns into its opposite. By not being the other (B), this force is itself (not-B), which identifies this force (not-B) in terms of the other (B), and turns its being-for-self into being-for-another. In terms of content, different properties belonging to each other in a unit (the exclusive one) turn into a free-floating multiplicity of properties involved in contrast relations to a diversity of other properties in the field of perceptual data (the also) (*PhG* 86–8/M ¶140–1).[13]

So also the being-for-self structure of self-confident individuality shows itself to be necessarily connected to its being for others. The act that transforms the world into the self's own act identifies the other in terms of its relation to this self. The world of other self-conscious agents expresses my self referred back to me. But my act inevitably becomes absorbed into what the world is for other self-conscious agents. My act belongs to their self-expression. In terms of content, the purpose, action, and accomplished reality emerging from the self's original determinate nature, e.g.

13 See my discussion of the play of forces in chapter 12, §4. Notice that Hegel explains the play of forces in terms of force expressed and force actual. He also explains the determinate negation of self-confident individuality in terms of self-expression and self-actualization.

her musical career, inevitably breaks up in a multiplicity of contingently associated factors because of its connection to the complex world of other determinate natures. For example, her contribution to the world of music becomes transformed by the way it is affected by the world of business, industry, transportation, communications, education, law, health care, perhaps even religion, as well as by other participants in the world of music.

The determinate negation. Thus, self-confident individuality expands into a dynamic between the self-conscious individual, the independent being of the social world, and other self-conscious individuals – all connected by self-conscious action. Self-confident individuality begins by taking the truth to be a self-conscious self knowing the world as an element appropriate to the self's own original determinate nature. The self acts on this confidence by producing a work that transforms the independent being of the world into a world focused on this self-conscious agent identified by this set of talents and interests. The world, however, absorbs the work into the complexity produced by the works of other self-conscious individuals, and thereby claims the self's work as something of its own. This transforms the independent being of the world into a thing whose true essence is the action of self-conscious individuals. The world is a work produced by the encounter between different self-conscious agencies. The individual adjusts to this development by shifting from action focused on the individual's original determinate nature to action for the simple purpose of participating in the universal work that manifests the world's status as an expression of self-consciousness. This action, however, exposes a determinate negation. The individual self knowing the world as its own work and self-expression turns into a participant in producing the world as the work and self-expression of other self-conscious individuals.

The sameness of these opposites is articulated in social laws. Each self-conscious agent acts according to a law that identifies this agent's actions with the spirit that acts in the agencies of other agents. These laws have content derived from the encounter between different original determinate natures. Reason as lawgiver begins with a system of determinate laws diversified in different spheres of action or areas of interest, which Hegel calls "masses" (*PhG* 229/M ¶421). This transforms the self into a self identified with the universal spirit of the world. The true essence of the existing world is the act whereby each self-conscious agent expresses itself as a self identified with the spirit that acts in everyone. "Spiritual essence is, in its simple being, *pure consciousness*, and *this self*-consciousness. The originally *determinate* nature of the individual has lost its positive meaning of being *in itself* the element and the purpose of its activity; it is merely a superseded moment, and the individual is a *self* in the form of a universal self. Conversely, the *formal* 'matter in hand' gets its filling from the active, self-differentiating individuality; for the differences within the latter constitute the *content* of that universal" *(PhG* 228/M ¶419).

Thus, reason as lawgiver transforms the agency of the self-conscious individual into a complex commitment. The agent acts on her or his original determinate nature, and yet the purpose of the action is not the expression of the self's particular, differentiating character. The musician engaged in the world of music knows that her contribution to the music world does not define the whole world of music. She knows, too, that the world of music does not define the whole world of social relations. Her participation in the world of music expresses her felt identification with a spirit shared not only with other participants in the music world but also with other agents involved in other spheres of action and interest.[14]

Hegel also articulates the determinate negation of self-confident individuality in terms of subjectivity, actuality, substance, being, and the category. The subjectivity of the self's universal spirit identifies what the actual world fundamentally is. Substantial being, the independently existing reality of the social world, exists as the actions of self-conscious individuals expressing themselves as the same social spirit. The category, first introduced in idealism as the sameness of self-consciousness and being, becomes a self-

14 According to Pippin, Hegel's account of self-confident individuality demonstrates that "we can only know what we intended to do after we have actually acted and in a way dependent on the reactions of others" (2006, 136). McDowell challenges this claim. Pippin, he says, confuses intention with the way things turn out (2009, 180). Focusing on Hegel's proof procedure, however, adds another perspective to the debate about intentions. According to this procedure, each form of consciousness brings into its experience a truth criterion, and each truth criterion except the first involves a complex set of commitments derived from a series of determinate negations. Self-confident individuality, for example, expects the truth to be a rationality that the subjectivity of the agent and the independent being of the world have in common, and expects this rational attunement to be already established in the given state of affairs. When the agent's work vanishes into its being-for-others, therefore, the agent accepts this result as his own act, and subordinates the particular character of the action to the more general purpose of participating with others in the action that produces the given world of social relations. Thus, Hegel's proof procedure poses the question, how do the layers of presuppositions derived from prior determinate negations determine what an agent intends. Dean Moyar, in his study of Hegel on conscience, suggests a way in which we might conceive intention in layers. He describes a nesting in which specific purposes have value for others because these purposes belong to "standing purposes (commitments) that one has developed over the course of one's life" (Moyar, 2011, 68, 155). If the individual's personal commitments have been formed by commitments that others share, then the individual's intentions would implicitly call for a result in which others can recognize their own values.

conscious individual knowing the social world as the expression of the self's own universal spirit (*PhG* 227–9/M ¶418–20). Thus, self-consciousness knows itself as the being-for-self of the social world. Each self-consciousness plays the role of the world's own universal spirit knowing itself as the true essence of the world's substantial being (*PhG* 229/M ¶422).

7 REASON AS LAWGIVER

Reason as lawgiver begins with the individual self's felt identification with the universal spirit of the social world and with the system of laws in which this spirit is articulated. This is what Hegel means when he says that the object of self-consciousness, the "ethical (*sittliche*) substance," has unquestioned authority. The self feels bound by the spirit of the social world and its laws, without reasons given or asked for, because the self experiences these as its own true self. "We cannot ask for their origin and justification, nor can we look for any other warrant; for something other than essence that is in and for itself could only be self-consciousness itself" (*PhG* 229/M ¶421). Hegel introduces the term "absolute" to describe this felt identification with the universal spirit of the social world, and he identifies what is absolute in ways that refer back to the Introduction to the *Phenomenology* (*PhG* 56–7/M ¶80; 62/M ¶89). "It has the value of the Absolute, for self-consciousness cannot and does not want any more to go beyond this object, for in it, it is in communion with itself: it cannot, for it is all being and all power; it does not want to, for it is the self or the will of this self" (*PhG* 228–9/M ¶420).

Although reason as lawgiver does not retain its absolute status beyond its determinate negation, it shows us the general structure of what we can expect absolute truth to be: individual self-consciousness knowing itself identified with the universal spirit of a social world that has the status of "all being." We must ask, therefore, how a social world acquires the status of all being. We shall have to keep track of this issue as we follow the demonstration further, especially in the discussion of spirit proper, where the movement of history becomes explicit.

Reason as lawgiver knows itself as a self-consciousness immediately identified with the determinate laws of what is absolutely true. The self assumes that his or her "sound reason" knows immediately what is right and good. Moreover, the self takes for granted that what reason knows as true must be a law that identifies the universality and necessity of absolute truth, and therefore is valid and authoritative in virtue of itself, without depending on anything else to justify its authority (*PhG* 229–30/M ¶420–3). Hegel selects two examples for testing the truth expectations of reason as lawgiver. First, "everyone ought to speak the truth" (*PhG* 230/M ¶424). The self-conscious individual, however, must speak as truth whatever his or her rationality immediately, without reflection or deliberation, acknowledges as true. This transforms the truth spoken into a contingency. The truth becomes whatever happens to be true for me, i.e. whatever corresponds to my knowledge and felt convictions. When, therefore, the universal proposition in which the law is articulated is translated into the determinate content of what individuals actually know and speak as true, it becomes a content limited to the speaker, not a truth acknowledged as such by everyone. "The contingency of the content has universality merely in the propositional form in which it is expressed; but as an ethical proposition it promises a universal and necessary content, and thus contradicts itself by the content being contingent" (*PhG* 230/M ¶424). As a law that articulates the universal spirit of a social world, the content of the law ought to be the same for everyone. This ought, however, detaches the universally necessary form required for the truth and authority of a law from the specific content in which it becomes actual.

"Love thy neighbour as thyself" provides a second example of a law that emerges from the dynamics of reason as lawgiver (*PhG* 230/M ¶425). Since truth here takes the form of making something actual, the law calls for an active loving, not just a fond feeling. Love here means actively willing something good for the beloved or actively willing the removal of something evil, which requires discernment regarding precisely what will really turn out well for him or her. The content of the individual's act, however, must be released into the power of the social world and the encounter with the actions of society at large. What the loving act aims to accomplish may be frustrated by the power of the state. The individual may not know the circumstances and social dynamics well enough to take action in an effective way. If the lover settles for being a help in need, the love act becomes dependent on whether a need happens to arise, and whether the help in the circumstances of the actual world persists as something good or gets twisted into something bad. An ethical law ought to be the same in the spirit of the individual agent and in the actuality of the world at large. The determinate content in which the law becomes active, however, turns this requirement into a contingency. Maybe it will turn out that way, and maybe not.

The examination of the two examples demonstrates that the necessity and universality of a social law is compromised when it is translated into the determinate content of real action. The examination also shows how the dynamics of reason as lawgiver distinguishes the form of the action, what it ought to be, from the content of the action. This result calls for a shift to a different form of reason, which Hegel calls reason testing law. Reason testing law challenges the authority of the determinate laws that actually govern the dynamics of the social world. It detaches the form of law from the content in which it appears, and asks whether established laws preserve the universality, necessity, and selfsameness required for a law binding on everyone (*PhG* 231–3/M ¶426–9). "The ethical nature (*Das sittliche Wesen*), therefore, is not itself simply as such a content, but only a standard for deciding whether a content is capable of being a law or not, i.e. whether it is or is not self-contradictory" (*PhG* 231–2/M ¶428).[15]

8 REASON TESTING LAW

Hegel reminds us that we are testing a law's validity as an "absolute" law, which he distinguishes from a law whose legitimacy depends on the way it serves some other end. Hegel offers as an example the case of property. Reason testing law does not ask whether property ought to be required by law because it is useful for some other purpose. Reason testing law asks whether property ought to be required by law just because property belongs to what a shared social spirit must be. Although Hegel does not explicitly talk about the appropriateness of this example, we could make a case for its appropriateness. Reason testing law takes the truth to be the individual self-conscious agent acting according to a law that expresses the universal spirit of the social world. According to this law, the same spirit must persist unchanged in the dynamic between the act of the individual agent and the realization of this act in the social world. Property is this selfsameness in its simplest form, the self knowing something in the world as its own.

In the discussion of reason testing law, Hegel represents the relation between self and world as a self related to a world that exists to serve the individual's needs, and restricts the term "property" to individual, exclusive ownership of a thing. Hegel tests a law that guarantees property by asking whether laws opposed to property are non-contradictory, and by asking whether the law of property itself can operate in the real world without becoming self-contradictory. He formulates the laws opposed to property thus: a law according to which no-one owns things, but rather acquires them as needed; a law according to which things are owned not by independent individuals but by everyone together. The testing of all three laws shows that neither property, nor non-ownership of things, nor

15 The Appendix at the end of this chapter provides a discussion of the Kantian response to Hegel's critique of reason as lawgiver.

communal ownership of things are self-contradictory in their formulations, because all three articulate the same law for everyone. If, however, we consider each one as a law activated in the agency of self-conscious individuals, all three become self-contradictory. Hegel locates the contradiction in the opposition between singularity (*Einzelnheit*) and universality, the relation between self and world dominated by the individual self and the same relation dominated by the world.

According to the law of non-ownership, the individual gets what he or she needs only if the dynamics of the world at large happen to provide it, and only when needed. The individual's needs, however, belong to the continuous life of a conscious self, and the subjectivity of rational thought is embodied in this life. By making the individual self dependent on the independent operations of the objective world, non-ownership of things acts against and contradicts the individuality and subjectivity of reason. The law of common ownership requires a law determining how things should be distributed for meeting the needs of individuals. If the principle is "to each according to need," the particular configuration of needs in each individual determines the way universal resources are distributed, and the law violates the all-inclusive selfsameness required for a valid law. If the principle governing the distribution of things is "to each an equal share," the law does not acknowledge the individual's particular, determinate nature as the embodiment of rational subjectivity. The law of property, however, is equally self-contradictory. Exclusive ownership depends on the contingency of being the first to make a claim, and hence lacks the necessity required for a law. It also contradicts the status of things as realities that belong to the world at large. My exclusive ownership, which focuses the externality of things on me, depends on everyone else acknowledging my ownership, which defines my ownership as a relation to the world at large (*PhG* 233–4/M ¶430–1).[16]

Reason testing law distinguishes the selfsameness of the law from the diversity of its actualization. By making this distinction, reason defines what spirit ought to be as the tranquil, undisturbed selfsameness of spirit remaining the same with itself in the self-consciousness of the agent, the reality of the social world, and the self-consciousness of other agents. This tranquil, undisturbed selfsameness belongs to the thought of a criterion according to which self-consciousness knows whether or not an established law is a valid law. Hegel also calls it "pure consciousness." This selfsameness, however, is

16 The Appendix at the end of this chapter provides a discussion of the Kantian response to Hegel's critique of reason testing law.

a formal universal. It has no content of its own. Its only determination is to command the form of selfsameness in whatever law-like arrangements of content happen to emerge from self-conscious agents with different determinate natures interacting with each other in the social world. Reason as the criterion of a valid law, therefore, cannot stand alone. It cannot become actual without the content of reason as lawgiver.

Reason as lawgiver, however, also cannot stand alone, since the validity and authority of its laws depends on the form of selfsameness. Hence, reason testing law has legitimacy only if it belongs to reason as lawgiver, and reason as lawgiver has legitimacy only if it belongs to reason testing law. The simplicity of reason's criterion turns out to be necessarily connected to its opposite, since becoming diversified and even opposed to itself in the dynamics of reason as lawgiver is a necessary condition of its actualization. Thought thinking the truth as the undisturbed, tautological selfsameness of self-consciousness and being must become actual. In order to become actual (1) it must determine itself as a universal spirit identified with the singularity of each self-conscious individual, (2) diversify itself in the different spheres of action and areas of interest given in the determinate natures of its members and in the determinate laws that emerge in their mutual relations, and (3) organize itself into a social world in which self-conscious individuals belong to the universality and substantial being of a social system (*PhG* 234/M ¶432; 235–7/M ¶435–6). Hegel calls this self-differentiating selfsameness "spirit."

9 RETREAT INTO A GROUND[17]

Hegel explicitly describes spiritual social existence as the unity of thought and being. He makes this point by distinguishing spirit from practical

17 Hegel analyzes the structure of spirit in two places: at the transition from reason as observation to practical reason; and at the transition from practical reason to spirit (*PhG* 193–6/M ¶347–52; 235–40/M ¶436–41). The earlier text, however, contains clues indicating that both analyses count as an analysis of the transition from practical reason to spirit. Hegel says explicitly that the earlier account anticipates the full reality of spirit, that the shift out of reason as observation produces as its immediate result only the beginning of the self's ethical experience of the world. This beginning belongs to the separate individuality of practical self-consciousness whose aim is to duplicate itself in the otherness of the world's objective being (*PhG* 196–7/M ¶356–7). Spirit proper conceives the whole relation between self and world as integrated into and existing within the shared spirit of a people. Both accounts of spirit in its full reality, therefore, have the same status in the demonstration developed in the *Phenomenology*. Spirit emerges from the full development of practical reason, not from the determinate negation of reason as observation.

reason. Practical reason knows the social world as an other confronting it, relates to the other as a field of action, and produces in it a rational order that reflects the rationality of the individual agent. Practical reason belongs to the subjectivity of thought asserting itself as the dominant element in the dynamics between thought and the objective world. The transition to spirit shifts to an underlying unity in which the subjective rationality of thought and the objective rationality of a world are one selfsame reality (*PhG* 234–5/M ¶436; 238–9/M ¶439).

This way of talking about social existence resembles the way Hegel talks about the unity of thought and being in the *Encyclopaedia*'s more abstract discussion of the immediate knowing position, which also applies with qualifications to the beginning of his own logic. In the *Encyclopaedia*, Hegel compares the immediate unity of thought and being to Descartes' *cogito.* The immediate knowing position asserts its intuition of the infinite as a cognition identified with the infinite itself. Hence the immediate intuition of the infinite demonstrates immediately the infinite actually existing, just as Descartes' "I think" immediately demonstrates the "I think" actually existing. Hegel analyzes this immediate unity by distinguishing its thought dimension from the subjectivity of thought and its being dimension from the givenness of sensible being. In the immediate knowing position, being exists in the form of thought, not as a sensible given, and thought is not the subjectivity of thinking, but the true essence of being.[18]

The *Phenomenology* describes spiritual social existence in the same way. Each citizen's "I think" asserts itself not as an isolated subjectivity, but as the spirit of a social substance. The individual knows his or her self immediately identified with the fundamental reality of the social world: "it is the universal 'I' of the category, the 'I' which is immediately the actual, and the world is only this actuality" (*PhG* 235–6/M ¶436). Social being exists not as a sensible given, but as a communal form of knowing; and communal self-consciousness thinks itself, not something else, as the reality of the social world. The shift from practical reason to spirit completely transforms the singularity of the self into the universal spirit of the social whole, not as a slavish surrender to a master, nor as belief in a truth that is other than the self, but as the self's immediate certainty of being a universal self. Social laws govern with unquestioned authority because they are "the absolute pure will of all which has the form of immediate being." As such these laws express the absolute, universal self-consciousness that each self recognizes as its own (*PhG* 235/M ¶436).

18 See chapter 5, §2.

This transformation of the self also transforms the relation between the subjectivity of thought and the objectivity of its other. At the end of reason as observation, the observer relates to the independent, objective existence of the world by focusing on the objective existence of self-consciousness. In phrenology, the inner spirit of the observed self presents itself as an independent, given objective thing. In the transition to spirit, self-consciousness as an observed thing becomes identified with the universal spirit of the whole. Thus, each self-conscious subject recognizes in another self this subject's own universal self reproduced as the independent being of the others. Spirit conceives the rational as the shared life of a people. "It is in fact in the life of a people or nation that the concept of self-conscious Reason's actualization – of beholding, in the independence of the 'other,' complete unity with it, or having for my object the free thinghood of an 'other' which confronts me and is the negative of myself, as my own being-for-*myself* – that the concept has its complete reality" (*PhG* 194/M ¶350). Note how strong Hegel's claim is here. The other members of my folk or country confront me as my own being-for-self. Even in their independence as a free thing that I am not, they stand before me as my other self. The spirit of the whole exists in each and all as universal custom identifying what they are and do. They get their being and essence from the objective being of the social whole, and also produce the whole as their universal work (*PhG* 193–5/M ¶347–50; 238/M ¶438).

Hegel explicitly interprets the transition into spirit as a retreat into a ground. In this transition, previous forms of consciousness are transformed into differentiations determined by and belonging to a ground. "It is the simple, spiritual essence which, in attaining consciousness, is at the same time *real Substance*, into which the earlier forms return as into their ground, so that, in comparison with the latter, they are merely <single> (*einzelne*) moments of its Becoming, moments which do indeed break loose and appear as independent forms, but in fact have existence and reality only as grounded in that Becoming, and possess their truth only in so far as they are and remain in it" (*PhG* 193–4/M ¶348). Each previous form of consciousness stands out and apart from the others not because they really are isolated, but because a communal spirit, which is their ground, differentiates itself in these different forms of experience.

> Spirit is thus self-supporting, absolute, real being. All previous shapes of consciousness are abstract forms of it. They result from Spirit analysing itself, distinguishing its moments, and dwelling for a while with each. This isolating of those moments *presuppposes* Spirit itself and subsists therein … In this isolation they have the appear-

ance of really existing as such; but that they are only moments or vanishing <magnitudes> (*die Größen*) is shown by their advance and retreat into their ground and essence; and this essence is just this movement and resolution of these moments. (*PhG* 238–9/M ¶440)

The determinate negations driving the moves that have carried the *Phenomenology* to this point demonstrate that the preceding forms of experience belong to and exist in a social world whose fundamental unifying principle is the spirit of a community.

With this shift into a ground, the investigation reverses direction. Spirit conceives the common ground that determines its own diversification in the subjectivity of self-consciousness and the objectivity of the social structure. Spiritual social existence also absorbs into the rationality of the actual world the factors previously identified as reason's opposite. It organizes the contingent particulars of life in a system of social roles and political frameworks so that their content belongs to and is derived from the unity of the communal spirit and the relational integration derived from it. Spirit preserves the pure singularity and givenness of the individual as a natural being with needs. The individual works to fulfill his or her given, natural needs within the context of a shared work system. This individual's work serves the needs of others, and the work of others serves this individual's needs. Within the work system, the individual unconsciously produces a universal work by participating in a system that directs the resources of society to the needs of its people. But the individual also explicitly and consciously performs the universal work, sacrificing his or her self for the good of the whole, and receives back from the social whole the universal spirit that is the individual's very self. Thus, even the being-for-self singularity of the self, and the natural givenness that comes with it, belong to and are derived from the self-determining dynamics of the social whole (*PhG* 194–5/M ¶351; 236–7/M ¶437). The rationality of social life exposes its true essence in the history of different national spirits. In this history, reason becomes more and more explicitly revealed to itself (*PhG* 239–40/M ¶441).

APPENDIX: THE RESPONSE TO HEGEL'S CRITIQUE OF KANT'S MORAL PHILOSOPHY

Over several decades Kant and Hegel scholars have argued about whether Hegel's critique of Kant's moral philosophy makes a good case. Some Kant scholars contribute to this debate by challenging the arguments Hegel develops in certain parts of the *Phenomenology*. Since, however, Hegel does not explicitly name Kant in these discussions, these challenges involve two different questions. The first question asks whether it is legitimate to interpret the text selected from the *Phenomenology* as an argument directed against Kant. The second question asks can Kant escape the problems exposed by Hegel's critique, and if so how.

John Silbur and David Couzens Hoy assume that reason as lawgiver belongs to Hegel's critique of Kant's moral principle.[19] Silbur defends Kant by showing that reason as lawgiver does not represent accurately Kant's position. But Silbur does not explain why he assumes that Hegel's critique of reason as lawgiver is proposed as a critique of Kant's moral principle. Hoy defends this assumption by calling attention to the way Kant insists that rational agents, in order to be fully autonomous, must give themselves the law according to which they act. We must ask, however, whether Hegel's account of reason as lawgiver is talking about giving the law in this Kantian sense.

My research suggests two reasons for rejecting the claim that reason as lawgiver is supposed to be a critique of Kant's moral principle. First, if we interpret reason as lawgiver as the result of a determinate negation exposed in self-confident individuality, then it does not resemble Kant's position enough to insist on the Kant connection, and Hegel certainly does not name Kant here. Self-confident individuality ends with a dynamic between the self-focused action of the rational agent necessarily connected to its opposite, i.e. to the agent's action absorbed into a world focused on the individuality of other agents. The laws of reason as lawgiver are the specific patterns established by the encounter between these different individual agencies. This suggests that reason 'gives' the law in the sense that each rational agent participates in the encounter that produces these law-like patterns. Second, we can make a plausible case for comparing reason as lawgiver to the determinate laws of understanding. Hegel himself compares self-confident individuality to sense certainty and perception. Perception ends with an opposition dynamic between the being-for-self separateness of a thing and the being-for-another relation that distinguishes it from other things. Self-confident individuality also ends in a dynamic between being-for-self and being-for-another. In understanding, this dynamic is rethought as a play of forces; and determinate laws, like the law of motion or electricity, are produced by this play of forces. In reason as lawgiver, the dynamic is rethought as an encounter between different individual agencies; and specific laws are produced by this encounter.

19 John Silbur (1974), 223–6. David Couzens Hoy (2009), 156–7.

Hegel's examination of reason testing law, read as an isolated selection, seems to be deliberately designed as a critique of Kant's categorical imperative and the contradiction test associated with it. In the general response to Hegel's critique of Kant's moral philosophy, Kant scholars tend to defend Kant by calling attention to the way he associates the contradiction test with universalization. Kant's moral philosophy tests a moral maxim by asking what would happen in the real world of actions if we willed the maxim as a universal law. If the universalization of the maxim results in self-contradiction, the maxim fails the test. This procedure brings the specific content of real circumstances into moral judgments, which challenges Hegel's claim that Kant's moral principle is too abstract to determine the moral rightness of specific moral norms.[20]

Silbur's version of this defense is especially relevant here, because it focuses on the critique of reason testing law that Hegel develops in the *Phenomenology*.[21] Silbur defends Kant by saying that although Kant's moral principle is indeed a formal principle, and does not function as a principle that derives the content of a right action from itself, it does determine the procedure according to which the form ought to be applied to content. Moral judgment reorders the content of sensibility so that it is never willed at the expense of a rational being.

If, however, we interpret Hegel's critique according to its role in the overall project of the *Phenomenology*, we find the content issue embedded in the more fundamental individuality dynamic first introduced as the determinate negation of virtue and the ways of the world. In this dynamic a self identified with a universal spirit becomes actual in an action that transforms the individual agent's self-expression into this agent's self existing for others. In self-confident individuality, which is defined by this determinate negation, the individuality dynamic plays itself out as an action that focuses the world and the agencies of other individuals on the agent's individual self. In the process, however, the dynamic becomes connected to its opposite, because it surrenders the individual's act into a world focused on the individual self of other participants in the same field of action. According to Hegel, the individuality dynamic functions as a necessary condition for the actualization of the universal. The universal cannot become actual unless it becomes real in this dynamic.[22]

20 See especially Lo (1981), Habermas (1990), 103, 195, 204.

21 Silbur (1974).

22 See §5 and §6 of this chapter.

This condition persists in Hegel's account of reason testing law. Hegel interprets the contradiction test as a theoretical tautology, an "A is A" proposition, in which the content of a moral maxim is compared to itself. This move is determined by the presuppositions of reason and the determinate negations of self-confident individuality and reason as lawgiver. These determinate negations show that in these forms of reason the rationality of self-consciousness is not the same as the rationality of the independent objective world. The presuppositions of reason, however, require this selfsameness. Hence, reason testing law conceives the selfsameness of the rational as a thought detached from the actual dynamics of self and world, because the dynamics of self and world do not measure up to what reason expects the truth to be. Conceiving the moral principle in this way may not represent correctly Kant's moral principle. But it does meet the requirements of Hegel's dialectical procedure.

The second part of Hegel's critique addresses the universalization issue. Hegel argues here that as a law actualized in the real world, all laws fail the contradiction test. The law must be actualized in the individuality dynamic between being-for-self and being-for-another, and thus the same law becomes identified with opposites playing off each other. This opposition dynamic, of course, is not what Kant means by contradiction. But it is what Hegel means by contradiction, and it preserves the results of the determinate negations exposed in the examination of self-confident individuality and reason as lawgiver. In order to defend Kant against Hegel's critique of reason testing law, therefore, the defence must address not just the content issue but also Hegel's analysis of rational action and the individuality dynamic.[23]

23 For a discussion of the way Hegel's critique of morality in the *Philosophy of Right* has been interpreted in the Kant-Hegel debate, see my article (2001b).

15

Spirit, Nature, and the Retreat into a Ground

SPIRIT CONCEIVES THE RATIONAL as a social whole whose communal self-consciousness, articulated in customs and laws, defines what a people or nation takes the truth to be. The self-conscious life of the whole diversifies itself in particular social roles, and organizes natural contingencies into a rationally organized social system. The irrational element introduced in reason as observation and developed in practical reason persists in the examination of spirit, but it takes three different forms: first, as naturally determined contingencies compromising the coherence of the social whole; second, as the given immediacy, the *de facto* existence, of the self-conscious individual; and third, as the independence of nature. All these appear in social existence as factors that resist the control of the concept. No rational necessity can explain them, and yet reason cannot be actual without them.

1 SPIRIT IN ITS IMMEDIACY: ANCIENT GREECE

The examination of spirit begins with spirit in its immediacy, communality in the form of "an objectively existent actuality." Hegel describes this social form as the form of consciousness (sense certainty, perception, understanding) persisting within the framework of social existence (*PhG* 238–9/M ¶440). He defines spirit in this form as self-consciousness identified with natural existence. The communality of the nation emerges as a natural element, the given communality of a common blood line (*PhG* 249–50/M ¶462; 250–1/M ¶464; 259–60/M ¶476). This is the domain of family life and divine law. Political action transforms nature by producing the nation's communal life as the act of the governing authority. This is the domain of human law (*PhG* 240–2/M ¶444–50). Human law differs from divine law only as the overt, conscious form of the communal spirit that remains hidden and unconscious in divine law. "Just as the Family in this way possesses in the community its substance and enduring being, so, conversely, the community possesses in the Family the formal element of its actual existence, and in the divine law its power and authentication" (*PhG* 248–9/M ¶460). Human law gets its legitimacy as the active, explicit articulation of the natural communality of family lineage.

The complete transformation of nature into self-conscious action, however, requires not only the communal self-consciousness of political action but also the communal self-consciousness of family action. Although the active life of a citizen transforms the individual's natural existence into something produced as a self-conscious spiritual act, an act for the community, the death that occurs in the natural course of things gives nature the upper hand by absorbing the individual into the universal natural process of life and death. Death, even death in the line of duty to the nation, has only a contingent association with what belongs to the communal self-consciousness of an action. In order to completely transform natural existence into the spiritual reality of communal existence, natural death must be transformed into something consciously done for the sake of the community.

> The duty of the member of a Family is on that account to add this aspect, in order that the individual's ultimate being, too, shall not belong solely to Nature and remain something irrational (*Unvernünftiges*), but shall be something *done*, and the right of consciousness be asserted in it ... The dead individual, by having liberated his *being* from his *action* or his negative unity, is an empty singular, merely a passive being-for-another, at the mercy of every lower irrational (*vernunftlosen*) individuality and the forces of abstract material elements ... The Family keeps away from the dead this dishonouring of him by unconscious appetites and abstract entities, and puts its own action in their place. (*PhG* 243–5/M ¶452)[1]

Here again Hegel characterizes nature as the irrational, reason's opposite. The family member, acting for the family's lineage, acts against nature's resistant otherness. She cheats nature of its victory by absorbing the dead individual into the spiritual continuity and universality of the family blood line.

Also, by assigning different genders to different areas of communal responsibility, the community transforms the natural diversification of human life in gender differences into an element in the diversification of

1 See also *PhG* 249–50/M ¶462.

the communal self-consciousness. Custom assigns male members of society to the domain of human law, and female members of society to the domain of divine law (*PhG* 247–9/M ¶457–9). The two, however, persist as differences within the same communal spirit. Each has the status and validity of the community itself; and neither has this status and validity without the other (*PhG* 249–51/M ¶460–3; 252/M ¶465). "The difference of the sexes and their ethical content remains, however, in the unity of the substance, and its movement is just the constant becoming of that substance ... Neither of the two is by itself absolutely valid; human law proceeds in its living process from the divine ... and equally returns whence it came" (*PhG* 248–9/M ¶460).

When, however, the individual acts dutifully, the difference that distinguishes human law from divine law shows itself as a conflict that puts the communal spirit in conflict with itself. The individual acts dutifully by asserting the law with which he or she is identified. Each asserts the law as the spirit of the community itself whose authority takes precedence over everything else. Divine law and human law, however, identify the communal spirit in opposite forms. Divine law defines the communal spirit identified with the individuality and particular interests of different families (*PhG* 249/M ¶461). Human law defines the same communal spirit produced and unified by a governing authority that acts against this disintegration. Each individual acting for the community asserts her or his law with the authority of the community itself. Hence, each dismisses the individual who opposes him or her as a mere individual asserting a singular self against the universality of the community. Each asserts his or her own law as the rights of the community itself, and by doing so becomes guilty of opposing the rights of the community asserted in the law of the other. This exposes a fundamental opposition at the heart of the communal spirit itself: between the diversification of the community in the individuality and particular interests of its members, and the unification of the community in the political action that acts against the divisiveness of individual and particular self-interest. Divine and human law become manifest as pure opposites, each identified by its opposition to the other, diversification opposed to unity and unification opposed to diversity (*PhG* 252–6/M ¶466–70).

Hegel tells us that the destructiveness of this opposition has its roots in the nation's dependence on nature. Individuality with its particular interests gets its communal form from its roots in the natural tranquility of blood kinship. Natural contingencies, however, persist as a perpetual threat to this tranquility. Hegel mentions the contingencies represented in the play *Antigone*: the contingency of two brothers born to the reigning monarch, the contingency of being the first born. We might mention others, e.g. Henry VIII of England without a male heir, in a nation with no tradition of female succession, a nation recently emerging from the wars of the roses in which the houses of York and Lancaster fought over whose bloodline could rightfully claim the throne. When contingencies like these transform divine and human law into opposing duties, the governing authority asserts its duty to human law in a form that acts against the authority of divine law. Thus, government finds itself acting against the given sense of community derived from family kinship, and thereby loses its ground in the given unity of the folk. [2]

As a result, government must find another way to overcome the divisiveness of family interests. The governing authority dissolves the independence of families in the universal action of war and claims the nation's young men for this universal action. This, however, makes the authority of human law appear as something other than and alien to the individuality and particularity of family interests, which makes an enemy of womankind. The irony of womankind derides and ridicules the government's action as an unworthy cause in its own right, as a mere vehicle for individual self-importance; female authority claims the family's young men for family interests. Moreover, the government depends on the family for male individuals to carry out its wars; and the family depends on the government for protection from foreign powers. The given harmony of a natural community dissolves in the internal conflicts between government interests and family interests, which gets the community involved in the larger conflicts between different warring peoples (*PhG* 256–60/M ¶473–5).

2 Hegel's use of *Antigone* in the *Phenomenology*'s examination of spirit's immediate form has provoked an ongoing debate. This debate focuses on the way the discussion of the play reveals Hegel's position on the role of woman in social life (see *The Owl of Minerva*, volume 33:2 for a set of articles representing some of the views that have emerged in this debate). Dahlstrom (2008) responds to the feminist debate by showing that the feminist concerns, although legitimate, are beside the point Hegel is trying to make with his interpretation of *Antigone*. "His overriding interest here is in illuminating how the dynamics of the ethical world emerge from the sexual difference" (145). My interpretation of the *Antigone* discussion shows that social roles based on gender difference belong to Hegel's more general concern with the role of natural determinations in the communal life of a people. They function as natural determinations integrated into social self-consciousness. Thus, Dahlstrom's interpretation and my own interpret Hegel's primary concern in similar ways. Moreover, my interpretation agrees with his when it calls attention to the way Hegel says explicitly and repeatedly that both gender roles are equally essential. Hyppolite's commentary (1946/1974) also focuses on the role of the natural element in this form of spirit.

2 LEGAL STATUS: THE ROMAN EMPIRE

The givenness of natural communal feeling, infected with natural contingency, becomes absorbed into a destructive process that negates its status as the persistent true essence of spiritual reality. This negation detaches communal self-consciousness from its involvement in the specific content of family lineage, naturally determined social roles, and inherited governing authority; detachment reduces the individual's identification with society to an empty form, the pure form of being recognized as a citizen with the right to claim the nation as "mine" (*PhG* 260–1/M ¶476–8). Hegel compares this detachment to stoicism. Like stoicism, it lets the other go free. The nation's content and resources exist as a separate, independent reality confronting the detached self-consciousness of each citizen. Here again, nature functions as the element that breaks free and exists on its own. Like stoicism, citizenship withdraws from the natural element and looks beyond it for the true essence of the social world. The natural content of external possessions or a person's naturally determined character does not matter. What matters is the citizen's right to claim society as her or his own and the social world acknowledging this right. Hegel says later that the equality of legal right is "that immediate recognition and validity of self-consciousness simply because it is," and refers to this as the individual's "natural being" (*PhG* 267–8/M ¶488–9). Even in its detachment from the natural content of its determinate nature, one natural element persists, namely the given existence of the individual self, which is sufficient in the spirit of legal status to establish the individual's right to claim society as "mine."

Yet self-consciousness cannot become identified with the being of society, and exist as the true essence of reality, unless it makes the independence of the nation's natural content its own. Hegel compares this to scepticism. Like sceptical thought, but with a positive rather than a negative aim, persons must become identified with a reality that maintains its independence of the self. Self-consciousness must externalize the self, send it out to exist in the independence of the social substance. The formal definition of citizenship, however, provides no principle for determining exactly how the content of the nation is to be appropriated by different individuals with the same right to property. Social self-consciousness makes the social substance its own by taking possession of its content in a random, disorganized way. The content of the social whole, including the determinate character and talents of its citizens, loses its organization and coherence when the spiritual status of its members becomes detached from the natural element. Nature set free loses its rational order. Its latent irrationality shows itself again. The coherence of society depends, therefore, on the dominant power of one individual, the emperor, who claims as his own all the nation's resources and thereby negates the divisiveness of competing property interests. Society as a whole, personified in a dominant individual, confronts the members of society as an alien power, not as each member's own social spirit (*PhG* 261–3/M ¶479–82).

Thus, the immediate unity of thought and being in the reality of social existence implies a diversification that distinguishes self-consciousness from the concrete content and independent existence of natural reality, and situates this concrete reality as a middle term between the unifying self-consciousness of the governing authority and the diversifying self-consciousness of individual citizens. Society exists as these two forms of individual self-consciousness making themselves actual in society's natural content and in the self-consciousness of those who claim society as their own. Social self-consciousness shows itself to be an unhappy consciousness, divided against itself in the unyielding exclusivity of individuality: the individuality of the ruler claiming for itself the content and resources of society, and imposing on his subjects the rule of his own exclusive will; the individuality of those ruled, who must somehow convert the alien power and society's wealth into something that expresses their own sense of self. From this point on, nature becomes a vehicle for the dynamics played out within the social structure between these opposed claims on the social world (*PhG* 263–5/M ¶483–4).

3 SELF-ALIENATED CULTURE: FEUDALISM AND THE ANCIEN RÉGIME

Hegel gives the name self-alienated culture to the social form that explicitly identifies itself as this unhappy social consciousness. The culture presupposes a fundamental alienation between the isolated individuality of the people and the universality of the social whole. In the previous form of spirit, legal status belongs to anyone acknowledged as a citizen, simply in virtue of the individual's immediate existence within the group of persons that society claims as its own. The determinate negation of this spirit, however, reduces the individuality of the citizen to a relation. In order to actualize the right of citizenship, a person must become involved in the universality and independent reality of the social world. Self-alienated culture endorses this development by defining membership in society in terms of the whole relation. Individuals become identified with society not in virtue of their given existence within its domain, but by surrendering their "natural being," their given individuality, to the otherness of the social world.

The individual self "alienates" its self, gives itself over to the culture, and becomes transformed into a universal self. This acculturation process actualizes both the individual self and the social world. It produces the individual as a universal self, and it brings the action of individuals into the dynamics that produce the reality of the social world (*PhG* 263–5/M ¶484–5; 267–8/M ¶488–90).

Hegel's account of self-alienated culture focuses on the role of language in the dynamics of the culture. The analysis of language here reappears later in the spirit of conscientiousness and plays an important role in explaining how a conscientious self becomes a shared self. My interpretation of self-alienated culture, therefore, highlights the language theme as well as the nature theme.[3] In self-alienated culture, the sacrifice of the self's natural being and its particular interests for the sake of the social whole functions as the norm that determines what is good. It is what spirit in this form takes the truth to be. This presupposition makes itself manifest in the noble life and in the way this life is acknowledged by others as "their own essence exemplified" (*PhG* 275/M ¶505). An individual sacrifices his own particular interests to serve the ruler, whom he acknowledges as the ruling element in the social order. Hegel calls the ruling element state power. It represents the universality of the social whole, which functions as its true spirit. If language has a role here, it functions only as counsel or advice concerning what best serves the good of the kingdom (*PhG* 274-5/M ¶503–5).

But the judgment implicit in the noble life separates what it judges as good from an element that persists as a significant force in the social structure. Particular interests are manifest in the way society breaks up into different classes and estates, each with its own specific concerns, interests, and values. This is the being-for-self element in the social whole, individuals serving their own individual self-interest. A noble individual who does not die for the cause continues to be a definite individual with a will of his own and interests specific to him. This renders his counsel ambiguous and suspect. Does it express a concern for the good of the kingdom, or only the particular interests of his class or estate (*PhG* 275–6/M ¶506; 280–1/M ¶519)? In order to achieve complete identification with society as a whole, the individual must somehow separate himself from particular interests. He achieves this in a form of speech that Hegel calls "language authoritative as language."

3 In Collins 2003a and 2006, I develop a more complete study of the way Hegel's project in the *Phenomenology* provides resources for discussing the role of language in social relations.

Hegel explains the dynamics of language in this form by distinguishing it from other ways in which language plays a role in the social order. Language articulates the laws and prevailing customs of a society in the form of commands. Language in the form of counsel speaks about the good of the kingdom. These forms of linguistic self-expression say too much and too little. They say too much because they express not only the self of the speaker but also the reality that gives the speech its subject matter or content. They say too little because they express the self only as related to something other than itself, not the self in itself. "Language authoritative as language," Hegel says, has the form of speaking itself as its content. What, then, is the pure form of speaking?

Speech expresses what the self experiences as its own consciousness, and consciousness belongs only to the one whose experience it is. Speech brings this inner consciousness out into a domain shared with others and delivers it over to them. Unlike work, the speech does not become existent outside consciousness in the objective reality of the world. It disappears into the consciousness of the one who hears it. This other consciousness has the same exclusivity as the first. It belongs only to the one whose experience it is. Thus, the inner, private consciousness of the speaker becomes existent as the inner, private consciousness of another self. What, then, does it mean for language to say nothing more than what the form of speaking itself does?

It means that the speaking surrenders the speaker's own exclusive singular self into the domain shared with others, to become existent as the exclusive singular self-consciousness of the one to whom the speech is spoken. The noble individual says to the ruler, "I am your man." Thus, he surrenders his very self, the singularity of self that he alone is, to the ruler. By doing so, he relates to the ruler no longer as an institution, as part of the social order, but as another self who hears what is spoken and thus takes it into his own singular self-consciousness. Since what is spoken is the very self of the speaker, this self lives now in the self of another. The noble individual says to the ruler, "I am your man, you are my king," and this speech gives the ruler his kingly self, his being the personification of society itself in whom the noble becomes universal. Thus, state power becomes the will of the king, and wealth becomes the king's gift (*PhG* 275–8/M ¶507–11).

By acknowledging the king as the personification of society itself, the noble's self-surrender transforms the universality of society into the singularity of the king's will. The exclusiveness of this will becomes manifest in the king's gifts of wealth. Wealth is a base thing. It has no purpose or value of its own. Its being is to be sacrificed, to serve and satisfy an individual's self-interest; and in this culture individual self-interest is itself base, since it is conceived as what must be sacrificed for the sake of the social whole. By acknowledging the noble's self-surrender with gifts of wealth, the king treats the noble as a self whose service can be purchased. Like wealth itself, the noble becomes for the king a thing with no purpose of its own, whose only being is to be sacrificed to the individuality of another. In the process, however, the king loses his status as the spirit of the social whole. The noble cannot find his true, universal self in this individual. The king becomes for the noble the exclusive, singular will of an individual who uses wealth, and the service he buys with wealth, as a thing sacrificed to his singular will, a singularity made manifest by arrogance, capriciousness, and whim. The noble's self-surrender transforms the universality of the ruler into the self-focused being-for-self that this culture condemns as base. The noble, therefore, withholds the complete commitment of his self. The language of self-surrender becomes base flattery. The oath of fealty masks rebellion waiting to happen (*PhG* 278–83/M ¶512–20).

The truth exposed in this development becomes a reality in the culture as judgments articulated in talk. These judgments take opposite forms. Honest consciousness talks about a tranquil universality in which each facet of the culture is one and the same essential spirit. But this is challenged by a disruptive consciousness that talks about a universal instability in which the good becomes bad and the bad good. Service to society as a whole, which is good, becomes service to the self-concern of the individual, which is bad; the isolated, arrogant will of an individual, which is bad, asserts itself as the will of society as a whole, which is good. The disruptive consciousness says that all talk of an unequivocal good is an empty abstraction. Actual existence itself perverts, destabilizes, divides the spirit of society. Honest consciousness responds with the claim that the good is still good, even if it is associated with what is bad, since this association is "its condition and necessity." Disruptive consciousness counters by saying that the good, then, exists only on the condition that it becomes identified with the bad and hence becomes the opposite of itself. Hegel's point is this: the unifying principle of real existence is necessarily connected to the conditions of real existence; and these conditions require a diversity in which different factors identify themselves by playing off what challenges or opposes them (*PhG* 281–5/M ¶520–4).

This development dissolves the whole structure of social reality into a process in which no factor involved in it stands firm. The system of social relations and social roles, the unified will of society, the diversified will of its members, the talk that defends their sameness of spirit, and the talk that attacks it – all these dissolve into mere factors in the whole process. The only thing that persists throughout is the self-consciousness that knows each and every factor as not what the spirit of society essentially is. The true spirit of society, therefore, is the negativity of this self-consciousness itself. The whole complicated social dynamic appears in its true form when it appears as not the really important thing. What makes this appear is the self's witty talk, which refuses to take any of it seriously (*PhG* 285–7/M ¶525–6; 292–3/M ¶539–40).

4 THE ENLIGHTENMENT

The Enlightenment spirit implicitly acknowledges this result by rejecting the values of the established social structure – state power and wealth, noble service and base self-interest, authority and rebelliousness – as it also rejects the social divisions caused by conflicting social roles and expectations. It seeks a higher value as the true essence and real meaning of the existing social order. Enlightenment faith finds this higher value in a transcendent kingdom of God, which restores the social world to harmony and peace; Enlightenment insight conceives the true essence as the universality of the self's own reason. Faith retains content and reality by conceiving the higher truth as an actual world, a world outside thought, but a world in harmony with itself, not the divided, discredited social order directly confronting us. Insight, to begin with, has no content. In order to detach itself from the divisive, discredited forces of the social order, the self must find its truest self not in service to the community, nor in particular projects and interests, nor in what it expects from society, but in a rationality detached from all these (*PhG* 287–9/M ¶529). Insight appropriates the content of social existence by taking over the content of faith.

Insight discredits faith by demonstrating that what faith represents as a transcendent other is really only a projection of the self's aspirations. Faith conceives a God in whom the self is not lost but found, whose acceptance gives the self its true worth. Faith's self-sacrifice signals the self's desire to detach itself from its worldly condition and attach itself to something more meaningful. Faith accepts the authority of unreliable historical texts only if and because its own inner witness acknowledges their message. Faith's sacraments and symbols represent the ordinary things of the world, like bread and wine, stone and wood, as if sensible realities could have a significance that transcends the ordinary conditions of life. All this shows that faith's transcendent world is only the otherness dimension of a reality that gets its true meaning by being a reflection of the self. Thus, insight appropriates the otherness dimension of faith, but reduces it to an empty principle that transforms the alien content of the social world into something appropriate to the true essence of the rational self (*PhG* 297–8/M ¶549; 299–303/M ¶552–6; 306–10/M ¶564–70; 310–11/M ¶572–3).[4]

This transforms the world of the Enlightenment into a world of utility. In the utility culture, the world's independent objective status finally and completely dissolves. The useful has a determinate character of its own, and hence has the appearance of objectivity. But the true essence of this appearance is its usefulness, and this reduces its objective character to its being useful for the self's concerns. Thus, the self runs through all the differentiated content of the world, and knows itself, this self, as the universal that is the simple essence of it all. The self experiences the world's otherness not as a substantial world existing in itself, but as a world existing for another self. Objects have no independence left. The self of pure insight and utility, however, knows itself not as a single self whose singularity excludes the self of others, but as a rational subject with the certainty of being the true essence of the actual. In the self of another, the self sees its own essential rationality doubled. Thus, everything dissolves in the object's being for the universal self of each and every citizen (*PhG* 313–17/M ¶579–83; 423–4/M ¶791).

5 ABSOLUTE FREEDOM AND TERROR: THE FRENCH REVOLUTION

The result is a social world without substance. It has no integrity and independence of its own. By itself, it is dispersed and destabilized by conflicting social forces. Only its existence as a reality existing for the self holds it together and gives it a unifying, stable orientation. In order to experience this truth, the self must do away with the independence of the established social structure. It must abolish the diversification of society into different spheres of action and interest, because this organizes society into an independent system and assigns individuals to a particular role in the dynamics of the social whole. To play a particular role in a social system, to be represented by another in the process of government, gives the self the experience of being limited to a particular part of the nation's life, dependent on its connection to the other parts of the system, and ruled by the dynamics of the system to which his or her sphere of action belongs. None of this organized independence has any legitimacy or truth for the self liberated by Enlightenment insight. In the culture of absolute freedom,

4 For an excellent study of the encounter between Enlightenment faith and insight, see di Giovanni 1995b.

the individual self takes itself to be not a participant with others in the spirit of the whole but the spirit of the whole itself. The self does not participate with others in the cooperative work of producing the nation's life. The subjectivity of the free self asserts itself as the will of the nation, and expects the nation's life to be a work produced immediately and directly by this individual's act (*PhG* 314–18/M ¶582–6).

Absolute freedom, however, cannot produce a work in the positive sense. A work exists as an object that has its own independent existence outside the self of the one who produces it. The agent lets his or her work go into the independent reality of the objective world. Absolute freedom takes the truth of the objective world to be the will of the individual completely liberated from the alien character of an independent, objective social order. It wills itself, therefore, precisely as free from everything else. It "lets nothing break loose to become a free object standing over against it" (*PhG* 318–19/M ¶588). Hence, it cannot make itself actual as a socially organized system of interests, social roles, and governmental structures. Social organization gives the objective world an independent objectivity that challenges the absoluteness of the individual's independent will. Absolute freedom makes itself actual, therefore, only as a will that negates not just the old order but any order that gives the social world an independent objective existence.

Since, however, absolute freedom takes the will of the nation to be the free will of each individual citizen, the nation's common will takes on the exclusivity of each individual self. This creates a contradiction between an individual will in the role of the government and the individual wills of the governed. Every attempt to govern is the exclusive, individual act of the governing will and thereby imposes on the people a will that is not their own. The people, therefore, become suspect. Their own status as individuals identified with the will of the nation necessarily opposes any act of government that is not their own doing. The nation falls apart in the exclusivity of each individual's free will asserted as the will of the nation itself. In this form, the independence of each individual's thought becomes an act of treason, since it asserts itself as a will that overrules and suppresses the will of the nation identified with the will of others. Such treason provokes and necessitates its own negation by the will of those whose freedom has been violated. Hegel calls this the spirit of absolute freedom and terror (*PhG* 316–21/M ¶584–92).

Hegel explains the result of this development by focusing on the role of death in the dynamics of the Terror. In this explanation, he refers to "individuals who have felt the fear of death, of their absolute master," and "the fear of the lord and master which has again entered men's hearts" (*PhG*

321/M ¶593-4). This wording invites us to compare the role of death in the Terror to the role of death in the opening moves of self-consciousness. Death in the prestige battle kills the self who loses, and thereby returns him to the independent, objective existence of nature. In the master-servant dialectic, fear of death takes over the self of the servant and transforms him into a worker absorbed into the dynamics of the natural order. Thus, death surrenders the self-conscious individual into an objective existence whose truth is a master self, a self completely independent of the objective order. So also the death-dealing culture of the Terror kills the self embedded in the determinate existence of a living individual and thereby returns the given, immediate existence of the self to the independent, objective existence of nature. So also the fear of death takes over the self attached to its own individual existence and transforms it into a self whose being and action serves a self-consciousness that is completely independent of determinate existence. In the Terror, the rational self finally emerges as a knowing and willing completely detached from its engagement in natural being. Even the immediate being, the *de facto* existence, of the individual self, loses its hold on the rationality that spirit knows as truth. The negativity of absolute freedom surrenders the determinate existence of the self into the dynamics of the independent social order, just as the servant worker self becomes an added force integrated into the independent dynamics of the natural world. Truth is the universal self-consciousness whose knowing and willing is completely independent of immediate existence in all its forms, even the immediate existence of the individual self. Truth is a knowing and willing that overrules these conditions and masters them, transforming them into a vehicle for its own universal, undivided selfsameness. This is the spirit of moral integrity and duty.

Analyzed as a determinate negation, absolute freedom ends with the will of the government and the will of the people reduced to pure opposites. The governing will wills nothing but the negation of the people's will, which is distributed in the exclusivity of each citizen; the people's will wills nothing but the negation of the government as an alien simple will. Each opposite has no will of its own except as a relation to the other. The truth implicit in this necessary connection transforms the opposites into participants in the same truth. The selfsameness of this truth requires a knowing and willing distinguished from the whole domain of immediate existence and the limiting conditions that isolate a will within the exclusive singularity of an individual self. This requirement justifies the shift to a social spirit that expects the truth to be a willing and knowing that overrules the exclusivity of the singular self and transforms the individual will into a willing and knowing that remains selfsame in each and every will (*PhG* 321–4/M ¶594–5).

6 THE MORAL VIEW OF THE WORLD

Hegel introduces the spirit of the moral world by returning to the theme with which he introduces the "Spirit" section of the *Phenomenology*. Hegel introduces spiritual social existence as the unity of thought and being. The rational individual knows his or her self immediately identified with the universal spirit of the social whole; and this spirit is an independently existing social world (being, substance) identified by the way a social self-consciousness conceives the truth (thought, subjectivity). We compared this interpretation of social existence to Hegel's discussion of Jacobi's immediate knowing position. According to Hegel's interpretation, Jacobi distinguishes the immediate intuition of the infinite from the immediate givenness of being presented in sensation, and also from the subjectivity of thought isolated in itself. Immediate knowing knows itself identified with thought existing as the essential character of being. In the *Phenomenology*, however, the identity of thought and being is conceived as the spirit of a social world, and the examination of spirit shows that the identity of thought and being takes different forms according to the way priority is assigned to its thought or being determination. Hegel says that the opposition between consciousness and its object emerges within spirit as an alien otherness between social self-consciousness and the independently existing social world in which the self expects to know itself. In the transition from absolute freedom and terror into the moral view of the world, the subjectivity of thought becomes completely detached from the whole domain of immediate existence and takes its own independent subjectivity to be the essential character and ground of "all being." "Absolute essential being is, therefore, not exhausted when determined as the simple essence of thought; it is all reality, and this reality is only as knowledge ... Into its conscious will all objectivity, the whole world, has withdrawn. It is absolutely free in that it knows its freedom, and just this knowledge is its substance and purpose and its sole content" (*PhG* 324–5/M ¶598). The moral will wills nothing but its own free self-conscious thought, and wills it as what all objectivity, all reality, fundamentally is (*PhG* 323–5/M ¶596–8).

The culture of morality carries with it the negations of the Enlightenment. Nothing in the reality of social existence has a worth of its own: neither the structure of authority and wealth, social roles and conflicting interests, personal enjoyment and prestige (negated in the dynamics of alienated culture), nor the inner truth of the actual world (Enlightenment faith and insight), nor the free will of individual persons (absolute freedom and terror). Morality restores meaning and truth to the social world by detaching the self from its involvement in these devalued realities, by giving the self a motive that transcends them. The moral view of the world expects individuals to universalize their self by acting according to principles not derived from natural conditions, or the socio-political structures of society, or thought attached to these conditions, or thought attached to the exclusive singularity of the self. Morality expects moral persons to overcome these divisive conditions by producing a world governed by principles that remain the same for all thinkers, and these are the principles of pure thought uncompromised by the isolated singularity of the individual thinker.

This way of conceiving the moral self, however, lets nature go free. It leaves to its own devices the independent existence of natural and social reality. Morality conceives nature in two forms: the independent existence of a world; and the natural determinations of the self in its relations to the world – its sensuous desires, given character, particular interests. According to the moral view, nature in both forms remains completely indifferent to morality. Moral action operates as a negation that overrules these natural forms. It transforms natural reality into a manifestation of the independent dutiful will of a moral self. In the process, however, moral action identifies the moral ideal with conditions that compromise its purity and universality. Moral action wills as duty a particular concern that the agent feels as her or his own; and it seeks the happiness of having achieved its purpose. Hence, the universality of dutiful intentions becomes inevitably mixed up with the exclusivity of this agent's will, this agent's accomplishment, this agent's cause, and becomes particularized in the specific duties of real life. Moreover, duty in action needs a world alien to it, a world that must be overruled by it, so that the moral agent can know the moral essence of the world as the agent's own act. Hence, the alienation between the subjectivity of the self and the objectivity of the world belongs to the necessary conditions of moral action (*PhG* 325–37/M ¶599–625).

In the God postulate, the moral view acknowledges the necessity of reconciling moral aspirations with the actual world of nature, sensuous inclinations, and particularized duty. The postulate conceives God as a holy will in which pure duty and the moral indifference of natural existence are reconciled. This, Hegel says, exposes the fundamental contradiction at the heart of the moral ideal. The God postulate conceives a transcendent moral perfection, a holy will that is completely free from the determinations of the actual world. Yet it conceives this same holy will sanctioning the particularized aims that morality is supposed to overrule with its dedication to universal duty (*PhG* 337–9/M ¶626–30).[5]

The morality of conscientiousness endorses this contradiction by conceiving the subjectivity of the moral agent identified with the unity of thought and nature conceived in the God postulate. In this new form of morality, God exists as the voice of conscience, and the self's involvement in the actual world becomes a reality derived from and sanctioned by the individual's conscientious conviction that a particular project is what duty requires of him or her (*PhG* 339–42/M ¶631–4). Conscience operates within the self as the universality of God's holy will differentiating and actualizing itself in the reality conditions of the self and its world.

In order to fully appreciate the dialectical justification of this shift, we must recognize in it another version of the systematic whole dynamic first introduced in the dialectic of understanding, repeated in the dialectic of unhappy consciousness, and repeated again in the transition from self-confident individuality to reason as lawgiver to reason testing law. In all these shifts, the *Phenomenology*'s examination of experience makes a distinction and then cancels it. In order to think the selfsameness of opposites, the moral view of the world distinguishes their sameness from the opposition that keeps them differentiated. The God postulate conceives a holy will in which moral thought and natural being are at one with each other, and it distinguishes this tranquil unity from the moral world of finite persons where morality and nature are in conflict. This, however, distinguishes the pure thought of a postulate from "real being and consciousness." It conceives the truth as a thought with no being, and it conceives real being and the consciousness involved in it as being without truth (*PhG* 339–41/M ¶631).

Morality moves to the God postulate, however, in the same way that understanding moves to simple force, unhappy consciousness moves to the

5 The vast literature focused on Hegel's critique of Kant's moral philosophy includes two debates that focus on the critique Hegel develops in the part of the *Phenomenology* entitled "The Moral View of the World." Jonathan Robinson (1977) detaches this part of the *Phenomenology* from its role in the phenomenological project as a whole, and studies Hegel's account of the moral view as a critique of the way Kant's moral philosophy makes a transition from morality to religion. According to Robinson, Hegel's critique of this move demonstrates the failure of Kant's whole moral theory. R. Z. Friedman (1986) defends Kant against Robinson's claims. Karl Ameriks (1987) analyzes the issues in the Kant-Hegel encounter on moral issues. Ameriks does not focus primarily on "The Moral View of the World" in the *Phenomenology*. But Kenneth Westphal (1991) responds to Ameriks by examining this text. Westphal's article examines carefully Kant's own world view, as well as Onora O'Neill's defence of it, and claims that Hegel's critique of the postulates is sound.

transcendence of the unchangeable, and practical reason moves to reason testing law. Understanding conceives simple force as the truth demanded by the play of forces. Unhappy consciousness conceives the divine self as the truth demanded by unhappy consciousness itself. Practical reason conceives the non-contradiction norm as the unity demanded by the connections played out in the dynamics of self-confident individuality. So also, the moral view conceives God as the truth demanded by the dynamics of moral action. God is the condition that enables a moral agent to accomplish what duty requires of her or him, and hence God makes it possible for reality to be what it truly is. Morality, therefore, must think the truth conceived in the God postulate as actually existent in the reality whose truth it is. It must cancel the distinction between them, and thus conceive being in the form of pure thought and pure thought as what exists. This justifies the shift to a form of morality that conceives the selfsameness of thought and nature in God as the inherent true essence of the real world (*PhG* 339–42/M ¶631–3).[6]

7 THE SPIRIT OF CONSCIENTIOUSNESS

The conscientious agent knows that the thought of duty is an empty abstraction, that it must be given reality in the personal conscience of the agent, in the concrete content of the agent's particular character, in the circumstances of the action, and in the self-consciousness of other moral agents acknowledging the conscientiousness of the action. In other words, the morality of conscientiousness knows conscience as the concern for universal duty determining itself as a reality distributed in the diversity of real life experience. The conviction that some particular course of action is the right thing to do gives the singularity and particularity of action the form of something good, and thus transforms individual decisions, particular interests and circumstances, established laws, customs, and social roles into universal duty actualizing and diversifying itself. Society exists precisely as the reality of conscientious conviction determining the content and relational forms of the social substance (*PhG* 340–5/M ¶632–9).[7]

6 Rebecca Comay's recent book, *Mourning Sickness: Hegel and the French Revolution*, interprets the account of conscience in the *Phenomenology* by relating it explicitly to the radical negativity introduced in the account of the French Revolution (Comay 2011). For a discussion of her interpretation, see the Appendix at the end of this chapter.

7 See the Appendix at the end of this chapter for a discussion of the different ways in which Hegel's position on the role of conscience has been interpreted.

In his account of the conscientious spirit, Hegel explicitly refers back to *die Sache selbst,* which emerges in the dynamics of self-confident individuality. The account of self-confident individuality analyzes rational action into different factors: purpose, means used, accomplished work, and given circumstances. All these factors are unified by the content of the agent's given particular character. The account shows, however, that the action breaks apart in the contingencies of the field of action, and the work vanishes in the world's relation to the agencies of other individuals. As a result, self-confident individuality focuses on the form rather than the content of the action. The heart of the matter (*Sache selbst*) is to transform the given world into the agent's own act. This, however, activates an opposition dynamic between different individuals, each claiming not only his or her own work, but the work of others as well.[8] The spirit of conscientiousness, Hegel says, finally masters this tendency to disintegration. Conscience wills all these factors, including the circumstances of the action, as vehicles and manifestations of its commitment to universal duty. The commitment to duty is a commitment to what identifies the agent with the other members of the moral fellowship. Action, however, brings the universal spirit of morality into the being-for-self structure of individual agency and thus transforms universal duty into something focused on the agent as an exclusive individual. The universal becomes active as my doing. I experience it as my accomplishment. It answers to my interests and concerns. Left to itself, therefore, the self-focused individuality of action actualizes the universal spirit that is the agent's true self in a form that excludes others and therefore compromises its universality. The universality of conscientiousness does not appear in the content of the action or in the individuality dynamic that is its form.

Conscientious action gets its universality not from the content and self-focused structure of action but from a self-consciousness that knows itself identified with the universal spirit that determines what is right and good, the spirit of God. This universality operates in moral action as an intention. The agent wills the action as a vehicle for making manifest the self's identification with the universality of the divine spirit. Conscience, therefore, is completely free to put into the action any content that is endorsed by the self's sense of itself identified with the universal spirit of God. By acting on this conviction, the individual expresses not only the individual's own spirit but the spirit that exists as the true self of every conscientious person (*PhG* 344–51/M ¶640–50).

8 See chapter 14, §6.

This form of conscience, however, is the spirit of a social world. The individuality of the agent's conscientiousness must actually exist as the will of society itself. The agent accomplishes this in a form of language that reproduces the self-sharing dynamic first introduced in the relation between the vassal and the king in self-alienated culture.[9] The speech of conscientiousness brings the inner, private self of the individual into a domain shared with others and gives it existence in those who hear the word and acknowledge it. The agent must say that the act is an act of conscience, that it is driven by the inner moral spirit that is the true self of the agent. But this is not enough. One who justifies an act to others by an appeal to the agent's conscience alone asserts blatantly that the act wrongs them. The agent must declare that the duty is an *acknowledged* duty. He or she must say to others that the action is intended as an act of conscience and hence manifests the spirit that inspires their own conscientiousness; and others must explicitly acknowledge the agent's conscientiousness. The moral ideal actually exists as a community in which persons mutually assure each other of their pure intentions, and thereby acknowledge each other as members of a moral fellowship whose communal spirit is the divine spirit of moral righteousness.[10]

Viewed in this way, conscientiousness concentrates itself in the perfectly transparent relation between the spirit of conscientiousness expressed as each self's own inner spirit and the same spirit acknowledged by others as their own. This collapses the otherness between self and world into the empty "I am I" in which the oppositions created by natural determinations have no role to play. The unity of thought and being exists as a community of beautiful souls; and this community exists in mutual assurances expressed and acknowledged in speech, a sound that immediately dies away. In this form, the unity of thought and being cannot become a thing, cannot produce itself as an independently existing real world (*PhG* 350–55/M ¶651–8).

It is important to notice that here again Hegel repeats a theme that appears in the *Encyclopaedia*'s examination of the third position on objectivity. The conscientiousness of the beautiful soul community is the com-

9 See §3 of this chapter.

10 Feldman (2006), chapter 2 provides a good description of the way language operates as a kind of rhetoric in the *Phenomenology*'s account of conscience. This discussion calls attention to the problem involved in keeping conscience present in its action once the action is released into a shared world. According to Feldman, language functions as a failed attempt to take care of this problem. Feldman's interpretation also fully appreciates the problems involved when conscience loses completely the reality of external existence.

munal form of the intuition described in the *Encyclopaedia* as the immediate intuition of the infinite. Both have the form of immediate intuition in which the self experiences its own identification with the divine. Hegel's use of Descartes' *cogito* to explain the third position on objectivity also helps us appreciate Hegel's account of the beautiful soul. The "I think" of the conscientious individual asserts the self-thinking of a universal divine spirit existing in and as the self-thinking of the conscientious individual. Like Descartes' *cogito*, this "I think" demonstrates the existence of the "I think" just by positing itself thinking. Unlike Descartes' *cogito*, however, it demonstrates the real being of the divine spirit identified with the real being of the individual's inner sense of self. "The consciousness that has risen above the thoughtlessness (*Gedankenlosigkeit*) that still holds these differences – which are none – to be differences, knows the immediacy of the presence within it of the absolute Being (*Wesen*) as the unity of that Being and its own self; it thus knows itself as the living in-itself, and knows that this knowledge is religion, which as knowledge that has a perceived or outer existence is the utterance of the community concerning its own Spirit" (*PhG* 354/M ¶656). The beautiful soul's way of thinking collapses the distinction that, according to the *Logic*, identifies the subject matter of the *Phenomenology*. The differences that ordinary phenomenal consciousness takes to be real differences "are none." Thought dependent on something other than itself for what it thinks collapses into thought simply asserting itself thinking. In the beautiful soul community, of course, thought must also speak. Some distinction between self and other exists in it. But speech does nothing more than speak the self-intuition of the speaker and surrender it into the self-intuition of the one who hears, and both speak the same spirit as their own and that of the other. "Looking at this submergence of consciousness within itself, we see that the *unexplicated substance* is, for consciousness, *knowledge* as *its* knowledge. As consciousness, it is divided into the antithesis of itself and its object which is, for it, essence; but it is just this object that is perfectly transparent, is its own *self*, and its consciousness is only this knowledge of itself. All life, all spiritual essentiality, has withdrawn into this self and has lost its difference from the *I* itself" (*PhG* 354–5/M ¶658). There is no true consciousness-of here, because there is no true otherness.

The *Phenomenology*, however, exposes a fundamental problem with this way of conceiving the identification of thought and being. "This absolute *certainty* into which substance has resolved itself is the absolute *untruth* which collapses internally; it is the absolute *self-consciousness* in which *consciousness* is submerged" (*PhG* 354/M ¶657). The untruth exposed in the collapse is not the untruth of a consciousness that depends on an other for its object, as the Maker-Winfield interpretation might claim. On the contrary, the collapse exposes the untruth of a self-consciousness in which the consciousness dimension, with its relation to a true other, "is submerged." "Just as little has consciousness an *outer existence*, for the objective aspect does not get as far as being a negative of the actual self, in the same way that this self does not attain to an actual existence. It lacks the power to externalize itself, the power to make itself into a Thing, and to endure being ... Its activity is a yearning which merely loses itself as consciousness becomes an object devoid of substance, and, rising above this loss, and falling back on itself, finds itself only as a lost soul" (*PhG* 354–5/M ¶658). The unity of thought and being requires thought existing as a substantial world, and this kind of existence requires an object that is "a negative of the actual self."

The spirit of conscientiousness, therefore, develops an opposition between the conscientiousness of action and the conscientiousness of the beautiful soul. Each form of conscientiousness negates the other. The conscience of the beautiful soul voices its negation in a judgment that accuses the conscientious agent of hypocrisy, because the agent's self-concerned actions do not manifest the universality expressed in the agent's conscientious speech. The conscientious agent accuses the beautiful soul of hypocrisy, because the beautiful soul substitutes its judgmental speech for real action. By doing so, it excludes the conscientiousness that gives the universal form of moral goodness to the singularity of the moral individual, the particularity of the self's natural determinations, and the given circumstances of the organized social world. Yet the duty to act, to transform being into the form of pure thought, belongs to the fundamental truth expectations of morality. Thus, the spirit of conscientiousness dissolves in a dynamic of opposites (*PhG* 354–60/M ¶659–67).

In words of confession, conscience engaged in action acknowledges the legitimacy of the beautiful soul's accusation that the action does not preserve the universality of conscientiousness expressed in the agent's speech. Thus, the conscientious agent throws away the self-concerned exclusivity of the agent's projects, and acknowledges that the essential thing is the shared conscientiousness expressed in these projects and asserted in the judgment that opposes their self-concerned structure. In words of forgiveness, the beautiful soul accepts the confession, acknowledges the conscientious spirit that operates in the action, and thereby gives up the isolated self-righteousness that separates pure thought from the reality of being. Thus, each form of conscientiousness acknowledges what stands opposed to itself as its other self. The unconflicted transparency of pure thought played out in the mutual assurances of the beautiful soul community acknowledges as a reflection of its own conscientious spirit thought surrendered into the divisions and tensions of individual, self-concerned action. And the conscientiousness of real action acknowledges as a reflection of its own conscientiousness the spirit of the beautiful soul that sets aside the antagonisms of active life and returns to the unifying spirit of the moral fellowship (*PhG* 360–2/M ¶668–71).

Here again the *Phenomenology* exposes a necessary connection between the tranquil, tautological universal and the divisive, self-opposed universal, between the unification of diversity and the diversification of unity. Here again Hegel explains the connection as the relation of pure opposites, each identified by its opposition to the other. Here again the contradiction demonstrates the necessity of reconceiving the truth as one selfsame principle distinguished from itself. In this case, however, opposition takes the form of thought isolated in a completely transparent relation to itself opposed to thought engaged in the reality of moral action. Moral agency brings with it the given particulars of the agent's psychological constitution and the circumstances given in the field of action. Hegel repeatedly refers to this element as "natural," thus recalling the resistant, irrational element exposed in reason as observation and identified as nature released, set free. Moral agency is contaminated by the "natural" element, the given contingencies, in which the moral agent accomplishes a moral purpose. The spirit of conscientiousness dismisses this element as unessential, reducing it to a vehicle for the subject's conscientious intentions. Yet without this content, knowing and willing cannot make itself true; it cannot actually exist as the true essence of the real world. Thus, the unity that collapses the otherness between thought and its object belongs to a larger truth in which consciousness confronting the given otherness of natural existence plays an equally essential role (*PhG* 338–40/M ¶628–30; 346–7/M ¶643; 354–5/M ¶659).[11]

11 Jay Bernstein uses Hegel's phenomenological account of conscience to challenge a morality of impersonal moral norms (Bernstein 1994, 61–4; 1996, 35). See the Appendix at the end of this chapter for a discussion of his Hegel-inspired position on the conscience issue.

8 THE TRANSITION TO THE CONCEPT OF RELIGION

The negation that emerges in the spirit of conscientiousness resembles the systematic whole dynamic that emerges in understanding.[12] The understanding dialectic ends with a unifying principle interacting with a diversifying principle. The spirit of conscientiousness brings itself to completion in a unifying spirit (beautiful soul conscientiousness) interacting with a diversifying spirit (conscientious action). The understanding dialectic reduces everything in the domain of the objective system to one element distinguished from others in the same system. Even the unifying force operates as one force distinguished from an opposed diversifying force. The conscience dialectic reduces everything in the domain of the social system to one element distinguished from others in the same system. Even the unifying spirit of the beautiful soul functions as one form of the moral spirit distinguished from an opposed form of the same spirit, the isolated spirit of pure moral intentions distinguished from the spirit of moral action engaged in the diversifying dynamics of individuality and the natural element. This resemblance between the understanding dynamic and the conscience dynamic helps us recognize two subtle elements in the dynamic of conscientiousness that an interpretation of its determinate negation must take into account.

First, the positive result of the understanding dialectic carries along with it an unresolved contradiction. Self-consciousness knows the objective world as a life system, which integrates into the selfsame system the separation and relation structures developed in the play of forces, and the unification-diversification structures developed in the system of physical laws. The dialectical development of perception and understanding has proved that these structures must exist in various sets of particulars given in perceptual experience. The life force that governs the structural dynamics of the objective system, however, does not explain why the particulars must be these particulars rather than some other particulars. Consciousness simply attributes to the forces operating in the system whatever particulars happen to appear in the required structural arrangements. Thus, the givenness of the particulars persists as an element in the structural system that consciousness acknowledges as a necessity of the system and yet does not comprehend in the principles according to which it knows the system. So also, the dynamic of confession and forgiveness, which integrates into the same spirit the unification and diversification forms of conscientiousness,

12 See chapter 12, §4–5.

acknowledges that the spirit of conscientiousness must become engaged in the natural element in order to transform the objective world into its own world. Conscientiousness, however, leaves the given particulars of the natural element unclaimed. They are accepted as a vehicle for the self's conscientious intentions, and are forgiven for the sake of the conscientiousness. But they are not determined by and derived from the internal necessities of conscientiousness itself. Thus, the spirit of conscientiousness, like understanding's system of natural laws, has the form of an abstract universal. The particulars that belong to the universal just happen to be the way it manifests itself. No principle or necessity explains why they must be these particulars rather than some other set of particulars. This is one of the forms that Dudley finds Hegel describing as "without concept" and therefore irrational. The universality of conscience, like the universality of understanding's system of forces, is not unconditional. It is conditioned by the unexplained givenness of the natural element.

Second, when the understanding dialectic transforms the objective system into a unification-diversification dynamic, it also changes the relation between consciousness and its object. The separation and relation dynamic that connects the objects of perception also transforms them into appearances of an inner unifying force. This distinguishes the objective system's appearance to consciousness from the independence of the system in the unifying force to which these appearances belong. The dialectic, however, also cancels the distinction by redefining the unifying force as that which appears in the perceptual field. This move transforms the independence of the objective system into that which relates itself to consciousness. In the shift to a consciousness that knows the objective system as a life system, consciousness knows the objective system as a separate reality that relates itself to consciousness, and as a unification-diversification dynamic that negates every element in the system as only one element among others. The system finds its wholeness principle in its relation to consciousness, which knows the various elements of the system as a connected whole. The system is a whole in its relation to a life, conscious life, that is outside the system.

So also the spirit of conscientiousness distinguishes the transparent unity of the moral fellowship (the community of beautiful souls) from its appearance in the diversified dynamics of moral action (egotistical moral action). But the same spirit of conscientiousness also cancels the distinction in confession and forgiveness. The spirit of conscientiousness dissolves into the opposition between the unifying spirit of the beautiful soul and the diversifying spirit of conscientious action. This move transforms the whole domain of social existence into a connected system in which no part of the social world functions as the spirit of the whole. Even the transparent unity of the moral fellowship is only one element engaged in a necessary relation to the diversification of the spirit in conscientious action. This result reduces the world of social existence to an appearance that finds its wholeness in its relation to a spirit that is outside the social system. This is the spirit of religion. Religion endorses the result of the conscience dialectic by conceiving the field of conscientious action as an objectively existent manifestation of the one spirit that is religion's own.

Hegel acknowledges that religion "as consciousness of *absolute Being* as such" has already appeared in forms of experience examined earlier in the *Phenomenology* (*PhG* 363/M ¶672). In general, therefore, religion in the *Phenomenology* refers to a consciousness that knows its object explicitly as the unqualified, unconditional truth of "what is." In previous forms of experience, however, religion has the form of consciousness, because consciousness knows "absolute Being," the true essence of all reality, as a truth that is other than the conscious self. The spirit of conscientiousness overcomes this otherness. The conscientious self knows the true essence of all reality as a divine spirit immediately identified with the individual self's own inner self-consciousness. Religion as absolute spirit represents the spirit of religion as a spirit that necessarily manifests itself in a self-consciousness that belongs to the reality and complexity of secular society (*PhG* 361–2/M ¶671; 363–5/M¶677–8; 367–8/M ¶682).

9 THE NATURE ISSUE

The irrationality issue associated with nature's independence, manifested in its resistance to rational organization, appears in various forms throughout Hegel's discussion of spirit. In its first form, spirit in its immediacy, Hegel explicitly uses the word "irrational" to describe the role of the natural element in the conflict between Antigone and Creon. Nature must not be allowed to claim for itself the body of Antigone's brother and the king's son. Natural contingencies – a king with two sons, the arbitrariness of being the first born – compromise the rational integrity of the social spirit. In the spirit of legal status, society loses its organization and coherence, allowing its natural resources to float free, and to become as a result a random state of affairs, which allows the emperor to claim them as his own. Self-alienated culture expects individuals to surrender their "natural being," and then provides resources for the satisfaction of natural inclinations as the arbitrary gift of the king. The Enlightenment ends with the Terror in which the givenness of natural life is dismissed as having no value, which finally and completely detaches the rational self from nature in all its forms.

In the account of the moral view and the spirit of conscientiousness, and in the analysis of the concept that identifies religion as absolute spirit, Hegel gives us a clue to what is required for completing the *Phenomenology*'s truth project. He points out that the moral view, the culture of conscientiousness, and the concept of religion accomplish the aims of knowledge by finding the true essence of objective reality in something that reflects the true spirit of the human self. Self-consciousness knows itself in its object when it knows the truth of the world as duty, when it knows the world as its own conscientiousness spoken and acknowledged in a moral fellowship, when it knows the secular world of moral action as the externalization and manifestation of the divine spirit. But in all of these, the form of free actuality, derived from the free standing objectivity of natural existence, does not get its due. According to the moral view, any involvement in the dynamics of nature compromises moral integrity. Duty demands action that acts against nature's moral indifference and overcomes it. The spirit of conscientiousness accepts the compromises of natural existence as a necessary element in the actualization of the moral fellowship. But it accepts them only as vehicles of universal conscientiousness. The otherness element is forgiven for the sake of the conscientiousness that cannot become real without it. Religion conceives the actual social world, in which thought remains attached to the content of natural existence, not as an independent reality with a spirit of its own, but as a reality completely absorbed by and in service to the unifying spirit of religion's God. Religion articulates the way a society conceives the spirit for whom the dynamic complexity of secular society exists and in which it becomes one and true. Revealed religion, however, exposes the necessity of restoring free actuality to true independence as the "absolute opposite" of this harmonious, transparent spirit (*PhG* 330–1/ M ¶611–12; 364–5/M ¶677–8; 367–8/M ¶682–3).[13]

APPENDIX: DIFFERENT INTERPRETATIONS OF HEGEL'S POSITION ON THE ROLE OF CONSCIENCE

Hegel explains the role of conscience in several different contexts, and this has raised questions about the consistency of Hegel's position on this issue. In the *Philosophy of Right*, conscience appears as a development within morality; and morality has a structure that fits the way the *Phenomenology*

13 See also *PhG* 26–7/M ¶32; 154/M ¶275.

describes practical reason. Morality belongs to the rationality of an individual agent whose moral intentions become actual in a field of action outside the self where other moral agents are also active (*PhR* §108–9, 115–18, 133, 136–8). Will Dudley examines the debate provoked by Hegel's different ways of interpreting the role of conscience.[14] He addresses the questions raised in this debate by distinguishing the project developed in the *Phenomenology* from the project developed in the *Philosophy of Right*. Dudley explains this distinction by emphasizing the character of the procedure that "is scientific in virtue of articulating all and only those determinations that are immanent in" the beginning concept.[15] The *Philosophy of Right* begins with the concept of free will; the *Phenomenology* "begins with the minimal assumptions that consciousness makes about itself as a knowing subject."[16] These differences, Dudley says, are "sufficient to explain the altered ordering of ethical life and morality," without resorting to some kind of change of mind on Hegel's part regarding the status of conscience.[17]

In the *Philosophy of Right*, however, Hegel tells us that we might use the conscience text from the *Phenomenology* to develop more fully the transition from morality to ethical life. But he cautions that in the *Phenomenology* the transition to a higher stage has a different character (*PhR* §140*Af*). I have followed Hegel's suggestion in an article that uses the conscience text in the *Phenomenology* to interpret the transition from morality to ethical life in the *Philosophy of Right*.[18] Dean Moyar, too, interprets themes developed in the *Phenomenology*'s account of conscience to support a theory that makes a case for what gives legitimacy to the norms of ethical life as these are interpreted in the *Philosophy of Right*. According to Moyar's theory, the language of conscientiousness is the language of rational claim making, the language of giving reasons. The recognition involved is indirect, focused on the accomplished action and the way it represents a value, a moral norm, to which others are themselves committed.[19] This way of interpreting Hegel's theory of conscience adapts the account developed in the *Phenomenology* to the dynamics of practical reason. Universality is conceived as a rational principle that belongs to the thought and commitments of each individual agent, not as a shared social identity, a communal spirit.

14 Dudley (2008), 130–40.
15 Ibid., 145–6.
16 Ibid., 147.
17 Ibid., 148–9.
18 Collins (2000b).
19 Moyar (2011), 68, 151.

In the *Philosophy of Right*, however, the transition from moral conscience to ethical life transforms the isolated individuality of moral conscience into a conscience that knows itself identified with the spirit of a shared social existence (*PhR* §151 + *A*). Hegel calls this form of conscience true or genuine conscience *(PhR* §137 + *A*). Daniel Dahlstrom asks whether true conscience leaves room for a conscientiousness that belongs to the individual's independence of society's established norms. He answers that ethical life must retain the "formal character" of conscience, which is "the process of deciding ... attributable to the subjective will alone."[20] Individuals must know that their personal commitment to particular ways of acting determines the existence of good or evil in their society. But they must also acknowledge that good must be actualized as a shared social existence.[21] According to Moyar, the conscientious agent wills the self-determined content of the individual's own ethical commitments. According to Dahlstrom, the conscientious agent wills the self-determined content of a communal spirit that both forms and is formed by the moral self-consciousness of its members. This is conscience in the form of ethical life.

The structure of ethical life in the *Philosophy of Right* appears in abbreviated form in the *Phenomenology*. At the transition from practical reason to spirit, the *Phenomenology* traces the general outline of a social dynamic that fits the way the *Philosophy of Right* analyzes ethical life. The outline describes two elements in the beginning structure of spirit: a universal work system in which the individual contributes to and draws upon resources for fulfilling individual needs, which resembles civil society in the *Philosophy of Right*; a universal work deliberately produced by the individual's willingness to sacrifice individual self-interest for the good of the whole, which resembles state life in the *Philosophy of Right* (*PhG* 194–5/M ¶351; 236–7/M ¶437; *PhR* §182, 188, 260). True conscience in the philosophy of right, therefore, belongs to a social structure that corresponds to the way the *Phenomenology* describes the beginning structure of spirit. George di Giovanni supports this point when he finds conscience implicit in the way Antigone deliberately acts against the established laws of the city. Antigone belongs to the first form of spirit examined in the *Phenomenology*.[22]

The *Phenomenology*, however, examines the way the beginning concept of spirit becomes more fully developed in the history of spirit from ancient times, through the Middle Ages and the Enlightenment, to the morality

20 Dahlstrom (2008), 160.

21 Ibid., 161–2.

22 di Giovanni (2009a), 233–4, 238.

culture of Hegel's own time. In the *Phenomenology*, therefore, morality is not an abstract moral law inherent in the rationality of an individual. As a form of spirit, conscientiousness acknowledges from the very beginning that it belongs to a community, that its true self is a self shared with others, that its engagement with others is a kind of belonging. But the moral view of the world and the spirit of conscientiousness do not belong to the undeveloped structure of spirit or ethical life. They identify spirit when its differences, tensions, and negations have been fully developed.

According to Jay Bernstein, the account of conscience in the *Phenomenology* demonstrates that there is no way of establishing objective criteria for determining whether conscience knows what is really right and good. Since it can never know completely the circumstances of the action, its moral judgments are fallible. Moreover, the consequences and meaning of an action involve factors that cannot be controlled or fully represented by the intentions of the agent, which leaves them open to a plurality of different, even conflicting, interpretations. Conscientious action is never beyond reproach. The spirit of conscientiousness, therefore, substitutes the universality of mutual recognition for the objectivity of universal principles, choices, and acts. Universality becomes actual not by conformity to some norm that defines what is right and good but by being acknowledged as one who acts conscientiously.[23]

Up to this point, my own interpretation agrees with Bernstein's. Bernstein, however, interprets confession and forgiveness as a conscientious self recognizing and acknowledging its dependence upon the conscientiousness of another who is separate and not bound by this self's conscientiousness. When the judging self rejects the conscientious agent's confession and refuses to forgive, the one who has confessed learns that "it does not necessarily speak with a universal voice, that nothing guarantees or underwrites its claims to generality," that its universality depends on whether others can find their self in its words and acts, and that its compromised conscientiousness cannot command this recognition.[24] The self confesses its fault, therefore, by throwing itself away, acknowledging that it does not ask for forgiveness as something owed, but as one totally dependent on the radical otherness of the self whose forgiveness alone can give it the completeness of finding itself in the other. If the other self rejects this confession, it also loses its self, since by its own hard heartedness, it cannot find

23 Jay Bernstein (1994), 61–4; (1996), 35.
24 Bernstein (1996), 44–8.

itself in the other and cannot be complete without it.[25] Bernstein insists, however, that freedom cannot be preserved unless the willingness to forgive is determined by the individual isolated in his or her individuality, and unless asking for forgiveness becomes a complete surrender of one's self to one who must be acknowledged as completely other. As a result, Bernstein interprets "united life" not as a shared universal spirit but as "ungraspable dependence."[26]

The structure of Hegel's proof procedure, however, derives the presuppositions of conscientiousness from the God postulate of the moral view reconceived as existent in and as the spirit of the moral subject. The conscientious self does not assert as truth the detached moral subjectivity of an individual self. It asserts as truth a moral authority derived from the self's identification with the universality of the divine spirit that derives from itself the authority of particular duties. Conscience asserts the divine spirit's authority to give particular courses of action moral legitimacy simply by giving them the endorsement of its own conscientious conviction. In order to give this conviction actual existence, however, it needs the expressed recognition of its conscientiousness from other moral subjects, and ultimately their forgiveness for the being-for-self exclusivity of moral action. To protect the freedom of the self, however, by insisting that the self's commitment to the other not be compelled or owed mistakes who the conscientious self takes his or her self to be. Forgiveness is owed not because my confession compels it, but because the spirit that is my true self and yours requires that we acknowledge in each other the same spirit shared, even when the sharing involves the otherness of an opposite. I do not throw myself away when I confess to you. I throw away the being-for-self exclusiveness that leaves you out of who I am. I acknowledge my self, my true spirit, in you, and expect you to acknowledge me in the same way.

Rebecca Comay's book, *Mourning Sickness: Hegel and the French Revolution*, discusses Hegel's phenomenological account of conscience in the context of the French Revolution's death culture. According to Comay, the *Phenomenology* interprets the French Revolution as a subjective self-consciousness that tolerates no objectivity or otherness. Not only does it wipe out the established social institutions of the old order, it also frustrates its own attempts to establish a new order and finally develops a culture of meaningless death that dismisses the very existence of other individuals. This creates a situation in which the subjectivity of self-consciousness must

25 Ibid., 49–52.
26 Ibid., 48–9.

create the objectivity of the other from nothing but itself, and yet its detachment from all engagement in objective determinations leaves the self empty of all content.[27]

Comay interprets Hegel's critique of Kantian morality in terms of this outcome. The moral view of the world transforms the radical negativity of the Revolution's death culture into the slavish sacrifice of all particularity. The moral self universalizes its self by acting against the particularity of natural conditions and recreating the natural world from nothing but the self's own pure subjectivity. But morality cannot succeed, it cannot become the master principle of the objective world, without being absorbed into the natural conditions it dismisses as completely worthless. Hence morality conceives its universalization as forever delayed.[28]

Conscience addresses this problem by casting itself in the role of a performative. Conscientious conviction – felt, declared, and acknowledged – creates the dutifulness of its moral act from nothing but the conviction itself and the words that declare and acknowledge it. But the certainty that declares the act dutiful becomes compromised by "the stain of contingency and partisanship contaminating the moral universality of every conscientious deed."[29] Conscience picks apart every finished work, obsessively finds fault with every project, and returns to its own empty, absolute beginning anew. Kant's forever delayed moral righteousness becomes the forever unfinished work of actualizing the universality of the conscientious community.[30] Although forgiveness heals these divisions and re-establishes communal connection, the speech of forgiveness says nothing and changes nothing. It simply says "yes," makes contact, establishes connection. It creates reconciliation as a pure performative. We are reconciled not because we have worked out our differences, but simply because we freely commit to being reconciled. This commitment returns the self to its engagement in the concrete work of the social substance; yet this engagement must "resubjectify" the objective world and perpetually reenact the "yes" of reconciliation and begin anew. Every established social world must be negated, mourned, released into the past, to free the spirit for the work of the future, which will again be negated, mourned, and released. Like Penelope's weaving, "the work is infinite and the shroud forever unfinished."[31]

27 Comay (2011), 42, 66–80.
28 Ibid., 88–93, 98.
29 Ibid., 106.
30 Ibid., 105–8.
31 Ibid., 131–8.

Up to a point, I find Comay's interpretation an interesting, imaginative, and fundamentally correct portrayal of the tensions that belong to the spirit of absolute freedom, the moral view, and the spirit of conscientiousness. Comay's interpretation of the conscientious spirit, however, remains fixed in its negative result. Interpreted according to the dynamics of Hegel's proof procedure, this negative result is a determinate negation; and determinate negations have a positive as well as a negative outcome. The spirit of conscientiousness expects the truth to be the subjectivity of the conscientious self identified with the divine spirit conceived in the God postulate. The God postulate conceives the subjectivity of universal duty reconciled with the conditions of objective existence. Hence, the spirit of conscientiousness acknowledges from the outset the necessity of actualizing the spirit of conscientiousness as the enduring otherness of a substantial world. But the examination of conscientiousness demonstrates that moral subjectivity cannot produce this enduring otherness unless it acknowledges the necessity of surrendering itself into the conditions of natural existence that moral subjectivity cannot completely dominate. This is why the judgmental stance of the beautiful soul collapses into forgiveness. Forgiveness does not leave everything unchanged and completely subjectified. Forgiveness acknowledges that the truth as moral subjectivity conceives it must be expanded to include its necessary connection to its opposite, i.e. to the natural conditions that persist as conditions belonging to the world's independence of moral subjectivity. Otherwise the spirit of conscientiousness cannot fulfill its own principles by becoming the spirit of an objective world. The spirit of religion conceives the unity of these opposites. Comay's interpretation of the conscientious spirit does not acknowledge that the negative outcome of the conscientious spirit calls for and justifies the transition into the spirit of religion and determines the way this spirit is conceived.

PART EIGHT

ABSOLUTE KNOWING

HEGEL HAS TOLD US in various texts that scientific procedure advances through determinate negations. These negations demonstrate the necessity of expanding a concept to include its necessary connection to its opposite. This result proves the necessity of reconceiving the opposites in terms of a common principle that determines both their necessary difference and their integration in the same differentiation dynamic. The common principle is the ground. The move into the ground is a retreat. It begins with what depends on the ground, and proves from what belongs to the derivative truth itself the dependence of this truth on the ground. In other words, the procedure backs up from what is derivative to what is primary, from the dependent truth into the ground on which it depends. In Part Seven, we have seen Hegel explain two major transitions as a retreat into a ground, the transition from practical reason to spirit, and from spirit to the concept of religion. In both explanations, he does more than analyze the determinate negation that immediately precedes the shift. He reviews the whole series of major transitions that precede it, and describes the way each form of cognition has been integrated into a larger perspective.

In the transition from practical reason to spirit, Hegel reviews the negations exposed in the examination of consciousness, self-consciousness, and reason. The preceding forms of cognition, he says, demonstrate their dependence on the ground by determining their own advance and retreat into it. When this dependence on a ground has been exposed, we find that the preceding forms of experience are not really isolated, each by itself. Rather they are one, selfsame communal spirit diversifying itself in these different forms of cognition. The examination shifts, therefore, to the immediate assertion of the ground as the primary truth, and proceeds to expose the way the determinations examined in consciousness, self-consciousness, and reason reappear as forms of social life (*PhG* 238-40/M ¶438–40).

Hegel explains the shift from conscientiousness to the concept of religion in a similar way. Each of the preceding forms of cognition taken on its own terms demonstrates its dependence on a ground that turns out to be the spirit of religion. Religion conceived as ground reconceives each derivative form of knowing as the actualization of religion, religion externalized in the free, independent existence of the secular world. In its separation from religion, the secular world breaks up in the four major forms of cognition previously examined in the *Phenomenology*: consciousness, self-consciousness, reason, and spirit. Moreover, each of these breaks up in differences that belong to the development of a whole. Hegel refers here to the way each form of cognition, each domain of inquiry or area of discourse, shows itself as a circular movement that begins with the immediacy of its subject matter, follows the necessary implications of this subject matter into a complex set of relations, and comes back to its starting point, now explicitly known as situated within this relational system. This circular movement forms the domain into a relational whole, and also demonstrates that the relational system has its ground in a unifying principle that identifies a different domain or area of discourse. For example, consciousness as cognition focused on an independent object distributes itself in sense certainty, perception, and understanding, each focusing on a different facet of the object existing in itself, independent of its relation to consciousness. The whole process completes itself in understanding's return to the object immediately presented in sense certainty, now situated within a whole complex system of law-governed, force-driven connections. And this development shows that the whole domain of objective independence is the diversification of a whole life system whose principle of wholeness is a life outside the system, namely the conscious life of a self. So also in the spirit of conscientiousness, the domain of spirit returns to the immediately given reality of the social world now known as a social dynamic between a unifying and diversifying spirit, which shows that the whole domain of social existence is the diversification of a social whole whose principle of wholeness is a religious spirit distinguished from the relational dynamics played out in social existence itself.

The different forms of religion are distinguished by being the ground of a different derivative form of knowing, and the phenomenological examination of religion follows the same order as the preceding examination of the derivative forms. The examination begins with religion in the form of consciousness (natural religion), proceeds to religion in the form of self-consciousness (the religion of ancient Greece), and ends with religion in a form that unifies consciousness and self-consciousness (revealed religion). In revealed religion, religion finally knows the ground in a form appropriate to the spirit of conscientiousness. It represents God, the absolute truth of all reality, in the form of spirit (*PhG* 365–7/M ¶679–81; 367–9/M ¶683; 419–20/M ¶786). In Part Eight, we will examine the way this form of religion retreats into a ground that completes the project developed in the *Phenomenology* and determines the transition into the beginning concept of philosophical science. In the process, we will relate this conclusion to the way Hegel interprets the role of the *Phenomenology* in his later works.

16

The Retreat into Absolute Knowing

THIS CHAPTER FOCUSES ON the dialectical strategy that governs the movement from the determinate negation of conscientiousness to the representations of revealed religion, and from the determinate negation of revealed religion to absolute knowing. The explanation of this movement pays special attention to the role of the irrationality issue in the way the *Phenomenology* finally reaches a truth criterion that completes the critical examination of experience.

1 THE POSITIVE RESULT OF THE CONSCIENCE DIALECTIC

Hegel says explicitly that the way revealed religion represents God meets the requirements implicit in the determinate negation of conscientiousness (*PhG* 361–2/M ¶671; 419–20/M ¶786). In order to interpret the dialectical function of revealed religion, therefore, we must look again at the negation of conscientiousness and expose exactly what kind of requirements it imposes on the form of religion that fulfills these requirements. Because we associate conscience with personal morality, it is easy to forget that Hegel's account of conscience in the *Phenomenology* belongs to spirit. It describes a social form of rational knowing. Reason expects the truth to be a common ground operating as the fundamental truth of independent thought and independent objective existence. Reason as spirit transforms the independent, substantial existence of the objective world into a world of knowing, a world unified and identified by the way the shared life of a people identifies and knows itself in the external reality of laws, institutions, and cultural forms and in the inwardness of each member's immediate sense of self.[1]

1 See chapter 14, §9.

The spirit of a morality culture conceives the shared life of a people as a social form of practical reason, which brings the particulars of social existence under the rule of a law, an obligation, a duty derived from the universality of human thought. Thus, a morality culture acknowledges explicitly and deliberately that the fundamental spirit of a particular society belongs to a spirit that transcends the limits of a specific social world, a spirit common to all rational beings. As a form of spirit, however, morality calls for the production of a social world in which the commitment to universal duty exists not as the private life of a rational individual but as a shared social commitment actualized in a complex system of social relations. The full implications of this actualization emerge in the spirit of conscientiousness.[2]

We have seen in Hegel's account of the life sciences that the givenness of particulars in a certain configuration is characteristic of nature let go, sent off on its own, nature as other than and liberated from thought.[3] This theme persists in the discussion of practical reason and spirit. The examination of practical reason exposes a lack of rational order in the contingent, unintended consequences of a self-confident individual's actions and in the given content of reason as lawgiver. In the forms of spirit, the irrational appears as the natural contingencies that provoke the conflict between Antigone and Creon, as the chaotic distribution of resources in the spirit of legal status, as negated in self-alienated culture's sacrifice of natural being, and as the negation of the individual's immediate being in the Terror. Finally, we have seen how the independence and irrationality of nature persist as a problem in the spirit of the moral world. The moral agent acts in the *de facto* reality of space-time, takes the stuff of moral existence from the givenness of natural particulars, and thus becomes entangled with the irrationality of nature.[4] Although the morality of conscientiousness addresses this problem, it nevertheless reduces the moral good to an empty form. Whatever conscientious conviction sanctions qualifies as good, no matter what the particular content is. Even conscientiousness lets the natural element go free. The world persists as a world of given particulars and contingencies that do not reflect the universality of thought (*PhG* 368/M ¶683). The determinate negation of conscientiousness preserves the natural element in this role. The natural element belongs to the spirit of confession and forgiveness not as an element integrated into the self-determining dynamics of conscientiousness, but as an element given to it

2 See chapter 15, §6–7.
3 See chapter 14, §1.
4 See chapter 15, §6.

by the independence of nature. The transition into the spirit of religion carries with it an element that stubbornly stands firm in its independence of rational thought.[5]

What requirements, then, does the determinate negation of conscientiousness impose on revealed religion? Since the negation shows how the spirit of conscientiousness retreats into a ground, revealed religion must know the absolute truth of all reality as a selfsameness that explains both the opposition and the necessary connection between the opposite forms of conscientiousness and integrates them into the same dynamic truth. In order to know the truth in this form, religion must take the truth to be the selfsameness of the opposites: thought isolated in its subjectivity, and thought surrendered into the independent objectivity of natural existence. Religion must represent the ground as the selfsameness of pure thought and independent being. In order to experience the ground as ground, religion must begin with the sameness of thought and being isolated in itself, and derive from this the diversity of the experience in which the opposites play out their necessary difference from each other. Since in the dynamic of conscientiousness thought has the form of spirit, religion must know the ground of this dynamic as spirit, which is a social form of knowing. Since

5 George di Giovanni interprets the spirit of conscientiousness and the transition into religion in terms of the problem posed by the irrationality of nature. "That there is (as is undoubtedly the case) an empirically apprehensible nature which resists the order of [reason] is a *de facto* situation for which there ultimately is no explanation ... Moral faith is introduced precisely in an effort to meet the existential difficulties encountered in the attempt to realize intentions in the context of a nature which is inherently antithetical to them" (di Giovanni 2009a, 238). We can assume that "moral faith" here refers to the God postulate, which acknowledges the necessity of sanctioning specific duties, thereby reconciling the universality of moral subjectivity with the particularity of natural conditions (see chapter 15 §6). Di Giovanni goes on to describe conscientiousness as an individual asserting together moral contradictories. The individual claims universal value for the particular content of his or her natural determinations. Conscience is a "contextualized voice" asserting itself with "universal authority"; it is "the 'beautiful soul' for whom the inner voice is the voice of God and the intuition of it the cult of God" (239). This provokes a moral battle to the death, in this case spiritual death. By asserting one's own natural determinations as a universal moral value, the individual inevitably does violence to others with the right to claim the same value for their own quite different particularity. This is the unavoidable violence, the inevitable evil and sin, that perpetually calls for confession and forgiveness. "The stage is set," di Giovanni says, "for the flowering of the religious community" (239–40). According to di Giovanni, spirit sets for itself a purpose not derived from nature, and by doing so, gives nature the power of the unpredictable. "Nature is the realm of the irrational, and religion is there to cope with it." Religion acknowledges the lord of nature with dread until human mortals come to terms with their finitude, and by acknowledging it are redeemed (241).

conscience conceives the truth as a spirit common to all rational beings, revealed religion must know the spirit of truth as a spirit not limited to a particular society or culture. Finally, since the determinate negation of conscientiousness preserves nature's independence of rational thought, religious self-consciousness must expand the concept of reason to include this independence as another dimension of rationality itself. The transition from the spirit of conscientiousness to revealed religion, therefore, identifies religion as (1) a social form of knowing, (2) that knows the truth as a spirit common to all humankind, (3) a spirit distinguished from the dividedness of the human spirit, (4) but also a spirit that lives in these divisions as the same spirit distinguished from itself.

2 REVEALED RELIGION AND THE CHRISTIAN EXPERIENCE

Hegel's account of revealed religion operates on two levels. It mentions here and there the way revealed religion itself articulates its doctrines and beliefs. On this level, the resemblance to Christianity is obvious. Hence, it is hard to deny that Hegel refers here to the reality of the Christian experience. Hegel also insists that this religious experience has the form of representation. Representation communicates what it means not in what it immediately expresses, but in the way this expression refers to some deeper meaning. For example, revealed religion uses the natural relations of father and son to express the self-sharing involved in conceiving God as spirit. Representation also leaves different facets of the truth distributed in different doctrines, without bringing them together in a coherent whole. Hegel's phenomenological examination of revealed religion, however, focuses primarily not on the way the Christian church articulates its doctrines and beliefs, but on the dialectical necessities implicit in the Christian experience. Although the examination shows that the form of representation has a dialectical function, the examination itself does not take the form of representation (*PhG* 410–11/M ¶771). Since the dialectical account does not exactly fit the way orthodox Christianity itself interprets its religious experience, we must ask whether this invalidates the point Hegel is trying to make in his account of revealed religion.[6]

6 For a discussion of the relation between Hegel's thought and the teachings of Christianity, see especially Cyril O'Regan (1994), (2001–02); Stephen Crites (1998); William Desmond (2003).

In order to address this question, I recall here a point made previously, in my discussion of issues raised by John McCumber and John Burbidge.[7] According to my interpretation of the task and method that Hegel himself proposes for the *Phenomenology*, the experiences selected for examination must have a certain loose appropriateness to the demands of the determinate negation, so that we can recognize the presence of dialectical necessities in our own experience. The requirements of the determinate negation, however, function as selection criteria that determine which elements in the experience belong to the demonstration developed in the *Phenomenology*. If there are other elements, other priorities, other ways of interpreting the experience, these have no status because they have not been justified by the series of determinate negations that brought the phenomenological demonstration to this point. The experience selected depends on the determinate negation for its legitimacy. Hence, it cannot function as a norm according to which the legitimacy of the determinate negation itself is judged. Since the project I am working on here focuses on the way the *Phenomenology* justifies the logical starting point of Hegel's philosophical system, my discussion of revealed religion focuses exclusively on the way the Christian experience meets the requirements of the determinate negation exposed in the examination of conscientiousness.

3 THE DIALECTICAL ACCOUNT OF REVEALED RELIGION

Revealed religion asserts as truth the "affirmative between these extremes." It affirms the selfsameness of the opposites exposed in the dynamics of conscientiousness: pure thought set off from the reality of conscientious action; conscientious action externalized in the independent conditions of the natural world (*PhG* 419–20/M ¶786). The account of revealed religion begins, therefore, with absolute being as the independent reality of a substance, what exists, what simply is. Hegel calls it "simple, self-identical, eternal essence" (*PhG* 409–10/M ¶769). Revealed religion represents this reality immediately identified with the form of spirit. In the process of simply being itself, simple eternal essence expresses all that it is in a word, leaving nothing of itself held back. The hearing of the word, and this alone, becomes the being (*Dasein*) of the one who hears (*PhG* 410-11/M ¶770). The otherness between the two, therefore, is "no difference; a loving recognition in which the two sides, as regards their essence, do not stand in an antithetical relation to each other" (*PhG* 411/M ¶772). Each recognizes

7 See chapter 11, §3.

in the other nothing alien, nothing resistant or opposed, nothing but itself shared as the very self of the other (*PhG* 410–11/M ¶770–2). Thus, revealed religion begins with immediate independent being represented as a tranquil, transparent form of spiritual self-sharing.

At this point, Hegel makes the same kind of move he has made many times before. A tranquil tautological unity, precisely because it relates itself to itself without conflict, posits with itself an other that it rules out or excludes. In a sense, this other belongs to what the tranquil self-sameness is, because to be a tranquil selfsameness, a difference that is not different, is to not-be the opposite, the anything-but-tranquil difference that divides and alienates. This connection to radical otherness is what revealed religion represents as the creation of the world. Hegel interprets the term "create" here not as a production that makes the world exist rather than not exist, but as a relation that derives what kind of reality the world is from what kind of reality God is. God conceived as the "loving recognition" in which each participant knows the other as in no way different from itself necessarily involves the conception of what God is not. The world conceived as God's absolute opposite belongs to the way God's own internal being is conceived. What the divine essence excludes or rules out determines what the world is. Thus, in revealed religion, religious self-consciousness experiences God as a transcendent other, and experiences itself belonging to a world fallen away from the completely tranquil and transparent selfsameness that is the divine being (*PhG* 411–13/M ¶772–5).[8]

What, then, constitutes the otherness of the world? In order to be truly other, it must take as its own exactly what the transcendent divine spirit excludes. Its differences must be not-the-same, set apart and indifferent to each other. It must dissolve all unity, dismember every whole. Hegel calls the alien character of the world "the natural spirit" (*PhG* 417/M ¶782). He explicitly analyzes the divisiveness of this spirit by focusing on the isolated separateness of self and nature. Human self-consciousness withdraws into itself to free itself from the divisiveness of natural existence. This in turn sets nature free to follow its own way, indifferent and even opposed to self-consciousness (*PhG* 417–18/M ¶782–3). Thus, revealed religion experiences the world as a conflict between the opposites exposed in the spirit of morality: the detached subjectivity of human thought that lets nature go free as a world indifferent to moral principle.

There are, then, two alienations implicit in the way revealed religion represents God. The first alienates the world from the tranquil, transparent

8 See also *PhG* 103–5/M ¶166–8; 330–1/M ¶611; 431/M ¶804.

selfsameness of divine spirit ("I am I"). The second alienates spirit in the world, which is the human spirit, from nature. The second alienation is the result of the first. The transparency of the divine spirit isolates the divine spirit in itself and thereby connects it by exclusion to a world alienated from God and alienated in itself. Since, however, both alienations belong to what is implicit in the conception of the transcendent God, the being of God encompasses within itself not only the tranquil, transparent selfsameness of the transcendent God but also its necessary relation to the divided world that is its opposite.

The fullness of God is the spirit that unites these opposites to each other and constitutes them as one and the same divine self-sharing. The word that speaks the very essence of God and generates God's self-expression in the divine other also surrenders God's self-expression into the alien otherness of the world. The Word of God becomes a human being, a sensuous reality immediately accessible to human self-consciousness, an individual isolated in his own singularity, subject to the limitations of space, time, and social context, immersed in the givenness of particular circumstances, vulnerable to the powers of nature. Thus, the absoluteness of God becomes identified with the conditions of human existence, and in the process makes itself known to human self-consciousness. By surrendering into the world the other who is the exact expression of the divine essence, God reveals to humankind the true essence of God. God is spirit. God is a being that lets itself go in the being of another, finds in the other its own self shared, and acknowledges this other self as a necessity of its own being (*PhG* 404–7/M ¶758–61; 414–15/M ¶779–80).

The divine spirit as it is represented in the Incarnation, however, does not reveal the spirit of God in its full meaning. God incarnate manifests the divine spirit as an individual self-conscious human being, a self isolated in its own singularity and separated from all others. God's other is the whole world of human existence. Hence, the divine spirit becomes fully manifest as a spirit shared with God's other only if the spirit of the God-man shows itself as the spirit of all the world. Revealed religion must represent God's incarnate Word as a self whose spirit is the spirit of every human self-consciousness. And revealed religion must represent this same universal spirit reconciled with the natural spirit that stands opposed to it, so that self and world can be known as the same divine spirit distinguished from itself (*PhG* 407/M ¶762; 411–12/M ¶775; 413–14/M ¶777–8).

The death of the incarnate God frees God's life-in-the-world from its isolation in the spatio-temporal individuality of a human self. Death negates individuality. In its natural meaning, it absorbs the individual into the universality of the natural life process; death identifies the God-man with the universality of the natural spirit. Death in its spiritual meaning absorbs the individual into the universality of communal life; death releases the spirit of the God-man to live as the spirit of the religious community. In the religious community, the spirit of God dies every day to the divisiveness of the natural spirit, and rises every day as the true spirituality of communal at-oneness. Death in its special meaning for revealed religion surrenders the life of God-in-the-world to the life of God in the transcendent divine spirit; the God-man surrenders his worldly self to the tranquil spirit of the transcendent God and thereby makes the world exist as God's other self (*PhG* 414–18/M ¶778–84).

If, however, the death of the incarnate God integrates the self-consciousness of the religious community into the absoluteness of God, it also integrates the absoluteness of God into the self-consciousness of the religious community. Absolute spirit surrenders its isolation, dwells within religious self-consciousness, and becomes identified with the inwardness and subjectivity of the religious self's immediate sense of self. The religious self knows itself integrated into the spirit of absolute truth (*PhG* 418–19/M ¶784–5). In this representation, religious representation becomes self-consciousness. The religious self knows the divine being as the human self's own spirit.

4 GOOD AND EVIL

Hegel's account of revealed religion includes a complicated and subtle discussion of good and evil. This discussion, like the whole discussion of revealed religion, bounces back and forth between representational and conceptual ways of articulating the content of revealed religion. The conceptual articulation of good and evil gives us Hegel's most explicit and complete analysis of the nature factor in absolute spirit.

Hegel introduces the notion of evil with the representation of humankind's fall. The story of the fall represents the status of humankind and its world as God's absolute opposite. As God's opposite, the human world falls away from the tranquil, transparent selfsameness of the divine spirit into radical separateness, complete dismemberment, alien otherness. Hegel develops the notions of good and evil from the dynamics of this opposition. "Good" refers to a simplicity completely at-one with itself, not confronted by anything alien. Such absolute simplicity is selfless, because a self knows itself in an other. Thus, Hegel says that the tranquil transparency of the divine spirit does not posit "otherness as such"; the simplicity of the divine spirit is a difference that is "immediately no difference," a "loving recognition in which the two sides, as regards their essence, do not stand in an antithetical relation to each other (*sich entgegensetzten*)" (PhG 411/M ¶772). Otherness as such resists, stands up against, what is different from itself. A self depends on this kind of otherness for its own being-for-self. A self knows itself from the way it is thrown back on itself by an other that opposes it. The other identifies the self as a knowing withdrawn into itself and differentiated from this other. Hence, the divine spirit becomes a self only when it knows itself in its opposite (*PhG* 411–12/M ¶774–5). "Good" refers to the divine spirit in its selfless simplicity (*selbstlose Einfache*).

Hegel defines evil, the opposite of good, as for-itself-being isolated in itself (*insichseinde Fürsichsein*). In other words, the term "evil" refers to the kind of being-for-self that keeps itself to itself, isolated in itself, cut off from relations that might expand its self-identity to include the other as another dimension of itself. Hegel names this principle of in-itself-ness nature, nature in general and human nature in particular. The human self, like all natural things, is an immediate existent, a singular that is simply itself being itself. Human nature, however, also brings knowing into the domain of the natural spirit as nature's other. The human self knows the divisiveness of the natural spirit as evil, which separates human consciousness from the natural existence it condemns and gives human cognition the form of a simple knowing withdrawn into itself (*das einfache Wissen*). In its isolation and separateness, however, human self-consciousness itself becomes evil (*PhG* 411–13/M ¶772–5; 415–16/M ¶780; 417–18/M ¶782–3).

Hegel analyzes the dynamics of good and evil in two forms: the dynamic in which the conflict remains unresolved; and the dynamic in which it is resolved by a determinate negation. In its unresolved form, good identifies the divine spirit, evil identifies the natural spirit, and the conflict between good and evil plays itself out in human self-consciousness. As a form of self-consciousness, a consciousness that knows itself in its other, human cognition belongs to spirit and hence to what is good. As a self-consciousness that separates itself from nature, its other, human self-consciousness isolates itself in itself, withdraws from its spiritual unity with its other, and thus reduces its spiritual character to a pure opposite. Spirit is reduced to what stands opposed to divisiveness; good is reduced to being the opposite of evil. The divisiveness of the human world, therefore, expands to include not only the dismemberment of the whole in the isolated being-for-self of each natural being, but also the isolation that separates the spirit of human self-consciousness from the natural spirit of the objective world. The human world is not an evil world pure and simple; the human world is a conflicted world in which good and evil play out their opposition to each other (*PhG* 412–14/M ¶776–7).

The divisiveness of the human world, however, emerges from the exclusivity implicit in the absolute at-oneness of the divine spirit. By being a selfless simplicity, the divine spirit identifies itself as not the opposite, i.e. as not a spirit of divisiveness and disintegration. Thus, the divine spirit conceived as absolutely at-one with itself is necessarily connected to its opposite, which is the divided world of nature and the human spirit. This is the determinate negation that resolves the conflict between good and evil by conceiving them as different elements within the same dynamic truth. The simple at-oneness of the divine spirit and the divisiveness of the created world belong to the same spirit distinguished from itself; good and evil are the same spirit necessarily related to and distinguished from each other. Good is good only by not being evil; evil is evil only by not being good (*PhG* 414–15/M ¶778–9).

Revealed religion comes close to recognizing this when it represents the selfsameness of God and nature in the doctrines of the Incarnation and the indwelling of the Holy Spirit. These representations express a conceptual issue. Essential being in its transcendence represents the absolute selfsameness of being, the selfless simplicity, in its absolute difference from its opposite. Its absolute other is spiritual unity torn apart by "nature in general" and "human nature in particular." Nature gets its definition from what it is not; it is not the tranquil, transparent selfsameness of essential being. Yet nature is. It is the isolated in-itself-ness of immediate being. Since, however, nature is defined by what it opposes, nature in general and human nature in particular are another dimension of selfless simplicity itself. They are its true set-free other. As such they function as the condition that confronts simplicity as an alien other, establishes it as a self set off from an other, and as spirit giving itself away to an other (*PhG* 415–16/M ¶780).

This analysis of good and evil reproduces a conceptual interpretation of the double alienation represented in creation, Incarnation, and the indwelling of the Holy Spirit. In the discussion of good and evil, however, Hegel explicitly identifies the role of nature in the content of revealed religion. Nature functions as a nothing that nevertheless is. It functions as the universal principle of dismemberment, isolation in immediacy, opposition to spiritual unity. In human nature, nature gives the human self its singularity, its isolated free being. Revealed religion boldly acknowledges God identified with this nature principle, this principle of not being absorbed and lost in the unity of absolute spirit.[9]

9 See Harris (1997), II, 677–98 where Harris probes the way revealed religion brings creation, evil precisely as evil, and the irrational into the necessary constitution of the divine spirit.

5 THE DEATH OF GOD

Hegel introduces the shift to absolute knowing by talking about the death of God, where the move into a new way of conceiving the truth retains the idiom of revealed religion's representations. Hegel interprets the death of the God-man not only as the natural death of God existing as a human individual but also as the death of God's transcendence, which Hegel calls "the abstraction of the divine being."

That death is the painful feeling of the Unhappy Consciousness that God Himself is dead. This hard saying is the expression of innermost simple self-knowledge, the return of consciousness into the depths of the night in which "I" = "I," a night which no longer distinguishes or knows anything outside it. This feeling is, in fact, the loss of substance and of its appearance over against consciousness; but it is at the same time the pure subjectivity of substance, or the pure certainty of itself which it lacked when it was object, or the immediate, or pure essence. (*PhG* 418–19/M ¶785)

In the death of God and the indwelling divine spirit, religious self-consciousness loses the substantiality of the truth, the truth as an other in which human consciousness finds the truth. Human self-consciousness is thrown back on itself, alone and isolated in its own sense of self. Thus, the otherness of God collapses into the pure subjectivity of human self-knowing. Yet religious self-consciousness knows its pure subjectivity as the subjectivity of substance itself. The death of God brings with it thought identified with the independent reality of being. Religious self-consciousness knows itself no longer as pure subjectivity set off from the reality of the objective world. Religious self-consciousness knows the spirit that dwells within it as the spirit of all reality. In this experience, reason's certainty of being all reality is finally confirmed.[10]

10 John Burbidge interprets the death of God as the collapse of all confidence in stable, dependable, eternal truth (Burbidge 2007, chapter 4). Burbidge interprets God as "that reality which ultimately underlies and explains everything that is." He interprets the mediator between God and human kind as "any actual, historical existence that 'mediates' this absolute essence by showing that it is not simply an abstract theory but actually works its influence in space and time" (63). The death of the mediator, therefore, represents the way any absolute essence entering the reality conditions of the human world becomes the victim of fate, contingency, the unpredictable. For excellent discussions of the ambiguities and complex relations involved in this issue, see Harris on the task of the *Phenomenology* (Harris 1997 I, xii–xiii, 8, 11, 14–16, 43, 110–14, 131), Harris, Dudley, and Fackenheim on the formula, "the rational is actual and the actual rational" (Harris 1997, I, 183–5, 188; Dudley 2003–04, 36–40; Fackenheim 1996, chapter 10). See also my discussion of Burbidge's position in chapter 19.

The dialectical legitimacy of this experience, however, depends on the way the spirit of conscientiousness retreats into a ground. The spirit of conscientiousness breaks up in an opposition dynamic between the isolated subjectivity of the beautiful soul and conscientious agency letting itself go in the conditions of an independent objective world. By reducing these forms of conscientiousness to pure opposites, the dynamic implies a unifying ground that determines and grounds the opposition dynamic and thereby transforms its participants into the same spirit distinguished from itself. This calls for a shift into the assertion of the ground as an independent, immediate principle, and the experience of the ground deriving from itself the divided spirit of conscientiousness. A religious form meets this requirement only if it represents the divine spirit necessarily surrendered into the dynamic of conscientiousness in which it makes itself manifest. The "death of God," therefore, is not just an unorthodox way of interpreting the Christian experience. It is dialectically required in some form if the religious experience is to qualify as the truth determined and justified by the determinate negation of the conscientious spirit.

6 THE FORM-CONTENT SHIFT INTO ABSOLUTE KNOWING

Hegel characterizes religion's collapse into human subjectivity as a shift in form without a shift in content. Revealed religion knows the absolute true content, but does not know it in its true form. What, then, is the absolute true content of revealed religion's truth experience? Revealed religion conceives absolute truth as a form of spirit. Spirit, as we have seen, is a communal form of knowing in which the singular self isolated within its own sense of self knows itself identified with the way a social world defines itself for itself in its cultural forms. If, therefore, the absolute truth of all reality is spirit, then in order to know the truth, we must conceive "all reality" as (1) a communal reality (2) that exists as a form of knowing, (3) in which the singular self's pure inwardness of knowing knows itself identified with (4) the way the whole social world defines itself for itself in its social institutions. How, then, does the social world of revealed religion define itself for itself?

First, it knows its spirit as a perfect self-sharing. This is not a slavish self-surrender in which spirit loses its self in the other. It is not a relation that appropriates what a self finds missing in its self. It is a perfect self-expression, a word, in which the divine spirit gives itself in all its fullness to the other, so that it lives in the other and knows the other as what answers perfectly to itself. Second, this spirit of self-sharing gives its self to its absolute opposite. The Word becomes flesh, and thus the perfect self-expression of the divine spirit becomes the very self of a human being. The human condition belongs to the self-sharing life of the divine spirit. Third, death absorbs the divine self into the life and death process of the natural system, into the movement and contingencies of human history, into the individuality conditions of human self-consciousness and the subjectivity-objectivity conditions of human conscientiousness. The spirit of God shares itself with humankind, and dwells in the self-consciousness of the human community as the divine self-sharing expressed in the other to which it gives itself.

This way of conceiving God transforms all the divisions of the human world into the same absolute spirit diversifying and reuniting with itself in the dynamics of human existence; and this absolute spirit is the spirit of self-sharing. The absolute truth of all reality is the spirit of self-sharing that knows itself in the self of its other, even when the self of the other is its absolute opposite. The human self knows the truth by knowing itself situated within the dynamics of this ground and identified with the absolute spirit of self-sharing that religion knows as God. Hence, the universality of the human self is not anything that can be isolated in the individual's self-determination. It is not a purpose or project, a thought, a principle, or a conviction that belongs to the self's exclusivity. The true universality of the human self is a conscientious self-expression that speaks its very self to others and acknowledges in the process that in their otherness, in the way their conscientiousness challenges its own, it finds its own spirit shared.[11]

Revealed religion knows the content of absolute spirit in the form of representation, the form of consciousness, as a beyond (*PhG* 419–21/M ¶787). Absolute knowing knows the same content in the form of a concept, the form of self-consciousness, as absolute knowing itself (*PhG* 427–8/M ¶798). The true content, Hegel says, is substance transformed into "the pure inwardness of knowledge," "the return of representation to self-consciousness" (*PhG* 420–2/M ¶787–8; 425–6/M ¶795).

What does Hegel mean when he says that revealed religion knows its true content in the form of consciousness? We have seen him distinguish

11 To use di Giovanni's way of speaking, the human self knows itself redeemed when it acknowledges its own finitude, when it recognizes that the spirit individuated in him or her is a limited manifestation of a larger spirit that lives just as truly in the differences that challenge him or her and carry this self's projects and works into unforeseen developments (di Giovanni 2009a, 241). Harris says the same thing another way. Religion, he says, transcends morality because it knows that moral disagreement is "the will of God," that moral judgments are always flawed, that even the unrepentant must be loved and understood, and that only this loving comprehension can bring the offender to recognize "what there is to repent for" (Harris 1997, II, 694).

revealed religion from natural religion, which has the form of consciousness, and from the religion of art, which has the form of self-consciousness. According to this distinction, revealed religion combines the form of consciousness with the form of self-consciousness (*PhG* 367–9/M ¶683). When Hegel distinguishes the different forms of religious experience, however, he focuses on the way each form represents the constitution of its object. Consciousness takes the object to be an independent reality, something existing in itself, independent of its relation to consciousness. Natural religion knows God in this form, as a natural thing, what simply is. Self-consciousness takes the object to be an independent reality existing for the conscious self. The religion of art knows God in this form, as a self-consciousness focused on itself. Reason takes the truth to be a common principle or ground that governs both the dynamics of independent thought and the dynamics of independent being. Revealed religion knows God in this form, as self-consciousness focused on an independent other whose spirit is the same as its own. Revealed religion has the form of consciousness not in what it takes God to be, but in the way it knows what it takes God to be.

Representation uses realities immediately present to human consciousness as references to some other truth. Consciousness, as a form of knowing different from self-consciousness, finds the truth in something outside consciousness, something independent of its relation to consciousness. Revealed religion represents the true content of absolute spirit as a transcendent being, an other that exists in itself, set apart from the religious consciousness that knows it. This transcendent otherness is the substance factor in religious experience. The absolute truth of all reality exists as an independent self-subsistent reality. Even the doctrine of the indwelling divine spirit, which transforms religious representation into self-consciousness, retains the form of consciousness. Revealed religion represents the integration of human self-consciousness into the life of absolute spirit as something accomplished by the transcendent other. God takes all the initiative. God's saving act overcomes the alienation between God and world. The world produced by human action persists in its alienated form and awaits some future time when God will accomplish its transfiguration. The spirit of the secular world, which is the human self's field of action, remains alienated from religious consciousness (*PhG* 420–2/M ¶787–8).

The religious way of knowing the absolute true content, Hegel says, fails to appreciate the way divine being "is drawn down from its abstraction" by religious self-consciousness itself (*PhG* 420–1/M ¶787). In order to experience absolute truth as spirit, human self-consciousness must experience the spirit of truth as the self's own spirit, the spirit known in the singular self's immediate sense of self; and it must experience this same spirit as the spirit of the self's social world. In order to know absolute spirit in its true form, therefore, human self-consciousness must know it as a spirit identified with and operating in human self-consciousness. The *Phenomenology* has shown that human self-consciousness reaches its true form in the spirit of conscientiousness; and the determinate negation of spirit in this form has shown that the conscience dynamic is "God manifested in the midst of those who know themselves in the form of pure knowledge" (*PhG* 362/M ¶671). When, therefore, the death of God collapses the transcendence of God back into the subjectivity of the human self, it brings the selfsameness of the divine spirit into the dynamic of conscientiousness (*PhG* 424–5/M ¶793).

7 THE TRANSFORMATION OF THE APPEARANCE

The shift from a determinate negation to its positive result always transforms the participants in the negation. In the determinate negation of perception, for example, consciousness finds that its experience of a thing's separateness dissolves in a separation and relation dynamic. Because perception takes the truth to be separate things, it dismisses this experience as untrue. It tries to avoid the opposition by distinguishing what belongs to the object from what belongs to the way consciousness experiences the object, or by distinguishing an essential factor from a necessary but unessential factor (*PhG* 75–8/M ¶119–24; 79–81/M ¶131). Because understanding's truth criterion endorses the relational dynamic exposed in perception, understanding knows the truth of perceptual objects not as an independent separateness, but as a play of forces. What perception dismisses as not true, understanding accepts as a positive factor in what the truth is (*PhG* 82–6/M ¶134–9). So also understanding experiences the opposition between the unifying law of attraction and the divisive law of repulsion as a development that compromises what understanding takes the truth to be. It tries to avoid the opposition by keeping each law isolated in a different domain. Self-consciousness, however, endorses the opposition by taking the objective system to be the unification-diversification dynamic of a life system (*PhG* 94–102/M ¶154–65; 104–7/M ¶169–73).

Self-consciousness, however, finds its own truth expectations challenged by the stubborn resistance of the objective life system and its relations to the opposed claims of other self-conscious individuals. Self-consciousness tries in various ways to preserve its dominance as the truth of the objective world: by means of a servant's work; by knowing the world as an intelligible world that corresponds to the self's independent thought; by a sceptical involvement that makes the world appear in its untruth; by surrendering its own compromised self to become identified with a transcendent unchangeable self-consciousness in whom thought and nature are one selfsame self. The self's surrender to the transcendent unchangeable self, however, identifies the human self with this selfsameness, which transforms self-consciousness into a universal self identified with a rationality that the independence of self-consciousness and the independence of the objective world have in common.[12]

The transition from revealed religion to absolute knowing requires a similar transformation of the elements in a determinate negation. The death of God in the dynamics of revealed religion shows that the transcendence of the divine spirit, which religion represents as the dominant truth, involves a necessary relation to and involvement in the broken world of the human spirit, which is the absolute opposite of the divine spirit. Religion tries to preserve its original truth expectation by preserving the dominance of the divine spirit in the dynamics between the spirit of the transcendent God and the broken spirit of the human world. Absolute knowing acknowledges in its truth expectation what religion resists, namely that identification with the broken world of the human spirit belongs to the necessities of absolute spirit itself. This transforms not only the way we know absolute spirit but also the way we know the broken world of the human spirit and the spirit of conscientiousness that belongs to it.

The spirit of moral conscientiousness takes the truth to be its own independent moral spirit overcoming the alien independence of the social world by actively transforming it into a reflection of the self's own moral subjectivity. In confession and forgiveness, conscientiousness tries to preserve its original truth expectation by forgiving the spirit's engagement in the natural element for the sake of the conscientiousness that this engagement expresses. Absolute spirit, however, is not the isolated subjectivity of thought. It is the ground that holds within its selfsameness all the diverse elements that belong to the world of conscientiousness, including the natural element that persists as the nothing that nevertheless is, the not-rational that remains as the independence condition of substantial reality. Absolute spirit is thought identified with the substantial independence of being, and as such transforms the isolated subjectivity of the beautiful soul into a self-consciousness identified with the self-subsistent reality of being (*PhG* 431–2/M ¶805; 432–3/M ¶807–8).

12 See chapter 13.

> [The beautiful soul] is not only the intuition of the Divine but the Divine's intuition of itself. Since this concept holds itself firmly opposed to its realization, it is the one-sided shape which we saw vanish into thin air, but also positively externalize itself and move onward. Through this realization, this objectless self-consciousness ceases to cling to the determinateness of the concept as against its fulfillment; its self-consciousness gains the form of universality and what remains to it is its true concept, or the concept that has attained its realization; it is the concept in its truth, viz. in unity with its externalization. (*PhG* 425–6/M ¶795)

The transformation of the beautiful soul transforms conscientious action into the agency of absolute truth itself. The absolute true content of revealed religion becomes the content of conscientious action. Conscience gives the secular world its true spirit when the conscientious self knows and wills the self's own identification with absolute spirit as the spirit of an independent, organized social world, embedded in the contingencies of natural existence. "The 'I' has neither to cling to itself in the form of self-consciousness as against the form of substantiality and objectivity, as if it were afraid of the externalization of itself: the power of Spirit lies rather in remaining the self-same Spirit in its externalization and, as that which is both in itself and for itself, in making its being-for-self no less merely a moment than its in-itself" (*PhG* 431–2/M ¶804).

What revealed religion represents as an other becomes in absolute knowing a concept within human thought (beautiful soul) that necessitates the actualization of truth thus conceived (conscientious action), so that the independence of pure thought knows the independence of the objective world as the same spirit of truth distinguished from itself (*PhG* 419–23/M ¶787–9; 426–7/M ¶796–8). "This last shape of Spirit – the Spirit which at the same time gives its complete and true content the form of the Self and thereby realizes its concept as remaining in its concept in this realization – this is absolute knowing" (*PhG* 427/M ¶798).

8 THE CERTAINTY OF BEING ALL REALITY

When the moral view conceives the truth as thought isolated in its own moral subjectivity, it lets nature go free and in the process detaches itself from the space-time conditions of the natural world. The examination of the moral view, however, exposes a determinate negation that cancels the distinction between pure duty and the concrete self of conscientiousness. This brings the universality of thought back into the conditions of a particular culture situated in a particular historical epoch. As long as moral subjectivity retains its dominance, the particularities of its historical conditions do not compromise its universality. Conscientiousness transformed by absolute knowing, however, integrates the natural element into the essential dynamics of absolute spirit. Hence, we must ask how conscience can produce a social world with the status of "all reality." What kind of social existence qualifies as the actualization of a spirit that is the absolute truth of all reality?

Hegel does not make a case for his response to this question, at least not in the *Phenomenology*. He simply assumes that the universality of absolute spirit becomes actual in the movement of history. History, he says, is "Spirit emptied out into Time," an externalization in which spirit slowly brings before itself what it is and digests "this entire wealth of its substance" (*PhG* 433–4/M ¶808). Thus, Hegel treats history as a social reality with some kind of coherence as a knowing process in which the spirit of all reality makes itself known to itself. The spirit of truth becomes the spirit of a social world by becoming the spirit of universal history. Conscientious action knows the truth as its own act by actualizing the concept of truth as the spirit of universal history (*PhG* 427/M ¶798). Absolute spirit cannot be known in its true form, therefore, unless it is known as the substantial social world transformed into the human self's own self-knowing, unless the spirit represented as a divine other shows itself as the human self's own self identified with and active in the human self's own world, unless the spirit of conscientiousness acknowledges its responsibility for history, not just for the moral character of a specific community (*PhG* 429–30/M ¶802). Absolute knowing calls human beings to the awesome task of giving the true spirit of all reality actual existence in the broken world of human experience.

Thus, absolute knowing expects the truth to be the whole dynamic in which the oppositions characteristic of phenomenal consciousness – consciousness and object, thought and being, subjectivity and objectivity, the rational and the irrational, self and world – bring out of their own internal necessities the selfsameness of pure thought and independent substantial being, only to turn around and develop these same dualities from the internal necessities of this selfsameness. In other words, absolute knowing takes the truth to be a movement that distinguishes the unity of spirit from the diversity of appearances by separating religious self-consciousness from the diversified dynamics of the secular world, and cancels the distinction in the purposiveness of human conscientiousness, which externalizes its unifying spirit in the secular world and knows itself therein (*PhG* 425–8/M ¶795–8).

17

The Infinity Dynamics of Absolute Knowing

HEGEL ANTICIPATES THE COMPLETION of the phenomenological project in his account of understanding, when he introduces a new concept as the result of the understanding dialectic. Understanding, Hegel says, justifies the concept of infinity, which will eventually emerge as the truth of consciousness (*PhG* 101–2/M ¶164). In the results of the understanding dialectic, however, consciousness does not yet recognize that the concept of infinity identifies the true essence of consciousness itself. Although the determinate negation of understanding justifies a shift into a form of self-consciousness, self-consciousness in this form does not yet know itself as "consciousness in general." As we have seen in the account of this cognitive form, the self comes before itself only as a singular self, not yet as the universality of consciousness as such.[1]

Also in the examination of understanding, Hegel tells us that the full exposition of infinity belongs to philosophical science (*PhG* 101–2/ M ¶164). Since, therefore, the *Phenomenology* is supposed to justify the beginning concept of philosophical science, we can interpret these comments to mean that the *Phenomenology* completes its task with a form of knowing that knows the singular self, the self with which the *Phenomenology* begins, as a self identified with the universality and infinity of consciousness as such. Absolute knowing should reproduce the infinity structure analyzed in the examination of understanding; and in this reproduced version, consciousness should know itself as the infinity of consciousness "in general."

In this chapter, I will analyze the structure of infinity that emerges at the end of the understanding dialectic, trace its development in each of the

1 See chapter 13.

major transitions of the *Phenomenology*, interpret absolute knowing in terms of this analysis, and explain how the concept of infinity emerges in absolute knowing as the true essence of consciousness itself with the status of consciousness in general. Section 1 explains how the infinity dynamic emerges in the dialectical development of understanding. Sections 2–4, show how each of the major transitions in the *Phenomenology* develops similar moves with similar results. Sections 5–7 explain and analyze the infinity dynamics of absolute knowing.

1 THE INFINITY OF LIFE

The analysis of infinity in the account of understanding develops in four moves. In the first move, the separateness and relatedness of perceptual things becomes a play of forces in which different elements belong to a dynamic that both distinguishes and connects them. In the second move, a distinction is made; understanding distinguishes simple force from the diversity of the play of forces, in order to become conscious of the necessity that integrates different forces into the same dynamic truth. In the third move, the distinction is cancelled. In order to become conscious of simple force as that which explains what appears in the play of forces, understanding conceives simple force as a unity that derives from itself the diversified form and content of the perceptual field. Cancelling the distinction brings the diversity of the perceptual field into the selfsameness of the explanatory principle, and thus transforms the selfsameness principle into that which diversifies itself in the play of forces dynamic, which transforms the play of forces into the same force distinguished from itself.

The result of these three moves expands understanding's truth criterion into a systematic whole distributed in the diversity of a unification-diversification dynamic. In the fourth move, this relational whole completes itself by being-for the simplicity, the selfsameness, of consciousness conscious of the whole's selfsameness. We shall see that infinity takes two different forms as we move through the *Phenomenology*. In understanding, it takes a being-for-self form. Being-for-self knowing knows the infinity dynamic played out in the object as a diversified relational whole that refers to a self-consciousness outside the relational system as the simple selfsameness of the whole and its true essence.[2] The transition from understanding to self-consciousness shifts from infinity as a mediated result to the immediacy of a new truth criterion asserting itself as ground. Self-consciousness begins

2 See chapter 13, §1.

with the conscious self asserting itself as the certainty of being the true essence of life. Self-consciousness in its immediate sense of self knows its relation to an other as no difference, as the "I am I" of self-intuition. Self-consciousness interprets its encounter with the natural world in terms of this intuition, and thereby knows its own conscious relation to the objective life system as derived from and a manifestation of this self-certainty (*PhG* 103–4/M ¶166–7).[3]

2 THE INFINITY OF UNHAPPY CONSCIOUSNESS

Self-consciousness begins as a relation between self and world with the self in the dominant role. The experience of self-consciousness, however, exposes an opposition dynamic between the independence of self-consciousness and the resistant independence of the objective life system. Stoic self-consciousness tries to preserve its dominance by redefining the dynamic in terms of self-conscious thought. Stoicism takes the truth to be the independent subjectivity of thought thinking the independent objectivity of the world as a fundamental intelligibility that corresponds to thought. Thus, stoic thought expects the independent objective system to be a reflection of thought itself, and to not be the tensions immediately presented in life. In order to know the objective world for what it truly is, therefore, thought must become involved in exposing the untruth of life. Thought takes the form of scepticism.

Something like a play of forces develops in scepticism. Thought by being itself, detached and independent, becomes engaged in negating the truth of the life-world; and thought, by becoming engaged in negating the life-world, establishes thought's detachment from and independence of that world. Thus, scepticism reduces the life-world to a pure negative, what is not-thought. Independent thought dominates the relation between thought and the objectivity of the life-world. As other, however, the life-world has its own independent character, carried over from the conclusion of the understanding dialectic; and thought gets its independence by pushing off from the independent otherness of this world. Thus, thought shifts into the dependent position, and identifies itself only as life's other. In this endless changing from one extreme to the other, thought negates its own claim to truth, because it cannot finally bring before itself either its own independence of life or life transformed into what corresponds to

3 See also chapter 13, §1.

thought. Thus, self-consciousness reproduces the play of forces dynamic as a development within self-consciousness itself.

Unhappy consciousness distinguishes its own divided self from the truth, and conceives the truth as thought remaining unchanged in its identification with objective existence. Since, too, the unchangeable is supposed to be the truth of the divided self, unhappy consciousness takes the truth to be the selfsameness of the unchangeable identified with a singular self-consciousness engaged in the life-world, but a self separated from the divided self of unhappy consciousness. Thus, the move into the truth criterion of unhappy consciousness imitates the second move of the understanding dialectic. It distinguishes the unifying principle from the diversity governed by it.

In asceticism, unhappy consciousness becomes conscious of all the subtle ways in which it asserts itself as truth, and becomes completely identified with the experience of this self-assertion as the self's untruth. Thus, self-consciousness experiences its self surrendered into the thought and life of the unchangeable, and experiences the unchangeable as the negation of the self's dividedness. The spoken assurances of the mediator, who acknowledges unhappy consciousness as a self reconciled with the unchangeable, transforms the unchangeable into that which exists in the divided self of unhappy consciousness, and transforms the dividedness of unhappy consciousness into the same unchangeable distinguished from itself. Thus, asceticism and the assurances of the mediator cancel the distinction between the unifying principle and the divided self, which imitates the third move, the distinction cancelled move, of the understanding dialectic.

The distinction cancelled move determines the transition from unhappy consciousness to the presuppositions of reason. Self-consciousness belongs to a selfsameness that transcends the limits of its own self-consciousness. Reason takes the truth to be the simplicity of a common ground that governs and determines the dynamics between independent thought and the independence of the objective world. Idealism asserts the ground in its immediacy, independent of the mediated relations in which it appears. Although reason begins within the independent subjectivity of thought, it does not reduce the truth of the object to its being-for the subjectivity of thought. Reason asserts itself as thought identified with being, as the common ground that operates as the fundamental truth of both thought in itself and the object in itself. This is the fourth move of the infinity dynamic in its systematic whole form. Reason begins with the simplicity and selfsameness of the rational asserted as the immediacy of a ground. Rational thought interprets its encounter with the natural world in terms of this immediacy, and thereby knows its own relation to the objective system as derived from and a manifestation of the certainty of being all reality.[4]

3 INFINITY RE-CONCEIVED IN PRACTICAL REASON

The examination of reason reproduces the movements of consciousness and self-consciousness interpreted by reason's truth expectations. A dynamic similar to the play of forces emerges in self-confident individuality. The individual self expects its original determinate nature to be the defining truth of the relation between self and world, and acts in order to make this truth explicit and overt. The action, however, surrenders the self's work into the dynamics of the objective world and the world's relation to other individuals; and these others are equally confident that their given nature is the defining truth of the relation between self and world. Each agent tries to play the role of the dominant member in the relation between self and world, and tries to reduce the others to participants in this self's world. Thus, the play of individualities is exposed as a mutual relation in which the being-for-self character of competing self-confident individuals shifts back and forth between the dominance of one and the dominance of others. The truth, therefore, is not a dominant self, but the unifying principle that integrates self, world, and other rational individuals into the same dynamic truth.

The distinction made and cancelled develops in reason as lawgiver and reason testing law. The examination of reason as lawgiver shows that the particular content of the laws that develop in self-confident individuality have only a contingent association, whereas the dynamic of self-confident individuality reveals a necessary connection. In order to conceive the necessity of the association, therefore, practical reason distinguishes the selfsameness, the non-contradictoriness, of the truth from the divisiveness of self-confident individuality and the contingent particulars of reason as lawgiver. Since, however, non-contradiction is supposed to function as the norm for what the individuality dynamic ought to be, the given laws of reason as lawgiver must be related to and tested by the norm. This testing shows that thought can think the laws as the same for everyone, which identifies the individuality dynamic and its content with a unity that negates its divisions and contingencies. It also shows, however, that this selfsameness contradicts itself when it becomes identified with the individuality dynamic. Real action focuses the otherness of objective existence on the singularity

4 See chapter 13, §1, 4–7.

of the rational individual, and in the process absorbs the rational individual into the independent dynamics of objective existence. Cancelling the distinction between the ought and the reality in which it ought to be actualized transforms the ought into a selfsameness that distributes itself in the divisions of self-confident individuality and the contingent content of reason as lawgiver; and it transforms these diversities into the same selfsameness distinguished from itself.

As a whole, this relational dynamic retreats into the selfsameness of a ground that determines and accounts for the coherence of the whole. This is the transition from practical reason to spirit and the fourth move in the infinity dynamic. Spirit is the self-consciousness of a society. In the spirit of the social whole, society identifies itself for itself, and this self-knowing exists as what identifies the substantial being of a social world.[5] Spirit begins, therefore, with social self-consciousness in its immediacy. The members of a society know themselves identified with the selfsameness of the social whole, and find themselves immediately identified with a social role. In these assigned roles, the spirit of the whole distributes itself in the individuality of its members, and reunites with itself in the unifying acts of government. Thus spirit reproduces the unification-diversification dynamic of practical reason transformed into the same spirit of the whole distinguished from itself.[6] Here again, infinity takes the form of a systematic whole.

4 THE INFINITY OF SPIRIT

The examination of spirit reproduces the movements of reason re-interpreted according to spirit's truth expectations. A dynamic similar to the play of forces emerges in the spirit of absolute freedom. This spirit takes the truth to be the will of the individual asserted as the will of the nation. The spirit of absolute freedom dissolves in a mutually destructive dynamic between the governing will acting against the treasonous resistance of the general population, and the resistant will of the people overthrowing and executing the members of the governing faction. Absolute freedom and terror reproduces the individuality dynamic as a social dynamic in which the individual asserts her or his own singularity as a self with universal status, only to be challenged by other individuals acting in the same world and claiming the same universal status. The spirit of absolute freedom dissolves in a mutual relation of opposites. The true essence of absolute freedom is

5 See chapter 14, §6–9.
6 See chapter 15, §1.

not the individual will of the citizen, whether governing or governed, but the spirit of moral duty, which conceives the necessary selfsameness of the opposites.[7]

In the moral view of the world, a distinction is made. The examination of the moral spirit shows that moral action identifies the universality of duty with the exclusivity of the individual and the contingencies of natural existence. Hence, the moral view distinguishes the true selfsameness of the moral spirit from the compromises of moral action. In the God postulate, it conceives the uncompromised selfsameness of universal duty identified with the conditions of objective existence. In the spirit of conscientiousness, the distinction is cancelled. The spirit of conscientiousness conceives the moral subject identified with the selfsameness of the divine spirit. Conscience actualizes itself as the selfsame divine spirit identified with the individuality dynamics of the actual world and the content of the natural element.

As a result of this move, the selfsameness of the divine spirit becomes identified with the unification-diversification dynamic of social existence. Beautiful soul conscientiousness clings to the tranquil at-oneness of its communality and preserves it by refusing to tolerate or acknowledge the conscientiousness of competing individualities and particular interests. In this form of conscientiousness, the divine spirit exists as a selfsameness that excludes diversity. Conscientious action claims for itself the universality of the communal spirit engaged in the work of producing a moral world. This form of conscientiousness defends its claim by challenging the way beautiful soul conscientiousness leaves out, rejects, excludes from itself the actualization of the moral spirit in the individuality of moral agents and the actions that transform the natural element into a vehicle for the moral spirit. The spirit of conscientiousness dissolves in a unification-diversification dynamic in which no part of the whole, not even the abstract selfsameness of the beautiful soul, qualifies as the selfsameness of the whole.

The transition from the spirit of conscientiousness to the concept of religion develops the fourth move in spirit's infinity dynamic. The diversified whole of conscientiousness retreats into the selfsameness of a ground, the spirit of religion distinguished from the relational system of the secular social world. Religion knows the diversified world of secular social relations as a world unified by its being-for religious self-consciousness. Religious self-consciousness experiences the diverse elements of the secular world as one and all belonging to its own religious spirit. This is a being-for-self version of

7 See chapter 15, §5.

the infinity dynamic. Religion asserts its experience of God as an immediate ground independent of the secular social dynamics that have retreated into it, and it represents the diverse elements of the social world as the manifestation of this religious spirit (*PhG* 365–8/M ¶679–82).[8]

5 INFINITY REPRODUCED AS THE RETREAT INTO ABSOLUTE KNOWING

Hegel begins the examination of religion with a survey that describes the whole domain of human experience as a movement that absorbs the different forms of experience into a relational system and retreats into the absolute spirit of religion as its ground. In the *Phenomenology*, the different facets of absolute spirit have been examined in their independence, their separation from each other; and the internal constitution of each has exposed its necessary connection to the others. This whole development culminates in a unification-diversification dynamic between beautiful soul conscientiousness and the conscientiousness of action (*PhG* 365–7/M ¶679–81; 367–9/M ¶683; 419–20/M ¶786). Thus, the whole domain of human experience shows itself as a relational system in which every participant, even the unifying conscientiousness of the beautiful soul, dissolves in relations to other participants in the same system. Nothing within the system persists as the selfsameness of the whole. The whole development of the phenomenological project is absorbed into a relational dynamic, just as the play of forces absorbs the whole perceptual field into the connectedness of a natural system of laws.

Revealed religion makes and cancels the distinction between the selfsameness of religion's absolute spirit and the divided spirit of the human world. It takes the truth to be the selfsameness of thought and being distinguished from their diversity and alienation in the human world. It represents this selfsameness as a form of spirit, spirit completely at one with itself in its other. It represents the human world as a world divided against itself in the withdrawal and resistance that separates the human from the natural spirit, and it takes this to be the absolute opposite of the divine spirit's tranquil, transparent at-oneness. Since the divine spirit is the truth of the human world, revealed religion represents the selfsameness of the divine spirit as the Word of God sent into the world to become identified with the human condition, which transforms the human world into God's other self.

8 See chapter 15, §6–8.

The human becomes integrated into the selfsameness and self-sharing of the divine spirit.

The death of God surrenders the otherness of the divine spirit into the pure subjectivity of human self-consciousness. Hegel explicitly associates this move into absolute knowing with "the painful feeling of the Unhappy Consciousness" (*PhG* 418–19/M ¶785). "The painful feeling of unhappy consciousness" refers to the way unhappy consciousness loses the otherness of the unchangeable, and collapses back into itself. The unchangeable turns out to be a rationality operating within human thought and the natural world. So also the transition from revealed religion to absolute knowing loses the otherness of the divine substance by conceiving the divine spirit as a spirit identified with human self-consciousness, operating in human action, surrendered into the irrational conditions of the human world. This transforms the tranquil at-oneness of absolute spirit into a unifying principle operating within the social world of conscientiousness.[9] In the process, the unifying spirit becomes a diversifying principle that distributes itself in each of the different participants belonging to this world, and thus transforms the diversities into the same spirit distinguished from itself.

The determinate negation of revealed religion, however, must be carefully distinguished from the determinate negation that emerges in the spirit of conscientiousness. In the spirit of conscientiousness, the opposites are pure thought and thought involved in the conditions of independent being, thought isolated in itself and thought surrendered into the independent externality of being, the subjectivity of pure thought set off from the independence of objective existence ("I am I") and the subjectivity of pure thought identified with the independence of objective existence ("I am the not-I").[10] The opposites that emerge in revealed religion's determinate negation are the selfsameness of thought and being in the divine spirit opposed to the duality that separates pure thought and natural existence in the spirit of the human world. In the spirit of conscientiousness, undivided, transparent selfsameness belongs to thought isolated in its own subjectivity. In the spirit of revealed religion, undivided selfsameness belongs to thought identified with being; and this selfsameness turns out to be necessarily connected to its absolute opposite, which is pure thought and independent being opposed to each other. Absolute knowing takes the

9 See chapter 16, §3–7.
10 See chapter 15, §7.

truth to be the spirit that drives this necessary connection and remains the same spirit throughout the whole dynamic.[11]

6 THE INFINITY OF ABSOLUTE KNOWING ITSELF

Hegel describes the relational dimension of absolute knowing both as the movement through the different forms of consciousness examined in the *Phenomenology* and as the dynamic of conscientiousness transformed by the determinate negation of revealed religion. Absolute knowing brings together the *Phenomenology*'s retreat into absolute spirit as its ground (the opposite that moves from diversity to unity) with revealed religion's experience of the ground as that which posits the differences of the diversified human world and exists in them as their fundamental truth (the opposite that moves from unity to diversity) (*PhG* 366–7/M ¶681; 422–5/M ¶789–94). Thus, absolute knowing moves through all the forms of cognition that precede it in the *Phenomenology*'s examination of experience, situates them all within the unification-diversification dynamic between the move into the selfsameness of absolute spirit and the move back from this selfsameness into the diversified whole.

Absolute knowing thinks the unity implicit in this process not as an indifferent unity, but as the driving spirit of the differentiation dynamic in which the differences, determined by their own internal constitution, necessitate their relations to each other and thus form a relational whole: "nor is Spirit a *tertium quid* that casts the differences back into the abyss of the Absolute and declares that therein they are all the same; on the contrary, knowing is this seeming inactivity which merely contemplates how what is differentiated spontaneously moves in its own self and returns into its unity" (*PhG* 431–2/M ¶804). This "seeming inactivity" is the knowing of the "we" that moves through the *Phenomenology* as a detached observer. By following the internal necessities of phenomenal knowing, the observer consciousness becomes conscious of itself as the still point that remains selfsame throughout all the complexity exposed in the demonstration.

It knows the whole domain of phenomenal knowing as an infinity dynamic in which absolute spirit identifies each diverse element, and from

11 For studies that examine Hegel's analysis of the true infinite in the *Science of Logic* and in the *Lectures on the Philosophy of Religion*, consult the works of Robert Williams and Robert Wallace. Wallace (2005) provides a book-length study of the topic. Williams (2012) includes his discussion in a book on Hegel and Nietzsche. Williams and Wallace discuss their different interpretations of the infinity issue in *The Owl of Minerva* (2010–11).

within each one's separate character drives it into connection with others (the play of forces move), absorbs all these elements into a selfsameness that negates their diversity (the distinction made), and surrenders the selfsameness back into the diversity (the distinction cancelled). This dynamic reduces every factor in the domain of phenomenal cognition to the status of a relational component among others, which shows that none of the relational components are the whole in itself. Like the self-consciousness of life, the self-consciousness of absolute knowing knows the systematic whole dynamic as a reality that turns itself into something "for" a knowing self distinguished from the dynamic itself. The observer consciousness knows the complexity of phenomenal cognition as the articulation and diversification of a selfsameness that exists as the observer's own thought. The observer consciousness knows its own thought identified with absolute spirit as the simplicity and selfsameness that grounds the infinity dynamics played out in the whole domain of phenomenal cognition. This calls for a shift into the priority of the detachment and selfsameness of the observer consciousness, a being-for-self version of infinity's fourth move. The observer consciousness asserts the selfsameness of absolute spirit in its immediacy, and derives from its own self-determination the determinations that in the *Phenomenology* have retreated into it (*PhG* 431–2/M ¶805).

Absolute knowing, like idealism, is the certainty of being all reality. It is the self-intuition that knows itself identified with the ground that diversifies itself in the infinity dynamics of experience. Absolute knowing differs from idealism, however, because the surrender involved in each case moves in opposite directions. The distinction made and cancelled in the examination of unhappy consciousness surrenders thought attached to life into the universality, stability, and selfsameness of the unchangeable. Although the transition into idealism redefines the unchangeable as a truth existing within human thought and the natural world, the transition preserves the dominance of the unchangeable. In reason's concept of truth, the singularity of the self and the tensions of life become completely subordinated to the structures and necessities of universal reason. In order to know the true essence of both self and world, reason must know the universal structures of thought appearing as the governing principles of the natural world and self-conscious individuals.[12] The distinction made and cancelled in the transition to absolute knowing reverses this surrender. Cancelling the distinction between ground and appearance surrenders the tranquil, transparent selfsameness of thought and being into the opposition between thought

12 See chapter 13, §7.

isolated in itself (the beautiful soul) and thought surrendered into and identified with the self-concerned exclusivity of the singular self and the contingent particulars given in the natural element (conscientious action).

Revealed religion represents this result in the doctrines of incarnation and the indwelling divine spirit. In these doctrines, the religious individual finds his or her self represented not as a servant self lost in service to another, but as a self accepted into the self-sharing that identifies God as spirit. Absolute knowing conceives this divine self-surrender as a necessity of absolute spirit itself and thereby acknowledges the necessary connection between the human world absorbed into the selfsameness of absolute spirit, and the selfsameness of absolute spirit absorbed into the diversity dynamics of the human world.

Absolute knowing also differs from idealism because it conceives differently both the selfsameness and the otherness of the rational. Absolute knowing, like idealism, is the certainty of being all reality. Absolute knowing, however, expects the truth to be a rationality that knows itself not only in what corresponds to the rational structures of thought but also in what absorbs these structures into the self-conscious movement of human history and "the form of free contingent happening" – a time, a place, a given association of particulars. Only by acknowledging the contingencies of nature and history as another dimension of itself can rational thought know itself as the fundamental truth of all reality (*PhG* 430–2/M ¶803–4; 432–3/M ¶806–8).

Finally, absolute knowing differs from idealism because it conceives the independence of the objective world as the substantial independence of a social world. In absolute knowing, the detached thought of the observer consciousness knows itself identified with the spirit that grounds the reality of the socio-historical phenomenal world. Hegel calls this ground, this whole in itself, the concept (*der Begriff*), which is thought withdrawn into itself thinking itself as the essence and ground of what appears as the world of human experience. Each participant in the unification-diversification dynamic of absolute knowing belongs to and is rooted in this ground: (1) the necessity that operates within different forms of real experience, which culminates in the pure thought of conscientiousness asserting itself as the true essence of social existence; (2) the determinate negation that distinguishes the abstract selfsameness of thought and being from the opposition between thought and being in the dynamics of history; (3) the surrender of this abstract selfsameness in the purposiveness of conscientiousness that accomplishes the unity of thought and being in the movement of history. The concept, therefore, is not the abstract selfsameness of thought and being that excludes and negates the diversity of historical reality, a self-sameness that is only one element in the dynamic of absolute knowing. The concept conceives the sameness of thought and being as the ground that originates from within its selfsameness the unification-diversification dynamic played out in the movement of history.

As its fulfillment consists in perfectly knowing what it is, in knowing its substance, this knowing is its withdrawal into itself in which it abandons its outer existence and gives its existential shape over to recollection. Thus absorbed in itself, it is sunk in the night of its self-consciousness; but in that night its banished outer existence is preserved, and this transformed existence – the former one, but now reborn of the Spirit's knowledge – is the new existence, a new world and a new shape of Spirit. In the immediacy of this new existence the Spirit has to start afresh to bring itself to maturity as if, for it, all that preceded were lost and it had learned nothing from the experience of the earlier Spirits. But recollection, the inwardizing, of that experience, has preserved it and is the inner being, and in fact the higher form of the substance. (*PhG* 433/M ¶808)

The withdrawal into "the night of self-consciousness" identifies the whole in itself, distinguished from its "outer existence" in the relational components of history. This part of the infinity dynamic exists as the spirit of a social world, as a "new world," a "new shape of Spirit," which the singular self knows as its own spirit. The "immediacy of this new existence" that must "start afresh" signals the shift from a knowing that retreats into a ground to a knowing that asserts the ground in itself, not determined by its relation to what it grounds, so that it can be known as the origin not the result of what it grounds. Thus, thought becomes an immediate knowing, an intuition, that knows itself identified with the immediacy of the infinite ground. In order to know the truth, a singular self existing in the world of human experience and identified with the spirit of history must withdraw into pure thought knowing itself as the ground that originates from within itself the articulation of self-thinking thought in the dynamics of history. The immediacy of being with which philosophical science begins is not an empty thought category. Rather it is the reality of a human thinker's self-intuition asserting itself as pure thought identified with the substantial reality of social-historical existence.

7 THE INFINITY OF CONSCIOUSNESS

In the *Phenomenology*'s account of absolute knowing, Hegel refers to the minimal form of consciousness with which the *Phenomenology* began, and identifies what this kind of knowing discloses about consciousness itself. The object showing itself to consciousness, the in-itself in its being-for consciousness, reveals consciousness to itself only as the immediate sense of its own consciousness-of condition. Hegel calls this immediate sense of itself "the certainty of itself" (*PhG* 428–9/M ¶801). The term "certainty," therefore, refers to the consciousness side of the consciousness-of-something experience. Certainty is the inwardness of consciousness immediately conscious of itself, distinguished from the way consciousness is conscious of the object, a distinction that persists even when consciousness knows the object as a reflection of consciousness itself.

The experience principle also appears in the absolute knowing chapter of the *Phenomenology*: "it must be said that nothing is known that is not in experience, or, as it is also expressed, that is not felt to be true, not given as an inwardly revealed eternal verity, as something sacred that is believed, or whatever other expressions have been used" (*PhG* 429–30/M ¶802). Thus, the *Phenomenology* acknowledges that the concept of truth justified by the *Phenomenology*'s examination of experience must be known not only as a conclusion produced by a proof procedure but also as an immediate experience in which its truth is a felt conviction. In other words, the truth concept that completes the task of the *Phenomenology* must take the form of an intuition in which the content of the truth is represented together with the certainty of its truth.

The Preface to the *Phenomenology* states this requirement explicitly: "Conversely, the individual has the right to demand that Science should at least provide him with the ladder to this standpoint, should show him this standpoint within himself. His right is based on his absolute independence, which he is conscious of possessing in every phase of his knowledge; for in each one, whether recognized by Science or not, and whatever the content may be, the individual is the absolute form, i.e. he is the *immediate certainty* of himself and, if this expression be preferred, he is therefore unconditioned *being*" (*PhG* 22–3/M ¶26).[13] Hegel suggests here that knowing absolute truth in its proper, "absolute," form requires an independent individual immediately conscious of his or her consciousness identified with "unconditioned being." The *Phenomenology* must provide a ladder to the absolute standpoint, the standpoint of philosophy, because knowing absolute, unqualified, unlimited truth in its proper form does not exist unless it exists as an individual's isolated, independent self-intuition.

13 See also *PhG* 29–30/M ¶36.

Here again Hegel exposes the audacity of the truth claim with which Hegelian philosophy begins. An individual consciousness, from within its own isolated sense of self, asserts itself as the reality, the unconditioned being, of infinite, absolute truth. This is the claim that the *Phenomenology* is supposed to justify. In order to accomplish this task, the *Phenomenology* must explain why knowledge of the truth must take this intuitive, subjective, experiential form. Indeed, it must explain more generally why an individual has a right to accept as true only what his or her own independent conviction acknowledges as true. In other words, the *Phenomenology* must justify the experience principle. In the process, the *Phenomenology* must connect the experience principle to a proof that distinguishes true and untrue, adequate and inadequate truth convictions. Finally, the *Phenomenology* must produce the intuitive, subjective, self-certainty that knows itself identified with the truth.

Let us review briefly, therefore, the moves in which this task is accomplished. The *Phenomenology*, through a long series of determinate negations, exposes the true essence of the object immediately presented to consciousness in the experience with which the examination begins. In the process, it fills out the certainty side of the experience. The determinate negations of consciousness and self-consciousness show that consciousness and its object are rooted in a common ground. The same rationality governs both the necessities of independent thought and the necessities of independent objective existence. Reason begins, therefore, as the certainty of being all reality. The inwardness, the subjectivity side, of rational knowing is immediately conscious of itself identified with the rationality that is the truth of all reality. This is idealism. And consciousness knows what the object truly is by finding in the object a structure that corresponds to what emerges in thought's immediate sense of itself thinking.[14]

The determinate negations of observational and practical reason define and redefine rationality until they expose the fundamentally social character of the common ground. Consciousness of something turns out to be consciousness of a social world. Consciousness knows the object as a society identifying itself and making itself known to itself in its laws, cultural norms, and institutions. The object itself is a world constituted as a form of knowing. Knowing the object in this way discloses consciousness to itself as a self immediately identified with the spirit of the objective world. The inwardness of spirit-consciousness, its immediate sense of self, takes the form of a felt identification with social custom. The determinate negations

14 See chapter 13, §5–7.

of reason and spirit, however, expose a fundamental opposition in rationality. Reason knowing the objective world as a rationality attuned to the rationality of pure thought, spirit knowing the social world as a universal spirit that remains the same in all its members, finds itself challenged by the self-focused singularity of self-conscious persons and by the givenness and unaccountability of the natural element.[15]

The spirit of conscientiousness exposes the full complexity of this challenge and in the process expands self-certainty to comprehend all aspects of this complexity. The determinate negation of the moral view determines the spirit of conscientiousness as the singular self's felt conviction that some particular course of action is right and good. Conscience knows in its immediate sense of itself what is concretely right. This brings together in one intuition the universality dimension of human thought, which is the concern for duty, the particular interests given in the individual agent's personal constitution, the circumstances given in the field of action, and the singularity of the self, whose felt conviction integrates the other three aspects into one intuition of what is right. Thus, conscience gives the particulars of an action the form of something willed as good. Since, too, conscience is a form of spirit, the conscientious self knows itself immediately identified with a culture of conscientiousness, and thus holds itself accountable to the concern for conscientiousness in society at large. Thus, the social world identifies itself as a world in which the self-certainty of conscientious conviction determines what is true and good. The immediate self-certainty of the conscientious subject knows the true essence of the objective world itself as this same conscientious self-certainty (*PhG* 342–8/M ¶634–44).

In conscientiousness, however, the self's immediate sense of self identifies the self only with the subjectivity and universality of the conscientious spirit. It reduces the given particulars of both self and world to a vehicle for the self's conscientious conviction. The particular content in which this conscientiousness gives itself reality does not matter. Thus, conscientiousness does not know itself identified with the spirit of natural existence, which persists as an alien element in its experience. Revealed religion, which articulates what is implicit in the determinate negation of conscientiousness, transforms the self-certainty of the human self into a felt identification with a spirit that transcends the detached subjectivity of morality and conscience. The religious self in its immediate sense of itself knows itself

15 See chapter 14; chapter 15, especially §9.

identified with a spirit in which the subjectivity of pure thought and the in-itself independence of substantial being are one and selfsame.[16]

In revealed religion, however, the self experiences its self integrated into the otherness and transcendence of this spirit. Absolute knowing acknowledges the reality of experience as a necessary condition of truth. The human self, embedded in the spatio-temporal free contingent happening of nature and history, engaged in the otherness of phenomenal consciousness, knows itself not as an unessential element surrendered into a spirit beyond itself, but as the duality in which the spirit of truth becomes actual and real (*PhG* 423–8/M ¶792–8).[17] This is why the human self has a right to acknowledge as true only what is felt as true in the individual's immediate sense of self. "Nothing is known that is not in experience," Hegel says, because truth is spirit. Truth exists as the isolated, singular self conscious of itself identified with the spirit of a social world, a spirit that conceives the truth as the sameness of thought and being realized in the absolute otherness of self and world (*PhG* 429–30/M ¶802; 432–3/M ¶807–8). Thus, the self-certainty of an individual who belongs to this spirit can assert itself as an intuition of absolute truth in which the reality of the self immediately manifests the reality of truth itself. In this intuition, self-consciousness knows the all-inclusive infinity of absolute knowing as its own true essence.

16 See chapter 16, §1–3.
17 See chapter 16 §4–7.

18

The Transition from Phenomenology to Philosophical Science

THE MOVE INTO ABSOLUTE KNOWING brings the *Phenomenology* to an end with an ambiguity. The *Phenomenology* completes its task by moving backwards to where it began and forward to something else. Absolute knowing returns the examination of experience to its starting point in sense certainty. Absolute knowing also sets aside the presuppositions of phenomenal consciousness and produces the concept that governs philosophical science, which is a different kind of knowing (*PhG* 429–30/M ¶802; 432–3/M ¶806). Setting aside the presuppositions of phenomenal consciousness requires a demonstration that overcomes the otherness between thought and being, consciousness and its object. In order to explain the way the *Phenomenology* brings its investigation to a conclusion, therefore, we must explain how a return to sense certainty overcomes the otherness between thought and being. Hegel gives us the key to this development when, in the account of absolute knowing, he talks about self-certainty and its limit.

In order to explain the transition from the *Phenomenology* to philosophical science, however, we must also construct an explicit account of the shift from absolute knowing as a form of experience to absolute knowing as the beginning of philosophical science. Hegel gives us the key to this move in the discussion of infinity, which is first introduced in the account of understanding. Both discussions, the one focused on the otherness of thought and being and the one focused on the infinity dynamics of absolute knowing, show how the end of the *Phenomenology* is connected to themes already examined in the introductory essays of Hegel's later works; and this shows us how to interpret the transition from the *Phenomenology* to the concept that defines the project of philosophical science.

1 THE COMPLETE APPROPRIATION OF THE OBJECT'S OTHERNESS

The *Phenomenology* begins with the minimal conditions for knowledge to appear, consciousness conscious of something (*etwas*). Conceived in this minimal way, consciousness is reduced to a dependent relation. It has no other determination than to be conscious of, depending on something else for a content that completes the relation by giving it an object to be conscious of. Since the object must provide what consciousness-of cannot get from itself, the object must stand on its own, in itself, independent of its relation to consciousness. This object, minimally conceived, simply is. Its only content is itself independently being. The examination of knowledge as an appearance, therefore, begins with truth conceived as an object, an *etwas*, whose being is independent of its relation to consciousness. Within this minimal structure, Hegel finds a minimal truth expectation. In order for consciousness to be conscious of the object, the object in its independence must become "for" consciousness. The object's independence of its relation to consciousness must make itself known in its relation to consciousness. Consciousness knows the truth by becoming conscious of what the object in its independence is. The task set for the *Phenomenology* is to examine the full implications of this beginning concept, to expose the determinate negations that repeatedly redefine what it means. The examination comes to a conclusion only when consciousness completely overcomes the otherness between itself and its object by knowing precisely and fully the true essence of what stands before consciousness as an independent other.[1]

This phenomenological examination of cognition shows that consciousness conscious of something (*etwas*), consciousness conscious of what confronts it immediately here and now, is situated within the dynamics of pure thought. Pure thought sets itself off from the conditions of givenness and spatio-temporal existence, then negates the separation by conceiving the given as the actualization and differentiation of pure thought itself. This actualization takes different forms. In the discussions of stoicism and reason, the *Phenomenology* introduces the form of thought as the independent subjectivity of thought recognizing itself in the independent objectivity of external existence. Reason conceives the form of thought as an attunement between thought and external objectivity. Thought knows itself in the intelligibility, the rationality, of its object, which corresponds to the rationality of

1 See chapter 9.

thought itself.[2] But Hegel insists that this externalization is still incomplete; and what it lacks is the object as that in which the spirit of rationality confronts its negative, its limit. This limiting factor he describes as space-time, "the form of free contingent happening," nature (*PhG* 432–3/M ¶807).

The appropriation of this limiting element also takes different forms. Consciousness brings the otherness of the natural world into its concept of truth when the moral view conceives nature as a world indifferent to moral principle and conceives the truth as the transformation of this world by dutiful action. Conscientiousness acknowledges that its concern for duty must become actually existent in the natural element, in the particulars of the self's interests and the given circumstances of the action, and also that these interests and circumstances must be integrated into the dynamics of conscientiousness spoken and acknowledged in a moral fellowship. The concept of religion acknowledges the opposition between nature and human self-consciousness while conceiving the truth as their reconciliation in the self-conscious life of the divine spirit. But in all of these, the form of free actuality, derived from the free standing objectivity of natural existence, does not get its due (*PhG* 330–1/M ¶611–12; 364–5/M ¶677–8; 367–8/M ¶682–3).[3] In other words, that which constitutes the object precisely as something not determined by its relation to consciousness persists as an element not appropriated by the way consciousness knows it.

In the determinate negation of conscientiousness, this problem becomes explicit. In the dynamics of conscientious action, the being-for-self exclusivity of the individual agent and the given particulars of both self and world become vehicles for a knowing that wills only its own identification with the universality of pure thought. Conscientious speech gives this pure knowing actual existence in relations among persons and situates the content of action within a framework of pure knowing. Thus, conscientiousness appropriates for the self of pure knowing all the realities involved in action. Pure knowing knows the true essence of the objective world as pure knowing itself existing as a morality culture. Conscientiousness, however, operates as an empty form. It wills its action only as the vehicle of its own subjective conviction. It does not appropriate the particular content that belongs to nature's independence, nature set free to exist on its own, in itself, independent of what thought demands of it (*PhG* 363–4/M ¶677). The independent "in-itselfness" with which the *Phenomenology* began remains resistant and unknown.

2 See chapter 13, §4–7.
3 See also *PhG* 26–7/M ¶32; 154/M ¶275.

Revealed religion, as the form of consciousness that acknowledges what is implicit in the determinate negation of conscientiousness, brings the independence of the natural element into the way the truth is represented. Revealed religion (1) represents the absolute truth of all reality as the immediate selfsameness of pure thought and substantial, self-subsistent being, (2) represents the human world as the absolute opposite of this selfsameness, (3) represents the opposite of selfsameness as the separation and opposition played out between human self-consciousness and natural existence, and (4) represents absolute selfsameness and its absolute opposite reconciled by the sameness of thought and being in the divine spirit surrendered into the opposition played out between them in the human world.[4]

Revealed religion, however, retains the form of representation, in which the divided human world remains an unessential element referring itself to something other than itself as its truth. For revealed religion, the creation and salvation of the world are contingent happenings initiated by God's free, contingent commitment; and the salvation of the world absorbs the world into a spirit not properly its own. The selfsameness of thought and being dominates the whole relationship between itself and the world (*PhG* 414–17/M ¶779–81; 419–21/M ¶787). Thus, revealed religion, which knows itself integrated into the life of the divine spirit, persists within the truth framework determined by the concept of religion. Even in this its final form, religion continues its commitment to the presupposition that truth belongs primarily to the unifying spirit of religion. The secular world gets its truth from its status as the spirit of religion made manifest in the realities of the objective social world (*PhG* 363–5/M ¶677–8).

Absolute knowing, however, knows that the divided world of human experience belongs to the internal necessities of truth conceived as the undivided selfsameness of thought and being. The sameness of thought and being, precisely by not being self-opposed, sets up the divided human world as a reality with its own self-identity, set off from the un-conflicted, transparent selfsameness of thought and being. The separation, however, also connects, since the selfsame and self-opposed are defined by the way they distinguish themselves from each other. This separating connection expands the concept of truth to include the selfsameness of thought and being knowing the opposition between thought and being as another, equally essential, dimension of the selfsame itself. The truth is the dynamic played out between them. In this dynamic, the sameness of thought and being distinguishes itself from the opposition dynamic that isolates thought

4 See chapter 16, §3.

in itself and separates it from the conditions of independent objective existence; then it cancels the distinction by becoming the fundamental truth of each opposite and the determining principle of their differentiation. The return to experience completes the selfsameness of thought and being and belongs to what it necessarily is.

This return to experience transforms the divided spirit of conscientiousness into the sameness of thought and being necessarily surrendered into the opposition between thought isolated in its subjectivity and thought surrendered into the absolute otherness of the objective world. Absolute knowing knows the sameness of thought and being transformed into a purpose accomplished by consciousness itself in the contingencies of natural existence. Rational thought accomplishes the truth by giving itself reality as an independent objective world; and this involves surrendering the rationality of thought into the contingencies and spatio-temporal limitations of nature and human history. Thus, absolute knowing takes the truth to be thought recognizing in the external world not only the rationality that corresponds to its own but also its own rationality let go, sacrificed, in the irrationality of what just happens to be the case – a time, a place, a given association of particulars.[5] Hegel describes this surrender as "the passage of the <concept> into consciousness," which means that thought knows the rationality of the objective world as something that belongs to the world's independence of its relation to consciousness (*PhG* 432–3/M ¶806). This brings the *Phenomenology* back to its starting point in sense certainty, to the here and now givenness of sense particulars. Thought cannot exist as the true essence of an independently existing object unless it exists in these particulars (*PhG* 432–3/M ¶806–7).[6]

In absolute knowing, cognition finally satisfies the truth criterion implicit in the minimal conditions required for knowledge to appear. Only in absolute knowing does the way the object is known completely reveal the object's independence. Only absolute knowing knows the last remnant of the object's otherness – the irrational unaccountability of its particulars, its distribution in different spaces and times – as a necessary condition of its truth. For absolute knowing, the truth is the spirit of rationality surrendered into the contingencies of nature and the movement of history (*PhG* 432–3/M ¶807–8).

5 See chapter 16, §4.
6 See also *PhG* 422–3/M ¶788; 425–7/M ¶795–6; 427–8/M ¶798–9; 430–2/M ¶804.

2 THE OTHERNESS THEME IN THE LATER WORKS

This same position on the relation between thought and the contingencies of experience shows up repeatedly in the introductory essays of the *Philosophy of Right* and the *Encyclopaedia*. Both texts interpret the formula, the rational is actual and the actual rational. Both interpretations belong to the standpoint defined by the presuppositions of philosophy proper. In other words, the interpretation of the rational-is-actual formula assumes the point of view that the *Phenomenology* is supposed to justify. In both texts, Hegel distinguishes the rational element in the real world from the contingencies in which it exists. In both texts, he insists that philosophy has a limited task, namely to identify the rational element in what is real. Working out the contingent arrangements that are most appropriate for the actualization of reason, identifying the empirical configurations in which reason shows itself – all this belongs to other knowledge areas, politics perhaps, and history, and the empirical sciences. Both the *Philosophy of Right* and the *Encyclopaedia*, however, also insist that the rational must be realized in these contingencies. This becomes explicit in the *Encyclopaedia*'s discussion of empiricism. Empiricism, Hegel says, makes a significant contribution to our knowledge of the truth because it insists that the truth must be known in the perceptual data presented in sense experience. Hegel interprets this as the reality principle required for truth. In sense experience, we know the reality of the rational.[7]

In the *Encyclopaedia*'s comments on Kant's third *Critique*, Hegel acknowledges the gap between the rational and the contingencies in which it becomes real; and he uses Kant's idea of purposiveness to address the issue. Hegel defines the idea thus: "an understanding in which the particular, which is contingent for the *universal* ([i.e. the] abstract identity) and cannot be deduced from it, would be determined through this universal itself" (*Enz* §55). Hegel finds in the idea of purposiveness a way in which the abstract selfsameness of the universal can determine contingent particulars without deriving them deductively from the necessary implications of the universal. Conceived according to the idea of purposiveness, contingent particulars belong to the universal as a purpose that it gives itself. In a sense, the universal invents a way to give itself existence as an integrated world distributed and diversified in the particulars of empirical reality.

7 See chapter 3, §2; chapter 4, §2. The *Science of Logic* touches on this same theme when it discusses logic embedded in language and the independence of logical thought recognizing in experience its own logical form (see chapter 6, §1–3).

Hegel objects, however, to the way Kant restricts the idea of purposiveness, reducing it to "a principle of judging that belongs only to *our* understanding" (*Enz* §58). According to Hegel, "the universality that is determined by reason – the absolute final purpose, *the good* – is made actual in the world, and this through a third, through the might that itself posits this final purpose and realises it – i.e., it is made actual by *God*, in whom, since he is the absolute truth, those antitheses of universality and singularity, of subjectivity and objectivity are resolved and declared to be not self-standing and untrue" (*Enz* §59).

The account of absolute knowing in the *Phenomenology* also interprets absolute truth as a purpose. According to this account, the spirit of truth existing in and identified with the conscientiousness of the human self brings about the unity of thought and being as the human self's own act. Conscientiousness, transformed by absolute knowing, acknowledges that the sameness of thought and being, which is truth, becomes actual and real only as a purpose accomplished. Conscientiousness achieves the truth, produces it, by surrendering the purity and selfsameness of conscientious thought into the diversity and contingencies of the empirical world, and by accepting this loss of selfsameness as a necessary component of the purpose it sets out to accomplish. Situated within the framework of absolute knowing, conscientiousness takes as its aim not the appropriation of the other but itself given away to the other. The purpose is not to overcome the world's otherness by transforming it into a reflection of the self but to identify thought with this otherness by becoming immersed in the externality and contingencies of the world's givenness. Thought gives itself reality as the true essence of the objective world by letting itself go in the contingent particulars that constitute the world as a reality independent of thought.[8]

The way Hegel in the *Encyclopaedia* criticizes Kant's idea of internal purposiveness confirms the way I have distinguished the *Phenomenology*'s account of absolute truth from interpretations that reduce the rational spirit to the rational subjectivity of the human self. In the *Encyclopaedia*, Hegel insists that the internal purposiveness conceived in Kant's idea does not belong to the conditions of *our* rationality, theoretical or practical, as Kant claimed. It belongs to the rationality and power of a spirit that transcends the limitations of our moral subjectivity. This spirit operates within the conscientiousness of the human spirit; and the achievement of the purpose belongs to the human spirit as its own act. But the human spirit has its ground in a spirit that comprehends not only the human spirit itself but

8 See chapter 16, §5–8; chapter 17, §5–7.

also the resistant otherness of the natural world. As Hegel himself says in the *Logic*, this is the *logos* of the ancient metaphysicians, not the transcendental rationality of Kant (*WL* 21:17–18/M 35; 21:29–30/M 39).

Thus, the introductory essays of the later works acknowledge what has emerged in the *Phenomenology*'s examination of experience. The *Phenomenology* exposes the rational element embedded in the contingencies of experience, and shows how the rational element itself calls for its realization in these contingencies. The *Phenomenology* also demonstrates that reason does not determine these contingencies, but rather surrenders itself into them. In the *Phenomenology*, the contingency element plays a general role, the role of nature's independence of thought.[9]

The "Subjective Logic" section of the *Logic*, where Hegel discusses the concept of the particular, repeats again, in a more explicit and succinct form, what the *Phenomenology* has claimed about the role of the irrational. According to this text, logic determines the particular only in its general form, in the difference between the undifferentiated universal and the particular in which the universal becomes differentiated from itself. Two particulars are sufficient for establishing this differentiation. Nature and spirit, however, do not respect the strictness of this concept.

> This is the impotence of nature, that it cannot abide by and exhibit the rigor of the concept and loses itself in a blind manifoldness void of concept (*begrifflos*). We can *wonder* at nature, at the manifoldness of its genera and species, in the endless diversity of its shapes, for wonder is *without concept* (*ohne Begriff*) and its object is the irrational (*Vernunftlose*). It is allowed to nature, since nature is the self-externality of the concept, to indulge in this diversity, just as spirit, even though it possesses the concept in the shape of concept, lets itself go into <representation> and runs wild in the infinite manifoldness of the latter ... Both [nature and spirit] indeed show traces and intimations of the concept on all sides, but do not exhibit it in trustworthy copy, for they are the side of its free self-externality; the <concept> is the absolute power precisely because it can let its difference go free in the shape of self-subsistent diversity, external necessity, accidentality, arbitrariness, opinion – all of which, however, must not be taken as anything more than the abstract side of nothingness. (*WL* 12:39/M 607–8)

Hegel shows here that the irrationality factor introduced in the *Phenomenology* does not get lost when he turns his attention to the *Logic*. Moreover, in this text from the *Logic*, he is clear and explicit in acknowledging that this

9 The whole of Part Seven traces this theme through the Reason and Spirit sections of the *Phenomenology*. Chapter 16, §3–4, follows the theme into the account of revealed religion.

factor belongs to the unintelligibility of nature and spirit. It provokes "wonder," which is "without concept." He also echoes here the way the analysis of good and evil, in the *Phenomenology*'s account of revealed religion, has defined the role of nature as a nothing that nevertheless is.[10] The irrational element, with all its superfluous content, functions as an abstract 'not,' the dismemberment of spirit's integrity in self-subsistent diversity, which is isolated in-itselfness, the "free outside itself being" in which a concept becomes an independent reality outside thought.[11]

3 CERTAINTY AND THE EXPERIENCE PRINCIPLE

As we have seen, the account of absolute knowing in the *Phenomenology* identifies absolute knowing as a form of certainty. This account defines certainty as the inwardness of consciousness immediately conscious of itself, distinguished from its consciousness of an object. In absolute knowing, consciousness is immediately conscious of itself identified with the infinity of absolute spirit.[12] The *Encyclopaedia*'s examination of the three positions on objectivity calls the inwardness aspect of experience the experience principle. According to this principle, a subject has a right to accept as true only what is confirmed by the subject's immediate sense of itself. The truth must be experienced, immediately felt, as true. The *Encyclopaedia*'s discussion finds the experience principle operating in empiricism, where it is applied to sense experience, and in Jacobi's immediate knowing position, where it is applied to the immediate intuition of the infinite, a supersensible experience (*Enz* §38*A*, §64*A*). Hegel endorses Jacobi's intuition of the infinite at least as the fulfillment of the experience principle. The intuition of the infinite, as Jacobi describes it, provides the experience in which the subject's own felt conviction acknowledges the concept of truth that defines philosophical science as Hegel himself interprets it.[13] As we have seen, the account of absolute knowing in the *Phenomenology* also acknowledges that absolute knowing must honour the experience principle (*PhG* 429–30/

10 See chapter 16, §4.

11 The irrationality factor in all its superfluous multiplicity becomes an explicit object of philosophical science in the philosophy of nature and the philosophy of spirit. Hence, interpretations of the move out of logic into these subsequent parts of Hegel's system must ask how the necessities of logic are related to this development. For an excellent discussion of this issue, see Burbidge, Halper, Maker, Winfield, Dudley, and Houlgate in *The Owl of Minerva* (2002–03). See also Dudley (2003–04).

12 See chapter 17, §5–7.

13 See chapter 5, §1–2.

M ¶802). The truth concept that completes the task of the *Phenomenology* must take the form of an intuition in which the content of the truth is represented together with the certainty of its truth. It is important, therefore, to look again at Hegel's discussion of the immediate knowing position in the light of what Hegel says about certainty and truth at the end of the *Phenomenology*.

The immediate knowing position claims that we know the truth not in a step-by-step reasoning process but in an immediate intuition of the infinite. Hegel compares this intuition to Descartes' *cogito*. The *cogito* does not begin a reasoning process that moves from the immediate experience of oneself thinking to the conclusion that this self exists. Rather, the immediate sense of oneself thinking is the immediate experience of oneself existing. Jacobi transforms this immediate sense of self into an intuition of infinite truth existing. Hegel analyzes the way the intuition represents this truth: not as being alone, which would be the immediate here and now givenness of sensible being; not as thought alone, which would be the isolated subjectivity of thinking; but as being whose essential character is thought, and thought existing as the independent reality of being (*Enz* §70, 77). Yet Hegel criticizes the immediate knowing position as a truth claim supported by the subjectivity of the knower's isolated conviction, which provides no way of distinguishing a true conviction from an evil or false conviction. An experience being felt as true is not enough to justify its claim.[14] Before we return to the proof issue, however, let us look carefully at what Hegel's criticism implies about the intuition itself. The intuition is an isolated, subjective experience. Yet it knows intuitively a truth not limited to this isolated subjectivity, a truth known as thought identifying reality itself in all its infinite scope. The subject of the intuition, therefore, is a knower isolated in his or her own subjective experience whose immediate sense of self counts nevertheless as an intuition of infinite truth. The self experiences itself immediately identified with the infinite in which thought and being are the same.

The *Logic* makes the same point when it describes absolute knowing as certainty no longer separated from truth: "Absolute knowing is the truth of every mode of consciousness, because, as the course of the *Phenomenology* showed, it is only in absolute knowing that the separation of the object from the certainty of itself is completely eliminated: truth is now equated with certainty and this certainty with truth" (*WL* 21:33–4/M 49). When, therefore, philosophical science begins in the *Logic*, it begins with a certainty, an

14 See chapter 5, §1–3. See also chapter 4, §1, especially the discussion of *Enz* §7+*A*, 8, 12+*A*.

intuition, that claims for itself the status of absolute truth. In other words, a finite human thinker, a thinker immersed in the spatio-temporal conditions of experience, a consciousness isolated in the exclusivity of its own subjective sense of itself, asserts its own 'I think' as the immediate intuition of unlimited, absolute truth. There is no way we can accept this claim without proof. Hegel's critique of Jacobi's immediate knowing position makes this clear, as does the *Logic*, which says repeatedly that the *Phenomenology* provides the proof needed.[15] The discussion of certainty and the experience principle, however, exposes another dimension of this proof. The proof must not only provide evidence that justifies the way Hegelian philosophy conceives the truth. In the process, it must produce in the individual thinker an intuition, an immediate sense of self, that feels itself identified with this truth.

4 THE HISTORY THEME REVISITED

In the concluding chapter of the *Phenomenology*, Hegel relates the experience principle to the history theme introduced in the Preface and the Introduction. According to Hegel, human history has worked its way through various spirits until it reveals in Hegel's own time a spirit, a culture, that knows what the truth absolutely is. Distributed in the externality of time, this development belongs to the contingencies of history. The true spirit appears, comes on the scene, as one spirit happening after others. The Preface to the *Phenomenology* describes this appearing as an intuition of the absolute detached from the concreteness and diversity of empirical cognition.[16] The Introduction describes it as one truth claim simply assuring us that its knowing is the truth and other forms of knowing are not.[17] The *Phenomenology* concludes, however, with this same spirit exposed as the necessary outcome of historically conditioned concept development. Hidden away in the historical appearance of absolute spirit is the recollection of other spirits that have retreated into this spirit as their ground. They belong to what is implicit in the spirit that asserts itself absolutely. The "Science of Knowing in the sphere of appearance," which is the *Phenomenology of Spirit*, brings this recollection to consciousness. It exposes the way the preliminary spirits organize themselves into necessary connections whose ground and unifying principle is the concept of truth that identifies the spirit of Hegel's

15 See chapter 5, §3; chapter 7, §1.
16 See chapter 8, §1.
17 See chapter 9, §2.

time. In the process, it integrates the reader of the *Phenomenology* into the educational process that produces in the reader's own consciousness the immediate sense of itself identified with the spirit of absolute truth (*PhG* 430–1/M ¶803; 433–4/M ¶808).

In the *Encyclopaedia,* Hegel says that the development of thinking in the externality of history belongs to philosophy itself "but freed from that historical outwardness, i.e., purely in the element of thinking" (*Enz* §14). In other words, philosophy demonstrates the same movement through different truth concepts not as a temporal succession but as a development determined by the necessities of free, independent thought. In its conclusion, the *Phenomenology* talks about yet another way in which the externality of history is transformed into a conceptually determined development. The *Phenomenology* begins with the fundamental structure of experience and the concept of truth implicit in this structure, which identifies the fundamental constitution of any conscious self. It proceeds by exposing the determinate negations that connect different forms of experience governed by different truth expectations into a whole whose ground is absolute spirit. Hegel concludes this process by saying that external history together with the *Phenomenology*'s examination of knowledge as an appearance produces "comprehended History," which forms "the inwardizing and the Calvary of absolute Spirit" (*PhG* 433–4/M ¶808). Comprehended history negates the lifeless isolation of the absolute and brings it into the inwardness of human experience. The human self immersed in the spatio-temporal contingencies of nature and history, isolated in its own sense of self, knows itself as the universality and infinity of truth surrendered into the givenness and concreteness of the natural element and the dismemberment of the whole in each singular self-consciousness. Thus, the *Phenomenology* demonstrates the legitimacy of assuming as philosophy does that the independent necessities of pure thought reveal not only the true essence of thought itself but also the true essence of human history. It also explains why Hegel in his later works insists that thought developing the necessities proper to thought in its independence of experience must return to experience and know its own structure realized in experience.[18]

5 INTUITION, MEDIATION, AND PROOF IN THE ENCYCLOPAEDIA

The preceding sections have exposed certain similarities between the way the *Phenomenology* ends and the way the later works describe the relation

18 See chapter 3, §1–2; chapter 4, §1–2; chapter 6, §1–3.

between philosophy and experience. With these themes in mind, we now turn to the fundamental epistemological question involved in the role Hegel assigns to the *Phenomenology*. What kind of proof demonstrates the truth of the concept with which philosophy begins? The later works explore this question most explicitly and thoroughly in three discussions: in the *Encyclopaedia*, (1) the critique of Jacobi's immediate knowing position, and (2) a critique of traditional arguments for the existence of God; in the introductory essays of the *Logic*, (3) the discussion of the way philosophy begins. We have examined these discussions on their own in previous chapters.[19] We examine them again here in relation to the way the *Phenomenology* itself completes its critical examination of experience and suggests the move into philosophical science.

Hegel criticizes Jacobi's immediate knowing position because it separates the intuition of the infinite from the mediation involved in demonstrating the truth of the intuition. By excluding mediation, intuitive cognition isolates itself in the subjectivity of a single consciousness, and bases its truth claim on nothing but the felt conviction of this consciousness. As a result, cognition in this form has no way of distinguishing true from untrue intuitive certainties, and no way of making the necessity of its truth known to others. Hegel agrees with the immediate knowing position, however, about the inadequacy of mediated cognition for knowing infinite truth. Mediated cognition knows the truth as something determined by its relations to what is other than itself. If we know the infinite by relating it to an other, we do not know what it truly is, because we do not know it as infinite, all-encompassing, restricted by nothing that is other than itself.[20]

Hegel's critique of traditional proofs for the existence of God clarifies this point. According to Hegel, these proofs take the form of understanding. A proof in this form begins with finite realities known for what they are in themselves, in their own being. The proof demonstrates that these realities are mediated by their dependence on an infinite ground. The demonstration produces a conclusion that conceives the infinite as a relation to the finite, and hence as mediated by something other than itself. Knowledge of God, Hegel says, is either pantheism, which knows a unifying substance related to finite realities as its modes, or dualism, which knows the infinite in terms of its separation from, its being "beyond," the finite.

In order to identify more precisely the way Hegel's criticism exposes a weakness in traditional proofs, I have examined the structure of Aquinas'

19 See chapters 5 and 7.
20 See chapter 5, §2.

argument from contingency, which is not quite as simplistic as Hegel's critique of the traditional proofs might lead us to believe. Aquinas, like Hegel, exposes the distortion involved in conceiving the infinite as a relation to the finite. If the infinite is constituted by a real relation to something other than itself, then the infinite would be dependent on and limited by this other and would not be infinite. Hence, Aquinas argues that the relation between the contingent world and the infinite God is a real relation in the world but not a real relation in God. According to Aquinas, however, the proof from contingency gives us only what Hegel would call a mediated knowledge of the infinite. We know it positively in terms of the finite by knowing it as that which explains the existence, order, and purpose of the contingent world. We know it negatively in terms of the finite by knowing it as beyond everything that our concepts of finite realities can comprehend. Aquinas acknowledges that human cognition cannot completely fulfill its natural movement toward truth until it knows the infinite in itself, in an immediate intuition. But only the direct presence of God to human intuition can accomplish this, and only in the afterlife. Like Jacobi, Aquinas would deny that human reasoning can produce an intuition of the infinite. Moreover, Aquinas conceives the infinite as an infinite content, all possible perfection, everything that being can possibly be.[21]

Hegel's position differs from this more subtle version of the traditional proofs because it claims that human reasoning can produce an intuition of the infinite, and because it conceives the infinite in a more modest form derived from the determinate negations of finite reality. Hegel calls his proof a rational proof. This kind of proof resembles the traditional proofs in its starting point. It begins with a finite reality immediately accessible to our knowing and known for what it is in itself. The proof uses this knowledge as evidence that demonstrates the dependence of finite reality on an infinite ground. In the domain of knowing with which the proof begins, knowledge of the infinite emerges in the way we know fully what the finite is. Knowledge of the infinite depends on our knowledge of the finite.

As a retreat into a ground, however, the proof demonstrates the necessity of shifting priorities. It shows that in the domain of being the infinite as ground has priority, and the finite gets its reality from the ground. Our knowing, therefore, distorts the truth demonstrated by the proof if it persists in a cognition that knows the infinite as a result of the finite. In order to make our knowing conform to what has been demonstrated in the proof, we must think the infinite by itself, on its own, so that we can think it as

21 *Summa Contra Gentiles* III, Part One, 51–4.

the origin or ground of the finite. Hence, we must know the ground in an unmediated, intuitive cognition and derive from this our knowledge of the finite. Hegel identifies a threefold mediation in this kind of proof: (1) the step-by-step movement that exposes the way the finite depends on an infinite ground, a movement that produces in the knower the concept of the infinite together with the certainty of its truth; (2) the separating mediation that identifies the infinite as something not determined by its relation to the finite; (3) a mediation within the infinite itself, which Hegel describes as spirit mediated by its relation to itself and also as the selfsameness of two different determinations, thought and being.[22]

6 INTUITION, MEDIATION, AND PROOF IN THE PHENOMENOLOGY

Now that we have examined the highlights of the demonstration Hegel develops in the *Phenomenology*, we can show how the *Phenomenology* provides the kind of proof Hegel proposes in his examination of Jacobi's immediate knowing position. Hegel's critique of the immediate knowing position suggests that the intuition of the infinite could be justified for all knowers by a rational proof that examines the nature of consciousness as such. The *Phenomenology* begins with a concept that reduces consciousness to its minimal conditions, consciousness of something (*etwas*). Hegel says explicitly that every appearance of consciousness, whatever other determinations it may have, appears with this minimal structure (*PhG* 58–9/M ¶82). The structure is determined by "the very fact that consciousness knows an object at all" (*PhG* 59–60/M ¶85). In other words, consciousness cannot be a consciousness, consciousness cannot appear, without being consciousness of something (*etwas*). This minimal concept, therefore, identifies a structure present in any consciousness, and whatever follows necessarily from this concept is necessarily true for each and every knower. The *Phenomenology*, however, must expose the necessities that connect the minimal structure of consciousness to the concept that completes its conceptual development, in order to produce in the knower the certainty that acknowledges the final version of this concept as absolute truth. The *Phenomenology* accomplishes this exposition in a series of determinate negations that repeatedly justifies conceiving the truth as infinity, a concept introduced in the transition from understanding to self-consciousness, and brought to completion in the dynamics of absolute knowing.[23]

22 See chapter 5, §3.
23 See chapter 16, §6 and the whole of chapter 17.

In chapter 17, we have shown how absolute knowing reproduces the structure of infinity first introduced in the account of understanding. In the infinity dynamic, we recognize the three mediations that Hegel describes in his discussion of the proof needed to support Jacobi's immediate knowing position. (1) The step-by-step process that proves the truth of absolute knowing exposes the mediated status of human experience as a whole, and shows that everything in the domain of human experience belongs to a system of relations, a whole. (2) This demonstration produces a negative mediation by showing that the selfsameness of the whole is a truth not contained within the dynamics of the relational system. True cognition must separate itself from its engagement in experience, even from the experiential form of absolute knowing itself. In its experiential form, absolute knowing operates within the dynamics of conscientious purposiveness and hence belongs to the dynamics of history. (3) The separating mediation demonstrates the necessity of conceiving the selfsameness of the whole in itself, independent of the mediations that prove its truth. As a result determined by a series of determinate negations, the demonstration proves the necessity of conceiving the whole as a simplicity in which the different determinations of absolute knowing are one and selfsame. As a retreat into a ground, it proves the necessity of reversing direction, asserting the concept of the ground in itself, and developing from its necessary implications the determinations that previously retreated into it.[24]

7 RETURN TO THE LOGIC

The same three mediations described in the critique of Jacobi's immediate knowing position appear again in the introductory essays of the *Logic*, and here Hegel explicitly associates these with the project developed in the *Phenomenology*. In "With What Must the Beginning of Science Be Made?" Hegel says:

> Here we have only to consider how the *logical* beginning appears. The two sides from which it can be taken have already been named, namely either by way of mediation as result, or immediately as beginning proper ... A beginning is *logical* in that it is to be made in the element of a free, self-contained thought, *in pure knowledge*; it is thereby *mediated*, for pure knowledge is the ultimate and absolute truth of *consciousness*. We said in the Introduction that the *Phenomenology of Spirit* is the science of consciousness, its exposition; that consciousness has the *concept* of science, that

24 See chapter 5, §3.

> is, pure knowledge, for its result. To this extent, logic has for its presupposition the science of spirit in its appearance, a science which contains the necessity, and therefore demonstrates the truth (*den Beweis der Wahrheit*), of the standpoint which is pure knowledge and of its mediation. (*WL* 21:54–5/M 68–9)

At the end of the *Phenomenology*, pure knowledge emerges as a result of the mediation that encompasses the whole domain of phenomenal consciousness and refers it to pure knowing as its ground. This is the first mediation, the step-by-step process that demonstrates the truth of pure knowing.

The first mediation demonstrates the necessity of the second, separating mediation. "Simple immediacy is itself an expression of reflection; it refers to the distinction from what is mediated ... Being is what makes the beginning here; it is presented indeed as originating through mediation, but a mediation which at the same time sublates itself, and the presupposition is of a pure knowledge which is the result of finite knowledge, of consciousness" (*WL* 21:55–6/M 69). This is the mediation that detaches thought from its involvement in the self-world dynamic of human experience.

As a retreat into a ground, this second mediation proves the necessity of shifting into an unmediated beginning. Philosophical science must begin with the independence of the ground. Pure knowing asserts itself in itself, in its freedom and independence, not mediated by anything, not determined by any ground, itself the ground in which determinations have their origin.

> But if no presupposition is to be made, if the beginning is itself to be taken *immediately*, then the only determination of this beginning is that it is to be the beginning of logic, of thought <for itself> (*für sich*). There is only present the resolve, which can also be viewed as arbitrary (*einen Willkür*), of considering *thinking as such*. The beginning must then be *absolute* or, what means the same here, must be an abstract beginning, and so there is *nothing* that it may *presuppose*, must not be mediated by anything or have a ground, ought to be rather itself the ground of the entire science. (*WL* 21:55–6/M 70)

The resolve to consider thought focused on itself posits the singular self's certainty of itself as pure thought identified with the immediacy of pure being.

In the *Encyclopaedia*, Hegel finds mediation within immediate knowing's intuition of the infinite. This intuition knows the infinite not as being alone, which would be the immediacy of a sense datum, and not as thought alone, which would be the isolated subjectivity of thought, but as the immediacy of being in the form of thought. The intuition contains two different determinations and in this sense is mediated. In "With What Must the Beginning of Science Be Made," however, Hegel says that the beginning cannot contain any mediation within itself. "Just as it cannot have any determination with respect to an other, so too it cannot have any within; it cannot have any content, for any content would entail distinction and the reference of distinct moments to each other, and hence a mediation. The beginning is therefore *pure being*" (*WL* 21:56/M 70). The *Encyclopaedia*, however, does not represent immediate knowing's intuition as a relation between being and thought, only as being and thought identified with each other. The *Logic* takes the same position.

> [Pure science] contains *thought in so far as this thought is equally the <thing>* (*die Sache*) *as it is in itself*; or the *<thing> in itself* in so far as this *is equally pure thought.* As *science*, truth is pure self-consciousness as it develops itself and has the shape of the self, so that *<in and for itself being is the known concept, but the concept as such is in and for itself being>* (*an und für sich Seiende gewurßter Begriff, der Begriff als solcher aber das an und für sich Seiende ist*). (*WL* 21:33–4/M 49)

Pure self-consciousness does not know itself as the isolated subjectivity of thinking, which is only "for itself." Nor does pure self-consciousness know its own being as a given sense-datum, which is only "in-itself." Pure self-consciousness thinks itself, posits itself, as pure thought identified with the independent reality of being.

In the *Encyclopaedia*, however, Hegel adds another element to his interpretation of the infinite's self-mediation: "God can only be called spirit inasmuch as he is known as inwardly mediating himself with himself ... and that is why the *knowing* of God as spirit contains mediation within it" (*Enz* 74). The *Phenomenology*'s account of absolute knowing suggests a way of sorting out these ambiguities. The demonstration developed in the *Phenomenology* proves that the whole domain of real experience belongs to the infinity dynamics of absolute spirit, which distributes itself in human self-consciousness, natural existence, and human history, and remains the same with itself in this self-sharing. In the element of experience, absolute knowing remains immersed in the mediating dynamics of absolute spirit. In the element of logic, absolute knowing shifts into its identification with the immediacy and undistributed selfsameness of the ground from which the mediations of the spirit are derived.

19

The Absolute Knowing Debate

IN A RECENT SET OF ARTICLES, six scholars have engaged in a debate focused on the interpretation of absolute knowing as the end of the *Phenomenology* and the beginning of the *Logic*. The debate began as a disagreement between Stephen Houlgate and Joseph Flay, and then expanded to include Simon Lumsden, Robert Williams, John Burbidge, and Rob Devos. The participants in this debate have each focused on a different part of Hegel's complicated discussion, and as a result have given priority to different factors in Hegel's analysis of absolute knowing. By examining briefly the contribution of each participant, and by situating it within the context of my own interpretation, I hope to identify more explicitly and precisely the position I am taking on this issue.

I have selected these articles for special consideration because they address more explicitly than others the questions addressed in the project I have developed in this book. Each participant explains the relation between the end of the *Phenomenology* and the beginning of the *Logic* by analyzing explicitly and carefully the structure of sameness and otherness with which the *Phenomenology* completes its project, and by asking explicitly how this structure affects the constitution of knowing with which the *Logic* begins. Hence, these contributors address questions regarding the precise way in which the move from the *Phenomenology* to the *Logic* is constituted, which is also a primary question addressed in my study of the *Phenomenology*. Also, the dialogue between the different articles creates a direct encounter between different interpretations of absolute knowing developed in articles and books published separately. Thus, it situates significant contributions to the discussion of absolute knowing in a context that asks each contributor to explain where his interpretation stands on questions raised by the others. Finally, the dialogue brings into the same discussion different facets of the issue, so that the full complexity of the relation between absolute knowing and the beginning of logic becomes exposed. By bringing my interpretation of the issue into an encounter with this dialogue, I hope to show how my study of the *Phenomenology* integrates the different facets of absolute knowing, and the different roles it plays, into a coherent, complex position.

1 SIMPLICITY VERSUS RELATIONAL OTHERNESS

The disagreement between Houlgate and Flay asks whether the otherness of thought and being is preserved in absolute knowing. According to Houlgate, it is not preserved: "the distinction between thought and being which once characterized consciousness has given way to the unity or identity of thought and being which constitutes the element of the *Science of Logic* ... the task of the *Phenomenology* is to undo the distinction upon which the idea of a relation between thought and being rests, and so to bring thought to the recognition that it has the capacity to determine by itself the meaning of being (in the *Science of Logic*)."[1] According to Flay, however, "the distinction between knowing and being is not 'undone,' and there is no simple unity or identity of thought and being." Rather, "knowing and the categories are embedded in a real relation with an independent world or being."[2] Flay analyzes this real relation by distinguishing the otherness or duality of the related from the unity of the relation. In a relation, the related factors remain other, each itself and not the other, and yet both belong to the same relation. Moreover, the duality of the participants and the unity of the relation mutually determine each other. The related factors constitute the unifying relation, and the relation constitutes the differentiated factors.[3] Absolute knowing shifts the focus from the way knowing knows its other, the object, to the way knowing knows the relation between knowing and its object, a relating that grounds the related factors *as relational.* In absolute knowing, the separation of knowing and being collapses, but their relational otherness persists, because the relation cannot be separated from the factors whose relatedness is determined by it.[4]

Both Houlgate and Flay agree that the *logos,* which is the subject-matter of philosophical science, is not thought alone or being alone. For Houlgate, however, the *logos* is a simplicity in which the relation between thought and

1 Houlgate (1993), 160.
2 Flay (1998), 71.
3 Ibid., 77.
4 Ibid., 74–6, 80–1.

being collapses and thought and being are identical. For Flay, the *logos* is the relation itself in which knowing and being mutually determine each other. The categories of philosophical science are not categories of thought, nor are they categories of being. They are categories of the relation between thought and being, and the independent otherness of the world persists in this relation.[5]

According to Simon Lumsden, Houlgate's interpretation takes as its primary concern Hegel's claim that absolute knowing overcomes the otherness between consciousness and its object, whereas Flay seeks to preserve the dynamic relation between the thinking subject and its object. In the process, each loses what the other retains. Houlgate loses the subjectivity of the thinking self and its concrete embeddedness in an inter-subjective context. Flay loses the insight that being can only be known in terms of thought. Lumsden offers an alternative interpretation that preserves the dynamic between the subjectivity of thought and its object, but finds therein no absolute otherness between thought and being.[6]

At the end of the *Phenomenology*, Lumsden says, consciousness knows the determinations of the object as "the totality *of its own* cognitive relations and experience."[7] Consciousness has an object confronting it, something standing before the subjectivity that is conscious of it. But the object is nothing more than the conditions that make it possible for the object to be known.[8] In absolute knowing, consciousness recognizes that these conditions are the structure of its own knowing. The knowing subject's own conceptual structure stands before the subjectivity of consciousness as the determinations of the object. Consciousness of an object shows itself as self-consciousness.[9] In another article, Lumsden describes this self-consciousness thus: "At the end of the *Phenomenology*, that which the natural consciousness had assumed to be the determinations of the object of its experience has become understood not as conditions of an external object but as the conditions of its own cognitive relations and experience."[10] In other words, absolute knowing knows the conditions of the relation between consciousness and its object, as Flay claimed. But according to Lumsden, absolute knowing knows these as the conditions of knowing related to an object that is itself nothing but a relation to knowing. The object for absolute knowing is the

5 Flay (1993), 150–2. Houlgate (1998), 61.
6 Lumsden (1998), 5–8, 11, 14, 21–2, 26–7, 29–30.
7 Ibid., 14.
8 Ibid., 17. See also Lumsden (2000), 89.
9 Lumden (1998), 17, 25.
10 Lumsden (2000), 88–9.

object as known, the object belonging to the knowing subject's own experiential relations to what is known. The object is not something independent of knowing, as Flay claims.

Lumsden insists, however, that this conceptual structure is not the abstract structure of Kantian self-consciousness.[11] Rather, it emerges from conceptual relations that are the product of "history, language, culture and so on."[12] Lumsden agrees with Houlgate that thought in the logic is released from the particularity of the subject. He insists, however, that the particularity of the subject is itself the condition of this release. The objective conditions of being show themselves as the conceptual structure of thought in a knowing that belongs to a particular self immersed in the dynamics of the inter-subjective context.[13] The transition into the *Logic* reorients this knowing to focus on the determinations of the conceptual structure "in their purity as the categories of thought."[14]

Houlgate, however, denies the distinction between absolute knowing and logical science, and rejects Lumsden's claim that the move from the end of the *Phenomenology* to the beginning of the *Logic* involves a transition. Houlgate supports this objection with texts in which Hegel explicitly acknowledges that the knowing with which the *Phenomenology* ends is the same pure knowing with which the science of logic begins. Houlgate insists as well that this pure knowing is not a relation to anything, not even to its own conceptual determinations as constitutive determinations of the object. Thought thinks itself not as a *consciousness of* itself but as thought asserting itself and deriving from itself the essential categories of being.[15] Houlgate acknowledges that the absolute knower "remains a particular, concrete person" and that absolute knowing is a form of self-consciousness.[16] But he insists that absolute knowing is not "unalloyed self-consciousness," because the self knows "the structure of self-determining rationality that the self shares with being as such."[17] In other words, the self-consciousness of absolute knowing suppresses its particularity, surrenders to a truth not restricted by the subject's limiting conditions, and lets itself be carried along by the

11 Lumsden (1998), 14.
12 Ibid., 27, 29. See also Lumsden (2000), 89.
13 Lumsden (1998), 5, 11.
14 Ibid., 27. See also Lumsden (2000), 93, 95.
15 Houlgate (1998), 54–5.
16 Ibid., 60.
17 Ibid., 59.

necessary determinations of the *logos*, the rational, the truth that self-conscious thought and being have in common.[18]

Lumsden in response insists that "there is no pure singular self into which the conscious subject can retreat."[19] The self, like its object, belongs to the relation between knowing and being known. The transition from the *Phenomenology* to the *Logic* simply shifts from the perspective of the finite self engaged as one factor in the relation between consciousness and its object to the perspective of the knowing-known relation itself and the conceptual determinations that belong to it.

2 DIFFERENT FORMS OF RELATIONAL OTHERNESS

Rob Devos, Robert Williams, and John Burbidge also interpret absolute knowing as a relational dynamic between self-consciousness and an object confronting it. They challenge Lumsden's interpretation, however, by insisting that this dynamic preserves an otherness that cannot be reduced to a likeness between the subject's own conditions and these same conditions existing as the constitutive determinations of the object. The relation between the knowing subject and the object known involves mutual, reciprocal determinations played out between the participants. The object precisely as other than, not the same as, the knowing self plays an equally essential role in the way the conditions of the subject's experience are determined.

Williams agrees with Lumsden that there is no absolute difference between the knowing self and its object. The relation is not an external relation that leaves the participants unaffected by and independent of the relation. Nor is it an internal relation that reduces otherness to the same entity related to itself. Rather, the otherness between different entities belongs to the relation.[20] Williams explains this claim by comparing absolute knowing to the dynamics of love commitments, and by analyzing it in terms of the forgiveness that transforms the spirit of conscientiousness into absolute spirit appearing in it. Marriage based on love transforms the alien otherness of two separate individuals into a belonging in which each self expands to include the other as its other self; the I becomes We.

18 Ibid., 61.

19 Lumsden (2000), 91.

20 Williams (1998b), 87–90; (1998a), chapters 10–13. See also the debate between Williams and Houlgate in Houlgate (1994) and Williams (1995a). This debate focuses on issues raised in Williams (1992), chapter 11.

But this belonging allows the other to be other, so that the very otherness of each is preserved in it. Each lover belongs to the other precisely as an *other* self.[21] So also, when the conscientious agent confesses the compromised, impure conscientiousness of the agent's action, and when the beautiful soul forgives it, each lets go of the self-righteousness that separates it from the other, while also allowing the other to keep its otherness in their acceptance of each other.[22] Williams interprets both models and the absolute knowing that resembles them as "self-emptying," "allowing the other to be," "a refusal to impose any scheme of its own on the object," "allowing the object to generate its own criteria and categories."[23] Absolute knowing determines itself because it freely gives its acceptance of the other as other. Absolute knowing does not create the world, does not bring out of itself what the world is. Absolute knowing "fits us into the world."[24]

Williams gives an account of absolute knowing that depends on the recognition model, which relates the self-consciousness of one individual to the self-consciousness of another.[25] In love and forgiveness, a self acknowledges the self of another person as its other self. Rob Devos and John Burbidge, however, raise a question that exposes a more radical kind of otherness in absolute knowing: "How could the freedom of absolute Spirit manifest itself in what is spiritless and not free?"[26] "Subjects," Burbidge says, "have self-consciousness, but the world of nature is notoriously not self-conscious at all."[27] Nature brings with it the contingency of what merely happens, the spatio-temporal conditionedness of the singular self, the unexpected, the opaque. Moreover, these random, non-transparent contingencies cannot be dismissed or overlooked as superfluous to the real truth of the matter. They belong to the necessities of the truth itself. According to Devos, absolute knowing knows "the externality and contingency of mere happening" as a necessity of the concept. Truth demands "openness to unpredictable happening."[28]

According to both Devos and Burbidge, this relation to the contingencies of the unexpected belongs to absolute knowing because absolute knowing is a form of action. According to Devos, absolute knowing "both knows

21 Williams (1998b), 89.
22 Ibid., 93.
23 Ibid., 97.
24 Ibid., 91, 97–9. See also Williams (1992), 206–11.
25 Williams (1998b), 93.
26 Burbidge (1998), 114. Devos (1998), 37–8.
27 Burbidge (1998), 114. See also Devos (1998), 44.
28 Devos (1998), 46–7.

and acts," because "the self takes up as its own the effort of the Concept itself."[29] The concept realizing itself in the phenomenal world becomes the self's own act, and what experience took to be "a mere happening," absolute knowing knows as a necessity of the concept itself. Devos interprets this necessity of the concept as an "option-for-meaning," as the capacity to synthesize, to transform "the externality and contingency of mere happening" into something that makes sense.[30] Burbidge goes one step further. The structure of action, by releasing thought into the contingencies of the phenomenal world, surrenders thought into a realm that stands opposed to "thought's total achievement," lies outside its "capacity for appropriation." The contingencies of the phenomenal world inevitably twist the intentions of practical thought into something unaccountable, even evil, something that does not "make sense." Thought does justice to the other not by "trying to appropriate it imperialistically, but by surrendering to it."[31]

3 ANALYSIS OF THE DEBATE ISSUES

The debate articulated in the previous sections breaks up into six different debate issues:

1 absolute knowing as the simple identity of thought and being (Houlgate) versus absolute knowing as relational (Flay, Lumsden, Williams, Devos, Burbidge);
2 the move from the end of the *Phenomenology* to the beginning of the *Logic* as a transition (Lumsden) versus no transition (Houlgate);
3 the beginning of the *Logic* as a self-consciousness that preserves the social-historical subjectivity of the self (Lumsden) versus a self-consciousness that withdraws from its social-historical conditions into the self-determined rationality that thought and being have in common (Houlgate);
4 relational absolute knowing conceived as the sameness that persists between the conceptual conditions of the thinking subject and conditions constitutive of the object known (Lumsden) versus relational absolute knowing conceived as thought related to an other with its own independent determinations (Flay, Williams, Devos, Burbidge);

29 Ibid., 42.
30 Ibid., 45–7.
31 Burbidge (1998), 111. See also 105–10, 113; Burbidge (1997), especially 28–34; Burbidge (2007), chapters 4–5.

5 relational absolute knowing as a dynamic between the unity and the duality of the relation (Flay), as the spiritual otherness of a self set free within the relation to another self (Williams), as the otherness involved in action, which releases conceptual thought into the domain of external, contingent happening (Devos, Burbidge);
6 absolute knowing in action conceived as a synthesis that makes sense of the contingent and unexpected (Devos), absolute knowing in action conceived as thought surrendering to the inevitable unaccountability of what happens (Burbidge).

In order to explain my own stand on these issues, I must first call attention to an ambiguity in the way the Houlgate-Flay debate uses Hegel's technical terms. Flay picks up from Houlgate the terminology of the *Logic*, which defines its beginning concept as a sameness of thought and being. Flay, therefore, talks about the relational dynamic of absolute knowing as a relation between thought and being. He uses this terminology to analyze a relation between the subjectivity of the knower and the objectivity of what the knower knows. The term "thought" refers to thinking, knowing, a certain way of being conscious-of; the term "being" refers to the object of this knowing. My interpretation of the self-consciousness dialectic, however, shows that this way of using the terms is misleading.

The *Phenomenology* introduces the form of thought in the account of stoic self-consciousness. Stoic self-consciousness detaches itself from life's unstable relations in order to know the truth that stands firm throughout all these vicissitudes. Stoicism takes the truth to be thought knowing the objective world as an intelligibility that is attuned to thought itself, as truth and goodness. From the very beginning, therefore, thought is conceived as a subject-object relation, thought as thinking related to thought as the intelligibility of the object.[32] Moreover, the account of unhappy consciousness expands the being of thinghood to encompass the whole complicated subject-object dynamics of thought and life. What exists is the whole dynamic between thought detaching itself from life and thought negatively engaged in life. This subject-object thinghood becomes true by becoming absorbed into the subject-object simplicity of the rational. From this point on, both subjectivity and objectivity belong to thought identified with being, which is the rational.[33]

32 See chapter 13, §4.
33 See chapter 13, §5–7.

In order to avoid confusion, therefore, I will interpret Flay's position on the relationality of absolute knowing as the relationality of subject and object rather than as the relationality of thought and being.

4 FIRST RESPONSE: RELATIONAL OTHERNESS RETREATS INTO A SIMPLICITY

My analysis of absolute knowing focuses on the retreat into a ground that determines the truth criterion of absolute knowing, and on the infinity dynamic that follows as a result. This approach preserves both the relational dimension of absolute knowing and the simplicity in which relational otherness collapses. Houlgate is right to claim that the *Phenomenology* ends and the *Logic* begins with the same absolute knowing. This does not prove, however, that there is no transition in the move from the *Phenomenology* to the *Logic*. The *Phenomenology* leads into and justifies the presuppositions of absolute knowing by way of the derivative forms of knowing whose internal determinations demonstrate their dependence on absolute knowing as their ground. This produces a mediated way of knowing the ground. We know the ground in terms of what depends on and is explained by it. In order to know it in a form proper to what the *Phenomenology* has proved it to be, we must reverse direction. We must assert the ground as the originating principle, and hence as independent, completely immediate, dependent on nothing other than itself. The transition from the end of the *Phenomenology* to the beginning of the *Logic* brings about this direction shift. The *Phenomenology* ends with the retreat from phenomenal knowing into absolute knowing as its ground. The *Logic* begins with absolute knowing asserted in its immediacy as ground, which the *Logic* also refers to as "pure knowing" (*WL* 21:33/M 48–9; 21:54–5/M 68–9).

The retreat into a ground defines the truth as an infinity dynamic. The infinity structure, first introduced in the transition from consciousness to self-consciousness, begins with a field of appearances integrated into a relational system, refers the relational components to a simplicity that identifies the whole in itself, in its selfsameness, and reconceives the relational system as this same truth differentiated from itself. In the infinity dynamic of absolute knowing, pure knowing moves through all the forms of cognition examined in the *Phenomenology*, and situates them all within the framework of a dynamic between the beautiful soul's self-intuition and the conscientious agent's purposiveness. Absolute knowing knows the selfsameness of the relational system by referring the relational components to the observer consciousness that holds them all together in its consciousness of their necessary connections, and knows the whole dynamic as the relationality of the same absolute spirit. Thus, the transition from the truth as a system of relations to the same truth as a simplicity develops within absolute knowing itself. At the end of the *Phenomenology*, absolute knowing knows itself in the mediation that drives the different forms of experience into necessary connections, in the negative mediation that separates the simplicity of the whole from the relationality of its components, and knows itself set free as the immediacy and in-itselfness of the whole. At the beginning of the *Logic*, absolute knowing shifts into the priorities of the truth revealed in the *Phenomenology*. The *Logic* begins with the priority of the ground in all its immediacy and simplicity, and sets out to know the way the simplicity of the ground determines the differentiation of the relational components.

Flay and Lumsden interpret the retreat into a ground as a shift from the perspective of one relational participant to the perspective of the relation itself as ground. My interpretation disagrees with this view and supports Houlgate's claim that the *Logic* begins with a thought that is in no way relational. In my judgment, however, Houlgate's interpretation of this beginning does not preserve everything that has been proved in the *Phenomenology*. Houlgate interprets the beginning concept of the *Logic* as if it were the conceptual framework of idealism, which the *Phenomenology* introduces as the dialectical result of self-consciousness, as the beginning concept of reason, and as a truth criterion negated in subsequent phenomenological moves. Idealism inherits the surrender accomplished in unhappy consciousness. It assumes that its thinking has withdrawn from the limitations and conflicts of the thought-life dialectic into a rationality not restricted by the singularity of the self, not unsettled by the opposition between thought thinking itself and thought identified with the conflicts of life, a rationality that is being in the form of thought thinking itself.

Absolute knowing, however, inherits a negation in which universal, ahistorical rationality surrenders its dominance over the singular self embedded in the reality conditions of human experience. With the death of God, rationality reveals itself as a timeless rationality necessarily involved in the time-bound reality of human self-consciousness. The *Logic* does not begin with the thought of a singular self surrendered to a rationality not properly its own. It begins with rationality surrendered into the reality and subjectivity of the singular self.[34] It begins with the singular self making a decision, deciding to posit itself thinking and to follow where this leads. It begins with thought as the singular self's *cogito* asserted with all the confidence and

34 See chapter 16, §5; chapter 17, §5–6.

audacity of Jacobi's intuition, which knows the being of its own thinking as the being of the infinite. Hence, the *Logic* does not begin with thought focused on the meaning of being. It begins with thought simply being, which exists nowhere except in a singular self's thinking identified with the real being of this thinking. This *cogito* can assert itself as truth, however, only because the *Phenomenology* has demonstrated that thought becomes identified with being in a singular self knowing itself identified with the universal spirit of an actually existing natural, social, and historical world.[35]

The Preface to the *Phenomenology* anticipates this result:

> But that an accident as such, detached from what circumscribes it, what is bound and is actual only in its context with others, should attain an existence of its own and a separate freedom – this is the tremendous power of the negative; it is the energy of thought, of the pure "I." Death ... is of all things the most dreadful, and to hold fast what is dead requires the greatest strength ... But the life of Spirit is not the life that shrinks from death and keeps itself untouched by devastation, but rather the life that endures it and maintains itself in it. It wins its truth only when, in utter dismemberment (*in der absoluten Zerrissenheit*), it finds itself ... This tarrying with the negative is the magical power that converts it into being. This power is identical with what we earlier called the Subject, which by giving determinateness an existence in its own element supersedes abstract immediacy ... and thus is authentic substance. (*PhG* 26–7/M: ¶32)

Spirit is converted into being by the "death" that surrenders its circumscribing unity and universality into the separateness and subjectivity of the pure "I," the singular self.[36] This interpretation of absolute knowing shows how the simplicity and immediacy of logic's beginning does not lose the subjectivity of thought, as Lumsden's critique of Houlgate claims. The *Logic* begins with the simplicity and immediacy of the singular self's subjectivity. This subjectivity is not one-sided because it is a subjectivity identified with the substantial reality of a social world.

This interpretation of absolute knowing also answers the challenge posed by Lumsden when he says "there is no pure singular self into which the conscious subject can retreat."[37] At the beginning of the *Phenomenology*, the observer consciousness, the "we," takes a position detached from all truth expectations. It simply observes the various forms of phenomenal consciousness and the self-critical dynamics determined by their various

35 See chapter 18, §5–7.

36 Compare to chapter 16, §5.

37 Lumsden (2000), 91.

truth criteria. In this detached position, the observer consciousness is "pure," uncommitted to the presuppositions that color the experiences of phenomenal consciousness in its various configurations. Because of this uncommitted status, the observer can become conscious of the negations that connect the different forms of phenomenal knowing to each other. At the end of the *Phenomenology*, therefore, the observer consciousness holds within the selfsameness of its knowing the whole system of necessary connections developed in the examination of phenomenal consciousness, and knows them all as relational components that belong to its own simplicity.[38] The observer consciousness is the "pure singular self" into which phenomenal consciousness can retreat.

5 SECOND RESPONSE: THE UNITY-DIVERSITY STRUCTURE OF RELATIONS

In the preceding section, I have shown how my interpretation of absolute knowing preserves both the simplicity of thought identified with being and a relational dynamic that retreats into this simplicity as the selfsameness of the relational whole. A response to the absolute knowing debate, therefore, requires an account of how my interpretation of the relational dimension in absolute knowing compares to the various ways in which the participants in this debate have interpreted the relationality of absolute knowing.

According to Flay, absolute knowing is a mutually determining dynamic between the unity and duality of a relation, with the duality conceived as the subjectivity of knowing and the objective reality of what it knows. According to Flay, therefore, the relatedness of knowing and known establishes an otherness that differentiates them, and the difference between knowing and known determines the way they are related. My analysis of absolute knowing finds a similar dynamic in the unification-diversification dynamic between the beautiful soul and conscientious action. In the conscientiousness of the beautiful soul, pure knowing operates as the unifying spirit of the community, isolated in the subjectivity of mutual acceptance and recognition, negating the diversification of the communal spirit in the self-focused concerns of conscientious action. In conscientious action, pure knowing operates as a communal spirit identified with the exclusive singularity of its members, engaged in appropriating the concrete realities of the objective world, thereby negating the detachment that preserves the undisturbed at-oneness of the beautiful soul. Confession and forgiveness

38 See chapter 17, §5–6.

acknowledge the legitimacy of the negations that separate each form of spirit from the other while also recognizing that true universality requires their necessary relation to each other. The related factors in this dynamic are not the differences themselves, but the unity of the relational system related to the diversity of the relational system.

According to my interpretation, however, the unification-diversification dynamic cannot stand alone as Flay suggests. In this dynamic, no member of the relational system identifies the whole, not even the unity that operates within the system, since each member is not the others. Even the unifying beautiful soul is other than and defined in relation to the diversifying conscientiousness of action. In order to become conscious of the wholeness of the whole, the selfsameness that persists throughout the relations must be distinguished from the limited character of its various participants, even if this distinction must also be cancelled so that the various participants can be and be known to be the same whole distinguished from itself.[39]

6 THIRD RESPONSE: THE OTHERNESS OF SUBJECT AND OBJECT

The disagreement between Flay and Lumsden shifts the focus of the absolute knowing debate to the relational otherness of the participants in the relation. Flay insists that objective reality operates as an independent factor in the knowing relation, which seems to support the claim that the object brings its own independent determinations to the dynamic between itself and the knowing subject. Lumsden seems to disagree with this interpretation. According to Lumsden, the same conceptual conditions determine both the thinking subject and the object of its thinking. Moreover, Lumsden's interpretation gives the subjectivity of thought the dominant role in defining the relation between knower and known. The object has no other determinations than those that make it intelligible to a knower.

Devos and Burbidge are on Flay's side of this disagreement; and they add to Flay's general claim an explicit account of how the independent otherness of objective reality operates in absolute knowing. They interpret absolute knowing as a form of action. Action transfers the thought of absolute knowing into conditions alien to thought: the contingencies of space and time; the *de facto* status of what just happens to be the case; unexpected consequences brought into play by nature and by the decisions of other agents. Burbidge calls this release into the unexpected an inevitable consequence of action. Both Devos and Burbidge claim that the contingency

39 See chapter 17.

factor belongs to the necessities of absolute knowing's truth concept. My analysis of absolute knowing supports all these claims by highlighting earlier moves in the *Phenomenology* that determine and justify the role of the contingency factor in absolute knowing.

The contingency factor appears in a necessary role as early as the examination of perception. The account of the perception dialectic demonstrates that the structure of the self-identity dynamic is the true essence of the perceptual object. Self-identity, however, cannot be perceived unless its dynamic structure exists in contingent arrangements of particular properties. Indeed the examination of perception explicitly argues against the possibility of reducing the perceptual object to a general form. Without the given particulars, perception cannot perceive the difference between each perceived thing and hence cannot perceive the self-identity that perception takes the truth to be. The self-identity structure requires its embeddedness in a given set of distinguishing properties without determining exactly which properties in what arrangements different things must have. The determinate negation of perception also exposes the way self-identity belongs to a separation and relation dynamic that integrates the field of perceptual objects into a connected system. These connections appear in perception as contrast relations between particular sets of properties, which transforms the perceptual field into a space-time continuum. The same form-content ambiguities persist in understanding. Again and again understanding must simply accept given arrangements of particulars as carriers of law-governed connections: in the play of forces, in the specific determinations of determinate laws, in the content of simple force.[40]

Self-consciousness experiences the independence of the objective life system as a spatio-temporal element that provides a continuum or context outside the self to which individual organisms belong, in which they find life support, and into which they become absorbed in death. The particularity dimension of the contingency issue appears in self-consciousness as desire, which can experience the world as its own only by repeatedly satisfying particular desires related to different resources derived from the independent operations of the objective system.[41] In the dynamics of scepticism, Hegel emphasizes the way thought loses itself in the contingencies and instability of the objective life world (*PhG* 120–1/M ¶205). The random character of space-time becomes explicit in unhappy consciousness. When unhappy consciousness knows its truth as unchangeable thought identified with the

40 See chapter 12, §2–3.

41 See chapter 12, §4; chapter 13, §1.

conditions of human self-consciousness, it takes this truth to be another singular self separated from the human self by belonging to a long ago, far away time and space (*PhG* 123–4/M ¶212). For unhappy consciousness, the thought and life of human self-consciousness belongs to the randomness of a particular time and place.[42]

The *Phenomenology* explicitly formulates the contingency issue in idealism and reason as observation. The transition from self-consciousness to reason brings the independence of the object back to an essential role in what the truth is. Reason expects the truth to be the same rationality governing the independence of pure thought and the independence of the objective world. When, however, idealism thinks the forms of pure thinking, it finds these entangled in particulars not determined by or corresponding to the structures of the thinking subject. This shows that these determinations belong not to the thinking subject but to the alien otherness of a thing-in-itself.[43] Reason as observation addresses the issue again when it cannot find a necessary law operating in the way particular functions are associated with others in the life of an organism. Nor can it find laws determining the relation between the inner and outer particulars of the self. Hegel explicitly calls this contingent element the "irrational" and "concept-less"; and he says that the irrational element belongs to nature's independence. The contingently given arrangement of particulars identifies the natural element's independence of its relation to a knower; and reason expects the independence of the objective world to be an essential factor in what rationality is. Hence, rationality is reconceived as the rational structures of pure thought identified with the irrational dimension of objective existence.[44]

In the examination of practical reason, the contingency element becomes explicit again in the analysis of self-confident individuality. The rational agent's action loses its coherence in contingent connections between its purpose, means, and accomplished work. Reason as lawgiver loses the necessity of law in the contingency of its content, and the necessary self-sameness of law cannot become real without becoming identified with this content.[45] In the examination of spirit, the contingency element appears first as the contingencies of birth and gender that compromise the integrity of a social world dependent on naturally given family lineage for its unity.[46]

42 See chapter 13, §5.
43 See chapter 13, §7.
44 See chapter 14, §1.
45 See chapter 14, §6–8.
46 See chapter 15, §1.

The contingency element appears again in the moral view of the world. The moral view takes the truth to be the moral subject's pure thought of duty, which lets both nature and the natural determinations of the self go free. The moral purity of the thinking self implicitly abandons the natural element, lets it go its own way indifferent to what morality requires of it.[47]

In the determinate negation of conscientiousness and in the account of revealed religion, the *Phenomenology* finally reaches a form of knowing that explicitly acknowledges the intransigence of natural existence as a necessary factor in what it expects the truth to be. In the spirit of conscientiousness, objective reality persists as something set off from and opposed to the human self because its natural contingencies cannot be completely absorbed into the thought structures of the human subject. The moral subject acts in this world in order to transform the world's otherness into another dimension of the self's own universal truth, since for the moral view only the universality of the self counts as the truth of the world itself and other self-conscious individuals. Action, however, compromises the universality of the moral subject. Action requires a self committed to a particular project carried out in a world shared by other agents. Hence, the self must bring its universal concern for what is right into the particulars of the self's interests and talents and the particular circumstances given in the field of action. As a result, the action takes on the form of the agent's exclusive being-for-self, since it satisfies this self's interests, favours this self with the sense of accomplishment, focuses the circumstances of the objective world on this self's concerns. If, however, the moral subject refuses to get involved in the compromises of the objective world, then it lets the world go free and fails to claim the world for moral purposes.

In confession and forgiveness, each side of this dilemma acknowledges the other as different from and yet necessary to itself. The harmonious at-oneness of the communal spirit, whose reality is limited to the intersubjective speech of mutual acceptance and recognition, acknowledges that engagement in the singularity of individual agents and in the contingent particulars of their projects is a necessary condition of spirit's existence as an independent, substantial world. Thus, the universality of thinking subjects loses its dominance, and the independent reality of natural existence becomes an equally essential factor in what the truth is. So also, the communal spirit surrendered into the independence conditions of the objective world acknowledges that the singular self's conscientious concerns and

47 See chapter 15, §6.

projects belong to a spirit and fellowship not limited to this self's interests and causes, not even to this self's nation or time in history.[48]

Revealed religion, whose truth expectations are justified by the determinate negation of conscientiousness, represents absolute spirit as a self-sameness of thought and being in which the opposites of the human world – spirit and nature, good and evil – are reconciled.[49] Absolute knowing brings this representation of absolute spirit back to the dynamics of conscientiousness. In this transformation of conscientiousness, nature persists as a pure negative that nevertheless is, as a world whose being necessarily retains a not-spirit character. In absolute knowing, the conscientious subject knows itself identified with the cause of absolute truth working itself out in history, knows its action motivated by this cause, and knows that the cause becomes a real world, a real community of spirit, only when real individuals act on it. Absolute knowing knows, too, that action inevitably realizes the truth in the circumstantial givenness of space-time, the ever changing contingencies of the natural world, the tangle of individually determined decisions and purposes, the unpredictable outcomes of human inventiveness, the surprising ways in which humans respond and adjust to each other, to the world, to their heritage, to the challenges of an unknown future. Without the self's engagement in these contingencies, the truth becomes an empty, unrealized concept.[50]

This interpretation of absolute knowing's relationality supports the interpretations offered by both Devos and Burbidge without completely rejecting Lumsden's interpretation. According to Devos, absolute knowing acts in a world full of contingencies in order to make sense of it, whereas Burbidge speaks of the action as absolute knowing letting itself go, surrendering to the world's contingency conditions. Absolute knowing "makes sense" of the world by inventing ways of configuring the world's contingent particulars so that they become integrated into the human spirit's absolute truth project. The human agent, motivated by the cause of absolute truth, transforms the alien otherness of natural existence into materials for actualizing the spirit of truth in the reality conditions of an independent substantial world. In order to achieve this, however, the rational subject must be willing to lose the clean, uncluttered form of its thinking in the messiness of the world's superfluous particulars and to accept the irrationality of these particulars as the nothingness, the not-being-spirit, required for a world able to sustain

48 See chapter 15, §7–9; chapter 16, §1.

49 See chapter 16, §4–5.

50 See chapter 17, §5–6.

its independent existence and not get lost in the subjectivity, or even intersubjectivity, and the thinking self.

Lumsden's interpretation seems at first to be very different from the Devos-Burbidge position, because Lumsden emphasizes the sameness of the conditions that determine both the thinking subject and the object of this thinking. Lumsden insists, however, that these conditions are determined by the realities of social-historical existence. In absolute knowing, the thinking subject knows that the subject's way of thinking and the object's way of being have been formed by the same social-historical conditions. If Lumsden is willing to acknowledge that the contingent, the unexpected, the circumstantial givenness of space-time belong to these conditions, then his interpretation seems to differ from the Devos-Burbidge position only in its emphasis. It retains, however, one significant difference that distinguishes it from the Devos-Burbidge interpretation and my own. Lumsden says repeatedly that the object has no other determinations than those that make it intelligible to a knower. Devos and Burbidge call attention to the radical otherness of nature, which is spiritless, without self-consciousness, opaque, and according to Burbidge, beyond thought's "capacity for appropriation."[51] My interpretation finds Hegel talking about the natural element as irrational, without concept. According to Devos, Burbidge, and myself, therefore, the natural element retains a whole host of conditions that make it unintelligible to a knower; and these conditions are the inevitable conditions in which action must achieve its purposes.[52]

7 FOURTH RESPONSE: THE OTHERNESS OF SELF AND SELF

Williams offers an interpretation of absolute knowing that focuses exclusively on the relation between one self-conscious individual and another, without discussing the role of the natural element in this relation. According to Williams, absolute knowing preserves within its relation the independent integrity of each self without reducing the relation to a mere attachment belonging to an isolated self indifferent to others. The relation preserves the true otherness of each self while keeping different individuals involved with each other. Williams applies this analysis to confession and forgiveness in Hegel's account of conscience. As an interpretation of absolute knowing, however, the analysis needs a more careful account of confession and forgiveness, as well as explicit attention to the role of the natural element

51 Burbidge (1998), 11.
52 See especially chapter 18, §2.

in the dynamics of conscientiousness. Absolute knowing preserves the form of conscientiousness transformed by confession and forgiveness and by the determinate negation of revealed religion. Hence, the interpretation of absolute knowing must remain faithful to the way conscientiousness has been determined by the sequence of determinate negations that precede it in the *Phenomenology*, by the way the determinate negation of conscientiousness determines the function of confession and forgiveness, and by the way the determinate negation of revealed religion exposes the full meaning of this negation.

In this context, conscience has the form of spirit. As such, it identifies the shared truth criterion of a society or culture. Each member of the community expects to recognize in the others his or her own conscientious spirit. The participants in confession and forgiveness, therefore, belong to the same spirit. The otherness that sets them apart belongs to the truth criterion that unites them.[53] The conscientious agent must confess the hypocrisy of the agent's action because the inter-subjective universality of conscientiousness requires it. The self-focused, self-interested structure of action betrays the shared spirit of the community. It appears as an exclusive preoccupation with the agent's own causes, concerns, and sense of accomplishment, and hence does not show the universal conscientiousness the agent's speech claims for it. So also the beautiful soul must forgive the compromises of conscientious action because the reality required of conscientiousness requires it. The spirit of conscientiousness cannot become the universal truth of a social world if it does not get involved in the realities of objective existence and the particulars of each member's distinctive character. The participants in confession and forgiveness, therefore, do not allow the other "to generate its own criteria and categories," as Williams claims.[54] Each form of conscientiousness acknowledges the opposite form of conscientiousness as a necessity that belongs to the truth criterion that they share.[55]

If, however, we shift the analysis proposed by Williams to the dynamics of conscientious action, and if we pay attention to the role of the natural element in these dynamics, the analysis exposes more interesting possibilities for the way self-to-self relations belong to absolute knowing. Conscientious action needs forgiveness because it surrenders the shared spirit of the community into conditions that work against the unifying spirit of the moral

53 For another defense of this claim, see di Giovanni (1995b).
54 Williams (1998), 97.
55 See chapter 15, §7; chapter 16, §1.

fellowship. The conscientious agent acts with the authority and legitimacy of the communal spirit. Yet action inserts this universal spirit into the being-for-self separation and relation dynamics of the singular self. And the singular self, like the perceived thing, must play out its self-identity structure in the given particulars of the individual's properties related to the particulars given in the relational field. These given particulars constitute the natural element in conscientious action; and this element manifests the objective world's independence of its relation to the subjectivity of the conscious self. Conscientiousness preserves the dominance of moral subjectivity by confessing and forgiving the natural element for the sake of the conscientiousness manifested in it. Since, however, it cannot give itself objective existence without getting involved in this element, the independence and absolute, irrational otherness of the natural element belongs to the determinate negation that determines the shift into the concept of religion, and becomes an explicit element in the dynamics of revealed religion. The death of the spirit, accomplished in the determinate negation of revealed religion, surrenders the selfsameness of absolute spirit into the opposition dynamic between the human spirit and the natural element, so that absolute knowing must acknowledge both the human spirit and the irrational element that stands opposed to it as the same absolute spirit distinguished from itself. Absolute knowing acknowledges that moral subjectivity belongs to a larger purpose. The human spirit must do more than touch the natural element with its intentions. The human spirit must live in the independence conditions of the objective world as well as in the subjectivity and intersubjectivity of self-consciousness.

How, then, does this affect the self to self relations of absolute knowing? It identifies the source of another self's otherness. It exposes the stubborn resistance of this otherness. It gives this resistant otherness an absolute claim on those who belong to absolute spirit's truth project. Each self has a natural element different from others. Each self forms its own and the world's particulars according to this self's opportunities and choices. Even if each person acknowledges that his or her project belongs to the same spirit of truth, the realization of this truth requires its translation into a particular content that the shared concept of truth does not determine. Individual agents acting in a world shared with other agents must invent and negotiate ways of giving the truth reality in the random, unexpected, circumstantial fabric of natural existence. Williams talks about letting the other self go free within the self's relation to the other. Hegel talks about thought letting nature go free, letting it be what does not completely conform to what thought expects of it. I am saying here that nature, in the natural world and in the natural constitution of the self, is the source of the otherness that Williams is talking about. We let others pursue their own interests and concerns, form their own opinions, devise their own ways of serving the cause of truth because absolute spirit cannot be a truly universal spirit if it does not live in this diversity; and we cannot be true to our own spiritual ground if we do not acknowledge the radical difference of others as another version of our own spirit.

Williams also says that the relational otherness of absolute knowing involves "a refusal to impose any scheme of its own on the object," that it does not create the world but "fits us into the world."[56] This way of speaking, in my judgment, must be qualified. I agree with the Devos-Burbidge interpretation when it interprets absolute knowing as a human knowing that takes upon itself the task of the concept that defines absolute truth. The concept of truth imposes certain norms and expectations: recognition of the fundamentally social character of the human spirit; preservation of free individuality within social existence; commitment to the spirit of human history, which involves acknowledging our responsibility to the past, to the future, to our own cultural spirit and that of others; the call to be rational in our thinking and in our acting; the willingness to take on the task of devising with others ways of letting our rationality become realized and embodied in the non-rational conditions of natural existence. Absolute knowing, therefore, has a scheme of its own. This scheme identifies thought with reality conditions opposed to the dependable, rationally ordered structures of the thinking subject. But the aim is to transform these reality conditions into vehicles, embodiments, of thought structures, and in the process transform thought into the independent existence of an objective world. I would say, therefore, that absolute knowing both creates the world and fits us into the world. By acting for absolute spirit, absolute knowing creates the world as a world belonging to this spirit. In the process, however, it must fit the norms and expectations of the rational spirit into the non-rational conditions of natural existence.

8 CONCLUSION

When, therefore, a knower enters Hegel's *Logic* by way of the *Phenomenology*, he or she takes a stand on two all-important questions: what is truth, and what does the truth require of me. In the transition from experience to philosophy, Hegel shows us that we belong to the truth aspirations of the

56 Williams (1998), 97–9. See also 91.

human spirit and exposes our involvement in something bigger than ourselves, our culture and heritage, our time in history. This challenges us to do our part not just by becoming engaged in conscientious causes but also by a disciplined thinking that brings to consciousness the full complexity of humanity's truth project. In the process of making his case, Hegel mentions repeatedly the responsibility imposed by our engagement in truth pursuits. A truth claim must demonstrate its truth both by proving its claim to other minds and by showing its truth in the realities of human experience. In order to accomplish the truth, we must think it correctly and realistically. In order to think the truth correctly, we must question everything, prove everything, including accepted ways of making a case, established prejudices for or against certain ways of thinking or acting, cherished social norms, accepted philosophical principles. In order to think the truth realistically, we must test every concept by examining the conditions of its realization. These are the lessons we can learn from a study of Hegel's *Phenomenology of Spirit* and its relation to philosophy.

Bibliography

THE WORKS OF G.W.F. HEGEL

Critical Edition

Gesammelte Werke, Rheinisch-Westfälischen Akademie der Wissenschaften and Hegel-Archiv der Ruhr-Universität Bochum. Hamburg: Felix Meiner, 1968ff.

German Editions of Particular Works

Differenz des Fichte'schen und Schelling'schen Systems der Philosophie (1801). In *Gesammelte Werke*, Band 4, *Jenaer Kritische Schriften*, edited by Hartmut Buchner and Otto Pöggeler. (1968).

Enzyklopädie der Philosophischen Wissenschaften im Grundrisse (1830). In *Gesammelte Werke*, Band 20, edited by Wolfgang Bonsiepen and Hans-Christian Lucas. (1992).

Glauben und Wissen. (1802) In *Gesammelte Werke*, Band 4, *Jenaer Kritische Schriften*, edited by Hartmut Buchner and Otto Pöggeler (1968).

Grundlinien der Philosophie des Rechts. Edited by Johannes Hoffmeister. Hamburg: Felix Meiner, 1955.

Phänomenologie des Geistes. Edited by Hans-Friedrich Wessels and Heinrich Clairmont, according to the text of *Gesammelte Werke* Band 9, edited by Wolfgang Bonsiepen and Reinhard Heede (1980), Hamburg: Felix Meiner, 1988.

Vorlesungen über die Beweise vom Dasein Gottes. In *Gesammelte Werke*, Band 18, *Vorlesungsmanuskripte II (1816–1831)*, edited by Walter Jaeschke (1995), 228–317.

Wissenschaft der Logik: Die Lehre vom Sein. (1832) Edited by Hans-Jürgen Gawoll, according to the text of *Gesammelte Werke* Band 21, edited by F. Hogemann and W. Jaeschke (1985). Hamburg: Felix Meiner, 1990.

Wissenschaft der Logik: Die Lehre vom Begriff. (1816) Edited by Hans-Jürgen Gawoll, according to the text of *Gesammelte Werke* Band 12, edited by Friedrich Hogemann and Walter Jaeschke (1981). Hamburg: Felix Meiner, 1994.

English Translations

The Difference Between Fichte's and Schelling's System of Philosophy. Translated by H.S. Harris and Walter Cerf. Albany: SUNY Press, 1977.

Elements of the Philosophy of Right. Edited by Allen W. Wood. Translated by H.B. Nisbet Cambridge & New York: Cambridge University Press, 1991.

Encyclopedia of the Philosophical Sciences in Basic Outline, Part I: Science of Logic. Translated by Klaus Brinkmann and Daniel O. Dahlstrom. Cambridge & New York: Cambridge University Press, 2010.

The Encyclopaedia Logic. Translated by T.F. Geraets, W.A. Suchting, H.S. Harris. Indianapolis & Cambridge: Hackett, 1991

Hegel's Philosophy of Nature. Translated by A.V. Miller. Oxford: Clarendon Press, 1970.

Faith and Knowledge. Translated by H.S. Harris and Walter Cerf. Albany: SUNY Press, 1977.

Lectures on the Proofs of the Existence of God. Edited and translated by Peter C. Hodgson Oxford: Clarendon Press, 2007.

Hegel's Phenomenology of Spirit. Translated by A.V. Miller. Oxford & New York: Oxford University Press, 1977.

The Phenomenology of Mind. Translated by J.B. Baillie. New York & Evanston: Harper and Row, 1967.

Hegel's Science of Logic. Translated by A.V. Miller. London: Allen and Unwin; New York: Humanities Press, 1969.

The Science of Logic. Translated by George di Giovanni. Cambridge: Cambridge University Press, 2010.

GENERAL BIBLIOGRAPHY

Allison, Henry E. 1983. *Kant's Transcendental Idealism.* New Haven: Yale University Press.

Ameriks, Karl. 1987. "Hegelian Critique of Kantian Morality." In *New Essays on Kant,* edited by Bernard den Ouden and Marcia Moen. New York: Peter Lang, 179–212.

Aquinas, Thomas. 1961–67. *Summa Contra Gentiles,* Textus Leoninus. Rome: Maretti.

– 1955–57. *On the Truth of the Catholic Faith.* Garden City: Doubleday.

Beiser, Frederick C., ed. 1993. *The Cambridge Companion to Hegel.* Cambridge & New York: Cambridge University Press.

Bernasconi, Robert. 1999. "'We Philosophers': *Barbaros medeis eisito.*" In *Endings: Questions of Memory in Hegel and Heidegger,* edited by Rebecca Comay and John McCumber. Evanston: Northwestern University Press, 77–96.

Bernstein, Jay M. 1994. "Conscience and Transgression: The Persistence of Misrecognition." *Bulletin of the Hegel Society of Great Britain* 29: 55–70.

– 1996. "Confession and forgiveness: Hegel's poetics of action," In *Beyond Representation: Philosophy and Poetic Imagination,* edited by Richard Eldridge. Cambridge: Cambridge University Press, 34–65.

Braun, H. 1968. "Zur Interpretation der Hegelschen Wendung: frei entlassen." In *Hegel, l'esprit objectif, l'unité de l'histoire,* actes du II-me congres international de l'association pour l'étude de la philosophie de Hegel, (Lille), 51–64.

Burbidge, John. 1981. *On Hegel's* Logic: *Fragments of a Commentary.* Atlantic Highlands: Humanities Press.

– 1992. *Hegel on Logic and Religion: The Reasonableness of Christianity.* Albany: SUNY Press.

– 1997. "Hegel's Absolutes," *The Owl of Minerva* 29, no. 1: 23–37.

– 1998. "Absolute Acting," *The Owl of Minerva* 30, no. 1: 103–18.

– 2001–02. "Secondness," *The Owl of Minerva* 33, no. 1: 27–39.

– 2002–03. "Chemism and Chemistry," *The Owl of Minerva* 34, no. 1: 3–17.

– 2003. "The 'Infinite Agony' of Spirit," *The Owl of Minerva* 34, no. 2: 171–86.

– 2006. *The Logic of Hegel's* Logic. Peterborough: Broadview Press.

– 2007. *Hegel's Systematic Contingency.* Basingstoke: Palgrave-Macmillan.

Chiereghin, Franco. 1984. "Hegels Konzeption der Wahrheit als Ganzes." In *Hegel's Logik der Philosophie: Religion und Philosophie in der Theorie des absoluten Geistes,* edited by Dieter Henrich und Rolf-Peter Horstmann. Stuttgart: Klett-Cotta, 213–23.

– 1994. *La Fenomenologia dello spirito di Hegel: Introduzione alla lettura.* Roma: La Nuova Italia Scientifica.

– 2003. "Principio e inizio in Hegel." In Ruggiu and Testa, 523–43.

Claesges, Ulrich. 1981. *Darstellung des Erscheinenden Wissens: Systematische Einleitung in Hegels* Phänomenologie des Geistes. *Hegel-Studien,* Beiheft 21. Bonn: Bouvier.

Collins, Ardis B., ed. 1995. *Hegel on the Modern World.* Albany: SUNY Press.

Collins, Ardis B. 1982. "Hegel's Redefinition of the Critical Project." In M. Westphal, ed. (1982), 1–14.

– 1989. Commentary on Carl Vaught's "Hegel and the Problem of Difference." In Desmond, ed. (1989), 49–55.

– 1990. "Contradiction and Relations: Hegel and the Tradition," *American Catholic Philosophical Quarterly* LXIV, no. 4: 509–41.

– 2000a. "Hegel's Unresolved Contradiction: Experience, Philosophy, and the Irrationality of Nature," *Dialogue: A Canadian Philosophical Journal* XXXIX: 771–96.
– 2000b. "Hegel on Citizenship, Language, and the Educational Function of the Workplace: Answering the Marxist Challenge," *The Owl of Minerva* 32, no. 1: 21–43.
– 2001a. "Justification and Time in Hegel's *Phenomenology*," *Bulletin of the Hegel Society of Great Britain* 43/44: 15–43.
– 2001b. "Hegel's Critical Appropriation of Kantian Morality." In *Beyond Liberalism and Communitarianism: Studies in Hegel's* Philosophy of Right, edited by Robert R. Williams. Albany: SUNY Press, 21–39.
– 2002. "The Role of Religion in Hegel's Epistemology." *Bulletin of the Hegel Society of Great Britain* 45/46: 36–55.
– 2003a. "Il ruolo del linguaggio nella critica hegeliana della conoscenza (The Role of Language in Hegel's Critique of Knowledge)." Translated by Andrea Sartori and Elisabetta Terzariol. In Ruggiu and Testa (2003), 373–99.
– 2003b. "The Task and Method of Hegel's *Phenomenology*." Review Article on Michael Forster's *Hegel's Idea of a* Phenomenology of Spirit (Chicago & London: University of Chicago Press, 1989), *Bulletin of the Hegel Society of Great Britain* 47/48, 72–87.
– 2006. "Work, Language, and Community: A Response to Hegel's Critics." In *The New Hegelians: Politics and Philosophy in the Hegelian School*, edited by Douglas Moggach. Cambridge & New York: Cambridge University Press, 275–99.
Comay, Rebecca. 2011. *Mourning Sickness: Hegel and the French Revolution*. Stanford: Stanford University Press.
Crites, Stephen. 1998. *Dialectic and Gospel in the Development of Hegel's Thinking*. University Park: The Pennsylvania State University Press.
– 2001–02. "Notes on *Hegel's Ladder*," *The Owl of Minerva* 33, no. 1: 97–105.
– 2002. "Harris's Escalator," *International Studies in Philosophy* 34, no. 4: 147–54.
Dahlstrom, Daniel O. 1981. "Hegel's Principia." *New Scholasticism* 55: 421–37.
– 2006–07. "Challenges to the Rational Observation of Nature." *The Owl of Minerva* 38, nos 1–2: 35–56.
– 2008. *Philosophical Legacies: Essays on the Thought of Kant, Hegel, and Their Contemporaries*. Washington: The Catholic University of America Press.
Deligiorgi, Katerina, ed. 2006. *Hegel: New Directions*. Montreal: McGill-Queen's University Press.
Denker, Alfred and Michael Vater, ed. 2003. *Hegel's* Phenomenology of Spirit. Amherst: Humanity Books.
De Nys, Martin J. 1982. "Force and Understanding: the Unity of the Object of Consciousness." In M. Westphal, ed. (1982), 57–70.

– 1995. "Self-consciousness and the Concept in Hegel's Appropriation of Kant." In Collins, ed. (1995), 148–53.

Descartes, René. 1964–76. *Meditationes de Prima Philosophiae* (*Meditations on First Philosophy*). In *Oeuvres de Descartes*, edited by Ch. Adam and P. Tannery. Vol. VII Paris: L. Cerf.

Desmond, William, ed. 1989. *Hegel and His Critics: Philosophy in the Aftermath of Hegel.* Albany: SUNY Press.

Desmond, William. 2003. *Hegel's God: A Counterfeit Double?* Aldershot Hants & Burlington: Ashgate.

Devos, Rob. 1998. "How Absolute is Hegel's Absolute Knowing?" *The Owl of Minerva* 30, no. 1: 33–50.

Di Giovanni, George. 1992. "The Category of Contingency in the Hegelian Logic." In *Selected Essays on G. W. F. Hegel,* edited by L. Stepelevich. Humanities Press, 41–59.

– 1993. "Reflection and Contradiction: A Commentary on Some Passages of Hegel's *Science of Logic*." In *G.W.F. Hegel: Critical Assessments,* IV vols, edited by Robert Stern. Vol. III, No. 68. London: Routledge.

– 1995a. "Hegel's *Phenomenology* and the Critique of the Enlightenment: An Essay in Interpretation," *Laval théologique et philosophique* 51, no. 2: 251–70.

– 1995b. "Hegel, Jacobi, and 'Crypto-Catholicism' or Hegel in Dialogue with the Enlightenment." In Collins, ed. (1995), 53–72.

– 1997. "Review of *Hegel: Phenomenology and System* by H.S. Harris." *The Owl of Minerva* 29, no. 1: 91–5.

– 2003. "Faith without Religion, Religion without Faith: Kant and Hegel on Religion." *Journal of the History of Philosophy* 41: 365–83.

– 2005. *Freedom and Religion in Kant and His Immediate Successors: The Vocation of Humankind, 1774–1800.* Cambridge & New York: Cambridge University Press.

– 2009a. "Religion, History, and Spirit in Hegel's *Phenomenology of Spirit*." In K. Westphal (2009a), 226–45.

– 2009b. "Jewish and Post-Christian Interpretations of Hegel: Emil Fackenheim and Henry S. Harris," *The Owl of Minerva* 40, no. 2: 221–37.

Di Giovanni, George and H.S. Harris, trans. 1985. *Between Kant and Hegel: Texts in the Development of Post-Kantian Idealism.* Albany: SUNY Press.

Dove, Kenley. 1982. "Phenomenology and Systematic Philosophy." In M.Westphal, ed. (1982), 27–40.

Dudley, Will. 2002–03. "Systematic Philosophy and Idealism," *The Owl of Minerva* 34, no. 1: 91–105.

– 2003–04. "Impure Reason: Hegel on the Irrationality of the Rational." *The Owl of Minerva* 34, nos 1–2: 25–48.

– 2004–05. "The Systematic Context and Structure of Hegel's Social Theory: A Response to Frederick Neuhouser," *The Owl of Minerva* 36, no. 1: 3–14.
– 2008. "Ethical life, morality, and the role of spirit in the *Phenomenology of Spirit*." In Moyar and Quante, eds (2008), 130–49.
Dulckeit, Katharina. 1998. "Can Hegel Refer to Particulars?" In Stewart (1998), 105–21.
– 1986. "Can Hegel Refer to Particulars?" *The Owl of Minerva* 17, no. 2: 181–94.
Fackenheim, Emil L. 1996. *The God Within: Kant, Schelling, and Historicity*. Edited by John Burbidge. Toronto: University of Toronto Press.
Feldman, Karen S. 2006. *Binding Words: Conscience and Rhetoric in Hobbes, Hegel, and Heidegger*. Evanston: Northwestern University Press.
Ferrini, Cinzia. 2009a. "The Challenge of Reason: From Certainty to Truth." In K.Westphal, ed. (2009a), 72–91.
– 2009b. "Reason Observing Nature," in K. Westphal (2009a), 92–135.
Fichte, Johann. 1981. *Die Bestimmung des Menschen* (1800). In Johann Gottlieb Fichte, I. *Werke,* Band 6, Werke 1799–1800, edited by Reinhard Lauth and Hans Gliwitzky. Stuttgart-Bad Cannstatt: Friedrich Frommann.
– 1987. *The Vocation of Man,* trans. Peter Preuss. Indianapolis & Cambridge: Hackett.
Flay, Joseph C. 1970. "Hegel's 'Inverted World,'" *The Review of Metaphysics* XXIII: no. 4, 662–78.
– 1984. *Hegel's Quest for Certainty*. Albany: SUNY Press.
– 1993. "Hegel's Metaphysics," *The Owl of Minerva* 24, no. 2: 145–52.
– 1998. "Absolute Knowing and the Absolute Other," *The Owl of Minerva* 30, no. 1: 69–82.
– 1998. "Hegel's 'Inverted World,'" in Stewart (1998), 138–52.
Fleischhacker, Louk. 1990. "Gibt es etwas Außer der Äußerlichkeit? Über die Bedeutung der Veräußerlichung der Idee." In *Hegel-Jahrbuch 1990,* edited by H. Kimmerle, W. Lefèvre, R. W. Meyer, Bochum: Germinal, 35–41.
Forster, Michael N. 1998. *Hegel's Idea of a Phenomenology of Spirit.* Chicago & London: University of Chicago Press.
Friedman, R.Z. 1986. "Hypocrisy and the Highest Good: Hegel on Kant's Transition from Morality to Religion." *Journal of the History of Philosophy* XXIV, no. 4: 503–22.
Fulda, Hans and Dieter Henrich, ed. 1998. *Materialien zu Hegels* Phänomenologie des Geistes. Frankfurt am Main: Suhrkamp.
Fulda, Hans Friedrich. 1965. *Das Problem einer Einleitung in Hegels* Wissenschaft der Logik. Frankfurt am Main: Vittorio Klostermann.
– 1998. "Zur Logik der *Phänomenologie* von 1807." In Fulda and Henrich, eds (1998), 391–425.

– 2008. "Science of the *Phenomenology of Spirit*: Hegel's program and its implementation." In Moyar and Quante, eds (2008), 21–42.

Gaarder, Jostein. 1996. *Sophie's World: A Novel About the History of Philosophy.* Translated by Pauline Moller. New York: Berkeley Books.

Gadamer, Hans-Georg. 1976. *Hegel's Dialectic: Five Hermeneutical Studies.* Translated by P. Christopher Smith. New Haven & London: Yale University Press.

Guyer, Paul. 1993. "Thought and Being: Hegel's Critique of Kant's Theoretical Philosophy." In Beiser, 171–210.

Habermas, Jürgen. 1990. *Morality and Communicative Consciousness.* Cambridge: Polity Press.

Halper, Edward C. 2002–03. "The Idealism of Hegel's System." *The Owl of Minerva* 34, no. 1: 19–58.

Harris, H. S. 1994. *Hegel: Phenomenology and System.* Indianapolis & Cambridge: Hackett.

– 1997. *Hegel's Ladder.* Indianapolis & Cambridge: Hackett. Two Volumes.

Hartnack, Justus. 1987. "Categories and Things-in-themselves." In Priest, ed. (1987), 77–86.

Henrich, Dieter. 1971. "Hegels über den Zufall." In *Hegel im Kontext,* edited by Dieter Henrich. Frankfurt am Main: Suhrkamp, 157–86.

Heinrichs, Johannes. 1974. *Die Logik der* Phänomenologie des Geistes. Bonn: Bouvier.

Hoff, Shannon. 2006–07. "Restoring Antigone to Ethical Life: Nature and Sexual Difference in Hegel's *Phenomenology of Spirit.*" *The Owl of Minerva* 38, nos 1–2: 77–99.

Hoffheimer, Michael H. 2001. "Translating *Knechtschaft.*" *The Owl of Minerva* 32, no. 2: 169–75.

Houlgate, Stephen. 1991. "Thought and Being in Kant and Hegel." *The Owl of Minerva* 22, no. 2: 131–40.

– 1993. "A Reply to Joseph C. Flay's 'Hegel's Metaphysics.'" *The Owl of Minerva* 24, no. 2: 153–61.

– 1994. "Hegel and Fichte: Recognition, Otherness, and Absolute Knowing." *The Owl of Minerva* 26, no. 1: 3–19.

– 1995. "Necessity and Contingency in Hegel's *Science of Logic.*" *The Owl of Minerva* 27, no. 1: 37–49.

– 1998. "Absolute Knowing Revisited." *The Owl of Minerva* 30, no. 1: 51–67.

– 2002–03. "Logic and Nature in Hegel's Philosophy: A Response to John Burbidge." *The Owl of Minerva* 34, no. 1: 107–25.

– 2006. *The Opening of Hegel's* Logic*: From Being to Infinity.* West Lafayette: Purdue University Press.

– 2009–10. "McDowell, Hegel, and the *Phenomenology of Spirit.*" and "Response to John McDowell." *The Owl of Minerva* 41, nos 1–2: 13–26, 39–51.

Hoy, David Couzens. 2009. "The Ethics of Freedom: Hegel on Reason as Law-Giving and Law-Testing," in K. Westphal (2009a), 153–71.

Hume, David. 1977. *An Enquiry Concerning Human Understanding.* Edited by Eric Steinberg. Indianapolis & Cambridge: Hackett.

Hyppolite, Jean. 1946. *Genèse et structure de la* Phénoménologie de l'esprit *de Hegel,* 2 vols. Paris: Aubier, Éditions Montaigne.

– 1974. *Genesis and Structure of Hegel's* Phenomenology of Spirit. Translated by Samuel Cherniak and John Heckman. Evanston: Northwestern University Press.

Jacobi, F.H. 1787. *David Hume über den Glauben, oder Idealismus und Realismus, Ein Gespräch.* Breslau: Gottl. Löwe.

– 1994. *David Hume on Faith, or Idealism and Realism, A Dialogue.* In *The Main Philosophical Writings and the Novel* Allwill. Translated by George di Giovanni. Montreal: McGill-Queen's University Press, 253–338.

Kant, I. *Kants Werke,* Akademie Textausgabe. Berlin/New York: Walter de Gruyter.

– 1903. *Kritik der reinen Vernunft,* 1. Auflage 1781, *Kants Werke,* Band IV.

– 1904. *Kritik der reinen Vernunft,* 2. Auflage 1787, *Kants Werke,* Band III.

– 1961. *Immanuel Kant's Critique of Pure Reason.* Translated by Norman Kemp Smith. London: Macmillan and Co, Ltd; New York: St. Martin's Press.

– 1998. *Critique of Pure Reason.* Translated by Paul Guyer and Allen W. Wood. Cambridge & New York: Cambridge University Press.

Kojève, Alexandre. 1947. *Introduction à la lecture de Hegel.* Edited by Raymond Queneau. Paris: Gallimard.

– 1969. *Introduction to the Reading of Hegel.* Abridged and edited by Allan Bloom. Translated by James H. Nichols, Jr. New York & London: Basic Books, Inc

Kolb, David. 1986. *The Critique of Pure Modernity: Hegel, Heidegger, and After.* Chicago & London: University of Chicago Press.

– 2004–05. "Beyond the Pale: The Spectre of Formal Universality." *The Owl of Minerva* 36, no. 1: 15–30.

Lauer, Chris. 2006–07. "Reason at Play: The Place of Schellingian Childishness in the *Phenomenology*'s Dialectic of Reason." *The Owl of Minerva* 38, nos 1–2: 57–75.

Llewellyn, John. 1987. "Kantian Antinomy and Hegelian Dialectic." In Priest, ed. (1987), 87–102.

Lo, Ping-cheung. 1981. "A Critical Reevaluation of the Alleged 'Empty Formalism' of Kantian Ethics." *Ethics* 91: 181–201.

Locke, John. 1979. *Essay Concerning Human Understanding.* Oxford & New York: Oxford University Press.

Ludwig, Walter. 1989. "Hegel's Conception of Absolute Knowing." *The Owl of Minerva* 21, no. 1: 5–19.

– 1992. "The Method of Hegel's *Phenomenology of Spirit.*" *The Owl of Minerva* 23, no. 2: 165–75.

Lumsden, Simon. 1998. "Absolute Knowing." *The Owl of Minerva* 30, no. 1: 3–32.
– 2000. "A Subject for Hegel's Logic." *International Philosophical Quarterly* 40, no. 1: 85–99.
– 2003. "The Problem of Beginning Hegel's *Phenomenology* and *Science of Logic*." *International Studies in Philosophy* 35: 83–103.
Maker, William. 1981. "Hegel's *Phenomenology* as Introduction to Science," *Clio* 10, no. 4: 381–97
– 1982. "Does Hegel Have A 'Dialectical Method'?" *The Southern Journal of Philosophy* XX: 75–96.
– 1987. "Reason and the Problem of Modernity." *The Philosophical Forum* XVIII, no. 4: 275–303.
– 1990. "Beginning." In *Essays on Hegel's Logic*, edited by George di Giovanni, Albany: SUNY Press, 27–43.
– 1992. "Hegel's Blasphemy?" *History of Philosophy Quarterly* 9, no. 1: 67–85.
– 1994. *Philosophy Without Foundations: Rethinking Hegel.* Albany: SUNY Press.
– 2002–03. "Idealism and Autonomy." *The Owl of Minerva* 34, no. 1: 59–75.
Marx, Karl. 1968. "Auszüge aus James Mills Buch *Élémens d'économie politique*," *Geschrieben im ersten Halbjahr 1844 Nach der Handschrift.* In Karl Marx and Friedrich Engels, *Werke*, Ergänzungsband: Schriften, Manuskripte, Briefe bis 1844, Erster Teil. Berlin: Dietz.
– 1994. *Excerpt Notes of 1844.* In *Karl Marx: Selected Writings.* Edited by Lawrence H. Simon. Indianapolis & Cambridge: Hackett.
McCumber, John. 1989. *Poetic Interaction: Language, Freedom, Reason.* Chicago & London: University of Chicago Press.
– 1993. *The Company of Words: Hegel, Language, and Systematic Philosophy.* Evanston: Northwestern University Press.
McDowell, John. 2003a. "L'idealismo di Hegel come radicalizazzione di Kant." In Ruggiu and Testa, 451–77.
– 2003b. "The Apperceptive I and the Empirical Self: Towards a Heterodox Reading of 'Lordship and Bondage' in Hegel's *Phenomenology*." *Bulletin of the Hegel Society of Great Britain* 47/48: 1–16.
– 2006. "The Apperceptive I and the Empirical Self: Towards a Heterodox Reading of 'Lordship and Bondage' in Hegel's *Phenomenology*." In *Hegel: New Directions*, 33–48.
– 2009. *Having the World in View: Essays on Kant, Hegel, and Sellars.* Cambridge & London: Harvard University Press.
– 2009–10. "Response to Stephen Houlgate" and "Response to Stephen Houlgate's Response." *The Owl of Minerva* 41, nos 1–2: 27–38, 53–60.
Mendola, G. 2006. "L'impossibile immediatezza Sull'originarietà del pensiero e il ruolo della mediazione in Hegel." *Verifiche* XXXV, no. 1–2: 21–50.

Moyar, Dean and Michael Quante, eds. 2008. *Hegel's* Phenomenology of Spirit: *A Critical Guide.* Cambridge: Cambridge University Press.

Moyar, Dean. 2011. *Hegel's Conscience.* New York: Oxford University Press.

Mure, G.R.G. 1950. *A Study of Hegel's Logic.* Oxford: Clarendon Press.

Neuhouser, Frederick. 1986. "Deducing Desire and Recognition in Hegel's *Phenomenology of Spirit.*" *Journal of the History of Philosophy* 24, no. 2: 243–62.

– 2009. "Desire, Recognition, and the Relation between Bondsman and Lord." In K. Westphal, ed. (2009a), 37–54.

Nuzzo, Angelica. 1994a. "Metamorphosen der Freiheit in der Jenenser Kant-Rezeption (1785–1794)." In *Evolution des Geistes: Jena um 1800,* edited by F. Strack. Stuttgart: Klett-Cotta, 484–518.

– 1994b. "Transformations of Freedom in the Jena Kant Reception (1785–1794)." Translated by A. Bunch. *The Owl of Minerva* 32, no. 2: 135–67.

– 2003. "The Truth of *Absolutes Wissen* in Hegel's *Phenomenology of Spirit.*" In Denker and Vater, eds, 265–94.

O'Regan, Cyril. 1994. *The Heterodox Hegel.* Albany: suny Press.

– 2001–02. "The Impossibility of a Christian Reading of the *Phenomenology of Spirit*: H.S. Harris on Hegel's Liquidation of Christianity," *The Owl of Minerva* 33, no. 1: 45–95.

Peperzak, Adriaan Th. 1987. *Philosophy and Politics: A Commentary on the Preface to Hegel's* Philosophy of Right. Dordrecht & Boston & Lancaster: Martinus Nijhoff Publishers.

Pinkard, Terry. 1988. *Hegel's Dialectic: The Explanation of Possibility.* Philadelphia: Temple University Press.

– 1990. "How Kantian Was Hegel?" *Review of Metaphysics* 43: 831–38.

– 1994. *Hegel's* Phenomenology: *The Sociality of Reason.* Cambridge & New York & Melbourne: Cambridge University Press.

Pippin, Robert B. 1978. "Hegel's Metaphysics and the Problem of Contradiction." *Journal of the History of Philosophy* XVI, no. 3: 301–12.

– 1989. *Hegel's Idealism: The Satisfactions of Self-Consciousness.* Cambridge & New York & Melbourne: Cambridge University Press.

– 1990. "Hegel and Category Theory." *Review of Metaphysics* 43: 839–48.

– 1993. "You Can't Get There from Here: Transition Problems in Hegel's *Phenomenology of Spirit.*" In Beiser, ed., 52–85.

– 2005. "Brandom's Hegel." *European Journal of Philosophy* 13, no. 3: 381–408.

– 2006. "Recognition and Reconciliation: Actualized Agency in Hegel's Jena *Phenomenology.*" In Deligiorgi, ed., 125–42.

– 2011. *Hegel on Self-Consciousness: Desire and Death in the* Phenomenology of Spirit. Princeton & Oxford: Princeton University Press.

Priest, Stephen, ed. 1987. *Hegel's Critique of Kant.* Oxford: Clarendon Press.

Priest, Stephen. 1987. "Subjectivity and Objectivity in Kant and Hegel." In Priest (1987), 103–18.
Quante, Michael. 2008. "'Reason ... Apprehended Irrationally:' Hegel's Critique of Observing Reason." In Moyar and Quante, 91–111.
Robinson, Jonathan. 1977. *Duty and Hypocrisy in Hegel's* Phenomenology of Mind: *An Essay in the Real and Ideal.* Toronto: University of Toronto Press.
Rockmore, Tom. 1986. *Hegel's Circular Epistemology.* Bloomington: Indiana University Press.
Rosen, Michael. 1982. *Hegel's Dialectic and Its Criticism.* Cambridge & New York & Melbourne: Cambridge University Press.
Ruggiu, Luigi and Italo Testa, eds. 2003. *Hegel Contemporaneo: La ricezione americana di Hegel a confronto con la tradizione europea.* Napoli: Guerini e Associati.
Russon, John. 2004. *Reading Hegel's* Phenomenology. Bloomington & Indianapolis: Indiana University Press.
Sarlemijn, Andries. 1975. *Hegel's Dialectic.* Translated by Peter Kirschenmann. Dordrecht & Boston: D. Reidel.
Sartre, Jean-Paul. 1957. *L'être et le néant; essai d'ontologie phenomologique.* Paris: Gallimard.
– 1994. *Being and Nothingness.* Translated by Hazel E. Barnes. New York: Grammercy Books.
Schrader-Klebert, Karin. 1969. *Das Problem des Anfangs in Hegels Philosophie.* Wien: R. Oldenbourg KG.
Sedgwick, Sally S. 1992. "Hegel's Treatment of Transcendental Apperception in Kant." *The Owl of Minerva* 23, no. 2: 151–63.
Siep, Ludwig. 2000. *Der Weg der* Phänomenologie des Geistes: *ein einführender Kommentar zu Hegels* Differenzschrift *und zur* Phänomenologie des Geistes. Frankfurt am Main: Suhrkamp.
Silbur, John. 1974. "Procedural Formalism in Kant's Ethics," *The Review of Metaphysics* 28, no. 2: 197–236.
Speight, Allen. 2006. "Hegel on conscience and the history of moral philosophy." In Deligiorgi, ed., 17–31.
Stiehler, Gottfried. 1964. *Die Dialektik in Hegel's* Phänomenologie des Geistes. Berlin: Akademie.
Steinberger, Peter J. 1988. *Logic and Politics: Hegel's* Philosophy of Right. New Haven & London: Yale University Press.
Stern, David. 1989. "A Hegelian Critique of Reflection." In Desmond, ed., 179–90.
– 1990. "The Immanence of Thought: Hegel's Critique of Foundationalism." *The Owl of Minerva* 22, no. 1: 19–33.
Stewart, Jon, ed. 1998. *The* Phenomenology of Spirit *Reader: Critical and Interpretive Essays.* Albany: SUNY Press.

– 2000. *The Unity of Hegel's* Phenomenology of Spirit*: A Systematic Interpretation.* Evanston: Northwestern University Press.

Wallace, Robert. 2005. *Hegel's Philosophy of Reality, Freedom, and God.* Cambridge: Cambridge University Press.

– 2010–11. "True Infinity and Hegel's Rational Mysticism: A Reply to Professor Williams." *The Owl of Minerva* 42, nos 1–2: 123–35.

Walsh, W. H. 1987. "The Idea of a Critique of Pure Reason: Kant and Hegel." In Priest, ed., 119–34.

Wandschneider, Dieter. 1985/86. "Die Absolutheit des Logischen Und Das Sein der Natur." In *Zeitschrift für Philosophische Forschung,* Band. 39, Heft 3, 331–51.

– 1991. "Dialektik als Antinomische Logik." In *Hegel-Jahrbuch,* edited by Heinz Kimmerle and Wolfgang Lefèvre. Fernwald [Annerod]: Germinal, 227–42

– 1992. "Nature and the Dialectic of Nature in Hegel's Objective Idealism." *Bulletin of the Hegel Society of Great Britain* no. 26: 30–51.

Westphal, Kenneth R., ed. 2009a. *The Blackwell Guide to Hegel's* Phenomenology of Spirit. Chichester & Oxford & Malden: Wiley-Blackwell.

Westphal, Kenneth R. 1989a. *Hegel's Epistemological Realism.* Dordrecht & Boston & London: Kluwer.

– 1989b. "Hegel's Attitude Toward Jacobi in the 'Third Attitude of Thought Toward Objectivity,'" *The Southern Journal of Philosophy* XXVII, no. 1: 135–56.

– 1991. "Hegel's Critique of Kant's Moral World View." *Philosophical Topics* 19, no. 2: 133–76.

– 1992. "Dialectic (Hegel)." In *A Companion to Epistemology,* edited by E. Sosa and J. Dancy. Oxford: Blackwell, 98–9.

– 1993. "Hegel, Idealism, and Robert Pippin." *International Philosophical Quarterly,* 33, no. 3: 263–72.

– 1998a. "Hegel's Solution to the Dilemma of the Criterion." In Jon Stewart ed., 76–101.

– 1998b. "Hegel, Harris, and the Spirit of the *Phenomenology.*" *Clio* 27, no. 4: 551–72.

– 1998c. *Hegel, Hume und die Identität: wahrnehmbarer Dinge.* Frankfurt: Klostermann.

– 1999. "Hegel's Epistemology: Reflections on Some Recent Expositions," *Clio* 28, no. 3: 303–23.

– 2000a. "Hegel, Harris, and Sextus Empiricus." *The Owl of Minerva* 31, no. 2: 155–72.

– 2000b. "Is Hegel's *Phenomenology* Relevant to Contemporary Epistemology?" *Bulletin of the Hegel Society of Great Britain* 41/42: 43–85.

– 2000c. "Hegel's Internal Critique of Naïve Realism," *Journal of Philosophical Research* XXV, 173–214.

– 2003. *Hegel's Epistemology: A Philosophical Introduction to the* Phenomenology of Spirit. Indianapolis & Cambridge: Hackett.
– 2006. "Contemporary Epistemology: Kant, Hegel, McDowell." *European Journal of Philosophy* 14, no. 2: 274–301.
– 2009b. "Hegel's Phenomenological Method and Analysis of Consciousness." In K. Westphal, ed. (2009a), 1–36.
Westphal, Merold, ed. 1982. *Method and Speculation in Hegel's* Phenomenology. Atlantic Highlands: Humanities Press.
Westphal, Merold. 1998. *History and Truth in Hegel's* Phenomenology (Third Edition). Bloomington & Indianapolis: Indiana University Press.
Williams, Robert. 1985. "Hegel and Transcendental Philosophy." *Journal of Philosophy* 82: 595–606.
– 1992. *Recognition: Fichte and Hegel on the Other.* Albany: SUNY Press.
– 1995a. "Discernment in the Realm of Shadows: Absolute Knowing and Otherness," *The Owl of Minerva* 26, no. 2: 133–48.
– 1995b. "The Other: F. H. Jacobi and German Idealism." In Collins, ed. (1995), 73–92.
– 1998a. *Hegel's Ethics of Recognition.* Berkeley: University of California Press.
– 1998b. "Towards a Non-foundational Absolute Knowing." *The Owl of Minerva* 30, no. 1: 83–101.
– 2010–11. "Hegel's Concept of the True Infinite," and "Hegel's True Infinity as Panentheism: Reply to Robert Wallace," *The Owl of Minerva* 42, nos 1–2: 89–122, 137–52.
– 2012. *Tragedy, Recognition, and the Death of God: Studies in Hegel and Nietzsche.* Oxford: Oxford University Press.
Winfield, Richard Dien. 1989. *Overcoming Foundations: Studies in Systematic Philosophy.* New York: Columbia University Press.
– 2002–03. "Objectivity in Logic and Nature." *The Owl of Minerva* 34, no. 1: 77–89.
Wolff, Michael. 1981. *Der Begriff des Widerspruchs: Eine Studie zur Dialektik Kants und Hegels.* Königstein im Taunus: Hain.
– 1986. "Über Hegels Lehre vom Widerspruch." In *Probleme der Hegelschen Logik,* edited by Dieter Henrich. Stuttgart: Klett-Cotta, 107–28.
– 1999. "On Hegel's Doctrine of Contradiction." Translated by Erin Flynn and K. Westphal, *The Owl of Minerva* 31, no. 1: 1–22.
Wood, Allen W. 1990. *Hegel's Ethical Thought.* Cambridge & New York & Melbourne: Cambridge University Press.
Yeomans, Christopher. 2010–11. "Hegel and Analytic Philosophy of Action." *The Owl of Minerva* 42, no. 1–2: 41–62.

Index